Personnel

Contemporary Perspectives
and Applications

The West Series in Management

Consulting Editors

DON HELLRIEGEL, Texas A & M
JOHN W. SLOCUM, JR., Southern Methodist University

Personnel

Contemporary Perspectives and Applications

Third Edition

ROBERT L. MATHIS
University of Nebraska at Omaha

JOHN H. JACKSON
University of Wyoming

West Publishing Company

St. Paul   New York   Los Angeles   San Francisco

A study guide has been developed to assist you in mastering
concepts presented in this text. The study guide reinforces
concepts by presenting them in condensed, concise form.
Additional illustrations, examples, and exercises are also
included. The study guide is available from your local
bookstore under the title, *Study Guide to Accompany
Personnel: Contemporary Perspectives and Applications*,
third edition, prepared by Sally A. Coltrin.

Copy editing: Rosalie Koskenmaki
Text design: Rick Chafian
Chart design: CHARTEX/Boston
Composition: Grafacon
Cover design: Peter Thiel

Library of Congress Cataloging in Publication Data

Mathis, Robert L., 1944–
    Personnel : contemporary perspectives and applications.

    (West series in management)
    Includes bibliographical references and indexes.
    1. Personnel management. I. Jackson, John Harold.
II. Title. III. Series.
HF5549.M3349   1982   658.3   81-16159
ISBN 0-314-63270-0   AACR2

1st Reprint—1983

To

Jo Ann Mathis
who manages me

R. D. and M. M. Jackson
who have been
successful managers of
people for many years

Contents

Comprehensive Cases

Preface

We Need Education in the Obvious
More Than Investigation of the Obscure

OLIVER WENDELL HOLMES

This third edition, like the previous two, approaches the study of personnel management from the position that *both* the practical aspects of personnel and the underlying reasons and theories behind the practices are important. Certainly not everyone who reads this book will be a personnel manager. In fact, most students who take a personnel course never become personnel specialists. However, everyone who works in any organization comes in contact with personnel management—both good and bad. Further, anyone who does become a manager must be able to manage personnel activities. We feel every manager is a personnel manager, and his or her actions in this area can have major consequences for the organization.

A unique feature of the book is specifying the "contact" between operating managers and the personnel unit. This is a way to view the division of labor between operating managers and the personnel unit. This division will vary depending on the size of the organization, its technology and history, and other factors; there are clearly a group of personnel activities for which individuals in the organization *have to take responsibility*. How this responsibility is divided is the "interface" concept used throughout the book.

This book examines the major activities in personnel or "Human Resources" management completely but concisely. We are gratified by the reception the first two editions received and feel the changes and additions suggested by users of the second edition have made the book even better.

NEW AND REVISED FEATURES

Personnel is a rapidly changing area of study. Two of the most important forces causing such changes are court decisions and revision of governmental regulations. We have made a concerted effort to include the most up-to-date legal information possible, and as a result, can honestly say that at this writing, the book is the most up-to-date personnel text available.

This edition has many new features including a greatly expanded *Instructor's Manual* and student *Study Guide.* In the text itself, each section is opened with an item of contemporary interest in the personnel area to set the tone for the material that follows. These include topics such as: employee recognition, sexual harassment, the new breed of employees, job burnout, day care, employee assistance programs, etc.

All chapters contain new material. Every effort was made to totally update statistics, projections, and other materials of that kind. To illustrate: Chapter One now contains material previewing what follows in the book's later chapters. All of the material relevant to the organization itself, as a system, has been consolidated in Chapter Two, including organizational development. The EEO chapters have been completely updated in keeping with new court decisions and EEO regulations. Person/job fit has been expanded in Chapter Six and a job analysis example form added. Human resource planning has been expanded in Chapter Seven and selection testing in Chapter Eight. Training evaluation has been expanded to include evaluation designs, and management development and career planning now constitute Chapter Ten.

The performance appraisal material has been reorganized and rewritten, and Behaviorally Anchored Rating Scales have been expanded. The legal aspects of performance appraisal are examined as well.

The last several chapters contain similar changes. These changes are all viewed by the authors as part of the continuous updating and polishing necessary to keep a book absolutely current and optimally organized to present information clearly.

A major contribution to this edition is the inclusion throughout of "real world" cases. Students want real world application of academic material and we have tried to provide that. In addition, several long cases are now available at the end of the book to be used for discussion, exams, or term projects.

Many instructors utilize cases in teaching. To further aid this instructional orientation, a short case that poses a problem opens each chapter in this edition with case "solutions" at hand. Another case problem is presented at the end of the chapter for analysis. Other features included are learning objectives, chapter-ending questions that focus on mastery of the material, and "idea check" questions after major learning segments.

The availability of an excellent study guide, written by Sally Coltrin, further enhances this book as a learning tool. The study guide contains chapter summaries, review questions, and exercises.

We feel that this edition contains a practical view of personnel management that integrates both the contributions from the behavioral sciences and the legal issues that have raised personnel or human resources management from a narrow record-keeping function to a mainstream organizational activity.

ACKNOWLEDGMENTS

Producing any book requires assistance from other people. Some of the cases included in the book reflect the reality of modern personnel management because they summarize the experiences of practicing managers and former students who contributed ideas. Case ideas were contributed by David Anderson, Donald Browers, Mike Hlavacek, Patricia House, David Jahrous, George Kahlandt, Jocelyn Kersten, Sandra Miller, Craig Parker, Jill Sass, Pam Stanek, Robert Stevens, and Frances White.

Helpful comments came from a number of persons. Reviewers who assisted included Mildred Butterfield (Mt. Hood Community College), Eugene Evans (Western Kentucky U.), Leo Osterhaus (U. of Texas at Austin), Richard Robinson (Portland State U.), Jack Warren (Jackson State Community College), and James Wilson (U. of Central Florida). In particular, the authors thank Walter Bogumil (U. of Central Florida) for his suggestions. Special thanks are also due to Sally Coltrin (U. of North Florida) author of the study guide to accompany the text, and Daniel R. Hoyt (Arkansas State University), who contributed substantially to the instructor's manual. Cynthia Evahn and Penny McCord, graduate students at the University of Nebraska at Omaha, provided valuable assistance in a number of areas. The illustrations provided by Andrew Somogyi demonstrate his contributions to the book. Jackie Mulherin and Carol Welch provided valuable secretarial assistance. Special recognition for secretarial support is deserved by Vicki Premis, whose continuing support was invaluable to the senior author. Finally, the comments of numerous former students helped the authors make the text a more effective learning resource.

The authors wish to note that many of the examples used to illustrate concepts are real situations but specific references to existing organizations or people is merely coincidental. We feel this edition has fulfilled what we perceive to be a real need in the study of Personnel Management.

Robert L. Mathis   John H. Jackson
Omaha, Nebraska   Laramie, Wyoming

To the Reader

This book is designed to aid you, the reader, as you learn more about personnel management. As you use this book, you may find value from the following tips:

1. Familiarize yourself with the learning objectives at the beginning of each chapter. The learning objectives indicate what you should know after reading and studying a chapter.

2. Outline each chapter for study purposes by noting the main, second level, and in-paragraph headings.

3. Read the case at the beginning of the chapter which illustrates the type of problems the information in the chapter would help you resolve.

4. As you read the chapter, notice the idea check questions and see if you can answer them. Each idea check relates directly to one of the learning objectives. If you cannot correctly and completely answer an idea check, go back and re-read the section immediately preceding the idea check.

5. After reading the chapter, answer the review questions. Also, if your instructor has requested you to use the student supplement, read the summary in that supplement and answer the sample questions in it.

6. Read the short ending case and answer the questions on it by applying ideas from the chapter.

7. For additional study assistance, you might wish to purchase the study guide written to accompany this text, which is authored by Dr. Sally Coltrin.

If you let this book and the learning features in it aid you, your study of personnel management will be easier and more enjoyable. With the knowledge you acquire, you will be able to become more effective in your chosen career field.

Personnel

Contemporary Perspectives
and Applications

Perspectives on Personnel Management

EMPLOYEE RECOGNITION: UNTAPPED RESOURCE FOR THE 1980s

Over $8 billion per year! That's the cost of various watches, plaques, luxury trips, jewelry, radios, glasses, and clothing bought by U.S. employers as tangible recognition of accomplishments and as encouragement for future performance.

A major manufacturer in New York spends over $300,000 for the annual company dinner at which employees are given 5, 10, 15, 20, and 25-year service awards. Mates or dates are invited to a lavish meal, guests are entertained by a band, and door prizes are given. Why are such sums being spent? The answer is *recognition*.

RECOGNITION

Recognition can be as simple as a verbal "pat on the back" by a supervisor who tells an employee, "You did a good job on that project." Or it can be as elaborate as a formal safety program that gives gifts to all employees in accident-free departments. The potential value of recognition can be seen in the results of several independent studies of employee attitudes sponsored by the Balfour Company, a Massachusetts-based manufacturer of jewelry and other recognition products.[1]

Employees surveyed generally indicated that they felt management did not appreciate the employees' efforts. Also, it's *how* the recognition is given, not just *what* is given that counts when recognizing employees for years of service or performance. The ultimate "tacky" gesture belonged to the company that mailed a $300 diamond watch to a 20-year service employee through the inter-company mail!

Interestingly, the personnel administrators surveyed reflected their employees' thoughts. Over 80% felt that their companies did not fully respond to the recognition needs of their employees.

Black & Decker, Control Data, and Parker Brothers (*Monopoly* game

[1] Much of the data has been provided by the Balfour Company, 25 County St., Attleboro, MA 02703.

manufacturer) are just a few of the employers that have established effective employee recognition programs. Honeywell Corporation has an outstanding system that uses both cash and merchandise awards to reward suggestion submitters.

The untapped potential for recognition has led numerous organizations to set up formal employee recognition programs to enhance productivity and develop good employee relations. Achieving both *productivity* and effective *employee relations* is the true challenge of personnel management in the 1980s.

This first section (1) examines the nature of personnel management, (2) defines and places personnel management in an organizational context, and (3) examines basic human considerations of motivation, leadership, group behavior, and communication.

Chapter 1 provides a basis for understanding what personnel management is and why it differs in various organizational situations.

Chapter 2 places personnel management in an organizational context and views an organization as an open system.

Chapter 3 examines the human resource by considering four basic intraorganizational processes: motivation, leadership, group behavior, and communication. Knowledge of each of these behavioral processes is fundamental to managing people.

CHAPTER 1

The Nature of Personnel Management

When you have read this chapter, you should be able to:

1. Discuss the three sets of issues about the nature of personnel management.

2. Reconcile the different views into a definition of personnel management that emphasizes managing the human resource.

3. List and in one sentence identify the seven personnel activities.

Pulled Both Ways

William Anderson, plant personnel manager for Amalgamated Products in Dallas, Texas, is the center of a controversy—and he does not even know it. The vice-president of personnel and the vice-president of manufacturing are arguing over an issue that will affect him. The company had received attention from the Occupational Safety and Health Administration (OSHA) because of its excessive accident rate, especially at the Dallas plant. The vice-president of personnel feels William must be told in no uncertain terms that the plant must be ready to pass a safety inspection at any time and that William, as plant personnel manager, will be held responsible for the results.

Unfortunately, the vice-president of manufacturing does not agree. He has continually emphasized that safety is the job of the line supervisors and is not a Plant Personnel Department job. As he put it to the personnel vice-president last week: "You Personnel people do the hiring and put up the safety posters, and the supervisors will run their departments."

Comments:

William has a problem, and it's even greater than he thinks. It illustrates how a misperception by management can cause problems.

The vice-president of manufacturing is working from a *narrow functional* view of personnel. Because safety is related to production efficiency, the vice-president of manufacturing has some valid reasons for his view. On the other hand, the vice-president of personnel appears to have a somewhat more professional view of personnel. Clearly, safety does have some "people" dimensions and the vice-president of personnel probably feels that the personnel manager should have the responsibility for safety activities.

What has been overlooked is that the safety activity must be handled by someone and a coordinated effort is necessary. All parties involved need to focus on the *activity* and who can best perform the various components of a good safety effort. Unless the personnel manager can generate that form of cooperation and understanding, continued confusion and ambiguity are likely to continue. There is no "right" answer as to who should *always* do these things. But *someone* must.

THE successful management of human resources is one of the keys to the effective operation of an organization. Numerous public relations documents describe people as "the most important resource" a firm has. As an example, IBM has been extremely successful in the computer industry due, in large part, to its ability to attract and retain skilled employees and managers. It is significant that IBM also has the reputation of having sound, forward-looking personnel management policies and practices.

Some managers feel that personnel management is primarily a "business" profession or activity. However, managers in both the private and public sectors must tap their human resources if they are to be successful. Large corporations, banks, universities, advertising agencies, small retail stores, hospitals, manufacturing firms, and governmental agencies all must tap the talents of their people if the organizations are to accomplish their objectives. A production supervisor, a hospital administrator, a grocery store manager, a mayor—any manager in any organization—will succeed in getting the job done only if that manager can deal with people.

But the days when a "concern for people" was all that was necessary for success in personnel matters are long past. Dealing with people's needs, expectations, and legal rights in work organizations has become more demanding and complex. Laws and regulations at federal, state, and local levels impose limitations on what managers can and cannot do as they manage employees. Nondiscriminatory recruiting, selection, and promotion criteria must be identified and used. Designing appropriate programs for training people to perform their jobs requires knowledge of both human and organizational concerns. Sound, coordinated, and legal wage and salary systems must be designed and implemented so that employees feel fairly compensated for their efforts. Personnel policies that help rather than hinder the accomplishment of work must be implemented. These areas are a few of the concerns of personnel management.

MAJOR CHALLENGES IN PERSONNEL FOR THE 80s

Productivity in the United States and all over the world has declined. A survey of the top 2,500 U.S. companies found 95% of the chief executives expressing concern about productivity gains.[1] Some 88% of them said they believed a compensation program could raise productivity. One of the problems suggested by the survey is management itself.

Some changes and trends in personnel management in the mid-1980s include:

• More government intervention in personnel activities;

- Changing expectations of the work force;
- New developments in work scheduling (job sharing, compressed work weeks, flex-time).

These and other trends as yet undetected will raise the importance of personnel-related activities. A survey of top executives found that 65% of the non-personnel executives predicted that personnel executives will become more heavily involved in developing corporate strategy and policy in the years ahead.[2] Also, the cost of personnel work is rising rapidly. In 1980 it cost companies an estimated $410 per employee, up from $375 in 1979, to perform personnel-related activities.[3]

The movement of personnel to the forefront in the years ahead is clearly indicated. However, many personnel practitioners *do not* have any formal and specific training in personnel.[4] The same can be said for operating managers with whom personnel specialists must cooperate. As Figure 1-1 shows the number of personnel jobs has increased dramatically since 1950. Yet the rate at which personnel professionals are being trained is slow.

This book provides you with a basic understanding of the tools and concepts of personnel management. Whether or not you ever make personnel your career, information on personnel management will be important to you in the years ahead. But who is a personnel manager? What exactly is personnel management? Which managers should do what jobs in managing people? These questions will help define the subject area. A usable definition of personnel management will be developed through the following discussion of different views of personnel.

VIEWS OF PERSONNEL MANAGEMENT

The opening case shows that not everyone agrees on what personnel management includes. One reason is that in different organizations personnel includes somewhat different activities or different amounts of responsibility for activities. For example, in one medium-sized bank all new non-management employees are hired by the personnel department. In another equally successful company new employees are screened by the personnel department and actually selected by the supervisors for whom they will work. Which is right? The answer seems to be that if it is working well for that company it is right for them.

Historical, philosophical, and other differences result in a slightly different emphasis being given to personnel in each organization. The way a given organization views personnel management can be determined by its response to three key issues:

1. Who is a personnel manager?

Figure 1–1. Growth in personnel jobs in the United States.

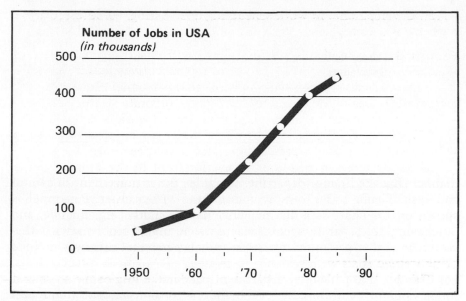

(Source: H. G. Heneman, Jr. *"Quo Vadis* PAIR," *Personnel/Human Resource Division Newsletter, Academy of Management,* March 1980, p. 3.)

2. How do you design personnel systems?
3. How do you learn personnel management?

To illustrate the various views, extreme positions on both sides of each issue will be presented in the following sections. In most situations when two distinctly different views are voiced, there are sound points made by each. Resolution incorporates the sound points made at the extremes but rejects the notion that one view is totally correct.

Who Is a Personnel Manager?

On this issue one side contends that personnel management is limited to only one part of the organization, the *personnel department.* This department handles "people" problems. The other side believes that all managers are personnel managers, and that it is only through the effective use of human resources by all managers that work gets done.

Personnel Specialists. As Figure 1–2 shows, the continuum of answers ranges from personnel specialists to every manager. Those who hold that the personnel specialist is best qualified to handle all personnel problems feel that personnel activities should be performed at one place in the organization. The personnel department "handles people," in the same

Figure 1–2.   Who is a personnel manager?

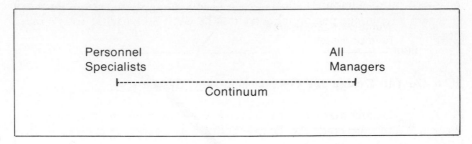

manner that the finance department handles the management of capital and cash. Figure 1–3 shows a typical organization chart. Personnel is shown on the chart as a distinct unit, just as marketing, finance, and purchasing are separate specialized units. A major problem with this structure is that personnel management may become narrowly defined as *only* those areas with which a "personnel" department directly deals. For example, the personnel department may make wage surveys, but it might not work with middle-level managers on allocation of production bonuses because that is "the production department's job."

Figure 1–3.   Personnel as a special unit in Amalgamated Products.

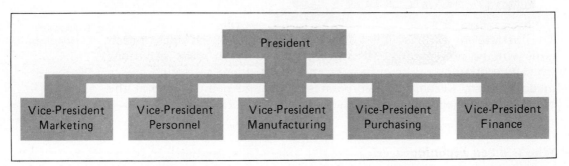

Every Manager.   The other side of this argument suggests that personnel management is spread throughout the organization. All managers are viewed as personnel managers. Sales managers, head nurses, manufacturing supervisors, corporate treasurers, college deans, and retail store managers are personnel managers because their jobs are closely tied to their employees' effectiveness. However it is unrealistic to expect an accounting department supervisor to be extremely knowledgeable about equal employment laws and various benefit plans.

The "all managers" view may preclude having a personnel department at all and suggests that the scope of personnel management is much broader than what one department can handle. As will be emphasized later, personnel specialists and operating managers must work together to manage personnel activities by each doing what they can do best.

How Do You Design and Operate Personnel Systems?

A second disagreement has to do with the way personnel systems are designed and operated. As Figure 1–4 shows, one extreme says that management can use standardized techniques for handling *all* people. These techniques will be effective because people will do what is expected of them for their own benefit. For example, if a training program has been well designed, it will be effective because people will benefit from it, and therefore will welcome it.

The other view holds that individual human nature and processes must be incorporated in the design and operation of personnel management activities. For example, establishing a rationally designed training program would not *necessarily* guarantee that the trainees would understand or approve of the training.

Figure 1–4.   How do you design and operate personnel systems?

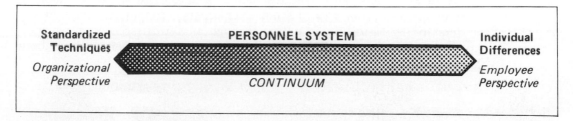

Standardized Techniques.   Principles or standard techniques *can* be the basis for making certain personnel decisions *if* they are based on consideration of scientific fact. But overuse of principles emphasizes organizational uniformity, conformity, and predictability. The use of principles also assumes that people will be just as rational and predictable as the organization expects them to be. The rational view can be summarized as "everything from the perspective of the organization and nothing from the worker's perspective."

Individual Differences.   The other side of this issue focuses solely on the people in organizations. Some criticize the rational approach for being rigid and too prescriptive. They argue that the type of organization, the type of position, and the employees' individual qualifications and personalities have such a great impact on personnel decisions that management principles have very little value. At a minimum, human nature will disrupt or alter orderly rational principles.

An extension of the logic applied here can be made. If standardization and uniformity are bad, they should be minimized. Carried to its logical extreme, the personnel systems in an organization should be designed to maximize employee individuality and satisfaction. This view is "everything from the employee's perspective."

The resolution of these extremes recognizes that organizations need a reasonable degree of standardization and uniformity. However, what is appropriate for one organization and its employees may not be best suited to another. Adjusting to individuals clearly must be done, but this must be balanced with the overall needs of the organization as well.

How Do You Learn Personnel Management?

A final question must be dealt with: *How do you learn personnel management?* One side of this debate claims that personnel management is a very practical and applied field. Thus it should focus on the development of very practical techniques for meeting personnel problems. Academic approaches are of little use.

The opposing side holds that personnel management should not be considered a field at all. This argument challenges the idea that personnel management as an area of study even exists. Proponents feel that understanding basic human nature through analytical studies in psychology, sociology, or anthropology is more appropriate than talking about techniques. Figure 1–5 illustrates this continuum.

Figure 1–5.   How do you learn personnel management?

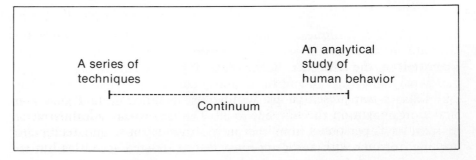

Techniques.   Learning about personnel only as a series of techniques can lead to a loss of the "big picture" as to why the techniques are followed. Without some understanding and ability to predict the effects of new personnel policies and practices, problems will not be solved as they arise. Technique lists typify an overconcern with doing and not enough concern with understanding. A good example of the extreme technique approach follows:

Five Steps for Handling Contract Grievances[5]

1. Check for procedural compliance.

2. Perform preliminary research.

3. Conduct an orderly first-step meeting.

4. Research the problem, then decide.

5. Present your decision.

Analytical Study.   Certain behavioral scientists fault the techniques approach to personnel as being excessively concerned with "how to" issues which do not consider "why". Techniques are sometimes viewed as "recipes" for dealing with any and all personnel problems.

Some holding this view challenge the idea that personnel management is even a field of study. They see it as being involved only in day-to-day problems. It is not "scientific" or even perhaps an art. The extreme side of this view contends that personnel professionals should be concentrating on the "humanization" of work, the creation of a climate of "openness," and the demise of the "bureaucratic structure" instead of job descriptions, application blanks, and company handbooks.

To resolve these differing views, it is vital to see personnel management as a combination of analytical studies from which specific applications are derived. The rather bland "list-following" urged by some techniques must be tempered with the knowledge gained from good scientific studies. In a similar manner, analytical studies that are not easily applied are of little value to personnel specialists and other managers.

Can you discuss three sets of issues about personnel management?

Summarizing the Different Viewpoints

The debates just presented are summarized graphically in Figure 1–6. The view shown on the left side focuses on day-to-day administration of traditional personnel activities in a rather rational and technique-oriented manner with authority for personnel-related activities limited to the personnel department. On the right side of Figure 1–6 personnel management is seen to be based on an analytical evaluation of people, their behavior in the organization, and all managers are personnel managers because they must interact with people on a continual basis.

In reality, successful personnel management contains elements of

Figure 1–6.   Reconciling differing viewpoints.

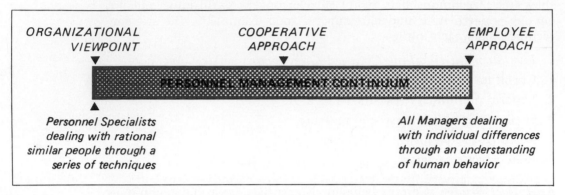

all these viewpoints. The specific blend that occurs in a given organization depends on its strengths, weaknesses, history, and other variables. It is important to realize that all contact with an organization's human resources cannot be limited to a personnel department. All managers are involved. Yet the personnel unit provides expertise in some areas that other managers probably do not have. Therefore, cooperation between the personnel unit and the other managers is very important for successful human resources management.

THE INTERFACE CONCEPT

This book uses a device, *the interface concept*, to emphasize the importance of cooperation between personnel specialists and other managers. The point of contact or *interface* between the two takes place in the seven major activities that focus on an organization's employees.

Figure 1–7.   Interface between personnel unit and other managers.

These activities are ones that *must be addressed by someone anytime an organization has employees.* For example: Who will do what jobs? How much will they be paid? Who is doing a good job?

INTERFACES are areas of contact between the personnel unit and other managers in an organization that occur within critical personnel activities.

Unless the contact between the personnel unit and the operating managers is based on who is most qualified to perform various parts of a personnel activity, the activity is likely to be mismanaged. In the opening case the conflict between vice-presidents is not likely to lead to effective management of safety activities. Only by cooperatively deciding who can best perform what will the safety activities themselves be sound.

Personnel activities should be performed by those who can do them most effectively. Who is "most appropriate" may vary from organization to organization based on such items as size, tradition, and the person who has specific expertise. However, *someone* must manage the "people-related" activities. They cannot be left to chance. Clearly, personnel management is a concern of *both* the managers *and* the personnel unit in an organization.

The size of an organization is often a key consideration in determining who will do what. In a very small organization, such as a small retail store, no specialized personnel unit may exist. Instead, the owner-manager will hire the clerks, handle the payroll, train new employees, and perform any other needed personnel activities. However, a large retail chain will usually have a specialized personnel unit.

Value of the Interface Concept

The major intent of the interface approach that this book uses is to *identify people-oriented activities* that must be performed in all organizations. The responsibility for proper management of personnel activities such as interviewing, training, or performance appraisal in a given situation is placed on both managers and personnel specialists. The interface device is applied in Figure 1–8 to illustrate how some of the concerns in employment interviewing might be divided between the personnel unit and other managers.

A manager must consider both the situation and the people involved to determine the most appropriate approach for handling problems. For example, assume that the appraisal of a nurse's performance is the activity under consideration. The interface approach suggests that various

Figure 1–8. The selection interviewing interface between the personnel unit and other managers.

Personnel Unit	Manager
Develops legal, effective interviewing techniques	Decides whether to do own final interviewing
Trains managers in selection interviewing	Receives training from personnel in interviewing
Provides interviews and testing	Does actual *final interviewing* and hiring where appropriate
Sends qualified employees to managers who want to do final interview	Provides feedback to personnel on hiring decisions and reasons for not hiring
Does final interviewing and hiring for certain managers and job classifications	

methods of appraisal might be used; but there are analytical considerations as well as considerations in technique. The head nurse and/or personnel administrator must choose the most appropriate appraisal method, given the situation and the nurse involved. This approach differs greatly from prescribing an appraisal technique for "any situation," or from examining appraisal problems in the absence of having to solve them. It also requires cooperation between the head nurse and personnel specialists, but the end result is a much more adaptable and effective personnel system.

Use of the Interface Concept

The interface idea will be developed throughout the book in each chapter with an interface showing particular personnel activities and who *typically* performs what portion of them. However, these interface illustrations are not attempts to indicate "the one way" all organizations can or should perform the activities. They illustrate how these activities *can* be divided. We now have enough information to define personnel management and discuss the seven major personnel activities that require attention in any organization.

Personnel Management Defined

The reconciliation of the various viewpoints emphasizes that personnel management is a *set of activities* that must be effectively managed.

> **PERSONNEL MANAGEMENT** is a set of activities focusing on the coordination of human resources in an organization.

The definition emphasizes the personnel activities themselves, and *not* who performs them. All organizations with people in them must deal with the specific personnel activities of *work analysis, staffing, training and development, appraisal, compensation, maintenance,* and *union relations.*

PERSONNEL ACTIVITIES

The major personnel activities that must be covered by the personnel unit and/or other managers are presented in the center portion of Figure 1–9. These activities are:

- Work Analysis
- Staffing
- Training and development
- Appraisal
- Compensation ⟩ EX & INT.
- Maintenance
- Union relations

The personnel unit, if one exists, and individual managers must cooperate to effectively manage the employees and their work within each of the seven activities.

Environmental forces which affect every aspect of any organization are shown in Figure 1–9 as an external boundary surrounding the organization. These forces include legal, societal, and interorganizational factors. The development of an organization as a system, open to environmental factors, and the relationship of the personnel unit to the total organization are concepts discussed in chapter 2. One critical environmental force, equal employment legislation, is described in chapters 4 and 5.

Intraorganizational forces of leadership, motivation, and group behavior are organizational processes of special interest to personnel focusing on human behavior. These forces are behavioral processes rather than specific personnel activities and are discussed in chapter 3.

Figure 1–9.　Model of personnel activities.

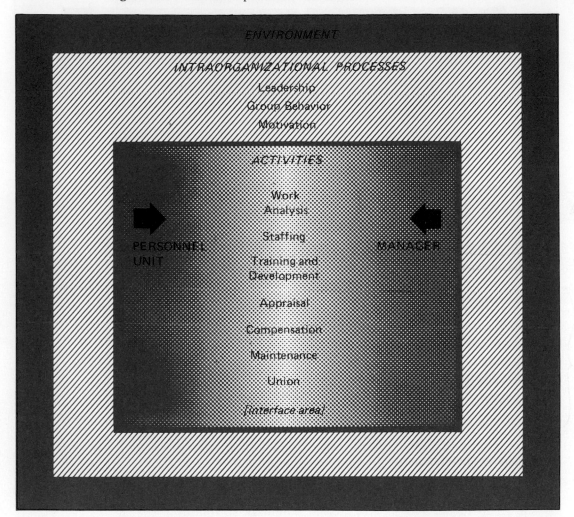

Work Analysis

The focus of work analysis is on a job as a unit of work. The specialization of narrow jobs versus the humanization of broader jobs is one consideration in *job design*. Once the unit of work is established, jobs can be analyzed and *job descriptions* and *job specifications* can be written. The nature of these activities and their implications for human behavior are discussed further in chapter 6. A good working relationship between people and their jobs does not just happen. It requires analysis of the job to be done and proper design of the work people do. Job design that considers people's behavioral desires will become increasingly important.

Analyzing jobs properly has implications for equitable pay systems as well. Why does a word processing specialist earn more pay than a keypunch operator? The answer has to be that one job requires more knowledge, skills, and abilities than the other. But without good job analysis it is difficult to explain the reasons to the keypuncher who is earning less.

Staffing

Staffing emphasizes the recruitment and selection of the human resources for an organization. Human resource planning and recruiting precede the actual *selection* of people for positions in organizations. Choosing the right person for the job involves the use of such data sources as application blanks, interviews, tests, background investigations, and physical examinations. The staffing interface is examined in chapters 7 and 8.

Human resource planning, affirmative action, equal employment opportunity, and *test validity* are terms slightly used 20 years ago. Yet, these concepts form the cornerstone of modern staffing practices. They affect personnel managers, as well as production, marketing, and finance managers. All these managers have to staff their jobs with people in such a way as to live with current legal and social expectations.

Probably no one area has changed as much in personnel as staffing. Much of the change is for the better because it has forced a more professional approach to matching people and jobs. There are major costs to both the organization and the individual associated with a mismatch.

Training and Development

Training and development includes the orientation *of the new employees, the* training *of employees to perform their job, and the* retaining *of employees as their job requirements change. The* development *and* growth *of more effective employees is another facet.* All these aspects of training and development are examined in chapters 9 and 10.

Training needs assessment, training evaluation, career planning, and management development have grown in importance. However, training costs—like everything else—are increasing, and management has a right to know whether or not it is receiving a dollar's worth of benefit for a dollar spent in this area. Further, as women and minorities with special training needs become more predominant in organizations of all kinds, a greater need for specialized types of training and development will continue to grow.

Training has always been a little like the flag, motherhood, and apple pie—you just don't question its value. That is changing. Even though training has been viewed as good, it is usually the first cost that gets reduced in an organization when budgets get cut. Increasingly in the 1980s managers are asking if training is cost effective. Will the company get more out of it than it will cost?

Appraisal

Performance appraisal focuses on how well employees are doing their jobs. An appraisal is useful in making *wage and salary decisions*, in specifying areas in which additional *training and development* of employees is needed, and in making *placement* decisions. Knowledge of the approaches to appraisal and the types of appraisal methods are integral to implementing an appraisal system. The behavioral consequences of appraisal are also a primary concern and are discussed in chapter 11.

Performance appraisal is typically very poorly done in most organizations because of ignorance about appraisal and a reluctance to be negative. Yet, as the cost of keeping poor employees continue to grow, performance appraisal will become even more critical. The cost associated with having unrecognized excellence and potential is at least as great. Well-designed, properly implemented appraisal systems, perhaps more than any of the other activities, require the cooperative efforts of the personnel unit and operating managers in an organization. The importance of performance appraisal can be summed up in one very simple thought: If employees don't know how they are doing, how can they improve?

Compensation

Compensation deals with rewarding people through *pay, incentives,* and *benefits* for performing organizational work. The behavioral side of compensation and the meaning of equity and reward to the employee are underlying considerations. Building on job analysis, the *job evaluation* activity determines the relative worth of each job. Also, special types of compensation fall within this interface. Compensation activities are discussed in chapters 12 and 13.

Pay is of great importance to employees. Although they obviously need it to purchase life's necessities, the motivating (or demotivating) effect of pay is a major concern as well. Productivity has been a national concern for some time. One possible way to increase productivity is to tie compensation to production. Yet, compensation administration is becoming increasingly complex, legislation has greatly changed benefit plans, and increasing unionization in white-collar jobs will make the tie between productivity and compensation even more complex. New approaches, new ideas, and a professional approach to compensation and benefits are vital if strides are to be made in this area.

Maintenance

The emphasis of maintenance activities is somewhat different than the others. Maintenance activities emphasize consistency, stability, continuity, and an acceptable work environment. The physical and mental health and safety of employees are key parts of this interface.

The Occupational Safety and Health Act of 1970 (OSHA) has forced management attention on the *health and safety* areas. The effects of various substances in the environment on employees at work is just being discovered. Developing a safe and healthy work environment will be an evolving process for most organizations. Largely because of OSHA, but also because of increasing management awareness of its social responsibilities to the public and its employees, personnel health and safety will continue to grow in importance.

Maintenance also includes *personnel coordination* and *personnel records and research*. In addition to developing and implementing policies, managers must communicate with employees and keep abreast of the state of the personnel activities in their organizations. These aspects of the maintenance interface are presented and discussed in chapters 14, 15, and 16.

Union Relations

Union-related activities are considered last because unions are organized, semi-external forces which influence the organization, the personnel unit, managers, and all the other activities. An understanding of unions requires an overview of the development of an organized labor movement in the United States, the current state of unions, and the international dimension of unions.

The prime union/organization contact occurs at two levels. One is at the formal organizational level and occurs when the union becomes the agent representing the employees of an organization. Once an organization is unionized, a contract must be negotiated through union/organization discussions and collective bargaining in which behavioral considerations play a vital role. At another level, a continuing union/organization relationship focuses on settling disputes and grievances which arise during the labor agreement. Because effective union relations may play a significant role in the management of human resources, a discussion of unions is vital. The union relations interface is discussed in chapters 17 and 18.

Labor unions will increase in importance in the years ahead for some organizations. In other organizations and industries a rethinking and reformulation of existing relationships may be necessary for the industries to grow and remain viable. The construction industry is an example of an industry where this reexamination appears to be occurring. Yet unions are becoming more of a force to be dealt with in the white-collar areas.

Can you briefly identify the seven major sets of
personnel activities?

A SURVEY OF PERSONNEL ACTIVITIES

A cost analysis can reveal the relative degree of responsibility for various activities that a specialized personnel department holds within the total organization. If a firm assigns costs to an activity, then the percentage of costs assigned to the personnel unit may be one means of measuring the extent of that unit's involvement in the organization.

A 1980 survey of 240 organizations, taken by the American Society for Personnel Administration and the Bureau of National Affairs, collected data on the relative allocation of the cost of the various personnel activities between the personnel unit and the rest of the organization. Figure 1–10 shows a comparison of these personnel unit costs.

In the survey, about half the organizations are manufacturing firms, about 30% are nonmanufacturing companies, and the remaining ones are health-care, education, and government organizations. In the survey the typical personnel department has one employee for every 100 employees on the employer's payroll. In Figure 1–10 over 90% of the costs for personnel records and reports are allocated to personnel department budgets. However, only 68% of the costs of recruiting/interviewing/hiring are allocated to personnel department budgets.

The survey also demonstrates clearly that what is as important as who does these activities is that they do get done. That is the theme of this book. For certain activities the personnel department in smaller organizations is less likely to be involved, and one can assume that if they are being done, other managers are doing some of them. In conclusion, the survey reinforces the importance of viewing personnel management using the interface approach.

REVIEW AND PREVIEW

The objectives of this chapter are to provide an examination and definition of personnel management and to present a brief overview of personnel activities. The effective management of human resources is absolutely necessary for the growth of all types of organizations—business firms, hospitals, governmental entities, and others. Therefore, a workable accommodation between the organizational necessities of productivity and coordination and the employees' needs and goals must be developed.

Figure 1–10. Percent of companies allocating money to the personnel unit for these activities.

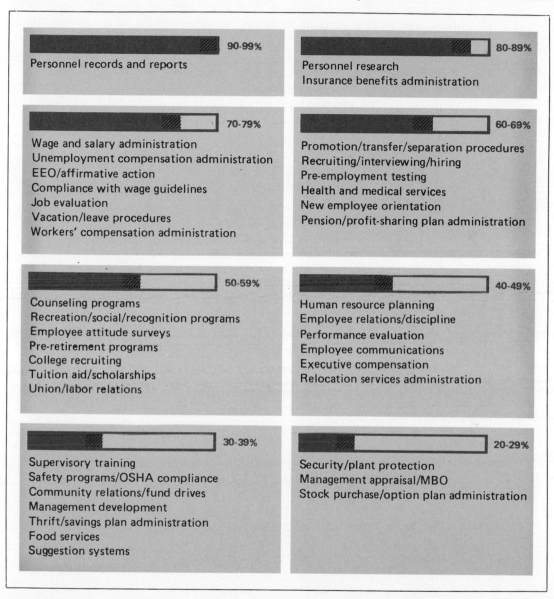

(Source: American Society for Personnel Administration and the Bureau of National Affairs survey, "Personnel Activities, Budgets and Staffs. 1979–1980," *Bulletin to Management #40*, (June 5, 1980, p. 2.) Reprinted by special permission from *ASPA/BNA Survey #40*, copyright 1980 by The Bureau of National Affairs, Inc., Washington, D.C.

Conflicting views about the essence of personnel management have been advanced and examined. The three sets of different viewpoints discussed in this chapter focus on separate aspects of personnel management. These divergent views can be reconciled by emphasizing that personnel management is a *set of activities which must be performed* if people are to accomplish work in modern organizations.

The theme of this chapter and this book is effective management of the activities and points of contact between personnel specialists and the management group. Seven activities form the core of personnel management: *work analysis, staffing, training and development, appraisal, compensation, maintenance,* and *union relations.*

Before turning to these activities, personnel management should be placed in an organizational context. Chapter 2 provides this organizational perspective.

Review Questions

1. Each set of differing viewpoints on personnel management is concerned with a slightly different issue. What are the three issues and what are the extreme viewpoints of each?

2. Define personnel management and explain how the three sets of differing viewpoints can be reconciled into your definition.

3. What are the seven personnel interfaces and what is the nature of each?

Case: Phillips Furniture

Ten years ago Albert Phillips opened his own retail store and sold unpainted furniture. His store was located in Lakeside, a small city in the southeastern part of the United States. Although his business was somewhat slow at first, it grew steadily.

Many more sales, stock, and clerical personnel were hired. However, it soon became evident that Mr. Phillips was not able to effectively service all potential customers. Warehouse space was also badly needed.

Phillips Furniture Store was situated in a central location, and Mr. Phillips was hesitant about relocating. As an alternative to relocating, Mr. Phillips opened a satellite store in an outlying district to attract a new source of customers, as well as to provide better service to his current customers. Mr. Phillips eventually expanded his business into several neighboring towns until he had a total of six stores. When Martin Furniture, a small manufacturing firm which supplied some of the furniture for Phillips, became financially unstable, Mr. Phillips was able to gain control of the manufacturing plant.

At the end of last week, you were called into Mr. Phillips' office, and Mr. Phillips said, to you, "I have been pleased with your progress with us as a management trainee since you graduated six months ago." He explained that he felt that the company had gotten large enough to need a personnel manager. Previously, all managers handled most of their own personnel activities, usually on a "casual" basis. Mr. Phillips told you that with the acquisition of the manufacturing firm, "It's time for us to get our personnel activities organized, and you're the person to do it."

When asked why, he said, "I reviewed your personnel file and noticed you had a course in personnel management listed on your transcript." Faced with both the challenge and the promotion, you accepted. Now you are trying to decide, "What am I, now that I'm a personnel manager?"

QUESTIONS

1. How would the interface concept help you in defining your role at Phillips Furniture?

2. On what activities would you tell Mr. Phillips you intend to focus? Why?

3. What would be your first actions, and why?

NOTES

1. John Cunniff, "Management Cited in Production Drop," *The Denver Post* (AP), November 16, 1980, p. 54.
2. *Wall Street Journal*, February 12, 1980, p. 1.
3. *Wall Street Journal*, July 29, 1980, p. 1.
4. H. G. Heneman, Jr., "*Quo Vadis* PAIR", *Personnel/Human Resources Division, Newsletter, Academy of Management*, March 1980, p. 3.
5. Keith B. Krinke and Jerome M. Nelson, "Five Steps For Handling Contract Grievances," *Supervisory Management*, September 1977, pp. 14–20.

CHAPTER 2

The Organization and Personnel

When you have read this chapter, you should be able to:

1. Tell what an organization is and why it should be viewed as an open system.

2. Identify issues affecting the nature of work systems.

3. Define and discuss as a part of the organization design subsystem the concepts of authority and line-staff.

4. Define Organization Development (OD) and identify two approaches to OD.

5. Explain why resistance to change occurs and how it can be managed.

6. Describe personnel's role in organizations.

7. Discuss personnel's role in public and matrix organizations.

8. Discuss three personnel concerns that exist in international environments.

Where Do You Find the Bodies?!

Milt Konrath has just received an assignment of questionable excitement. Milt is a management trainee for a large retail store chain. After graduation from college his first assignment was as assistant manager in the Automobile Service Center in Boomtown, Colorado.

Boomtown sits in the middle of a huge, newly developed coal field and a great deal of oil and gas exploration is going on as well. Boomtown has grown from 30,000 to 60,000 in three years and the unemployment rate in town is less than 3%. Those not working simply would rather not.

The Auto Service Center is normally staffed with three mechanics, two "grease monkeys" who do less skilled work, and three tire changer/clean-up persons. The wages paid these people are dictated from corporate headquarters in an effort to maintain common rates between stores.

Unfortunately the wages offered (although very competitive elsewhere) are well below what people can make in either the coal mines or with the exploration companies. The last mechanic (who made $20,000 a year) quit Wednesday to go to work repairing diesel earth-moving equipment at $38,000 a year plus overtime. The store had also been unable to replace the grease monkeys and clean-up persons. The last one quit a $5.80/hour job two weeks ago to work in the mines at $14.52/hour.

Milt's boss, the Automotive Manager, has just given him the assignment of recruiting and filling the vacant positions. The service department has almost ground to a halt without employees and the manager would like the problem fixed quickly.

Comments:

The situation described in Boomtown is very typical in several parts of the western United States. Unfortunately there are no easy solutions that Milt can adopt. He might try recruiting mechanics from economically depressed areas elsewhere and Milt might design an incentive system for use with shop personnel. Another alternative is to start renting space in the center for individuals to work on their own vehicles. Also, Milt and his boss must convince headquarters that there must be greater flexibility available to the managers in Boomtown. In summary, the case emphasizes the need for planning, flexibility, and creativity in dealing with personnel problems, and that organizations are truly affected by environmental forces.

MANAGING human resources is a part of every managerial job in every organizational unit. Personnel activities typically performed by managers include appraising people's performance, designing jobs, and orienting and training employees. Managers in all types of organizations—business, government, military, nonprofit, and others—need a working knowledge of personnel management.

Because personnel management takes place in organizations, an understanding of the nature of organizations is necessary, even though the role of a personnel unit may vary from organization to organization. This chapter describes how personnel fits into the organization. Although it is somewhat different in different organizations, all organizations share certain characteristics that are important in understanding personnel management and how it is practiced.

THE ORGANIZATION

To move toward organizational goals, the coordination of the activities of a number of people is necessary. Some means must be developed to divide the work. Also, members of the organization must accept guidance by certain other members to realize the benefits of coordination.

For example, a hospital is an organization attempting to provide health care through the combined efforts of administrators, doctors, nurses, and technicians. Administrators primarily act to direct and coordinate the efforts of the hospital employees. An organizational structure is established by staffing a hospital with an administrator, director of nursing, director of housekeeping, and chief surgeon to guide the hospital's efforts to provide quality health care. The number of beds and the type of laboratory and X-ray equipment also affect the overall organization and operation of the hospital.

Organization Defined

An ORGANIZATION is a set of stable social relations deliberately created with the intention of accomplishing some goal or purpose, generally existing with an authority structure, and influenced considerably by its technology and the environment in which it operates.

This definition does not include spur-of-the-moment social arrangements with short-term purposes, such as a group of passengers trapped in a bus in a snowstorm who must reach safety to survive. That is not an organization as defined here.

What is an "organization"?

Organizations as Systems

Many approaches have been used in the past to try to understand organizations and how they operate. At one time, organizations were thought of in terms of a "universal organizational design," complete with a set of principles. Those ideas have generally been combined under the title of "Classical Organization Theory."

Classical theory is criticized for being too restrictive and inadequate because of the environment in which a modern organization operates. The current trend in organization design is to build the organization to fit the situation, so that the organization can deal successfully with its environment. Some of the classical "principles" may apply and some may not, depending on the circumstances. No one universal organizational design will fit all situations. As an example, in some manufacturing firms a quality-control inspector reports to the plant manager. In others, quality control may not be a separate job because employees check the quality of their own work.

Systems Approach.   The systems approach is currently popular because it provides a useful way to emphasize the whole organization and the interrelationships of its parts. The major implication of the systems approach is that an organization must be examined as a whole, including its parts or "subsystems," and as a part of the environment around it. For example, a public university is a system with subsystems (colleges of business, arts, engineering, etc.) and is part of a state system including other public universities in the state.

System Components.   Regardless of size, purpose, or makeup, a system, whether biological, such as the human body, or social, such as a business organization, has four major components: *inputs, transformation processor, outputs, and feedback.* Figure 2–1 shows the relationship of these components to each other and the organization as it might apply to a bank.

Open Systems.   The basic difference between an open system and a closed system is that the open system affects and is affected by its environment. The closed system tries to operate as a self-contained unit with little regard for its environment. Note in Figure 2–1 some examples of external forces that affect the internal operations of a bank.

Using the systems approach, the organization is an open system, or

Figure 2–1. Simple bank system and its components.

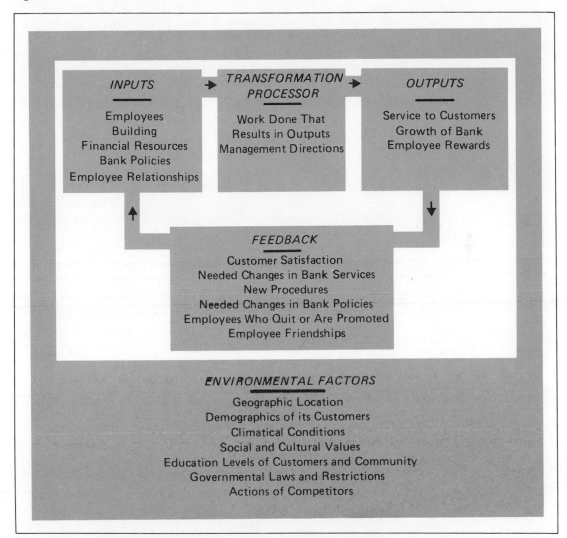

a "living" entity which takes energy from its environment, processes it, and returns outputs to the environment. In other words, it is a "transformation system" which changes inputs into outputs.

It is important to realize that as an open system, the organization is continually dependent upon inputs from the environment. Too much managerial concern with the internal aspects of an organization, such as coordination, control, or job design, ignores the system's relation to its environment. This nearsightedness may be fatal to the existence of the organization. For example, a bank that does not consider a free checking account plan offered by another bank may lose customers.

The most important argument for an open systems approach to studying organizations is the increasingly complicated and unstable environment in which most organizations exist. For example, the passage of laws on equal employment opportunities (EEO) and occupational safety and health (OSHA) has had significant impact on the selection and promotion of employees and working conditions in many organizations. With the rapid growth of technology, geographical expansions into foreign countries, and rapid social and political change, organizations and their personnel activities are constantly pressured to adjust to changing environments.

Why view an organization as an open system?

ORGANIZATIONAL SUBSYSTEMS

One way to view an organization is to see it as a system composed of interrelated parts or *subsystems* in which everything interacts with everything else. Figure 2–2 shows three interacting characteristics of an organization. The interrelated nature of the three components, indicated

Figure 2–2.   Organizational Subsystems.

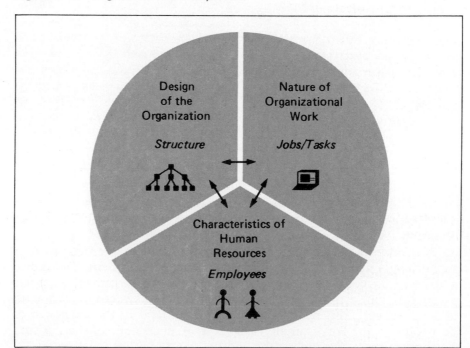

by the arrows, reflects the fact that change in one of the variables can result in a change in any or all of the others. The characteristics of the people who are employed in an organization, for example, depend on the nature of the work and the design of the organization. In turn, the characteristics of the people affect each of the other components as well.

This model emphasizes that an organization is a dynamically linked whole, not just a collection of parts. A manager can change any of the variables but must realize that all components are interrelated. For this reason, changes in one part *will probably affect* the other parts.

As adjustments in the nature of the work are made, other portions of the organization may need to be restructured or redesigned. Consider the payroll department of Coastal Petroleum Company when a computer was introduced to process payroll. First, people had to be trained. New specialists were hired, which resulted in new social groupings—new carpools, lunch groups, and so on. New facilities were needed to accommodate more equipment. In addition, the department was reorganized and a new layer of management was needed. The design which worked well with 25 bookkeepers simply did not work well with the new computer staff.

The subsystem focusing on characteristics of human resources is examined in chapter 3. The other two subsystems are discussed below.

Nature of Organizational Work

The work done by an organization includes such factors as: work schedules followed; materials and equipment used; and work layout and work flow. The nature of the work to be done helps determine the *technology* to be used. Technology can affect the shape and complexity of an organization. The technology needed to package a deodorant spray is different than the technology required to manufacture color televisions. More time, money, parts, and machines are needed to make a color television. Changes in tasks or products may require considerable expenditures to change the technology used. However, refusal to keep up with technological changes may hurt the success of an entire organization. The plight of the U.S. steel industry, with its many obsolete or old factories, illustrates the importance of keeping up with technological advances.

Work Schedules. Working arrangements are a part of technology as defined here. One area of working arrangements that has been in transition is the traditional eight-hour, five-day week work schedule. Organizations have been experimenting with a great many different possibilities for changing work schedules: the four-day, 40-hour week; the four-day, 32-hour week; the three-day work week; and flexible scheduling. Changes of this nature require some major adjustments for organizations.

✗ FLEX-TIME refers to starting and quitting time variations but assumes that a constant number of hours (usually eight) are worked each day.

Basically, flex-time requires each person to work the same number of hours. However, the traditional eight-hour work shift is lengthened by the addition of one or more hours at the beginning and end of the normal work day. This total span of possible work hours is labeled *bandwidth time.*

As shown in Figure 2–3, these hours include a *core time* when all employees must be present. Bandwidth and core times can be adjusted to fit the particular needs of an individual employer or operation.

Figure 2–3.   Flex-time illustrated.

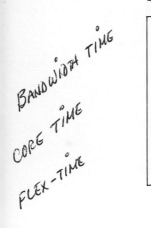

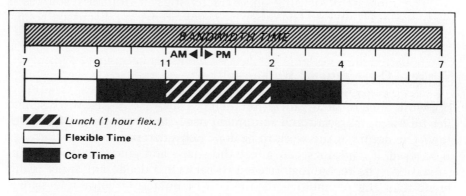

Flex-time allows management to relax some of the traditional "time clock" control of personnel. The system, which has grown in the United States, has been applied in heavy industry, department stores, banks, insurance companies, and a wide variety of other businesses. Although the flex-time system has been confined mainly to white-collar workers (clerical jobs) within these organizations, it has also been successfully applied to manual production work.

One organization that has made effective use of flex-time is the Social Security Administration (SSA), a part of the U.S. Government. Some interesting results two years after implementation are:

- At least 70% of the employees liked flex-time better than the traditional work schedule.

- 90% of the employees liked helping to decide their work hours.
- 80% of the employees were able to have better child-care arrangements.
- Annual leave usage and tardiness were generally decreased.
- As measured in a variety of ways, productivity of employees rose.[1]

Productivity Management.   One of the hottest issues during the mid-1980s is increasing the productivity of U.S. organizations. A number of new work design concepts are being tried as part of productivity management programs.

Quality Circles (QC) and *work teams* are two strategies that have been used. QCs are small groups of employees that meet on a regular basis to discuss ways to improve productivity and to cut costs. Where QCs have been used workers often receive a part of their savings and output increases as productivity bonuses. Northrop Corporation, a manufacturer of aircraft and defense-related items, has set up QCs in production and office areas.[2] Many other firms have also made use of similar programs, including Nucor Steel, Nashua Corporation, and International Harvester.

Modern organizations are so complex that it is not surprising that their employees often see only their own small organizational segment. Employee responsibilities may be so demanding that they give little attention to the organizational system as a whole. This "worm's-eye" view rather than a systems perspective may keep employees from performing in keeping with the system's best interest.

Japanese organizations try to provide this system orientation to their employees. Sharp of America's plant in Memphis assembles color televisions for the Japanese organization. All new employees complete an 18-hour course covering such topics as "Sharp Philosophy and History" and "Employee Cooperation."

Computerization.   Another common work-based technological change is the introduction or conversion to computerization. Many organizations have had to computerize their operations to remain competitive. Bringing the computer into an organization may be a great trauma for the people who will be affected by the technological change. Many companies have handled changes of this nature very well with a minimum of disruption, but others have had miserable experiences with such changes. The difference is in the way the innovation was planned and implemented.

Work changes also require both specialized human resources, which result in the need for more organization, and more planning. The overall result is the increased need for organizations to do what individuals alone cannot do; thus organizations grow and require the redesign of their structures.

What are some issues affecting the nature of work?

Design of the Organization

ORGANIZATION DESIGN results in a structure for the organization.

Structure serves the same purpose as the skeleton does for the human body: to hold it together to function well. Just as the human skeleton has various bones, an organization is composed of structural units, such as divisions and departments.

Structural Growth. All organizations have structure. The growth of an organization's structure generally begins when a very small organization adds more people. Suppose an individual has an idea: stores carrying merchandise selling for 5¢ and 10¢. The stores are enthusiastically received and the entrepreneur must eventually move to a larger building, hire more employees, and open new stores. Soon the founder becomes overburdened because it is impossible for one person to direct effectively all of the stores. The entrepreneur must get organized! Figure 2–4 contains a brief story of such an entrepreneur—Frank W. Woolworth. Eventually conditions may be such that more managers must be hired to manage the additional stores. Thus, some sort of division of duties begins.

Figure 2–4.

F.W. WOOLWORTH CO.

Frank W. Woolworth, founder of the world's most famous five-and-ten-cent stores, once indicated that the turning point in his career came when he suffered a breakdown that confined him to a hospital. "Before that," he said, "although I had several stores, I felt it was up to me to do everything myself. I was sure that there was nothing I couldn't do better than any of my employees—even dressing windows and opening boxes of merchandise. During my long absence, I found things had gone along quite well. After that, I changed my tactics. I let others attend to the ordinary running of the business and devoted myself to working out plans for expansion—and we made much greater progress.

(Source: Forbes, February 6, 1978, p. 95.)

Organizations "coordinate" the efforts of human resources by placing some direction on people's behaviors. Whenever two or more people get together—for any purpose—there must be someone "in charge." Thus, the foundation of an organizational structure based upon formal authority is laid.

What is organization design?

Authority

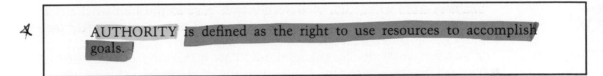

4   AUTHORITY is defined as the right to use resources to accomplish goals.

Authority can be derived in two ways: through *formal* designation or through *informal* designation. Formal authority exists originally in the governing body of an organization. For example, if the organization is a corporation, ultimately the stockholders hold formal authority for making decisions. However, this formal authority is delegated to the board of directors and to the president, who then delegates some of this authority to various vice-presidents, who in turn delegate authority to operating managers, and so on. Figure 2–5 illustrates a variety of organizational authority structures.

LEADERSHIP
1.- FORMAL
2.- INFORMAL

Figure 2–5.   Organizational hierarchies.

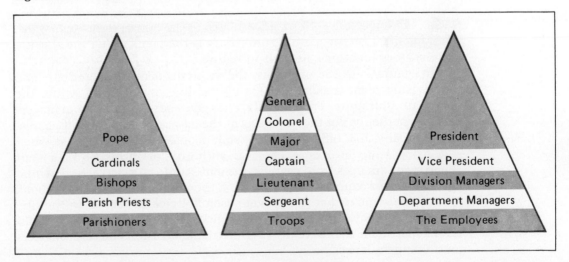

Formal Authority.   A manager attains formal authority by accepting a position as a manager. Unquestionably, when Carolyn Carter agrees to become manager of the accounting department, she acquires the right to direct it. It is even possible under certain circumstances for her to fire anyone who will not accept her formal authority. Although this action seems rather harsh, it may be a weak alternative in many situations. Even in military organizations where absolute authority and right to command have traditionally been a basis for issuing orders, there is a growing recognition that formal authority and commands are not the only way to guide people.

Informal Authority.   Informal authority is a concept often used along with formal authority in describing leadership. Instead of having a formally designated position, an "authority figure" emerges from the group or is given authority by subordinates. This dimension of authority is explored in some depth in chapter 3 in the discussion on leadership.

Line and Staff

A distinction can be made between two types of formal authority. The traditional distinction between *line* and *staff* refers not only to differences in formal authority, but to differences in types of work as well.

Line.   Line authority is usually described as the right of a manager to demand accountability from subordinates for their performance. It includes the right to command subordinates. The line is generally considered to be the operating branch of the organization or that portion directly concerned with producing the product or service.

Staff.   Staff authority commonly refers to an advisory or supportive relationship. The line part of a university is the faculty, and the athletic and business functions are staff in nature.

In Figure 2–6, the president, the vice-president of operations, and the division plant managers make up the line organization, while the others are staff units. Traditionally, staff gives advice, but line managers decide whether or not they will accept the advice offered by staff people.

Typically, line officials consult staff people for their expertise when a decision is to be made. The real authority or influence of a staff department emerges from that department's ability to make worthwhile and significant contributions to solving the problems facing line people. A staff department that can provide useful advice or service to the line departments may soon do more than just advise. For example, a staff legal department may actually begin to make decisions on legal matters for a company president.

Figure 2–6. Line and staff authority on an organizational chart.

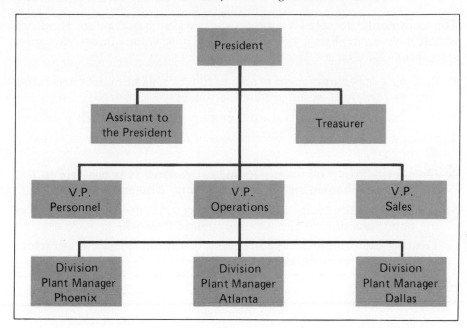

How are line and staff authority different?

ORGANIZATION DEVELOPMENT AND CHANGE

Even in the absence of rapid organizational change, a program to improve effectiveness or change attitudes and values may be necessary. A collection of ideas and techniques has emerged called Organization Development (OD) which can help organizations deal with changes. OD attempts to help organizations better understand current and potential problems and provides alternative methods of solving them.

> ORGANIZATION DEVELOPMENT is a value-based process of self-assessment and planned change, involving specific strategies and technology, aimed at improving the overall effectiveness of an organizational system.[3]

Value-Based

The commonly accepted view of OD as value-based refers to efforts which have an explicitly humanistic bias. The values underlying most attempted OD changes are:

1. Providing opportunities for people to function as human beings rather than as resources in the productive process;
2. Providing opportunities for each employee to develop full potential;
3. Seeking to increase the effectiveness of the organization in terms of all its goals;
4. Attempting to create an environment in which it is possible to find exciting and challenging work;
5. Providing opportunities for employees to influence the organization, the environment, and the way they relate to work;
6. Treating each employee as a person with complex needs, all of which are important at work and in life.[4]

Can you define OD?

Approaches to Organization Development

Improvements in the effectiveness of the organization can be made by changing people, or through technology, as shown by Figure 2–7. For

Figure 2–7. Organization Development model.

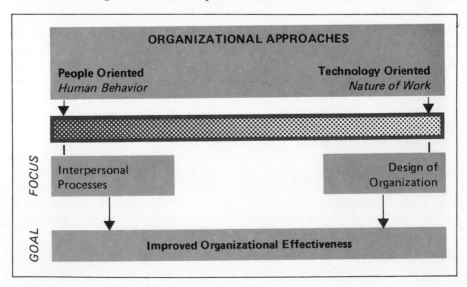

example, in the Bennett Supply Company, the productivity of the work force has been low, costs have been rising, and the absence and turnover rates are rising. Mr. Bennett is trying to decide how to reverse these trends and help the organization work better. He might appropriately begin with *action research*, an attempt to gather information on problems and make appropriate changes. He can either do this research himself or hire a consultant to help him. After changes are carefully planned, the effects on the variables under consideration can be monitored.

From this research Mr. Bennett might try to make changes in the interpersonal *processes* of his firm. Actions to build more team spirit and to develop a climate where employees can express their feelings more openly and honestly might be taken.

Or, Mr. Bennett might want to change *technology* by bringing in a new means of performing jobs in the company. He might also change *structure* variables by adding another level of management to the hierarchy. All these "targets" for OD intervention or change are legitimate. The ones appropriate for Bennett Supply depend on that firm's particular situation and management's assessment of it.

People Approaches

OD techniques can include several types of intervention. The *survey feedback method* is a process in which data are systematically collected (usually by analysis of questionnaires from members of the organization), summarized, and the results are fed back to employees.

Team building (group development) means developing a good working relationship among group members. Techniques such as T-group or laboratory training are useful in team building.

Intergroup development attempts to solve problems of contact between groups in an organization. For example, intergroup development might focus on minimizing or resolving conflicts between departments. These approaches (survey feedback, team building, and intergroup development) can have a number of positive effects on the attitudes of those involved.

Technological Approaches

Organization Development may focus on changes in the nature of work and the design of the organization, or both. In this case, the OD approaches are deeply rooted in engineering, sociology, psychology, and economics.

One *technological approach* would be exploring the possibilities of job redesign. Organizational design changes include removing levels of the management hierarchy and giving lower units in the organization more opportunity for self-direction. Creating new authority and responsibility patterns are other design change possibilities.

What are two general approaches to OD?

Successful changes, especially those concerned with personnel administration in an organization, do not simply happen—they are carefully planned. Planning for change requires an understanding of why people resist change.

 Resistance to Change in Work Organizations

Employees resist change in many ways. Wildcat strikes, quarrelling between employees and supervisors, requests for transfers, absenteeism, frequent job changes, and reduction in output are all ways employees can resist change.

Most people have a need to maintain stability with their environments. When a person's stability is threatened by changes, a number of concerns can cause resistance.

Economic Loss. Employees who are concerned about possible changes in income are prone to resist change. For example, the employees of a clock manufacturer feared they would lose their jobs if the company changed to manufacturing electronic clocks instead of mechanical clocks.

Status Loss. Another fear is that a change will detract in some way from an employee's status. For example, if a change meant a new job but a smaller office, a manager might resist because he or she viewed the smaller office as a loss of status or importance.

Uncertainty. Resistance may be caused by a fear of uncertainty. Employees may be unwilling to learn something new because they are uncertain they will be able to do the required operations. A cashier at a supermarket resisted the change to an electronic cash register because he feared he would not be able to operate the new register rapidly and accurately.

Inconvenience. Another cause of resistance to change is inconvenience. All people develop habits which provide security in a day-to-day existence. When they are thrown into a new situation, the old habits and old ways of operating may no longer apply. New patterns of behavior may have to be developed.

Interpersonal Disruptions. A final cause for resistance to change is a perceived threat to interpersonal relationships. When a change means becoming part of a new work group or being separated from close friends in the existing work group, a person is likely to balk. For this reason a person may hesitate at being transferred to a new job, even though it would mean a promotion and a raise. The disruption of old friendships and the effort involved in establishing new ones may cause resistance.

What are some reasons why people resist changes?

Positive Aspects of Resistance to Change. Resistance to change is not *necessarily* bad. Obviously, too much resistance to change can be disruptive for the organization and can even lead to extreme acts such as sabotage or efforts to disrupt production. However, managers can make a mistake by assuming that because people resist change, they must always be *forcing* change upon people. This is not necessarily the case.

Too much resistance to change is an indication that something is wrong in the way the change is being introduced, just as fever indicates infection in the human body. Likewise, a complete lack of resistance to change may indicate that employees are so afraid to oppose change that they are unwilling to express their concerns and an unfavorable organizational climate.

Strategies for Reducing Resistance to Change. If, despite good planning and consideration of the human and social factors involved, resistance still appears likely, what can a manager do to handle such resistance to change? Several strategies are available.

One possibility is to make change tentative, that is, on a *trial* basis at first. This approach is especially appropriate if the employees have had an opportunity to participate in the decision-making process. If the employees have not participated in the decision, resistance may be greater. Careful *two-way communication* can help reduce resistance. Many times resistance is based on a lack of understanding, and if managers will really listen to employees' suggestions, problems can be reduced.

Another possibility is to provide an *economic guarantee* to employees. If an employee refuses to move to a new job, a guaranteed reimbursement for all relevant costs could be offered. It is quite common in union contracts for management to guarantee that no union member will suffer economic loss as a result of technological change. Although guarantees are extremely useful in removing such opposition, they can also be expensive. However, when the cause of resistance to change is economic in nature, a manager should consider some type of economic incentive as a way to gain employee cooperation.

How can resistance to change be managed?

Assessment of OD

As a field of study, OD has made both academicians and practitioners aware of the need for planned change. However, much more research is needed for OD to become the systematic body of knowledge OD practitioners would like it to be. Therefore, OD should be seen as a very useful strategy for changing organizations, provided that change is systematic and many organizational units and members are involved. Continued research on OD may reveal new and more precise means for effectively changing organizations. Also, OD emphasizes that understanding the nature of the subsystems of an organization is basic to analyzing the operation of the entire organization.

PERSONNEL'S ROLE IN ORGANIZATIONS

Personnel management is often considered a staff function. As a functional part of the organization, personnel activities are localized into one department. In Figure 2–6, note that personnel is a separate specialized department. However, the authors of this text feel that personnel management is a set of activities which cannot be neatly segmented into one department.

Even though the personnel department has normally been considered a staff department, the distinction is becoming more clouded. In some organizations certain duties, often considered line in nature, have been delegated to the personnel department. For example, hiring management trainees to work in the line organization could be considered a line activity because the success of hiring directly affects future operations. However, hiring is very often done by the personnel department. This delegation of some line authority to a staff department is neither unusual nor a problem as long as both sides agree on who is to do what, as emphasized in the first chapter. However, line managers and personnel specialists have not always agreed on exactly what the role of the personnel specialists should be.

Personnel in Organizations: Historical Perspective

Personnel as the managing of people in organizations is as old as mankind. Minimum wages have been around since at least 1800 B.C. Division of labor, span of control, hierarchy, and incentive plans have been viable nearly as long.

But personnel management as a specialized area in organizations really began its growth at the beginning of the 20th century. Prior to that time most hiring, firing, training, and pay adjustment decisions were made by first line supervisors. Early personnel departments were primarily clerical in nature. Such exciting work as payroll and retirement records, stockholder visits, school relations, and the company picnic were often the major tasks of the personnel departments. It was often referred to as "the garbage can function," and was staffed accordingly.

With the growth in importance of collective bargaining because of unions in the 1940s and 1950s and the social legislation of the 1960s and 1970s, that attitude was changed in many organizations. A great many pieces of legislation now directly affect any organization employing people. As a result of the large fines and other penalties that can be levied, personnel departments are becoming much more professional.

Personnel and Line Managers' Views

In one study,[5] a group of personnel executives and a group of line managers from different organizations were asked to rank the importance of a list of activities the personnel department could perform in their organizations. The results are interesting. As Figure 2–8 shows, there is considerable disagreement between the personnel executives and line managers on the involvement of the personnel department in certain activities. Of the most important activities ranked by personnel executives, line managers did not include five (layoffs, vacations, transfers, job analysis, and recreation/social) in the top 15. On the other hand, some activities the line managers thought were important did not make the top 15 for the personnel directors: orientation, pay structure design, wage surveys, performance appraisals, and training and development.

From this study, it is clear that the "proper" role of personnel has not been agreed upon. Further, it is inappropriate to say that all management people want the personnel unit to perform a given activity. The division of personnel activities obviously depends upon which specific activities are included in the personnel specialists' domain.

As pointed out in the first chapter, the degree of each activity performed by specialists varies from company to company. A study such as the one reported here can be done easily in any organization to determine what personnel specialists and other managers think the ideal division of duties should be. To compound the difficulty in identifying "the proper role" of personnel, consider the wide variety of organizational settings in which personnel activities occur.

Figure 2–8. Ranking of personnel's roles.

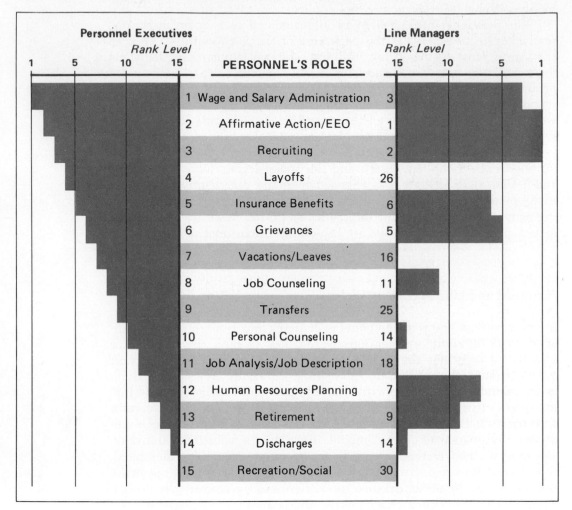

(Source: H. C. White and M. N. Wolfe, "The Role Desired for Personnel Administration," *Personnel Administrator*, June 1980, p. 90–91.)

Where does personnel "fit" in the organization?

PERSONNEL IN VARIED ORGANIZATIONAL ENVIRONMENTS

Personnel activities are managed in a wide range of organizations facing widely varied environments. Personnel management in three environments has grown in importance: *public organizations, matrix organizations,* and *international environments.* These three illustrate the expanding nature of personnel in organizations today. Growth in each of these areas creates special problems and challenges.

Personnel in Public Organizations

Even though a slightly different environment exists in the public sector, personnel activities must be managed if effective utilization of human resources is to occur. Building on the U.S. Civil Service System, established in the 1880s to reduce patronage and favoritism in the selection of governmental employees, many state and local governmental bodies have established "merit systems" and formal personnel policies and procedures.

Civil Service Reform Act of 1978.   To make the U.S. Federal Government operate more efficiently, the Civil Service Reform Act was passed in 1978. The Act eliminated the Civil Service Commission and replaced it with the Office of Personnel Management (OPM) and the Merit Systems Protection Board (MSPB).

Several major revisions brought the Federal personnel system closer to practices prominent in the private sector. For example, government executives have an opportunity to earn *pay bonuses* for outstanding work. Under the old system, standard pay raises were almost automatically granted to all employees. Also, ineffective performers in the upper levels can now be demoted more easily. An improved system of appraising employee performance, coupled with a less cumbersome appeals process, allows greater flexibility in removing poor performers. Unions representing federal workers gained additional rights too.

Public Personnel Challenges.   Increasingly in the 1980s complaints are being voiced about governmental personnel systems at all levels. The rules and regulations developed to protect state and local governmental employees are being criticized for preventing flexibility in the management of public organizations. Personnel professionals in public organizations must be able to translate their expertise into creative solutions to a number of problems faced by public agencies. Likewise, other managers in public organizations need to recognize the importance of effective personnel administration on the success of their agencies. The manager of a group of welfare claims clerks might use the expertise of personnel specialists to increase effectiveness in the claims office and thereby provide better service to welfare claimants and taxpayers alike.

Those personnel specialists who will be dealing with these challenges are not significantly different from private personnel directors. A study of the characteristics of public personnel directors in Iowa found great similarities with those in the private sector. The public sector directors tended to have more education but less experience than their private counterparts.[6]

What is personnel's role in public organizations?

Personnel in Matrix Organizations

A new, nontraditional form of organization, the *matrix organization*, offers a different environment for personnel management. In a matrix organization two organization structures exist at the same time—a conventional functional organization and a "project team"-oriented organization. The result of the overlay of the project teams on the conventional structure is a grid or "matrix." The project teams are created and dissolved as the situation demands. People may join a project team for a certain project, retain their position in the conventional organization, and return full time to it when the project is completed. A project manager is in charge of the team which draws expertise from wherever he/she finds it in the organization.

Starting in the defense and aerospace industries, the matrix organization form has spread to many other areas. Industrial firms using a matrix format in some or all areas of operation include Dow Corning, TRW Systems, General Electric, Equitable Life Insurance, Shell Oil, and Citicorp.[7] Nonindustrial users include CPA firms, hospitals, real estate development companies, law firms, and various governmental agencies.[8]

The ultimate result of the matrix format is that a functional personnel specialist may report to two bosses—the director of the personnel function and the project manager. The personnel specialist is responsible for coordination of all personnel activities performed on the project. As is evident, the potential for conflict is heightened, especially if the director of personnel and the project manager disagree on how a personnel activity is to be managed. The personnel specialist may be left in the middle of such a conflict. Recognition that conflict is possible makes it especially important to manage the organizational interface between the functional manager and the project manager so that needed personnel activities are performed on the project, but in a manner that considers the personnel requirements of the entire organization.

U.S. Personnel Goes International

More personnel specialists and operating managers in the 1980s may manage in many countries outside the United States. The growth of the American-based multinational corporation (MNC) typifies the importance of viewing an organization as a system affected by environmental factors such as culture, language, climate, politics, and social upheavals. The importance of international awareness is illustrated when one considers that firms such as Gillette obtain a large percentage of their sales and profits overseas.

The character of personnel activities varies significantly according to the location of the company. Some countries, such as Zambia and Japan, expect top management positions to be filled by executives from their countries. Other countries have requirements on the percentage of jobs which may be filled by foreigners. U.S. citizens who transfer to Saudi Arabia, for example, must adjust to cultural and religious codes on the role of women, the prohibition of liquor, and many other factors.

These and other problems lead a growing number of people to turn down overseas jobs. As the number of working spouses increases, overseas transfers often mean income losses. As a result, companies must offer rich perquisites. Alcoa pays a 20% salary bonus on top of other foreign expenses and Westinghouse subsidizes rent and education expenses. Chicago's Continental Illinois National Bank pays a bonus in Beirut because of shooting.

Multinational corporations face many problems in sending employees abroad. One major concern is the cost of making a mistake. It has been estimated that it costs $16,000 to $20,000 to place a person overseas, and another $10,000 to bring that person home if he or she quits prematurely.[9]

One study of multinational staffing policies revealed that a variety of other problems exist. Some of the personnel problems identified include: (1) blocking of promotions by reserving certain slots for host-country nationals, (2) anxiety caused by transfers and adjusting to a different setting, (3) using inappropriate decision-making styles which do not fit cultural norms.[10] There are three other major problems: selection, compensation, and return (or repatriation) of the expatriate employee.

An EXPATRIATE is an employee transferred out of his or her native country.

Selection. Many companies have the misguided notion that a good domestic employee will make a good expatriate. This idea has cost companies many thousands of dollars in mistakes. One study of expatriate failure found poor selection as the cause in 80% of the cases.[11]

The procedure for avoiding failure is a multi-step process. First, a comprehensive description of the job to be done should be prepared. Responsibilities that would be unusual in the home nation should be noted, such as: dealing with public officials; handling local work codes; responding to ethics, morals, and personal issues such as religious prohibitions and personal freedoms.

Next, recognition of the limitations of interviewing as a means of valid selection is important. In the selection interview an interviewer may try to evaluate the level of:

- empathy
- self-awareness
- role differentiation
- dogmatism
- tolerance for ambiguity
- respect for equality
- nonverbal communication skills
- self-esteem.

These personality items have been related to success in adapting to alien cultures, but are not easily measured in an interview.

The goal of selection should be to provide a real picture of the life, work, and culture to which the expatriate is considering going. Cross-cultural orientation programs can be useful for both the expatriate and the spouse and family. The U.S. State Department can help acquaint the family with the social, economic, and political conditions.

Another obvious and related problem is the promotion and transfer of foreign citizens to positions in the United States. Special training to ease the adjustment of foreign managers and their families may be required. The acceptance of a foreign boss by a U.S. worker is another concern.

Compensation.   Compensation can be a significant problem also, especially if overseas living costs are significantly higher than those in the United States. For example, the cost of living in Tokyo is much above comparable costs in most U.S. cities. A decision must be made as to how to adjust a person's salary to compensate. Also, should a firm reduce the pay of someone who is transferred from overseas to the United States or Canada?

Many organizations feel a detailed understanding between the organization and expatriate is critical for success. This agreement specifies all compensation issues and is signed by both parties. A listing of the issues that should be included is shown in Figure 2–9.

The income tax laws for a U.S. citizen living abroad must be a compensation consideration. A 1981 tax law removed some penalties that were previously in existence. Effective in 1982, a U.S. citizen can exclude the first $75,000 earned abroad from U.S. income taxes, and the exclusion rises to $95,000 in 1986. Also, U.S. expatriates can reduce their U.S. tax bill by deducting foreign income taxes up to the maximum

Figure 2–9. Items for an expatriate compensation agreement.

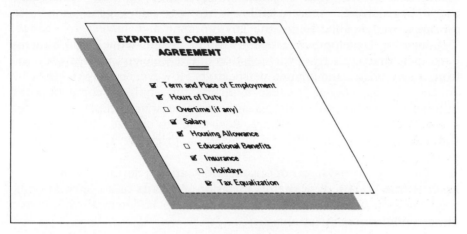

U.S. rate of 50%. Tax laws for expatriates are often complex and subject to revision.[12]

Repatriation. Another major difficulty can arise when it is time to bring expatriates home. While they have been away, many changes may have occurred. At Economic Laboratory (a cleaning products firm) overseas work can mean "out of sight, out of mind," and G.D. Searle and Company admits it has trouble finding jobs for returning overseas workers. Studies have shown that returning employees face anxiety in three areas: (1) personal finances, (2) reacclimatization to U.S. life style, and (3) readjustment to the company.[13]

Most of the benefits enjoyed overseas (special bonuses and allowances) are taken away when the expatriate returns. Many companies give special aid in relocating to help ease the strain on family budgets. Psychological counseling has been used to help readjustment to both the culture and the company.

Personnel activities must be changed to deal with the demands of an international organization. As more and more firms engage in cross-national trade, managing personnel activities in an intercultural environment will be of increasing importance.

Can you discuss personnel in the international environment?

REVIEW AND PREVIEW

In this chapter, the organization has been described as a vehicle for accomplishing cooperative human efforts. Basic ideas for managing organizations have evolved and many of these ideas are still widely used today. Currently the most useful way to view each organization is as an open system affected by the environment and subject to change. Organization Development is a body of knowledge, values, and humanistic goals that approaches the question of effectiveness in organizations from a systematic and applied perspective. However, managers must be concerned with change because it ultimately requires people to work differently than before. For this and other reasons, people may react strongly and negatively to change. Resistance to change can be reduced through good planning efforts and, where appropriate, through Organization Development.

Two major subsystems of organizations are: (1) nature of work (technology), and (2) design of the organization. As parts of an open system, their components are interrelated and basic to understanding the role of personnel in organizations.

Questions about the nature of the work to be done and the nature of the authority to be given to the personnel unit are often raised. Personnel is usually described as a staff department, but there is little agreement between line managers and personnel managers as to exactly what activities should be directed by the personnel department.

Personnel management exists in several varied environments that affect the way its activities are managed. Especially important in the 1980s is the practice of personnel management in international environments.

Because the nature and characteristics of human resources form another organizational subsystem, every manager needs some basic understanding of human behavior. Motivation, leadership, group behavior, and communications are the basics of human behavior discussed in the next chapter.

Review Questions

1. What is an organization? Why must organizations be viewed as open systems?

2. Discuss the following statement: "The nature of work will change significantly between now and 1990."

3. What is authority? What are the concepts of line and staff? How do these ideas relate to personnel management?

4. Suppose you are a management consultant called in to assist in an Organization Development effort. What approaches would you use?

5. Why does resistance to change occur and how would you attempt to manage it?

6. Why should personnel be seen as an organizational interface? How does this view help understand personnel's role in public and matrix organizations?

7. Personnel management in international settings is increasingly important to U.S. firms. What are some issues?

Case: Credit Service Company

Harold Stanley started Credit Service Company about three years ago. The company is a data processing service bureau that primarily handles charge account billings, charge card production, and credit record processing. The firm started small but has now grown to 75 employees. Harold has done all the recruiting and selection since the firm began. Most of the personnel activities had been handled on a very informal and haphazard basis by Mr. Stanley or the supervisors. Because of the time pressures and the many other demands on him, Harold hired Vic O'Donnell, a recent college graduate, as the firm's first personnel manager.

Vic was determined to set up a true personnel department. Since the firm has grown rapidly, Vic could see that the firm would probably have to add 75 to 100 more employees over the next two years to keep up with the projected sales increase. Within a short period of time Vic had redesigned the application blank and had established a personnel file for each employee. He discovered that the firm had many women employees but no female supervisors. Also, there was a noticeable lack of employees from racial minorities. Therefore, Vic developed a detailed plan to head off potential equal employment problems. He also developed a revised selection procedure in which he did most of the selection interviewing.

Mr. Stanley voiced support for Vic's selection efforts. However, he was very adamant that he wanted to be able to have the final say over any new employee hired. Also, Mr. Stanley voiced strong feelings about the government telling him who he could hire or not hire. As he said, "I'll hire whoever I damn well please." Vic was quite concerned by this reaction, since it looked as if he was not going to be given the flexibility he needed to do what he felt should be done.

QUESTIONS

1. Discuss why it is important to look at Credit Service Company as an open system.
2. Identify the authority and structural problems that exist.
3. If you were Vic, how would you proceed in trying to implement your plans?

NOTES

1. Cary B. Barad, "Flexitime Under Scrutiny: Research on Work Adjustment and Organizational Performance," *Personnel Administrator*, May 1980, pp. 69–74.

2. Earl C. Gottschalk, Jr., "U.S. Firms, Worried by Productivity Lag, Copy Japan in Seeking Employees' Advice," *Wall Street Journal*, February 21, 1980, p. 40.

3. This definition is taken from Newton Margulies and Anthony P. Raia, *Conceptual Foundations of Organizational Development*, (New York: McGraw-Hill, 1978), p.24.

4. Newton Marguiles and A. P. Raia, *Organization Development: Values Process and Technology* (New YOrk: McGrqw-Hill, 1972), p.3.

5. H. C. White and M. N. Wolfe, "The Role Desired for Personnel Administration," *Personnel Administrator*, June 1980, pp. 90–91.

6. Myron D. Fottler and Norman A. Townsend, "Characteristics of Public and Private Personnel Directors," *Public Personnel Management*, July-August 1977, pp. 250–258.

7. "How to Stop the Buck Short of the Top," *Business Week*, January 16, 1978, pp. 82–83.

8. Stanley M. Davis and Paul R. Lawrence, *Matrix* (Reading, MA: Addison-Wesley, 1977).

9. "International Employment is a World Apart," *PMA News*, February 1981, p. 3.

10. Yoram Zeira and Ehud Harari, "Genuine Multinational Staffing Policy: Expectations and Realities," *Academy of Management Journal*, June 1977, pp. 327–333.

11. W. Holmes and F. Piker, "Expatriate Failure—Prevention Rather than a Cure," *Personnel Management*, December 1980, pp. 30–32.

12. "A Cut in the Cost of Expatriate Workers," *Business Week*, August 31, 1981, p.87.

13. L. Clague and N. B. Krupp, "International Personnel: The Repatriation Problem," *The Personnel Administrator*, April 1978, pp. 29–33.

CHAPTER 3

Human Behavior and Personnel

When you have read this chapter, you should be able to:

1. Define motivation and discuss several problems involved in defining and learning about motivation.

2. Identify and discuss four ideas about why people behave as they do.

3. Identify and compare the three major leadership approaches.

4. Define what a work group is and discuss at least four characteristics of groups.

5. List three barriers to successful communication.

Shifting Stan

Stan Wharton had been a member of the loading dock crew for 15 years. His performance had always been above average, but he had never wanted to move to another job although the opportunities had been offered to him. Last year, Stan got married for the first time. He has shown some behavior changes that have puzzled his supervisor.

Stan no longer seems to be part of the work group as he once was. In fact, for many years he was the informal leader and the member to whom the favor of the group seemed most important. Now he doesn't even eat lunch with them. He leaves the plant at lunch to go home to his new child and wife. His work is still good, however.

Stan has just asked to be considered for the next supervisory slot available, which was a great surprise after 15 years of refusing to change jobs. His supervisor isn't sure whether to recommend him or not based upon his seeming distance from the work group.

Comments:

Stan Wharton typifies that motivation is a force in the individual that must be adjusted to by a manager. Stan's marriage would be one significant factor to consider when attempting to identify why he has changed his behavior. Instead of looking primarily to the work group for interpersonal satisfaction, he appears to have a greater orientation to off-the-job interpersonal satisfaction. The new family responsibilities and attendant financial consideration might be one reason for his desire to become a supervisor. Also, his wife may be "pushing" him to assume a higher level job. This case emphasizes the impact of human behavior on personnel management.

Many different perspectives are available for studying people at work, ranging from the academician's research on people and their work problems to the practitioner's "practical" approach to solving such problems. Although the difference between these two approaches can be great, advocates of each agree that a basic understanding of organizational behavior (the behavior of people in work organizations) is a very important part of personnel management. For example, how can you design compensation systems, or predict the effect of incentives if you do not study motivation? How can managers consider management development activities designed to improve leadership ability if they do not understand leadership? How can you deal with work restriction from group members or job design if you have no understanding of group dynamics? How can a manager deal with rumors, formal company communication programs, and interviewing without a knowledge of the basics of communication?

The purpose of this chapter is not to provide the reader with a detailed examination of human behavior—that is best left for a course on organizational behavior. Rather, some key considerations in viewing personnel from a behavioral vantage point are highlighted. Interpreting and using research insights on human behavior are essential for effective human resource management. The areas of human behavior emphasized here are the concepts of *motivation, leadership, group behavior,* and *communication.*

MOTIVATION

Motivation is concerned with the "whys" rather than the "hows" or "whats" of human behavior. Motivation attempts to account for the "drives" or "wants" inside an individual rather than describing the individual's actions or behavior.

What is Motivation?

> MOTIVATION is derived from the word *motive* and is an emotion or desire operating on a person's will and causing that person to act.

This definition emphasizes that motivation is an action device. People usually act for one reason: to obtain a goal. Thus, motivation is a goal-directed drive and, as such, it seldom occurs in a void. The words "need," "want," "desire," and "drive" are all semantically similar to "motive."

Importance of Motivation

Most managers will agree with the statement that "The success of any organization is determined by the efforts of the people in it." And managers often say that problems relating to employee behavior are the most perplexing. Questions such as the following are often asked: "How do you get people to do what you want them to do?"; "How can one be sure that people will do their work without a supervisor constantly watching them?" Because human resources are a crucial determinant of how well an organization performs, the effective motivation of people to acceptable behavior and performance is necessary.

What is motivation?

Approaches to Understanding Motivation

It is often difficult to determine why employees behave as they do simply by observing their behavior. People's actions cannot always be directly related to their conscious or subconscious thoughts. Nor are these actions always related to obvious daily occurrences. For example, if an employee has an argument with her supervisor and fails to report to work the next day, it may appear that her behavior is a result of the confrontation. However, that behavior may be motivated by a combination of factors including overwork, family illness, or some other problems.

Multiple Causes.   Different people may have different reasons for behaving in the very same manner. For example, one manager may join a service club because it is a good place to make business contacts; another may join because of the social environment; still another joins because of the interesting programs and speakers at the club. Thus, three different "whys" can underlie the same behavior, which further complicates inferring motivation from behavior.

Multiple Behaviors.   In addition, the same motive may result in different behavior. For example, if Jan Welch wants a promotion, she may work at performing her job exceptionally well. But Bill Proust, who also wants a promotion, might take a different approach. He may try to "apple polish" the boss to get the promotion. Another manager, who also wants the promotion very badly, may be afraid to do anything at all for fear he will fail. The motivation for these three behaviors is the same, but it cannot be determined simply by viewing the behavior of the three managers.

Motivation as a Subject.   In this chapter the discussion will attempt to stay away from extremes, but it is important to understand that the subject matter is somewhat complex. Approaches to understanding motivation differ because individual theorists have attempted to develop their own views of motivation. They approach the problem from different

starting points, with different ideas in mind, and from different backgrounds. Different viewpoints include Herzberg's theory of work motivation, Maslow's approach to motivation, and Porter and Lawler's model
of motivation, among others. This variety of views does not mean that
only one approach is correct. It does mean that each has made a different
contribution to the understanding of human behavior. The perspective
taken in this text is to provide a practical view of the important approaches to motivation.

Many managerial views of motivation are based upon assumptions
about what goals people are expected to achieve as employees. For example, if a sales manager says he wants to "motivate" his employees,
he is really saying he wants his employees to select the goals that *he*
wants them to seek—goals related to what he considers proper for persons selling in his division. His employees are undoubtedly motivated
but perhaps not toward doing what he would have them do. Figure 3–1
illustrates such a manager's model of motivation. However, this view
is too restrictive a view of motivation, as will be shown.

Figure 3–1. Managerial model of motivation.

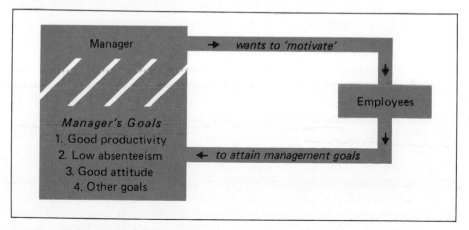

MOTIVATION AND VIEWS OF HUMAN NATURE

The study of motivation over the last century has been focused on
answering the question, *What is the basic goal of man?* Managers have
operated with their own preconceived ideas of basic human goals. Over
time, four major assumptions about human nature and the mainsprings
of motivation have emerged.[1] These assumptions have been translated
into managerial philosophies and views of employee motivation. One
of the most long-lived approaches is based on the assumption that people
are rational-economic beings.

Rational-Economic View

This idea basically suggests that humans reasonably, logically, and rationally make decisions that will result in the most economic gain for themselves. Therefore, employees are motivated by the opportunity to make as much money as possible and will act rationally in such a manner as to maximize their wages. The assumption is that *money* is the most important motivator of all people.

This explanation of human motivation is weak because a great deal of behavior does not reasonably follow from the rational-economic assumption made about human nature. For example, if employees are primarily interested in maximizing their economic return, why do some of them restrict piece-rate production and others refuse to take overtime? Obviously, the rational-economic assumptions have some limitations.

Social View

The social view of human nature suggested that all people can be motivated to perform if a manager appeals to their social needs. A predominant emphasis in the management literature became "happiness and harmony in the group leads to productivity" or "a happy worker is a productive worker."

Human Relations.   The social view of human nature brought about the *human relations approach.* Humans were viewed as a bundle of attitudes, sentiments, and emotions. Managers were told that to be effective they should use "image management" to convince workers of their importance to the company. Employee participation in the decision-making process (as long as they could not hurt anything) was supposed to lead to a feeling of harmony, loyalty, and satisfaction. Unfortunately, proponents of this view went too far in trying to explain motivation with their one variable, as earlier proponents of money as a motivator had done. Not everyone is motivated by harmony and cooperation, and many found the insincerity of the human relations approach to be repulsive.

Self-Actualizing View

During the late 1950s and early 1960s the ideas of another group of management thinkers, many of whom were trained in the behavioral sciences, became very popular. They assumed that people are beings striving to reach *self-actualization.* This concept means that a person desires to reach his or her full potential and is illustrated by the ideas of Abraham Maslow, Douglas McGregor, and Frederick Herzberg.

Abraham Maslow. A clinical psychologist, Abraham Maslow, developed a theory of human motivation which continues to receive a great deal of exposure in the management literature.[2] Maslow classified human needs into five categories. He suggested that there is a fairly definite order to human needs, and until the more basic needs are adequately fulfilled, a person will not strive to meet higher needs. Maslow's well-known hierarchy includes (1) physiological needs, (2) safety and security needs, (3) belongingness and love needs, (4) self-esteem needs, and (5) self-actualization needs.

An assumption often made by those using Maslow's hierarchy is that workers in modern industrialized society have basically satisfied their physiological, safety, and belongingness needs. Therefore, they will be motivated by the need for self-esteem and the esteem of others and by the need for self-actualization. Consequently, items to satisfy these needs should be present at work: the job itself should be internally meaningful and motivating.

Douglas McGregor. The concepts behind the self-actualization view were perhaps best expressed by Douglas McGregor, who presented two opposite sets of assumptions which he believed were basic to most managers. Summarized in Figure 3–2, one set was labeled Theory X and the other Theory Y. McGregor felt that managers typically held one of these sets of assumptions about human nature and acted in keeping with those assumptions. However, McGregor argued that people are really more like Theory Y than like Theory X. A key point in McGregor's Theory Y is that work is in and of itself a motivator.

Figure 3–2.   A summary of Theory X and Theory Y (McGregor).

Theory X	Theory Y
People dislike work and will try to avoid it.	People do not inherently dislike work.
People have to be coerced and threatened with punishment if the organization's goals are to be met.	People do not like rigid control and threats.
Most workers like direction and will avoid responsibility.	Under proper conditions, people do not avoid responsibility.
People want security above all in their work.	People want security but also have other needs such as self-actualization and esteem.

(Source: Douglas McGregor, *The Human Side of Enterprise.* New York: McGraw-Hill, 1960, pp. 33–45.)

Frederick Herzberg.   In the late 1950s Frederick Herzberg and his research associates conducted interviews with 200 engineers and accountants who worked in different companies in the Pittsburg area. The result of this research was a theory that, like Maslow's, has been widely discussed in the management literature.[3]

Herzberg's Motivation/Hygiene theory assumes that one group of factors, *motivators*, accounts for high levels of motivation to work. Another different group of factors cause discontent with work. These factors are labeled *hygiene,* or maintenance factors. The motivators are *achievement, recognition,* the *work itself, responsibility,* and *advancement.* The hygiene factors are *company policy and administration, supervision, salary, interpersonal relations,* and *working conditions.*

The implication of this research for management and personnel is that the hygienic or maintenance factors provide a base which must be carefully considered if dissatisfaction is to be avoided. But even if all these maintenance needs are taken care of, people will still not necessarily be motivated to work harder. Only those factors called motivators cause more effort to be exerted and more productivity to be attained.

Herzberg's work has been the subject of much controversy, which revolves around his research method and later attempts to replicate his findings. The controversy still continues.

The self-actualizing school of thought, with its sometimes moralistic requests to improve the job and let the individual achieve self-actualization, has given way to the recognition that everyone is somewhat different and that job situations vary. To comprehend motivation and human behavior, one must understand the interactions between individual characteristics and characteristics of the situation. The fourth approach to motivation and human behavior recognizes that people are "complex."

Complex View

The complex view basically suggests that each person is different and that a variety of items may be motivating, depending upon the *needs* of the individual, the *situation* the individual is in, and what the individual *expects* in the way of rewards for the work done. Theorists such as Victor Vroom, Lyman Porter, and E. E. Lawler do not attempt to fit people into one category but accept human differences.

Victor Vroom.   Vroom noted that people act to obtain goals.[4] But whether or not they will act at all depends on whether or not they believe their behavior will help them achieve their goal. In choosing a path to a goal, people establish preferences among various acts based upon their prediction of the outcome of each act. For example, will hard work lead to more money in the pay envelope? Some people will conclude that it does, and others will conclude that it does not, depending upon past experiences with hard work and more money.

Another critical element is how much the person wants the outcome. If Lisa Harmon does not really want a promotion, offering her a promotion that requires relocation to another city will not be highly valuable to her. To put it another way, a person's motivation depends on: (1) his or her *expectation* that a particular behavior will result in a desired outcome or goal, and (2) the *value* the person assigns to that outcome. Numerous other researchers have added to Vroom's model.

Lyman Porter and E. E. Lawler.   Porter and Lawler contend that the above relationship is expanded by including *perceived equity* as a variable influencing job behavior. Perception is the way an individual views the job. Figure 3–3 contains a simplified Porter and Lawler model.

Suppose that a male department store clerk is motivated to expend effort on his job by selling men's wear. From his job he receives two types of rewards, *intrinsic* (internal) and *extrinsic* (external). To this salesclerk, intrinsic rewards could include a feeling of accomplishment, a feeling of recognition, or other motivators (Herzberg's terminology). Extrinsic rewards might be such items as pay, benefits, good working conditions, and other hygiene factors (as Herzberg labeled them). The salesclerk compares his performance to both types of rewards he receives. This comparison is made from his perception of his performance and his rewards. He then reaches some level of satisfaction or dissatisfaction. Once this level is reached, it is difficult to determine what he will do. If he is dissatisfied, he might put forth less effort next time, or he might work harder to get the rewards he wants, or he might just accept his

Figure 3–3.   Porter and Lawler motivation model.

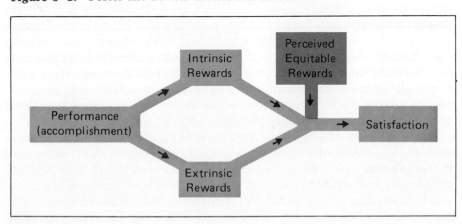

(Source: Edward E. Lawler, III, and Lyman W. Porter, "The Effect of Performance on Job Satisfaction," *Industrial Relations* 7, October 1966. Used with permission.)

dissatisfaction. If he is highly satisfied, it does not mean he will work harder. He may emphasize quality or he may say, "I got what I wanted."

The essence of the Porter and Lawler view of motivation is the important role of perception. They also show that performance leads to satisfaction rather than satisfaction leading to performance.

Equity as a Motivator. People want to be treated fairly, not just in the rewards they receive, but also in such areas as vacations, work assignments, and even penalties assessed. Fairness in management literature is referred to as equity.

EQUITY is defined as the perceived fairness of what the person does (inputs) compared with what the person receives (outcomes).

Inputs are what a person brings to the organization and include educational level, age, experience, productivity, and other skills or efforts. The items received by a person, or the *outcomes*, are the rewards obtained in exchange for the inputs. Outcomes include pay, benefits, recognition, achievement, prestige, and any other rewards received. Note that the outcome can be either actual and tangible (that is, the economic meaning) or intangible (that is, internal to the person).

The individual's view of fair value is critical to the relationship between performance and job satisfaction because equity is an exchange and comparison process. Assume you are a laboratory technician in a hospital. You exchange your talents and efforts for the tangible and intangible rewards the hospital gives. You then compare your inputs— what you did—to your outcomes—what you received—to determine the equity of your compensation. As Figure 3–4 shows, the comparison process also includes the individual's comparison of inputs/outcomes to the inputs/outcomes of other individuals. Thus you will also compare your talents, skills, and efforts to those of other laboratory technicians or other hospital employees. Your perception—correct or incorrect—significantly affects your valuation of your inputs and outcomes. *Inequity* occurs when there is an imbalance between the inputs and the outcomes as a result of the comparison process.

If inputs exceed outcomes. One view of equity theory research suggests that if an employee is under-rewarded (more inputs than outcomes), the employee will tend to reduce his or her inputs.[5] If, like the lab technician mentioned above, you feel that you have received fewer rewards than your inputs, you will attempt to resolve the inequity. Your reactions can include some or all of the following: increased dissatisfaction, attempts to get compensation raised, quitting the job for a more equitable one, changing your perceptual comparison, or reducing your productivity. All these actions are attempts to reduce the inequity.

Figure 3–4.   Equity evaluations.

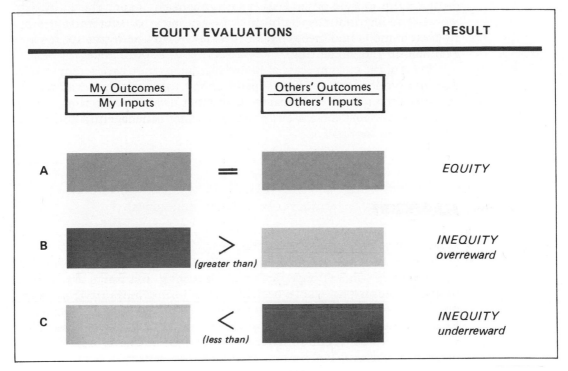

If outcomes exceed inputs. One obvious way a person may attempt to resolve this type of inequity is by putting forth more effort. If you feel that you received more rewards than you deserved, you might work harder in order to justify the "overpayment." Or, you might process the same number of laboratory samples, but do so more accurately and produce higher quality results. Other actions could include a recomparison, whereby you might decide that you evaluated your efforts inaccurately and that you really *were not* overpaid.

Regardless of the action taken, you will make some attempt to relieve the inequity tension. Research evidence on the type of action you are most likely to take is mixed. Feelings of inequity have important implications for the design and administration of compensation programs, staffing, training, and performance appraisal. They can clearly affect motivation.

> *What are four views about why people behave as they do?*

Importance of Complex View. The complex approach to motivation is important in that it gets away from the simplistic assumptions of the three other views. Work motivation really is very complex. It depends on both the individual and the environment in which the individual works. The important aspect of this view is that a manager must attempt to match individual needs and expectations to the types of rewards available in the job setting.

In sum, the current state of knowledge about motivation emphasizes that motivation really does "depend upon" the individual and the individual's job situation. Managers who must direct or lead these "complex" people must have a basic understanding of leadership and its relationship to motivation.

LEADERSHIP

Management and leadership are not exactly the same concepts. *Management* implies the existence of formal authority, while *leadership* may not have any connection with formal authority. Managers are in their positions because they have been given the formal authority to perform their jobs, including directing the actions of others. The responsibility for seeing that the job gets done accompanies this authority. Leadership, however, does not require a delegation of formal authority from "above" in an organization. It does not even have to occur in a formal organizational environment. A street gang, for example, will have a leader, though perhaps not a formally appointed one. This leader is not a "manager" in the common sense of the word.

The distinction between leadership and management is not always clear. Employees obey or follow managers partially because they must. If employees consistently refused to cooperate, they typically would not be employed very long. People may obey or follow leaders for entirely different reasons. A group may follow a leader because the individual is physically attractive or knowledgeable, or for any number of other reasons.

The manager does not always have to be a leader to be effective, but some key ideas about leadership can be useful to the manager. For example, Jessica Harbeck, a new accounting supervisor, may rely on command rather than persuasion with Fred Abbott, a 60-year-old employee. If Jessica does not understand the difference between being a manager (having a position) and being a leader (having followers), she may find that after a while command may not work with Fred and a different kind of relationship is needed.

The successful manager's concern with leadership focuses on obtaining the very best performance from employees. Some employees do only the minimum number of tasks required of them. But most managers prefer effective and creative employees who are willing to put extra effort into doing a job.

Leadership Approaches

Many different approaches have been taken to understand leadership. For centuries leadership has been studied with varying degrees of rigor.

Trait Approaches.   Many early studies on leadership were done by psychologists who examined personality traits of leaders. Leaders were thought to be dominant extroverts who possessed the traits of self-confidence, empathy, and intelligence.

This approach is closely connected with the "Great Leader" theory of leadership. This approach assumed that a better understanding of leadership could be gained by studying the personalities and behavior of famous leaders. The implication is that if you study these people, "you too can become a great leader." Such study certainly can be interesting, but what worked for Susan B. Anthony, George Washington, or Benito Juarez years ago may not necessarily be applicable in today's world or in a different set of circumstances. Although numerous famous leaders had these traits, many other individuals with the same traits failed to become leaders.

"Style" Approaches.   During the last few decades several attempts to classify leadership into two basic dimensions have been made. The Ohio State Leadership Studies have significantly affected our knowledge of leadership. Through the use of sophisticated statistical techniques two basic dimensions of leader behavior were isolated: *initiating structure* and *consideration*.

> INITIATING STRUCTURE refers to efforts on the part of the leader to get the job done.

Initiating structure may involve scheduling, maintaining, and communicating standards of performance; emphasizing that deadlines be met; and assigning group members to particular tasks—in other words, a concern with productivity, costs, and getting the work done. It has also been called the "production-oriented" style.

> CONSIDERATION refers to behavior indicating warmth, trust, friendship, and mutual respect between the leader and the group members.

Behavior which shows consideration includes explaining why decisions were made, consulting group members before making decisions, listening to group members' problems, doing personal favors for group members, and performing other such actions. Leaders high on consideration have been called "people-oriented" leaders.

Managers who score high on *initiating structure* may be very effective and successful on performance measures such as productivity, profit, and efficiency. They are commonly rated very well by their superiors. Managers who are high on *consideration* tend to have high morale in their work group, lower employee turnover, and lower grievance rates than those who are low on consideration.

The general view that accompanies this "style" approach to leadership is that effective leaders are high on both initiating structure and on consideration (see Figure 3–5) and that they are concerned with their people and concerned with getting the job done. However, viewing leadership only as initiating structure and consideration presents a problem because there is little evidence showing how successful a leader with either a "people" or "production" orientation, or both, will be in different situations.

Figure 3–5. Leadership style approach.

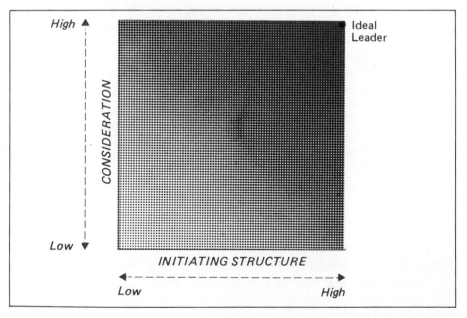

Situational Approaches. Situational differences, such as the size and climate of the organization, the nature of tasks, and how well the leader gets along with the followers, all may make a difference in the effectiveness of a given leadership style. Consequently, the situational approach to the study of leadership evolved.

The question of which leadership style yields the best results is really determined by the conditions under which the leader is operating. Production-oriented leadership may be more effective under some conditions and people-oriented leadership under others. These issues are still being researched, but some general guides are available.

Fred Fiedler.   Since the 1950s Fiedler and his associates have been researching leadership by studying nurses, steel crews, consumer sales cooperatives, church groups, athletic teams, factories, aviation cadets, and others. The main conclusion of all this research is that the effectiveness of the leader depends upon both the leadership style and the favorableness of the situation. Fiedler concludes that in either very favorable situations or very unfavorable situations production-oriented leadership works best. In other situations where poor leader-member relations, weak position power, or unstructured tasks combine to make the situation moderately unfavorable, the people-oriented leader is more effective.[6]

Path-Goal Approach.   Another researcher, Robert House, has tried to identify those situations in which a leader's consideration or initiating-structure behavior affects employee performance or satisfaction.[7] His approach is based upon the path-goal motivation ideas of Vroom and Porter and Lawler mentioned earlier. House argues that a leader can affect (1) intrinsic rewards of work, (2) intrinsic rewards associated with achievement, (3) extrinsic rewards associated with achievement, (4) the clarity of the "path" an employee will follow to achievement, and (5) the probability that achievement will be rewarded.

This theory predicts that a considerate leader is important if the work itself is boring and uninteresting. "If you have a bad job you don't need a bad boss too." When the job itself is stimulating, the importance of consideration is less.

Initiating structure by the leader is important when the job is unstructured or ambiguous or when a crisis occurs. If the job is already well structured, a high degree of structure from the leader is unnecessary and irritating.

This approach to the situational nature of leadership represents another attempt to identify what leadership style is most appropriate in a given situation. As more research on the path-goal approach and similar theories is done, a better grasp on improving leadership effectiveness will become available.

Vroom and Yetton.   Vroom and Yetton propose an approach to leader decision-making situations. Their model consists of a set of questions about the situation to which a manager must answer yes or no. On the basis of answers to the sequence of questions certain decision styles are rejected as inappropriate. After the entire sequence of questions has been answered one or more styles will remain that meet all requirements for quality and acceptability.

The model itself resembles a complex tree and requires extensive discussion to explain. If you are interested in learning more, allow considerable time to review a good source of explanation of the model.[8]

Can you discuss the three major leadership approaches?

Leadership Effectiveness

Certain kinds of leadership skills can be learned and are an important part of many management training programs. Successful leadership also depends upon an individual's personality. Because changing leadership styles is often very difficult, placing individuals in a situation more compatible with their leadership styles may be more effective. It is much easier to move a manager to a job which fits his or her leadership inclinations than it is to try to change the individual's way of leading.

Recognizing that certain kinds of behavior are inappropriate in certain situations, it follows that some individuals may be incapable of providing the proper behavior in every situation. When a manager is improperly placed, the appropriate leadership style may require behavior he or she simply cannot provide. In such a case it is better for both the manager and the organization if the manager is moved into a more appropriate situation.

An important part of effective leadership is a basic understanding of how individuals behave as members of groups. Group forces can generally affect management operations. The impact of work groups on productivity and operations demands that group behavior be discussed when considering behavioral foundations of personnel.

GROUP BEHAVIOR

Groups of employees can make a manager's job easy or impossible. Managers must understand the behavior and characteristics of groups to effectively direct progress toward organizational goals.

A WORK GROUP is a collection of individuals brought together to perform organizational work.

Work groups frequently have varied and overlapping social arrangements. For example, a work group of 20 people in a government agency office may have several subgroups, which may develop because of such items as social considerations, carpools, and physical location. Figure 3–6 shows the overlap that often occurs in the membership of groups at work. Regardless of the type of work situation, a work group shares certain basic characteristics in common with groups in many other settings.

Figure 3–6. Overlap in group memberships.

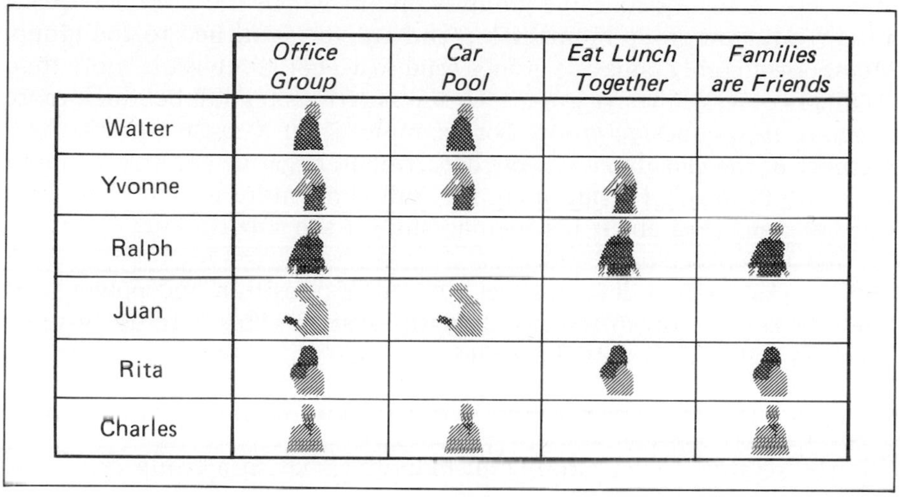

	Office Group	Car Pool	Eat Lunch Together	Families are Friends
Walter	●	●		
Yvonne	●	●	●	
Ralph	●		●	●
Juan	●	●		
Rita	●		●	●
Charles	●	●		●

What is a work group?

Group Characteristics

Informal groups frequently develop common "codes of behaviors" to help attain group goals. During the growth, development, and maturity of a group, a "collective mind" develops which guides members' attitudes and actions as a group. This group understanding is called a *norm*.

NORMS are expected standards of behavior, usually unwritten and often unspoken, that are generally understood by all members of a group.

Norms.   Norms may develop in any group as a group's "code of behavior" for many reasons. They deal with such behaviors as which other groups to associate with, how other groups are to be viewed, and what appropriate behavior or expressions are within the group. For example, the employees in the detective division of a police department may have a group norm that implies that officers on parking patrol are to be viewed as inferior. As numerous studies have revealed, norms can even dictate acceptable productivity rates, and group "quotas" may be different from the formal quotas posted by management.

Cohesiveness.   Groups differ on "cohesiveness" or closeness among members. A highly cohesive group is one in which the members place a high value on group membership and are very attached to the group. Members of highly cohesive groups tend to accept group goals more than members of less cohesive groups. Group sanctions tend to be much more effective in a cohesive group. For example, if an X-ray technician is a member of the closely knit X-ray department, negative comments about his attire from other group members will carry more weight than if he were unconcerned about his membership in the department.

Status.   As a group develops, each member's position and power in it tends to become organized into a status system. This "status system" becomes the structure of the group.

> STATUS is the relative social ranking an individual has in a group or organization.

Even in work groups, status usually results in a "pecking order" comprised of an informal leader and perhaps second- and third-level members. Status symbols may include dress, office size, desk size, number of pictures in the office, or a private office with a door and a window. These symbols serve a purpose in that they allow people knowledgeable about the status system to identify a person's "place" in that system.

Group Composition.   The success of a group is partially determined by the individual characteristics of group members. Age, sex, ethnic background, marital status, experience, and educational levels are important considerations. If the individual characteristics of a group's members are very similar, higher individual member satisfaction will usually result than in a group with diverse members. In homogeneous groups, members tend to be more friendly and have higher group spirit. However, groups whose members have quite different characteristics (heterogeneous groups) tend to be more productive.

Groups composed of diverse individuals are likely to be superior in arriving at inventive solutions and new ideas because many different approaches to problems are presented by different people. For instance, when the product line supervisor for a ski-wear firm needed some new ideas for next year's product line, she called in people with very different backgrounds to brainstorm the problem: people from engineering, sales, design, and public relations. They did not always agree on an idea, but they provided quite a variety of new ideas on the product line.

Size. The size of a group tends to affect individual performance in the group. Although size certainly affects the speed with which decisions can be made in a group, the relationship between size and performance is not completely clear. For example, at one university the department of management has only six faculty members; at another, the department of management has 25. Decisions about course assignments and curriculum will probably be easier in the smaller department. Also, as the number of members in a group increases, role definitions must be clearer because face-to-face communication is reduced. Generally, it is safe to say management becomes more difficult as group size increases and communication becomes more important.

What are four typical characteristics of groups?

Status
cohesiveness
group composition
size

COMMUNICATION

Communication is a behavioral process that affects motivation, leadership, and group effectiveness. Interpersonal communication occurs both formally and informally in organizations in written, spoken, and other forms.

The basic communications process is represented in Figure 3–7. Before a message can be conveyed, formally or informally, it is *encoded* or converted to symbolic form (made into words, for example); then it is passed by way of a *channel* (or medium) to the receiver who *decodes* (or retranslates) it. The desired result is the transfer of reasonably accurate meaning from one person to another. However the process is subject to many failures.

Communication Barriers *(3 ea)*

Communication problems are often mentioned by managers as being the biggest ones. Better communication comes about when people are aware of *semantic, technical,* and *perceptual* barriers.

Figure 3–7. Basic communication process.

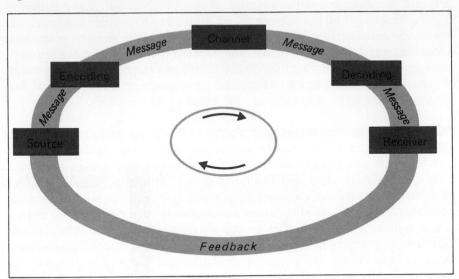

(1) **Semantic Barriers.** The *semantic* barrier is a barrier of words. Communication can be difficult because words or symbols have different meanings. The word "fire" can mean either a flame or to discharge an employee.

(2) **Technical Barriers.** *Technical* problems can prevent a message from conveying the intended meaning. If you were in a room talking with friends and a rock band was playing loudly, you might not accurately hear what was said. A message can be interrupted by noise before it reaches the receiver. Noise and physical barriers can be technical problems in oral communication.

(3) **Perceptual Barriers.** *Perceptual* problems occur because people have different mental frameworks. If Maria attempts to tell Paul about a dog, Paul conjures a visual image of a dog. Maria may be talking about a chihuahua, while Paul may be thinking about a German shepherd.

Informal Personnel Communication

An important part of organizational communication is done through informal channels. These channels interweaving throughout an organization are referred to as the *grapevine.* Just as jungle drums in old Tarzan movies indicated trouble, the grapevine often reflects employee and organizational problems. A well-known expert on the organizational grapevine, Keith Davis says that effective supervisors and managers should monitor the grapevine as a supplement to formal channels.[9] The absence of a grapevine in a company might be evidence that employees are too scared to talk or that they care so little about the company that they do not want to talk about it. Managers should be aware of current grapevine messages and listen for major distortions. Activity in the grapevine depends on how important a topic is and the presence (or absence) of official communication on it.

Figure 3–8.   Communications matching.

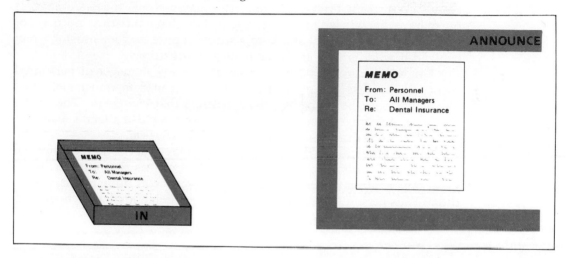

Both formal and informal communication should be matched to the receiver. The message should be transmitted over appropriate media using the right symbols at a level meaningful to both the sender and the receiver. Personnel communication also must match the message to the purpose, as Figure 3–8 shows. If the personnel unit wants to tell managers about a change that will affect their relations with union stewards, they send a memo to the managers. If the personnel unit did not care whether or not managers received the message, they could post it on the bulletin board in the cafeteria.

What are three barriers to successful communication?

REVIEW AND PREVIEW

This chapter has been concerned with selected basic processes necessary to understanding the human resource. Four major views of basic human nature—*rational-economic, social, self-actualizing,* and *complex*—have evolved over time and still exist. The complex view appears to recognize the current realities of people in organizations.

Leadership is an important part of managing people in organizations. The trait approach and leadership style approach are two past approaches to studying leadership. Contemporary situational theorists emphasize that effective managers must be diagnosticians. They must be able to determine which leadership style is appropriate in a given situation and to match leadership styles and situations as much as possible.

The importance of group behavior has been reviewed. Because work groups are present throughout modern organizations, today's managers must have knowledge of some basic group characteristics: norms, cohesiveness, status, size, and composition. These factors must be recognized if work groups are to be managed effectively.

Finally, communication is important to any manager or personnel specialist. Because communications is an information transfer process, a manager must be concerned about barriers that can occur. The grapevine as an informal communication network may also affect a manager, especially in dealing with groups in the organization.

The next section of this text builds upon an understanding of human behavior and turns specifically to external concerns that affect *staffing* in an organization. To emphasize the importance of human behavior as the various personnel activities are examined, behavioral aspects of each activity will also be highlighted.

Review Questions

1. What is motivation? Why is it so difficult to identify the causes of behavior?
2. What are the four sets of views about basic human nature? Which one do you see as most compatible with your own values?
3. What is leadership? What are the three general approaches that have been used in studying leadership?
4. "An effective leader must be a good diagnostician." Discuss.
5. What is a work group and why would awareness of group characteristics help a manager?
6. Discuss how communication barriers and informal communication problems can be interrelated.

Case: A Failure to Communicate

"I'm here for an interview with the manager." Those are the words Barb McCann had echoing in the back of her mind. Barb is the secretary for Tom Cane, regional manager of Carson Insurance Company. Along with Barb and Tom are five agents who all share a branch office and handle business surrounding and including the Boston area.

Barb's job entails answering the phone, taking dictation, typing, filing, and numerous other activities which maintain efficiency in the office. She has been with Carson Company full time for one and a half years. She was hired as a receptionist and shortly afterward assumed the responsibilities of office secretary.

Barb's concerns started one afternoon when her office door opened and a young woman, with an air about her that was very professional, entered. She looked at Barb with strong eye contact and said, "I'm here for an interview with the manager."

Barb panicked. "He's replacing me? He's not satisfied with my work? He wants someone with more experience? My office skills aren't professional? Why didn't he even tell me?" These were all questions that raced through Barb's mind before she could even blink. After she caught her breath, she proceeded to confirm that the woman was in the right office, for the right interview, with the right manager. Once confirmed, Barb notified Mr. Cane that the interviewee had arrived.

The interview lasted longer than Barb was scheduled to work, so she left the office while the meeting was still in progress. Needless to say, she didn't sleep very comfortably that night. Her boss didn't acknowledge the interview for three days, so Barb had many restless nights worrying if she would have a job the next day.

Finally, the anxiety and paranoia reached its peak and Barb confronted Mr. Cane. She mentioned the interview and inquired about it. Before he could respond, she told him about her willingness to work hard, her continual desire to improve, her dedication to maintaining office efficiency, and her excellent absentee record. Mr. Cane nodded and replied, "The interview was to hire an additional agent for the Wilmington branch office. The interviewee currently lives in Boston, so I handled the meeting." All of a sudden, Barb was breathing a sigh of relief. "He's not replacing me. He is satisfied with my work. He doesn't want someone with more experience. My office skills are professional." The answers all seemed to appear. Before Barb could say a word, embarrassment set in. She thanked Mr. Cane for the explanation and resumed her normal duties as office secretary.

QUESTIONS

1. Where did communication break down?
2. Outline other major areas of "misunderstanding" that occur frequently in office situations.

NOTES

1. The authors acknowledge the influence and contributions of Edgar Schein, *Organizational Psychology*, 2nd ed. (Englewood Cliffs, NJ: Prentice-Hall, 1970), in framing and structuring the various assumptions and approaches to motivation.

2. A. H. Maslow, *Motivation and Personality* (New York: Harper & Row, 1954, chapter 5.

3. F. Herzberg, B. Mausner, and B. Snyderman, *The Motivation To Work* (New York: John Wiley & Sons, 1959).

4. Victor H. Vroom, *Work and Motivation* (New York: John Wiley & Sons, 1964).

5. For a concise explanation of equity theory, see Michael R. Carrell and John E. Dittrich, "Equity Theory: The Recent Literature, Methodological Considerations, and New Directions," *The Academy of Management Review*, April 1978, pp. 202–210.

6. Fred E. Fiedler, "Engineer the Job to Fit the Manager," *Harvard Business Review*, September-October 1965, p. 119.

7. Robert House, "Path Goal Theory of Leader Effectiveness," *Administrative Science Quarterly*, 16, 1971, pp. 321–338.

8. R. J. Aldag and A. P. Brief, *Managing Organizational Behavior*, (St. Paul: West Publishing, 1981), p. 268–274.

9. Keith Davis, *Human Behavior at Work* (New York: McGraw Hill, 1977), pp. 278–286.

Equal Employment Opportunity

SEXUAL HARASSMENT: NEW FRONTIER ON AN OLD PROBLEM

In a 1980 *Time* magazine advertisement placed by the National Organization of Women (NOW) a woman dressed in a tailored business suit is pictured with a man's hand on her leg. The caption reads, "He calls it fun, she calls it sexual harassment." This ad, a number of court cases, and some guidelines issued by the Equal Employment Opportunity Commission are all signs that male-female relationships at work are a new frontier for equal employment compliance efforts.

In the first year after the EEOC issued its guidelines, over 300 sexual harassment complaints were filed by women workers. An official of the EEOC testified that of 118 charges that were substantiated, 106 were caused by supervisors or other managers. Women who refused sexual advances were fired, transferred to less desirable jobs, or faced such continuing harassment that they resigned.

Most people would agree that sexual harassment is inappropriate for a work environment. But what is sexual harassment? The EEOC guidelines indicate that unwelcome sexual advances, requests for sexual favors, or verbal or physical acts of a sexual nature that affect decisions about employment conditions, promotions, and pay raises constitute sexual harassment.

Mary H. was pressured by a senior vice-president of a large company to have an affair with him. When she refused, she was fired. When she filed a complaint, the court supported her. The company settled with Mary for $100,000 and kept the vice-president on the payroll.

Judy U. was a graduate student at a major university who was told that if she wanted an A in a class she would have to go to bed with the professor. She refused and filed a complaint. The professor resigned and Judy graduated, having had her course grade changed to an A after her complaint was upheld.

Sexual harassment can work the other way too. A woman U.S. Army officer was disciplined after a male private filed harassment charges against her. The private was promised "easy duty" if he succumbed to the sexual advances of the officer.

To protect themselves from sexual harassment charges employers must take affirmative action to avoid sexual harassment. Some actions suggested by the EEOC guidelines include:

1. Disciplining offenders using organizational sanctions, up to and including firing them.

2. Communicating to all employees, especially to supervisors and managers, sexual harassment concerns and regulations and the importance of creating and maintaining a work environment free of sexual harassment.

3. Developing means whereby individuals who feel they have been harassed can report the incidents without fear of retaliation and means to ensure that complaints are satisfactorily investigated and acted upon.

Without knowledge of the numerous equal employment regulations and concerns in this area and others, it is difficult for an organization to truly be an "Equal Opportunity Employer." In this section the nature of Equal Employment Opportunity (EEO) regulations is examined. Chapter 4 examines the legal constraints presented by EEO on the organization and how they developed. Then chapter 5 describes issues associated with implementing EEO as an individual employer.

Equal Employment and Staffing

When you have read this chapter, you should be able to:

1. Explain four reasons why effective staffing is important.

2. Discuss the nature of Title VII of the Civil Rights Act of 1964.

3. Identify the governmental agencies enforcing equal employment regulations.

4. Briefly explain the importance of four landmark court cases on equal employment.

5. Explain the two strategies to comply with the 1978 Uniform Guidelines.

6. Define and explain three types of validity.

Keep on Truckin'?

Tim Rowe owns a small trucking firm that specializes in local and metro-area delivery in a large city in the United States.

All employment activities are handled by Tim who has always hired employees on the basis of three qualifications:

1. they must have a high school diploma;
2. they must pass a short paper-and-pencil test which is given to all applicants; and
3. they must have a valid driver's license if applying for the position of driver.

The short test is interesting, as it was devised by Tim from sample questions found on a GED (General Education Degree) Equivalency Test. The test consists of 33 vocabulary and mathematical questions, each worth 3 points. Anyone scoring below 70 is automatically rejected.

Last month two drivers quit, so Tim advertised in the local paper for two new drivers. Ten people applied for the openings, but Tim rejected four applicants because they were not high school graduates. Three others were rejected because of test scores below 70. The two white males hired scored the highest on the test, had high school degrees, and also had valid driver's licenses.

This week Tim was notified that two equal employment complaints had been filed against him and his firm. One complainant, a woman, alleges that the test does not measure a person's ability to drive and is not a valid predictor of job success. The other complainant, a minority man, alleges that the high school diploma requirement is not related to ability to do the job and unfairly discriminates against minorities. Tim is trying to decide how to respond to these complaints.

Comments:

Tim Rowe is on shaky ground with his selection procedure. He will be hard pressed to demonstrate that his selection instrument (pencil-and-paper test) is job-related. Also, in light of a 1971 case, unless a high school diploma can be shown to be related to the job performance of a truck driver, it is not a legal criterion for selection. Tim might be better off to try to settle these complaints than to fight them through the courts. Of the three requirements, only the driver's license "test" appears to be job-related.

AN important part of personnel management is providing the organization with a staff of employees to do its work. The components of staffing and some external constraints that affect those components are depicted in Figure 4–1. At the heart of that figure are three distinct general activities—work analysis, recruiting, and selection. *Work analysis* is concerned with analyzing and defining jobs so that a clear picture is obtained of job duties and the qualifications needed for individuals to perform those duties satisfactorily. *Recruiting* focuses on generating an adequate number of qualified applicants for managers to review. *Selection* is the stage at which individuals are actually screened and either rejected or hired.

Each of the components is affected by a wide range of external environmental constraints. Some of the most important of these constraints are identified in the outer portion of Figure 4–1. The absence or presence of *labor unions,* good *economic conditions,* and current

Figure 4–1 External constraints and staffing.

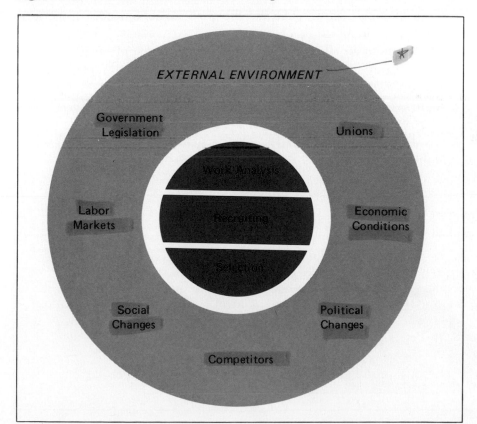

political forces and changes all must be considered. In addition, the actions of *competing employers*, the appearance of *social changes*, and the composition of *labor markets* could all affect each of the staffing components.

The opening case provides a good example of another external environmental constraint, *governmental legislation*. The trucking firm manager faces two challenges to part of his staffing activities as a result of equal employment opportunity (EEO) legislation. Because of the importance of EEO requirements mandated by federal, state, and local governments, most of this chapter and all of the next one focus on the impact of this external environmental constraint. Before examining equal employment requirements, the nature of effective staffing is highlighted.

EFFECTIVE STAFFING

Objectives of an effective and legal staffing program are shown in Figure 4–2. Those objectives are:

1. To accurately identify jobs and the qualifications needed to perform them;
2. To maintain an adequate supply of appropriate applicants;
3. To select those applicants best qualified for employment in the organization;
4. To verify selection and placement by a follow-up of employees to see how well they fit the jobs they are performing;
5. To do the above efficiently and in a manner which promotes good public relations;

Figure 4–2 Staffing objectives.

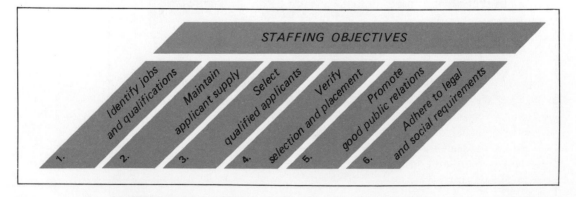

6. To perform these functions within the constraints of the law and social expectations.

These objectives may not seem difficult to achieve. However, many problems are involved which may not be evident at first.

Before actual recruiting and selection can begin, the employer must know what jobs need filling and the nature of those jobs. Whether a job is for a computer programmer or for a systems analyst would significantly affect the screening of applicants and the content of a recruiting advertisement. By becoming familiar with the job, it is easier to identify the minimum qualifications needed for someone to satisfactorily perform the job.

To maintain a good supply of applicants, an organization must deal with a variety of changes over which it has little (if any) control. The organization must draw from essentially the same labor market that supplies all employers—private, public, and military. Significant changes in wages, working conditions, and demand in other sectors of the labor market can radically change the availability of job applicants. When a large new employer comes into a community, all organizations drawing employees from that market are affected.

Also, an organization must keep accurate records of its labor requirements in order to take steps to fill them. Recruiting methods should be planned to stimulate an increase of applicants when needed. The organization also needs to know where possible sources of labor are, including the approximate number and quality of potential workers from each source.

Matching Process

Sound selection and placement is important for both the employer and the applicant. How well an employee is matched to a job affects the amount and quality of the employee's work. This matching also directly affects training and operating costs. Workers who are unable to produce the amount and quality of work expected can cost an organization a great deal of money, time, and trouble.

Proper placement is also important to the individual applying for a job. The wrong choice of a vocation or improper job placement can result in wasted time when the employee could be getting useful experience in a more suitable field. Poor placement can result in an unhappy individual or dismissal if the employee cannot do the job.

Effective staffing also requires constant monitoring of the match between person and job. It is not just a one-time effort ending with initial placement.

Can you explain the importance of staffing activities?

Specific External Forces in Staffing

The days are past when a manager could handle hiring people in any manner that seemed convenient. Within the last 20 years both federal and state governments have become more involved because of social demands that organizations be more responsible in their staffing processes. Government pressure, however, is only one of several external staffing constraints.

Public Opinion.   The public is a very important external factor. Public opinion in recruiting and hiring practices cannot be ignored. Recruiting qualified people may be very difficult if the public's opinion of an organization is that it is a poor place to work, that it treats employees unfairly, or that it hires only certain "types" of people.

Competing Employers.   Competitors are another important external force in staffing. Failure to consider the competitive labor market and to offer pay scales and other benefits competitive with organizations in the same general industry and geographical location can be a mistake. Underpaying or "undercompeting" may result in a much lower quality work force.

Unions.   In some instances unions can control or influence recruiting and staffing needs. An organization with a strong union may experience a reduction in its flexibility in deciding who will be hired and where he or she will be placed. Unions can also work to an employer's advantage through cooperative staffing programs. Examples are to be found in the building, trade, and printing industries. Such cooperativeness has not been the case in manufacturing. Union shops have typically given management a free hand in hiring while insisting on strong seniority provisions for promotion.

Government.   One of the major external forces which must be considered in staffing is governmental influence. Historically, certain minority groups and women have been discriminated against in staffing. As a result, government stepped in to see that discrimination did not continue. Staffing is no longer a simple process; it must be handled by someone knowledgeable about numerous legal requirements. Most operating managers usually do not have time to become involved with the intricacies of all the regulations. Consequently, many employers have equal employment specialists in their personnel units.

Figure 4–3 External forces affecting staffing.

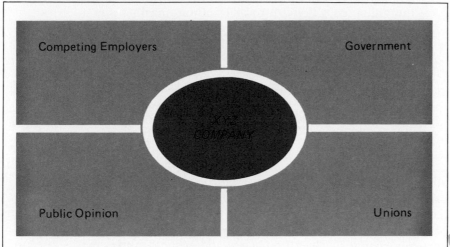

With all the external forces bearing on the staffing activities in organizations, managers cannot afford to leave the process to chance. Managers must first be *aware* of the external forces relevant to their organization and how these affect them. Next, they must plan both immediate and future needs for employees. Then they must maintain an active and effective recruitment and selection program that complies with governmental restraints on staffing.

EQUAL EMPLOYMENT: GOVERNMENTAL RESTRAINTS

The purpose of this section is to describe important government influences on staffing. Because the topic is so extensive, it is not possible to treat it in a totally comprehensive manner. This discussion is intended to provide a basic understanding and specific coverage of some of the most important areas.

Title VII, Civil Rights Act

Discrimination against many minority groups is now clearly prohibited by law. The keystone of the structure of antidiscrimination legislation is the Civil Rights Act of 1964.

Section 703A, Title VII, of the 1964 act states that:

It shall be an unlawful employment practice for an
employer (1) to fail or refuse to hire or to discharge any
individual or otherwise to discriminate against any
individual with respect to his compensation, terms,
conditions, or privileges of employment because of such
individual's race, color, religion, sex, or national origin; or
(2) to limit, segregate or classify his employees in any way
which would deprive or tend to deprive any individual of
employment opportunities or otherwise inadvertantly affect
his status as an employee because of such individual's race,
color, religion, sex, or national origin.[1]

The Civil Rights Act was passed by Congress to set up the mechanism for bringing about equality in hiring and job opportunity. As is
often the case, the law contains ambiguous provisions which give great
leeway to the agencies who enforce the law. In addition, interpretations
of these ambiguous provisions in laws change as the membership of the
agencies change. Title VII language and agency rulings may sometimes
cause confusion since they may seem to be in conflict at times. However,
the power that agencies have in interpreting the law explains the potential for such a situation to occur.

Who Is Covered?

Title VII as amended by the Equal Employment Opportunity Act of 1972
covers:

1. All private employers of 15 or more persons,
2. All educational institutions, public and private,
3. State and local governments,
4. Public and private employment agencies,
5. Labor unions with 15 or more members,
6. Joint (labor-management) committees for apprenticeship and training.[2]

Any organization meeting one of these criteria is subject to rules and
regulations of governmental agencies set up to administer the act.

*What does Title VII of the 1964 Civil Rights Act
cover?*

Enforcement Agencies

Several governmental agencies have the power to investigate illegal and
discriminatory practices. The most prominent of these agencies are the

Equal Employment Opportunity Commission and the Office of Federal Contract Compliance Programs.

Equal Employment Opportunity Commission (EEOC).   The EEOC was created by the Civil Rights Act of 1964 to be the agency responsible for enforcing the employment-related revisions. There are five members on the EEOC, all appointed by the president and confirmed by the U.S. Senate. The agency initiates investigations, responds to complaints, and develops guidelines to enforce Title VII regulations. The EEOC has been given expanded powers several times since 1964 and is the major agency involved with employment discrimination.

The powers of the EEOC are not to be taken lightly. Where the courts have upheld the EEOC's finding of discrimination they have ruled that remedies include back pay and remedial "affirmative action". Some examples include:[3]

> Ford Motor Co.—$23 million settlement to 14,000 women and minority applicants.
> I. Magnin—$1.9 million to three former retailing executives fired in violation of the age discrimination law.
> Western Electric—$7 million to 1700 women who were victims of sex discrimination in job placement.

When a discrimination charge is received by the EEOC it is processed as shown in Figure 4–4. Notice that there are a number of decision stages and points. The three stages represent increasingly more involved actions in which a complainant and an employer continue to disagree. The rapid charge processing system was introduced in 1977 to try to eliminate the extremely long delays that had occurred in the past.

Office of Federal Contract Compliance Programs (OFCCP).   Beginning with President Franklin D. Roosevelt and continuing through the passage of the Civil Rights Act of 1964, numerous executive orders and actions have been issued that require employers holding federal government contracts to be nondiscriminatory. During the late 1960s, the Office of Federal Contract Compliance (OFCC) in the Labor Department was established with the responsibility of enforcing nondiscrimination in government contracts. Under Executive Order 11246, the Secretary of Labor was given the power to

1. publish the names of noncomplying contractors or unions,
2. recommend suits by the Justice Department to compel compliance,
3. recommend action by the EEOC or the Justice Department to file suit in federal district court,
4. cancel the contract of a noncomplying contractor or blacklist a noncomplying employer from future government contracts.

Figure 4–4 Rapid charge processing system.

TIME LAPSE	EEOC ACTION	PROBLEM RESOLUTION
	1 INTAKE INVESTIGATION	
Immediate Action	Complainant Initial Inquiry • Mail • Telephone • Drop in	If Non-Jurisdictional, Refer to Appropriate Agency
	⬇	
Immediate Action Subject to Complainant Availability	If EEOC Matter Require In-Depth Interview at EEOC Office or via Telephone • Obtain Full Story and Names of Witnesses and Comparitive Data • Prepare Detailed Charge • Post-Charge Counseling RE: EEOC Process and to Promote Settlement Interest	If Non-Jurisdictional or not valid Title VII claim refer to appropriate Agency
	⬇	
2-3 Days	Docketing, Deferral to 706 Agency where Appropriate or Request for 706 Waiver under Work-Sharing Arrangement; Assignment to Investigator.	
	⬇	
2-3 Days	Charge Served on Employer with Notice of Fact-Finding Conference, Interrogatory and Invitation to Settle on 'No Fault Basis'	If Employer Responds to Settlement Overture, Negotiate Settlement and Close
	2 FACT FINDING CONFERENCE -- INVESTIGATION/SETTLEMENT	
Held within One Month from Date of Charge	Fact-Finding Conference Held if No Pre-Conference Settlement • Sort Out Disputed and Non-Disputed Facts • Clarify Issues • Identify Additional Documentation Needed • Continue Settlement Efforts	If Settlement Succeeds, Execute Settlement Agreement and Close
	(Continued on opposite page)	

Fig. 4–4   (continued)

TIME LAPSE	EEOC ACTION	PROBLEM RESOLUTION
	3 POST-CONFERENCE ACTIONS	
Completed within Three to Four Months from Date of Charge	If Continued Settlement Efforts Fail and Case has Merit and/or Investigation is Incomplete • Prepare Investigative Report • Identify Areas of Further Inquiry ↓ Refer for Extended Investigation	*Close* Charge has No Merit: No Cause Further *Settlement* Effort Succeeds Complainant Fails to Cooperate Complainant Requests Rt. to Sue Complainant Requests Withdrawal

(Source: U.S. Equal Employment Opportunity Commission, *Mission*, 5 (1977), p. 13.)

What are the agencies that enforce equal employment regulations?

Landmark Court Cases

In March of 1971, the Supreme Court's decision in the case of *Griggs* v. *Duke Power Company* put some teeth in the Civil Rights Act. As a result, companies must be able to *prove* that their selection procedures do not tend to discriminate.

Griggs v. Duke Power.[4]   The Griggs case dealt with a promotion and transfer policy which required individuals to have both a high school diploma and to obtain a satisfactory score on two professionally developed aptitude tests, one of which was the Wonderlic Intelligence Test. Blacks failed the tests at a higher rate than whites. In addition, fewer blacks had high school diplomas than whites.

The U.S. Supreme Court ruled that Title VII of the Civil Rights Act prohibits not only overt discrimination but also practices which are fair in form but discriminatory in operation. The court also stated that *if an employment practice cannot be shown to be related to job performance, the practice is prohibited.* This decision established two major points: (1) it is not enough to show a lack of discriminatory intent if the selection tool discriminates against one group more than another; (2) it is the employer's responsibility to prove that any employment requirement is directly job-related.

Albemarle Paper v. Moody.[5] In the Supreme Court case *Albermarle Paper* v. *Moody* in June 1975, the Court *reaffirmed* the idea that *any* "test" used for selecting or promoting employees must be a valid predictor of performance measure for a particular job. The term "test" includes such items as *performance appraisals* used for promotion decisions. The Court also found that if it can be shown that any selection test has an *adverse impact* (evidenced by hiring, promotion, etc., that does not result in a pattern similar to minority representation in the population), the burden of proof for showing that test is valid falls upon the *employer*. Thus, if some tests appear to have an adverse impact on blacks, for example, the employer must be prepared to demonstrate that the selection/promotion instruments measure what they are supposed to measure. Also, employment tests must be sound predictors of a person's future job success.

Washington v. Davis.[6] A 1976 Supreme Court decision in a case involving the hiring of police officers in Washington, D.C., represents a slight shift in emphasis. In this case the issue was a reading comprehension and aptitude test given to all applicants for police officer positions. The test contained actual material that the applicants would have to learn during a training program. Also, the city could show a good relationship between success in the training program and success as a police officer. The problem with the test was that a much higher percentage of women and blacks failed this aptitude test.

The court ruled that the city of Washington, D.C., did not discriminate unfairly because the test was very definitely job-related. The implication of this case was that if a test is clearly related to the job and tasks performed, it is not illegal just because a greater percentage of minorities or women do not pass it. The crucial issue is that a test must be specifically job-related, and not solely judged on its adverse impact.

University of California Regents v. Bakke.[7] In this case Bakke, a white man, applied to the University of California at Davis Medical School and was denied admission. The university had set aside sixteen places in each beginning class for ethnic minority persons. Bakke was denied admission even though he had scored higher on the admissions criteria than minorities who were admitted. Thus, Bakke felt he suffered "discrimination in reverse" and sued for admission.

REVERSE DISCRIMINATION may exist when a more qualified person is denied an opportunity because of guarantees given to protected group individuals who may be less qualified.

The Supreme Court reached a somewhat nebulous decision by ruling 5–4 that Bakke should be admitted but that admission plans that consider race as a factor are not illegal. The nine justices wrote six different opinions, with the swing decision being written by Justice Powell, who said: "Equal protection cannot mean one thing when applied to one individual and something else when applied to a person of another color." However, Powell also ruled that preserving racial diversity was a legitimate goal of the university. But, having a specific number of reserved slots was illegal. Powell stated that "race or ethnic background may be deemed a 'plus' in a particular applicant's file, yet it does not insulate the individual from comparison with all other candidates for the available seats." The ultimate effect of the Bakke decision was to set up further court tests in order to clarify the legal status of reverse discrimination concerns.

Kaiser Aluminum v. Weber.[8]   In this case Brian Weber, a white steelworker, charged Kaiser Aluminum and his union, the United Steelworkers, with "reverse discrimination." Under an agreement between the company and the union 50% of the slots in a crafts training program were reserved for blacks. Weber sued because he was denied admission to the training program even though he had more seniority than some black workers admitted to the program.

The U.S. Supreme Court ruled that because the affirmative action plan that gave blacks a preference was voluntarily agreed to by the company and union, the plan did not violate Title VII provisions. The key portion of the decision said that "the inference that Congress did not wish to ban all voluntary, race-conscious affirmative action being further supported by its use of the word 'require' rather than 'permit' in Title VII." The relevant sentence from Title VII said that "nothing in Title VII shall be interpreted to '*require*' any employer to grant preferential treatment to any group, because of that group's race...." Also, because the preference did not require discharging white workers and replacing them with black workers, the plan was a temporary measure used to eliminate racial inequality.

Some experts have indicated that the Supreme Court really "ducked the issue" by using one word as the basis for the decision. The Weber case did provide some guidance, but it did not settle the legal status of "reverse discrimination" once and for all.[9]

County of Washington v. Gunther.[10]   This focused on the issue of "equal pay for men and women performing "comparable" jobs. The major issue involved was labeled "comparable worth."

Comparable worth is the concept that jobs requiring comparable knowledge, skills, and ability should be paid similarly.

In this case Gunther and other women were prison matrons who were paid less than prison guards. The U.S. Supreme Court reached a very narrow decision, based upon a 5-to-4 decision. The decision specifically stated that the court was not ruling on the "comparable worth" issue. However, the majority opinion stated that Gunther could file a sex discrimination suit under the Civil Rights law even if the jobs involved were not equal jobs. The Court emphasized that it was not defining what must be done to prove sex discrimination on the "precise" contours of lawsuits challenging sex discrimination in compensation. The ultimate result of this case was to set up further court cases in order to specifically clarify the legal status of comparable worth and equal pay issues.

Undoubtedly, a number of the issues raised in the above cases, such as reverse discrimination and comparable worth, represent significant potential legal concerns. Each case regarding discrimination is considered on its own merit, and while precedents such as these certainly do apply, they are not guarantees that an employer will or will not be charged and found guilty of discrimination. Employers must be aware of precedents and the intent and interpretation of the law itself by the EEOC and other enforcement agencies.

Can you identify and discuss at least four important cases on EEO?

EQUAL EMPLOYMENT GUIDELINES

To implement the provisions of the Civil Rights Act of 1964, the Equal Employment Opportunity Commission (hereafter referred to as EEOC) and other federal agencies developed compliance guidelines and regulations. What became apparent was that each governmental entity had a slightly different set of rules and expectations. Finally in 1978 the major government agencies involved agreed upon a set of uniform guidelines.

Uniform Guidelines on Employee Selection Procedures

The 1978 guidelines apply to the EEOC, the Department of Labor's OFCCP, the Department of Justice, and the Office of Personnel Management.[11] They provide a framework used to determine if federal laws on discrimination are being adhered to by employers.

Tests and other selection procedures used in making employment decisions include but are not limited to:

• Hiring
• Promotions
• Recruiting
• Demotion
• Labor union membership requirements
• Licensing and certification requirements
• Training
• Performance appraisals.

These guidelines affect virtually all phases of personnel. There are two major means of compliance that are identified in the guidelines.

No "Adverse Impact" Strategy.   The first compliance strategy identified is for employers to have no adverse impact in their employment procedures. Generally, when courts have found that there is discrimination, they have found that what is important is the effect of employment policies and procedures regardless of their intent. Any practice, however harmless in intent, which has an "adverse impact" on members of a "protected group" is considered discrimination.

ADVERSE IMPACT occurs when there is a substantial under-representation of protected group members in employment decisions.

Under the guidelines, adverse impact is determined using the *4/5ths Rule.*

The 4/5THS RULE is that discrimination generally occurs if the selection rate for any protected group is less than 80% of the selection rate of majority groups.

An example of the 4/5ths rule is shown in Figure 4–5. Assume that Standard Company interviewed both men and women for manufacturing assembly jobs. Of the men who applied, 40% were hired; of the women who applied, 25% were hired. As shown, the selection rate for women is less than 80% (4/5ths) of the selection rate for men. Consequently, Standard Company does have an "adverse impact" in its employment process.

A percentage of women or minority workers in any job classification which is not in relation to their representation in the general population or workforce constitutes strong evidence of discriminatory practices and

Figure 4–5   Determining adverse impact.

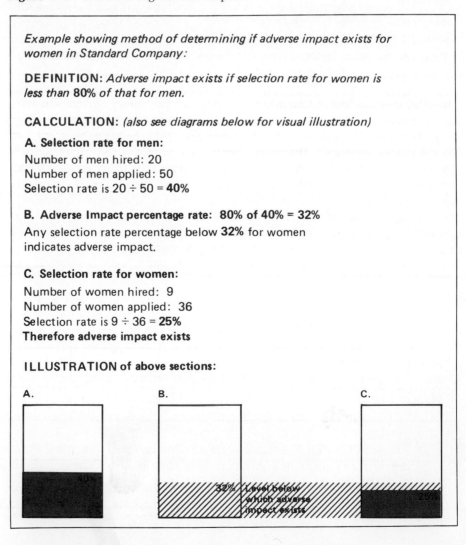

Example showing method of determining if adverse impact exists for women in Standard Company:

DEFINITION: *Adverse impact exists if selection rate for women is less than **80%** of that for men.*

CALCULATION: *(also see diagrams below for visual illustration)*

A. Selection rate for men:

Number of men hired: 20
Number of men applied: 50
Selection rate is 20 ÷ 50 = **40%**

B. Adverse Impact percentage rate: 80% of 40% = 32%

Any selection rate percentage below **32%** for women
indicates adverse impact.

C. Selection rate for women:

Number of women hired: 9
Number of women applied: 36
Selection rate is 9 ÷ 36 = **25%**
Therefore adverse impact exists

ILLUSTRATION of above sections:

A.   B.   C.

40%   32% Level below   25%
         which adverse
         impact exists

adverse impact. A company which has only 3% minority employees when the minority workforce in the area is 15% will have to show that its hiring is truly nondiscriminatory.

One strategy for complying that the EEOC guidelines identify is to have *no adverse impact.* Thus, if Standard Company hired at least eight women for every ten men hired, there would be no adverse impact. Some have skeptically referred to this approach as "getting your numbers in line." Others have stated that this approach may have the effect of imposing quotas on employers.[12] One caution for employers attempting to use this approach is that there must be no adverse impact at all levels and job groups and for all of the different "protected group" minorities. Consequently, taking the easy way out and "getting the numbers in line" is not really as easy as it appears.

The major advantage of the 4/5ths rule is that it is a yardstick that employers can use to determine if they are having adverse impact. For areas in which adverse impact exists, employers may then turn to the other compliance strategy of validating that employment decisions are based on job-related information.

Job-Related Validation Strategy.   The idea that personnel staffing practices must be valid includes such instruments as job descriptions, application blanks, interviews, employment tests, promotion tests, and performance appraisal practices. Hence, validity touches many of the common sources used to make employment and promotion decisions.

> VALIDITY means that a "test" actually measures what it says it measures.

For a general intelligence test to be valid, it must actually measure intelligence, not just a person's vocabulary. Therefore, an employment test that is valid must measure the person's ability to perform the job for which he/she is being hired. However, a test is useful only if it is *valid* and *reliable.*

> RELIABILITY refers to the consistency with which a test measures an item.

For a test to be reliable, an individual's score should be about the same every time that individual takes it, excluding practice effects. Unless a test measures a trait consistently (or reliably), it is of little value in predicting job performance. Consequently, the reliability of a test must be established before it is used.

A test is said to be valid for selection purposes if there is a significant relationship between performance on the test and performance on the job. The better a test can distinguish between satisfactory and unsatisfactory performance of the job, the greater its validity. Applicants' scores on valid tests can be used to predict their probable job performance. Acceptable reliability coefficients are quite high—a correlation of .80 or better. On the other hand, acceptable validity coefficients are considerably lower because of intervening variables, perhaps as low as .30 for "practical significance." Because of the importance of the validation strategy, it is examined in greater detail next.

What are two strategies to comply with 1978 uniform guidelines?

VALIDITY AND EQUAL EMPLOYMENT

If a charge of discrimination is brought against a company, the company must be able to demonstrate that its tests are valid. Tests of any kind attempt to predict performance on the job. The test is the *predictor,* and the job behavior is called the *criterion variable.* Careful job analysis determines exactly which behaviors are needed for each particular task. Predictors are then validated against behaviors as criteria to measure job performance. Some court cases have pointed out the difficulty in using subjective supervisory performance ratings as the criteria against which tests are validated. However, if the predictors do accurately predict job performance behavior, they are legally acceptable and quite useful in selection.

General aptitude and psychological tests, such as those dealing with mental abilities, are becoming increasingly difficult to validate, because a test must measure the person for the job and not the person in abstract (*Griggs* v. *Duke Power*). Current EEOC guidelines recognize four types of validity which may be used.

Types of Validity

The four basic types of validity are: (1) predictive validity, (2) concurrent validity, (3) content validity, and (4) construct validity. Each type is discussed as it relates to employment.

Predictive Validity. This method of validating employment practices is calculated by giving a test and then comparing the test results with the job performance of those tested. Figure 4–6 shows predictive validity.

Figure 4–6   Predictive validity.

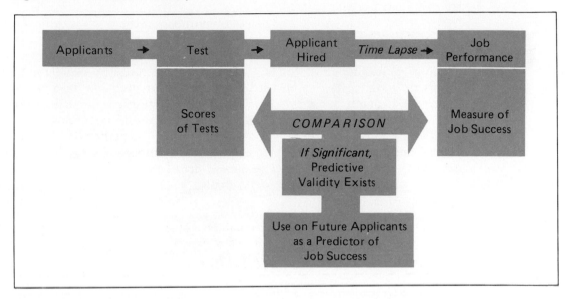

To illustrate how a predictive validity study might be designed, consider the following. A retail chain, Eastern Discount, wants to establish predictive validity for a pencil-and-paper arithmetic test it plans to use to hire cashiers. Obviously, it wants a test that will do the very best job of separating those who will do well from those who will not. Eastern Discount first hires 30 people and gives them all the pencil-and-paper test. Sometime later (perhaps six months) the scores on the test are compared with the 30 employees' success on the job. The test items that correlate highly with success on the job are considered valid predictors of performance and may be used to hire future employees.

However there are several problems with using predictive validity even though it is considered sound in a statistical sense. For example, a relatively large number of people have to be hired at once, and the test scores cannot be considered. Obviously the firm may hire both good and bad employees initially. Because of these and other problems, another type of validity is often used—concurrent validity.

Concurrent Validity.   Concurrent essentially means "at the same time." Figure 4–7 shows how concurrent validity is determined.

Using concurrent validity, current employees instead of those newly hired are used to validate the test. The test is given to current employees and then the scores are correlated with their performance ratings. A high correlation suggests that the test is able to differentiate between the better and the poorer employees.

Figure 4–7 Concurrent validity.

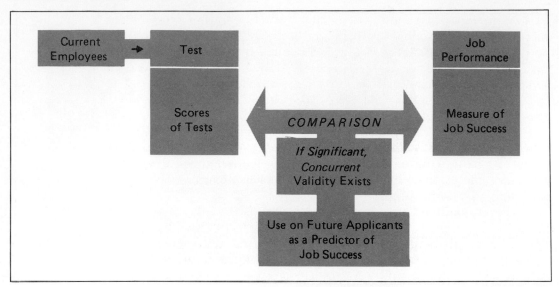

A major potential drawback with concurrent validity is that the extremely poor employees are no longer with the firm to be tested and the firm does not really have a representative range of people to test. Another problem is that the learning that might have taken place on the job has influenced the test score, and applicants taking the test without the benefit of the job experience might score low on the test, but might be able to do the job.

Content Validity.   This type of validity uses a logical and less statistical approach. In content validity a person would perform a test which is an actual sample of the work done on the job. Thus, an arithmetic test for a cashier would contain some of the calculations that a cashier would have to make on the job. Content validity is especially useful if the workforce is not large enough to accommodate better statistical designs.

Construct Validity.   This type of validity is somewhat more difficult to deal with than the others. In psychology a *construct* is an idea or characteristic inferred from research. In a sense, it is a figment of scientific imagination, something that cannot be seen but is assumed to be there. Most tests are designed to measure something; that something is typically a hypothetical construct, such as Intelligence Quotient (IQ), which attempts to measure a person's basic intelligence. Construct validity is more likely to run into difficulties with measuring the person in abstract than the other three validities.

Validity—Current Directions

Of the four types of validity, two stand out as being the most useful and preferred in personnel staffing activities: *predictive* and *content*. In the past, predictive validity has been preferred by EEOC because it is presumed to give the strongest tie to job performance. However, because predictive validity requires (1) a fairly large number of people and (2) a time gap between the test and the performance, content validity is increasingly being used.

Growth of Content Validity. Content validity is a solid alternative because its basic requirement is a good analysis of what tasks one performs in a job. By knowing exactly what is done, a test can be derived using an actual work sample.

In a metropolitan U.S. city a personnel specialist analyzed and rated the tasks of current firefighters to establish a test for firefighter applicants. Then a test was devised at a training center that reflected a realistic sample of a firefighter's job. Instead of having applicants lift weights to test strength, all applicants were required to drag a 75-pound hose up three flights of stairs in a four-minute period. This test represented the average amount of time that firefighters actually have in a real fire.

Many practitioners and specialists alike see content validity as a way to validate staffing requirements using a common sense approach. In the *Washington* v. *Davis* case discussed earlier, the Supreme Court also appeared to give support to the content validity approach because the training course test represented actual training materials used by police officers.

Can you explain predictive, concurrent, and content validity?

Using a modern view of personnel management, the governmental legislation and court decisions mentioned earlier are forcing employers to make changes that should have been made earlier. Using an invalid instrument to select, place, or promote an employee is not good management practice, as well as now being illegal. Management should be concerned with using valid instruments from the standpoint of the efficiency of operations. Many organizations are increasing the use of instruments that have been demonstrated to be valid. In one sense, the current requirements have done management a favor in that they are now forced to do what they probably should have been doing previously.

REVIEW AND PREVIEW

This chapter is primarily concerned with the effects of legal constraints on staffing. Forces such as the general public, competitors, and unions are major external forces; however, governmental influence is the most immediate concern for most personnel decisions. A manager involved with the staffing activities of an organization must be familiar with these external constraints.

There have been a number of landmark cases in which employers were found guilty of discrimination in their personnel practices. These court cases have helped define what really is considered discrimination and have emphasized the importance of reliability and validity of selection instruments or "tests."

In the next chapter the issues associated with implementing equal employment laws in an organization are considered. Affirmative action, as well as a number of other areas, such as sex discrimination, handicapped employees, and age discrimination, are discussed.

Review Questions

1. Discuss the following comment: "Staffing is too important to leave to chance if it is to be done effectively."
2. What is equal employment opportunity and how is it enforced?
3. Identify the impact of each of the following court cases:
   a. *Griggs* v. *Duke Power*
   b. *U.S.* v. *Georgia Power*
   c. *Albemarle Paper* v. *Moody*
   d. *Washington D.C.* v. *Davis*
   e. *U. of California Regents* v. *Bakke*
   f. *Kaiser Aluminum* v. *Weber*
   g. *County of Washington* v. *Gunther*
4. Why is validation considered to be a more business-like strategy of complying with the 1978 uniform guidelines in employee selection procedures?
5. Explain what validity is and differentiate among content, concurrent, and predictive validity.

Case: A Problem of Tardiness

Jack Canton, the foreman of the assembly department of the Sledge Tool Company is in charge of 25 employees. Of these employees, 24 are white—Andrew Caldwell is the only black man in the department.

Caldwell is 39, a divorcé with custody of his four small children ranging from two to seven years. Caldwell is considered by his superiors to have the best working knowledge in the department. Unfortunately he is tardy many mornings. He finds it hard to get his children up, ready for school or the babysitter's, and get himself to work on time. The problem has been discussed with Caldwell numerous times.

Andrew Caldwell did work very hard at his job. He stayed late in the afternoons and into the evenings to make up any time that he might miss in the mornings. There was little question in Canton's mind that Andrew Caldwell worked as hard as anyone in the department. The assembly operation was individual rather than a group work. The problem occurred on rush orders.

One Thursday, Caldwell's tardiness was holding up a particular job that had to be completed by 11:00 that morning. It was already 8:45 A.M., and no matter how hard Caldwell might work it would be impossible for him to finish it. Canton had thought about assigning the job to someone else, but he felt that Andrew was the most qualified man to do it.

At 9:30 A.M. Caldwell walked in the door and explained that his two-year-old was very sick and he had to call the doctor to get a special prescription for her. He would have called in, but with the turmoil at home, he had forgotten. Caldwell told Canton that he would work throughout his lunch hour and into the evening to make up for this lost time.

Several of the workers heard this conversation at their work stations. Their discussion was quite loud. The general nature of the conversation focused on such statements as: "Why should Caldwell get preferred treatment around here? He's always late but the boss never does a damn thing about it. Just because he's black, he gets special treatment."

Canton knew he had to do something about the situation quickly. It was beginning to get out of hand, but he did not exactly know what to do. He thought about what his next move should be.

QUESTIONS

1. What are the issues here?

2. What would you do?

---

* Adapted from: R. L. Hilgert, S. Schoen, and J. Towle, Cases and Policies in Human Resources Management, 3rd. ed., (Boston: Houghton Mifflin, 1978).

NOTES

1. Civil Rights Act, 1964, Title VII, Section 703A.

2. *Affirmative Action and Equal Employment*, U.S. Equal Employment Opportunity Commission, Washington, D.C., 1974, p. 12–13.

3. *Fair Employment Digest* (Berea, OH: American Society for Personnel Administration), September 1980, and March 1981, issues.

4. *Griggs* v. *Duke Power Co.*, 401 U.S. 424 [1971].

5. *Albemarle Paper Co.* v. *Moody*, 74-389 [1975].

6. *Washington, Mayor of Washington, D.C.* v. *Davis*, 74-1492 [1776].

7. *University of California Regents* v. *Bakke*, 438 U.S. 265 [1978].

8. *Kaiser Aluminum and Chemical Corp.* v. *Brian F. Weber*, 78-435 [1979].

9. David E. Robertson and Ronald D. Johnson, "Reverse Discrimination: Did *Weber* Decide the Issue?" *Labor Law Journal*, 31, November 1980, pp. 693–699.

10. *County of Washington* v. *Gunther*, 80-429 [1981].

11. "Adoption by Four Agencies of Uniform Guidelines on Employee Selection Procedures (1978), *Federal Register*, August 25, 1978, Part IV, pp. 38295–38309.

12. Charles F. Schonie and William L. Holley, "Interpretive Review of the Federal Uniform Guidelines on Employee Selection Procedures," *Personnel Administrator*, June 1980, pp. 44–48.

CHAPTER 5

Implementing Equal Employment

When you have read this chapter, you should be able to:

1. Explain the importance of good recordkeeping to EEO compliance.

2. Define affirmative action and identify its relationship to EEO.

3. Give examples of six different potential areas for discrimination.

Bob Wilson Versus the Feds

Bob Wilson works for International Paper Suppliers, a small paper whole-saler in a large city in the North-Central United States. Bob is the general manager and usually does most of the hiring. Selection is not an over-whelming burden since International Paper Suppliers has only 45 em-ployees, and Bob generally hasn't had to hire more than four or five people a year.

Three weeks ago Bob rejected three applicants and hired a fourth for the position of route driver with the company. One of the four applicants was Emilio Gonzales, a Hispanic man about 35 years old. Bob didn't feel that Emilio would feel "comfortable" with the rest of the work group. Bob had no personal biases, but he knew that some of the other drivers did have strong prejudices. Also, Emilio would have been the only Hispanic in the company, so he was rejected.

This morning in the mail Bob received a notification from the Equal Employment Opportunity Commission that Emilio Gonzales filed a complaint with the commission against International Paper Suppliers alleging that they are discriminatory in their hiring practices. Bob doesn't know very much about the EEOC or what his responsibilities are, but he does know that this is a problem he doesn't need during this busy time of the year.

Comments:

The days when hiring could be done on a hit and miss basis are pretty well gone. Even small organizations like International Paper Suppliers must concern themselves with government regulations regarding the selection and recruiting process. Bob's reasons for not hiring Emilio Gonzales may have made sense to him. But a more important question is, are they legally defensible? If Bob has told Emilio that he was not being hired because he was Hispanic, the EEOC is likely to use that fact in its case. Bob is probably on shaky legal footing and must now go through the EEOC complaint process. It is important that he know what his rights and obligations under the law really are.

T HE previous chapter dealt with the relationship between the staffing process and external constraints on that process, especially equal employment considerations. But what exactly does the EEOC expect from an employer in complying with the somewhat general guidelines in Title VII? And what actions on the part of the employers have led to findings of discrimination? These and other questions will be examined in this chapter.

EEO RECORDS

To aid enforcement of the equal employment opportunity (EEO) laws, the federal government through the enforcement agencies has required employers to survey workforces and maintain records on the distribution of minority individuals in the work force. All employers with at least 15 employees are required to keep records that can be requested by the Equal Employment Opportunity Commission (hereafter the EEOC) and the Office of Federal Contract Compliance Programs (hereafter the OFCCP). One small manufacturing firm in the Southwestern U.S. with 40 employees did not keep any EEO-related records. Because it was located in a small town, the owner of the company, Mr. Ryan (a name given to protect the guilty), felt that keeping such records was a waste of time and a government imposition. However, a woman applied for a manufacturing job, was told that "women did not belong in the plant," and then filed a discrimination complaint with a state equal employment agency. When the investigator checked on the complaint, he asked Mr. Ryan how many women worked in the company the previous three years, what jobs they held, the number of women who had applied for plant jobs in those three years, and other data. Obviously without any records Mr. Ryan had no defense. The end result was a substantial penalty imposed on Mr. Ryan and his firm in the form of back pay and penalties, in addition to having to give the woman complainant a job with retroactive seniority. In this situation discrimination was obvious, but without adequate records on past practices Mr. Ryan and his firm were subjected to greater pressure and penalties. It is for such reasons that all employers should maintain adequate employment records.

Annual Reporting Form

The most basic report that is filed with the EEOC is the annual report. The report is *not voluntary*. All employers with 100 or more employees (except state and local governments) or subsidiaries of another company that would total 100 employees must file the reports. Also, federal con-

Figure 5–1

Standard Form 100
(Rev. 12-76)
Approved GAO B-180541 (R0077)
Expires 12-31-78

EQUAL EMPLOYMENT OPPORTUNITY
EMPLOYER INFORMATION REPORT EEO-1

Joint Reporting Committee

- Equal Employment Opportunity Commission
- Office of Federal Contract Compliance Programs

Section A — TYPE OF REPORT
Refer to instructions for number and types of reports to be filed.

1. Indicate by marking in the appropriate box the type of reporting unit for which this copy of the form is submitted (MARK ONLY ONE BOX).

(1) ☐ Single-establishment Employer Report

Multi-establishment Employer:
(2) ☐ Consolidated Report
(3) ☐ Headquarters Unit Report
(4) ☐ Individual Establishment Report (submit one for each establishment with 25 or more employees)
(5) ☐ Special Report

2. Total number of reports being filed by this Company (Answer on Consolidated Report only) _____

Section B — COMPANY IDENTIFICATION *(To be answered by all employers)*

OFFICE USE ONLY

1. Parent Company
   a. Name of parent company (owns or controls establishment in item 2) omit if same as label

Name of receiving office | Address (Number and street)

a.

City or town | County | State | ZIP code | b. Employer Identification No.

b.

2. Establishment for which this report is filed. (Omit if same as label)
   a. Name of establishment

c.

Address (Number and street) | City or town | County | State | ZIP code

d.

b. Employer Identification No. | (If same as label. skip.)

Multi-establishment Employers: Answer on Consolidated Report only

3. Parent company affiliation
   a. Name of parent—affiliated company | b. Employer Identification No.

Address (Number and street) | City or town | County | State | ZIP code

---

Section C — EMPLOYERS WHO ARE REQUIRED TO FILE *(To be answered by all employers)*

☐ Yes ☐ No 1. Does the entire company have at least 100 employees in the payroll period for which you are reporting?

☐ Yes ☐ No 2. Is your company affiliated through common ownership and/or centralized management with other entities in an enterprise with a total employment of 100 or more?

☐ Yes ☐ No 3. Does the company or any of its establishments (a) have 50 or more employees AND (b) is not exempt as provided by 41 CFR 60-1.5, AND either (1) is a prime government contractor or first-tier subcontractor, and has a contract, subcontract, or purchase order amounting to $50,000 or more, or (2) serves as a depository of Government funds in any amount or is a financial institution which is an issuing and paying agent for U.S. Savings Bonds and Savings Notes?

NOTE: If the answer is yes to ANY of these questions, complete the entire form; otherwise skip to Section G.

Fig. 5–1 (continued)

Section D — EMPLOYMENT DATA

Employment at this establishment--Report all permanent, temporary, or part-time employees including apprentices and on-the-job trainees unless specifically excluded as set forth in the instructions. Enter the appropriate figures on all lines and in all columns. Blank spaces will be considered as zeros.

JOB CATEGORIES	OVERALL TOTALS (SUM OF COL B THRU K) A	NUMBER OF EMPLOYEES									
		MALE					FEMALE				
		WHITE (NOT OF HISPANIC ORIGIN) B	BLACK (NOT OF HISPANIC ORIGIN) C	HISPANIC D	ASIAN OR PACIFIC ISLANDER E	AMERICAN INDIAN OR ALASKAN NATIVE F	WHITE (NOT OF HISPANIC ORIGIN) G	BLACK (NOT OF HISPANIC ORIGIN) H	HISPANIC I	ASIAN OR PACIFIC ISLANDER J	AMERICAN INDIAN OR ALASKAN NATIVE K
Officials and Managers											
Professionals											
Technicians											
Sales Workers											
Office and Clerical											
Craft Workers (Skilled)											
Operatives (Semi-Skilled)											
Laborers (Unskilled)											
Service Workers											
TOTAL											
Total employment reported in previous EEO-1 report											

(The trainees below should also be included in the figures for the appropriate occupational categories above)

Formal On-the-job trainees	White collar											
	Production											

1. NOTE: On consolidated report, skip questions 2-5 and Section E.
2. How was information as to race or ethnic group in Section D obtained?
   1 ☐ Visual Survey   3 ☐ Other — Specify ....
   2 ☐ Employment Record   ....
3. Dates of payroll period used –

4. Pay period of last report submitted for this establishment

5. Does this establishment employ apprentices?
   This year? 1 ☐ Yes   2 ☐ No
   Last year? 1 ☐ Yes   2 ☐ No

Section E — ESTABLISHMENT INFORMATION

1. Is the location of the establishment the same as that reported last year?
   1 ☐ Yes   2 ☐ No   3 ☐ Did not report last year   4 ☐ Reported on combined basis

2. Is the major business activity at this establishment the same as that reported last year?
   1 ☐ Yes   2 ☐ No   3 ☐ No report last year   4 ☐ Reported on combined basis

OFFICE USE ONLY

3. What is the major activity of this establishment? (Be specific, i.e., manufacturing steel castings, retail grocer, wholesale plumbing supplies, title insurance, etc. Include the specific type of product or type of service provided, as well as the principal business or industrial activity.

e.

Section F — REMARKS

Use this item to give any identification data appearing on last report which differs from that given above, explain major changes in composition or reporting units, and other pertinent information.

Section G — CERTIFICATION (See instructions G)

Check one
1. ☐ All reports are accurate and were prepared in accordance with the instructions (check on consolidated only)
2. ☐ This report is accurate and was prepared in accordance with the instructions.

Name of Certifying Official	Title	Signature		Date
Name of person to contact regarding this report (Type or print)	Address (Number and street)			
Title	City and State	ZIP code	Telephone Area Code	Number	Extension

All reports and information obtained from individual reports will be kept confidential as required by Section 709 (e) of Title VII tractors who have a contract of $50,000 or more and financial institutions in which government funds are held or savings bonds are issued must file the annual report. The annual report must be filed by March 31 for the preceding year. A copy of the basic annual report form (EEO-1) is shown in Figure 5–1. Notice that this form requires employment data by job category, classified according to various protected groups.

Application Flow Data

Under EEO laws and regulations employers may be required to show that they do not discriminate in the recruiting and selection of protected groups. How many women applied versus the number hired can be compared to the selection rate of men to determine if adverse impact exists. Because racial data are not permitted on application blanks or other preemployment records, the EEOC allows a "visual" survey or a separate "applicant information form" that is not used in the selection process. The fact that minority group identification is not present on company records is not considered a valid excuse for failure to provide the data required. An example of such a form is shown in Figure 5–2. Notice that this form is filled out voluntarily by the applicant and the data must be maintained separately from all selection-related materials.

EEO Record Retention

All employment records must be maintained as required by the EEOC and "employer information reports" must be filed with the federal government. Further, any personnel or employment record made or kept by the employer must be maintained for review by the EEOC. Such records include application forms and records concerning hiring, promotion, demotion, transfer, layoff, termination, rates of pay or other terms of compensation, and selection for training and apprenticeship. Even those application forms or test papers completed by unsuccessful applicants may be requested. The length of time documents must be kept varies.

Notice Posting.   Under the Civil Rights Act employers are required to post an "officially approved notice" in a prominent place where employees can see it. This notice should state that the employer is an equal opportunity employer and does not discriminate.

Keeping good records, whether required by the government or not, is simply good personnel practice. Complete records, including individual records, are necessary for responding when a charge of discrimination has been made. If proper documentation is lacking, it may lead to an employee being given back a job which was performed poorly.

Figure 5-2 Applicant flow data form.

THE C COMPANY

THE FOLLOWING STATISTICAL INFORMATION IS REQUIRED FOR COMPLIANCE WITH FEDERAL LAWS ASSURING EQUAL EMPLOYMENT OPPORTUNITY WITHOUT REGARD TO RACE, COLOR, SEX, NATIONAL ORIGIN, RELIGION, AGE OR HANDICAP AS WELL AS THE VIETNAM ERA READJUSTMENT ACT. THE INFORMATION REQUESTED IS VOLUNTARY AND WILL REMAIN SEPARATE FROM YOUR APPLICATION FOR EMPLOYMENT.

A. MONTH `06` DAY `06` YEAR `84` APPLICATION DATE
1   6

B. `529` – `50` – `6356` `A` APPLICANT SOCIAL SECURITY NUMBER
7   16

C. `G` FIRST INITIAL   D. `R` MIDDLE INITIAL
17   18

E. `DRABNER` LAST NAME
19   32

STREET
F. `12184 E KEPNER PLACE` ADDRESS
33   58

G. CITY `AURORA` STATE (first 2 letters) `CO` ZIP `80012`
59   71   72 73   74   78

H. `A` 1/ EEO CODES

EEO CODES 1/
A—White Male
B—White Female
C—Black Male
D—Black Female
E—Hispanic Male (Spanish Origin)
F—Hispanic Female (Spanish Origin)
G—American Indian/Alaskan Native Male
H—American Indian/Alaskan Native Female
I—Asian or Pacific Islander Male
J—Asian or Pacific Islander Female

I. MONTH `10` DAY `15` YEAR `38` BIRTH DATE
80 81   82 83   84 85

J. ☐ ARE YOU HANDICAPPED—Impairment which substantially limits one or more of a person's life activities
86
NO —LEAVE BLANK
YES—ENTER 'Y' Ask for Form 2

K. ☐ ARE YOU A DISABLED VETERAN—
87
30% V.A. Compensation or discharged because of disability incurred in line of duty
NO —LEAVE BLANK
YES—ENTER 'Y'
Ask for Form 2

L. `Y` ARE YOU A VIETNAM ERA VETERAN—
88
180 days Active Duty between Aug. 15, 1964 & May 7, 1975
NO —LEAVE BLANK
YES—ENTER 'Y'
Ask for Form 2

JOB YOU HAVE APPLIED FOR (see reverse side) _SAFETY & OCCUPATIONAL HEALTH SPEC._

LOCATION APPLICATION IS MADE FOR _DENVER_ _COLORADO_
(City or Town)   State

TO BE COMPLETED BY OFFICE ACCEPTING APPLICATION

☐ DIVISION

DEPT. APPLICATION IS MADE FOR

EEO STAFF USE ONLY
90   99

M. ☐ REFERRAL SOURCE
89
A—Walk in/Write in
B—Ad Response
C—State Employment Agency
D—College Placement Office
E—Minority Referral Agency
F—CETA Referral
G—Private Employment Agency

Applicant's Signature

Used with permission.

What records are a part of EEO compliance?

AFFIRMATIVE ACTION

Affirmative action basically means *results*. This effort requires continuing commitment by an employer to improve its equal employment opportunity posture, rather than make merely a one-time effort to comply with certain standards.

Nature of Affirmative Action

Under an affirmative action plan, an employer will specify targets and steps that will be taken to guarantee equal employment opportunities for minority group personnel.

> AFFIRMATIVE ACTION refers to efforts by organizations to identify problem areas in their minority employment and to identify goals to overcome those problems.

Affirmative action programs often include specific timetables and goals for hiring of minority members where there are deficiencies.

As an example, in a settlement involving American Telephone and Telegraph (AT&T) affirmative actions included:

1. Hiring and promotion targets for women and minorities in each job classification. These targets are to be reviewed by OFCC regularly.
2. Goals for employing men in previously all-women jobs.
3. Assessment of all female college graduates hired since 1965 to determine interest and potential for higher level jobs.[1]

Who Must Have?   Affirmative Action Plan requirements are enforced by the OFCCP. Employers who meet OFCCP regulations must have a formally prepared Affirmative Action Plan (AAP).

The two major conditions that are considered are (1) the number of employees the employer has, and (2) the size of the contract. As a result of concerns about the paperwork demands on employers, adjustments in the requirements have been made since 1981. To identify correct requirements, an employer should check with a labor attorney or the OFCCP.

Development of an Affirmative Action Plan (AAP)

There are a number of suggested steps for developing an effective AAP. See Figure 5–3 for an example of these basic steps. The most important step is the first one, developing a policy that indicates a commitment to affirmative action. In a survey of Contract Compliance officers the two most important parts of compliance efforts are: (1) evidence that top management is seriously committed to EEO policies and (2) violations of those policies are enforced.[2]

Figure 5–3 Basic steps to develop an effective affirmative action program.

---

1. Issue written EEO policy and Affirmative Action Commitment.
2. Appoint a top official with responsibility and authority to direct and implement the program.
3. Publicize the policy internally and externally.
4. Survey present minority and female employment by department and job classification.
5. Develop *goals* and *timetables* to improve utilization of minorities, males and females in each area where underutilization has been Identified.
6. Develop and implement specific programs to achieve goals.
7. Establish internal audit and reporting systems to monitor progress.
8. Develop supportive in-house and community programs.

Contents of an AAP

An Affirmative Action Plan is a formal document that is available for review by employees and enforcement officers. Also, the contents of the plan and the policies flowing from it must be reviewed with operating managers and supervisors as part of managerial training programs.

Many plans are very long and require extensive staff time to prepare. One small firm with 150 employees has a plan that is 48 pages long, while the plan for Mutual and United of Omaha Insurance Companies is over 1000 pages long. The table of contents of a plan for a small employer is shown in Figure 5–4.

Figure 5–4 Affirmative action plan (sample).

TABLE OF CONTENTS

I	Policy Statement
II	Dissemination of Policy
	A. Internal
	B. External
III	Responsibilities
IV	Required Utilization
V	Goals and Time Tables
VI	Identification of Problem Areas
VII	Dissemination of AAP
VIII	Audit and Reporting
IX	Sex Discrimination
X	Support of Action Programs
IX	Consideration of Minorities
XII	Religious and National Origin Guidelines
XIII	Handicapped Policy
XIV	Veteran and Vietnam Policy

What is the relationship of affirmative action to EEO?

EQUAL EMPLOYMENT AND MANAGEMENT PRACTICES

A wide variety of managerial practices have been affected by equal employment and affirmative action regulations. To provide a broad picture of the current impact of equal employment, the following overview of selected management practices indicates some which have been upheld and some which have been found to be illegal. It is difficult to draw general conclusions from court decisions because the court approaches each factual situation with a straightforward legal analysis of *that particular situation*, rather than trying to establish ideological patterns. However, this analysis will highlight some recent court decisions in the discrimination area.

Sex Discrimination

Title VII of the Civil Rights Act prohibits discrimination in employment on the basis of sex. However, as with racial discrimination, it has taken a series of court decisions and EEOC rulings to determine exactly how broad that prohibition really is.

Bonafide Occupational Qualifications and Sex Discrimination.   Some of the difficulties encountered in enforcing the abolition of sex discrimination center around the Bonafide Occupational Qualification (BFOQ) mentioned in the Civil Rights Act. What constitutes a BFOQ is subject to different interpretations in various courts across the country. Employment can be reasonably restricted to one sex on the basis of "authenticity." An example of this authenticity is women actresses portraying women characters. Also BFOQ's exist on the basis of "community standards of morality" or "propriety," such as male restroom attendants in men's restrooms.

A BFOQ was found to exist in the following case:

> A college woman whose major is statistics, marketing, and survey work decided she wanted to spend the summer working for a poll-taking firm. She planned her course of action carefully, writing the government bureaus to learn where concentrated centers of surveying activity might be. She picked several large metropolitan areas where polls were taken and watched newspapers from these areas for employment ads. When one appeared she wrote and requested a job. She received no answer. Because summer was near she traveled to that city to visit the company. She was told that the two areas that were being studied required work and travel in rough neighborhoods. The company had a policy of not hiring women for such assignments.

> The woman knew that the Civil Rights Law prohibited discrimination because of sex. She decided she would attack this company's decision through the EEOC which agreed to investigate. The company in question reiterated its position and said that it had two territories left open, both in slum neighborhoods. The surveyors had to travel on foot a good part of the time they were in the area, and interviews were sometimes held at night. In fact, one of their regular workers had been beaten by a gang of youths and was recuperating at home. The worker, a woman, had quit, saying the area made her too nervous. The company therefore felt it had a right to specify the sex of employees for these areas. It was looking for a man, one who was both diplomatic and able to take care of himself. Because of the

dangers involved, interviewers for these areas were being paid time and a half.

The student countered that during the day a woman alone in a house would be more receptive to another woman. She expressed confidence that she could handle any situation that developed. The commission said it felt there were no legal grounds for further action. It based its decision on the dangerous conditions which prevailed in the surveying area and concluded that hiring a man for the position made good sense and was not necessarily wrongful discrimination.[3]

It should be noted, however, that the definition of a BFOQ has been increasingly narrowed as a result of court rulings over the years.

Restrictive State Laws.   Many states have laws to "protect" women by requiring that they be restricted to a certain number of working hours a week or by specifying the maximum weight a woman is allowed to lift (25 pounds in several states). The EEOC has disputed these laws, and in many cases they have been ruled invalid in court because they conflict with federal law and are not reasonable grounds for denying jobs to women.

Discrimination in Job Assignments.   Title VII was violated when an employer (1) established job categories designated "male" or "either" and refused to consider women under any circumstances for jobs designated as male jobs, (2) established weight limitations that had the effect of continuing male and female job classifications that previously existed, and (3) subsequently adopted a policy of designating jobs as either "heavy" or "light" and failed to consider women for jobs designated as "heavy" unless women specifically requested such jobs. Since the employer had historically classified its employees on the basis of sex (in violation of Title VII), it could not rely on word-of-mouth notice of job vacancies.[4]

A qualified woman who unsuccessfully applied for a position of resident trainee mortician established sex discrimination by showing that (1) the funeral home shortly thereafter hired a man for that position; (2) licensed embalmers and morticians, both nationally and locally, were, in overwhelming preponderance, men; (3) the funeral home had never employed a woman as a licensed embalmer, licensed mortician, or resident trainee mortician; and (4) the funeral home did not employ both men and women to do the same work in any of its job categories.[5]

Equal Pay and "Comparable Worth".   An amendment to the Fair Labor Standards Act enacted in 1963 forbids employers to pay lower wage rates to employees of one sex than to the other sex for equal work performed under similar working conditions. The "comparable worth" issue, discussed in chapter 4, was not clarified by the Gunther case. This Equal Pay Act, enforced by the EEOC, applies only to employees subject to the minimum wage provisions of the Fair Labor Standards Act. An exception to this law is a difference in pay based on some factor other than sex.

To illustrate, a country hospital in Kentucky violated the Equal Pay Act by paying female aides and male orderlies substantially different salaries for the same work. The hospital could not show that the higher paid orderly positions required substantially greater effort, greater skill, or assumption of greater responsibility.[6] In another case, three women employed by the Fargo Police Department as "car markers" showed that, because their salaries were 50% lower than their male predecessors, there was a violation of the Equal Pay Act. Even though the men were trained as patrol officers, they seldom, if ever, performed any duty other than car marker.[7]

In summary, the critical aspect of differences in pay is that the *jobs must be substantially different.* Tasks performed only intermittently or infrequently do not make jobs different enough to justify significantly different wages. This point is best clarified by the decision in a case involving male and female managers working for Sears Roebuck. A wage difference between male and female managers was not justified merely because two of the male managers did "extra duties." Other managers did "extra duties" at about the same rate, which was infrequent and sporadic. Different wages may not be paid male and female managers who are performing essentially the same job.[8]

Pregnancy Discrimination Act and Maternity Leaves.   In 1978 a federal law, the Pregnancy Discrimination Act (PDA), was passed. This act requires that women employees "affected by pregnancy, childbirth, or related medical conditions will be treated the same for all employment related purposes."[9] The major impact of the act was to change maternity leave policies and employee benefit systems. Under the PDA pregnancy must be treated just as any other medical condition. The same provisions regarding disability insurance and leaves of absences must apply to pregnant employees as would apply to male workers who were injured in a car wreck. In some situations male employees have been given paternity leave by their employers.

Sexual Harassment.   In 1980 the EEOC issued guidelines designed to curtail sexual harassment. As the commentary opening section 2 indicated, sexual harassment is an age-old problem that was finally addressed. Sexual harassment ranges from sexual innuendoes and lewd remarks to physical actions.

Under the guidelines employers are expected to have specific policies prohibiting sexual harassment and to discipline offenders. In one case in Minnesota an employer had to pay $5000 in damages and lost wages to a black female employee. The woman quit her job after informing the company that several men verbally and physically harassed her at work, but the company ignored her complaints.[10]

Sexual harassment by supervisors and managers who expect sexual favors if an employee is to be granted a raise or promotion is totally inappropriate in a work environment. This view has even been supported in a situation in the U.S. Army in which a woman officer was punished for sexually harassing an enlisted man. Also, a few sexual harassment cases have been filed involving a manager and an employee of the same sex. However, the vast majority of situations have involved harassment of a woman by a man.

The Handicapped and Discrimination

Disabled and handicapped people have special discrimination problems in that often they are not considered for jobs for which they are qualified. To deal with their concerns, in 1973 Congress passed the Vocational Rehabilitation Act, and in 1974 it passed twelve amendments officially titled The Rehabilitation Act of 1974. These acts constitute the basis for federal intervention into employment of the handicapped.

Generally, the net effect of the law and subsequent executive orders is as follows:

1. Federal contractors and subcontractors with more than $2,500 contract must take affirmative action to hire qualified handicapped people.
2. Contractors have an obligation to inform all employees and unions about their affirmative action plans and to survey their internal labor forces to locate qualified handicapped.
3. The Architectural Barriers Act of 1968 attempts to ensure that buildings financed with public money are accessible to the handicapped.

Many companies have recognized the advantages of hiring the handicapped without any pressure from the law or courts. McDonnell Douglas Corporation and Inland Steel were leaders in the area before the laws were enacted.[11]

Seniority and Discrimination

The U.S. Supreme Court has ruled that seniority systems are not invalid just because they perpetuate the effects of past discrimination. The decision involved alleged discrimination by a trucking company against blacks and Spanish-surnamed persons who sought employment as line drivers. Those who were hired were given lower-paying and less-desirable jobs as servicemen or city drivers and, when they sought to transfer to line jobs, they could not carry over their seniority. The Court concluded that the seniority system was entirely bonafide, applying equally to all races and ethnic groups. To the extent it locked employees into non-line-driver jobs, it did so for all.[12]

Religion and Discrimination

The EEOC proposed guidelines on religious discrimination in 1979. However, they were extremely controversial and were not adopted. Consequently, the general rule established in a U.S. Supreme Court case involving TransWorld Airlines represents the guide in this area.

In that case, *TWA* v. *Hardison,*[13] Hardison worked for TWA in Kansas City and was a member of the World Wide Church of God, which forbids working on Saturday. However, under the terms of a union contract, low seniority workers such as Hardison could be called to work special assignments on Saturdays. TWA offered to change the work assignment, but the union objected. Then TWA tried other alternatives, but none were acceptable to Hardison and the union. Ultimately, Hardison refused to work on Saturday, was discharged, and filed suit.

The ruling by the Supreme Court was that an employer is required to make reasonable accommodation of an employee's religious beliefs. Because TWA had done so, the ruling denied Hardison discrimination charges.

Offering alternative work schedules, making use of compensatory time-off, or otherwise adjusting to employee religious beliefs are recommended. However, once "reasonable" (a somewhat vague standard) accommodation efforts have been made, the employer has abided by the law. It must be stressed that refusing to hire individuals because of their religion or religious beliefs is illegal.[14]

Employment Uses of Conviction and Arrest Records

Generally, courts have held that conviction records may be used if the offense could be considered job-related in nature. For example, a bank could use an applicant's conviction for forgery as a valid basis for rejection. However, some decisions have held that only convictions which could be seen as job-related occurring within the most recent five years are allowed. Consequently, employers often have a phrase added to an inquiry about conviction, such as, "Indication of a conviction will not be an absolute bar to employment."

Arrest records have been generally viewed with suspicion by courts. Statistics indicate that in some geographic areas a greater number of minorities are arrested than nonminorities. Consequently, using arrests, not convictions, may have an adverse impact on some groups protected by Title VII.[15]

Discrimination because of Grooming and Appearance

A variety of appearance features has been examined for discriminatory impact. Some of the common areas that have been ruled on are hair length, beards, and dress codes. Employer grooming codes which require different hair lengths for male and female employees bear such negligible relation to the purposes of Title VII that it cannot be concluded that they violate the act.[16] Regarding beards, an employer that maintained a rule forbidding employees at its produce warehouse to wear beards did not violate Title VII's ban on sex discrimination when it discharged a warehouse employee for refusing to shave off his beard.[17] Likewise, regarding dress codes, an employer did not violate Title VII's ban on sex discrimination when it discharged a male employee for refusing to wear a tie. There was no merit found in his contention that it enforced unequally separate dress and grooming codes for male employees and female employees.[18]

Discriminatory Use of Height-Weight Restrictions

Many of the cases involving discriminatory use of height-weight restrictions were actually sex or race discrimination cases. Employers tried to prohibit women or traditionally short minority individuals from being employed. For example, the state of Alabama violated Title VII in setting height and weight restrictions for correctional counselors. The restrictions (5 feet, 2 inches and 120 pounds) would exclude 41.13% of the female population of the country but less than 1% of the men. The Supreme Court found that the state's attempt to justify the requirements as essential for job-related strength failed for want of evidence. The Court suggested that if strength were the quality sought, the state could have adopted a strength requirement.[19]

Age Discrimination

The Age Discrimination in Employment Act of 1967, amended in 1978, makes it illegal for an employer to discriminate in compensation, terms, conditions, or privileges of employment because of the employee's age.

It is unlawful (1) to fail or refuse to hire or to discharge or otherwise discriminate against any individual, applicant, or

employee 40 to 70 years old as to compensation, terms,
conditions, or privileges of employment because of age, or
because he has opposed an unlawful employment practice
or taken part in asserting his rights against an employer
who has unlawfully so discriminated, (2) to limit, segregate,
or classify employees so as to deprive any employee 40 to
70 years old of employment opportunities or adversely
affect his status as an employee because of his age, (3) to
use printed or published notices or advertisements
indicating any preference, limitation, specification, or
discrimination based upon age, (4) to reduce the salary rate
of any employee in order to comply with the act.[20]

The act does not apply if age is a Bonafide Occupational Qualification. Nor do the prohibitions against age discrimination apply when
an individual is disciplined or discharged for good cause, such as poor
job performance.

For many years racial and sex discrimination cases overshadowed
age discrimination cases. However, in May 1975, Standard Oil of California agreed to a $2 million settlement for 160 older workers laid off
during a reduction-in-force beginning in 1970. In June of 1974, the U.S.
Labor Department filed a $20 million suit on behalf of 300 older em-
ployees laid off when the B & O Railroad merged with the C & O
Railroad.[21] With these cases as forerunners, the number of age discrimination cases has increased significantly. This act is discussed in more
detail in chapter 13 because it relates directly to retirement-related
benefits.

Child Labor

Child labor laws, found in Section XII of the Fair Labor Standards Act,
set the minimum age for most employment at 16 years. For "hazardous"
occupations, 18 years is the minimum. A list of 17 hazardous occupations
is contained in Figure 5–5.

The law is quite strict for 14- and 15-year olds, who may essentially
hold only clerical, office, and retail food service jobs, pump gas, or do
errand and delivery work. They can work only between 7 A.M. and 7
P.M. during the school year and are restricted to an eight-hour day and
a 40-hour week. These provisions do not apply to newspaper delivery,
theater performances, and children working for their parents in such
non-hazardous occupations as farming.

Many organizations require *age certificates* for employees because
the Fair Labor Standards Act places the responsibility on the employer
to ascertain an individual's age. Asking for an age certificate helps an
employer avoid unknowingly hiring someone who is too young to per-

Figure 5–5 Child labor and hazardous occupations.

1. Manufacturing or storing explosives
2. Driving a motor-vehicle and being an outside helper
3. Coal mining
4. Logging and sawmilling
5. Power-driven wood-working machines*
6. Exposure to radioactive substances and to ionizing radiations
7. Power-driven hoisting apparatus
8. Power-driven metal-forming, -punching, and -shearing machines*
9. Mining, other than coal mining
10. Slaughtering, or meat packing, processing, or rendering*
11. Power-driven bakery machines
12. Power-driven paper-products machines*
13. Manufacturing brick, tile, and related products
14. Power-driven circular saws, band saws, and guillotine shears*
15. Wrecking, demolition, and shipbreaking operations
16. Roofing operations*
17. Excavation operations

* *In certain cases, the law provides exemptions for apprentices and student learners, in these occupations.*

(Source: Employment Standards Administration, Wage and Hour Division, U.S. Department of Labor, *A Message to Young Workers about the Fair Labor Standards Act, as Amended in 1974.* WH Publication #1236, Revised, 1976, p. 2.)

form a hazardous job. These certificates may be issued by a representative of a state labor department, education department, or by a local school official. In various states these certificates may be referred to as age certificates, employment certificates, work permits, or working papers.

MANAGERIAL GUIDE TO EQUAL EMPLOYMENT INQUIRIES

The variety of areas in which discrimination may occur is quite broad, as the discussion has indicated. To narrow the focus, Figure 5–6 contains guidelines for lawful and unlawful preemployment inquiries. All those inquiries labeled as "discriminatory" have been so designated because of findings of adverse impact in court cases. Although many different questions are often asked in interviews and on application blanks, all of them may not be permitted under existing equal employment regulations. This list, developed by an equal employment enforcement

Figure 5–6 Guidance to lawful and unlawful pre-employment inquiries.

Subject of Inquiry:	It is not discriminatory to inquire about:	It may be discriminatory to inquire about:
1. Name	a. Whether applicant had ever worked under a different name	a. The original name of an applicant whose name had been legally changed. b. The ethnic association of applicant's name
2. Birthplace & Residence	a. Applicant's place of residence, length of applicant's residence in Nebraska and/or city where employer is located.	a. Birthplace of applicant b. Birthplace of applicant's parents c. Birth certificate, naturalization or baptismal certificate
3. Race or Color	a. General distinguishing characteristics such as scars, etc.	a. Applicant's race or color of applicant's skin
4. National Origin & Ancestry		a. Applicant's lineage, ancestry, national origin, descendants, parentage or nationality b. Nationality of applicant's parents or spouse
5. Sex & Family Composition		a. Sex of applicant b. Dependents of applicant c. Marital status
6. Creed or Religion		a. Applicant's religious affiliation b. Church, parish or religious holidays observed
7. Citizenship	a. Whether the applicant is in the country on a visa, which permits him to work or is a citizen	a. Whether applicant is a citizen of a country other than the United States.
8. Language	a. Language applicant speaks and/or writes fluently	a. Applicant's mother tongue, language commonly used by applicant at home
9. References	a. Names of persons willing or proved professional and/or character references for applicant	a. Name of applicant's pastor or religious leader
10. Relatives	a. Names of relatives already employed by the Company b. Name and address of person or relative to be notified in an emergency	a. Name and/or address of any relative of applicant
11. Organizations	a. Applicant's membership in any union, professional service or trade organization	a. All clubs, social fraternities, societies, lodges, or organizations to which the applicant belongs where the name or character of the organization indicates the race, creed, color, or religion, national origin, sex or ancestry of its members
12. Arrest Record & Convictions		a. Number and kinds of arrests and convictions unless related to job performance.
13. Photographs		a. Photographs with application or before hiring b. Resume with photo of applicant.
14. Height & Weight		a. Any inquiry into height and weight of applicant, except where it is a bona fide occupational requirement
15. Physical Limitations	a. Whether applicant has the ability to perform job related functions	a. Whether an applicant is handicapped, or the nature or severity of a handicap
16. Education	a. Training an applicant has received if related to the job applied for	a. Educational attainment of an applicant unless there is validation that having certain educational backgrounds (i.e., high school diploma or college degree) is necessary to perform the functions of the job or position applied for
17. Financial Status		a. An applicant's debts or assets b. Garnishments

(Source: Used with permission of Omaha, Nebraska, Human Relations Department.)

agency, illustrates the care that managers must take to avoid the appearance as well as the actual act of discrimination.

It should be clearly understood that this guide is not a complete list of questions. Employers can obtain all needed information about applicants as long as the information cannot be used for discriminatory purposes. As additional court decisions are made, employers should keep informed of changes that occur.

Once an employer tells an applicant he or she is hired (the "point of hire"), earlier prohibited inquiries may be made. *After* hiring, medical examination forms, group insurance, and other enrollment cards containing inquiries relating directly or indirectly to race, color, religion, or national origin may be filled out. Photographs or other evidence of race or religion and national origin may be requested *after* hire for legal and necessary purposes, but not before. However, such data may need to be maintained in a separate personnel records system in order to avoid its use when making promotion decisions.

REVIEW AND PREVIEW

This chapter has dealt with some of the implementation issues surrounding the EEO. In addition to surveying the workforce and keeping good records, many employers must develop Affirmative Action Plans. Finally, a number of areas of management practice affected by EEO were described.

The number of court cases mentioned indicate that managers must stay current in this field, since it is changing rapidly. Areas such as equal pay, maternity, and seniority policies have all been affected by court decisions.

The next section builds upon this general understanding of equal employment and turns specifically to activities involved in staffing the organization. Chapter 6 looks at the process of analyzing jobs and work, a critical prelude to recruiting and selecting employees.

Review Questions

1. Discuss: "How can I report race to the EEOC when I cannot ask it on my application blank?"
2. What is affirmative action? Why is it important?
3. Evaluate the following statement by the president of a small conpany: "I can hire or promote whomever I please, as long as I get someone who can do the job."
4. Why do some employers require age certificates?

Case: Discrimination?

Ms. Ruth Wittman, a black woman, was employed as an operator of a check reader-sorter machine in a bank. After two years on the job, Ms. Wittman was discharged for being habitually absent and tardy. She filed an official charge of discrimination with the District Office of the Equal Employment Opportunity Commission (EEOC). She listed the following allegations.

1. Although the bank had terminated her employment because of excessive absenteeism, a white employee in her department, who had as many absences as she, was not terminated or reprimanded by the department manager.

2. A white worker in the department was allowed to leave the building during working hours, whereas she was not allowed to leave the building during working hours.

3. A white employee was assigned lighter blocks of work for processing.

4. She was restricted by the assistant department manager from having conversation with her co-workers. When she discussed this problem with the department manager, he did not seem to understand the problem and failed to correct it.

The bank made the following responses to the allegations.

1. No employee in the entire bank had a combined absence-tardiness record as poor as that of Ms. Wittman. Written documentation was furnished demonstrating that Ms. Wittman had been counseled on 54 separate occasions in a two-year period concerning excessive absenteeism and tardiness.

2. Bank policy prohibits employees from leaving the building during working hours except under unusual circumstances and then only with management permission. The department manager stated that he administers this policy in a completely fair manner without regard to race or color.

3. All blocks of work in the department are assigned on a random basis without regard to race or color. Employees in training programs normally have lighter work loads until the training period has been completed.

4. A grievance procedure is outlined in the employee handbook. If an employee is not satisfied after talking with the department manager, he or she is encouraged to talk with the personnel officer or another officer of the bank.

QUESTION

Is this discrimination on an illegal basis?

NOTES

1. *Affirmative Action and Equal Employment* (U.S. Equal Employment Opportunity Commission, 1974), p. 10.

2. Kenneth E. Marino, "Conducting an Internal Compliance Review of Affirmative Action," *Personnel*, March-April 1980, pp. 24–34.

3. *Dynamic Management Series, 106*, p. 9. Used with permission of Bureau of Business Practice, Waterford, Connecticut.

4. *Nance* v. *Union Carbide Corp.*, 13 FEP Cases 211/39 F. Supp. 436 (W.N.C. 1975).

5. *Sharp* v. *Brown and Co. Funeral Home*, _____F. Supp. _____ (E. Mich. 1977).

6. *Brennan* v. *Owensboro-Daviess County Hospital*, 523 F.2d 1013 (6th Cir. 1975).

7. *Peltier* v. *City of Fargo*, 533 F.2d 374 (8th Civ 1976).

8. *Brennan* v. *Sears, Roebuck and Co.* 410 Supp. 84 (ND Iowa 1976).

9. Public Law 95-555, 92 Stat. 2076, October 31, 1978.

10. *Fair Employment Digest*, (Berea, OH: American Society for Personnel Administration), September 1980, p. 4.

11. Gopal C. Pati, "Countdown on Hiring the Handicapped," *Personnel Journal*, 57, March 1978, p. 149.

12. *International Brotherhood of Teamsters* v. *U.S.*, 45 L.W. 4506, 1977.

13. *TransWorld Airlines* v. *Hardison*, 432 U.S. 63 (1977).

14. For a more detailed discussion, see John D. Blackburn and Kathryn P. Sheehan, "Recent Developments in Religious Discrimination: The EEOC's Proposed Guidelines," *Labor Law Journal*, 31, June 1980, pp. 335–339, and John M. Norwood, "But I Can't Work Saturdays," *Personnel Administrator*, January 1980, pp. 25–30.

15. See Ralph J. Zatskis, "The Legality of the Arrest-Conviction Record Inquiry Under Title VII," *Labor Law Journal*, 28, September 1977, pp. 572–582.

16. For example, see *Barker* v. *Taft Broadcasting Co.* 14 FEP Cases 697, 549 F.2d 400 (6th Cir. 1977); *Druia* v. *Delta Airlines*, 13 FEP Cases 1167, 410 F. Supp. 513 (E. Mich. 1976).

17. *Kearney* v. *Safeway Stores*, 14 FEP Cases 55, _____F. Supp.__ (W. Wash. 1975).

18. *Fountain* v. *Safeway*, 15 FEP Cases 96, 555 F.2d 753 (9th Cir. 1977).

19. *Dothard* v. *Rawlinson*, 45 LW 4888.

20. Employment Act of 1967, as amended in 1978.

21. "The Courts Reinterpret Old-Age Discrimination," *Business Week*, February 24, 1975, p. 91.

Staffing the Organization and Its Work

THE NATURE OF THE "NEW BREED" OF EMPLOYEE

In the following interview, the editor of *Personnel Journal* talked with a number of personnel executives about major issues in personnel today. This portion of that discussion deals with the executives' opinions about the changing nature of the work force that their companies must recruit, select, and place in jobs.[1]

Douglas H. Marr, Assistant Vice President, Equitable Life Assurance Society of the U.S., New York, NY

Marr: There is an emerging work population which is beginning to internalize the issues and "expectation of involvement" which appeared in the 1960s. These workers want to help run the company. We hire many MBAs in an analytical capacity, and they fully expect to quickly influence corporate policy and investments.

It was different 20 years ago. You paid your dues and worked your way up the corporate ladder. I see a growing stress between the expectations of younger workers, who want greater participation, and older workers, who are setting policy.

In the insurance industry, we have a whole populace of generally conservative people who are facing a new group of workers who expect a freedom of choice, to have a say in the organization, and to manage their own careers.

I think it is important to help both groups in the work force cope with the stress of our changing and temporary society—professionally as well as personally.

PJ Editor: What do you mean by a "temporary society"?

Marr: By a temporary society, I am referring to changing organizational structures, changing corporate policies, and new government regulations. We have a whole work populace continually trying to cope with these changes.

Jayson B. Strode: Assistant Administrator, Personnel, Rehabilitation Institute of Chicago, IL

Strode: There is evolving evidence that workers are less inclined to devote their lives to companies. This is evident in the increasing inclination not to relocate and with the increased emphasis on reducing job stress and professional burnout. Many employees are not willing to tolerate the same level of involvement with work and the same commitment as in the past.

Our job is to find ways to retain and recharge these people, to get the work done, and to still keep productivity up.

I see worker participation as partially offsetting reduced employee job commitment. If employees can play a greater part in the general management of an organization, then there is a greater probability that they can maintain job satisfaction.

We need to continually offer opportunities for employees to contribute ideas to the organization and in ways which are not just prescribed by the job description. We need to develop new ways and systems so that employees can make their full contribution to the organization. Right now we are wasting talent and the opportunity for involvement.

Strode: For the 1980s, I see a shift from a recruitment focus to retention. I know that reducing turnover is not a new idea, but we will find that there are simply not enough students coming out of the schools to meet our labor needs. One of the most effective ways of dealing with this problem is to retain existing personnel.

This section deals with staffing, which involves three distinct processes: work analysis, recruiting, and selection. The first phase of staffing any organization is understanding the components of jobs. When a person is hired, both management and the individual must have a clear understanding of the job the new employee will perform. A job is an organizational unit of work, and chapter 6 examines job design and its effects on people.

Chapter 7 examines the planning for and development of an appropriate group of persons to be considered for possible employment. Once a pool of applicants has been accumulated, the actual selection of persons for employment takes place. The selection can be made using a variety of data sources as a basis for selection decisions. Chapter 8 presents the information on selection.

---

[1] Excerpts from "Personnel Issues: Some Readers' Views," *Personnel Journal* 59, September 1980, pp. 723–732. Reprinted with the permission of *Personnel Journal*, Costa Mesa, California; all rights reserved.

CHAPTER 6

Analyzing Jobs and Work

When you have read this chapter, you should be able to:

1. Define what a job is and its three components.

2. Explain the difference between job simplification and job enlargement.

3. Define job analysis and indicate three uses of job analysis information.

4. List and briefly discuss four common methods of conducting a job analysis.

5. Discuss the impact of behavioral and legal concerns on the job analysis process.

6. Identify the three parts of a typical job description and the relationship of a job description to a job specification.

The Reluctant Receptionist

Superior Products Company has recently hired a new personnel assistant, Virginia Fisher, who just received a college degree. Frederick Mills, the personnel director, was extremely pleased to find someone who had some familiarity with basic management concepts because he was the entire personnel department, except for a clerk-typist. During the interview Frederick emphasized that he planned to have Virginia function as his assistant and that she would be doing some interviewing and be responsible for maintaining employee records. Because Superior has over 300 employees, Frederick had been too busy to prepare anything resembling a job description except for some scrawled notes on the back of an envelope.

Everything went fine for the first week for Virginia. On Monday of the second week, Frederick called Virginia into his office and explained that there was another minor duty that he had not mentioned to her. Frederick said, "In order to get approval to hire you from the president, I had to agree that whoever was hired would be the relief receptionist from 11:30 to 12:30 every day. The switchboard is usually quite busy and we wanted to be sure someone who is capable would be the backup." Virginia was not very happy about this assignment being sprung on her, but she agreed to try it for a while.

Within two weeks she was beginning to dread having to work the switchboard an hour everyday. Also, she discovered that she was expected to be the relief if the receptionist was sick or unable to work. On Wednesday and Thursday of the third week the regular receptionist was sick and Virginia filled in for her. On that Friday, Virginia told Frederick she was quitting in two weeks. When asked why, Virginia replied, "You misrepresented the job to me. You never said anything about my receptionist duties. If you had, I probably would not have taken the job."

Comments:

The importance of job descriptions and job specifications is highlighted in this case. Lack of a prepared job description has led to the firm's losing an employee after only a short time because the personnel director misrepresented the job. By seeing a job description, an applicant can gain a more accurate picture of the expectations associated with a job. Preparation of a job description would also provide the basis for developing a clear job specification that the personnel manager could use in recruiting, selecting, and training a personnel assistant.

PERSONNEL management is concerned with effective work performance by the organization's employees. As the opening case indicated, managers should have a thorough understanding of jobs and the responsibilities that go with them before people are recruited and hired for jobs. This chapter is primarily concerned with the processes of dividing the total work of an organization into the work to be performed in individual jobs, and the identification of qualifications needed by employees to perform those jobs satisfactorily. The activities involved are job design and job analysis.

WORK ACTIVITIES AS AN INTERFACE

The twin activities of *job design* and *job analysis* together form the work interface. Designing and analyzing jobs requires cooperation and coordination by personnel specialists and operating managers. Use of the interface concept puts the focus on who can best perform various aspects of job design and job analysis.

Figure 6–1 is a typical work interface that can be found in organizations having a specialized personnel unit. In small organizations managers have to perform all the work interface activities. In Figure 6–1,

Figure 6–1. Work interface.

Personnel Unit	*Managers*
Monitors and researchs effects of job design on turnover, absenteeism, and attitudes	Design jobs with assistance from specialists
	Supervise performance of jobs as designed and make adjustments as needed
	Monitor productivity and its relationship to job design
Prepares and coordinates job analysis procedures	Complete or assist in completing job analysis
Prepares job descriptions and job specifications	Review and maintain continuing accuracy of job descriptions and job specifications
Periodically reviews and assists managers in maintaining current job descriptions and job specifications	
	Develop performance standards with assistance from specialists

notice that the managers are the individuals mainly responsible for developing work procedures, performance standards, and designing and supervising the performance of work in jobs. The personnel unit attempts to determine the effects of job design and to suggest changes when research discovers job design is having negative effects. The analysis of jobs is coordinated by the personnel unit, which also provides special assistance in actually writing job descriptions and job specifications. Managers provide or assist in providing job analysis information.

WHAT IS A JOB?

Every job is composed of *tasks,* *duties,* and *responsibilities.* Although the terms "position" and "job" are often used interchangeably, there is a slight difference in emphasis. A *position* is a collection of tasks, duties, and responsibilities performed by one person.

A JOB is an organizational unit of work.

A job may include more than one position which is very similar to another. Thus, if there are two persons operating postage meters in a mail room, there are two positions (one for each person) but just one job (postage meter operator).

A government manual notes that a task is composed of motions and "is a distinct identifiable work activity," whereas "a duty is composed of a number of tasks and is a larger work segment performed by an individual."[1] Because both tasks and duties describe activities, it is not always easy or necessary to distinguish between the two. If one of the employment supervisor's *duties* is to "interview applicants," one *task* which is a portion of that duty would be "asking questions."

RESPONSIBILITIES are obligations to perform accepted tasks and duties.

When a person becomes a manager, he or she also accepts responsibilities for the performance of the work unit. Closely related to responsibility is authority. As noted in chapter 2, *authority is the right to direct resources.* An authority relationship statement for a sales manager might be: "Has authority to place advertisements costing less than $500." Thus, the extent of the authority that goes with that job is identified.

What are the three components of a job?

Person/Job Fit

Not everyone would be happy as a physician, or as an engineer, or as a dishwasher. But certain people like and do well at each of those jobs. The person/job fit is a simple but important concept that involves matching characteristics of people with characteristics of jobs. Figure 6–2

Figure 6–2   Person-Job fit.

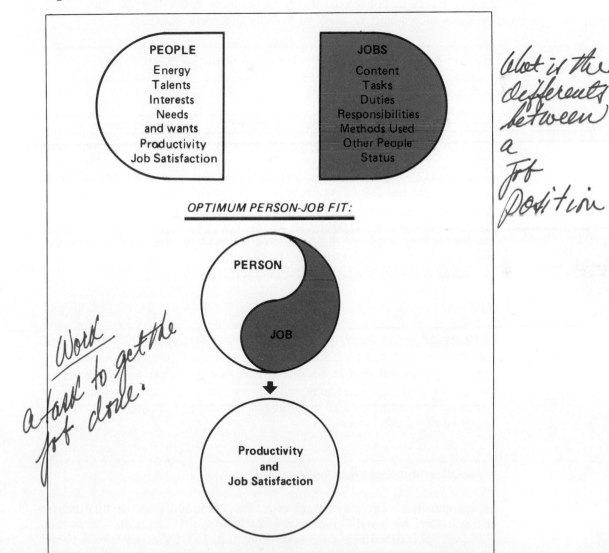

[handwritten: What is the differents between a Job Position]

[handwritten: Work a fork to get the job done!]

shows the relevant dimensions of the person/job fit. Obviously, if a person does not fit a job either the person can be changed or replaced, or the job can be changed. In the past it was much more common to make the round person fit the square job. However, "reshaping" people does not seem easy to do. Consequently, by redesigning jobs the person/job fit can be improved. Jobs may be designed when they are first established or redesigned later. But, in either case, the term used is usually *job design*.

JOB DESIGN refers to conscious efforts to organize tasks, duties, and responsibilities into a unit of work to achieve a certain objective.

Nature of Job Design

Identifying the components of a given job is an integral part of job design. Designing or redesigning jobs encompasses many considerations, and many different techniques are available to the manager. It has been equated with job enrichment, a technique developed by Frederick Herzberg, but, as the following discussion of considerations and techniques will demonstrate, job design is much broader than job enrichment alone.

Job design must consider (1) the *content* of the job, (2) the *methods* or technology used, (3) their combined *effects* on the people doing the job, and (4) the relationships with other people at work that are likely to develop through interpersonal contact.

JOB DESIGN CONSIDERATIONS AND TECHNIQUES

There are several considerations and techniques that can be used in designing or redesigning jobs. The following is not intended to be an exhaustive treatment of all possibilities but rather to acquaint the reader with some of the issues.

Specialization/Simplification

Specialization suggests that greater efficiency and productivity result from having a job with only a very limited number of tasks. The people holding specialized jobs can learn them more easily and perform them more efficiently. They can become a "specialist" in a simplified job. *Job simplification is* an extension of scientific management and the division of labor framework discussed in earlier chapters. This approach emphasizes the industrial engineering techniques of motion-and-time study and work sampling. *Motion-and-time study* is a precise observation and clocking of the actions performed in a job to determine the most efficient way to get it done.

Work Sampling.   *Work sampling*, a somewhat different approach, does not require observing each detailed action throughout an entire work cycle. Instead, a manager can determine the content of a typical workday through statistical sampling of certain actions rather than timing all actions. Work sampling is particularly useful for clerical jobs.

However, work sampling is not always well received. For example, in the Idaho Department of Health and Welfare, work sampling was instituted to increase efficiency. Seven random times a day a whistle was blown. The 30 workers were required as part of the study to fill out forms describing what they were doing at the moment the whistle went off. Data was then collected and analyzed to determine better ways to design the jobs.

However, the workers reactions were that the process was insulting, degrading, and disruptive. One secretary fumed, "It is insulting to my intelligence the way they go about these things." Another noted, "Yesterday morning there wasn't a single whistle. They all blew in the afternoon and everyone was sitting on pins and needles afraid to take a break or go to the bathroom." Another said the study doesn't bother her but the focus on secretaries does. "I think everyone should be a part of it, not just the clerical staff," she said.[2] Because of such reactions the study was ultimately dropped. It must be noted that work sampling methods can include random observations without the whistle blowing.

Advantages and Disadvantages of Specialization.   Specialization and simplification are very powerful concepts for improving productivity. Without the application of specialization to manufacturing, the cost of televisions, automobiles, appliances, and many other products would be so high that very few people could afford them. However, there are costs associated with using these techniques as well.

In recent years there have been problems noted regarding extensive specialization and simplification of jobs. Critics say that it has gone too far, to the extent of deliberately ignoring or inadequately considering the human element. By creating extremely specialized jobs, managers find some employees who react negatively to them. Boredom, lower quality, absenteeism, turnover, and increased coordination costs may accompany too much specialization.

Another major problem is coordinating all the various highly specialized parts of the organization. Specialists may have difficulty seeing the "big picture," and may define the organization and its objectives in terms of their own small specialty. Specialists even develop their own language or jargon that makes communication among specialists difficult.

What is job specialization?

Job Enlargement/Job Enrichment

Attempts to alleviate some of the problems encountered with excessive job simplification fall under the general heading of job enlargement.

JOB ENLARGEMENT is the concept of broadening the scope and/or depth of a job.

Some authors contend that job enlargement means only increases in job scope and that increases in both job scope and job depth are different and should be called job enrichment. Nevertheless, the above definition of enlargement (as encompassing scope and/or depth) reflects a general view.

JOB DEPTH is the amount of planning and control responsibility in a job.

JOB SCOPE refers to the number and variety of tasks performed by the job holder.

An assembly line worker is very restricted in choosing what is done and when it is done and would therefore have very little depth in the job. In contrast, the vice-president of purchasing would have a wide job scope whereas the purchasing file clerk would have a much narrower job scope. *Enlarging job scope means that more operations are added to a job.* More tasks of a similar nature are added, or the employee is allowed to rotate to a different unit of work on a similar level. This latter technique, known as job rotation, can be a way to break up an otherwise routine job.

JOB ROTATION is the process of shifting a person from job to job.

For example, one week on the auto assembly line, John Williams attaches doors to the rest of the body assembly. The next week he attaches bumpers. The third week he puts in seat assemblies and then rotates back to doors again the following week. Job rotation need not be done on a weekly basis. John could have spent one-third of a day on each job or one entire day, instead of a week, on each job. It has been argued, however that rotation does nothing to get at the *real root* of the boredom with routine problems. Rotating a person from one boring job to another may help somewhat in the short run, but the jobs are still perceived to be boring.

Increasing job depth refers to increasing the influence and self-control employees have over their jobs. A manager might increase job depth to add variety, require more skill and responsibility, and provide more autonomy and opportunities for personal growth in a job. Methods include giving an employee more planning and control responsibilities over the tasks to be done. Simply adding more tasks does not increase job depth.

Supporters of the idea that more job depth is a positive step contend that higher productivity, lower absenteeism, and higher motivation will result because of the additional challenge and responsibility. They say that work will be more meaningful and satisfying and therefore employees will be more productive. However, some recent research has shown that while job enrichment results in substantial improvements in employee attitudes, it may not necessarily lead to greater productivity.[3]

Not all employees *want* their job enlarged in scope or depth. It depends on the motivations, expectations, and rewards the employees want. For example, when a towel rack manufacturer attempted to enlarge some jobs by giving workers the latitude to assemble, package, and label five-piece towel racks, the experiment was unsuccessful. The work force was primarily older, long-service employees who felt secure with the routine to which they had become accustomed. They were successful in resisting the change in job design, even though some of the younger workers would have agreed to the change.

Professionalization

Some jobs can be designed such that "professionals" are used to do the work. This "professionalization" presents some interesting advantages and disadvantages. Lawyers, accountants, physicians, as well as master plumbers, electricians, and medical technicians, come equipped with the necessary knowledge to do certain kinds of work as a result of their training. Consequently, they often require less direct supervision in getting that work done. In essence, they design the jobs themselves.

However, using professionals may present some problems as well. They tend to relate to their profession rather than to the employer. Also, they may have different expectations about treatment and pay. Still, when the situation is right, designing a job so that professionals can be used can offer some real advantages.

Performance Feedback

There is increasing evidence that a job that can provide the worker with feedback on how he or she *is* performing relative to how he or she *ought to be* performing has some advantages. In many situations these opportunities for feedback on performance can be designed right into the job.

For example, a job may be designed so that the worker keeps records on the number of units he or she produces daily and a record of rejects or quality errors. This recording and reporting is built right into the job duties and not added in afterward. Such feedback on performance against expected standards has been shown to improve productivity in several instances.

Social Ecology: The Physical Setting of Work

Designing jobs properly requires that the layout of the work or the setting in which a job must be done is considered. The way the work space surrounding a job is utilized can influence the worker's performance of the job itself. Several different job-setting factors have been identified, including size of work area, kinds of materials used, sensory conditions, distance between work areas, and interference from noise and traffic flow.[4]

Group versus Individual Jobs

Typically a job is thought of as being something one person does. However, where it is appropriate, jobs may be designed for groups. The use of groups or "work teams" has been found to increase satisfaction with the job and decrease turnover, as pointed out in chapter 2.

The Volvo plant at Kalmar, Sweden, has made very successful use of work teams in building automobiles. A work team has responsibility for a complete component of a car, such as the engine or the body. The team can become expert on a whole subassembly of a car, and members can influence work procedures and work rates.[5]

Job Design Summarized

For innovations such as those discussed above to be successful, they must be a part of the original design of jobs or a part of a rather complete redesign. Further, such considerations as pay (individual incentives versus group incentives) and time requirements (shift, eight-hour day, flexitime, four-day work week) are best built into the job design.

Job design involves the consideration of specialization and simplification, job rotation, professionalism, and enlargement of scope and depth relative to the organization, the personal desires and motivations of the employees, and many other situational factors. Job design is crucial and requires perceptive understanding and analysis of employees and organizational work.[6] One way to begin to understand organizational work is a formal program of job analysis, which examines the tasks, duties, and responsibilities contained in an individual unit of work.

Can you compare job simplification and job enlargement?

JOB ANALYSIS: GETTING INFORMATION ON JOBS

Job analysis is the most basic personnel activity because it focuses on what people are expected to do.

> JOB ANALYSIS is a systematic investigation of the tasks, duties, and responsibilities of a job, and the necessary knowledge, skills, and abilities someone needs to perform the job adequately.

For example, if a supervisor tells an employee, "You are a grocery clerk," that clerk may not know what behavior is expected, because there are many different tasks and duties a grocery clerk could do. But when an individual is hired for a job with specific duties and responsibilities, the manager can then expect certain work to be done.

Job analysis usually involves collecting information on characteristics of a job that differentiate it from other jobs. Information that can be helpful in making that distinction includes:

- Work activities
- Behavior required
- Machines and equipment used
- Performance expected
- Working conditions
- Personnel requirements

What is job analysis?

End Products of Job Analysis

Job analysis identifies the components of a job which can be communicated to employees so they know exactly what to do. Figure 6–3 shows that job analysis serves as the basis from which job descriptions, job specifications, and job evaluations are prepared.

Figure 6–3 Job analysis: most basic personnel activity.

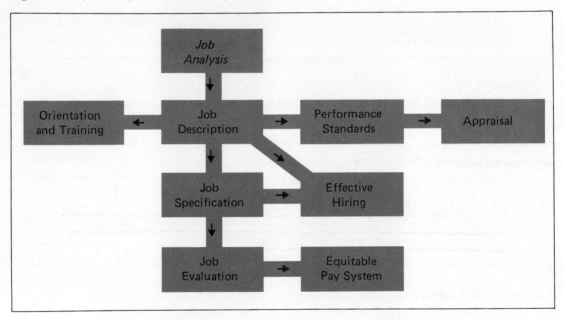

Job Description. Basically, the job description indicates what is done, why it is done, where it is done, and briefly, how it is done.

> A JOB DESCRIPTION is a summary of the tasks, duties, and responsibilities in a job.

Performance standards should flow directly from a job description, telling what the job accomplishes and the satisfactory performance expected in each area of the job description. The logic here is very clear. If employees know what is expected and what is good or poor performance, they have a much better chance of performing acceptably. Unfortunately, performance standards, while beneficial, are often omitted from most job descriptions.

Job Specification.   The job description describes the job; the job specification describes the person needed for the job. The major use of job specifications is to guide in the recruiting and selecting of people to fill jobs.

A JOB SPECIFICATION lists the various knowledge, skills, and abilities an individual needs to do the job satisfactorily.

An example of a job specification for a clerk-typist might be: "Types 50 words per minute with no more than two errors, successful completion of one year of high school English, or passing of an English proficiency test."

Job Evaluation.   A job evaluation uses the other parts of job analysis information to determine the worth of a job in relation to other jobs so that an equitable and meaningful wage and salary system can be established. Because job evaluation is such an integral component in the compensation of human resources, a detailed discussion is postponed until chapter 12.

Uses of a Job Analysis

Good personnel management requires both the employee and the manager to have a clear understanding of the duties and responsibilities to be performed on a job. Job analysis facilitates this understanding by focusing on a unit of work and its relationship to other units of work by identifying what composes a job. Job analysis has several key uses.

Employee Selection.   Selecting a qualified person to fill a job requires knowing clearly the work to be done and the qualifications needed for someone to adequately perform the work. Without a clear and precise understanding of what a job entails, a manager cannot effectively select someone to do the job. If a retail store manager has not clearly identified what a clerk is to do, it is difficult to know, for example, if the person hired must be able to lift boxes, run a cash register, or keep the books.

Recruitment.   Closely related to selection is the use of job analysis for planning how and where to obtain employees for openings anticipated in the future. An understanding of the types of skills needed and types of jobs that may be open in the future enables managers to have better continuity and planning in staffing their organization. For example, in Witlow Corporation, a recent job analysis showed that the "Accountant II" job which traditionally required a college-trained person could be handled by someone with high school bookkeeping. As a result, the company can select from more available candidates and may save a considerable amount of money in salary costs.

Compensation.   While the established and unwritten assumption is that people are to be compensated for their work, more difficult jobs should pay individuals more for doing them. Job analysis information is used in a job evaluation to give more weight, and therefore more pay, to jobs with more tasks, duties, and responsibilities.

Training and Orientation.   By providing a definition of what comprises a job through job analysis, the supervisor can easily explain to a new employee the boundaries of the employee's unit of work. It is difficult for an employee to perform well if there is confusion about what the job is and what is supposed to be done. The case that opened the chapter illustrates the problems caused by a poor job analysis.

Performance Appraisal.   By comparing what an individual employee is supposed to be doing (based on job analysis) to what an individual has actually done, the value of the individual's performance and competency can be determined. The ultimate objective for any organization is to pay people for performance. To do this fairly, a comparison of what individuals should do, as identified by performance standards, with what they have actually done is necessary.

What are three uses of job analysis information?

METHODS OF ANALYZING JOBS

Job analysis does not have to be a complicated process. However, the systematic investigation of jobs should be done in a practical, logical manner. The process of collecting and using information about a job is aimed at determining what work is done, how it is done, why it is done, and what skills and abilities are needed to do it.

Gathering information about jobs can be done in several ways. Four common methods used are: (1) functional job analysis, (2) observation,

(3) interviewing, and (4) questionnaires. Some combination of these approaches may be used depending upon the situation and the organization.

Functional Job Analysis (FJA)

Functional job analysis attempts to analyze jobs by building standardized task statements and job descriptions which can be used in a variety of organizations. A functional definition of what is done in a job can be generated by examining the fundamental components of *data, people,* and *things.*

Within each of these classifications a hierarchy of functions exists that can be identified by numbers. Figure 6–4 shows the levels and numbers associated with the dimensions of a job. The lower the number under data, people, and things, the more involved the job is in dealing with those functions. These numbers, as well as numbers providing other information, can be used to identify and compare jobs on their important elements by using the *Dictionary of Occupational Titles* [DOT], a standardized data source provided by the federal government.

Figure 6–4 Work functions from *Dictionary of Occupational Titles.*

DATA (4th Digit)	PEOPLE (5th Digit)	THINGS (6th Digit)
0 Synthesizing	0 Mentoring	0 Setting Up
1 Coordinating	1 Negotiating	1 Precision Working
2 Analyzing	2 Instructing	2 Operating-Controlling
3 Compiling	3 Supervising	3 Driving-Operating
4 Computing	4 Diverting	4 Manipulating
5 Copying	5 Persuading	5 Tending
6 Comparing	6 Speaking-Signalling	6 Feeding-Offbearing
	7 Serving	7 Handling
	8 Taking Instructions- Helping	

Dictionary of Occupational Titles (DOT).[8]   The DOT describes a wide variety of jobs. Specifically, over 20,000 jobs are classified and described using standard occupational categories (SOC). The DOT classifies and numbers jobs in a nine-digit code. Using this method a manager would look up a general analysis contained in the DOT, and then FJA can be used to sharpen the standardized DOT information. The job descriptions in Figure 6–5 are taken from the current DOT.

Figure 6–5 Sample job titles and descriptions from *Dictionary of Occupational Titles.*

090.117-022 DIRECTOR, ATHLETIC (education)

Plans, administers, and directs intercollegiate athletic activities in college or university. Interprets and participates in formulating extramural athletic policies. Employs and discharges coaching staff and other department employees on own initiative or at direction of board in charge of athletics. Directs preparation and dissemination of publicity to promote athetic events. Plans and coordinates activities of coaching staff. Prepares budget and authorizes department expenditures. Plans and schedules sports events, and oversees ticket sales activities. Certifies reports of income produced from ticket sales. May direct programs for students of physical education.

151.047-010 DANCER (amuse. & rec.)

Dances alone, with partner, or in group to entertain audience: Performs classical, modern, or acrobatic dances, coordinating body movements to musical accompaniment. Rehearses dance movements developed by CHOREOGRAPHER (amuse. & rec.) May choreograph own dance. May sing and provide other forms of entertainment. May specialize in particular style of dancing and be designated according to specialty as ACROBATIC DANCER (amuse. & rec.); BALLET DANCER (amuse. & rec.); BALLROOM DANCER (amuse. & rec.); BELLY DANCER (amuse. & rec.); CHORUS DANCER (amuse. & rec.); INTERPRETATIVE DANCER (amuse & rec.); STRIP-TEASE DANCER (amuse. & rec.); TAP DANCER (amuse. & rec.).

160.162-010 ACCOUNTANT, TAX (profess. & kin.)

Prepares Federal, state, or local tax returns of individual, business establishment, or other organization: Examines accounts and records and computes tax returns according to prescribed rates, laws, and regulations. Advises management regarding effects of business, internal programs and activities, and other transactions upon taxes and represents principal before various governmental taxing bodies. May devise and install tax record systems. May specialize in particular phase of tax accounting, such as income, property, real estate, or Social Security taxes.

166.117-018 MANAGER, PERSONNEL. (profess. & kin.)

Plans and carries out policies relating to all phases of personnel activity. Recruits, interviews, and selects employees to fill vacant positions. Plans and conducts new employee orientation to foster positive attitude toward company goals. Keeps record of insurance coverage, pension plan, and personnel transactions, such as hires, promotions, transfers, and terminations. Investigates accidents and prepares reports for insurance carrier. Conducts wage survey within labor market to determine competitive wage rate. Prepares budget of personnel operations. Meets with shop stewards and supervisors to resolve grievances. Writes separation notices for employees separating with cause and conducts exit interviews to determine reasons behind separations. Prepares reports and recommends procedures to reduce absenteeism and turnover. Contracts with outside suppliers to provide employee services, such as canteen, transportation, or relocation service. May keep records of hired employee characteristics for govermental reporting purposes. May negotiate collective bargaining agreement with BUSINESS REPRESENTATIVE LABOR UNION (profess. & kin.)

709.684-026 BIRD-CAGE ASSEMBLER (wirework)

Fabricates wire birdcages, using handtools and drill press: Cuts wire to specified length, using wirecutter. Positions metal plate in *jig*, and drills holes around circumference of plate, using drill press. Fits ends of wires into holes in plate, and fastens upper ends of wire together to form cage.

(Source: U.S. Department of Labor, *Dictionary of Occupational Titles*, 4th ed. Washington, D.C.: United States Government Printing Office, 1977.)

Using the identification code from the Director of Athletics, (090.117–022), a brief explanation can be given of how the DOT is used. The first three digits (090) indicate the occupational code, title, and industry designations. The next three digits (117) represent the degree to which a director of athletics *typically* has responsibility and judgment over *data, things,* and *people.* The final three digits are used to indicate the alphabetical order of titles within the occupational group having the same degree of responsibility and judgment.

The value of the DOT is in the wide range of jobs described. A manager or personnel specialist confronted with preparing a large number of jobs can use the DOT as a starting point. Then the job descriptions contained in the DOT can be modified to fit the particular organizational situation. The importance of the DOT is demonstrated by the fact that job descriptions based on the DOT are considered satisfactory by federal employment enforcement agencies.

FJA is advocated as being easy to learn and use because statistical percentages can be assigned to each of the three dimensions (things, data, people) following the preparation of a task statement. A detailed explanation of the procedures in the FJA is not appropriate here, but it is relevant to note that use of DOT and FJA can be helpful to managers who are *not* personnel specialists. FJA can be used in developing occupational "career ladders" by identifying jobs requiring progressively more skill or responsibilities. This identification can clarify promotion and career progress. Also, because FJA is standardized, statistical data can be developed for personnel decision-making areas such as test validation.

Observation

The observation method of job analysis requires the manager to begin without any standardized information sources such as the DOT. The manager watches and observes the individual performing the job and takes notes to describe the tasks and duties performed.

Use of the observation method is limited because many jobs do not have complete and easily observed job cycles. For example, to analyze the job of a pharmaceutical sales person would demand that the observer follow the sales person around for several days. Furthermore, many managers may not be skilled enough to know what to observe and how to analyze what they do see. Thus, observation may be more useful in repetitive type jobs and in conjunction with other methods. Managers using other methods may watch the performance of parts of a job to gain a general familiarity with the job components and the conditions in which it is performed. This observation will help them better apply some of the other job analysis methods.

Interviewing

The interview method of job analysis requires that the manager or personnel specialist visit each job site and talk with the employee performing each job. Usually a structured interview form is used to record the information. Such a form is shown in Figure 6–6. Frequently the employee and the employee's supervisor must be interviewed to obtain a complete understanding of the job. During the job analysis interview the manager or personnel specialist must make judgments about the information to be included and its degree of importance.

The interview method can be quite time consuming. If Jones Computing Service has 30 different jobs, and the job analysis interviewer

Figure 6–6 Job Analysis interview form.

I. PERSONAL INFORMATION	
1. Name (Last, First, Middle)	8. Department
2. Social Security Number	9. Board, Commission, Bureau, Institution (Where applicable)
3. Official Title of Position	10. Division, Section, Unit

4. Work Title of Position
    Part-time___Permanent___
    Full-time___Temporary___
    Seasonal___
	11. Work Address (Mailing Address)

5. Years in Present Position	12. Regular Schedule of Hours and Shift Rotation. If any
6. Name and Class of Immediate Supervisor	DATE ANALYST
7. Name and Class of Next Higher Level Supervisor	CLASSIFICATION TITLE

Fig. 6–6 (continued)

II. DIFFICULTY OF WORK

Percent of Time	TASK STATEMENTS 13. Performs what action? To whom or what? To product what? Using what tools, equipment, work aids, processes?

14. What *KNOWLEDGES,* procedures, practices, policies, and other guidelines do you use in the performance of the duties you listed? (Include any subject areas, technical knowledge or specialized knowledge. Qualify the knowledges as much, some, general, extensive.)

15. What *ABILITIES/SKILLS* are required for the position (Explain the abilities and/or skills required to perform the position, such as ability to write reports, ability to train new employees, ability to type, operate a bulldozer, etc.)

16. What minimum level or education/training and experience is needed for successful performance of the duties and responsibilities of the position? (Include licenses and/or certificates, special courses, etc.)

17. How much time did it take you to reach a satisfactory level of efficiency in the position and what kind of training did you receive to reach this level?

III. RESPONSIBILITY

18a. List name and class titles of employees under your *immediate supervision.* (If more than ten list only class titles and number in each class.)

18b. Extent of Supervision:
___Assign work   ___Train workers   ___Discipline
___Oversee and review   ___Performance rating   ___Plans methods, procedures,
   work   ___Recommend hiring, firing,   work flow
___Approve work   promotion   ___Others (explain)

---

19. What guidelines are used in completing your tasks? (references, manuals, precedents, oral and written instructions, text books, standard methods, procedures, etc.)

20. *Who* reviews or checks your work? *How* is it reviewed? *When* is it reviewed

21. What happens when an error is found? How would it be found? How soon would it be found? Give specific examples.

22. Does this position require unusual physical demands such as standing, stooping, pulling, climbing, lifting or any special physical requirements such as eye-hand coordination, keen hearing, etc.?

23. In what working conditions is this position performed? Are there any hazards? Is work done in extreme weather conditions?

24. Does this position entail responsibility for the safety of other employees or the public?

25. Describe any contact (in person, by telephone, or by letter) with people other than your supervisors or subordinates you make as a regular part of your work. Include how often, with whom and why you have these contacts.

26. Does this position involve travel? Describe.

151

spends at least 10–15 minutes on each interview, the time involved for just interviewing and obtaining the analysis information will be extensive. The time problem will be compounded if the interviewer talks with two or three employees doing the same job. Furthermore, professional and managerial jobs are more complicated to analyze and usually require a longer interview.

For these reasons, combining the interview with one of the other methods is suggested. For example, if Lorraine Bowen has observed an employee perform a job, she then can check her observation data by also interviewing the employee. Likewise, the interview as a follow-up means is frequently used in conjunction with the questionnaire method.

Questionnaire

The questionnaire is a widely used method of analyzing jobs and work. A survey instrument is developed and given to employees and managers to complete. *At least* one employee per job should complete the questionnaire, which is then returned to the supervisor or manager for review before being used for the preparation of job descriptions.[9]

The major advantage of the questionnaire method is that information on a larger number of jobs can be collected in a relatively short period of time. However, some follow-up observation and discussion is necessary to clarify inadequately completed questionnaires and interpretation problems. The questionnaire method assumes that the employees can accurately analyze and communicate information about their jobs. That may not be a good assumption in all cases. For these reasons, the questionnaire method is usually combined with interviews and observations to clarify and verify the questionnaire information.

Position Analysis Questionnaire.   A specialized questionnaire method is the *Position Analysis Questionnaire* (PAQ), a structured instrument for job analysis. Each job is analyzed in terms of the 194 job "elements" contained in the PAQ. A manager using the PAQ checks either applicable elements or the appropriate place on a six-point rating scale. The PAQ attempts to identify the occupant behavior involved in jobs. The nature of the PAQ job elements makes it possible for almost any type of position or job to be analyzed. It is easily quantified and can be used to conduct validity studies on tests. The PAQ can be translated into a job evaluation system to ensure internal pay fairness, which considers the varying demands of jobs. It also has been suggested as a method for generalizing job component validity.[10]

What are four job analysis methods?

BEHAVIORAL AND LEGAL ASPECTS OF JOB ANALYSIS

When systematically analyzing jobs, managers must be aware of two general concerns. One is the reaction of employees to such an intensive look at their jobs. The other concern is the impact of governmental constraints, especially equal employment, on job analysis and its outcomes. First the impact of human behavior on the job analysis process must be considered.

Behavioral Side of Job Analysis

A detailed examination of jobs, while necessary, can be a demanding and threatening experience for both managers and employees. For example, in one shoe manufacturing firm, Phil Goetz had worked very hard in the packing department for many years. Everyone knew Phil worked hard, but because he was a hard worker no one ever really questioned what he did. When a new manager came to the packaging department, he felt a job analysis was in order. Phil violently resisted any attempt to analyze his job and refused to cooperate with the analyst. Phil was sure he would be put back to packing shoes eight hours a day instead of working on many different projects as he was presently doing.

Employee Fears.   One fear that some employees have is that clearly analyzing, specifying, and defining their jobs will put a *straitjacket* on them. Just like the shoe packer, they feel creativity and flexibility may be limited by formalizing the duties, responsibilities, and qualifications needed for a job. But, it does not necessarily follow that analyzing a job will limit job depth.

Another concern that some employees have is a fear about the *purpose* of a detailed investigation of their jobs. The attitude that "As long as someone doesn't know precisely what I am supposed to be doing, then I am safe" may generate attempts to hide the uniqueness of a job. The employee's concern is that somebody must feel they did something wrong if such a searching look is to be taken of their jobs. Consequently, explanation of the job analysis process and why it is being done should be part of any job analysis.

Resistance to Change.   As jobs change, there is a continual need to update and revise job descriptions and job specifications to make them more meaningful. As would be expected, people become used to working within defined boundaries of responsibilities. When an attempt is made to change those "job fences," fear, resistance, and insecurity are generated. Suggesting it is time to revise job descriptions provokes anxiety because the employees' safe and secure job world is threatened. Their jobs may be changed and they may have to take on new and difficult responsibilities.

Because resistance in this situation is a natural reaction, effective managers should expect it and be prepared to deal with it. Perhaps the most effective way to handle this problem is to involve the individual in the revision process. Allowing Diane Morris, a purchasing analyst, to help reexamine her job and play a vital role in writing up the new job description and job specification can help overcome a certain amount of this fear and anxiety. However, this uneasiness may not completely diminish until the individual becomes accustomed to working under the new set-up. Because jobs change, supervisors and managers should expect to continually strive to overcome resistance as changes in jobs and work occur.

In addition, as work is changed and becomes more complex, especially at managerial and administrative levels, it is more difficult to analyze and determine exactly what constitutes the job. For example, trying to write a job description for the president of a corporation is very difficult because of the general and often varied actions required. Likewise, clearly identifying the tasks, duties, and responsibilities for a head nurse or for a university dean is difficult because of the wide scope, flexibility, and complexity of the activities in which they engage.

Overemphasis on Current Employee.   A good analysis and the resulting job descriptions and specifications do not describe only what the individual currently holding the job does and that individual's qualifications. That person may have unique capabilities and the ability to expand the scope of the job to assume more responsibilities. The company would have difficulty finding someone exactly like that individual if he or she left. Therefore, the job description and job specification should indicate duties, responsibilities, and *key* qualifications needed, but should not be merely a description of what the person currently filling the job does.

Managerial "Straitjacket."   Through the information developed in a job analysis, the job description is supposed to capture the scope of a job. However, some individual employees may use job descriptions in order to limit managerial flexibility, thus putting a "straitjacket" on a manager. Consequently, some nonunion employers refuse to show job descriptions to their employees. This refusal makes it difficult for an employee to say, "I don't have to do that because it is not in my job description." In some organizations with a unionized work force, very restrictive job descriptions may be encouraged or even demanded by union representatives as a mechanism to keep employees from having to accept additional work assignments.

A good example of using job descriptions to restrict work occurred when air traffic controllers followed "the book" and caused havoc with airplane departures and landings at major airports. The attitude, "It is not in my job description," can become very burdensome for a management involved in changing an organization, its technology, and jobs in response to changing economic or social conditions.

Legal Aspects of Job Analysis

In addition to behavioral concerns, managers must also be aware of the importance of the legal impact of job analysis. The equal employment discussion in the previous chapter continually made reference to the need for "job-relatedness" in staffing activities. A job analysis provides the basis for job relatedness through the development of job descriptions and job specifications.

Federal employment agency enforcement guidelines clearly indicate that a sound and comprehensive job analysis is required for selection criteria to be validated. Without a systematic investigation of a job, an employer may be utilizing requirements that may not be specifically job-related. For example, if a trucking firm requires a high school diploma for a dispatcher, that firm must be able to indicate how such an education requirement matches up to the tasks, duties, and responsibilities of a dispatcher. The only way the firm might be able to justify that requirement would be to identify that the knowledge, skills, and abilities needed by the dispatcher could only be obtained through formal education.

In summary, it is extremely difficult for an employer to have a legal staffing system without performing a sound job analysis. Consequently, job analysis truly is the most basic personnel activity, primarily because it focuses on the jobs employees perform.

What are some behavioral and legal aspects of
job analysis?

JOB DESCRIPTIONS AND JOB SPECIFICATIONS

The job description is compiled and prepared to concisely summarize the job analysis information for each job. Job descriptions should be accurate, readable, understandable, and usable.

Job Description Components

The typical job description, such as the one in Figure 6–7, contains three major parts. These parts are described below.

Figure 6–7 Sample job description: Benefits Manager.

Date: March, 1978	Job Title: Benefits Manager	
Div. Administration	Dept: Personnel	Sect:
Reports to: Personnel Director		
Supervises: N/A		

Education: College degree in Personnel or Business Administration preferred but not essential

Experience: Considerable experience with employee group insurance programs preferred

Major Accountabilities

1. Insures ERISA compliance and reporting for all pension and welfare benefits, keeping a current knowledge of IRS and DOL regulations.
2. Coordinates employee benefits and services.
3. Counsels employees regarding benefit problems.
4. Manages the office in the absence of the Personnel Director.

Duties and Responsibilities

1. Maintains ERISA reporting calendars for TSA, Retirement Plan, LTD and Life Insurance, Health Insurance.
2. Prepares and files appropriate reports to IRS, DOL, and employees, including gathering and verifying information from all insurance companies and/or other sources.
3. Maintains ERISA records for Retirement Plan. Correlates and insures accuracy of records with Trustee, Actuary, and legal counsel.
4. Calculates retirement benefits and processes forms, including Vested Terminations, Early, Normal, and Late Retirement, including Joint and Survivor and Lump sum cash-out benefits.
5. Counsels employees regarding benefits at the time of transfer in status, termination and retirement. Monitors pay period benefits reports insuring accuracy.
6. Processes garnishments on employees.
7. Approves requests for Educational Assistance and makes payments and receives reimbursements to the Hospital.
8. Administers absence control program, monitoring excused and unexcused absences, records and insures proper disciplinary action is being executed according to established policy and procedures. Maintains records and distributes reports on absenteeism to Department Heads and Personnel Director.
9. Manages salary security program, including processing of claims insuring proper reporting to insurance companies and employee understanding of life and LTD benefits and procedures.
10. Manages health insurance program including counseling employees regarding benefits and claim procedures, pays billings and insures proper payroll input for deductions.
11. Administers TSA program, including conducting annual reopenings with broker, counseling employees regarding benefits and maintains records insuring correct salaries, deductions and billing procedures.
12. Receives and processes unemployment compensation claims and verifies and pays quarterly billings.
13. Ensures accurate and timely payment of terminal benefits.
14. Conducts and analyzes benefits surveys in order to maintain pay competitiveness with area hospitals.
15. Recommends changes in benefit policy and practices.
16. Performs other duties as assigned.   [Used with permission.]

Identification.   The first part is the identification section. In this part the employee's job title, department, and the reporting relationship are presented. Additional information such as the date of analysis, a job number, the number of employees holding the job, and the current pay scale of the job occupants can also be included.

General Summary.   The second part, the general summary, is a concise summarization of the general responsibilities and components that make the job different from others. One personnel specialist has said about the general summary statement: "In 25 words or less describe the essence of the job." In the example the listing of major accountabilities serves as the general summary.

Specific Duties.   The third part of the typical job description, the specific duties section, contains clear and precise statements on the major tasks, duties, and responsibilities performed. The most time-consuming aspect of writing job descriptions is this listing of specific duties.

Writing Job Descriptions

In writing job descriptions it is important to use *precise action verbs* which accurately describe the employee's tasks, duties, and responsibilities. For example, avoiding the use of vague words such as "does" or "handles" is important. Also, the specific duties should be *grouped and arranged* in some sensible pattern. If a job requires an accounting supervisor to prepare several reports and to perform other functions, those statements relating to the preparation of reports should be grouped together.

A guide to writing a job description statement for a social welfare job is shown in Figure 6–8. The manager preparing the job description should use precise and clear language but should not fall into the trap of writing a motion analysis. The statement, "Walks to filing cabinet, opens drawer, pulls folders out, and inserts material in correct folders," is a motion statement. The specific duty statement, "Files correspondence and memoranda to maintain accurate customer policy records," is sufficiently descriptive without being overly detailed.

It is not the intent of this section to provide a detailed guide to writing job descriptions, but only to highlight some of the key ideas a manager should remember in writing or revising job descriptions.[11] Some job descriptions contain other sections about materials or machines used, working conditions, or special tools used. This information often is included in the specific duty statements or in a comments section. Also, the final statement in many job descriptions is often the *miscellaneous clause.* This statement is included to cover the abnormal and unusual situations that comprise a very small part of an employee's job. Having

Figure 6–8   Writing a job description of a social welfare job.

Performs What Action? (verb)	To Whom or What? (object of verb)	To Produce What? (expected output)	Using What Tools, Equipment, Work Aids, Processes?
Asks Questions/ listens Records answers	To/of applicant On eligibility form	In order to determine eligibility	Eligibility form Eligibility criteria in manual Interviewing techniques

This task statement can be more readable in this way: "Asks client questions, listens and records answers on standard eligibility form, using knowledge of interviewing techniques and eligibility criteria in order to gather information from which client's eligibility for food stamps can be determined."

(Source: *Job Analysis: Developing and Documenting Data, A Guide for State and Local Governments*, U.S. Civil Service Comm., BIPP 152–35, December 1973, p. 6.)

such a statement is an attempt to prevent an employee from saying, "It's not covered in my job description."

One of the challenging aspects of writing job descriptions involves describing executive and upper management level jobs. Because of the wide range of duties and responsibilities, those jobs often are described in more general terms than jobs at lower levels in the organization.

What are the three components of a job description and how do you write them?

Job Specification

The job specification, a logical outgrowth of a job description, attempts to describe the key qualifications someone needs to perform the job satisfactorily. Specific factors identified often can be grouped into three categories: *Knowledge, Skills,* and *Abilities* (KSAs). Factors within these categories include education, experience, work skill requirements, personal requirements, mental and physical requirements, and working conditions and hazards. A job specification for a remote visual display terminal operator might include such items as a required education level, a certain number of months of experience, typing ability of 60 wpm, high degree of visual concentration, and ability to work under time pressure.

A job specification can be written by talking with the current holder of the job about the qualifications needed to perform the job satisfactorily. But caution should be exercised so that the characteristics of the current job occupant are not used as the sole basis for the job specification statements. Checking the job requirements of other organizations and businesses with similar jobs is another means to obtain information for preparing job specifications.

Critical KSAs.   In writing any job specification, it is important to list only those KSAs essential for satisfactory job performance. Only directly job-related items which are nondiscriminatory should be included. For example, a high school diploma should not be required for a job unless the manager can demonstrate that an individual with less education cannot perform the job as well. Because of that concern, some specification statements read: "high school diploma, or equivalent acceptable experience." In some technical jobs the exact educational skills can be indicated: "Must have thorough knowledge of PL-1 and COBOL computer languages." Figure 6–9 is one example of this approach.

A process for developing relevant KSAs has evolved very recently in the public sector. Using a content validity approach that focuses only on critical job-related criteria, this process uses a group of experts in a job, including employees holding the job, to identify clear, recognizable, and ratable KSAs. These KSAs then become the basis for selecting employees using only job-related KSAs.[12]

How is a job description and a job specification
closely linked?

Using Job Descriptions and Job Specifications

Once the job descriptions and specifications are prepared, the manager should provide feedback to the current job holders, especially those who assisted in the job analysis. One feedback technique is to give employees a copy of their own job descriptions and specifications for review. Giving the current employees the opportunity to make corrections, ask for clarification, and discuss their job duties with the appropriate manager or supervisor enhances manager-employee communications. Questions about how work is done, why it is done that way, and how it can be changed as topics that arise. When employees are represented by a union, it is essential that union representatives be included in reviewing the job descriptions and specifications. Otherwise, the possibility for future conflict is heightened.

Performance Standards.   An important use of job descriptions and specifications is to generate performance standards for each of the job re-

Figure 6–9 Management data processing: Job description/specification combination.

CLASS TITLE: Systems Project Leader

CHARACTERISTICS OF THE CLASS:

Under direction, is responsible for work of considerable difficulty in supervising a project team in the plan, design, and implementation of a major data processing project.

Incumbents are responsible for supervising a team of programmer/analysts in the design, installation, and implementation of a system and functions with complete independence within the framework of the assignment. This level is distinguished from the EDP Programmer/Analyst III by having responsibility for planning, designing and implementing a total project and may assign responsibility at the job level to EDP Programmer/Analyst III. This level is distinguished from the EDP Systems Project Manager who has the responsibility for managing several project teams.

EXAMPLES OF DUTIES:

Supervises and participates as a member of a project team in systems design and implementation; plans and designs automated processes determining applications and computer requirements, conducting feasibility studies, scheduling projects and implementation of activities; coordinates the development and implementation of projects working with users and DP personnel to maintain schedules, to identify/resolve problems, and to maintain effective communication with users and DP management; assists users in planning and the development of new systems and maintenance, modification and enhancement of existing systems to identify/resolve problems, assure that schedules are being met, provide better service, and maintain effective communication links; prepares written instructions/descriptions for use in developing user procedures and programming specifications; supervises the activities of programming staff in the development of coded instructions for digital computer processing and may perform programming functions as required; plans and develops test data files, testing sequence and reviews test results for adherence to programming and operations standards.

KNOWLEDGE, ABILITIES AND SKILLS:

Considerable knowledge of electronic data processing equipment capabilities; considerable knowledge of application systems design techniques and procedures; considerable knowledge of project organization, management and control; good knowledge of the principles and techniques of programming and digital computers; good knowledge of the principles of supervision; some knowledge of statistics. Ability to analyze data and situations, reason logically, draw valid conclusions and develop effective solutions to systems problems; ability to design procedures for processing data with digital computers; ability to prepare comprehensive reports; ability to analyze and evaluate the progress of the system being developed; ability to speak and write effectively.

MINIMUM QUALIFICATIONS:

Two years experience equivalent to an EDP Programmer/Analyst III

---

sponsibility statements. Because performance standards list what is satisfactory performance in each area of the job description, the employee has a clear identification of what is expected on the job. Thus, the development of clear and realistic performance standards can intercept some problems which often arise when employees' performances are appraised.

Staffing.   A good job specification is useful when staffing because it provides a specific set of qualifications for an individual to be hired for a specific job. Clarifying what type of person is to be recruited and selected definitely helps a manager, supervisor, or personnel specialist. Likewise, the well-written job description can be used to give applicants an initial statement of what they will be doing if they are hired. Thus, the type of job, job requirements, and job expectations can be identified more effectively to prospective or new employees.

As is evident, job descriptions and job specifications are valuable tools for managers and employees in any organization. The development and use of job descriptions and job specifications is a time-consuming process, but one that is necessary for effective organizational staffing and operation.

REVIEW AND PREVIEW

The major thrust of any organization is to move toward goals or objectives by performing the work of the organization in a logical and coordinated fashion. To do so, the work of the organization must be divided into jobs. A job has the dimensions of scope and depth and forms an integrated unit of work. The expectations and rewards desired by the individuals performing the jobs should be considered when jobs are designed. A successful matching of individual expectations and organizational needs is important.

Once jobs are designed they must be analyzed. The job analysis process generates information used in the development and utilization of job descriptions, job specifications, and job evaluation. The job description delineates the key tasks, duties, and responsibilities of a job; job specifications translate those job requirements into the human knowledge, skills, and abilities needed to perform the described job satisfactorily.

There are several uses that can be made of the job description and job specification information obtained by analyzing jobs and work. One of the most beneficial of these uses is in recruiting and selecting the people to fill the analyzed jobs. The next chapter examines recruiting activities, and chapter 8 explores the nature of personnel selection.

Review Questions

1. What do you do when you design a job? What are some key considerations?
2. Distinguish the relationship or lack of it between job simplification and job rotation. What is a criticism of each?
3. Clearly define and discuss the relationship between job analysis, job descriptions, and job specifications.
4. "Job analysis is the most basic personnel activity." Discuss.
5. In two sentences each, describe the four common methods of analyzing jobs.
6. How do human behavior and governmental considerations affect the job analysis process?
7. Construct a form for a sample job description. Why is a job description necessary before developing a job specification?

Case: College Bookstore

The College Bookstore is located on the campus of a large southern university. The university classes operate on a quarter system, which requires the bookstore to order textbooks for the beginning of a new term. The number of new textbooks to be received, priced, and shelved at the start of a new term is extensive.

There are basically five different operations involved in getting books from the receiving dock to the retail shelves. They are:

1. Transporting the boxes from the receiving dock to the pricing area using a two-person system.
2. Unboxing and sorting the books in each shipment.
3. Checking a shipment against the purchase order to ensure that the correct titles and quantities were shipped for each publisher.
4. Placing a price tag on each book.
5. Shelving books in appropriate locations using one-person book carts.

Because of the volume of books involved at the beginning of each term, student helpers are usually hired for about two weeks before each term to process the incoming books. These temporary employees usually work six to eight hours a day on the textbook receiving process.

QUESTIONS

1. How does job design apply to this case?
2. a. How many jobs would you have under a job simplification approach?
   b. Why might job rotation be considered?
   c. Why might a job enlargement strategy be considered?
   d. How would job analysis, job descriptions, and job specifications be useful to the textbook department manager?

NOTES

1. *Job Analysis for Improved Job-related Employee Development.* U.S. Civil Service Commission, BIPP 152-69, August 1976.
2. *Omaha World Herald*, February 22, 1981.

3. C. Orpen, "The Effects of Job Enrichment on Employee Satisfaction, Motivation, Involvement, and Performance: A Field Experiment," *Human Relations* 32, 1979, pp. 189–217.

4. E. Sundstrom, R. E. Bunt, and D. Kamp, "Privacy at Work: Architectural Correlates of Job Satisfaction and Job Performance," *Academy of Management Journal*, March 1980.

5. For more information see Richard Steers and Lyman Porter, *Motivation and Work Behavior*, 2d ed. New York: McGraw-Hill, 1979, chapter 9.

6. J. R. Hackman and G. R. Oldham, *Work Redesign*, Reading, MA: Addison-Wesley, 1980.

7. A concise but detailed explanation of FJA is contained in *ASPA Handbook of Personnel and Industrial Relations: Volume I, Staffing Policies and Strategies*, Dale Yoder and Herbert G. Heneman, Jr., editors. Washington, D.C.: The Bureau of National Affairs, 1974, pp. 4–58 through 4–63.

8. U. S. Department of Labor, *Dictionary of Occupational Titles*, 4th ed. Washington, D.C.: United States Government Printing Office, 1977.

9. Adapted from *Wage and Salary Administration: A Guide to Current Policies and Practices*. Chicago: The Dartnell Corporation, 1969. Used with permission.

10. E. J. McCormick, J. D. Shaw, A. S. Denist, "Use of the PAQ for Establishing the Job Component Validity of Tests," *Journal of Applied Psychology*, vol. 64, no. 1, 1979, pp. 51–56.

11. For a detailed guide on preparing and writing job descriptions see *Job Analysis*, U.S. Civil Service Commission, or R. I. Henderson, *Compensation Management*. Reston, VA: Reston Publishing Co., 1979, chapter 7.

12. For detailed information, see Robert Otteman and J. Brad Chapman, "A Viable Strategy for Validation: Content Validity," *The Personnel Administrator*, November 1977, pp. 17–22.

Human Resource Planning and Recruiting

When you have read this chapter, you should be able to:

1. Explain the nature of the Human Resource Planning process.

2. Discuss several controllable and uncontrollable variables affecting the supply and demand of human resources.

3. Identify and briefly explain at least three internal sources of employees.

4. Name and briefly discuss at least four external recruiting sources.

5. List three advantages and disadvantages of internal and external recruiting.

Midwestern Bank Corporation

Midwestern Bank Corporation is a large bank holding company that owns and operates 27 banks in a midwestern state. The bank's growth has been great. Starting with one bank ten years ago, the holding company (thanks to a big infusion of capital) has purchased 26 other banks in the primarily rural towns of the state. In the past these banks have had local ownership and management. The holding company is now trying to reap some of the economies of scale by centralizing many policies and functions and providing more dynamic management for many of the banks.

Until this year Midwestern had no personnel department per se. Frank Franklin had taken care of what little personnel work had been done at headquarters but now Frank was retiring. No one had shown any particular interest in taking his place so the company had gone to the west coast and had hired an experienced personnel manager from a large bank holding company there. He was to report May 1st. The president had provided a list of some of the areas that he felt had been neglected and would probably need work, and some of the company's three-year plans.

The areas of neglect were as follows:

- Hiring: we are shorthanded in several positions.
- Management development: we need more college graduates.
- EEO: our percentage of women at higher levels is too low.

Future plans identified included three items:

1. We plan to offer an attractive early retirement option for older bank officers to bring in new blood.

2. We plan to open six *new* banks (not purchase existing banks) in the next five years.

3. We predict increases in business of 10% per year for the next five years.

Comments:

The importance of planning for the future is stressed in this case. Human Resource Planning (HRP) is the tie between personnel planning and organizational long-range plans and objectives. Midwestern Bank arrived at its current state of affairs over a long period of time. It will take time to resolve the areas of neglect and to respond to future plans. For any progress to be made the president must give the personnel manager "clout" and emphasize that personnel planning and recruiting are of major importance throughout the organization. Solid planning will then enable the new personnel manager to target this recruiting effort.

To develop an effective work force an organization must first determine the skills and number of people it will need and then find and hire them. Such actions require (1) Human Resource (HR) planning to determine the needs and (2) a knowledge of appropriate recruiting sources and methods.

In most large organizations the HR planning and recruiting functions are coordinated through a personnel department. It is the responsibility of this department to maintain and analyze HR plans with other departments as part of a perpetual recruiting effort.

Often other managers help in the recruiting effort by determining the skills and qualifications needed in individuals who will fill vacancies in their areas. Figure 7–1 shows a typical interface between the personnel department and managers for HR planning and recruiting. In small organizations, and even in some divisions of large organizations, several different managers may work on recruiting.

Figure 7–1. Human resource planning/recruiting portion of staffing interface.

Personnel Unit	Managers
Proposes objective for HR planning	Determine qualifications and anticipate needs
Designs HR planning data systems	Identify and monitor career plans of employees
Collects data from managers to prepare HR Plans	Determine management succession
Forecasts recruiting needs	Assist in recruiting effort
Assists in career planning and training to accomplish planned goals	Provide management review and discussions
Plans, coordinates and evaluates recruiting efforts	

HUMAN RESOURCE PLANNING

As in other operational areas, planning is important in personnel. HR planning is tied in with generally accepted planning methods and efforts in finance, marketing, and production.

> HUMAN RESOURCE PLANNING consists of determining what must be done to ensure the availability of employees required for an organization to meet its objectives.

Ensuring the type and number of employees needed can include many elements. A good example of what can result from HR planning can be found in Sears, Roebuck's efforts to inject youth into its merchandising management. Sears found that they had experienced a large increase in the number of executives holding their jobs past age 63 after the 1978 change in retirement laws. Most observers felt that Sears was top-heavy with older managers and that this concentration had limited the company's flexibility and innovation level.

The company's HR planning operations evidently came to the same conclusion because Sears offered a "limited time special sale on early retirement." It allowed executives who were 55 or older and who had 20 years of service to retire early and to receive special incentive pay in addition to normal retirement benefits. Sears felt the normal attrition rate of 6% in that group was insufficient to meet company objectives. The company expected 500 to 600 executives to take advantage of the "special." [1]

The Process of HR Planning

The general process of HR planning is illustrated in Figure 7–2. Notice that the first stage of HR planning is an examination of *organizational objectives and plans.* If a retail chain plans to double its number of stores from 100 to 200 in a three-year period, that firm must also identify how many, and what types of, new employees will be needed to staff these new stores. These are *staffing* plans.

Staff management can then identify how many employees will be needed and can *inventory* its existing employee work force. This check on HR availability identifies the skills and capabilities of current employees so that the firm can build on its existing reservoir of workers, as well as on what might be available outside the organization.

A *HR needs forecast* can be made by comparing the number of people and the skills that will be needed to what the firm anticipates will be available. Using this data as a base, the firm then must develop HR plans/programs to expand, contract, or change.

Why Plan?

HR planning must be viewed *over time* because it allocates human resources to jobs over long periods, not only for the next month, or even the next year. It concerns the *current* level of skills in an organization, expected vacancies due to retirements, promotions, transfers, sick leaves, discharges, or other reasons. Also, through this type of planning, expansions or reductions in operations and projected technological changes can be analyzed. On the basis of such analysis, plans can be made for shifting employees internally, laying off and otherwise cutting back, or

Figure 7–2. HR planning process.

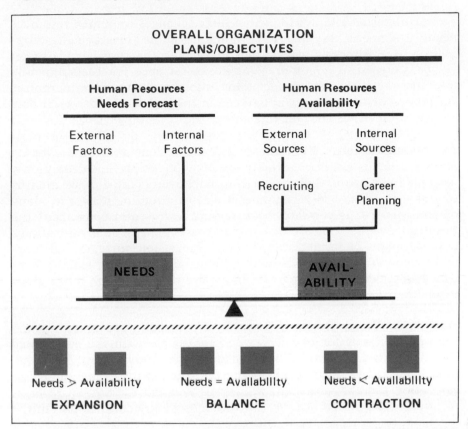

for training present employees, as well as for recruiting and hiring new people.

What is HR Planning?

Benefits of Planning.   Some of the potential benefits of an effective HR planning system are:

1. Upper management has a better view of the human resources dimensions of business decisions.
2. Personnel costs may be less because management can anticipate imbalances before they become unmanageable and expensive.
3. More time is provided to locate source talent.
4. Better opportunities exist to include women and minority groups in future growth plans.
5. Better planning of assignments to develop managers can be done.

Nature of Forecasting

Forecasting is an attempt to predict future changes in human resources needs. It is not an easy undertaking, and has some "crystal-ball gazing" aspects to it. Although some rather advanced techniques have been developed, forecasting is far from being an exact science. Forecasts generally take historical data and project them into the future. This method is adequate, but the manager must keep in mind that the historical data are based on trends that may be changing.

Forecasting Periods.   HR forecasting should be done over three planning periods: *short-range, intermediate,* and *long-range.*[2] The most commonly used planning period is short-range, usually over a period of six months to one year. This level of planning is almost a routine matter in many organizations. It is common because very few assumptions about the future are necessary. These short-run forecasts indicate an organization's best estimates of immediate personnel needs. Intermediate and long-range forecasting is a much more difficult process. Intermediate plans usually project one to five years into the future and long range plans extend beyond five years.

Forecasting Human Resource Demand.   HR planning attempts to match the organization's forecasted *demand* for people with the anticipated *supply* of available workers. To identify the demand, two basic approaches can be used: (1) calculating the demand for people on an organization-wide basis, using the *average demand* for the entire organization over a period of time; (2) considering individual "units" in the organization rather than the entire organization.

For example, a forecast that Apex Corporation needs 75 new employees next year might mean less than a forecast that Apex Corporation needs 25 new people in sales, 25 in production, 10 in accounting, 5 in personnel, and 10 in the warehouse. This unit breakdown obviously allows for more consideration of specific necessary skills than the aggregate method.

Models are available for forecasting human resources needs that range from a manager's guess to a very rigorous and complex determination. Simple models may be quite accurate in certain instances, but the complex models may be necessary in other circumstances. For example, complex models are required in work-load scheduling, military staffing, or airline staff scheduling.[3]

Forecasting Internal Supply

For some time managers have recognized the need for periodic financial audits. Auditors' reports are generally used to pinpoint areas of potential problems, such as excessive cost overruns, inadequate reporting techniques, or fraud. The same technique can be used to check the use of personnel in an organization and to determine the supply available.

Human Resource Inventory.   One of the first steps in conducting a *Human Resource Audit* is a performance appraisal for each individual in a department that identifies each person according to the quality of his or her work. This information is then combined by work group to pinpoint the level of performance in a work unit. For example, combining the performance ratings of the eleven people in one company's management group shows that the company has a high percentage of very qualified managers; nine of the eleven are rated good or excellent overall.

Charts giving an overview of the department's employee situation may be plotted for each department in an organization. When overall data are charted, the accumulated information can show where there are few internal candidates for future positions. Likewise, the HR inventory can indicate where there is a reservoir of trained people that the employer can tap as it meets future conditions.

A part of internal inventorying must consider some factors over which there is little control. Some employees will die, quit the firm, retire, or otherwise reduce the current employee force. Likewise, new employees will be hired. Thus, internal planning must utilize forecasts about these factors when an internal audit is conducted.

Human Resource Information System.   Most managers feel they have a good idea of the talent available in their organization. But that information is not always current or complete. Perhaps even more important, the information is not in a form that can be used to forecast future needs.

Many employers have developed computerized information systems to help manage HR inventories in large organizations. Such systems usually include data on:

- individual demographics
- career progression
- appraisals
- skills
- interests
- training/education
- target positions
- geographic preferences
- promotability ratings

These data can be used to generate system output that provides a useful inventory of talent when vacancies occur.

Several reports on analyses of the data can be made to provide information on both supply and demand of HR internally. For example, it is possible to determine the following:

- open positions
- hard-to-staff positions
- "blocked" career paths
- useful training positions
- attrition data
- affirmative action information

Forecasting External Supply

Except for some qualified individuals already in the organization, most new employees must be obtained from outside the organization. A great many factors can affect the supply of labor available to an employer and to the economy in general.

Economic Conditions.   The general business cycles of recessions and boom times can make labor readily available or dry up a good source of recruits. There is a considerable difference between finding qualified applicants in a 5% unemployment market and in a 9% unemployment market. In the 5% unemployment market, very few qualified applicants are likely to be available for any kind of position. Those who *are* available may be basically unemployable because they are uneducated, unskilled, or unwilling to work. As the unemployment rate rises, the number of qualified candidates available rises.

Government Policies.   Government pressure on organizations to hire more minority group members has increased the difficulties involved in finding qualified minority group members for many high-skill positions. The effect of affirmative action pressures to hire minorities and women for certain jobs has been a real shortage of such potential employees in those areas.

Job Mobility and Work Force Participation.   Another important, documented trend affecting the supply of labor is *job mobility*. While people changed jobs more regularly during the 1960s than in the past, they changed jobs less frequently in the 1970s. In the 1980s it appears mobility will not reach to levels of the 1960s either. This mobility may not be reflected in the unemployment figures, because many people look for job changes while still on their present job.

A company also cannot control *people's decisions to leave or enter the job market*. A significant factor in the available work force is that more women are entering or reentering the job market. It is estimated that well over 60% of all women in the United States will be in the labor force by 1990. Figure 7–3 indicates this increase graphically.

In addition, many people have chosen recently to delay retirement, keeping themselves in the work force longer than before. The percentage of men over 65 still in the work force has declined from 50% at the end of World War II to around 20% now. But it has stopped declining and some experts predict that it might rise again.

Population and Job Availability Changes.   In the next two decades the United States will have a gradually aging labor force reflecting both the aging of the post-World War II "baby boom" and increased longevity. Yet the work force has expanded dramatically with the increased number of women in the work force. By 1985, a reduction in the labor force growth rate is likely. After that a relatively smaller number of people will be looking for entry level jobs.

Figure 7–3.   Civilian labor force participation rates of women, by age, 1970, 1980, and 1990.

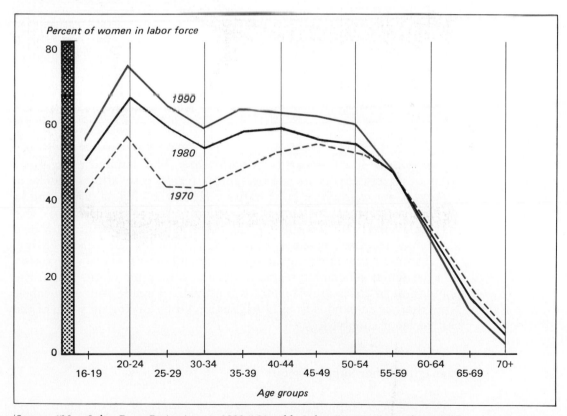

(Source: "New Labor Force Projections to 1990," *Monthly Labor Review*, December 1976.)

The number of high-skill jobs and white-collar jobs are expected to grow at a much more rapid rate than jobs in general. But a surplus of college graduates is expected until the mid 1980s, as shown in Figure 7–4. The picture is one of a gradually changing gap between jobs and people who want to work.

Figure 7–4. Gap between workers and jobs.

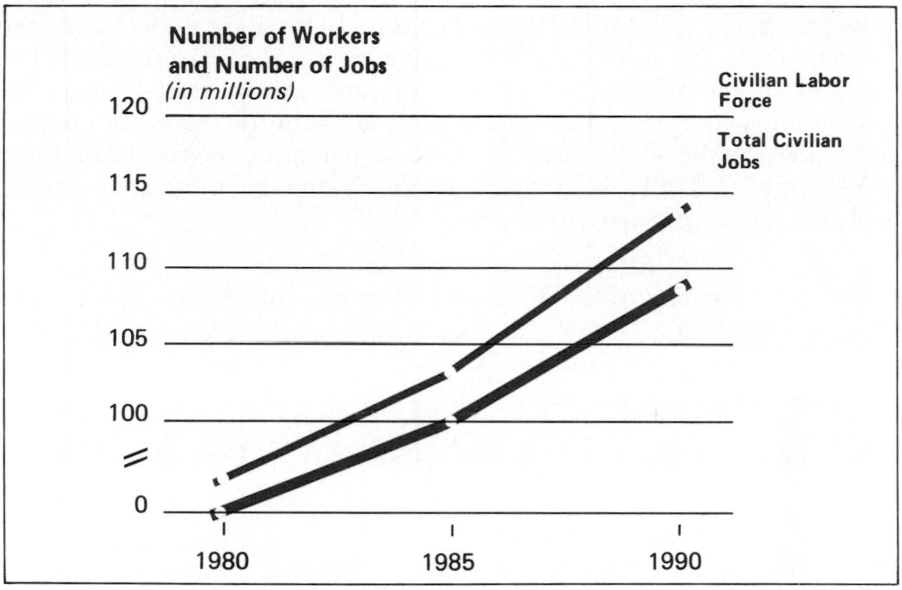

Geographical and Competitive Conditions. The demand for workers from other employers in a geographical region also affects the labor supply. If, for example, a large military facility is closing or moving to another geographical location, a large supply of very good civilian labor may be available for a while. On the other hand, the opening of a new plant may decrease the supply of labor in a given market for some time.

Another factor affecting the supply of manpower is the net migration in a particular geographic region. For some time after World War II the population of cities grew rapidly and provided a ready source of labor. Now there is an exodus from Northeastern cities, drying up some of the skilled labor supply.

Managing Labor Supply Factors

There are numerous factors affecting the supply of labor. Figure 7–5 illustrates the interrelationship in the labor supply of variables that an organization *can control* and the variables that are *uncontrollable.*

Figure 7–5. External supply of manpower.

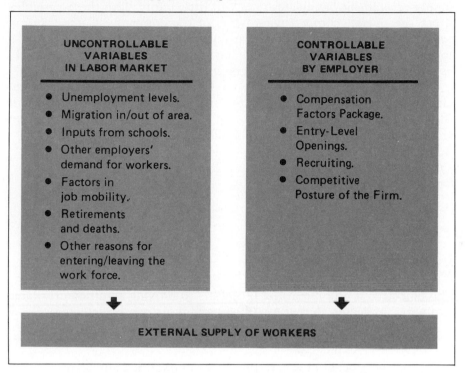

(Source: Adapted from N. S. Deckhard and K. W. Lessey, "A Model for Understanding Management Manpower Forecasting, and Planning," *Personnel Journal*, 54, March 1975, p. 171. Reprinted with permission of *Personnel Journal*) copyright, March 1975.)

Uncontrollable Supply Variables.   Uncontrollable variables in the labor markets include *retirement and deaths* since they reduce the overall number of people available to work. Another variable is *job mobility,* which largely depends on the economy. In a high unemployment market, people are less apt to leave a job without having another job available. They might be looking, but probably will not leave a sure thing without some sort of security. The effects of *other employers' demands* for employees on a given organization have been previously discussed in this chapter.

   Input to the labor market from schools is an uncontrollable variable which changes somewhat with time. For example, those born during the "postwar baby boom" graduated and reached the job market in the mid-1960s. There was a reduction in the number of young people graduating from school during the 1970s corresponding to a reduced birthrate in the 1950s.

Controllable Supply Variables   Variables that *can* be controlled are the *kind of recruiting efforts* made by the firm and the *number of entry-*

level job openings. A vigorous recruiting effort will turn up a larger supply of available candidates than will little effort. Both these variables affect the overall *competitive posture* of the company. *Compensation package factors* affect competitive posture, too. Employers offering a competitive compensation package have less difficulty securing a supply of workers than do those employers who are not competitive.

In summary, HR planning is vital. The extent to which an organization attempts to plan and control its need for human resources will determine whether the firm *shapes* its participation in the labor market or *is shaped by* the labor market situation.

Can you list six factors that must be considered in making HR forecasts?

NATURE OF RECRUITING

The objective of the recruiting process is to provide a sufficiently large group of candidates so that qualified employees can be selected.

RECRUITING is the process of generating a pool of qualified applicants for organizational positions.

If the recruitment process does not provide an adequate group of candidates for selection, good employees may not be hired. If the number of available candidates equals the number of people to be hired, there is *no selection*—the choice has already been made. The organization must either leave some jobs unfilled or take all the candidates.

In addition to *general* recruiting, an organization must engage in *specialized* recruiting. Such recruiting efforts are directed at the particular type of individual the organization wants to hire. For example, recruiting college-educated electronics engineering employees is a more specialized process than recruiting drafting clerks.

While extensive recruiting efforts are usually associated with tight labor markets and a high organizational need for employees, recruiting efforts should not be limited to such difficult periods. Even during periods of reduced hiring, long-range Human Resource plans should include contacts with outside recruiting sources to maintain visibility and maintenance of employee recruiting channels within the organization. These activities are essential so that the recruiting activity can be stepped up on short notice when needed.

Recruiting Activities

Important activities for proper recruiting include:

1. Determining and categorizing long-range and short-range needs by job title.
2. Staying informed of conditions in the employment market.
3. Developing effective recruiting material.
4. Recording the number and quality of applicants from each recruiting source.
5. Following up on applicants to evaluate the effectiveness of the recruiting effort.

When a vacancy occurs which must be filled, internal sources of qualified applicants are generally considered first. Employees can be promoted or transferred into the position, or sometimes an individual may be demoted into the vacant position. A good HR planning program maintains information on present employees for internal transfers. In the normal course of events employees resign, retire, die, or are fired. Without proper planning, unforeseen vacancies can hamper the organization's operation, especially if a new employee is not promptly found and trained.

RECRUITING SOURCES

Recruiting efforts often have a shorter time focus. Building upon HR plans, employers must translate plans into action. They must also fill openings when unexpected vacancies occur.

There is a wide variety of sources for recruiting applicants. It is tempting to evaluate these various sources on the basis of effectiveness or some similar criterion. Such an effort would be hard to justify because the sources can vary greatly and because different organizations have vastly different needs.

Internal Sources

There are numerous internal recruiting sources: present employees, friends of employees, former employees, and former applicants. Also, promotions, demotions, and transfers can provide additional people for a given organizational unit, if not for the entire organization. Using internal personnel sources has some advantages over external sources. First, it allows management to observe an employee over a period of time and to evaluate that person's potential and specific job behavior.

These factors cannot be as easily observed off the job. For an organization to promote its own employees to fill job openings may be motivating; employees may have little motivation to do a good job or to do more than just what the job requires if management's policy is to promote externally.

If the skill level needed does not exist in the present work force, employees may be trained in the new skill. For example, one organization, unable to hire computer programmers, decided to train its own programmers on a pilot project basis. The managers for whom the programmers went to work rated their retrained employees as meeting or bettering job requirements. Such programs can be costly and time-consuming. However, internal retraining can be considered if the necessary skills are not available in the organization's work force.

Job Posting and Bidding.   One procedure for moving employees into other jobs within the organization is a *job posting and bidding* system. Employees can be notified of all job vacancies by posting notices, circulating publications, or inviting employees to apply for jobs. In a unionized organization, job posting and bidding can be quite formal and usually is spelled out in the labor agreement. Such action gives each employee an opportunity to move to better positions within the organization. Without some sort of job posting and bidding, it is difficult to find out what jobs are open elsewhere in the organization.

A survey of employee promotion policies and practices revealed that the most common method of notifying current employees of openings is by posting notices on bulletin boards. However, professional job openings were posted on bulletin boards much less frequently than clerical and blue-collar openings.[4]

Job posting and bidding systems can become ineffective if handled improperly. Jobs should be posted *before* any external recruiting is done. A reasonable period of time must be allowed for present employees to check notices of available jobs before considering external applicants. When employees' bids are turned down, they should be informed of the reasons.

Many other potential problems must be worked out. What happens if there are no qualified candidates on the payroll to fill new openings? Is it necessary for employees to inform their supervisors that they are bidding for another job? How much lead time should an employee be required to give? When should job notices not be posted? These questions must be adequately anticipated. In any event, a mechanism such as job posting and bidding helps an employer tap the talents of current employees.

Recruiting through Current Employees.   A good source of people to fill vacancies can be reached through the organization's current staff. Employees can develop good prospects among their families and friends by acquainting them with the advantages of a job with the company, furnishing cards of introduction, and encouraging them to apply. This source is usually one of the most effective methods of recruiting because many qualified people are reached at a very low cost to the company. In an organization with a large number of employees, this approach can provide quite a large pool of potential organization members. Most employees know from their own experience about the requirements of the job and what sort of person the company is looking for. Often employees have friends or acquaintances who meet these requirements. A word of caution is appropriate here. When the organization has an *underrepresentation* of a particular minority group, word of mouth referral has been considered a violation of Title VII of the Civil Rights Act.

There are two principal plans for employee recruiting. One plan is the *campaign method*, which is a concentrated drive for a short period of time. It is used principally when large numbers of new people are required quickly. For example, when a large resort motel needed several dishwashers and busboys, the manager asked current employees if they knew of anyone to fill these places. Several of those suggested were hired the next day.

The second and preferable plan is a *continuing program* which anticipates the need for qualified individuals. This plan may generate fewer applicants than the first, but the continuing program brings far better results. A good arrangement is to have each first-level supervisor contact his or her own work group about possible recruits because they know the employees best, and contacts on recruiting are very natural. A continuing program needs to provide incentives to help maintain the enthusiasm necessary for good results. One incentive is knowing that management and supervisors support the recruiting effort and that all employees are invited to participate. One firm gives a $25 savings bond to each employee recommending someone who is eventually hired.

Former Employees.   Former employees are also an internal source of applicants. Some retired employees may be willing to come back to work on a part-time basis or may recommend someone who would be interested in working for the company. Sometimes people who have left the company to raise a family or finish a college degree are willing to come back to work. Individuals who left for other jobs might be willing to come back for a higher rate of pay. An advantage with this group of former employees is that their performance is known.

A senior vice-president at New York's Chemical Bank says, "The days of discriminating against people who previously left are gone." The concept of corporate loyalty has long kept many firms from rehiring those who left. American General Insurance Company of Houston, however, regards returning employees as among its most loyal workers. And Kentucky Fried Chicken hired a former junior officer as its new president even though in the interim he had worked for Church's Fried Chicken.[5]

Previous Applicants.   Another source of applicants is the organization's applicant files. Although not truly an internal source, those who have previously applied for jobs can be recontacted by mail, a quick and inexpensive way to fill an unexpected opening. Although "walk-ins" are likely to be more suitable for filling unskilled and semi-skilled jobs, some professional openings can be filled by applicants for previous jobs. One firm that needed two cost accountants immediately contacted qualified previous applicants and was able to hire two individuals who were disenchanted with their current jobs.

Can you identify three internal recruiting sources?

External Institutional Sources

If internal sources do not produce an acceptable candidate, several types of external sources are available. These include schools, colleges and universities, employment agencies, temporary help firms, labor unions, media sources, and trade and competitive sources.

School Recruiting.   Public schools may be a good source of new employees for many organizations. A successful recruiting program with these institutions is the result of careful analysis, thorough training and planning, and continuing contact on an individual school basis.

Major considerations for such a recruiting program are as follows:

1. School counselors and other faculty members concerned with job opportunities and business careers for their students should be contacted regularly.
2. Good relations should be maintained with faculty and officials at all times, even when there is little or no need for new employees.
3. Recruiting programs can serve these schools in ways other than the placement of students. For instance, the organization might supply educational films, provide speakers, or arrange for demonstrations and exhibits.
4. It should be recognized that numerous organizations compete for their share of the capable graduates. Continuing contact and good relations provide an organization a better opportunity to secure the best graduates.
5. The extent and scope of this recruiting program will depend on needs. However, a long-range view of recruiting is desirable to avoid a campaign approach if possible.
6. Some larger schools have a centralized guidance placement office.

Contact can be established and maintained with the supervisors of these offices, as they are in a good position to help plan and conduct recruiting activities.

School counselors are generally interested in the employer's policies and working conditions and will usually cooperate with an organization that treats its employees fairly. Promotional brochures to acquaint students with starting jobs and career opportunities can be distributed to counselors, librarians, or others to help public relations. Participation in career days and giving tours of the company to school groups also aid in maintaining good contact with school sources.

College and University Recruiting.   At the college or university level the recruitment of graduating students is a large-scale operation for many companies. Most colleges and universities maintain placement offices where employers and applicants can meet. However, college recruiting presents some interesting and unique problems.

There is a great deal of competition for the top students in a college and much less competition for those farther down the ladder. One study pinpointed attributes that recruiters seem to value most highly in college graduates; poise, oral communication skill, personality, appearance, and written communication skills all came in ahead of grade point average.[6]

College recruiting provides American employers with about two out of three new hires on the college level. Three groups are especially in demand: (1) engineers and other technical personnel, (2) computer scientists, and (3) fast-track management trainees.[7]

College recruiting can be very expensive. Therefore an organization should determine carefully if the positions it is trying to fill with college graduates *really* require a college degree. A great many positions do not; yet many employers insist upon filling them with college graduates. The result may be a disgruntled employee who must be paid more and who is likely to leave if the job is not sufficiently challenging.

Employment Agencies.   Every state in the United States has a *state* employment agency. These agencies operate branch offices in many cities throughout the state. Such agencies can be a potential source for recruiting applicants.

Also, *private* employment agencies are found in most cities. For a fee collected from either the employee or the employer, these agencies will do some of the preliminary screening for an organization and put the organization in touch with applicants. These agencies differ considerably in terms of their level of service, costs, policies, and the types of applicants that they provide. An employer can determine from the Better Business Bureau or Chamber of Commerce which agencies are reputable. Employers can reduce the range of possible problems with these sources by giving an employment service a good definition of the position to be filled, including such details as job title, skills needed, experience and education required, and pay ranges available.

Temporary Help.   Perhaps the most easily accessible and immediate source of certain types of help is the temporary help agency. These agencies supply secretarial, clerical, or semi-skilled labor on a day-rate basis. As Figure 7–6 indicates, temporary employees are used for a variety of reasons. The use of temporary help might make sense for an organization if the work it does is subject to seasonal or other fluctuations. Hiring temporary help may be more efficient than hiring to meet peak employment needs. In the latter case, the employer either has to find something to keep employees busy during less active periods or resort to layoffs.

Labor Unions.   Labor unions are a source of certain types of labor. In some industries, such as construction, unions have traditionally supplied

Figure 7–6.   Use of temporary help.

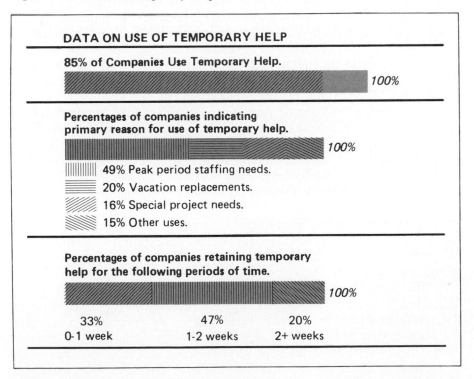

Note: Results based on survey of 1083 companies.

(Source: *Central New York Business Review*, reported in Sam Dickey, "The Generalist," *Management World*, December 1980, p. 24.)

workers to employers. A labor pool is generally available through a union, and workers can be dispatched to particular jobs to meet the needs of employers. The hiring hall is usually the contact point.

Media Sources. Media sources are widely used and familiar to many people looking for a job: newspapers, magazines, television, radio, and billboards. Almost all newspapers carry help-wanted sections and these are frequently a source of applicants for many organizations. Newspapers are useful because there is usually a two- or three-day lead time to place the ad. For positions which must be filled quickly, newspapers may be a good source. However, with newspaper advertising there can be a great deal of waste circulation and often applicants are only marginally suitable, primarily because employers do not describe their jobs and the relevant needed qualifications well. Many employers have found it is usually not economically advisable to schedule newspaper ads on days *other* than Sunday.

Media ads can also be helpful. At a window manufacturing company an affirmative action program suggested by the EEOC required the company to advertise all positions in the local newspaper as "public announcements." Therefore, the company used the newspaper as their main media source.

A representative of Hughes Aircraft Corporation has reported some interesting findings regarding newspaper and magazine advertising for applicants.[8] He suggests that conditions of the labor market exert quite an influence on ads. For example, during a recession a four-inch, one-column classified ad for electronics technicians experienced with radar and fire control systems produced 437 replies. At a time of labor shortages, this same ad expanded to two columns brought just two responses. Consequently, it is suggested that *records* be kept of the success of ads.

Two recent studies shed some light on the use of ads. In one, the Bureau of National Affairs found that eight out of ten companies do use newspaper advertising to recruit professional, managerial, technical, and plant personnel.[9] However, another study rating the effectiveness of sources of recruitment found newspapers and college placement poorer sources of employees (based on performance, absenteeism, and work attitudes) than journal/convention contacts and self-initiated contacts.[10]

Other media sources include general magazines, television and radio, and billboards. These sources might be less suitable for frequent use, but may be useful for one-time campaigns aimed at providing specially skilled workers quickly. General Electric once used a billboard at a major plant to advertise its openings for welders. Radio ads have also been tried by some employers.[11]

Trade and Competitive Sources. Other sources for recruiting are *trade associations*, *trade publications*, and *competitors*. Trade associations usually publish a newsletter or magazine containing job ads. Such publications may be a good source for specialized professionals needed within an industry. Also, by placing ads in specialized publications or by listing at professional meetings, openings for professional personnel can be publicized.

In addition, an employer may meet possible applicants currently employed with a competitor at trade associations and industry meetings. Some employers directly contact individuals working for a competitor. Employees recruited from these sources spend less time in training because they already know the industry.

What are four general external sources for applicants?

INTERNAL VS. EXTERNAL SOURCES: A COMPARISON

There are pros and cons associated with both promotion from within (internal) as a source of employees and resorting to hiring outside the organization (external) to fill openings. Figure 7–7 summarizes some of the most commonly cited advantages and disadvantages of each source.

Generally speaking, promoting from within is thought to be a positive force in rewarding good work. However, if followed exclusively,

Figure 7–7.   Internal versus external sources.

INTERNAL	
Advantages	Disadvantages
1. Morale of promotee	1. Inbreeding
2. Better assessment of abilities	2. Possible morale problems of those not promoted
3. Lower cost for some jobs	3. "Political" infighting for promotions
4. Motivator for good performance	4. Need strong management development program
5. Causes a succession of promotions	
6. Have to hire only at entry level	

EXTERNAL	
Advantages	Disadvantages
1. "New blood", new perspectives	1. May not select someone who will "fit"
2. Cheaper than training a professional	2. May cause morale problems for those internal candidates
3. No group of political supporters in organization already	3. Longer "adjustment" or orientation time
4. May bring industry insights	

it has the major disadvantage of perpetuating old ways of operating. Recruiting externally for professionals such as lawyers and CPAs may be cheaper than training them. It also infuses the organization with new ideas that are needed from time to time. But recruiting from outside the organization for any but entry-level positions has the problems of "adjustment" time for the new persons. A serious drawback to external recruiting is the impact of selecting an outsider instead of promoting a current employee.

Most organizations combine the two methods. In organizations that exist in rapidly changing environments and competitive conditions, a heavier emphasis on external sources might be necessary. However, for those organizations existing in environments that change slowly, a heavier emphasis on promotion from within would be more suitable.

What are three advantages and disadvantages of
internal and external recruiting?

REVIEW AND PREVIEW

HR planning is basically an attempt to determine an employer's short, intermediate, and long-term demand for people and to predict the availability of the supply of manpower. By attempting to match these elements, an organization can determine potential problems and move to take care of those problems.

Two general groups of recruiting sources exist: (1) internal sources, (2) external sources. A basic decision must be made whether to look within the organization or to use external sources for new employees, or to some combination of each. The particular source to be used should be determined according to the number of positions open, the qualifications needed of applicants, and other environmental factors.

The selection process requires a large number of applicants. If there are only as many people applying for jobs as there are jobs, there is *no* selection process. Therefore, recruiting activities aim at providing an adequate number of qualified applicants for the selection process, which is discussed in the next chapter.

Review Questions

1. "Recruiting has a time-frame." Discuss this statement. *177*
2. What is Human Resource planning? Why is it important? What information would you need to develop such a plan? *161*

3. Suppose you had to locate a new sales representative and you wanted to recruit within your organization. How would you proceed?

4. You need a computer programmer. What external sources would you use and why?

5. You are vice-president of administration in an insurance company and need to hire a controller. Discuss what considerations you would have in deciding to go outside versus promoting someone from inside your firm.

Case: Northwest State College

Northwest State College (a disguised name) is a four-year regional state college and has an enrollment of about 3,500 students. Its business department has a faculty of seven full-time instructors, and other part-time instructors are used as needed. Currently about 900 students are majoring in business. The college is located in a medium-sized northern community of about 70,000. Most of the faculty recruiting is done by one person, the department head, who makes the initial contact with prospective faculty members at various professional meetings held during the school year. If the department head cannot attend a meeting, recruiting is done by an instructor from the business department.

Projections are that enrollment at Northwest State will increase about 25% in the next five years. Most of the increase is expected in the business area. The ideal faculty size would be about 16 full-time instructors to handle the load and to eliminate the need for part-time instructors. Most of the full-time instructors currently in the Department of Business Administration hold MAs or MBAs from various northern colleges. The salary scales and fringe benefits are considered to be slightly lower than the compensation available at similar colleges in the region. In addition to any increase in faculty members needed due to enrollment, three replacements are needed for this fall in the business area to replace individuals who have gone elsewhere.

Northwest State has a recruiting policy that requires final approval of candidates by the department head, the vice-president for academic affairs, and the president of the college. In addition, the school has a policy requiring that at least two candidates be invited to the campus before any candidate can be hired so that adequate screening can take place. Often the result is a waiting period of two months between initial contact, application, and campus interview for most applicants. Some other small colleges in the area pay full travel expenses for potential candidates, while the majority of the others pay at least half. Northwest State does not pay any travel expenses if the candidate is *not* hired. Only if the candidate is offered a position and accepts is full reimbursement for travel expenses given. Usually the payment comes about two months after the campus interview.

In the past Northwest State has not been very successful in filling empty positions. The president is concerned and wants to evaluate the recruiting program so that a better one can be designed.

QUESTIONS

1. List the reasons why you would not consider a position at Northwest State if you were a potential applicant.
2. Evaluate the approval procedure for applicants.
3. What would be the components in a recruiting system you design?

NOTES

1. "Aging Americans," *Wall Street Journal*, November 5, 1979, p. 1.

2. James W. Walker, *Human Resource Planning* (New York: McGraw-Hill, 1980).

3. *Ibid.*, p. 107.

4. *Employee Promotion and Transfer Policies*, PPF Survey No. 120 (Washington, D.C.: The Bureau of National Affairs, January 1978), p. 2.

5. "Rehiring Employees. . . ." *Wall Street Journal*, December 4, 1979, p. 1.

6. A. Blitstein, "What Employers are Seeking in Business Graduates," *Collegiate Forum*, Winter 1980/1981, p. 7.

7. S. J. Wilhelm, "Is Campus Recruiting on Its Way Out?" *Personnel Journal*, 60, April 1980, p. 302.

8. R. A. Martin, "Employment Advertising: Hard Sale, Soft Sale, or What?" *Personnel*, May-June 1971, pp. 33–40.

9. "Remember the Classifieds," *Personnel Journal*, 59, November 1979, p. 736.

10. J. A. Breaugh, "Relationships between Recruiting Sources and Employee Performance, Absenteeism and Work Attitudes," *Academy of Management Journal* 24, March 1981, pp. 142–147.

11. Rick Stoops, "Radio Advertising as an Effective Recruitment Device," *Personnel Journal*, 61, January 1981, p. 21.

CHAPTER **8**

Selecting Human Resources

When you have read this chapter, you should be able to:

1. Identify at least four reasons for having a unit specializing in employment.

2. Diagram a typical selection process in sequential order.

3. Discuss the reception and application blank phases of the selection process.

4. Identify several key ideas to remember when using selection tests.

5. Contrast the initial screening interview and the in-depth selection interview.

6. Construct a guide to interviewing based upon the interviewing suggestions in the chapter.

7. Describe the need for and the privacy considerations of the background investigation of applicants.

8. Tell why medical examinations are a useful part of the selection process.

The Super Management Trainee

Kathy Morelli had been employment office manager for just ten weeks for a large corporation employing about 10,000 persons. The employment office handled the recruiting and screening of about 10,000 people a year and hired 10–15% of those screened. Kathy noticed a position requisition for a management trainee for one of the offices on the south side of the city that had been on file for six weeks and had remained unfilled. Two days later, a very likely looking candidate for the position applied: Bruce Williams, an aggressive young man of 22. When questioned, Bruce revealed that he had quit college within one semester of graduating to support his terminally ill mother after his father had died of cancer. Bruce was an impressive young man and his firm handshake, pleasant smile, and quick wit impressed Kathy immediately. His scores on the aptitude test were not as high as Kathy would have liked, but she felt that personal qualities exhibited by Bruce overcame these difficulties and saw no need to contact Bruce's former employers. Kathy sent Bruce to the manager of the office where the position was located. Shortly thereafter, Kathy received a phone call from the manager indicating that he shared her high opinion and Bruce was hired.

Three weeks later Kathy received a telephone call from the manager who angrily suggested that Kathy be a bit more careful in the selection of management trainee prospects. Bruce had been discovered stealing from the company and had been fired last week.

Kathy was mystified and amazed that she could have misjudged someone so badly. She decided to check with Bruce's former employers and found that he had falsified his positions and length of time at each employer. She also found out that Bruce's father and mother were alive and well. Kathy spent a rather melancholy day reflecting on the difficulty of selecting good employees.

Comments:

Many people feel that they are good judges of people and resort to the use of "hunch," "gut-feeling," or "intuition." Unfortunately, these bases do not always hold up under close scrutiny. Therefore, certain steps, including checks and balances, are built into an effective selection procedure. One of these important checks is a background investigation. Former employers provide good sources of information about potential employees. Therefore, careful adherence to the checks and balances designed into an effective selection program will result in minimizing the kinds of problems that Kathy encountered in this case.

SELECTION usually begins when a manager or supervisor sends a request to the employment office, if one exists, that a person is needed to fill a certain vacancy. A job description, a part of job analysis, is contained in the request to identify the vacancy. A job specification may accompany the request to describe what kind of person is wanted to fill the vacancy. The employment specialists then use the job description and the job specification to begin the recruiting process. The pool of applicants generated by recruiting activities must be narrowed down and one person selected to fill the job.

NATURE OF SELECTION ACTIVITIES

When a person applies for a job, that individual brings many expectations, desires, and emotions to the employment situation. Selection is a very important concern of personnel management because its objective is to match a person to a job. As the opening case illustrates, many perils exist in the process of selecting employees.

> SELECTION is the process of picking individuals who have relevant qualifications to fill jobs in the organization.

Selection Activities and Public Relations

In addition to matching qualified people to jobs, the selection process has an important public relations impact. Discriminatory hiring practices, impolite interviewers, unnecessarily long waits, or inappropriate testing procedures can produce very unfavorable impressions.

Poorly handled selection can considerably damage the image other departments have worked hard to build. In one situation, a student who applied for a part-time clerical job was treated rudely and waited 45 minutes for an interview, after being told that she would be interviewed immediately. She finally left without being interviewed and made it a point to tell her friends not to apply for a job at that firm.

Selection Interface

The selection portion of the staffing interface is shown in Figure 8–1. In different organizations these activities are done to a greater or lesser degree by the two organizational entities. Some organizations maintain

Figure 8–1. Selection portion of staffing interface.

Personnel Unit	Managers
Provides employment process and facilities	Request employees with certain qualifications to fill jobs
Evaluates success of selection process	Provide information to allow evaluation of selection process
Applies selection criteria	Help develop and perhaps apply selection criteria

the traditional practice that the personnel unit initially screens the candidates, and the appropriate managers or supervisors make the final selection.

Until recently, the basic hiring process was performed in a rather unplanned manner in many organizations. In some companies each department screened and hired its own employees. Many managers insisted upon selecting their own people because they were sure no one else could choose employees for them as well as they could. This attitude still prevails in many organizations and may create a difficult relationship between managers and the personnel unit.

This practice has been reexamined in some larger organizations because of the need to maintain equitable, nondiscriminatory hiring practices. For example, in the San Francisco Bay Mercantile Company (disguised name) the personnel office screened applicants and sent them to the individual job supervisor to be hired or not. William J. Smythe, the supervisor in charge of dock operations and delivery, made it a point to insist that no "minority" person could work for him. He would reject all applicants the employment office sent unless they were white, Anglo-Saxon, and Protestant. One day the employment office was notified by the EEOC that a Mr. Fernando Martinez had filed a complaint against the company because Mr. Smythe had rejected him for employment. After an EEOC hearing found Mr. Smythe's behavior to be blatantly discriminatory, Mr. Martinez was ordered hired and he was given back pay to the date the discrimination occurred.

Multiple government regulations on hiring practices have removed the possibility of managers doing their own hiring in many organizations. However, careful relations between the department doing the hiring and other parts of the organization are still needed. Many organizations have established a specialized part of the personnel unit to handle employment.

The Employment Office

Selection activities may be centralized into a specialized organizational unit that is part of a personnel department. This specialization depends to a large extent on the size of the organization. In smaller organizations, a full-time hiring specialist or unit may be impractical.

Advantages.   Some of the more important reasons for coordinating the employment function within such a unit, as much as is realistic, are:

1. It is easier for the applicant because there is only one place to apply for a job.
2. It facilitates contact with outside sources of applicants because issues pertaining to employment can be cleared through one central location.
3. It frees operating managers to concentrate on their operating responsibilities. This release is especially helpful during peak hiring periods.
4. It can provide for better selection because hiring is done by specialists trained in staffing techniques.
5. The applicant is more assured of consideration for a greater variety of jobs.
6. Hiring costs may be cut because duplication of effort is avoided.
7. With increased government regulations on the selection process, it is important that people who know about these rules handle a major part of the hiring process.

What are some reasons for having a unit
specializing in selection?

The employment section of the personnel unit is generally concerned with the following operations: (1) receiving applicants, (2) interviewing applicants, (3) testing applicants, (4) arranging for physical examinations, (5) checking references, (6) placing and assigning new employees, (7) follow-up of these employees, (8) termination interviewing, and (9) maintaining adequate records and reports. These activities are at the heart of the selection process.

SELECTION PROCESS

Certain steps are taken to process applicants for jobs in most organizations. Variations on this basic progression depend upon organizational differences, including factors such as size of the organization, nature of the jobs to be filled, the number of people to be selected, and the pressure of outside forces such as EEO considerations.

The process shown in Figure 8–2 is a typical selection process and Pete Dickens is a typical applicant. He comes to the organization and is directed to the employment office where he is received by a receptionist. Some firms conduct a very brief interview to determine if an applicant is qualified before the applicant is given an application form.

Figure 8–2. A typical selection process.

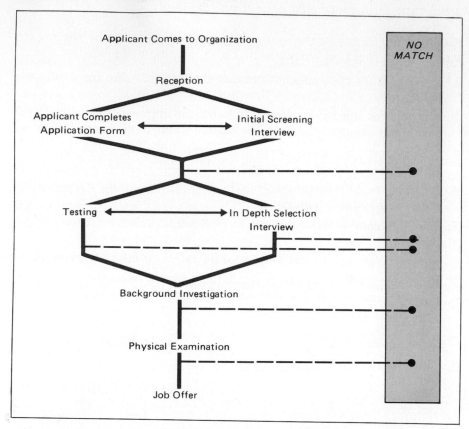

In Pete's case, the receptionist gave Pete an application form to complete. This completed application form serves as the basis for an initial screening interview, after which Pete may be told that he does not fit any positions the company has available.

If Pete is deemed to have the minimum necessary qualifications, he may go to an in-depth interview or to testing, depending upon the ease and cost of testing. If he is applying for a job which requires typing, he may be given a typing test before he has an in-depth interview. However, if he is applying for a job as a lab technician, he will probably have the in-depth interview before any tests are given. If he does not meet the minimum validated test scores or is deemed unsuitable through the in-depth interview, he is rejected.

If everything is in order to this point, his references and background may be investigated. If favorable feedback is received, Pete may be asked to take a physical exam. Based upon the results of the physical exam, he is either given a job offer or rejected. Some firms might wait to give a physical until after he has accepted the job, especially if the job has no specific physical requirements.

This process can take place in a day or over a much longer period of time. If the applicant is processed in one day, checking references usually takes place after selection. If the process takes longer, checking references may be done before the selection decision is made. Often one or more phases of the process are omitted or the order is changed depending upon the job applied for, the size of the employer, and many other factors.

It is important that the selection process be seen as a series of data-gathering activities. The employer wants to generate as much *job-related* information as possible to aid in choosing an individual to fill a job. The model in Figure 8–2 of the selection process represents the various data-gathering steps that can be used. The rest of the chapter examines each of these steps separately.

What is a typical selection process?

Reception

A person's first impression of the organization is made at this initial stage of selection. The importance of making a favorable impression at this time cannot be overemphasized. The person's attitudes about the organization and even the products or services it offers can be influenced at this encounter.

Whoever meets the applicant initially should be tactful and able to offer assistance in a courteous, friendly manner. If few jobs are available, applicants can be so informed at this point. It should be made clear that the applicant is welcome to fill out an application blank, but employment possibilities must be presented honestly and clearly.

Why is applicant reception important?

Initial Screening Interview

In some cases, before the applicant has filled out the application blank for an available job, it is usually appropriate to have a brief interview to see if the applicant is likely to match any of the jobs available in the organization. In other situations, the applicant will have completed an application form before the short interview. This brief interview is called an *initial screening interview*.

Questions can be asked to determine if the applicant is likely to have the ability to perform available jobs. Typical questions might concern job interest, location desired, salary expectations, and availability for work. The *structured interview*, in which the interviewer has a list of questions that require short answers, is the most suitable method.

The Application Form

Application forms are a widely used selection device. Properly prepared, such as the one in Figure 8–3, the application form serves three purposes: (1) it is a record of the applicant's desire to obtain a position, (2) it provides the interviewer with a profile of the applicant which can be used in the interview, and (3) it is a basic personnel record for applicants who later become employees.

EEO Considerations and Application Forms.

While application forms may not usually be thought of as "tests," the data requested on application forms must conform to EEOC guidelines and be validated as a predictor of job-related behavior. One review of applications from 151 of the largest corporations revealed that all but two firms had at least one "legally inappropriate" question on their application blanks. Fifty-seven of the firms had more than ten "inappropriate" questions.[1] This data indicates that many employers need to "clean up" their application blanks.

One interesting point to remember is that an employer must collect data on the race and sex of those who apply for reporting to EEOC, but the application blank cannot contain these items. As pointed out in chapter 5, the solution picked by a growing number of employers is one in which the applicant provides EEOC reporting data. This form is then filed separately and is not used in any other personnel selection activities.

Weighted Application Blank.

One way to make the application blank more precise is by developing a weighted application blank. A job analysis is used to determine ability, skills, and behavioral characteristics needed to do the job. Then weights or numeric values are placed on different responses to application blank items.

There are several problems associated with weighted application blanks. One difficulty is the time and effort required to develop such a blank. For many small employers and for jobs that do not have numerous employees, the cost of developing the weights would be prohibitive. Also, the blank must be updated every few years to ensure that the factors previously identified are still valid predictors of job success. Finally, and probably most importantly, many of the items that earlier studies identified as predictors could not be asked because of EEO restrictions. For example, asking about family responsibilities (married, number of children) and age is likely to cause the employer difficulty because of the need to show the job-relatedness of those inquiries. In a survey of almost 200 firms, only 4% were using a weighted application blank.[2]

Figure 8–3. Application blank sample.

The C Company

AN EQUAL OPPORTUNITY EMPLOYER

PLEASE PRINT ALL INFORMATION

Name

Present Address (Number, Street, City, State and ZIP Code)	Telephone Number	Alternate Phone Number

Relatives working for The C   Company (Name, relationship and department in which they work)

Type of work preferred	Are you willing to work:			Work skills you possess	
		Yes	NO		
Work location preferred	Over 40 hours per week?	☐	☐	Typing	___ WPM
	Irregular shifts?	☐	☐	Shorthand	___ WPM
Would you accept any other positions?	Nights?	☐	☐	Keypunch	___ SPH
☐ YES ☐ NO	Saturdays or Sundays?	☐	☐	License(s) _____	
	Holidays?	☐	☐	Other _____	
Date Available for Employment	Travel?	☐	☐	_____	

ADDITIONAL WORK SKILLS

Circle highest grade completed:

High School _____   9 10 11 12   Graduated? ☐ YES ☐ NO
College _____   13 14 15 16   Degree Received _____ Major _____
Graduate School _____   Other schools (Vocational, Military, etc.) _____

Have you ever been employed by The C   Company before?   ☐ YES ☐ NO

If Yes, Position	From	To	Reason for Leaving
Department	Supervisor Name & Title		Location

IF YOU ARE NOT A U.S. CITIZEN, DOES YOUR VISA OR IMMIGRATION STATUS PERMIT LAWFUL EMPLOYMENT? ☐ YES ☐ NO ☐ N/A	IF EMPLOYED, CAN PROOF OF CITIZENSHIP, VISA OR ALIEN REGISTRATION NUMBER BE PROVIDED? ☐ YES ☐ NO ☐ N/A

List current and previous employers: (List most current first, next most current second, etc.)
May we contact your current employer? ☐ YES ☐ NO

Position	Employer		Location	
Supervisor	Telephone Number	Dates Worked From To		Pay Rate $
Position	Employer		Location	
Supervisor	Telephone Number	Dates Worked From To		Pay Rate $
Position	Employer		Location	
Supervisor	Telephone Number	Dates Worked From To		Pay Rate $

Have you ever been convicted of a crime within the last seven years, or have you been imprisoned for the conviction of a crime within the last seven years?   ☐ YES ☐ NO   The existence of a record of convictions for criminal offenses is not considered an automatic bar to employment

Date of conviction _____ Describe Circumstances _____

Military service? ☐ YES ☐ NO	If Yes, From To	Branch of Service	MOS/Duties
Highest Rank Obtained	Reserve status ☐ NATIONAL GUARD ☐ ACTIVE RESERVE ☐ NONE		

Using Application Forms.   Many employers use only one application blank. This practice may not be "targeting" the application form to specific occupational groups as much as is possible. A hospital might have one form for nurses and medical technicians, another for clerical and office employees, another for managers and supervisors, and one for support persons in housekeeping and food service areas.

The information received on application blanks may not always be completely accurate. In one study an examination of application blank responses provided by prospective applicants and the applicants' previous employers showed that there was substantial disagreement. In two categories, length of previous employment and previous salary earned, the two sources disagreed in 57% of the cases. The typical applicant *overestimated* both the duration of the prior employment and the previous salary. Further, there was substantial disagreement on the reason for leaving the previous job.[3]

In an attempt to correct the inaccuracies, many application forms carry a statement at the bottom of the form which the applicant is to sign: "I realize that falsification of this record is grounds for dismissal if I am hired." Whether or not this phrase reduces inaccurate information on the application blank is not known. Requesting the names of previous supervisors on the application blank may be extremely useful for future use in investigating the application, and is perhaps a better idea than having an applicant sign an "oath."

If the applicant shows no obvious disqualifications, testing can be scheduled or the applicant can be given an in-depth interview. As mentioned earlier, the choice of using the interview or a test next would depend upon the nature of the job applied for, the cost of the test, and other related factors.

Why are application forms important?

SELECTION TESTING

Many people claim that when properly used and administered, formal tests can be of great benefit in the selection process. Considerable evidence supports this. However, because of EEO pressure, many employers reduced the use of tests during the 1970s. A 1975 study of 2,500 companies by Prentice-Hall, Inc., and the American Society for Personnel Administration found that 36.5% of the companies sampled did not test at all. Of those that were still using tests, three out of four had reduced their use, and nearly 14% indicated that they would soon stop.[4] However, with the adoption of new EEOC guidelines that allow content validity, it appears that increasing use of tests may be occurring.

Types of Tests

There are many different tests that could be used for selection screening. Some employers purchase already prepared tests. One listing of tests contains information on over 1,000 tests.[5] Other employers develop their own tests; some of these are very crude while others are prepared by staff industrial psychologists.

Aptitude and Proficiency Tests.   Aptitude tests are used to measure an applicant's ability to handle the work for which he or she is being considered. Included are tests of "general aptitude," such as mental ability, and "specific aptitude," such as finger dexterity. Mental aptitude and general intelligence tests were used more extensively before the *Griggs* v. *Duke Power* decision in 1971. Tests that measure mechanical ability and mathematical aptitude can be shown to be job-related much more easily. An example of a mathematical aptitude test for retail sales clerks, such as those who work at K-Mart or J.C. Penney's, is illustrated in Figure 8–4.

A proficiency test is a more specific skills-oriented test. The typing test that many firms give to secretarial applicants is a commonly used proficiency test. Work sample tests that require an applicant to perform part of the job that is being applied for are especially useful because of their close tie to the job. The 40-yard dashes and blocking drills used in pro football training camps are examples. Having a truck driver applicant actually back a truck up to a loading dock would be a proficiency test. If you have ever rented a trailer and tried to back your car and trailer into a driveway, you can understand why such proficiency would be important to a truck driver.

General Personality and Psychological Tests.   General psychological tests attempt to measure personality characteristics. The legendary Rorschach "ink blot" test and the Thematic Apperception Test (TAT) are examples. In the TAT test an applicant is shown a picture and asked to create a story about the picture. A picture might show an executive sitting at a desk cluttered with papers who appears to be gazing at a photograph of family members sitting on the desk.

As would be expected, such tests are difficult to validate as being job-related for many jobs. Also, the possibility of applicants "faking" responses exists with such tests. One joke about the "ink blot" test is that you should indicate that you see the same thing in every ink blot. There are two psychological tests that are used in the selection process that are extremely controversial. They are a *polygraph* and *graphology*.

Polygraph.   The polygraph, more generally and incorrectly referred to as a "lie detector," is a mechanical device that measures the galvanic skin response, the heart and pulse rate, and the breathing rate of a person.

Figure 8–4. Smith Discount Store sales test.

Please answer the following questions. These are examples of problems sales employees face when serving customers. Assume that there is no sales tax on any item.

1. Work the following amounts

$ .79	$ .89	$10.00	$.79	$11.00	$4.98
1.39	4.31	− 8.63	× 4	−10.35	× 5
2.81	10.49				

$15.00	$5.00	$20.00	$1.09	$3.90	$1.79
−11.41	−4.98	− 7.98	× 3	× 2	× 2

2. A customer makes the following purchases:

   2 pair of socks at $1.79 each   _____
   1 shirt at $9.98   _____
   2 pair of slacks at $17.95 each   _____

                              Total   _____

   The customer hands you $50.00. How much change do you give? _____

3. A customer buys the following items:

   3 packages of paper towels at $1.29 each   _____
   5 records at $2.95 each   _____
   2 boxes of nails at $3.49 each   _____

   What does the customer owe?   _____

4. A man returned a shirt that had cost $12.99 and exchanged it for one that sold for $15.49. He gave you a twenty dollar bill. What is his change?

   _____

5. A customer wanted to buy four items that totaled $37.14. She discovered she didn't have enough money, so she didn't buy one item for $9.85. How much did the other three items cost? _____

6. A little boy gave you three dimes, four nickels, two one dollar bills, five quarters and 14 pennies. How much did he give you? _____

7. An employee buys a lamp for $40. He receives a 15% discount. How much does he save? _____

8. Elastic sells for 39¢ a yard. The customer buys five yards. How much do you charge her? _____

Once a person is hooked up to the machine, an examiner asks questions and the person's physiological response is charted by the machine. The theory behind the polygraph is that if a person answers incorrectly, the body will "reveal" the falsification through the polygraph's recording mechanisms.

The extent of usage of the polygraph is shown in the fact that one-fifth of the largest employers in the United States use polygraphs.[6] Banks and retail firms concerned about employee theft are common users of the polygraphs. Employers use polygraphs both when selecting new employees and with current employees. A drugstore chain uses it to try to control employee theft. A pharmaceutical manufacturer uses it to screen potential employees who may try to conceal personal drug problems. Another manufacturer uses the polygraph to identify applicants trying to conceal prior worker's compensation claims.[7] Organizations involved in security and law enforcement are also heavy users of the polygraph.

Serious questions about the usage of polygraph in employment settings have been raised, especially questions about its constitutionality and the invasion of privacy. Such concerns are clearly captured in the description given by an applicant for a job at a brewery in the Western United States, as shown in Figure 8–5, even though the description may be a bit extreme.

Another criticism is the heavy reliance placed on the polygraph examiner who interprets a person's responses. There has been little control exercised over the qualifications of these examiners.

As a result of these concerns, 12 states have passed laws banning the use of polygraph tests for employment purposes. Nineteen states have laws about licensing required for operators, with Illinois having the most restrictive regulations.[8] Also, several bills have been introduced in the U.S. Congress to regulate or outlaw polygraph usage in employment situations.

In spite of these criticisms and the difficulty of identifying the job-relatedness of some of the questions used in some polygraph examinations, the usage of polygraphs will probably continue until or unless further legislation restricting its usage is passed. It has been said that the cost/benefit argument often used to justify polygraph usage should include the legal and public relations "cost."[9]

Graphology (Handwriting Analysis).   This test is similar to a polygraph in that it relies heavily on the person, in this case a graphologist, who analyzes the responses and attempts to discern personality characteristics as revealed in a person's handwriting. One graphologist claims to be able to identify over 100 personal traits from a handwriting sample.[10]

The problems with such a test are similar to those with the polygraph. Much depends upon the graphologist who interprets the results but who may be relatively untrained. Also, as with many personality tests, an employer might have difficulty identifying the relationship between a series of personality traits and job performance.

Figure 8–5. Polygraph applicant description.

'How Does This Test Apply to Making Beer?'

... "Then came the biggest shock. I was scheduled for a lie detector test. When I reported, the polygraph operator was a heavy set man dressed in white. He looked like a guard in a mental institution. He attached straps around my chest, stomach and arms. I felt helpless and wondered why all this was necessary to make beer.

"When the polygraph operator began the test he dealt with questions I had answered on the employment application. However, it didn't take long before the operator began asking extremely personal questions. Like 'Are you having sexual relations with your girl friend?' 'Have you had sex with more than one person?', 'What kind of sex?', 'Are you a Communist?', 'Have you ever done anything in your past that if known could bring embarrassment upon this company?'

"And further: 'Have you ever committed an undetected crime?' 'Have you ever participated in a march or riot or demonstration?' 'Have you ever stolen anything from anyone in your life?' 'What?' 'What was it worth?' 'What is the total worth of what you have stolen in your life?'

"It is hard to put into words the anger I felt at being forced to go through an interrogation which had absolutely nothing to do with employment . . .

Source: Andrew Kahn, *et. al.* "The Intimidation of Job Tests," *AFL-CIO Federationist,* January, 1979, p. 3. Used with permission.

Test Usage. The most important factor to consider when choosing and using a formal test is the validity of that test. As emphasized in the chapters on Equal Employment Opportunity regulations, unless the test measures what it is supposed to measure (validity) on a consistent basis (reliability), it should not be used. Finally, individuals trained in testing and test interpretation should be involved in the establishment and maintenance of a testing system.

Given the above provisions, it is easy to see why some employers, especially small ones, dropped tests. The result is that much more weight and emphasis is placed on the in-depth interview.

*What should you remember when choosing and
using tests in the selection process?*

SELECTION INTERVIEWING

An in-depth selection interview is designed to probe areas of interest to the interviewer to determine how well the applicant will work for the organization. The in-depth interview is designed to integrate all the information from application blanks, tests, and perhaps reference checks, so that a selection decision can be made. There may be conflicting information at this point, so the interviewer must obtain as much pertinent information about the applicant as possible during the limited interview time and then evaluate this information against job standards.

Equal Employment and Interviewing

The interview, like a pencil-and-paper test and an application blank, is a type of predictor and must meet the standards of job-relatedness and nondiscrimination. Some court decisions and EEOC rulings have attacked the interviewing practices of some firms as being discriminatory. In one EEOC case the court ruled that by relying on questions not related to the job applied for, interviewers violated EEOC guidelines.[11] Many experts feel that the safest and fairest type of interview to use is a structured interview, one of several types of interviewes.[12]

Types of Interviews

Structured Interview.   The purpose of a structured interview is to generate data on applicants that can be compared. If an interview asks Mary Mazzaro one question and does not ask the same question of Steve Smith, the interviewer has no similar basis for evaluating each of the applicants.

A STRUCTURED INTERVIEW is conducted using a set of standardized questions that are asked all applicants for a job.

This type of interview also allows an interviewer to prepare questions in advance that are job-related and to then complete a standardized interviewee evaluation form. Completion of such a form provides some documentation if anyone, including an EEO enforcement body, should question why one applicant was selected over another.

Even though a series of patterned questions are asked, the structured interview does not have to be rigid. The predetermined questions should be asked in a logical manner, but the interviewer should avoid reading the questions and rigidly continuing down the list of questions. The applicant should be allowed adequate opportunity to clearly explain the answers given. Also, the interviewer should probe until an adequate understanding of the applicant in each area has been gained.

Nondirective Interview.   The nondirective interview is heavily used in psychological counseling but is also widely used in selection. The interviewer asks general questions designed to have the applicant discuss himself or herself. The interviewer then picks up on an idea in the applicant's response to one question to phrase the next question. For example, if the applicant says, "One aspect of my last job that I enjoyed was my supervisor," the interviewer might ask, "What type of supervisor do you most enjoy working with?"

Difficulties with a nondirective interview include maintaining its job-relatedness and obtaining comparable data on each applicant. A manager may indicate a preference for the nondirective interview as a way to hide a lack of preparation for the interview. Also, by not having the same data from each applicant, a manager may hire one applicant instead of another because of "general attractiveness" of the applicant. Although not just physical appearance, the general attractiveness is often a result of an interviewer's subjective perceptions and biases, which may not have a direct relationship to a person's ability to perform the job. While these biases can enter into a structured interview also, they are not as well restricted in the nondirective interview.

Stress Interview.   The stress interview is a special type of interview. It is designed to create anxiety and pressure on the applicant to see how the applicant responds. In the stress interview the interviewer assumes an extremely aggressive and insulting posture. Those who utilize this approach often justify its use when interviewing individuals who will encounter high degrees of stress on the job, such as a consumer complaint clerk in a department store or an air traffic controller.

The stress interview appears to be a "high risk" approach. The typical applicant is already somewhat anxious in any interview. The stress interview can easily generate a very poor image of an interviewer and an employer, thus creating resistance by applicants who might be offered a job.

Can you compare and contrast the screening and in-depth interviews?

Interviewing Suggestions

Many people think the ability to interview is an innate talent. This contention is difficult to support. Just because someone is personable and likes to talk is no guarantee that the person will be a good interviewer. Interviewing skills are developed through training and through following some of the suggestions below.

Planning the Interview.   Effective interviews do not just happen; they are planned. Pre-interview planning is essential to a well-conducted in-depth selection interview. The interviewer should review the application blank and other data before beginning the interview.

Using a Chronology.   A useful planning tool to probe an individual's past history, especially unexplained gaps in an individual's past work or school record, is plotting a chronology.

A CHRONOLOGY is a structured review of activities during a period of time.

For example, when Herb Ellis applies for a job as a management trainee, the in-depth interviewer asks Herb, with the help of his application blank, to recall his past work experience. Questions such as those in Figure 8–6 are good for developing a chronology.

Figure 8–6.   Chronology Questions.

"Why did you choose that particular job?"
"What were the qualifications for the job?"
"What were your duties specifically?"
"What did you like and what did you dislike about the job?"
"What kind of training did you receive?"
"Describe the supervision you received."
"What promotions and raises did you receive?"
"What are some reasons you had for leaving the job?"

All the jobs that Herb has had for the last five years are arranged into a time-frame which allows the interviewer to see any gaps in the chronology. By questioning Herb about the dates of his employment, the interviewer determines that two years ago there was a four-month period during which Herb did not work, nor was he going to school. Careful questioning about this fact that had not appeared on the application blank revealed that Herb had been involved in an automobile accident and had suffered a back injury. He had not noted this fact on the application blank.

Problems in the Interview

There are a number of pitfalls that interviewers should avoid. Operating managers and supervisors most often use poor interviewing techniques because they do not interview often and have not been trained to interview. Some of the most common problems in the interview are highlighted next.

Snap Judgments. Ideally, the interviewer should collect *all* the information possible on an applicant before forming a judgment. Reserving judgment is much easier to recommend than to do. It is very difficult not to form an early impression. Too often interviewers form an early impression and spend the balance of the interview looking for evidence to support it. Research on the interview confirms this and indicates that interviewers make a decision within the first four to five minutes of an interview. Also, decisions about high-quality applicants usually take longer.[13]

Negative Emphasis. Research studies show that unfavorable information about an applicant is the biggest factor in decisions about overall suitability. Unfavorable information is given roughly twice the weight of the favorable information received. It has been found that a single negative characteristic may bar an individual from being an accepted candidate, but no number of positive characteristics will guarantee a candidate's acceptance.[14]

Halo Effect. Interviewers should strictly try to avoid the "halo effect," which occurs when an interviewer allows some very prominent characteristic to overshadow other evidence. The halo effect would be present if an interviewer let a candidate's alma mater overshadow other aspects and lead the interviewer to hire the applicant because "all state university grads are good employees."

Biases. An interviewer must be able to face up to personal biases. For example, studies on the interview process have found that women are generally rated lower, by both female and male interviewers.[15] An indication that personal bias has influenced a selection decision is the selection of an applicant who falls below standards or the rejection of an applicant who meets standards. An interviewer should be able to honestly write down the reasons for selecting a particular applicant. The solution to the problem of bias lies not in claiming that a person has no biases, but in demonstrating that they can be controlled.

Cultural Noise. The interviewer must learn to recognize and handle "cultural noise." Applicants want a job; to get it they know they have to get by the interviewer. They may feel that if they divulge any of the "wrong things" about themselves, they may not get the job. Consequently, applicants may be reticent to tell the interviewer all about themselves. Instead they may try to give the interviewer responses which are *socially* acceptable but not very revealing. These types of responses are *cultural noise*—responses the applicant believes are socially acceptable rather than facts.

An interviewer can handle cultural noise by not encouraging it. Any support of cultural noise by the interviewer is a cue to the applicant to continue those answers. Instead, the applicant can be made aware that the interviewer is not being taken in. An interviewer can say, "The fact that you were the best flag handler in your Scout troop is interesting, but tell me about your performance on your last job."

Interviewer Believability.   Interviewers represent their employer and must be believable. Glowing accounts of the company and rambling testimonials are a form of cultural noise given by interviewers. One study found that applicants see interviewers as the least credible source. Also, providing negative information about a job increased the credibility but, as expected, providing negative information decreases the likelihood of the applicant accepting a job offer.[16]

Control.   Another very important part of the interview is control. If the interviewer does not control the interview, the applicant usually will. Control involves knowing in advance what information must be collected, systematically collecting it, and stopping when everything needed is collected.

Control of the interview should not be equated with the interviewer talking. The interviewer should talk no more than 15% to 20% of the time in the in-depth interview. If the interviewer talks more than that, the interviewer is being interviewed. The purpose of the interview is to have the interviewee provide information, and the interviewee is the one who should be doing the talking.

The interviewer can lose control by the type of question he or she asks. Lou Markley, an interviewer, might ask, "Can you tell me about your part-time jobs?" The applicant might take off on a 30-minute discussion. Control of the interview is lost if the interviewer cannot break in. Letting the applicant know what is to be accomplished during the interview and how it is to be accomplished helps establish control because the applicant understands his or her role in the interview.

Questioning Techniques

Good Questions.   Many questions an interviewer asks assume the past is the best predictor of the future, and it usually is. An interviewer is less likely to have difficulty when questioning the applicant's demonstrated past performance. For example, at the racetrack there are many ways to pick a horse. You can guess a winner, you can ask someone, you can stick a pin in your program, or you can study the track record of the horses. Unless you are very lucky, you are likely to lose the least amount of money in the long run by using the last method. While the applicant who has had seven jobs in the last two years *may* settle down and stay on this job, the chances are much greater that this will not occur.

Some types of questions provide more meaningful answers than do others. Good interviewing technique is dependent upon the use of open-ended questions directed toward some particular object. An open-ended question is one which cannot be answered "yes" or "no." *Who, what, when, why, tell me, how, which* are all beginnings for questions that will produce longer and more informative answers. "What was your attendance record on your last job?" is a better question than "Did you have a good attendance record on your last job?" The latter question can be answered simply, "Yes."

Poor Questions.   Certain kinds of questions should be avoided:

1. *Questions which rarely produce a true answer.* For example, "How did you get along with your co-workers?" This question is almost inevitably going to be answered, "Just fine."

2. *Leading questions.* A leading question is one in which the answer is obvious from the way the question was asked. For example, "You do like to talk to people, don't you?" Answer: "Of course."

3. *Illegal questions.* Questions which involve race, creed, sex, national origin, and so on, are obviously illegal and are just as inappropriate in the interview as they are on the application blank.

4. *Obvious questions.* An obvious question is one for which the interviewer already has the answer, and the applicant knows it. Questions already answered on the application blank should be probed, not reasked. If an interviewer asks, "What high school did you attend?", Joyce Sauer is likely to answer, "As I put on my application blank, South High School in Caveton." Instead, ask questions that probe the information: "What were your favorite subjects at South High, and why?"

There are certain question areas that an interviewer may minimize. These can be referred to as the "EGAD" factors. These are questions about the applicant's *e*xpectations, *g*oals, *a*spirations, and *d*esires. While the answer to an EGAD question *may* produce a meaningful answer, usually the applicant will respond with cultural noise. For example, in answer to the question, "What are your aspirations?", the college graduate will often tell you that he or she wants to become a vice-president.

The person settles for vice-president instead of president because the applicant does not want to appear egotistical. Yet it is considered "culturally acceptable" in our society to demonstrate a certain amount of ambition and the vice-presidential level appears to be appropriate.

The applicant is not likely to be able to answer an EGAD question realistically. Consequently, the answer an interviewer will receive is probably the applicant's idea of what the interviewer wants to hear. Many times the answer is straight from the organization's advertisements and recruiting brochures. For example, "I am looking for a job that provides a challenge and an opportunity for advancement."

The answer to an EGAD question is not likely to be very predictive. The attainment of a B+ average in school is a fact, is verifiable, and is likely to be more predictive.

Listening Responses.   The good interviewer avoids listening responses such as nodding, pausing, casual remarks, echoing, and mirroring. Listening responses are an essential part of everyday, normal conversation. While they are necessary to maintain rapport, they do provide feedback to the applicant. Applicants may try to please the interviewer and look to the interviewer's listening responses for cues. Even though the listening response may be subtle, it does provide information to the applicant.

While the total absence of listening responses can create stress, listening responses may be overly supportive and foster cultural noise as well. For example, one interviewer used the casual remark, "That's nice," constantly. After every statement the applicant made, the interviewer would comment, "That's nice," while trying to think of the next question. This habit had a tendency to encourage the interviewee to talk about things that were really not pertinent to the interview and the job at hand. As a result, the interviews took much longer than necessary.

The Interview Process Reviewed

The following is a summary of procedures for the in-depth selection interview. These techniques are appropriate for most interviews; however, for highly skilled positions or professional or managerial positions, different techniques may be more appropriate.

Interview Summary.   The interviewer should set the stage for the interview by letting the applicant know what is going to happen and what is expected of him or her. For example, the interviewer might suggest: "The purpose of this interview is to determine whether there is a match between your interests and qualifications and what we have to offer. To do this, I'd like to briefly review your history from 1977 to the present, paying particular attention to your school and work activities; and then I'd like to come back and have you cover some of the areas in greater detail."

Exchange of Information.   After the stage has been set, the interviewer can review the chronology presented in the application form. For example, "You worked for Orbus Company from January 1979 to September 1981 as a clerk"; "What did you do between September and November 1981?"

The interviewer can then probe important areas. Questions might include: "Let's discuss your job at Orbus Company." "What were your responsibilities?" "How did you get the job?" "What were several reasons you had for leaving?"

The applicant's questions also must be answered and the job situation should be explained. Whether hired or not, the applicant should feel that he or she has been given fair consideration and treatment.

Close the Interview.   And finally, the interviewer closes the interview. One question has proved very useful for closing an interview: "Is there anything else about you I should know before we close this interview?" Many times interviewees will use this opportunity to bring out something that may have been bothering them through the course of the interview. It also indicates that this is the *last* question before the interview closes.

The Turndown.   A large percentage of applicants are not hired. The manner in which they are turned down can have a personal effect on the individual and on that person's impression of the organization. Most people can perform successfully in *some kind* of job in *some* organization—it is simply a question of finding a match. The best interest of the applicant is served if the applicant is *not* placed in an unsuitable position. The interviewer does well to direct attention to this fact.

A standard turndown phrase can be quite beneficial if properly developed. One company uses the turndown phrase, "In my judgment, we do not have a match between your qualifications and the needs of the job for which you have applied so as to use your qualifications to their best advantage."

It is generally good practice *not* to give reasons beyond a turndown phrase for not hiring someone. Considerable experience in this area has indicated that giving reasons for not hiring encourages argument or comparison of the applicant with a present employee. Reasons may be misquoted by the applicant when talking with other individuals, resulting in many other problems. In addition, such reasons may be taken as advice or counseling on the part of the interviewer. Vocational advice or counseling is inappropriate at this point. Interviewers should be trained to recognize qualifications for their own particular organization, but these qualifications may not hold for other occupations or organizations. Also, the applicant should not be encouraged to hope for a job with the company if there is no future possibility that he or she would even be hired.

Such phrases as "Try back again in six months" or "We'll keep your application in our files and call you if something comes up" when untrue are unjustifiable. Utmost care must be taken not to hold out hope where none exists. It simply is not fair to the applicant, although it might be more comfortable for the interviewer.

Written Record of the Interview.   During or immediately after the interview, the actual decision is made whether or not to further consider the applicant. It is important that the interviewer make notes regarding interview data so that the information can be reevaluated later if necessary.

A written evaluation of interview data gives an overall view of findings, provides a check for consistency, and points up items that need further investigation. More important, the interviewer must use the information to support a final decision. Requiring written records forces the interviewer to justify the decision.

What would be in a guide for interviewing an applicant?

What Interviewers Look For.   Overall, interviewers attempt to see evidence of competence and success. One study determined that there *was* a core of information looked for by interviewers in the seven occupations investigated. One cluster is similar to a "personal relations" variable, and the second cluster seems to represent the "attributes of a good citizen." Included were trustworthiness, dependability, conscientiousness, responsibility, and stability.[17]

In another study, interviewers rated résumés which portrayed applicants with *average* grades, *excellent* work experience, and *appropriate* interest lower than résumés which portrayed people with *poor* work experience, *inappropriate* interests, but *high* scholastic standing. The information about scholastic standing in this study was so overwhelmingly important that the latter résumés received good evaluations.[18] Certain items are obviously more important to interviewers; but to the extent that these are not based on valid reasons, their use must be guarded.

Assessment of Interviews.   Despite its widespread use, the interview is probably one of the *weakest* tools for predicting an applicant's job performance. First, no one is sure that much of the information covered in an interview is predictive of performance on the job. Second, of the information that is predictive, much of it cannot be measured reliably in an interview.

Why, then, bother? The interview does provide *some* information which cannot be obtained in other ways, such as communicative ability and attitudes. Also, personal contact reassures both applicants and interviewers.

BACKGROUND INVESTIGATION

Background investigation, as noted earlier, may take place either before or after the evaluation (in-depth) interview. Checking a person's background is highly recommended, considering that a good deal of the information accumulated on the application blank and in the interview may be incorrect. Background checks may require investing a little time and money, but they are generally well worth the effort.

Types of References.

Background references can be put in several categories: school references, prior work references, credit check references, or personal references. Often personal references are of little value and probably should not even be required. No applicant will ask somebody to write a recommendation who is going to give a negative response. Therefore, personal references from relatives, ministers, or family friends are likely to be a weak source of selection information.

Problems in investigating applicants' backgrounds arise because managers must contact people in other organizations they may not know. Often people are hesitant to give a negative reference, *especially in written form*, for a former employee. Some employers have a policy to give only the essential information such as dates of employment, title of the last job, and perhaps salary. Although this information can be used to verify the applicant's statements, it has very little other use.

Impact of Privacy Legislation

A variety of federal and state laws designed to protect the privacy of personal information has been passed. The major law is the Federal Privacy Act of 1974, which applies primarily to governmental agencies and units. However, bills to extend the provisions of the privacy act to other employers have been regularly introduced. Employers should be aware of the impact pending privacy legislation could have on their employment practices, especially background investigations.

One proposed privacy provision would require signed written release from a person before information could be given to someone else. Also, either a copy of the information would be given to the individual, or the right of the person to inspect the personnel file would be established. Another person or employer who gave information that could not be documented and which prevented someone from obtaining a potential job could be sued. Other privacy provisions that would affect personnel files and records are discussed in chapter 16.

It must be emphasized that many of these provisions were not law at the time this book was prepared. Figure 8–7 provides guidelines for reference information.

Figure 8–7. Guidelines for reference information.

When asking for information:

1. Request job-related information only.
2. Obtain written release from job candidates prior to checking references.
3. Stay away from subjective areas.
4. Continue to use reference checks.
5. Evaluate who provides any subjective reference material received.

When responding to reference requests:

1. Do not blacklist former employees.
2. Fully document all released information.
3. Make no subjective statements.
4. Obtain written consent from employees prior to providing reference data.
5. Use a telephone "callback" procedure when verifying application blank data.
6. Do not offer reference data over the telephone.
7. Release only the following general types of information:
   Dates of employment
   Job titles during employment and time in each position
   Promotions and demotions
   Attendance record and salary
   Reason for termination (no details, just reason)
8. Do not answer the rehire question ("Would you rehire this person?")

(Source: Developed from information in John D. Rice, "Privacy Legislation: Its Effect on Pre-employment Reference Checking," *The Personnel Administrator*, (February 1978), pp. 46–51.)

Contacting References

In spite of the potential limitation imposed by privacy concerns, many employers do contact references. A study found that 77% of the employers responding used some combination of a letter and a telephone call as the main means of verifying background information.[19]

Successful contact can sometimes be made by telephone. In many ways telephone contacts are superior to written ones because the former employer is more likely to provide information over the phone that would not be provided in a permanent written form. Some suggestions for checking references by phone are:

First, place the telephone call to the applicant's former supervisor rather than to the personnel office.

Second, it is important that checks not be made with an applicant's present employer unless the applicant agrees that it is acceptable.

Third, identify yourself immediately. Emphasize that you are verifying information given by a former employee who is applying for a position. It acts as an opening wedge to obtain additional information.

If it is necessary to use a letter to obtain reference information, the reference could be asked to determine to what extent the former employee could meet specific job requirements. These requirements should be based on job analysis and be very clearly defined so that the reference can react to them.

How do privacy considerations affect background investigations?

Medical Examination

A medical examination may be given to all applicants who otherwise meet the hiring requirements. Often this examination is one of the last steps in the employment process. A medical examination is usually given in a company medical office or by a physician approved and paid by the organization. The purpose of a medical examination is to obtain information on the health status of the applicant being considered for employment. Medical information is useful in:

1. Assigning workers to jobs for which they are physically and emotionally fitted and are capable of performing in a sustained and effective manner.

2. Providing data about an individual as a basis for future health guidance.

3. Safeguarding the health of present employees through the detection of contagious diseases.

4. Protecting applicants who have had health defects from undertaking work that could be detrimental to themselves or might otherwise endanger the employer's property.

5. Protecting the employer from workers' compensation claims that are not valid because the injuries or illnesses were present when the employee was hired.

Physical standards for jobs should be realistic, justifiable, and geared to the job requirements. Many very good potential employees can be rejected inappropriately by unnecessarily rigid medical standards. Physically handicapped workers can perform quite adequately in many jobs. These individuals, if they have the ability, can be among the best workers the organization can have. However, in many places, they are rejected because of their handicaps, rather than being carefully screened and placed in a job where their handicaps will not matter. In summary, handicapped workers can provide an untapped source of potential if placed in jobs compatible with their handicaps.

Some firms use a preemployment health checklist that the applicant completes. Then, depending upon the responses given, a physical examination may be scheduled with a physician. With the cost of a very simple physical examination being $50 or more per person, it is easy to see the potential savings available by using a questionnaire.

Why might physical examinations be useful in selection?

ASSESSMENT CENTERS

An assessment center is not a place but is a selection and development means composed of a series of evaluative exercises and tests. In one assessment center candidates go through a comprehensive interview, pencil-and-paper test, individual and group simulation, and work exercises. The candidates' performance is then evaluated by a panel of trained raters.

A number of state and local governments use the assessment center when selecting department or division heads because of the potential charges of political favoritism that could be leveled using a typical selection process. One major city has used the assessment center to select a director of public works, the fire chief, the city engineer, and the employee relations administrator.

Assessment centers are especially useful in determining promotable employees and in helping to develop them. These issues are discussed in chapter 10. Our purpose in this brief section is to indicate that assessment centers can be used in selection.

REVIEW AND PREVIEW

Important activities in the selection process have been covered in this chapter. From the reception of an applicant, through the application and initial screening process, to testing, in-depth selection interview, background investigation, and the physical examination, the entire process must be handled by trained, knowledgeable individuals.

Selection, if properly done, ensures that high-quality people can be brought into the organization. The government, however, has severely limited what can be done in the selection process. This limitation has forced many employers to examine and improve their selection processes to focus on predicting performance.

During the selection process the employer must make a decision about who is hired. In the next chapter the importance of training the individuals who have been hired is discussed. Initial orientation to the work situation, as well as the general nature of training, is discussed in the next section.

Review Questions

Validity is most important →

1. You are starting a new manufacturing company. What phases would you go through to select your employees?

2. Agree or disagree with the following statement: "A good application blank is fundamental to a good selection process."

3. Discuss the following statement: "We stopped giving tests altogether and rely exclusively on the interview for hiring."

4. Make two lists. On one list indicate what information you would want to obtain from the screening interview; on the other indicate what information you would want to obtain from the in-depth interview.

5. Develop a structured interview guide for a 20-minute interview with a retail sales clerk applicant. Include specific questions you would ask.

6. How would you go about investigating a new college graduate's background? Why would this information be useful to you in making a selection decision?

7. List the advantages and disadvantages of having a complete medical examination given to all new employees.

Case: Selecting a Programmer

Marie Pendergrass has been data processing supervisor for two years. She is in the process of selecting a candidate for a programmer trainee position she has created. Her plan is to develop the trainee into a systems analyst within two years. Since this is a fast track, she needs a candidate whose aptitude and motivation are high.

Fourteen candidates applied for the job at the employment section of the Personnel Department. Six were women, eight were men. An employment specialist screened the candidates for Mary using a carefully prepared interview format, including questions to determine job-related skills. Six candidates, three women and three men, were referred to Marie.

Marie then conducted a structured in-depth interview and further narrowed the selection down to one woman and two men. Her boss, a company vice-president, agrees with her judgment after hearing Marie's description of the candidates. However, Marie's boss feels particularly unsure of the abilities of the female candidate. From the selection interview, past job experience, and education, there is no clear indication of the candidate's ability to perform the job. The vice-president is insistent that Marie test the candidate with a programmer aptitude instrument devised by a computer manufacturing firm. The test had been given four years ago, and some of the most successful current analysts had scored high on it.

Marie went to the Personnel Department and asked them to administer the test to the "questionable" candidate. The personnel manager informed her that the company policy had been to do no testing of any kind during the last two years. Marie explained the request had come from a vice-president and asked that she be given a decision on her request by Friday.

QUESTIONS

1. Identify and evaluate the stages of the selection process reflected in the case.
2. If you were Marie, what would you do?

NOTES

1. Ernest C. Miller, "An EEO Examination of Employment Applications," *Personnel Administration*, March 1980, pp. 63–69 + .

2. *Selection Procedures and Personnel Records*, PPF Survey # 114 (Washington, D.C.: The Bureau of National Affairs, September 1976), p. 3.

3. I. L. Goldstein, "The Application Blank: How Honest Are the Responses?" *Journal of Applied Psychology* 55, 1971, p. 491.

4. *Personnel Management: Policies and Practices Report #22*, (Englewood Cliffs, NJ: Prentice-Hall, 4-2-75).

5. O. K. Buros, *Eleventh Mental Measurements Yearbook* (Highland Park, NJ: Gryphon Press, 1981).

6. John A. Belt and Peter B. Holden, "Polygraph Usage Among Major U.S. Corporations," *Personnel Journal*, 57, February 1978, pp. 80–86.

7. "Business Buys the Lie Detector," *Business Week*, February 6, 1978, pp. 100–104.

8. John A. Belt, "The Polygraph: A Questionable Personnel Tool," *Personnel Administrator*, in press.

9. *Ibid.*

10. Jitendra M. Sharma and Harsh Vardhan, "Graphology: What Handwriting Can Tell You About an Applicant," *Personnel*, March-April 1975, pp. 57–63.

11. Richard A. Arvey, *Fairness in Selecting Employees* (Reading, MA: Addison-Wesley, 1979), p. 165.

12. Elliott D. Pursell, et al., "Structured Interviewing: Avoiding Selection Problems," *Personnel Journal*, 59, November 1980, pp. 907–912.

13. William L. Tullar, et al., "Effects of Interview Length and Applicant Quality on Interview Decision Time," *Journal of Applied Psychology*, 64, December 1979, pp. 669–674.

14. T. W. Dobmeyer and M. D. Dunette, "Relative Importance of Three Content Dimensions in Overall Suitability Ratings of Job Applicant Resumes," *Journal of Applied Psychology*, 54, 1970, p. 69.

15. Arvey, *Fairness in Selecting Employees*, pp. 174–176.

16. Cynthia Fisher, et al., "Source Credibility, Information on Favorability and Job Offer Acceptance," *Academy of Management Journal* 22, March 1979, pp. 94–103.

17. M. D. Hackel and A. J. Shuh, "Job Applicant Attributes Judged Important across Seven Diverse Occupations," *Personnel Psychology* 24, 1971, p. 50.

18. Dobmeyer and Dunette, "Content Dimensions of Resumes," p. 70.

19. George Beason and John A. Belt, "Verifying Applicants' Backgrounds," *Personnel Journal*, July 1977, pp. 345-348.

Training and Development

BURNOUT!!!

C. J. is Sales Manager for the West Coast region of a large parts manufacturer. He has always been considered bright and a hard worker. He got promotions at a rapid rate, bought a big house, membership in the country club, and sent his kids to college. He works long hours, but his productivity is now very low. For escape, he occasionally slips away for a continuation of a noon-time affair with a woman from the office. C. J. is a victim of a newly recognized syndrome affecting many employees in different positions—job burnout.

Kate is the Office Manager for a large electronics firm in the Northeast. She has always had the reputation for getting her work done, done right, and done on time. In fact, as recently as eight months ago, Kate was a serious candidate for Administrative Vice-President. Today, she is listless, her mind wanders, and her irritability is a topic of conversation in the office. Like C. J., Kate is a victim of burnout.

Joe D. was one of the best workers on the floor. His daily ticket always exceeded everyone else's. His quality was the model used by management to instruct new employees. Today, Joe D. is different. His absenteeism rate is triple the next worst in the plant. Things slide by without making quality adjustments. Joe is burned out, too.

There was a time when burned-out people were viewed as simply "tired." The cure was a little rest or "getting away for a few days." In fact, the original argument for employees taking vacations recognized this need to "get away." But job burnout will not be cured by a few days off.

Psychologists say that burnout is characterized by low energy, irritability, and a negative attitude toward self and job. It seems to affect certain occupations more than others: nurses, divorce and criminal lawyers, police officers, teachers, and staffers in mental hospitals and hospices.

It does seem to occur most often around a person's mid-life years but can occur very early in a career as well. Reports of persons 28 years old and younger suffering burnout have been noted. Burnout seems to be brought on by severe or chronic stress in *the job* at which a person works. Jobs that allow very little time free of pressures seem to cause burnout. Nursing may be the classic example. Erratic hours, little room for advancement, deep emotional involvement, and low pay all contribute.

Psychologists suggest that burnout has three phases. The first is a feeling of emotional exhaustion, a feeling of being drained. Next comes cynicism and an insensitivity toward people around you. Finally, the person believes that he or she is a failure and the effort they have put into the job has been a waste.

The cost to business of job burnout has not been calculated or even estimated. However, it seems safe to assume that it is considerable. The "cure" is not entirely clear at this point. However, a partial solution is for the person to be allowed changes in routine. Varying job assignments or working on projects with a *definite end point* seems to help. Sabbatical leaves or leaves of absence may be appropriate in some cases.

Finally, the employee suffering burnout must come to understand his or her feelings about the job and may need to make changes to avoid the syndrome. These changes may include a regular exercise program such as running or tennis, a change of location, doing things *you* want to do, or outside interests.

Burnout has only recently been identified as a source of symptoms many of us have seen or felt. Personnel's role may be to monitor the problem and, through flexible career planning, help burnout-prone employees to adjust.

In this section, we note that people must receive some training to perform jobs, and to advance to better jobs. Training programs provide employees with the opportunity to learn new skills and ideas so that the organization develops its internal talent for the future.

Training and orientation are the topics of chapter 9. Orientation is the first organizational training an employee receives. Before a person can perform well on the job, he or she must be properly introduced, or oriented, to the organization.

Chapter 10 deals with methods of developing employees. Development is a broad and longer-range type of training. By developing employees, especially managers, an organization prepares itself for the future. Another part of this chapter focuses specifically on the importance of career planning for employees.

CHAPTER 9

Orientation
and Training

When you have read this chapter, you should be able to:

1. Explain five aspects of an effective orientation system.

2. Define training and discuss at least five learning principles that relate to training.

3. Discuss the three major phases of a training system in an organization.

4. Identify three ways to determine training needs.

5. List and discuss at least four training methods.

6. Give an example of each of the four levels of evaluating training and how to design evaluation efforts.

Confused Claims Clerks

The claims department has been causing continual problems at the Mutual Aid Insurance Company (MAIC). Employees in the claims department review the adjuster's reports, check the policyholder's records, and then type up a claim report and a claims voucher. Using the claims voucher, the accounting department draws up the payment to the policyholder. Before the check is mailed, however, the claims department clerk must verify the check against the claims report and the claims voucher. If you are confused so far, you can understand why new clerks had problems.

In the past, turnover had been quite high in the claims department. During exit interviews the claims clerks often said that they were reprimanded for making mistakes, but they really did not know how to do the job well. Janet Hollenbeck, the assistant personnel manager, decided to check into the training the claims clerks received. Janet found that the claims supervisor had about 25 clerks to supervise. Consequently, she had very little time to spend training new claims clerks. The on-the-job training was really "sink or swim" in nature. A new clerk was shown the forms and was told, "Ask someone if you have any problems, but don't make any mistakes." Janet has decided that the on-the-job training that is now done is the major cause of the mistakes and turnover.

Comments:

The on-the-job training in the claims department is obviously inadequate and the lack of a systematic approach to training has resulted in more severe organizational problems. Also, the supervisor has such a wide span of control that there is little or no time that can be used to do true on-the-job training. The critical factor is for the assistant personnel director and the supervisor together to devise a systematic and well-conceived training program, including formal orientation of new employees to MAIC and to their jobs.

IN order to be an asset to the organization, new employees must know organizational policies and procedures. Also, new employees need training in how to perform their jobs. But learning does not stop after this initial introduction. Working in an organization is a continuous learning process, and learning is at the heart of training and development activities.

ORIENTATION

In orientation, an attempt is made to "install" a new employee so that he or she is sufficiently acquainted with the company to feel comfortable and learn the job. This does not mean that orientation should be the mechanical process described in the opening case. A sensitive awareness to employees' anxieties, uncertainties, and needs is important.

> ORIENTATION is the planned introduction of employees to their jobs, their co-workers, and the organization.

Purposes of Orientation

The orientation process has several important purposes. The overall goal is to help new employees learn about their new work environment.

Initial Favorable Impression.   A good orientation program will create a favorable impression of the organization and its work. Just as a favorable initial impression of an individual helps you to form a good relationship, so a good initial impression of a company, co-worker, or supervisor can help a new employee adjust. The lack of a good orientation program may be responsible for a high turnover rate among employees during their first months on the job. One study concluded that the effectiveness of an orientation approach had a lasting effect on absenteeism and turnover.[1]

Enhance Interpersonal Acceptance.   Another purpose of orientation is to ease the employee's entry into the work group. Meeting new people can create anxiety and concern, even in social situations such as a party. Similarly, new employees are concerned about meeting the people in their work unit. Some worries might be, "How will I get along with the people I will work with?" "Will people be friendly?" As pointed out in chapter 3 on group behavior, one of the characteristics of work groups is group norms or codes of behavior. New employees must be "instructed" or "socialized"; that is, they must be introduced to what the group expects of them. The expectations of a group of employees may not always parallel the management's formal orientation. However, if a manager does not have a well-planned formal orientation, the new employee may be oriented only by the group.

Aid Adjustment. An effective orientation program will reduce the adjustment problems of new employees by creating a sense of security, confidence, and belonging. So another purpose is to sustain or build up a new employee's self-confidence. Research suggests that new employees are afraid they will not be able to perform well and are anxious in front of the experienced employees.[2] Orientation can aid in minimizing such problems.

Why is orientation important?

Orientation as an Interface

Orientation requires cooperation between individuals in the personnel unit and other managers and supervisors. In a very small firm without a personnel department, such as a machine shop, the new employee's supervisor or manager has the total orientation responsibility. In large organizations with personnel departments, managers, supervisors, and the personnel department should work as a team in employee orientation.

Figure 9–1 illustrates a common orientation interface in which managers work effectively with personnel specialists in orienting a new employee. Together they must develop a planned, comprehensive, and effective orientation program to communicate what the employee needs to learn.

Certain types of information can probably be presented best by the immediate supervisor, while providing other orientation information is the task of the personnel specialist. A supervisor may not know all the details about the organization's health insurance or benefit options, but he or she can usually present information on safety rules, allowing the

Figure 9–1. Orientation interface.

Personnel Unit	Managers
Places employee on payroll	Prepare co-workers for new employee
Designs formal orientation program	
Explains benefits and company organization	Introduce new employee to co-workers
Develops orientation checklist	Provide overview of job setting and work rules
Evaluates orientation activities	

personnel department to explain insurance and benefits. As the data in Figure 9–2 clearly indicate, both personnel unit specialists and operating managers have responsibilities in a formal orientation program.

ESTABLISHING AN EFFECTIVE ORIENTATION SYSTEM

A systematic approach to orientation requires attention to attitudes, behaviors, and information that new employees need. Unfortunately, orientation is often rather haphazardly conducted. The general ideas mentioned next highlight some ideas that are components of an effective orientation system.

Prepare for New Employees

New employees must initially feel that they belong and are important. Therefore, both the supervisor and the personnel unit should be prepared to receive the employee. It is very uncomfortable for a new employee to arrive at work and have a manager say, "Oh, I didn't realize you were coming to work today" or "Who are you?" This depersonalization obviously does not create an atmosphere of initial acceptance and trust.

Furthermore, co-workers need to be aware that a new employee is arriving. This awareness is especially important if the new employee will be assuming certain duties which might threaten a current employee's job status and security. The manager or supervisor should prepare the current employees by discussing the new worker and the purpose for hiring that person.

Determine Information New Employees Want to Know

The overriding question guiding the establishment of an orientation system is, "What does the new employee need to know now?" Often new employees receive a large amount of information they do not immediately need, but they fail to get vital information needed during the first day of a new job.

In a large organization, it is especially important that managers and personnel specialists try to coordinate the information to new employees. Such coordination is a further indication of the importance of the interface idea. In a small organization the manager or supervisor determines what is to be explained.

Some organizations systematize this process by developing an orientation checklist. Figure 9–3 indicates the items to be covered by the personnel department representative and the new employee's supervisor.

Figure 9–2. Responsibility for formal orientation program.

| | % of Companies with Formal Programs | | | | | |
| | By Industry | | | By Size | | All |
	Mfg.	Nonmfg.	Nonbus.	Large	Small	Companies
Person Responsible for Coordinating Program:						
Personnel Director	100	85	86	87	100	91
Training & Development Director	19	28	27	30	12	25
Line Manager	19	7	0	11	9	10
Participants in The Program Include:						
Personnel Department Representative	54	60	81	53	82	62
Company Officers Division Heads	21	26	31	26	23	25
Training, Education & Development Personnel	21	30	4	23	17	21
Immediate Supervisors &/or Employee's Department Head	28	21	0	22	14	20
Safety Supervisor	19	6	13	15	5	12

Note: Percentages add to more than 100 because of multiple responses

(Source: "ASPA-BNA Survey 32: Employee Orientation Programs," *Bulletin to Management...*August 28, 1977, p. 6. (Washington, D.C.: Bureau of National Affairs).) Used with permission.

Figure 9–3. Orientation checklist.

Name of Employee _____ Name of Employee _____
Starting Date _____ Starting Date _____
Department _____ Department _____
                                   Position _____

PERSONNEL DEPARTMENT

Prior to Orientation

_____ Complete Form A and give or mail
to new employee
_____ Complete Form B
_____ Attach Form B to Orientation
Checklist–Supervisor & give to the
supervisor

Employee's First Day

*Organization and Personnel Policies
and Procedures*

_____ History of XYZ Inc.
_____ Organization Chart
_____ Service to Community—Purpose of
the Co.
_____ Employee Classifications

Insurance Benefits

_____ Group Health
_____ Disability
_____ Life
_____ Workmen's Compensation

Other Benefits

_____ Holidays
_____ Vacation
_____ Jury and Election Duty
_____ Death in the Family
_____ Health Services
      _____ Professional Discounts
      _____ Appointments
End of Orientation—First Day
_____ Make Appointment for Second Day
_____ Introduce Employee to Supervisor

Other Items

_____ Job Posting
_____ Bulletin Board—Location & Use
_____ Safety
_____ No Drinking
_____ Where to Get Supplies
_____ Employee's Records—Updating

At the end of the employee's first two
weeks, the supervisor will ask if the
employee has any questions on the
above items. After all questions have
been satisfied, the supervisors will sign
and date this form and return it to the
Personnel Department.

SIGNATURE _____

DATE _____

SUPERVISOR

Employee's First Day

_____ Introduction to Co-workers
_____ Tour of Department
_____ Tour of Co.

Location of

_____ Coat Closet
_____ Rest Room
_____ Telephone for Personal Use and
Rules Concerning it

Working Hours

_____ Starting and Leaving
_____ Lunch
_____ Breaks
_____ Overtime
_____ Early Departures
_____ Time Clock

Pay Policy

_____ Pay Period
_____ Deposit System

Other Items

_____ Parking
_____ Dress

During Employee's First Two Weeks

Emergencies

_____ Medical
_____ Power Failure
_____ Fire

Employee's Second Day

_____ Pension Retirement Plan
_____ Sick Leave
_____ Personal Leave
_____ Job Posting
_____ Confidentiality
_____ Complaints and Concerns
_____ Termination
_____ Equal Employment Opportunity

ORIENTATION CONDUCTED BY _____

(Used with permission.)

Using a checklist, the manager and the personnel representative can be sure all necessary items have been covered. However, the presentation should not resemble a military briefing. The important concern is that the new employee understand the items covered. Much of the information on retirement, withholding, and insurance will be forgotten in the confusion of the first day anyway. Attempts to reduce this overload will result in better retention later.

Present Three Types of Information

There are three general types of information usually included in the orientation process. The first type of information concerns the normal workday and the employee's job.

Normal Workday. The immediate supervisor or manager is probably better prepared to outline a normal day for the employee. The manager/supervisor should devote some time during the first morning solely to covering daily routine information with the new employee. This information would include the following: introducing the new employee to other employees, showing the employee the work area, letting the new employee know when and where to take coffee breaks and lunch, indicating what time work begins and ends, identifying where to park and where the restrooms are, and indicating whether the custom is to "brown bag it" or not.

Nature of Organization. A second type of information is a general organizational orientation. This might be a brief review of the organization's history, its structure, who the key executives are, what its purpose is, its products and/or services, how the employee's job fits into the big picture, and any other information of a general nature. If an annual report for a firm is prepared, giving an employee a prepared annual report is an effective aid in providing a general overview of an organization and its components.

Organizational Policies, Rules, and Benefits. Another important type of information is the policies, work rules, and benefits employees have. Typically this information is presented by both the personnel unit and the supervisor. Employee policies about sick leave, tardiness, absenteeism, vacations, benefits, hospitalization, parking, and safety rules are important facts that the new employee should know.

Determine How to Present the Information

Managers and personnel representatives should determine the most appropriate way to present orientation information. For example, rather than telling an employee verbally, information on company sick leave and vacation policies may be presented better on the first day in an employee handbook. The manager or personnel representative can review this information a few days later to answer any of the employee's questions.

Information Overload.   One of the common failings of many orientation programs is *information overload.* This occurs when so many facts are presented to new employees that they ignore important details or inaccurately remember much of the information. By providing a handbook, the employee can refer to information when needed.

Employees will retain more of the orientation material if it is presented in a manner which encourages them to learn. The proper materials, handbooks, and information leaflets must be available and should be reviewed periodically for updates and corrections. Some organizations have successfully used filmstrips, movies, slides, charts, and teaching machines. However, one caution is that the emphasis should be on the information presented, not just "entertaining" the new employee.[3]

Evaluation and Follow-Up

A final point which needs emphasis is that a systematic orientation program should have an evaluation and follow-up. Too often, typical orientation efforts assume that once oriented, employees are familiar with everything they need to know about the organization forever.

A personnel department representative or a manager can evaluate the effectiveness of the orientation by follow-up interviews with new employees a few weeks or months after the orientation. Employee questionnaires can also be used. Some firms even give new employees a written test on the company handbook two weeks after orientation.

Reorientation.   A reorientation program in which all employees are periodically given a refresher "introduction" should be a part of follow-up. In 28% of the firms in one survey a second orientation is conducted.[4] Reorientation is especially important if significant changes in organizational policies or structure have occurred. For example, if one company is purchased by another, a reorientation of employees of both firms may be necessary because of changes in operating relationships and policies caused by the merger. Orientation is a never-ending process of "introducing" both old and new employees to the current state of the organization.

Although orientation introduces or reintroduces the organization to employees, they also need information about their jobs and how to perform them. Orientation is one *special* type of training. The next section examines the general nature of training.

What are the components of an effective orientation system?

TRAINING

Many types of training exist besides orientation. Job skill, supervisory, sensitivity training, and management development are a few of the types of training.

Training Defined

Training can be defined either narrowly or broadly. In a limited sense, *training* is concerned with teaching *specific* and *immediately usable* skills. In a broad sense, *training* provides *general information* used to *develop* knowledge for future long-term applications.

In a personnel management context, the narrow definition of training means that it explores job-related skills, while development often denotes the broad scope of training. To illustrate: a person can receive training to improve skills on a new word-processing machine, whereas developmental training may come from a management course on effective leadership. The hope is that over time the trainee will develop into a better leader. However, this distinction between training and development can be an artificial one because both focus on learning. Training in this text will be used to include both the job-related and developmental dimensions.

> TRAINING is a learning process whereby people acquire skills, concepts, attitudes, or knowledge to aid in the achievement of goals.

Training as an Interface

Training as an interface is shown in Figure 9–4. Notice that skill training, developmental training, and Organization Development are all included. In the sample interface shown, the personnel unit serves as an expert source for training assistance and coordination. Also, the personnel unit typically has a longer range view of employee careers and the importance of developing the entire organization than do individual operating managers. This is especially true at lower levels in the organization.

Figure 9–4. Training interface.

Personnel Unit	Managers
Prepares skill training materials	Provide technical information
Coordinates training efforts	Monitor training needs
Conducts or arranges for off-the-job training	Conduct the on-the-job training
Coordinates career plans and personnel development efforts	Continually discuss employees' future potential and monitor employees' growth
Provides input and expertise for Organizational Development	Participate in organizational change efforts

On the other hand, managers are likely to be the best source for providing the technical information used in skill training and for determining when employees need training or retraining. Because of the close and continual interaction they have with their employees, a major part of a manager's job is to determine and discuss employees' career potentials and plans. Also, organizational development and change efforts will fail without active managerial participation and involvement.

If an organization is small, managers may have to cover the activities normally performed by personnel specialists in larger organizations. In small organizations, nearly all types of training are often done by managers. Regardless of the size of an organization, employee training is extremely important.

What is training?

Importance of Training

Training has current and future implications for the success of an organization. It is a learning process, whether its focus is orientation, initial job-skill training, developing employee potential, or retraining employees because of changes in technology or job assignments.

The goal of all types of personnel training is short- and long-term improvement of employee performance. Training can contribute to higher production, fewer mistakes, possibly greater job satisfaction, lower turnover, and the ability to cope with organizational, social, and technological change. Effective training is an *investment* in the human resources of an organization with both immediate and long-range returns. Regardless of whether training is called *education* (to denote conceptual learning) or *job-related* (to denote skill learning), learning has to occur for training to be successful. A basic understanding of some psychological learning principles is necessary for managers to become effective trainers.

LEARNING PRINCIPLES: THE PSYCHOLOGY OF TRAINING

Learning is a psychological process which has been intensely researched for many years. Managers can use information from this research to make total training efforts more effective. It is beyond the scope of this text to extensively review all learning concepts and supporting research. Instead, some of the major considerations guiding personnel training efforts will be presented.

Intention to Learn

Motivation, which is heavily influenced by values, attitudes, and perceptions, underlies all learning. People best learn information they think is beneficial, if it is presented *when* they want to learn it. For learning to take place, *intention* to learn, even if subconscious, increases *attention* to what is being said, done, and presented. Motivation to learn is expressed in such questions as "How important is my job to me?" "How important is it that I learn that information?" "Will learning this help me in any way?" "What's in it for me?"

It should be emphasized that learning is a very complex psychological process which is not fully understood by practitioners or research psychologists. Often, trainers or supervisors present information and assume it has been learned. However, learning takes place only when information is received, understood, internalized, and some change or conscious effort has been made to use the information.

Reinforcement

The notion of reinforcement is based upon the *law of effect*, which states that if a behavior is positively rewarded, it probably will be repeated. Providing positive rewards for certain behavior is called *positive reinforcement*. Learning theories that revolve around the idea of reinforcement state that people tend to repeat response patterns which give them some type of positive reward and to avoid repeating actions associated with negative consequences.

The rewards or reinforcements an individual receives can be either external or internal. For example, Jean Lane, R.N., receives an external reward in learning how to use a new electrocardiogram machine; if she performs the proper operations, Jean will get a certificate of completion.

An internal reward appeals to the trainee's internal needs. A machinist learned to use a new lathe in the machine shop. Although he made many mistakes at first, he was beginning to do well. One day he knew he had mastered it and was quite pleased with himself. This feeling of accomplishment is a type of internal reward.

Many training situations use both internal and external rewards. If a new salesclerk answers her supervisor's question correctly and is complimented for giving the correct answer, she may receive both an internal and an external reward.

Behavior Modification

A comprehensive approach to training based upon reinforcement has been developed. This approach is known as behavior modification. Built upon the theories of psychologist B. F. Skinner, behavior modification (called BMod) has become increasingly popular. BMod makes use of four means of changing behavior, labeled *intervention strategies.*[5]

Intervention Strategies.   The four strategies used in BMod are *positive reinforcement, negative reinforcement, punishment,* and *extinction.*

POSITIVE REINFORCEMENT occurs when a person receives a desired reward.

If an employee is on time every day during a week, that employee receives extra pay equivalent to one hour of normal work. That employee has received positive reinforcement of his or her good attendance by receiving a desired reward.

With NEGATIVE REINFORCEMENT an individual works to avoid an undesirable reward.

An employee who is at work on time every day does so to avoid criticism of a supervisor. Thus, the potential for criticism leads to the employee taking the desired action.

> PUNISHMENT is action taken to repel the person from the undesired action.

A grocery manager punishes a stock clerk for leaving the stockroom dirty by forcing him to stay after work to clean it up. Behavior can also be modified through extinction.

> EXTINCTION refers to a situation in which no response is given the trainee.

Assume an employee dresses in a new style to attract the attention of her superior. The supervisor just ignores the dress. There is no reinforcement, positive or negative, and no punishment is given. With no reinforcement of any kind and no clear confirmation, the likelihood of the employee extinguishing the new dress behavior is increased. The expectation is that behavior receiving no reinforcement will not be repeated.

Providing employees with direct information about their productivity, quality, and accuracy is a form of behavior modification and positive reinforcement. The idea behind positive reinforcement is that people behave in ways that they find most personally rewarding, and management can improve employees' behavior by providing the proper rewards.

Immediate Confirmation

Another learning concept closely related to reinforcement is immediate confirmation. This concept deals with the timing of feedback.

> IMMEDIATE CONFIRMATION indicates that people learn best if reinforcement is given as soon as possible after the training response.

To illustrate, a corporate purchasing department has developed a new system for reporting inventory information. The new system is much more complex than the old and requires a new recording form which is longer and more difficult to fill out. However, it does give computerized information much more quickly, and errors in the recording process delay the total inventory report. The purchasing manager training inventory personnel might not have the trainees fill out the entire inventory form when teaching them the new recording procedure. Instead the manager might explain the total process, then break it into smaller segments, and have each trainee complete the form a section at a time. By checking each individual's form for errors as each section is completed, the purchasing manager can give immediate feedback or confirmation before the trainees fill out the next section. This immediate confirmation corrects errors which, if made throughout the whole form, might have established a pattern to be unlearned.

Spaced Practice

Psychological research reveals that for certain kinds of tasks, practice spaced over a period of hours or days results in greater learning than the same amount of practice in one long period. For example, training a cashier to operate a new machine could be alternated with having him do a task he already knows how to do. Thus, the training is distributed instead of being concentrated into one period. For this reason some firms spread their orientation of new employees over an entire week by having an hour or two daily devoted to orientation, instead of covering it all in one day.

Whole Learning

The concept of whole learning suggests it is better to give an overall view of what the trainee will be doing than to go immediately into the specifics. Another term for whole learning is *Gestalt learning.*

Job training instructions should be broken down into small elements after the employees have had an opportunity to see how the elements fit together. For example, in a plastics manufacturing operation it would be good to explain to trainees how the raw chemical material gets to them in the plant and what is done with the plastic moldings after they finish their part of the manufacturing process. The information is explained as an entire logical happening, so that trainees can see how the various pieces fit together into the "big picture." After a supervisor goes over the entire operation, showing how all the parts fit together, he or she can break the information into its separate parts.

Active Practice

Active practice is more effective than learning by reading or passive listening. For example, serving a tennis ball demands attention and concentration; actual performance is necessary rather than just reading about it or hearing an explanation of how to do it. Once some basic instructions have been given, active practice should be built into any learning situation.

Jill McDonald is being trained as a customer service representative. After being given some basic selling and product details, Jill should be allowed to call on a customer to use the knowledge she has received. Mixing learning methods such as reading and listening with more active methods is effective.

Plateaus

During the learning process employees can reach a stage where they make little or no progress. At this point, the trainees should be encouraged and advised that these temporary plateaus are expected, common, and understandable. This encouragement is needed to prevent a feeling of despair or a desire to "give up."

Applicability of Training

Training should be as real as possible so that trainees can successfully transfer the new knowledge to their jobs. The training situation should be set up so that trainees can picture the types of situations they can expect on the job. For example, training managers to be better interviewers should involve role-playing applicants who can respond the same way that applicants would.

The learning concepts and training ideas discussed above can be used by managers, training specialists, and personnel representatives to make their efforts more effective. Whether the training is a formal course, an orientation course, on-the-job preparation, or a supervisory development seminar, building the above learning concepts into the effort can result in better performance of trainees.

What are five learning concepts?

SYSTEMS APPROACH TO TRAINING

The success of any training depends upon learning occurring. Too often, unplanned, uncoordinated, and haphazard training efforts significantly reduce the positive learning effects which are expected. Training and learning takes place whether an organization has a coordinated training effort or not, especially through informal work groups. Employees learn from other employees, but without a sound system of training, effective learning from the organization's viewpoint may not occur. Figure 9–5 depicts the components of such a system.[6] Notice there are three major phases in a training process: (1) *the assessment phase,* (2) *the implementation phase,* and (3) *the evaluation phase.*

In the *assessment phase,* the need for training is determined and the objectives of the training effort are specified. A simple example is an examination of the performance of clerks in a billing department which indicates their typing abilities are weak and that they would profit by having typing instruction. Then the objective of increasing the clerks' typing speed to 60 words per minute without errors could be established. The number of words per minute without errors is set as the criterion against which training success is to be measured and represents the way the objective is made specific.

In the next phase, *implementation,* the clerks would be given a

Figure 9–5. Model of training system.

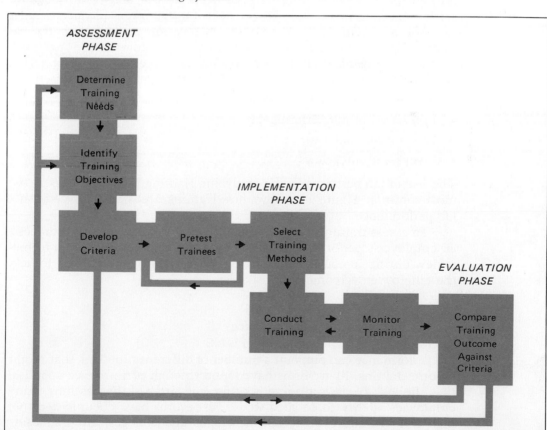

typing test, and the billing supervisor and a personnel training specialist would work together to determine how to train the clerks to increase their typing speed. A programmed instruction manual might be used in conjunction with a special typing class set up at the company. Then the training is actually conducted.

The *evaluation phase* is crucial and focuses on measuring how well the training accomplishes the desired objective. Monitoring of training serves as a bridge between the implementation phase and the evaluation phase.

What are the three phases in a training system?

DETERMINATION OF TRAINING NEEDS AND OBJECTIVES

All types of training are designed to help the organization accomplish its objectives. Determining training needs is the diagnostic phase of setting training objectives. To consider an analogy, a physician must examine a patient before prescribing medication to deal with the patient's ailments. Likewise, by examining the symptoms of the "patient," whether an organization or an individual employee, a course of action can be planned to make the "patient" healthier or function better.

Training needs can be assessed in several ways:

- observation of job performance
- organization analysis
- surveys and interviews

The use of job performance for analyzing training program needs is the most common. Figure 9–6 shows how training needs are analyzed using job performance.

To assess training needs through the performance appraisal process, an employee's performance inadequacies can be determined in a formal review during appraisal. Then some type of training is designed to help the employee overcome the weakness.

Pinpointing Needs: Job Performance

Job performance can pinpoint a number of different problems that might require training. Many firms have found through performance appraisal that the lack of basic reading, writing, and math skills has hurt many employees' ability to do good work. Test scores have documented that high schools, and even technical schools and colleges, are graduating students deficient in English and math. For example, Continental Illinois

Figure 9–6. Using job performance to analyze training needs.

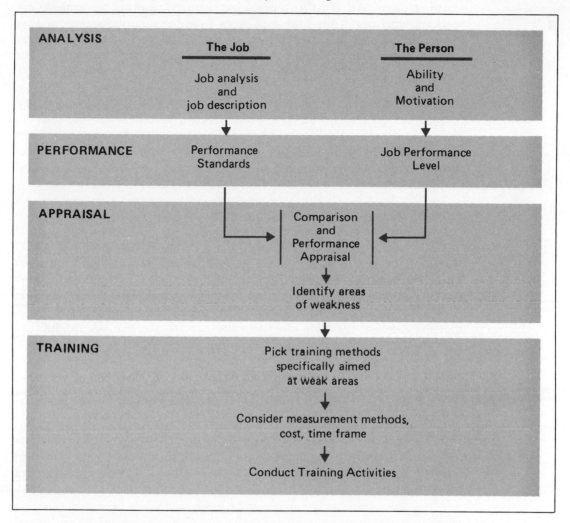

Bank and Trust Co. has begun offering remedial English courses to those who need it. One study found that 35% of the companies surveyed have to provide training in areas that schools provide.[7] That these firms are willing to do so indicates the serious consequences of errors made by deficiently educated people. For example, at JLG Industries (a manufacturer of cranes and aerial lifts) one employee who did not know how to read a ruler wasted $700 worth of sheet steel in one morning by mismeasuring. In addition, JLG had purchased electronic equipment to handle inventories and schedules. But poorly educated employees who kept feeding incorrect numbers into the computer cost the company nearly $1 million in corrections.

Employees have been injured or killed when they could not read warning signs. At Westinghouse Electric in California several young workers who could not read well were fired because management was fearful of such accidents around defense equipment. Failures in job performance can illustrate training needs quite graphically if management will monitor such training needs.

Job Requirements.   As part of assessing training needs it is necessary to examine job descriptions and job specifications. These sources provide information on the skills and abilities necessary for employees to perform jobs. The results of job analysis—job descriptions and job specifications— provide the basis for comparison of performance with expectations of management.

Pinpointing Needs: Organizational Analysis

Another way of diagnosing training needs is through organizational analysis. Organizational analysis considers the scope of an organization as a system. Both internal and external factors would need to be considered. For example, as part of a five-year business plan, a manufacturer of mechanical cash registers identifies the need to shift to the production of computer-based electronic point of purchase equipment. As the organization implements its plans, current employees will need to be retrained so that they can do electronic instead of mechanical assembly work. The analysis of the firm's business strategies and objectives helps identify training needs before those needs become critical.

On a continuing basis, detailed analysis of personnel data can reveal training weaknesses. Departments or areas with high turnover, high absenteeism, low performance records, or other deficiencies can be pinpointed. After these problems are analyzed, some training objectives can be developed.

Pinpointing Needs: Surveys and Interviews

Another way training needs may be assessed is through surveys or interviews of both managerial and nonmanagerial employees. Such tools can provide some insight into what employees believe their problems are and what types of action they recommend. Some surveys can be generalized to include more than one employer. A survey of first-level supervisors in state and local governments in North Carolina was useful in identifying that individualized training would be more useful than general programs because of widely varying needs identified by the supervisors themselves.[8]

A survey can take the form of questionnaires or interviews with supervisors and employees on an individual or group basis. The purpose is to gather information on problems as the individuals involved perceive them.

How can training needs be identified?

Setting Training Objectives

Once training needs are determined, objectives should be set to begin meeting these needs. As Figure 9–7 suggests, training objectives can be of three types. The first type of training objective is *regular* training, which is ongoing. Orientation is an example of regular training because it attempts to provide learning for all employees as they enter and work in the organization. The second type of training objective is *problem-solving*. The emphasis is on solving a particular problem instead of presenting general information on problem areas. The final type of objective is *innovation* or *change-making*, which is primarily developmental in nature and has a longer effect and return.

Figure 9–7. Types of training objectives.

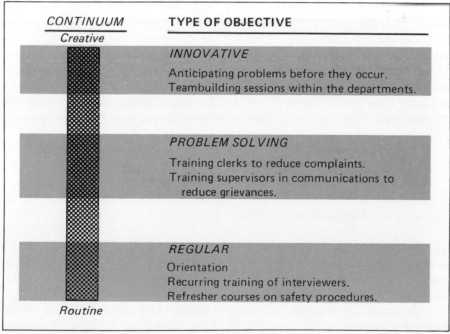

CONTINUUM	TYPE OF OBJECTIVE
Creative	
	INNOVATIVE
	Anticipating problems before they occur.
	Teambuilding sessions within the departments.
	PROBLEM SOLVING
	Training clerks to reduce complaints.
	Training supervisors in communications to reduce grievances.
	REGULAR
	Orientation
	Recurring training of interviewers.
	Refresher courses on safety procedures.
Routine	

TRAINING METHODS

Once needs and objectives have been determined, the actual training effort must begin. Regardless of whether the training is job-related or developmental in nature, some particular training method must be chosen. Some methods involve the use of various visual aids to enhance the learning experience. The following overview of common training methods and techniques classifies methods into several major groups.

On-The-Job Training

The most common type of training at all levels in an organization is on-the-job training. Whether or not the training is planned, people *do* learn from their job experiences, particularly if these experiences change over time. This type of training is usually done by the manager and/or other employees. A manager or supervisor training an employee must be able to teach, as well as show, the employee.

A special guided form of on-the-job training is Job Instructional Training (JIT). Developed during World War II, JIT is still used widely. The JIT method is a four-step instructional process involving *preparation, presentation, performance tryout,* and *follow-up.*[9]

Another on-the job method of training is *job rotation*, where the employee performs one job for a period of time and then moves to another job for another period of time. The intent is to provide employees with a broad exposure to their job-related responsibilities.

On-the-job training (OJT) is by far the most commonly used kind of training. It is flexible and obviously relevant to what the employee is doing. However, OJT has some problems as well. It can disrupt regular work, and the person doing the training might not be a very effective trainer. Unfortunately OJT can be the same as *no training* in some circumstances when the trainee is merely abandoned to learn the job.

Cooperative Training

There are two widely used cooperative training means. These are internships and apprentice training.

Internships.   One type of cooperative job-experiential training is an internship. Internship is a form of on-the-job training which usually combines job training with classroom instruction in trade schools, high schools, colleges, or universities.

In a typical internship, students receive educational credit for on-the-job experience. For example, William Jefferson, a junior petroleum engineering student at a state university, goes to school one semester and works for an oil company the next semester. He gets nine hours of independent study credit for his work semester. William's objective is to acquire *knowledge and skill*. The internship also helps him earn his way through school. It gives him a chance to look at the oil company as a future employer, and the firm can decide whether or not they want to offer him a job when he graduates.

Apprentice Training.   Another form of cooperative training involving employers, trade unions, and government agencies is *apprentice training*. An apprentice program involves on-the-job experience by an employee under the guidance of a skilled and certified worker. Certain requirements for training, equipment, time length, and proficiency levels may be monitored by a unit of the U.S. Department of Labor. Apprentice training is most often used to train people for jobs in skilled crafts such as carpentry, plumbing, photoengraving, type-setting, and welding. Apprenticeships usually last from two to five years, depending upon the occupation. During this time the apprentice receives lower wages than the certified individuals.

These cooperative methods emphasize "real world" learning by providing practical experiences to which classroom knowledge can then be applied. Further, they give both employer and employee an opportunity to evaluate each other for long-range employment opportunities.

However, for cooperative training in any form to work well certain factors must be considered. First, the training must provide good feedback so that knowledge of results can reinforce learning. Second, efforts must be made to be certain that individual rates of learning are accommodated. A slow learner and a fast learner should not be forced into the same schedule.

Simulated Training

Another type of training is done off-the-job but attempts to reproduce or simulate on-the-job experiences. Such training allows an employee to train using equipment or in a job setting similar to the actual work situation. In this way a trainee can learn in a realistic manner but may avoid some on-the-job pressures during the initial learning process.

Allowing Rose Hoffman to practice on a switchboard in a simulated setting before taking over as a telephone receptionist allows her to learn her job. Consequently, she is likely to make fewer mistakes in handling actual incoming calls. Airlines use simulators to train pilots and cabin attendants, and astronauts train in mock-up space capsules. One caution about simulated training is that it must be realistic. The equipment should be as similar to the type the trainee will actually use as possible so the transfer of learning can be made easily. If this can be done, simulation can overcome some of the problems associated with OJT.

Behaviorally Experienced Training

Some training efforts focus on emotional and behavioral learning. Employees can learn about behavior by *role-playing,* in which individuals portray an identity in a certain situation. *Business games, cases,* incomplete cases called *incidents,* and short work assignments called *in-baskets* are behaviorally experienced learning methods. *Sensitivity training* or *laboratory training* is personal emotional learning.

The critical issue in any situation using these methods is that the purpose of the exercise be clear. For instance, role-playing can be "fun" or "annoying" for some people. It is best that trainees understand what the exercise is attempting to teach.

Classroom and Conference Training

Training seminars, courses, and presentations can be used both in job-related and developmental training. Lectures and discussions are a major part of this training. The numerous management development courses offered by trade associations and educational institutions are examples of conference training.

Company-conducted short courses, lectures, and meetings are usually classroom training, while company sales meetings are a common type of conference training. This type of training frequently makes use of training techniques and media to enhance the learning experience. Films, tapes, cases, and other means may be used to stimulate the classroom and conference learning methods.

Training methods of this kind are familiar to trainees, as all have seen them in school. However, they are essentially one-way communication, and not appropriate for motor-skill acquisition.

TRAINING MEDIA

Several aids in presenting training information are available to the trainer. Some of these aids can be used in many settings and with a variety of training methods. The most common ones are *programmed instruction, computer-assisted instruction,* and *audiovisual aids.*

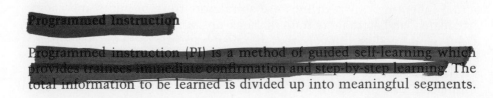

Programmed Instruction

Programmed instruction (PI) is a method of guided self-learning which provides trainees immediate confirmation and step-by-step learning. The total information to be learned is divided up into meaningful segments.

Using either a "teaching machine" or a book, an employee is presented small segments of information which progressively increase in difficulty. Trainees respond to each segment of information by answering a question or responding on a machine. The trainee receives an answer or looks up the answer. Correct responses allow the trainee to proceed to other material. If an incorrect response is given, the trainee is guided back to previous material for review.

Examination of the effectiveness of programmed instruction reveals that it reduces training time on the average by one-third, but it does not appear to be more or less effective in increasing retention than conventional training.[10] The logical conclusion is that managers or trainers should not expect programmed instruction to do their training better, only faster. Therefore, programmed instruction should be seen as an aid, not as a training end in itself.

The individualized characteristics of PI are attractive. Self-pacing and feedback make it inexpensive to use once it is developed. But it is expensive to develop, which is a major disadvantage. Also, trainees may not like PI as the sole learning method, but do accept it more favorably as a part of a combination of methods.

Computer-Assisted Instruction

Another medium using sophisticated modern equipment, *computer-assisted instruction* (CAI), focuses on trainees learning by interacting with a computer. This method offers a wide variety of exciting possible applications. For example, trainees learning about collective bargaining can play a bargaining game using the computer to generate moves and countermoves. This simulation gives the trainees some feel for the problems, difficulties, and strategies involved in union-management bargaining. As would be expected, the cost and programming knowledge required to use computer-assisted instruction in such a manner are factors which may limit its use.

Audio/Visual Aids

Other technical training aids are audio and visual in nature and include audio and video tapes, films, and closed-circuit television. These tools are especially useful if the same information must be conveyed to different groups at different times, such as information on new products for sales personnel in several states.

However, trainers must avoid becoming dazzled with the "machine gadgetry" and remember that the real emphasis is on learning and training. The effectiveness of the technologies and media need to be examined as a part of the evaluation of the training effort. When one-way communication is an acceptable way to instruct, these media are appropriate. They also allow presentation of information that cannot be recreated in a classroom—demonstrations of machines, experiments, examination of behavior, etc. However, they are not flexible methods and are usually especially designed for a given training program. Such specialized design takes more time and may increase the overall training costs.

What are four training methods?

EVALUATION OF TRAINING

To be justified, the training must make an impact on the performance of the employees trained. By determining how well (or *if*) trainees have learned, a manager can make decisions about the training and its effectiveness. Evaluation of training compares the post-training results to the objectives expected by managers, trainers, and trainees. Too often, training is done without any thought of measuring and evaluating how well the objectives are accomplished. Because training is both time-consuming and costly, evaluation of training should be built into any training effort.

For example, a training program designed to help minority students advance in the retail business was offered in Philadelphia. The training included such standard retailing items as business math and sales methods. But it went further to include coaching in dress, behavior, and language. Businesses involved in the training are evaluating its effectiveness. Several have decided it is worth doing again. Others are disappointed with the retention rate, and about 50% of the trainees are no longer with the companies sponsoring the training.[11]

Levels of Evaluation

The way in which training is to be evaluated is best considered before training begins to allow design flexibility in evaluating its success. Training can be evaluated at four levels, as shown in Figure 9–8.

Reaction.   *Reaction-level* evaluation can be measured by interviewing or by trainee questionnaires. The immediate reaction may measure how the people *liked* the training, rather than how it *benefited* them.

Learning.   *Learning-level* evaluation measures how well trainees have learned facts, ideas, concepts, theories, and attitudes. Tests on the train-

Figure 9–8. Levels of training evaluation.

1.	**Reaction**	*How well did the trainees like the training?*
2.	**Learning**	*To what extent did the trainees learn the facts, principles, and approaches that were included in the training?*
3.	**Behavior**	*To what extent did their job behavior change because of the program?*
4.	**Results**	*What final results were achieved (reduction in cost, reduction in turnover, improvement in production, etc)?*

(Source: Ralph F. Catalnello and Donald L. Kirkpatrick, "Evaluating Training Programs— The State of the Art," *Training and Development Journal,* May 1968, pp. 2–3. Reproduced by special permission from the May, 1968 *Training and Development Jopurnal.* Copyright 1968 by the American Society for Training and Development, Inc.)

ing material are commonly used for evaluating learning and can be given both before and after training to compare scores.

Behavior. Evaluating training at the *behavior level* attempts to measure the effect of training on job performance. This is more difficult to measure than learning. Interviews of trainees and their co-workers and observation of job performance are ways to evaluate training at the behavior level.

Results. The *results-level* evaluation of training measures the effect of training on the achievement of organizational objectives. Because results such as productivity, turnover, quality, time, sales, and costs are more concrete, this type of evaluation can be done by comparing records before and after training.

The difficulty with this measurement is the easy deduction that training caused the changes in results. This implication ignores the impact that other factors may have had. For example, Joe Riviera, a department manager for a shoe manufacturer, goes through a supervisory training program. By comparing turnover in Joe's department before and after the training, some measure of results can be obtained. However, turnover is also dependent on the current economic situation, demand for shoes, and the quality of employees being hired. Therefore, when using results evaluation, Joe's manager should be aware of the complexity involved in determining the exact effect of his training.

What are the four levels of evaluating training?

Evaluation Designs

There are many possible ways to design an evaluation of training to see
if training had an effect. The three most common are shown in Figure
9–9.

Post-measure.   The most obvious way to evaluate training effectiveness
is to determine after the training whether or not the individuals can
perform the way management wants them to perform. Assume that you,
as a manager, have 20 typists you feel could improve their typing speed.
They are given a one-day training session and then given a typing test
to *measure* their speed. If the typists can all type the required speed
after training, was the training good? At this point you could not really
know. Perhaps they could have done as well before the training. You
can't know whether the typing speed is a result of the training or could
have been achieved without training.

Pre/Post-measure.   By designing the evaluation differently, that issue
could have been considered. If you had measured the typing speed *before*

Figure 9–9.   Training evaluation designs.

Type of Testing	Pre Measure Testing T_1	Training TR	Post Measure Testing T_2	Result RES $(T_2 - T_1)$
Post Measure	—	●	●	●
Pre/Post Measure	●	●	●	●
Pre/Post Measure with Control Group	●	●	●	●
	●	—	●	○

Training/Evaluation Segments

and *after* training, you could have gotten a better idea of whether or not the training made any difference. However, a question remains. If there was a change in typing speed, was the training responsible for the change, or did these people just type faster because they knew they were being tested? It has been found that people often perform better when they know they are being tested on their results.

Pre/Post with Control Group.   A final evaluation design can deal with this problem. In addition to the 20 typists who will be trained you can test another group of typists who will not be trained to see if they do as well as those who are to be trained. This second group is called a *control group.* The final portion of Figure 9–9 shows the sequence for a pre/post design with a control group.

There are other designs that can be used, but these three are the most commonly used. It should be noted that where possible the pre/post or pre/post with control group designs should be used because they provide more accurate measurement than the post-measure alone.

How can training evaluation be designed?

REVIEW AND PREVIEW

A key part of personnel management is training. Training activities provide employees with information and encourage them to learn about the organization, their jobs, and their capabilities. This chapter has highlighted the importance of training as a planned activity. One type of training is orientation, which introduces a new employee into a work organization so that he or she adjusts quickly.

The main concern behind training is learning. Training can be narrow in scope, such as job-related training, or broad in scope, as in development, but it does not always equal learning. Familiarity with basic learning principles can guide managers and trainers in planning and evaluating training efforts.

A systems approach to training incorporates these learning concepts into planned training efforts. The first phase of planned training is to assess needs and determine objectives. Then a training program can be formulated and conducted using various methods and media. After the training program is completed, its effectiveness should be evaluated. This evaluation provides managers with information to determine future training needs and to revise current efforts.

This chapter has examined training as a general personnel activity. The next chapter deals with the longer-range aspects of training—personnel development. Chapter 10 looks at personnel development in general and career development in particular.

Review Questions

1. Identify the importance of orientation and tell how you would orient a new management trainee.

2. Differentiate between training and development. Indicate how learning is a part of each.

3. Why are learning principles so important to remember when designing training efforts? Be specific.

4. What are the three major phases in a training system? Identify the processes within each phase.

5. You are training keypunch operators. What training methods would you use?

6. You want to evaluate the training received by some keypunch operators. Give examples of how to evaluate their training at four different levels.

Case: The New Payroll Clerk

Irene Kemp has just completed her first day on a new job at Key Data Processing Co. (KDP). Although she had been out of the work force while raising a family, she was hired recently as a payroll clerk, based primarily on three years' experience she had 15 years ago. Quite naturally, she approached a job with more anxiety than the average person taking a new job.

That evening, Jim, her 15-year-old son, asked, "How did it go today?" Irene replied, "Oh, okay I guess, although I'm not really sure." She continued describing her day to her son and related that upon arriving at work, she went to the personnel department. The personnel assistant said, "Are you starting today? Have a seat while I get some forms for you to fill out." After spending 30 minutes having various hospitalization, retirement, and other benefits explained, Irene was thoroughly confused, but managed to complete all the relevant forms. The personnel assistant then told her to go to the accounting department.

After taking two wrong turns, Irene entered the accounting department and asked one of the clerks where Mrs. Schultz, the supervisor, was. "Oh, she's in a meeting and will be back in about an hour. Can I help you?" Upon learning that Irene was a new employee, Roy Harmon, the clerk, introduced Irene to the other six people in the department. Roy got Irene some coffee and began telling her "the true story" about KDP, including the fact that two supervisors had quit in other departments. He also told her how to "get along with Fran (the supervisor)".

About 10:15, Fran Schultz returned from her meeting, saw Irene and said, "Oh I'm sorry, I forgot you were starting today. Why don't you observe what Roy is doing while I return some calls." At 10:45 Fran called Irene into her office and spent 45 minutes reviewing work rules and the job responsibilities of payroll clerks. Then Fran left for lunch after asking one of the other clerks to "let Irene tag along with you for lunch."

After returning from lunch, Fran showed Irene the forms, where her desk was, and gave her some time cards which needed the hours computed. Irene spent most of the rest of the day completing the time cards, except for a break in mid-afternoon. At 4:10 Fran checked back with Judy, noted a few errors, and explained that she would have more time to spend with Irene tomorrow. Irene then punched out at 4:30 and went home.

Irene's son Jim, with the candor of a 15-year-old, said, "Man, they sound disorganized." Later that evening Irene told her son that she was having doubts about taking a job at KDP.

QUESTIONS

1. What problems can you identify with the orientation activities experienced by Irene?
2. How would you make changes in the orientation process? What changes would you make?

NOTES

1. J. P. Wanous, *Organizational Entry* (Reading, MA: Addison-Wesley, 1980), p. 8.

2. D. Reed-Mendenhall and C. W. Millard, "Orientation: A training and development tool," *Personnel Administrator*, August 1980, p. 41.

3. Murray Lubliner, "Employee Orientation," *Personnel Journal*, 57, April 1978, p. 208.

4. "ASPA-BNA Survey #32: Employee Orientation Programs," *Bulletin to Management*, August 25, 1978 (Washington, D.C.: The Bureau of National Affairs), p. 8.

5. Fred Luthans and Robert Kreitner, *Organizational Behavior Modification* (Glenview, IL: Scott, Foresman, 1975).

6. The model is an original one, but the authors acknowledge the stimulation provided by a model contained in Irwin L. Goldstein, *Training: Program Development and Evaluation* (Monterey, CA: Brooks/Cole Publishing, 1974).

7. "Remedial Bosses," *Wall Street Journal*, January 22, 1981, p. 1.

8. Thomas H. Jerdee and Richard P. Calhoon, "Training Needs of First-Level Supervisors," *The Personnel Administrator*, October 1976, pp. 23–24.

9. War Manpower Commission, *The Training within Industry Report* (Washington, D.C.: Bureau of Training, War Manpower Commission, 1945), p. 195.

10. Allen N. Nash, Jan P. Muczyk, and Frank L. Vettori, "The Relative Practical Effectiveness of Programmed Instruction," *Personnel Psychology*, 24, 1971, pp. 397–418.

11. *Omaha World Herald*, February 6, 1981.

CHAPTER 10

Employee Development and Career Planning

When you have read this chapter, you should be able to:

1. Define personnel development and identify two conditions for its success.

2. List and describe at least five on-the-job and off-the-job personnel development methods.

3. Discuss specific benefits and problems associated with assessment centers.

4. Explain issues involving the development of women managers.

5. Differentiate between organization-centered and individual-centered career planning.

Development Obligation?

Harvey Halm is 40 years old and has been an employee with Obris Corporation for 15 years. Obris Corporation is an employer of about 2,500 in the eastern part of Pennsylvania. Harvey has been a very good employee and has participated in a number of company-sponsored development experiences. He has enjoyed company-paid night school at the local college. He has participated in several in-house experiences designed to prepare him for a management job, and last year he went through the company assessment center. He passed with flying colors.

Last week Harvey was offered a first-level management job. Today he turned it down saying he was happy doing what he was doing and did not want the new job. His boss, Samuel Reitz, is flabbergasted. He feels the company has invested a good deal of time and effort preparing Harvey for this opportunity. Besides, Harvey is his best candidate for the job.

Samuel is considering suggesting to the president of the company that this expenditure for "development" be discontinued. He feels that situations such as this clearly indicate that the money is being wasted.

Comments:

This case illustrates that the organization had plans for Harvey, but these plans evidently had not been clearly discussed with Harvey. Nor had Harvey indicated his acceptance of the plans the firm had for him. However, the development funds were not wasted because Harvey has continued to be a good employee. The funds just did not accomplish the goal that appears to have caused their expenditure: development and promotion of a supervisor. Harvey could be viewed as ungrateful, but the firm probably deserves the greater share of the blame because the situation reveals an inadequate focus of its employee development efforts.

ULTIMATELY an organization's effectiveness depends on the abilities of its people. Although general abilities are screened in the selection process, many employee skills must be developed over time. Development occurs from the experiences people encounter as they grow older.

Managers in particular need a variety of experiences to develop. A planned system of developmental experiences for employees at any level can help expand the overall level of abilities contained in an organization and increase its potential and flexibility.

PERSONNEL DEVELOPMENT—WHAT IS IT?

The purpose of personnel development is to enlarge an employee's *capacity* to successfully handle greater responsibilities and/or to better handle current responsibilities. Development usually deals with improvement of intellectual or mental abilities needed to do a better job.

> **PERSONNEL DEVELOPMENT** focuses on increasing the capabilities of employees for continuing growth in the organization.

A person's development depends, to an extent, on the relationship with one's superior. By concentrating on the individual employee's goals and potential, a manager can significantly affect an employee's development. Performance appraisals obviously play an important role in development. Through discussions about an employee's past performance and current strengths, concrete proposals can be planned for future development. A performance appraisal can determine, for example, if employees are placed in jobs which exceed their abilities, or if they need additional training to improve performance. Then plans can be initiated to develop the required knowledge and skills. As shown in Figure 10–1, personnel

Figure 10–1. Personnel development interface.

Personnel Unit	Managers
Develops and coordinates employee and management development efforts.	Participate in management development programs
Maintains management replacement charts	Identify employees' development needs
Evaluates employee development efforts for the organization	Assign employees tasks designed to "stretch" them
Administers details of development programs.	Plan for their own development
Keeps abreast of new advances in development techniques	Evaluate subordinates' development

specialists typically takes a more guiding and coordinative stance on development. Managers at all levels must be deeply involved, however, for development to succeed.

What is personnel development?

Conditions for Successful Personnel Development

Personnel development is much more than just acquiring a specific skill, such as learning to type. For instance, progress can be made in developing (1) attitudes about the greater involvement of employees, (2) improved abilities to communicate, and (3) technical knowledge of a subject such as capital budgeting. Regardless of the objective, two conditions are critical for successful personnel development: *top management support* and the *interrelated nature of development*.

Top Management Support.   Top management support and belief in the importance of development efforts is necessary to give people the "room" they need to expand their capabilities. Top management must be willing to delegate some decision-making authority to lower-level positions in the organization to develop young managers. These efforts must be made even if some of them fail. For example, if top management is afraid or unwilling to relinquish control and authority to a younger manager for learning purposes, little management development is likely to result.

Personnel Developmental Interrelationships.   Important relationships exist between personnel development efforts and selection, placement, compensation, and appraisal activities. Neglect of any of these important links can lead to problems with development efforts throughout the whole system. The ultimate result may be the organization's failure to effectively use its human resources.[1]

What are two key conditions for successful personnel development?

Developmental Replacement Charts

With information from some of the interrelated sources mentioned above, replacement charts are drawn which are very similar to depth charts used by a football team. (Such charts show the back-up players at each position.) The purpose of replacement charts is to ensure that the right individual is available at the right time and has had sufficient experience to handle the job. In Figure 10–2 a replacement chart for the Rocky Mountain Manufacturing Company is shown. Replacement charts

Figure 10–2. Replacement chart for Rocky Mountain Manufacturers.

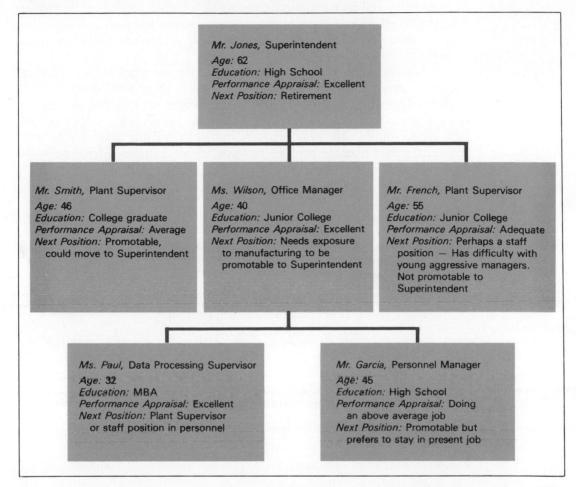

are an excellent basis for determining what kind of development is needed by which employees.

Note that the chart specifies the kind of development each individual needs to be promotable. Ms. Wilson needs exposure to manufacturing to be promotable to superintendent. Her job as office manager has not given her much exposure to the production side of the operation. Ms. Paul needs exposure to plant operations and personnel. Mr. French needs to learn how to handle young, aggressive managers. However, Mr. French's appraiser felt French would not be promotable to superintendent—even with additional training.

Replacement charts indicate where weaknesses exist. If some positions are without adequate back-up, then a decision or *assessment* must be made, either to develop someone to fill the position internally or to recruit outside. An individual must be selected, placed in the proper position, then trained, and receive a performance appraisal. This information then becomes feedback to the entire employee development system.

A problem with replacement charts is the potential for a person to become "stereotyped." On such a progression chart a person who has been placed in the "mediocre performer" category because of a mismatch with a given job may become unpromotable. Replacement charts can help those individuals who need assistance to become promotable, but it requires that management be realistic in its appraisal of the reasons they are considered promotable.

Problems in Personnel Development

Personnel development efforts are subject to certain common mistakes and problems. Managers at all levels, especially top managers, make these same mistakes. Most of these problems are the result of inadequate planning and narrow thinking about coordinated employee development.

Specific major problems include the following:

- Sloppy needs analysis
- Picking up fad programs
- Abdicating responsibility for development to staff
- Attempted substitution of training for selection
- No training of those who lead the development activities
- Using only "courses" as the road to development.
- Encapsulated development

Encapsulated Development.   Failure to consider how employee development fits the organization can result in encapsulated development. This occurs when an individual learns new methods and ideas in a development course and returns to a work unit which is still bound by old attitudes and methods. The reward system and the working conditions have not changed. Although the trainee has learned new ways to handle certain situations, these methods cannot be applied because of the status quo and the unchanged work situation. The new knowledge remains encapsulated in the classroom setting. Encapsulated development is an obvious waste of time and money because it is ineffective.

This and other mistakes are commonly made in development programs. They are usually enough to reduce the effectiveness of development efforts.

CHOOSING A DEVELOPMENT PROGRAM

There are many personnel development methods available. Before describing each, it is important to identify some criteria to indicate when each one should be used. The goals of the development effort can be *people-oriented, job-specific (technical),* or *planning and conceptual.* Different techniques serve these different goals. Figure 10–3 shows the extent to which each method is suited to each of the three goals. A discussion of each of these methods follows, organized around an on-the-job, off-the-job format.

Figure 10–3. Matching development goals and methods.

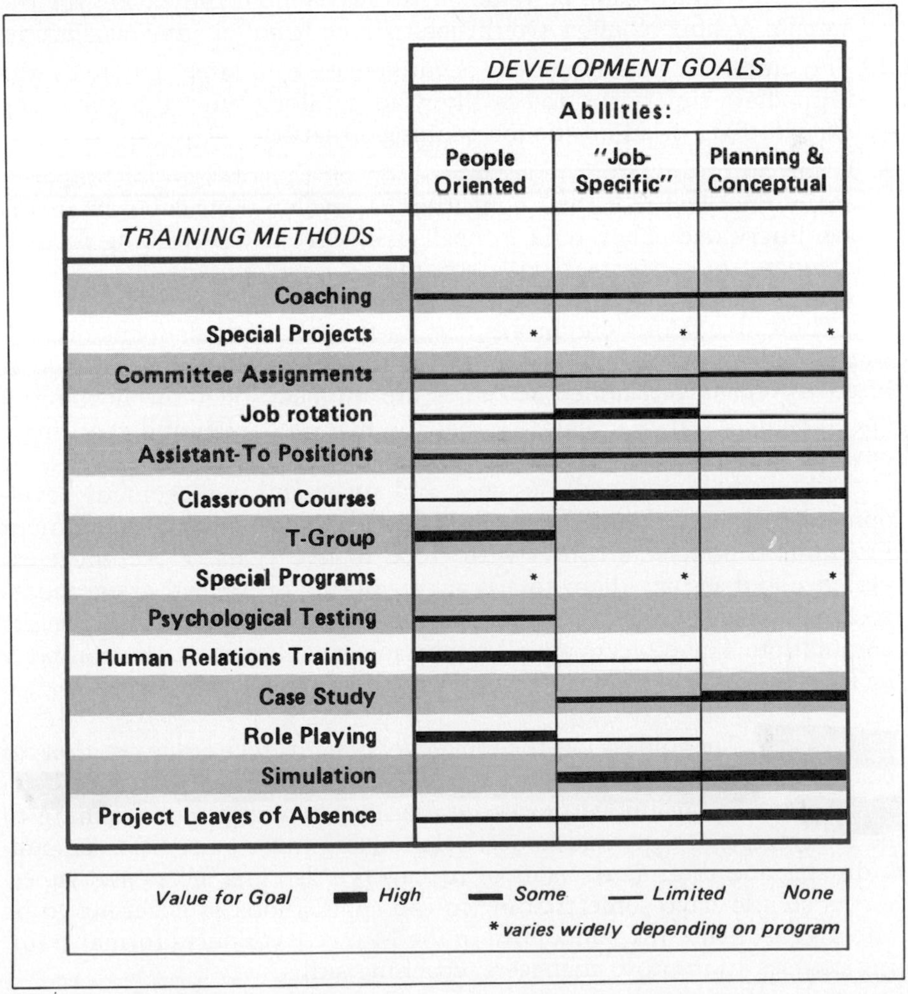

| | DEVELOPMENT GOALS | | |
| | Abilities: | | |
TRAINING METHODS	People Oriented	"Job-Specific"	Planning & Conceptual
Coaching	Some	Some	
Special Projects	*	*	*
Committee Assignments	Some		
Job rotation	Some	High	
Assistant-To Positions	Some		
Classroom Courses		High	
T-Group	High		
Special Programs	*	*	*
Psychological Testing	High		
Human Relations Training	High	Limited	Limited
Case Study		Some	High
Role Playing	High	Limited	Limited
Simulation		High	High
Project Leaves of Absence	Some		Some

Value for Goal ▬ High — Some _ Limited None
*varies widely depending on program

On-the-Job Methods

On-the-job methods generally are directly job-related, an advantage to the organization and to the personnel involved. Some of the most common advantages are:

1. Effective training can be *tailored to fit* each trainee's background, attitudes, needs, expectations, goals, and future assignments. Off-the-job training cannot usually be tailored as well to the exact measurement of each trainee.
2. The importance of *learning by doing* is well recognized in on-the-job training.
3. Some development programs can be very time-consuming and managers in training may be reluctant to leave the organization for the amount of time required. On-the-job training is *not as time-consuming.*
4. The employee's development is influenced to a large extent by the immediate supervisor and is likely to go along with the *superior's expectations* in an on-the-job training situation.
5. When an organization relies mostly on off-the-job training, supervisors do not feel that their obligation to develop their subordinates is a primary one. They tend to neglect it. On-the-job training *focuses a supervisor's attention on subordinates' development.*

These five points emphasize that on-the-job methods focus on day-to-day learning. The major difficulty with on-the-job methods is that often too many unplanned activities are lumped under the heading of "development." It is imperative that the managers plan and coordinate development efforts so that desired learning actually occurs.

An example of a well designed and successful management development program is Sun Chemical's General Management Development Program.[2] Sun selects MBAs with three to five years of technical experience and assigns them to a year of working on special assignments selected to give them well-rounded skills and a familiarity with the corporation. The projects are all important ones; however, the company lacks managerial resources to complete them.

Coaching. The oldest on-the-job development technique is that of coaching, the daily instruction of subordinates by their immediate superior. It is a continuous process of learning by doing. For coaching to be effective, a healthy and honest relationship must exist between subordinates and their supervisors or managers. Also, managers and supervisors should have some training in the applications of coaching to be effective. A major insurance firm in the Midwest conducts formal training courses to improve managers' coaching skills.

Subordinates will benefit from coaching only if they consider it a positive development tool. At the heart of an effective coaching relationship are mutual goals and objectives, including a personal career plan for the subordinates. This plan must then be followed up by regular discussions between the employee and the manager. For example, Marion Brewer, a management trainee, and her boss regularly discuss certain critical job behavior she has exhibited. During their last meeting, her boss discussed her good decision-making ability and pointed out her willingness to assist subordinates with their job problems. He then pointed out a situation in which Marion had been soundly chewed out by a manager of equal rank from another department. Her supervisor emphasized that Marion needs to develop more self-confidence and an ability to stand up to opposition when she knows she is right.

Unfortunately, like many on-the-job methods, coaching is easy to implement without any planning at all. Because someone has been good at a job or particular part of a job is no *guarantee* that they will be able to teach someone else to do it well. It is often too easy to neglect systematic guidance of the learner even if the "coach" knew which systematic experiences were best. Sometimes doing a full day's work gets priority over learning. Also, many skills have an intellectual component to them that might be better learned from a book or lecture before coaching occurs.

This discussion of the problems should not lead one to believe that coaching cannot work. It can, but it requires a knowledgeable coach and some planning.

Special Projects.   Special projects can be almost anything. The Sun Chemical example is one kind. Another is *conference leadership*, which usually requires that the trainee organize and chair problem-solving conferences. As an example, junior executives may be asked to plan and preside at meetings with other managers to solve problems, such as why the production department has been unable to meet a sales request on time. In so doing, the junior executives will learn more about sales and production problems, human nature, and how to organize a conference. Many other types of special projects can be devised.

Committee Assignments.   Assignment of a promising employee to important committees can be a very broadening experience. Employees who participate in committees which make important decisions and plans may gain a real grasp of personalities, issues, and processes governing the way the organization functions. Assigning persons to a safety committee may give them the safety experience needed to become supervisors. Also, they may experience the problems involved with maintaining employee safety awareness. This committee experience often helps employees emphasize safety to workers they would supervise. Caution should be exercised so that committee assignments do not become time-wasting nuisances.

Job Rotation.   Job rotation involves shifting employees from one position to another similar one. For example a promising young manager may spend three months in the plant, three months in corporate planning, and three months in purchasing. When properly handled, rotation encourages a deeper and more general view of the organization. The General Electric Co. uses job rotation during a 15-month sales training program. Trainees in this program work in at least three areas. Included are such assignments as contractor sales, retail sales, credit, advertising, and product training.

In some companies job rotation is unplanned; other companies have elaborate charts and schedules precisely planning the program for each employee. Managers should recognize that job rotation can be expensive because a substantial amount of managerial time is lost. The trainee must take time after each change of position to become reacquainted with different people and techniques in the new unit.

A disadvantage of job rotation is that it may discourage the trainee from taking a long-term perspective of the job. If a move is imminent, the employee may become more concerned with short-term problems.

Assistant-to Positions.   The assistant-to position is a staff position immediately under a manager. Through this job, trainees can work with outstanding managers they may not otherwise meet. Some organizations have "junior boards of directors" or "management cabinets" to which trainees may be appointed. Assignments such as these are useful if trainees have the opportunity to deal with challenging or interesting assignments.

What are four on-the-job methods of personnel development?

Off-the-Job Techniques

Off-the-job development techniques can be effective because an individual has an opportunity to get away from the job and to concentrate solely on what is to be learned. Meeting other people who are concerned with somewhat different problems and different organizations may provide an employee with different perspectives on old problems. There are a variety of methods which may be used.

Classroom Courses.   Many off-the-job development programs include some classroom instruction. The advantage of classroom training is that it is widely accepted because most people are familiar with it. Classroom training can be conducted by specialists who are either employed by the organization or outside experts.

A disadvantage of classroom instruction is that lectures often produce passive listeners and lack of participation. Sometimes trainees have little opportunity to question, clarify, and discuss the lecture material. Classroom effectiveness depends upon the size of the group, the ability of the instructor, and the subject matter.

T-group Training.   T-group training has also been called sensitivity training, encounter group, and laboratory training. It is a technique for learning about one's self and others by observing and participating in a group situation. These small groups may meet for two or three hours or more daily for a period of a week or longer, usually off the job site. The leader attempts to keep a free format of activities and group relationships.

At first, group members tend to be frustrated and do not understand why they are "wasting" their time. They may be openly hostile toward the leader and each other. The leader tries to encourage "openness" in the expression of feelings and reactions to other people in the group. Some topics of discussion are motives and impressions of other people. The participants may gradually open up and show themselves for what they are.

T-group training is supposed to develop an awareness of human, group, and personal behavior. Even though people may be changed by the training, findings suggest that the sponsoring organization does not always benefit from the changes. One study found that "sensitivity training ranks low as an effective management development tool when compared to several other common approaches."[3]

Special Programs.   A widely used personnel development method is to send employees to externally-sponsored courses or short courses. These programs are offered by many colleges and universities and professional associations such as the American Management Association.

Some larger organizations have established training centers exclusively for their own employees. For example, the federal government has created Executive Seminar Centers in Kingspoint, New York, and in Berkeley, California, and the Federal Executive Institute in Charlottesville, Virginia. Trainees in these courses are exposed to a variety of problems and learning materials. However, a common complaint about these programs is that they do not deal specifically with the realities of an individual's work place and a high percentage of the participants simply are not ready for the courses they attend. Some attend at the wrong time in their careers, while others are near retirement. Many have not had the preliminary training in management that the programs assume.

Psychological Testing.   Psychological pencil-and-paper tests have been used for several years to determine an employee's developmental potential. Intelligence tests, verbal and mathematical reasoning tests, and personality tests are often used. Such testing can provide useful information to employees in understanding such aspects as motivation, reasoning difficulties, leadership styles, interpersonal response traits, and job preferences.

The biggest problem with good psychological testing lies in interpreting the results. An untrained manager, supervisor, or worker cannot accurately interpret test results. A professional reports scores to someone in the organization, but then the interpretation is left essentially to untrained novices who may attach their own meanings. It should also be recognized that some psychological tests are of limited validity and can be easily faked. Psychological testing appears appropriate only when closely supervised by a qualified professional throughout the testing and feedback process.

Human Relations Training.   Human relations training originated in the well-known Hawthorne studies. Originally the idea was to prepare supervisors to handle the "people" problems brought to them by their employees. This type of training focuses on the development of human skills a person needs to work well with others. Many human relations training programs are aimed at new or relatively inexperienced first-line supervisors and middle managers. Human relations programs typically deal with motivation, leadership, communication, and humanizing the work place. Participation is emphasized and components of morale are carefully examined.

The major problem with such programs is the difficulty in measuring their effectiveness. The development of human skills is a longer-range goal. However, the tangible results associated with human relations training are hard to identify over the span of several years. Consequently, such programs are often measured using only the participant's reaction to them. As mentioned in the previous chapter, reaction-level measurement is the weakest form of evaluating the effectiveness of training.

Case Study.   A case study is a classroom-oriented development technique which has been used widely. Cases provide a medium through which the trainee can study the application of management or behavioral concepts. The emphasis is on application and analysis instead of mere memorization of concepts.

One common complaint about the case method is that the cases cannot be made sufficiently realistic to be useful. Also, cases may contain information inappropriate to the kinds of decisions that trainees would make in a real situation.

Role-playing.   Role-playing is a development technique which requires the trainee to assume a role in a given situation and act out behavior associated with that role. Participants gain an appreciation of the factors in a certain situation. Andrew McBride, a labor relations director, may be asked to play the role of the union vice-president in a negotiating situation to give him insight into the constraints and problems facing union bargaining representatives. Role-playing is a useful tool in some situations, but a word of caution: trainees are often uncomfortable in role-playing situations and care must be taken.

Simulation (Business Games).   Several different business games are available commercially. These may be computer interactive games where individuals or teams draw up a set of marketing plans for an organization, such as trying to determine the amount of resources to be allocated for advertising, product design, selling, and sales for effort. The participants make a decision and then the computer tells them how well they did in relation to competing individuals or teams. Other computer-based business games often have to do with labor/management negotiations. In one such simulation a player takes the role of either management or union and the computer takes the other role. The trainee and the computer bargain on such items as wages and benefits.

Simulation, when properly done, can be a useful management development tool. However, simulation receives the same criticism as role-playing. Realism is sometimes lacking and the learning experience is diminished. Learning must be the focus, not just "playing the game."

Sabbaticals and Leaves of Absence.   Sabbatical leaves are a very useful development tool. Sabbaticals have been popular for many years in the academic world, where professors take a leave to sharpen their skills and advance their education or research. Similar sorts of plans have been adopted in the business community. For example, Xerox Corporation gives some of its employees six months or more off with pay to work on "socially desirable" projects. Projects include training people in the ghettos or providing technical assistance to overseas countries.

Paid sabbaticals can be an expensive proposition, however. Also, the nature of the learning experience is not within the control of the organization and the exact nature of the developmental experience is left somewhat to chance.

What are some off-the-job development methods?

Assessment Centers

Assessment centers can help identify areas in employees that need development. They also are useful for selecting managers.

Operation of Center.   Essentially, an assessment center is a series of individual and group exercises in which a number of candidates participate. During these exercises, the participants are observed by several specially trained judges. For the most part these exercises are work samples of managerial situations that require the use of managerial skills and behavior. The "center" is a set of activities rather than just a physical location.

The assessment center approach was originally developed during World War II for selecting OSS agents. One major company, American Telephone and Telegraph, has since made large-scale use of the concept. Candidates may participate in a wide variety of standardized exercises such as management games, leaderless discussion groups, and in-baskets over a several-day period. Trained observers watch the candidates' behavior in detail and record impressions. Each assessor writes a report on each candidate which is given to the candidate's superior to use in selection and promotion decisions. The reports often identify guidelines for further development of the assessed employee.

Problems.   Assessment centers are an excellent means for determining management potential. However, one problem is that some managers may use the assessment center as a way to avoid a difficult promotion decision. For example, suppose a plant supervisor has personally decided that a subordinate is not a qualified candidate for promotion. Rather than stick by the decision and tell the employee, the supervisor sends the employee to the assessment center in hopes that the report will show that the employee is not qualified for promotion. The problems will be worse if the employee receives a positive report. However, if the report is negative, the supervisor's views are validated. Using the assessment center in this way is not recommended. Two other problems are (1) making sure the exercises in the assessment center are valid predictors of management performance and (2) properly selecting and training the assessors.

Validity of Centers.   The validity of assessment centers for selection has been the subject of many studies. These studies have generally suggested that assessment centers predict management success much better than other methods.[4] However, some researchers have been concerned with the very high validity coefficients found in these studies. They question whether the use of salary growth and advancement to measure the success of assessment centers is appropriate. It can be argued that these items may not be related to competence, effectiveness, or superior performance.

Finally, assessment centers are expensive. The actual cost varies from organization to organization, but it usually costs at least $600 for each candidate to go through a center. However, the cost of making a mistake with management selection is great too. One firm reported $19,000 worth of legal, salary, and benefit payments to terminate a department head.[5]

Even with the expense it is reported that more than 1,600 major firms have created assessment centers, including General Electric, Union Carbide, and IBM. AT&T operates more than 70 centers that evaluate 15,000 employees per year.[6]

What benefits and problems exist with assessment centers?

MANAGEMENT DEVELOPMENT: SPECIAL ISSUES

Two additonal areas of special interest when dealing with management development are (1) managerial modeling and (2) special problems of women managers. These areas will be examined to show the impact and importance of sound management development planning and implementation.

Managerial Modeling

There is an old truism in personnel management development that says managers tend to manage as they were managed. Another way of stating this idea is that much management is learned by modeling the behavior of other managers. This revelation is not surprising because a great deal of human behavior is learned by modeling others. Children learn by modeling parents and older children; they are quite comfortable with the process by the time they grow up.

Modeling, a very powerful management development tool, has been used successfully in industry in several ways. Over 2,700 first-line supervisors at General Electric have been trained in the use of modeling to help ease the hard-core unemployed into the work world.[7] As a supervisory development method, modeling has been used by firms such as Quaker Oats, Ford Motor, Xerox, Lukens Steel, Gulf Oil, and American Cyanamid.[8]

Modeling is a very natural way for managers to develop, since it will likely occur regardless of design, intent, or desire. Management development efforts can take advantage of the natural human behavior by matching young or developing managers with appropriate models and then reinforcing the desirable behaviors that are exhibited.

Management Development and the Woman Manager

Management development efforts for some groups may need a different orientation than for other groups. During the last several years, employers have experienced increasing pressure to promote women into management positions. Both legal and societal pressures have encouraged the movement of women out of traditional "women's" jobs and into the mainstream of management activity.

The biggest obstacle for a woman seeking advancement in management is the traditional attitude of both men and women towards masculine and feminine roles. Development of women managers seems to require an understanding of their special needs, as well as the requirements of the business. Research on women managers leads to the following recommendations for management development programs:

1. Women need to raise their self-esteem as managers.

2. Women need to learn new behavior for managing interpersonal conflict.

3. Women need to develop leadership and team-building skills.

4. Women need help with career planning.

5. Training for *women only* is desirable initially.[9]

Rather than resorting to special training for potential women managers, selecting those who are already qualified would be most efficient. However, the demand for qualified women managers sometimes precludes this solution, especially when there is an urgency to hire and promote qualified female managers under an affirmative action plan. The state of California developed a program to develop women employees for management jobs in such a situation.[10]

As the foregoing suggests, if special training for women is necessary, it is likely to be more attitudinal in nature than ability-oriented.[11] This factor and the popularity of assertiveness training with women managers suggest that the differences and special problems are more related to attitudes than to ability.

As with any social change, the initial introduction of women into management has been difficult for some organizations. Some male managers maintain that special training for women is "reverse discrimination." Organizations should take positive steps to ensure that a talented man has the opportunity to develop his managerial ability. The same treatment for talented women must also be available.

CAREER PLANNING AND GUIDANCE

In the past, career guidance has been considered a service for high school or college students. However, as the employee work role becomes more complex, more employers are providing career counseling. Exxon Corporation is just one of many employers that use career planning for many of its managers.

Certain common career concerns are frequently expressed by employees in all organizations. These concerns include the following:

"What do I really *want* to do?" "What do I *know* how to do?" "What career opportunities can I expect to be *available*?" "Where do I want to *go*?" "What do I *need to do* to get there?" "How can I tell *how well* I am doing?" "How do I get out of the box I am in?" Usually, in-house career planning and guidance is limited to what the organization has to offer. However, these opportunities may not always include all possibilities in a particular field.

Organization-Centered vs. Individual-Centered Career Planning

The nature of career planning can be somewhat confusing because two different types exist. Career planning can be either *organization-centered* or *individual-centered*.[12]

Organization career planning involves career paths which are the logical progression of people between jobs. These paths represent "ladders" that each individual can climb to advance in certain organization units. For example, one might enter the sales department as a sales counselor, then be promoted to account director, then sales manager, and finally vice-president of sales.

Individual career planning, on the other hand, focuses on individuals rather than jobs. People's goals and skills are the focus of analysis. Such analysis might include situations both within and outside the organization that can expand an employee's capabilities. It might even include movement to another organization. The points of focus for organization- and individual-oriented career planning are compared in Figure 10–4.

Figure 10–4. Two approaches to career planning.

Organization Career Planning (OCP)	Individual Career Planning (ICP)
future needs	self-awareness: abilities and interests
career ladders	planning goals: life and work
assessment of individual potential	planning to achieve goals
connecting organizational need/opportunity with individual need/desire	alternatives, internal and external to organization
coordination and audit of career system	career ladders, internal and external to organization

(Source: Elmer Burack, "Why All the Confusion About Career Planning?" *Human Resources Management*, Summer 1977, p. 21. Graduate School of Business Administration, University of Michigan, Ann Arbor, MI 48109.)

Human resource planning forms the basis for successful organizational career planning. Only by forecasting the demand for people needed in various jobs in the future and the current internal supply of people and their potentials can a career system be put together for the organization.

If careful matching of organizational needs and personal goals takes place, human resource planning will consider both the organizational and individual perspectives. Unfortunately many organizations often compile recruiting and career ladders or both without considering information about how current employees fit into those plans.

How Do People Choose Careers?

Studies indicate that four general individual characteristics help affect the career choices made.[13]

1. *Interests:* Persons tend to pursue careers that they perceive match their interests.
2. *Self-identity:* A career is an extension of a person's self image, as well as a molder of it.
3. *Personality:* This factor includes personal orientation (whether one is realistic, enterprising, artistic, etc.) and personal needs (including affiliation, power, and achievement needs).
4. *Social background:* Socioeconomic status and the education and occupation level of a person's parents are some of the factors included here.

Less is known about exactly how people choose specific organizations. One factor is the opportunity for and availability of a job when the person is looking for work. The amount of information available about alternatives is an important factor as well. Beyond these issues people seem to pick organizations on the basis of a "fit" between the climate of that organization *as they perceive it* and their own personal characteristics.

Effective Individual Career Planning.   Good career planning at the individual level first requires that a person accurately know himself/herself. One must face issues such as: How hard are you really willing to work? What kind of factors are important to you? What kind of trade-off between work and family or leisure are you willing to make? These questions and others must be dealt with honestly before personal goals and objectives can realistically be set. Professional counseling may be available to persons to help them make these decisions.

Supervisors and managers high in the organization can help a person determine what skills and talents are necessary for success at each organizational level. Other information on occupations or careers outside the employee's current employer often must be gathered by the employee. Once this material is gathered, decisions can be made.

Individual goal setting about the nature of a career is an important first step. Once goals have been set, planning for their achievement must be done. This planning consists of determining a series of actions that will lead to the goals. These steps may include a variety of training and development methods, such as those discussed earlier.

Career planning is still more an art than a science. However, the alternative of no career planning for both the organization and the individual is not a sound one either.[14]

> *What is the difference between organizational-centered and individual-centered career planning?*

REVIEW AND PREVIEW

Personnel development takes a longer range and broader view of training than does job-skill training. While development may include some skill development, it is more specifically oriented toward a person's capacity to handle future responsibilities. Development activities can include persons at all levels of the organization. Regardless of the level of the people involved, upper management support is important because development requires integration with other organizational activities.

A wide range of development methods are available. Some of these methods can be conducted on-the-job. Other methods often require an employee to be off-the-job when participating in personnel development activities.

Assessment centers are a special off-the-job development technique. By simulating actual work situations, the assessment center has been fairly successful at predicting future job success of those assessed. But they are expensive to initiate and operate and may not be measuring performance properly.

Career planning is one of several development methods mentioned in this chapter. It is a process for matching people and jobs. Career planning can be individual-oriented, organization-oriented, or both.

The next chapter considers all the dimensions of performance appraisal crucial to the development of employees. Performance appraisals also have an impact on the compensation employees receive.

REVIEW QUESTIONS

1. What is personnel development and why is top management support so important?

2. You are the head of a governmental agency. What two methods of on-the-job development would you use with a promising supervisor? What two off-the-job methods would you use? Why?

3. Why do you believe that many large companies have started assessment centers?

4. "Women managers should be treated like men when it comes to development activities. Neither group should receive special treatment or have unique activities planned for them." Discuss.

5. Discuss whether you would prefer organization-centered or individual-centered career planning.

Case: Developed Today, Gone Tomorrow?

Completed

A large midwestern firm maintains an organizational policy of promoting individual growth. By offering generous allowances for costs associated with tuition, books, and miscellaneous expenses, employees are supported in their efforts to gain a college or other institutional education. This program is also offered to persons whose individual goal is to continue their education through a graduate program if the field of endeavor is one that could prove to be advantageous to the corporation.

The computer programming department has a high rate of participation in the educational supportive program. It is generally accepted that this high rate is due to the above-average aptitudes of the personnel in the department and to the high personal goals set by them. In addition, the department has its own in-house set of training courses and purchases "space" in various seminar classes. These programs are geared to making the employee specifically more valuable to the department. The managers in the programming department have been very proud of the development of their personnel and feel that education (from all sources) has improved departmental performance.

Just recently, however, the system seemed to backfire in the programming department. Ezra Brooks, a very bright and aspiring young programmer for whom management had high hopes, quit. Ezra had found that the extensive intraorganization training, the invaluable work experience, and a newly awarded college diploma represented a fairly lucrative portfolio of credentials that he took to a large national accounting firm. Ezra had expressed a desire to stay, but he was told that there were no anticipated openings at managerial levels in the computer area.

Ezra's manager had a dilemma. Loss of Ezra meant a ten labor-month setback for the project he was working on. He also felt that the benefit of the extensive training Ezra had received at the company's expense was little utilized compared to what Ezra would have contributed had he remained with the company. However, the manager's greatest concern was that Ezra was the first in a group of several employees who would graduate from college in the near future. To the remaining group Ezra had shown that if the firm would not recognize his achievement and aspirations, other employment could be easily obtained. As Ezra's manager, what would you do to retain him and what changes would you recommend in the educational aid program?

NOTES

1. An excellent discussion of the interrelated nature of development can be found in: R. W. Walters "Developing Future Managers Systems Approach," *Personnel Administrator*, August 1980, p. 47.

2. E. E. Barr, "Experiencing Success: Breaking Them in at Sun Chemical," *Business*, September/October 1980, pp. 9–14.

3. William J. Kearney and Desmond D. Martin, "Sensitivity Training: An Established Management Development Tool?" *Academy of Management Journal*, 17, December 1974, p. 759.

4. R. J. Klimoski and W. J. Strickland, "Assessment Centers—Valid or Merely Prescient?" *Personnel Psychology* 30 (1977), pp. 353–356.

5. E. Yager, "Assessment Centers: The Latest Fad?" *Training and Development Journal*, January 1976, pp. 41–44.

6. John Koten, "Career Guidance," *Wall Street Journal*, July 11, 1978, p. 1.

7. R. F. Burnaska, "The Effects of Behavior Modeling Training Upon Manager's Behavior and Employee's Perceptions," *Personnel Psychology*, 29, 1976, p. 329.

8. "Imitating Models: A New Management Tool," *Business Week*, May 8, 1978, pp. 119–120.

9. J. Steven Heiner, Dorothy McGlauchlin, Constance Legeros, and Jean Freeman, "Developing the Woman Manager," *Personnel Journal*, 54, May 1975. Reprinted with permission of *Personnel Journal*, copyright May 1975.

10. Kristin Amundsen, "Key to Developing Managerial Women," *Management Review*, February 1979, pp. 55–58.

11. For further amplification, see Loretta M. Moore and Annette U. Richel, "Characteristics of Women in Traditional and Non-Traditional Managerial Roles," *Personnel Psychology*, 33, 1980, pp. 317–333; and O. C. Brenner and Joseph Tomkiewicz, "Job Orientation of Males and Females: One Sex Differences Declining?" *Personnel Psychology*, 32, 1979, pp. 741–750.

12. Elmer Burack, "Why All the Confusion About Career Planning?" *Human Resources Management*, Summer 1977, p. 21.

13. Douglas T. Hall, *Careers in Organizations* (Pacific Palisades, CA: Goodyear Publishing, 1976), pp. 11–13.

14. An excellent discussion of career planning from both the organization's and employee's perspective can be found in: J. W. Walker *Human Resources Planning* (New York: McGraw-Hill, 1980), chapters 13 and 14.

Appraising and Compensating Human Resources

DAY CARE: A BASIC BENEFIT?

Inflation, life style change, women's liberation. These trends and others have led to a dramatic increase in the number of mothers of preschool children who work. As more and more mothers of preschool children in this country enter the labor market, the need for child care is increasing. Employers and labor representatives are recognizing the child care need as a major concern of employees and are exploring ways to alleviate it.

In 1960, only 19% of mothers, husband present, with preschool children were in the labor force, but by 1979, labor force participation of these mothers had increased to 43%. In 1979, 45% of all women with children under age six were in the labor force, putting an estimated 7.2 million preschool children in need of child care services.

Finding reliable child care has been a problem for many working women. One survey of mothers working full time revealed that 30% had changed child care arrangements within two years because of undependable or poor quality care. In 1979, the National Commission on Working Women reported on a national survey of over 80,000 employed women; 33% of those with dependent children reported that child care was a problem.

Management and labor representatives are aware of the link between unsatisfactory child care arrangements and employee absenteeism. Some employers have helped solve their own absenteeism problems and their employees' child care problems by sponsoring or supporting reliable child care services.[1]

Corporate day care centers enjoyed a brief vogue ten years ago but most were closed because of high operating costs and employee apathy. Now, in some labor-short areas and industries, personnel people are finding day care can help recruit talent. Wang Laboratories, Xerox, Stride Rite, Measurex, Hewlett-Packard, and Polaroid provide day care in their own centers or help locate and pay for outside services.

[1] "Child Care Centers Sponsored by Employers and Labor Unions in the United States." U. S. Department of Labor, Office of the Secretary, Women's Bureau, 1980, p. 1.

The benefits resulting to employers from having day care facilities available for employees were summarized in one study[2] as follows:

1. Increased ability to attract employees.

2. Lower absenteeism.

3. Improved employee attitude toward employer.

For companies considering a child care facility, it is clear that good needs assessment is important. The number of employees *eligible* to use the service and the number *willing* to use it are not the same. In fact, that is one of the major reasons child care centers have been closed. Too few employees were using for them to break even.

An employer who hires many women in the child-bearing years might want to consider this option. It is not a glamorous benefit, but it works and it is certain to grow in importance.

This section is concerned with appraising and compensating performance. The process of examining employee performance is called *performance appraisal.* Appraisals are useful in solving some personnel problems, but the practice creates still other problems. Chapter 11 covers behavioral reactions to appraisals, common mistakes made in appraising performance, and some components of a successful appraisal process.

One major reason for appraising an employee's performance is to reward those who do more work with more *compensation.* To provide themselves with the necessities of life, most people "sell" their services to organizations for money (pay). Pay usually means more to people than just legal tender. It can be a reward or a status symbol. But it is still compensation for effort. People want to be compensated fairly and are concerned about equity—fair treatment in pay.

Equitable pay can be determined in a number of ways. Effective organizations use well-designed personnel systems, such as job evaluation, to see that employees are paid fairly. Systems to evaluate the worth of jobs are discussed in chapter 12, which also includes a discussion of the legal constraints on compensation practices.

People are not only paid in money. Incentives and extra benefits are also forms of compensation. Different kinds of incentives can be designed to achieve a variety of results. Some incentive systems and guides to designing incentive systems are discussed in chapter 13.

Now that benefits average over 35% of the payroll dollar, both employees and managers are concerned that benefit programs be well designed and that benefits be distributed equitably. Chapter 13 also provides details on this important area of personnel management.

---

[2] Ibid., p. 7.

CHAPTER 11

Appraisal of Human Resources

When you have read this chapter, you should be able to:

1. Identify the three major uses of appraisals.

2. Discuss three different raters that can be used.

3. Give examples of appraisal methods under three general types.

4. Explain three rater errors.

5. Discuss several concerns about the appraisal feedback interview.

6. Describe how to construct Behavioral Anchored Rating Scales (BARS).

7. Identify the nature of Management By Objectives (MBO).

8. Describe aspects of legal and effective appraisal systems.

Unequal-Equal Supervisors

Hubert Johnson is a department head. He has been with the company for 30 years and knows his way around quite well. He has two employees, Harriet Green and Neil White. Harriet has been with the company for 15 years and Neil has been with the company for six years. Harriet has always been cooperative, loyal, dependable, but not an especially good supervisor. Recently Hubert has noticed that Harriet has begun to "slip" in the performance of some of her duties. Neil, on the other hand, is a very ambitious, energetic, and dependable supervisor who grasps problems quickly and easily. Hubert has to complete performance appraisals on both individuals annually.

Ten months ago he did his appraising with a great deal of displeasure because he hated to face the unpleasantness of a negative performance appraisal review. As a result, he rated both the employees about the same. When a discussion about the ratings was conducted, both supervisors appeared to be satisfied with the rating they had received.

Six months ago business began to fall off and a reduction in force was put into effect. This week, after a number of other people were laid off or demoted, it became necessary to move either Harriet Green or Neil White from the position of a supervisor to that of a worker until sales picked up. Hubert wants to keep Neil on the supervisory job, but on the basis of the appraisals there is no difference between the two. In the past when two employees have had the same ratings, the person with the most seniority receives priority. Hubert must decide today what to do.

Comments:

Hubert is facing a very common problem. Having to distinguish between dependable, loyal service over a long period of time, and a higher quality of service from another individual over a shorter period of time is difficult. He has further complicated the unpleasant task by failing to face up to the differences in performance between the two earlier and communicating his feelings to them.

Demoting the more senior employee might be perceived by the rest of the people in the department, as well as by the individual involved, as a company slap at long-service, loyal employees. On the other hand, to demote an individual who was clearly a superior performer emphasizes longevity at the expense of performance. In addition, Hubert needs Neil on the job.

This case demonstrates the extreme need for doing performance appraisal properly. Performance appraisal can be used as the basis for making this decision, but it must be done right if it is to be both defensible and accepted by the parties involved. A poor job of performance appraisal has compounded this already difficult situation.

AFTER an employee has been selected for a job, has been trained to do it, and has worked on it for a period of time, his or her performance should be reviewed. Deciding how well employees do their jobs has been called employee rating, merit rating, employee evaluation, performance review, performance evaluation, and results appraisal.

PERFORMANCE APPRAISAL is determining how well employees do their jobs and communicating that information to them.

USES OF APPRAISAL

Appraisal attempts to measure how well employees are performing their duties and meeting their job responsibilities. The information provided by performance appraisal is useful in three major areas: compensation, placement, and training development (see Figure 11–1).

Figure 11–1. Uses of performance appraisal.

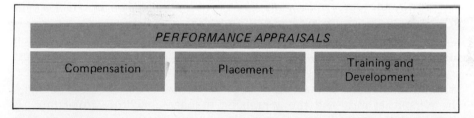

Compensation

The first and most common use of appraisal is as a basis for greater pay raises. Managers need performance appraisals to identify employees performing at or above expected levels. This approach to compensation is at the heart of the idea that raises should be given for merit rather than for seniority. *Merit* means an employee receives a raise based on performance.

Placement

Appraisal information is also used when placement decisions are made. When merit is the basis for reward, the person doing the best job receives the promotion. An individual doing a poor job may be subject to discharge or demotion. Either placement decision requires an appraisal of the employee's performance.

Training and Development

Performance appraisal information also has a training use. Appraisal identifies the weaknesses and potential of subordinates, and can identify training needs. Performance appraisal can inform employees about their progress and tell them what skills they need to develop to become eligible for a pay raise, promotion, or both.

How can appraisals be used?

INFORMAL VS. SYSTEMATIC APPRAISAL

Performance appraisal may occur in two general ways, *informally* or *systematically.* The informal appraisal is conducted whenever the supervisor or personnel manager feels it necessary. The day-to-day working relationship of a manager and an employee provides an opportunity for the employee's performance to be judged. This judgment is communicated through conversation on the job, over coffee, or by on-the-spot examination of a particular piece of work.

A systematic appraisal system occurs when the contact between manager and employee is formalized and a system is established to report supervisory impressions and observations of employee performance. When a formalized or systematic appraisal exists, the interface between the personnel unit and the appraising manager becomes important. A personnel unit can be of great assistance to a manager in seeing that appraisal is done effectively.

Appraisal Interface

The appraisal process is one that can be quite beneficial to the organization and individuals involved if done properly. It can also be the source of a great deal of discontent if not done equitably and well. In situations in which an employer must deal with a very strong union, performance appraisals may be conducted only on salaried, nonunion employees. The emphasis on seniority over merit is the major cause of this union resistance to appraisals.

Figure 11–2 shows that the personnel unit typically designs a systematic appraisal system. The manager handles the actual appraising of

Figure 11–2. Appraisal interface.

Personnel Unit	Managers
Designs and maintains formal system	Actually rate performance of employees
Establishes formal report system	Make formal reports
Makes sure reports are in on time	Review appraisals with employees
Trains raters	

the employee, using the systemized procedures developed by the personnel unit. As the formal system is being developed, the manager usually provides input on how the final system will work. Only rarely does a personnel specialist actually rate a manager's employees.

Timing of Appraisals

An important characteristic of a sound appraisal system is appraising employee performance on a regular basis. Typically, systematic appraisals are conducted every six months or annually. One study of 216 firms found that appraisals were most often conducted once a year (52%). The semiannual performance appraisals were used by 24% of the firms.[1]

This regular time interval feature of formal or systematic appraisals distinguishes them from informal appraisals. Both employees and managers are aware that performance will be reviewed on a regular basis and necessary adjustments planned. However, informal appraisal should be conducted whenever a manager feels it is necessary or will be useful.

WHO WILL DO THE RATINGS?

Performance appraisal can be done by:

- Supervisors who rate subordinates
- Subordinates who rate their superiors
- Peers who rate each other
- Combination of raters

The first method is clearly the most common. The results of a survey of 216 firms showed that the immediate superior has the sole responsibility for appraisal in 78% of the organizations. Approximately

63% of the firms have a practice of having the appraisal reviewed and approved by the appraising superior's boss.[2]

Superior Rating of Subordinates

This approach to appraising assumes that the superior or manager is the most qualified person to evaluate a subordinate's performance realistically, objectively, and fairly. The "unity of command" notion—that every subordinate should have only one superior—remains unchanged.

As with any rating system, the supervisor's judgment should be objective and based on actual performance. Toward this end many managers keep weekly logs of what employees have done during the past week. These provide examples when rating time arrives. They also serve as memory joggers for managers who cannot be expected to remember every detail of performance over a six-month or a one-year period.

A manager's ratings of his or her subordinates are typically reviewed by the manager's superior.[3] This is done to make sure the manager has done a proper job of appraisal, and to make sure the recommended salary increase is justified. Figure 11–3 shows this review process.

Figure 11–3. Appraisal process.

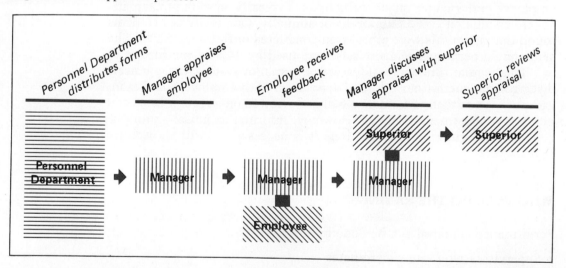

Subordinate Rating of Superiors

The concept of having superiors evaluated by subordinates is being used in a number of organizations today. A prime example of this type of rating is taking place in colleges and universities where students evaluate a professor's performance in the classroom. Industry has used some subordinate rating for developmental purposes. Results are used to help superiors improve themselves or to help assess a manager's leadership potential.

Advantages. There are some advantages to having subordinates rate superiors. First, in situations where the superior-subordinate relationship is critical, subordinates' ratings can be quite useful in identifying competent superiors. Combat soldiers rating their leader is an example. Also, this type of rating program can help make the superior more responsive to subordinates. This advantage can quickly become a disadvantage, however, if it leads to the superior's not managing his workers, but trying only to be a "nice guy." Nice people without other qualifications may not be good managers in some situations.

Disadvantages. A major disadvantage is the negative reaction many superiors have to being evaluated by subordinates. The fear of reprisal may be too great for employees to give realistic ratings. The principles of "proper" superior/subordinate relations may be violated by having subordinates rate superiors. Employees may resist rating their bosses because they do not perceive it as a "proper" part of their job. Also, subordinates may not be aware of the important parts of a supervisor's job. If this is the case, the subordinates might be rating the superior only on the way the superior treats them, and not on critical job requirements.

The problems and disadvantages associated with subordinates rating superiors seem to limit the usefulness of this appraisal approach. It might be useful in certain special situations such as in a university or research and development department. However, the traditional nature of most organizations seems to restrict the applicability of subordinate rating except for self-improvement purposes.

Peer Ratings

The use of peer groups as raters is a third type of appraisal system. The peer technique is seldom used in open committee form. If a group of salespersons met as a committee to talk about each other's ratings, future work relationships might be impaired. Therefore, the peer rating approach is best used by summarizing individual ratings. Also, it should be noted that most of the research on peer ratings was done on military personnel at the "management or pre-management" level (officers or officer candidates).

There are several likely reasons for the scarcity of peer ratings in industry. One is that members of peer groups in industry may not be as closely knit as peer groups in military training settings. Another reason is that peer ratings may be most useful at managerial levels for identifying leadership potential.

A final important reason for the absence of peer ratings in industry is the use of performance appraisal results in most nonmilitary settings. Performance appraisal results in industry are usually used as input to determine promotion or financial reward. Peer ratings are generally used for development and counseling in military situations, not for promotion or financial reward determinations.

In summary, the peer rating appears to have some limitations. Where there is an absence of closely knit groups and experience with this system, such ratings methods may not be appropriate.

Combination Approaches

Combinations and variations of the three methods already mentioned make an almost infinite number of different appraisal systems possible. Regardless of who is doing the rating a *method* for rating is necessary. Several methods are possibilities. Two have been selected to illustrate the combination approach: *committee of superiors* and *multiple rating systems*.

Committee of Superiors.   Because more people have had a chance to know and watch the individual being rated, more useful information on that person may be available if rating is done by a committee of superiors. If more information is available, an organization can pinpoint better employees for promotions or future job assignments.

However, as with any personnel technique, there are some disadvantages. Having *more* information does not necessarily mean *better* information. Without objective data to make appraisals, committees may simply be pooling their collective ignorance.

Other problems arise with committee group appraisal. It can be quite time-consuming. The choice of the committee chair can be the crucial factor determining the efficient operation of the appraising committee and the outcome. If the employee being rated thinks the committee members are hostile, that person will not benefit from the appraisal. Further, the committee members must realize the purpose of the appraisal session is to help an individual, not to "nail" the employee to the wall.

Multiple Rating System.   The *multiple rating system* for superior's ratings is very simple. It merely requires that several superiors separately fill out rating forms on the same subordinate. The results are then tabulated to come up with an appraisal of the person being rated.

Such rating of subordinates by superiors is especially appealing when the preservation of organizational status is important. A young loan officer in a bank who is responsible for loan judgments has her performance reviewed by a group of superiors comprising the bank's loan committee. This method preserves the role of judge for the superiors involved in the rating process.

Who can do appraisals?

METHODS FOR APPRAISING PERFORMANCE

Appraisals can be conducted using a number of methods. In Figure 11–4 the various methods are categorized into three major groups.

Figure 11–4. Performance appraisal methods.

Category Rating Methods
1 *Graphic rating scales*
2 *Checklist*
3 *Forced choice*

Comparative Methods
1 *Ranking*
2 *Paired comparison*
3 *Forced distribution*

Written Methods
1 *Critical incident*
2 *Essay*
3 *Field review*

Category Rating Methods

The simplest methods are those that require a manager to indicate how an employee rates on a form by marking a level of performance. The graphic rating scale, the checklist, and forced choice methods are common category methods.

Graphic Rating Scale. The graphic rating scale is the most commonly used method. Figure 11–5 shows a typical graphic rating scale form used by managers rating office employees. The rater checks the appropriate place on the scale for each duty listed. More detail is then added by providing space for comments following each factor rated.

There are some obvious drawbacks to the graphic rating scale. Often separate traits or factors are grouped together and the rater is given only

Figure 11–5. Sample performance appraisal form.

Date sent _____   Return by _____

Name _____   Job title _____

Department _____   Supervisor _____

Full time _____ Part time _____ Date of Hire _____

Period _____ From _____ to _____

Reason for appraisal (check one): Discharge _____

Regular interval _____ Probationary _____ Counseling only _____

_____
_____

Major job duties:

Job duty 1: _____

Lowest		Satisfactory		Highest
1	2	3	4	5

Explanation _____
_____
_____

Job duty 2: _____

Lowest		Satisfactory		Highest
1	2	3	4	5

Explanation _____
_____
_____

Job duty 3: _____

Lowest		Satisfactory		Highest
1	2	3	4	5

Explanation _____
_____
_____

Job duty 4: _____

Lowest		Satisfactory		Highest
1	2	3	4	5

Explanation _____
_____
_____

Attendance:

Lowest		Satisfactory		Highest
1	2	3	4	5

During rating period, number of absences _____

Comments: _____
_____
_____

Figure 11–5.   (continued).

OVERALL:
Consider a general view of the employee's job performance during the rating period:

Lowest		Satisfactory		Highest
1	2	3	4	5

Explanation _____

_____

_____

_____

_____

_____

Areas of Improvement: Please identify 2 or 3 areas in which the employee needs to improve. Also note specifically how the employee can make progress towards better performance: ____

_____

_____

_____

_____

Supervisor: _____   Date: _____

Please indicate the degree to which you agree or disagree with this performance rating.

Strongly agree	Mid Point	Strongly Disagree

Comments on your appraisal: _____

_____

_____

Employee signature _____   Date: _____

Director _____   Date _____
Comments _____

May not be reproduced without permission; Robert L. Mathis; Omaha, Nebraska.

one box to check. Another drawback is that descriptive words often used may have different meanings to different raters. Factors or categories such as "initiative" and "cooperation" are subject to many interpretations, especially when used in conjunction with words such as "outstanding," "average," or "poor."

Checklist.   The *checklist* is a simple rating method in which the manager is given a list of statements or words and asked to check statements representing the characteristics and performance of each employee. The checklist can be modified so that varying weights can be assigned to the statements or words. The results can then be quantified. Usually the weights are not known by the rating supervisor, but by someone else, such as a member of the personnel unit.

The difficulties with the checklist are: (1) as with the graphic rating scale, the words or statements may have different meanings to different raters; (2) the rater cannot readily discern the rating results if a weighted checklist is used; and (3) the rater does not assign the weights to each factor. These three difficulties limit the use of the information by a rater when discussing the rating with the employee. Thus, effective developmental counseling may be difficult.

Forced Choice.   The *forced choice* technique is a more complex version of the checklist. The rater is required to check two of four statements: one that the employee is "most like" and one that the employee is "least like." The items are usually a mixture of positive and negative statements. The intent is to eliminate or greatly reduce the rater's personal bias.

The difficulty of constructing and validating the statements is the major limitation of the forced choice method, especially for a relatively small organization. This method is also more difficult to explain in an appraisal interview than some other methods. Figure 11–6 shows an example of a forced choice item.

Figure 11–6.   Sample forced choice item.

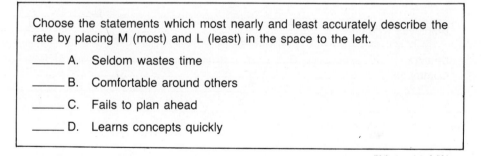

Choose the statements which most nearly and least accurately describe the rate by placing M (most) and L (least) in the space to the left.

_____ A.   Seldom wastes time

_____ B.   Comfortable around others

_____ C.   Fails to plan ahead

_____ D.   Learns concepts quickly

Comparative Methods

Another group of methods requires that managers directly compare the performances of their employees against each other. These techniques include *ranking, paired comparison,* and *forced distribution.* A key-punch operator's performance would be compared to other keypunch operators' by the computing supervisor as a part of appraisal.

Ranking.   The *ranking* method is relatively simple. The rater simply lists all his or her subordinates from highest to lowest in one total listing. With ten employees, they are ranked 1 through 10—best to poorest.

The primary drawback to the ranking method is that the size of the differences between individuals are not well defined. For example, there may be little difference in performance between individuals ranked second and third, but a big difference in performance between those ranked third and fourth. This can be overcome to some extent by assigning points to show the size of the gaps existing between employees.

Ranking also means that someone must be *last*. It is possible that the last-ranked individual in one group would be the top employee in a different group. Further, the basis for ranking could include rater bias or varying performance standards.

Paired Comparison   The rater using the *paired comparison* method formally compares each employee with every other employee in the rating group one at a time. The number of comparisons can be calculated using the formula $N(N - 1)/2$, where N is the number of people rated. For example, a manager with 15 subordinates would have to make 105 different comparisons on each rating factor. Use of the paired comparison method provides more information about individual employees than the straight ranking method. Obviously, the large number of comparisons that must be made is the major drawback of this method.

Forced Distribution.   The *forced distribution* method compares subordinates and overcomes the drawback involved in the paired comparison method. Using the forced distribution method, a head nurse ranks subordinate nursing personnel along a scale, placing a certain percentage of employees at various performance levels. This method assumes that the widely known "bell-shaped curve" of performance exists in a given group. Figure 11–7 shows a scale that was used with a forced distribution.

Figure 11–7.   Forced distribution on a bell-shaped curve.

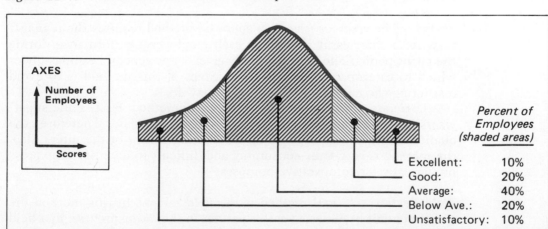

A drawback to forced distribution is that a supervisor may resist placing any individual in the lowest (or in the highest) group. Difficulties can arise when the rater must explain to the employee why he or she was placed in one grouping and others were placed in higher groupings. Further, with small groups there may be no reason to assume that a bell-shaped distribution of performance really exists.

Written Methods

Another group of methods requires a manager or a personnel specialist to provide written appraisal information. Documentation and description form the essence of the *critical incident*, the *essay*, and the *field review* methods.

Critical Incident. The *critical incident* method is slightly different from the previous methods because it is more a recording of employee actions than an actual rating. The manager keeps a written record of the highly favorable and highly unfavorable actions in an employee's performance. When something happens (a critical incident involving the employee), the manager writes it down. A list of critical incidents is kept during the entire rating period for each employee. Because the critical incident method does not necessarily have to be a rating system, it can be used with other methods as documentation of the reasons why an employee was rated a certain way.

There are several drawbacks to using the critical incident method. First, what is a critical incident is not always interpreted the same way by all supervisors. Next, daily or weekly writing about each employee's performance takes a lot of time. Further, the critical incident method can result in employees becoming concerned about what the superior writes about them. Employees may begin to fear the manager's "black book."

Essays. The *essay* or *free-form* appraisal method requires the manager to write a short essay describing each employee's performance during the rating period. The rater is usually given a few general headings under which to categorize comments. The intent of this method is to avoid restricting the rater as other methods may do.

There are some drawbacks to the essay method. First, some supervisors communicate in writing better than others do. Therefore, the quality of the ratings depends on the writing ability of the rater. Also, the method is very time-consuming and difficult to quantify or express numerically for comparative purposes.

Field Review. A final method is the *field review.* In this method the personnel unit becomes an active partner in the rating process. In a field review a member of the personnel unit interviews the manager about each employee's performance. The personnel representative then compiles the notes of each interview into a rating for each employee. The rating is then reviewed by the supervisor for needed changes. This method assumes that the representative of the personnel unit knows enough about the job setting to guide supervisors into giving more accurate and thorough appraisals.

The major limitation of the field review method is that the personnel representative has a large amount of control over the rating. While this control may be desirable from one viewpoint, supervisors may see this method as challenging their managerial authority. Some managers may "interpret" the information given the personnel specialist. In addition, the field review method can be very time-consuming, particularly if a supervisor has a large number of employees to be rated.

What are various appraisal methods?

RATER ERRORS

There are many sources for error in performance appraisal. One of the major sources is mistakes made by the rater. There is no single way to eliminate these, but making raters aware of them is very helpful.

Varying Standards Problem

When appraising employees, a manager should try to avoid using different standards and expectations for different employees performing similar jobs. For example, a student who received a lower grade than another student might become irate about the unfairness of the grading. The same reaction occurs when employees believe their boss uses different standards in appraising each individual's performance.

Even if an employee has actually been appraised on the same basis as other employees, the employee's perception is key. If Joe Batista, a student, felt a professor had graded his exam harder than another student's exam, he might ask the professor for an explanation. The student's opinion might not be changed by the professor's claim that he had "graded fairly." So it is with performance appraisals in a work situation. If performance appraisal information is to be useful, the rater must use the same standards and weights for every employee and be able to defend the appraisal.

Recency Problem

The recency problem occurs in appraisal when recent performance is given greater weight. Examples are giving a student a course grade based upon only performance in the last week of class or giving a drill press operator a high rating even though he made the quota only in the last two weeks of the rating period.

The recency problem is an understandable rater error because of the difficulty in remembering performance that is two or three months old. Also, employees become more concerned about their performance and behavior as formal appraisal time approaches. Some employees may attempt to take advantage of the recency problem by "apple polishing" their boss shortly before an appraisal is to be completed.

Rater Bias

Another error occurs when a rater's values, beliefs, or prejudices distort the ratings given. If John Annis, manager of a machine section in a tool plant, has strong dislikes for persons of certain races, this bias is likely to result in distorted appraisal information for some people. Age, religion, sex, appearance, or other arbitrary classifications may be reflected in appraisals if the appraisal process is not properly designed.

Rater bias is very difficult to overcome, especially if a manager is not aware or will not admit such bias is affecting appraisals. Examination of ratings by higher level managers may help this problem.

Rater Patterns

Students are well aware that some professors tend to grade more easily than other professors. Likewise, a manager may develop a similar "rating pattern." For example, Dolores Bressler, office manager, tends to rate all her employees as average or above. Even the poor performers receive an average rating from Dolores. However, Jane Carr, the billing supervisor, believes that if employees are poor performers, they should be rated below average. An employee reporting to Jane who is rated average may well be a better performer than one rated average by Dolores.

Another rater pattern is for appraisers to rate all employees within a narrow range (for example giving class grades which are nearly all Bs), regardless of actual differences in performance by the employees. This type of error is the *central tendency* error.

Rater pattern errors are often the result of the reluctance of a superior to give a low appraisal. Appraisers generally find evaluating others difficult, especially if negative evaluations must be given. In the same way, a professor experiences more uneasiness and reservation when having to give a student a course grade of F rather than B.

Making an appraiser aware that he or she has fallen into a pattern is one way to deal with the problem. Also, including precise and explicit definitions of categories on the rating form and allowing for considerable rating spread on each item are other means of handling rater patterns.

Halo Effect.   The halo effect occurs when a manager rates an employee high or low on all items because of one characteristic. For example, if a worker has few absences, his supervisor might give the worker a high rating in all other areas of work, including quantity and quality of output, because of the dependability, without really thinking about other characteristics separately. Giving a management trainee a high rating because she is attractive would also be a halo effect.

Halo effect

An appraisal that shows the same rating on all characteristics may be evidence of the halo effect. Clearly specifying the categories to be rated, rating all employees on one characteristic at a time, and training raters are means of dealing with the halo effect.

Can you discuss errors in appraisals?

THE APPRAISAL FEEDBACK INTERVIEW

Once appraisals have been made on employees, it is important that they be communicated. The results should be discussed with employees so that they have a clear understanding of how they stand in the eyes of the immediate superior and the organization. In the appraisal interview emphasis should be placed on counseling and development, not solely on telling the employee, "Here is how you rate and why." Focusing on development provides an opportunity to consider the employee's performance and its improvement.

Common Concerns

The appraisal interview presents both an opportunity and a difficult situation. It is an emotional experience for the manager and the employee. The manager must communicate both praise and constructive criticism. A major concern is how to emphasize the positive aspects of the employee's performance while still discussing ways to make needed improvements. If the interview is handled poorly, the manager should realize that resentment and conflict may result and will likely be reflected in future work.

Employees commonly approach an appraisal interview with some concern. They often perceive that performance discussions are very personal and important to their continued job success. At the same time they want to know how the manager feels they have been doing. Criticisms of performance may be taken as direct personal indictments of the individual and not just as a discussion about performance. Thus, Ralph Nagel, a bank teller, may see constructive criticisms as a commentary on his inadequacies as a person, and not a commentary on weaknesses in his performance as a bank teller.

It is fairly common for organizations to *require* that managers discuss appraisals with employees. One survey of 150 organizations found that approximately 97% of the surveyed firms required an appraisal interview.[4] Figure 11–8 summarizes hints for an effective interview.

Figure 11–8. Hints for the appraisal interview.

DO	DON'T
Prepare in advance	"Lecture" the employee
Focus on performance and development	Mix performance appraisal and salary or promotion issues
Be specific about reasons for ratings	Concentrate only on the negative
Decide on specific steps to be taken for improvement	Do all the talking
Consider your role in the subordinate's performance	Be overly critical or "harp" on a failing
Reinforce the behavior you want	Feel it's necessary that you agree on everything
Focus on the future performance	Compare the employee to others

Reactions to Performance Appraisal

The reaction of students to grades and tests (which are both forms of performance appraisal) illustrates the emotional and behavioral nature of appraisal. Students are typically very concerned with the equity of the grading process and the criteria on which they will be evaluated. Like students, employees are concerned about the fairness, consistency, and usefulness of appraisals.

Reactions of Managers.   Managers and supervisors who must complete appraisals on their employees often resist the appraisal process. The manager may feel he or she is "put in the position of playing God." Also, a major part of a manager's role is to assist, encourage, coach, and counsel subordinates to improve their performances. However, being a judge on one hand and a coach and counselor on the other causes the manager internal conflict and confusion.

The fact that appraisals may affect an employee's future career may cause raters to alter or bias their ratings. This bias is even more likely when managers know that they will have to communicate and defend their ratings to the employees, their bosses, or personnel specialists. From the manager's viewpoint, providing negative feedback to an employee in an appraisal interview can be easily avoided by making the employee's rating positive.

Reactions such as these are attempts to avoid unpleasantness in an interpersonal situation. Eventually this avoidance helps no one. A manager owes employees a well thought-out appraisal.

Reactions of the Appraised Employees.   A common reaction by employees is to view appraising as a zero-sum game (there must be a winner and a loser). Employees may well see the appraisal process as a threat and feel the only way to get a higher rating is for someone else to receive a low rating. This win-lose perception is encouraged by comparative methods of rating.

Appraisals can be both zero-sum and non- zero-sum (both parties win and no one loses) in nature. Emphasis on the developmental and self-improvement aspects of appraisal appears to be the most effective means to reduce some of the zero-sum reactions of those involved in the appraisal process.

Another common employee reaction can be related to the way students view tests. Simply because a professor prepares a test he or she feels is fair, it does not necessarily follow that the students will feel the test is fair. They simply see it differently. Likewise, employees being appraised will not necessarily agree with the manager doing the actual appraising.

These reactions of appraised employees highlight some of the behavior resulting from appraisal. Such reactions become important considerations as appraisal systems are developed, implemented, and operated.

What are some appraisal feedback concerns?

SPECIAL APPRAISAL SYSTEMS: BARS AND MBO

Two special attempts made to overcome some of the difficulties associated with appraisal are *Behaviorally Anchored Rating Scales* (BARS) and *Management By Objectives* (MBO). BARS seems to hold promise for situations in which many people are doing the same job and MBO is useful for management appraisals.

Behaviorally Anchored Rating Scales

A BARS system is designed to overcome the problems of category methods by describing examples of good or bad behavior. These examples are "anchored" against a scale of performance levels. Figure 11–9 shows a BARS for a college professor's attitude toward students. What constitutes various levels of performance is clearly defined in the figure. Spelling out the behavior associated with each level of performance helps minimize some of the problems noted earlier.

Figure 11–9. Behaviorally Anchored Rating Scale for professor's attitude toward students.

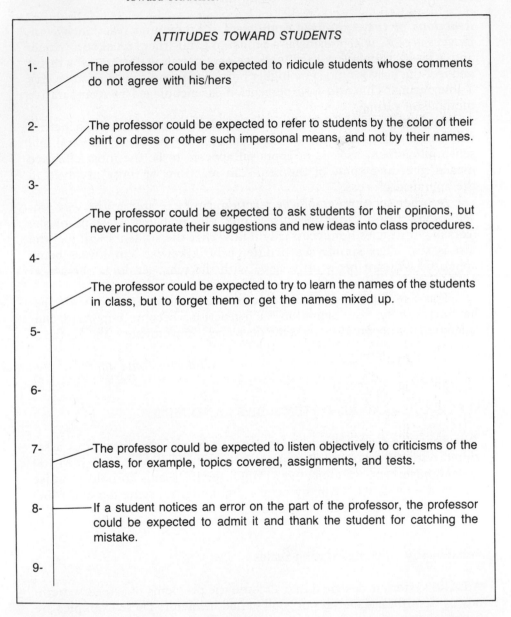

ATTITUDES TOWARD STUDENTS

1- The professor could be expected to ridicule students whose comments do not agree with his/hers

2- The professor could be expected to refer to students by the color of their shirt or dress or other such impersonal means, and not by their names.

3-

The professor could be expected to ask students for their opinions, but never incorporate their suggestions and new ideas into class procedures.

4-

The professor could be expected to try to learn the names of the students in class, but to forget them or get the names mixed up.

5-

6-

7- The professor could be expected to listen objectively to criticisms of the class, for example, topics covered, assignments, and tests.

8- If a student notices an error on the part of the professor, the professor could be expected to admit it and thank the student for catching the mistake.

9-

Constructing BARS. Construction of a BARS begins by identifying the important *job dimensions* associated with the job. These are the most important performance factors in an employee's job description. To continue with our college professor example, assume the major job dimensions associated with *teaching* are:

1. Course organization
2. Attitude toward students
3. Fair treatment
4. Competence in area.

Short statements such as critical incidents describing both good and bad behavior (anchors) are generated and are then "retranslated" or assigned to one of the job dimensions. This task is usually a group project and assignment to a dimension usually requires 60%–70% of the group to agree. The group then assigns each "anchor" a number representing how good or bad the behavior is. When numbered these anchors are fitted to a scale. Figure 11–10 shows a flow diagram of the construction process.

Figure 11–10.   Flow diagram of BARS construction.

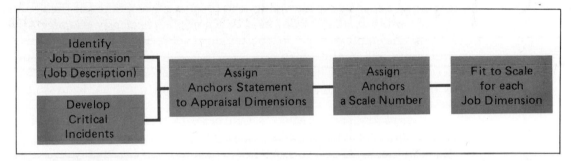

BARS require more time and effort to develop and maintain. They also require several appraisal forms to accommodate different types of jobs in an organization. In a hospital, nurses, dieticians, and admission clerks all have different jobs, and would require the development of separate BARS forms for each.

BARS represent an emerging area of research and application. However, there are enough problems and unanswered questions remaining to indicate that BARS may not represent the ultimate objective, job-related appraisal system.[5]

How are BARS constructed?

Management by Objectives

A system of "guided self-appraisal" called *Management by Objectives* (MBO) is useful in appraising managers' performance. Disenchantment with the previously discussed approaches for managers has increased

MBO's popularity. Other names for MBO include *appraisal by results, targeting-coaching, work planning and review program, performance objectives,* and *mutual goal setting.*

MBO specifies the results and performance goals an individual hopes to attain within an appropriate length of time. The objectives each manager sets are derived from the overall goals and objectives of the organization. Workable MBO should not be a disguised means for a superior to dictate the objectives individual managers or employees set for themselves.

Key MBO Ideas.   Three key ideas underlie an MBO appraisal system. First, if an employee is really involved in planning and setting the objectives, a higher level of commitment and performance may result. Instead of having the standards and ratings set by some other person, in MBO the employee plays the key role in setting the standards and determining the measurement scheme. Employee participation in determining the goals is believed to lead to greater acceptance of the goals.

Second, if what an employee is to accomplish is clearly and precisely defined, the employee will do a better job of achieving the desired results. Ambiguity and confusion may arise when superiors determine the objectives for an individual and may result in less effective performance. By having the employee set objectives, he or she gains an accurate understanding of what is expected.

A third key part of MBO is that performance objectives should be measurable and define results. Figure 11–11 contains some sample objectives. Vague generalities such as "initiative" or "cooperation" common in many superior-based appraisals should be avoided. MBO objectives are specific actions to be taken or work to be accomplished.

Figure 11–11.   Sample objectives for MBO.

> "Submit completed regional sales report no later than the third of every month."
> "Obtain orders from at least five new customers per month."
> "To maintain payroll costs at 10% of sales volume."
> "Have scrap loss less than 5%."
> "Fill all organizational vacancies within 30 days after openings occur."

The MBO Process.   Implementing the guided self-appraisal system using MBO is a four-stage process. These phases are common, regardless of the title of a guided self-appraisal system. The four stages are shown in Figure 11–12 and discussed next.

Figure 11–12. MBO process.

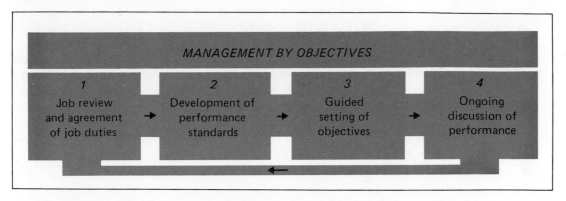

1. *Job Review and Agreement.* The employee and the superior review the job description and key activities comprising the employee's job. The idea is to agree on the exact make-up of the employee's job.

2. *Development of Performance Standards.* Specific standards of performance must be mutually developed. This phase specifies a satisfactory level of performance that is specific and measurable. For example, a salesperson's quota to sell five cars per month may be an appropriate performance standard. Selling that number of cars can be measured and is a satisfactory level of performance.

3. *Guided Objective Setting.* Objectives are established by the employee in conjunction with, and guided by, the superior. Continuing the example of the automobile salesperson, an objective might be set to challenge the employee to improve performance; the salesperson might set a new objective of selling six cars per month. Notice that the objective set may be different from the performance standard. Objectives should be set so that attainment is realistically possible.

4. *On-going Performance Discussions.* The employee and the superior use the objectives as bases for continuing discussions about the employee's performance. While a formal review session may be scheduled, the employee and the manager do not necessarily wait until the appointed time for performance discussions. Objectives are mutually modified and progress is discussed during the period.

What is MBO?

MBO Critique. No management tool is perfect, and MBO has been criticized. One of the most important cautions is that MBO is not appropriate for all employees or all organizations. Jobs with little or no flexibility, such as assembly-line work, are not compatible with MBO. An assembly-line worker usually has so little job flexibility that the performance standards and objectives are already determined. The MBO process seems to be most useful with managerial personnel and employees who have a fairly wide range of flexibility and self-control in their jobs.

Additionally, MBO may be seen as a disguised means for managerial manipulation since it requires a climate which supports openness and a mutual orientation. When imposed upon a rigid and autocratic management system, MBO may fail. Extreme emphasis on penalties for not meeting objectives defeats the developmental and participative nature of MBO.

What are some criticisms of MBO?

PERFORMANCE APPRAISAL AND THE LAW

Discussions of appraisal techniques often emphasize orderly gathering and recording of appraisal information. While this "record-keeping" aspect is useful and important, legal limitations must be considered when designing and using a performance appraisal system.

A growing number of court decisions have focused on performance appraisals, particularly as they relate to equal opportunity concerns. Guidelines issued by the Equal Employment Opportunity Commission (EEOC) and other federal enforcement agencies make it clear that performance appraisals must be job-related and non-discriminatory.

Court Cases and Appraisals

It may seem somewhat odd to emphasize that performance appraisals must be job-related because appraisals are supposed to measure how well employees are doing their jobs. Yet in numerous cases courts have ruled that performance appraisals in use by organizations were discriminatory and were not job-related. Three important cases are summarized below.

Brito v. Zia Company (1973). In this case, Zia Company used appraisal scores to determine which workers would be laid off; those with low performance appraisals were laid off. However, the court found that a disproportionate number of workers in protected classes were laid off. The court stated that appraisals were "tests" and subject to validation against the job duties the workers performed. Also, the court stated that appraisals were "not administered and scored under controlled and standardized conditions."[6]

Albemarle Paper v. Moody (1975). In this case, the U.S. Supreme Court again held that performance appraisals are "tests" that are subject to EEOC guidelines. There were two important issues in this case related to performance appraisal: *subjective supervisory ratings* and the *absence of job analysis.*

The problem of subjective supervisory ratings in appraisal is captured by the following quote from the court decision:

> There is no way of knowing precisely what criteria of job
> performance the supervisors were considering, whether each
> of the supervisors was considering the same criteria—or
> whether, indeed, any of the supervisors actually applied a
> focused and stable body of criteria of any kind.[7]

U.S. v. City of Chicago (1976). In this case, the courts found that the performance appraisal systems used by the Chicago Police Department discriminated against blacks and Hispanics. Also, the officer and sergeant exams were found to be discriminatory. The court ruled that "supervisory ratings are not a fair measurement of an employee's suitability for promotion."[8] The city was also prohibited from using tests or the appraisal system and was forced to hire nonminorities according to a court-established quota system until nondiscriminatory instruments could be developed.

A Legal Performance Appraisal System

By investigating existing case law, the elements of a performance appraisal system which can be expected to hold up in court can be determined:[9]

1. Absence of adverse impact evidence *or* presence of validity evidence.
2. Formal evaluation criteria that limit a manager's absolute discretion on appraisal.
3. Personal knowledge and contact with the person whose work is being rated.
4. A review process which prevents one manager acting alone from controlling an employee's career.

It is clear that the courts have had an interest in seeing that performance appraisal is both fair and nondiscriminatory. Employers must decide how to design their appraisal systems for the courts, enforcement agencies, and the employees.[10]

What is included in a legal appraisal system?

AN EFFECTIVE PERFORMANCE APPRAISAL SYSTEM

Regardless of the performance appraisal system in use, it is the understanding of what appraisal is supposed to do that makes or breaks the system. When performance appraisal is used for development of the employee as a resource it usually works. When management uses it as a whip or fails to understand its limitations, it fails. The key is *not* which form is used or which method. Performance appraisal depends upon managers' understanding of its purposes. In its simplest form it is a manager saying "Here are your strengths and weaknesses, and here is a way to shore up the weak areas."[11]

Training of Appraisers

Because appraisal is important and sometimes difficult, training of appraisers is valuable. Providing managers and supervisors with some insights and ideas on rating, documenting appraisals, and making appraisal interviews increases the value and acceptance of an appraisal program. As Figure 11–13 illustrates, the results of a survey of 216 organizations revealed that many supervisors have had little appraisal training. Training appraisers gives them confidence in their abilities to make appraisals and handle appraisal interviews. Training and performance appraisal share many common elements. It has been suggested that the training section of some personnel departments may be uniquely suited to overseeing performance appraisal in large organizations.[12]

What makes an effective performance appraisal system?

Figure 11–13.   Appraiser training.

Appraiser Training	None	Initial	Refresher	
Small Organizations	54	24	22	%
Large Organizations	56	17	27	%

(Source: Alan H. Locher and Kenneth S. Teel, "Performance Appraisal—A Survey of Current Practices," *Personnel Journal*, 56, May 1977, pp. 245–247 +. Reprinted with permission *Personnel Journal*, copyright May 1977.)

REVIEW AND PREVIEW

Appraising employee performance is vital in any organization. It not only allows managers to improve the level of performance in the organization, but it provides a basis for employees to improve themselves and their chances for career advancement.

Appraisal can take many forms; some are better suited to certain situations than others. The approaches can be classified into categories based upon who is doing the appraising: subordinates, groups of superiors, or peers. Three methods are available: *category-rating methods* such as graphic rating scales and checklists; *comparative methods* such as ranking, paired comparison, and forced choice; *written methods* such as critical incidents, essay, and field review. Behaviorally Anchored Rating Scales (BARS) and guided self-appraisal (MBO) are special approaches for special situations.

Review Questions

1. What are the three major uses that can be made of appraisals?
2. What are the three basic approaches to appraisal? Which method would you prefer as an employee? As a manager? Why?
3. Suppose you are a supervisor. What would be your concerns in appraising your employees?
4. Identify three rating errors.
5. Construct a plan for a post-appraisal interview with an employee who has performed poorly.
6. What are BARS and MBO? Identify some problems with each.
7. Discuss the following statement: "Most performance appraisal systems in use today would not pass legal scrutiny."
8. Your boss asks you to develop an appraisal system. How would you proceed?

Case: Congratulations, and Welcome Back?

Janet Janousek joined the Customer Information section of a large manufacturing company as a secretary in December 1978. Janet's transfer to Customer Information came after a previous transfer from the Market Analysis section to the Sales Department in an attempt to improve her performance.

On November 1, 1979, Janet was given a performance appraisal. The appraisal followed counseling sessions on July 3, 1979, July 30, 1979, and September 15, 1979, as well as numerous sessions between January 1979 and July 1979. The November appraisal indicated that Janet appeared to be making improvements in her job performance; however, her performance again deteriorated, as noted by her performance appraisal in January 1980.

Her supervisor felt that Janet's poor performance was related to her personal affairs, which led to a number of activities felt to be incompatible with the efficient and effective operation of the office. The supervisor noted such activities as the following: spends an inordinate amount of time making personal telephone calls; relates her personal problems to other employees in the office; appears preoccupied with her personal problems; and frequently reports to work in a very tired state.

The supervisor felt that Janet possessed positive attributes. She had the education and skills that matched well with her secretarial duties. She worked quickly when the task was clearly stenographic. The supervisor also observed that Janet's poor performance may have been a result of her pregnancy.

It was clear to the supervisor that Janet's problems at work were related to her personal affairs and that she did not have the ability to adapt rapidly to "uncertain environments" in which resourcefulness and initiative are required. On March 4, 1980, Janet left the company on a maternity leave of absence. The supervisor has just received word that Janet gave birth to a 7 pound, 6 ounce baby boy, and wants to return to work in six weeks.

QUESTIONS

1. What problems existed in this case?
2. Were additional courses of action open to the supervisor in order for Janet to improve her performance?
3. In what ways does the fact that the employee is a woman and pregnant affect the appraisal and the supervisor's choice of action?
4. As the supervisor, what would you do?

NOTES

1. Alan H. Locher and Kenneth S. Teel, "Performance Appraisal—A Survey of Current Practices," *Personnel Journal*, 56, May 1977, pp. 245–247 +.

2. Ibid.

3. Kenneth S. Teel, "Performance Appraisal: Current Trends, Persistent Progress," *Personnel Journal*, 59, April 1980, p. 301.

4. *Employee Performance: Evaluation and Control*, PPF #108, February 1975, p. 6 (Washington, D.C.: The Bureau of National Affairs).

5. For a review of BARS literature, see: Gary P. Latham and Kenneth N. Wexley, *Increasing Productivity Through Performance Appraisal* (Reading, MA: Addison-Wesley, 1981), pp. 51–64.

6. *Brito* v. *Zia Company*, 478 F2d. 1200 (1973).

7. *Albermarle Paper Co.* v. *Moody*, 74-389 (1975).

8. *U.S.* v. *City of Chicago*, 549 F2d 415 (1977) *Cert. denied* 434 US 875 (1977).

9. P. Linnenberger and T. J. Keaveny, "Performance Appraisal: Standards Used by the Courts," *Faculty Research Paper, The University of Wyoming* No. 317, January 1980, p. 9.

10. C. R. Klasson, D. E. Thompson, and G. L. Luben, "How Defensible is Your Performance Appraisal System?" *Personnel Administrator*, December 1980, p. 80.

11. P. J. McGuire, "Why Performance Appraisals Fail," *Personnel Journal*, 59, September 1980, p. 745.

12. R. B. McAfee, "Performance Appraisal: Whose Function?" *Personnel Journal*, 60, April 1981, p. 298.

CHAPTER. 12

Compensating Jobs and Work

When you read this chapter, you should be able to:

1. Identify the three meanings of compensation for employees.
2. Discuss the pay secrecy issue.
3. List the key provisions of the basic laws dealing with compensation.
4. Contrast and compare the time and productivity bases of compensation.
5. Define job evaluation and its purposes.
6. Explain briefly four methods of job evaluation.
7. Identify the stages involved in developing a pay system.

The Campus Store

The Campus Store is one of 15 stores in a chain of stores located in major university towns across the country. The home office of the Campus Store is located 800 miles away. This office handles most of the bookkeeping and payroll paperwork for all the stores in the company. Because the company operates nationwide, the stores are all subject to the federal wage and hour laws.

The home office has a company policy that the payroll figures for each store must not exceed 10% of a store's gross sales. Because the Campus Store is only two years old, its payroll has been running 12%. The home office usually allows each new store a two-year grace period before it demands that the 10% figure be met. The Campus Store must meet the 10% figure during the current year.

It is now February 1. The federal wage law required the company to raise the minimum wage on January 1. When the new wage law took effect, the wages of all employees who made above the minimum originally were raised to achieve the same relative level. The increased wage level resulted in the monthly payroll figure for the Campus Store jumping to 12.3% of gross sales.

In addition, the home office has a company policy of paying the minimum wage for six months, and then giving a raise if warranted. Because of this policy, the store has an extremely high turnover rate within the first year of an employee's service to the store. The store manager who must deal with the problems feels that if he cut the number of employees necessary to get down to the 10% ratio between payroll to sales, there will be a drop in service, more shoplifting, and lower sales.

Comments:

The problems in this case are severe because of the local manager's lack of control over the wages employees can be initially offered. Thus his ability to deal with the higher turnover and to keep trained employees is reduced. The federal minimum-wage increase should be taken into consideration by the home office as a factor over which managers have no control. Also, the wage structure in the area might be different from the wage structure in the home office area or in other areas of the country. One would hope that the logical arguments against current compensation policies would cause the home office to change them. Without significant changes, the store will continue to experience problems.

COMPENSATION costs are significant expenditures in most firms. As the opening case illustrates, compensation policies and practices may also be one of the biggest headaches for managers and personnel specialists. At one Norfolk, Virginia, hotel, the Omni employee payroll and social benefits compose about 50% of all costs of doing business. Group insurance costs increased over $120,000 in three years and the hotel's part of employee social security contributions increased $75,000.[1]

Figure 12–1.   Formal compensation components.

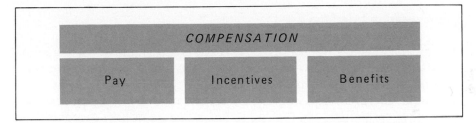

TYPES OF COMPENSATION

Formal compensation can be offered using three types of rewards (see Figure 12–1). Pay refers to the base wages and salaries employees receive. Compensation forms such as bonuses, commissions, and profit-sharing plans are designed to give employees an incentive to produce results. Health insurance, vacation pay, or retirement pensions are examples of benefits.

PAY is the basic compensation employees receive, usually a wage or salary.

INCENTIVES are rewards designed to encourage and reimburse employees for efforts beyond normal performance expectations.

> BENEFITS are rewards available to employees or a group of employees as a part of organizational membership.

This chapter deals with issues in the overall compensation process and the basic pay employees receive. Because incentives and benefits are special types of compensation, they are discussed in a separate chapter, chapter 13.

Compensation Interface

A typical compensation interface is illustrated in Figure 12–2. Personnel specialists usually guide the overall development and administration of an organization's compensation system by conducting job evaluations and wage surveys. Also, because of the technical complexity involved, personnel specialists are typically the ones to develop incentive and benefit systems. On the other hand, managers try to match employees' efforts with rewards, using the job evaluation and wage survey information as guidelines when recommending pay rates and pay increases. Much managerial activity goes into monitoring employee attendance and productivity. Because time and/or productivity are the bases for compensation, this monitoring is a vital part of any manager's job.

Figure 12–2.   Compensation interface.

Personnel Unit	Managers
Develops and administers compensation system	Attempt to match performance and rewards
Conducts job evaluation and wage survey	Recommend pay rates and pay increases
Develops incentive and benefit systems	Monitor attendance and productivity for pay and incentive compensation

BEHAVIORAL ASPECTS OF COMPENSATION

People work to gain rewards for their efforts. An employee's motivation is closely related to the compensation rewards given, whether the rewards are pay, benefits, or internal satisfaction. The behavioral dimensions of compensation cannot be separated from the process, nor can they be ignored by managers. When people work they expect to receive fair value (that is, equity) for their labors. This perception of fair value, briefly described in chapter 3, has a significant impact on the satisfaction and performance of employees. By exchanging their labors and talents for rewards, employees are induced to continue contributing to the organization.

Meaning of Compensation to Employees

The basic compensation or pay employees receive is often a prime reason for working. With the pay received, the necessities and luxuries of life in a modern society are bought. However, compensation usually has several other meanings to employees. There are three basic areas in which compensation has meaning: *economic, psychosocial, and growth.*

Economic. The *economic* meaning of base pay is the most obvious because pay serves as a way of obtaining the necessities and luxuries people need and want. Relatively few people have an independent source of income through inheritance, accumulation, or illegal action (such as bank robbery). Some disadvantaged individuals who are unable to work, or a few individuals who choose not to work, receive money from government agencies. For most people, however, employment in organizations is the way to obtain economic resources which can be exchanged for such items as food, a house, a car, clothes, furniture, vacations, and countless other goods and services.

Psychosocial. A second meaning of compensation is *psychosocial* in nature. Pay and other types of compensation provide means for "keeping score" and the psychological satisfaction of achievement. If Ed Schwinn receives a raise, he may see his change in compensation as recognition for his efforts and he may derive a sense of achievement from his work. This internal satisfaction may mean more to him than what he can buy with the additional money. Conversely, the absence of adequate compensation may cause Ed to become discouraged or dissatisfied. One author suggests that research on pay indicates that the satisfaction of psychological and social needs such as status, and recognition are affected by the pay a person receives.[2]

Status is the relative social ranking of a person to others. That compensation acts as a status symbol is well-known. As confirmed by research, people compare their base pay to determine how they "rank" in the social structure. As a measure of status, compensation gives highly rewarded individuals high social standing and importance. This relative "ranking" can significantly affect individuals' satisfaction, and possibly even their performance.[3]

Ranking can occur within work groups. A division manager might compare her pay to that of other employees in the division and with other division managers. She may be satisfied with her pay when comparing it to other division managers. Or, she may feel that, based on pay, there are higher status and lower status division managers.

Growth. Compensation is also a means to *growth and motivation.* From the viewpoint of the organization, people are compensated for performance. It is to be hoped that compensation can be used as one measure of how well employees have grown in their performance and capabilities. It can also serve as a means for motivating higher performance. Increased compensation can serve as a goal for which people will strive if they see that greater effort brings the increased pay, and if they want the increased pay.[4] However, the amount of money that serves to motivate one employee to produce more may not motivate another employee.

What are the three meanings of compensation?

The various meanings that compensation can have for employees and managers alike are quite complex and have been subject to continuing research. The multifaceted nature of financial rewards is summarized well by the following statement from an unknown employee:

"Some people are rich and some are poor—rich is better!"

Figure 12–3. "Closed" vs. "Open" pay system.

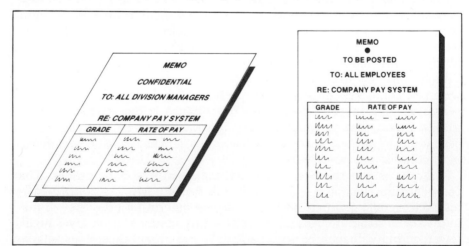

Pay Secrecy

Because comparison is such a critical part of the equity issue, some academicians and practicing managers have pointed out the need to provide pay information to employees. Pay information typically kept secret includes how much others make, what raises others have received, and the pay policies of the organization.

"Closed" Pay Systems.   One reason for secret or closed pay systems is the fear that open pay systems will create discontent, petty complaining, and tension. If an accountant knows for sure that he is paid less than another accountant, he may become dissatisfied and feel he is receiving "inequitable" treatment. Also, an open pay system forces managers to explain and justify pay differences. If there are not good reasons for the differences, personnel problems can increase.

"Open" Pay Systems.   A growing number of companies are opening up their pay systems to some degree. Some information that firms supply to employees includes compensation in policies, salary structures, a general description of the basis for the compensation system, and where an individual's pay is within a salary grade.[5] By being given pay information, employees do have the information needed to make more accurate equity comparisons. An open pay system requires that managers be able to explain satisfactorily any pay differences that exist. Consider this situation: You and a co-worker have the same education and length of service, but you feel you work harder than he does. When raises are awarded you both get exactly the same raise. You feel undercompensated. Your manager must be able to explain why you are paid the same or you may become more dissatisfied.

An open pay system provides the basis for discussion and accurate comparison. Research on pay secrecy has revealed that in some situations, open policies on pay are related to high motivation and performance. In other settings, open policies on pay have caused low satisfaction, low motivation, and conflict between managers and their employees. The implication is that an open pay system can be used if: (1) performance can be measured, (2) individuals work rather independently, and (3) there is a means to tie an individual's inputs and effort to the outputs and reward.[6]

To illustrate, pay openness between certain types of sales representatives might be appropriate. Sales representatives do have objective performance measures (amount of sales, number of customers contacted, etc.), they work independently, and their pay can be tied fairly closely to sales effort. Often, sales representatives are shown each month what the level of sales (and therefore commissions) of everyone in the sales group has been.

Policies that prohibit discussion of individual pay are likely to be violated. Co-workers do share pay information and may feel that an open pay system recognizes this fact. Also, by having the pay system explained in the open, distortions and other misinformation carried by the "grapevine" can be confronted. Managers should be aware of the pay secrecy issue and avoid keeping pay secret when it would be advantageous to use an open system.

What is pay secrecy vs. pay openness?

Behavioral Summary

The importance of the above behavioral dimensions of compensation should be evident. A manager who does not consider the meaning of compensation to employees, the perceived fairness (equity) of the compensation, and the pay secrecy issue cannot develop a sound compensation and personnel management.

LEGAL CONSTRAINTS ON COMPENSATION

Several legal constraints in the United States affect employee compensation and personnel management. Laws affecting minimum wage standards and hours of work are two important areas of governmental influence on compensation.

Fair Labor Standards Act of 1938

The major law on compensation is the Fair Labor Standards Act of 1938 (FLSA) and its amendments. This act has three major objectives: (1) establish a minimum-wage floor, (2) encourage limits on the number of weekly hours employees work through overtime provisions, (3) discourage oppressive child labor. The first two objectives are most relevant to current personnel management practices.

Minimum Wage. The FLSA set a minimum wage to be paid a broad spectrum of employees. Numerous groups were exempted from coverage under the 1938 Act. In 1966 the FLSA was amended to update the act and to include more employees and industries. Currently, most organizations and employees are covered, with the exception of executive, professional, and administrative personnel. Also, local and state government employees are not covered by the FLSA. The basic minimum wage effective January 1, 1981, is $3.35 per hour.

Overtime.   The FLSA also contains overtime pay requirements. Under the 1938 version and still in effect are provisions setting overtime pay at one and a half times the regular pay rate for all hours in excess of 40 per week except for executives, administrative, professional employees, and outside sales persons. Figure 12–4 contains a brief description of the administrative category abstracted from various government publications.

Figure 12–4.   FLSA category.

Administrative Employees

—Assume responsibility for office work related to management policies or general business operations

—Exercise discretion and independent judgment

—Provide assistance to executive or administrative employees

—Perform activities with minimal supervision

—Execute special assignments

—Devote no more than 20% of total hours worked to activities not related to managerial duties. (NOTE: 40% if employed by a retail or service establishment)

—Meet detailed salary/week earnings test levels identified in the law.

Source: *Executive, Administrative, Professional and Outside Sales Exemptions Under the Fair Labor Standards Act*, U.S. Department of Labor, Employment Standards Administration, Wage and Hour Division, W H Publication 1363, 1976.

The work week is defined as a consecutive period of 168 hours (24 hours × 7 days) and does not have to be a calendar week. Hospitals are allowed to use a 14-day period instead of the seven-day work week as long as overtime is paid for hours more than 80 in a 14-day period. Overtime provisions do not apply to farm workers, who also have a lower minimum wage schedule. No daily number of hours requiring overtime is set, except for special provisions relating to hospitals and other specially designated organizations. Thus, if a manufacturing firm has a four-day/ten-hour schedule, no overtime pay is required by the act.

Equal Pay Act of 1963 and "Comparable Worth"

As a part of amendments to the FLSA in 1963, 1968, and 1972, the Equal Pay Act is an attempt to prohibit wage discrimination on the basis of sex. As the Wage and Hour Division of the U.S. Labor Department states,

> The equal pay provisions of the FLSA prohibit wage
> differentials based on sex, between men and women
> employed in the same establishment on jobs that require
> equal skill, effort, and responsibility and which are
> performed under similar working conditions.[7]

Jobs must be "substantially" the same, but not necessarily identical. Pay differentials on the basis of merit or seniority are not prohibited if they are not based on sex discrimination. However, the "comparable worth" issue affects many pay policies and practices.

"Comparable Worth" Issue.   Although discussed in chapter 4 in detail, it seems appropriate to mention the issue here. To review, the concept of "comparable worth" is that jobs that require equal knowledge, skills, and abilities should be paid at comparable levels. Although it may be discriminatory to have such a situation, one view is that it is a reflection of the "going rate" for the jobs that creates the disparity, not discriminatory actions by an employer who "follows the market." Nevertheless, the ruling in the *County of Washington* v. *Gunther*[8] case did not clarify the situation and employers should be mindful of future cases and rulings when developing pay systems.

The lower pay that women have traditionally received for the same jobs that men perform can no longer be justified on the basis of future promotability. Paying a man more because the employer believes the man has a greater possibility of staying with the organization is not allowed. In the past some felt women should be paid less because they might quit to marry, become pregnant, or have to move because their spouses were transferred, but such concerns, even if true, cannot be used to justify pay differences.

The costs of settling claims under this act can have a significant financial impact on an employer. One Midwestern department store chain (whose identity is withheld to protect the guilty) was assessed $750,000 in back pay for paying women who managed women's ready-to-wear departments less than male managers of men's wear departments.

Walsh-Healey Act of 1936

Many of the provisions of the Walsh-Healey Act of 1936 were incorporated into the FLSA passed two years later. However, the Walsh-Healey

Act requires companies with *federal supply contracts* exceeding $10,000 to pay a minimum wage. This act applies only to those working directly on the contract or who substantially affect its performance. For example, if a company has a contract to supply shoes to the Army, those employees directly involved in making and supplying the shoes have to be paid a minimum wage. Executive, administrative, and maintenance employees are not covered by the act.

A difference between the Walsh-Healey Act and the FLSA is that the former requires overtime payment for hours over eight per day or 40 per week, but the latter requires overtime pay only for those over 40 per week and includes no clause about number of daily hours. As Figure 12–5 shows, an employee working on a federal contract with a four-day/ten-hour schedule would have to be paid overtime for two hours per day under the Walsh-Healey Act, even though the weekly hours would be kept to 40 hours.

Figure 12–5. Wage calculations.

Employee David Tomeski	Regular Pay Rate $5.00	Hours Worked 10 hrs/day Monday-Thursday = 40/week
Fair Labor Standards Act		Walsh-Healey Act
Regular Pay: 40 hrs/week × $5.00 Total Pay = $200.00 (no overtime due)		Regular Pay: 8 hrs/day × 4 days = 32 hrs ×$5.00 $160.00 Overtime Pay: 2 hrs/day × 4 days = 8 hrs (5.00 × 1½) ×$7.50 $60.00 Total Pay: $220.00

Davis-Bacon Act of 1931

The Davis-Bacon Act of 1931 affects compensation paid by firms engaged in federal construction projects valued in excess of $2,000. It deals only with *federal construction projects* and does not contain specific minimum wage provisions. However, it does require that the *prevailing wage rate* be paid on all federal construction projects. The prevailing wage actually may be, and frequently is, the average union rate for the local area where the construction is being done. Thus, if the average rate for carpenters in a city is $7 per hour, the carpenters building a new post office in the city must be paid at least $7 per hour.

The Davis-Bacon Act has been accused of causing higher costs on government projects. Even the Government Accounting office has cited the prevailing wage provisions as being in need of review and revision.[9] While many states have also had their versions of the Davis-Bacon, many of them are being dropped.

What are four laws that affect compensation?

State Laws

Modified versions of these compensation-related federal laws have been enacted by many states and municipal governmental bodies. These laws tend to cover workers included in intrastate commerce not covered by federal laws. If a state, such as Alaska, has a higher minimum wage set than that set under the Fair Labor Standards Act, the higher figure becomes the required minimum wage.

Most states formerly had laws which limited the number of hours women could work. However, these laws have generally been held to be discriminatory in a variety of court cases. Consequently, most states have dropped such laws.

COMPENSATION BASES

Several forms of compensation are available for managers and employees to use in developing an overall remuneration program for the organization. Minimization of cost and matching effort and reward to achieve equity are important in choosing a method of compensation. Because a method of payment can directly affect the equity perceptions of employees, managers should carefully choose a method consistent with both the tasks performed and the individuals performing them. There are three bases for compensation: time, productivity, and a combination of time and productivity.

Time

Employees may be paid for the amount of time they are on the job. One reason for paying on the basis of time is the ease of record keeping. A payroll clerk can compute pay from time-clock cards. Another reason for time-based payment is that it may be difficult in some positions to pay employees for what they produce rather than how long they work. Some clerical jobs may be of this nature.

There are three pay classes in many organizations, identified according to the way pay is distributed and the nature of jobs. The classifications are:

- *hourly,*
- *salaried nonexempt,*
- *salaried exempt.*

Hourly.   The most common means of payment based on time is hourly and employees paid hourly are said to receive wages. Wages are pay directly calculated on the amount of time worked. Hourly paid employees are paid overtime in most cases because they are not exempt from the overtime provisions of the Fair Labor Standards Act. To compute this type of pay, the number of hours an individual works is multiplied by the wage rate to determine gross pay.

Salaried Nonexempt.   Salary is another means of paying people for the time worked. Being on salary typically has carried higher status and importance for employees than being on wages. Salary is compensation that is consistent from period to period and is not directly related to the number of hours worked by the individual.

A fairly recent development is for those manufacturing and clerical personnel typically paid on an hourly basis to be paid a salary. One corporation has used an all-salaried approach in some of its plants with success. A common reason for this switch is to create a sense of loyalty and organizational commitment among employees who may not have that orientation. Putting blue-collar workers on salary is a drastic change from historical patterns of pay.

Under the provisions of the FLSA each salaried position must be identified as *salaried exempt* or *salaried nonexempt.* Employees in positions classified as salaried nonexempt are covered by the overtime provisions of the FLSA, and therefore must be paid overtime. Typical salaried nonexempt positions would include secretarial, clerical, or manufacturing positions. Figure 12–6 illustrates calculation of overtime for a nonexempt employee paid a salary.

Figure 12–6.   Computing salaried nonexempt overtime pay.

```
       Helen Gibson, a keypunch operator, receives $180/week.
         $180 ÷ 40 hrs per week = $4.50/hour
       Assume she works 44 hours; she is due 4 hours of overtime.
       Overtime rate (1½ × $4.50) = $6.75
         Total pay = 40 hours × $4.50 = $180
                      4 hours × $6.75 =   27
       Helen's gross pay for the week       $207
```

Salaried Exempt. Individuals holding salaried-exempt positions are exempt from the coverage of the FLSA overtime provisions and are not required by law to receive overtime payment. Salaried-exempt positions include executive, administrative, professional, and outside sales employees described earlier.

Productivity

Another basis of compensation, called *piece-rate*, is one of the oldest means of tying productivity and effort together. An employee who works in an electronics plant packaging radios is paid on the basis of productivity. If the employee is paid 50¢ for each radio packaged, and is expected to package 80 radios a day, the employee receives $40.

The piece-rate system can be easily explained to workers. Total pay can be calculated readily and effort is tied directly to productivity. If some individuals want to work faster than others, they can choose their own speed. Employees who want to earn more can produce more units or work at a faster pace.

A productivity-based pay system should be developed with caution so that quality is also encouraged. For example, paying the radio packager only on the basis of quantity might lead to some radios being carelessly packed, sacrificing quality. Another possible drawback to a piece-rate system is that the piece-rate, or productivity compensation rate, must be determined for each specific job. These rates are determined through motion and time studies, described in chapter 6. If minimum-wage requirements change or an individual's compensation must change, the productivity rate must also be changed. The piece-rate can also be applied to other types of jobs. For example, paying a door-to-door salesperson $1.50 for each magazine subscription sold is another form of piece-rate or productivity pay.

Other methods of piece-rate pay have been developed at various times. "Modified" piece-rate plans sometimes offer workers the opportunity to receive higher pay for units produced above a quota. For example, since the radio packager's standard is to package 80 radios per day, the employee might be paid 10¢ extra for each radio packaged above the standard.

Combination Methods

Employees can also be paid by combining time methods with a productivity method. The salary plus commission available to sales representatives is most familiar. Assume that a sales representative for a consumer products company manufacturing shaving cream is paid $1,000 a month plus 1% of the dollar value of all merchandise he sells. Combining a salary with a productivity reward is designed to motivate the sales representative to sell more but recognizes that not everything can be measured. Executive level managers typically receive a salary plus some type of bonus plan for sales, production, or profitability. These combination systems will be examined in more detail in chapter 13 on incentives.

What are three bases used in compensating employees?

Compensation and Task Structure

The type of task done should be matched with the type of compensation appropriate for it. Individuals paid on an hourly basis, such as production workers or clerical workers, typically have more routine and shorter job cycles. If the task is such that individual productivity can be determined, a piece-rate or some incentive type of system can be utilized.

A combination plan might be useful in a situation where income can fluctuate but it is also desirable to tie productivity to effort. For example, a sales representative's income can fluctuate significantly over the course of a year. By paying a base salary each month, the sales representative is assured a continuity of income each month; but adding a commission or productivity reward encourages extra sales effort.

The important point to be made in compensation and task structure is that the task and work done by individual employees should be examined and the compensation methods used should fit the types of tasks and the work done. The method of paying individuals should be fair and should reflect the different levels of effort and skills necessary to perform jobs. A useful system for identifying differences in jobs for compensation purposes is job evaluation.

JOB EVALUATION

The principal aim of job evaluation is to provide an equitable basis for the comparison of jobs. Systematic evaluation of jobs is an attempt to reduce favoritism and leads to a formal, coordinated pay system.

> JOB EVALUATION is the systematic determination of the relative worth of jobs within an organization.

Job Evaluation Process

Job evaluation flows from the job analysis process and uses job descriptions as its base. Figure 12–7 depicts the job evaluation process.

Figure 12–7. Job evaluation process.

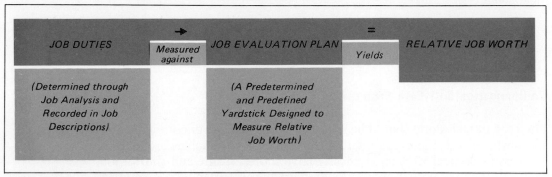

(Source: Reprinted by permission of the publisher from *Compensation* by Robert E. Sibson. © 1974 by AMACOM, a division of American Management Associations.)

The beginning point for job evaluation is the job description. As mentioned in chapter 6, a job description describes the job "in abstract," not the individual performing the job. When doing job evaluation, the job description of every job in an organization is examined by comparing:

1. the relative importance of the job,
2. the relative skills needed to perform the job, and
3. the difficulty of one job versus other jobs.

Although job evaluation uses a systematic approach, managers should be aware that job evaluation can never be totally objective. Subjective judgments cannot be avoided and must be explained to employees if the resulting compensation system is to be useful.

Job evaluation systems should be clearly communicated so that employee misunderstandings and complaints about perceived inequity will be reduced. Managers and personnel specialists should make sure the job evaluation system is not overemphasized and that the real meaning of what is being done is not underemphasized. Managers should also be aware that some individuals will always feel themselves to be treated unfairly, but that job evaluation is an attempt to overcome as much of this perception as possible. One study reported that union leaders viewed job evaluation with some distrust.[10] Managers of unionized employees must also deal with this concern, regardless of the job evaluation method used.

Can you define job evaluation and tell its purpose?

JOB EVALUATION METHODS

There are several methods used to determine internal job worth through job evaluation. All methods have the same general objective, but each method differs in its complexity and measurement means. Regardless of the method used, however, the intent is to develop a usable, measurable, and realistic system to determine compensation in an organization. A survey of employers revealed that some methods are more popular than others. In Figure 12–8 notice that the point system is the most widely used method and ranking methods the least used.

Figure 12–8.   Job evaluation procedures.

Evaluation Method Used	Exempt only or all employees (N = 84)	Nonexempt or office only (N = 63)	Plant only (N = 25)	All plans (N = 172)
Point system	46	56	68	53
Factor comparison	31	35	36	33
Job classification	24	22	32	24
Market pricing	15	11	0	12
Hay Associates plan	23	2	0	12
Simple ranking	17	13	4	9
Forced-choice ranking	5	8	0	5

(Source: "Personnel Policies Forum," *Job Evaluation Policies and Procedures*, PPF Survey # 113. Washington, D.C.: Bureau of National Affairs, June 1976, p. 4.)

Market Pricing

Although discussed as a job evaluation method, market pricing does not truly consider the relative internal worth of a job. Instead, it simply assumes that the pay set by other employers is an accurate reflection of a job's worth. One difficulty with this approach is the assumption that jobs are the same in another organization. Also, direct market pricing does not adequately consider the impact of economic conditions, employer size, and other variables. To illustrate, in one midwestern U.S. city, one of the major employers is a highly unionized company. The clerical pay is based on the pay scale in the unionized part of the company. A beginning secretary is paid $1100/month; consequently, the firm always has a waiting list of extremely experienced and qualified persons available. A small insurance agency manager who is hiring a secretary would have extreme difficulty justifying such an expenditure. That manager might hire someone with less experience for considerably less money. This example illustrates that using market pricing exclusively has some definite pitfalls and why more complex methods have developed.

Ranking Method

The ranking method is one of the simplest methods used. Managers and personnel specialists using the ranking method place jobs in order ranging from highest to lowest in value. The entire job is considered rather than the individual components. Variations on straight ranking can be used. *Alternation ranking* and *paired comparison* ranking are two common variations.

Advantages and disadvantages. Ranking methods are extremely subjective and managers may have difficulty explaining why one job is ranked higher than another to employees, especially since these rankings will ultimately affect the pay individuals on those jobs receive. Also, when there is a large number of jobs, the ranking method can be awkward and unwieldy. Consider a personnel specialist in an automobile parts manufacturing concern who must rank 250 different jobs. This method would be almost impossible to use in a way that could be justified to most employees. Therefore, the job ranking method is limited in use and is more appropriate to a small organization having relatively few jobs.

Classification or Grading Method

The job classification method of job evaluation was developed under the old U.S. Civil Service System for its civilian employees. A number of classes or GS grades for jobs are defined. Then the various jobs in the organization are put into the classes according to common factors found in jobs, such as degree of responsibility, abilities or skills, knowledge, duties, volume of work, and experience needed. The classes are then ranked into an overall system.

Steps in Classification. There are five basic steps to classifying jobs.[11] In the first step necessary information is taken from job descriptions and job specifications. The next step is to separate jobs into types (like sales jobs, manufacturing jobs, clerical jobs, etc.). The third step is to identify the job factors to be used to grade or classify the jobs. Several factors are often used. Fourth, descriptions of job classes are made by writing statements such as: "Jobs falling in this classification have the following characteristics." Finally, individual jobs are placed in the appropriate classification. Often the fourth and fifth stages are combined because it is difficult to write a grade description without also considering the job descriptions that are to be placed in that grade.

Advantages and Disadvantages. One of the major reasons that the job classification method is widely used in government and other organizations is that it is a system employees and managers can understand. Also, the classification method has some flexibility. As evidence of this flexibility to handle a wide variety of jobs, consider the U.S. Federal Government and the large variety and number of jobs classified according to GS grades.

The major difficulty with the classification method is the subjective judgment needed to develop the grade descriptions and to accurately place jobs in them. With a wide variety of jobs and generally written grade descriptions, some jobs may appear to fall into two or three different grades. Thus, some subjective judgments must be made. Another problem with the job grading or classification is that it relies heavily on job titles and duties and assumes they are similar from one organization to another. For example, a social welfare supervisor in a state governmental agency in one county might have different job responsibilities than a social welfare supervisor in a smaller county or a different governmental agency. If both are evaluated using a classification system, there may be some inappropriate grading of responsibilities involved. For these reasons a number of federal, state, and local governmental agencies are shifting to the use of a point system.

Point Method

The point method, the most widely used job evaluation method, breaks jobs down into various identifiable components and places weights or points on these components. The components are developed from a job analysis by identifying factors that are common to the jobs under study. Then the relative weights (or points) are assigned to each degree of the component using a mathematical calculation formula.

The point method is more sophisticated than the ranking and classification methods because of the way each job is broken down. Because the different job components carry different weights, each is assigned a numerical value. The values of the various components are then added for each job and compared to other jobs.

The individual using the point chart in Figure 12–9 takes the job description and then identifies the degree to which each element is necessary to perform the job satisfactorily. To minimize bias, this determination is often made by a group of people familiar with the job. Once all jobs have had point totals determined, they are ultimately grouped together into pay grades.

Advantages and Disadvantages.   The major reason the point method has grown in popularity is because it is a relatively simple system to use. It considers the components of jobs rather than just the total job, and it is a much more comprehensive system than either the ranking or classification method. Once points have been determined and a job

Figure 12–9. Point method charts.

Skill	Clerical Group				
	1st Degree	2nd Degree	3rd Degree	4th Degree	5th Degree
1. Education	14	28	42	56	
2. Experience	22	44	66	88	110
3. Initiative & ingenuity	14	28	42	56	
4. Contacts with others	14	28	42	56	
Responsibility					
5. Supervision received	10	20	35	50	
6. Latitude & depth	20	40	70	100	
7. Work of others	5	10	15	20	
8. Trust imposed	10	20	35	50	70
9. Performance	7	14	21	28	35
Other					
10. Work environment	10	25	45		
11. Mental or visual demand	10	20	35		
12. Physical effort	28				

The specific degrees and points for Education, Trust Imposed, and Work Environment are as follows:

Education   Education is the basic *prerequisite* knowledge that is essential to satisfactorily perform the job. This knowledge may have been acquired through formal schooling such as grammar school, high school, college, night school, correspondence courses, company education programs, or through equivalent experience in allied fields. Analyze the minimum *requirements of the job and not the formal education of individuals performing it.*

1st Degree   Requires knowledge usually equivalent to a two-year high school education. Requires ability to read, write, and follow simple written or oral instructions, use simple arithmetic processes involving counting, adding, subtracting, dividing and multiplying whole numbers. May require basic typing ability.

2nd Degree   Requires knowledge equivalent to a four-year high school education in order to perform work requiring advanced arithmetic processes involving adding, subtracting, dividing, and multiplying of decimals and fractions; maintain or prepare routine correspondence, records, and reports. May require knowledge of advanced typing and/or basic knowledge of shorthand, bookkeeping, drafting, etc.

3rd Degree   Requires knowledge equivalent to four-year high school education plus some specialized knowledge in a particular field such as advanced stenographic, secretarial or business training, elementary accounting or a general knowledge of blueprint reading or engineering practices.

4th Degree   Requires knowledge equivalent to two years of college education in order to understand and perform work requiring general engineering or accounting theory. Must be able to originate and compile statistics and interpretive reports, and prepare correspondence of a difficult or technical nature.

Responsibility for Trust Imposed   This factor appraises the extent to which the job requires responsibility for safeguarding confidential information and the effect of such disclosure on the Company's relations with employees, customers or competitors.

1st Degree   Negligible. Little or no confidential data involved.

2nd Degree   Some access to confidential information but where responsibility is limited or where the full import is not apparent.

3rd Degree   Occasional access to confidential information where the full import is apparent and where disclosure may have an adverse effect on the Company's external or internal affairs.

4th Degree   Regularly works with and has access to confidential data which if disclosed could seriously affect the Company's internal or external affairs or undermine its competitive position.

5th Degree   Full and complete access to reports, policies, records and plans of Company-wide programs, including financial cost and engineering data. Requires the utmost discretion and integrity to safeguard the Company's interests.

Work Environment   This factor appraises the physical surroundings and the degree to which noise is present at the work location. Consider the extent of distraction and commotion caused by the sounds.

1st Degree   Normal office conditions. Noise limited to the usual sounds of typewriters and other equipment.

2nd Degree   More than average noise due to the intermittent operation by several employees of adding machines, calculators, typewriters, or duplicating machines.

3rd Degree   Considerable noise generated by constant machine operation such as is present in the Data Processing section.

(Source: *Wage and Salary Administration: A Guide to Current Policies and Practices.* Chicago: The Dartnell Corp., 1969, pp. 135–141. Used with permission. Revision published every three years.)

evaluation point manual has been developed, the method can easily be used by nonspecialists. A definite advantage is that the system can be understood by managers and employees.

Another reason for the widespread usage of the point method is that it does not consider current pay for a job. It evaluates the components of a job and total points are determined before the current wage structure is considered. In this way some realistic assessment of relative worth can be determined instead of just relying on *past patterns* of worth.

One major drawback to the point method is the time needed to develop a point system. For this reason point manuals and systems developed by management consultants or other organizations are used by many employers. Another disadvantage is that even though the point system does attempt to be objective, managers must still make subjective judgments to determine how many points should be allotted for each element. Human error through misinterpretation or misjudgment is definitely a possibility. Even though the point system is not perfect, in several respects it is probably better than the two previous systems because it does consider and attempt to quantify job elements.

Factor Comparison

The factor comparison method, which is very quantitative, involves determining the key jobs, called *benchmark jobs*, in an organization. A *benchmark job* is often identified as one performed by many individuals or having special significance to the organization. For example, one key job in a retail store might be a clothing salesclerk.

A BENCHMARK JOB is a standard type of job that is correctly priced and representative of major factors in most jobs in the organization.

To develop this method, factors such as responsibility, mental demands, skills required, and working conditions are identified in 10–20 benchmark jobs. All benchmark jobs are then ranked factor by factor against each other. The factor comparison method is actually a combination of the ranking and point methods. Then the individual doing the evaluation compares these positions in terms of the above factors and ranks them according to the importance of the factors in each job. Monetary values are then assigned to each one of the factors and compared with the existing monetary scales for the benchmark jobs. Finally, evaluations of all other jobs in the organization are made by comparing them to the benchmark jobs.[12]

Hay Plan.   A special type of factor comparison method used by a consulting firm, Hay and Associates, has received widespread application. As noted in Figure 12–8, approximately 12% of the firms surveyed were using the Hay Plan. However, it is interesting that most usage of the Hay Plan is with exempt only or with all employees. The Hay Plan uses three factors: *know-how, problem-solving,* and *accountability* and numerically measures the degree to which each of these three elements is required in each job.[13]

Advantages and Disadvantages.   One of the major advantages of the factor comparison method is that it is tied very specifically to one organization. Each organization must develop its own key jobs and its own factors. For this reason buying a packaged system which may not be appropriate for an organization should be avoided. The factor comparison method does establish quantitative weights as the point method does, but requires the evaluator to make a specific comparative identification of the weights assigned. Finally, factor comparison not only tells which jobs are worth more, but it also indicates *how much* more, so the factor values can be more easily converted to the monetary wages.

The major disadvantage of the factor comparison method is its difficulty and complexity. It is not an easy system to explain to employees and it is time-consuming to establish and develop. A factor comparison system may not be appropriate for an organization with many similar jobs. As an example, some organizations have had difficulty using the Hay Plan with nonexempt employees, primarily because many clerical jobs vary very little on accountability.

Extensive space is not being devoted in this text to factor comparison because it is an extremely complex system. Managers attempting to use the method should consult a specialist or one of the more detailed compensation books or manuals.[14]

> *Can you identify and briefly discuss four job*
> *evaluation methods?*

DEVELOPING AND ADMINISTERING A PAY SYSTEM

Once internal equity is determined through job evaluation, the basis for developing a total pay system is available. The development of a pay system requires consideration of an organization's pay policies and how they are to be administered. As a part of the administration process, managers should compare the pay their organizations are offering to what other employers in the community and region are paying employees for similar types of jobs through a wage survey. Once wage survey in-

Figure 12–10. Pay system components.

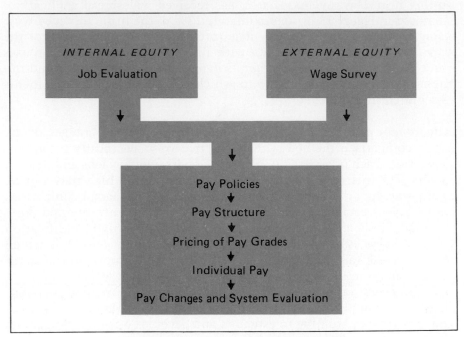

formation is collected, wage curves and labor grades can be developed and jobs can be priced.

Figure 12–10 shows the relationship of job evaluation and wage surveys to a total pay system. An employer may choose to use wage surveys conducted by other organizations or may decide to conduct its own survey.

A WAGE SURVEY is a means of gathering data on the existing compensation rates for employees performing similar jobs in other organizations.

Using Prepared Wage Surveys.   Several sources for pay information are available including government surveys, trade associations, unions, and consulting services. As an example, in numerous communities employers participate in a wage survey sponsored by the Chamber of Commerce. This information is also needed by new employers interested in locating in a community. National surveys on many jobs and industries are available through the U.S. Department of Labor, Bureau of Labor Statistics, or through national trade associations.

When using salary surveys from other sources, it is important to use them properly. Some recommendations that are appropriate include the following:[15]

1. Is the survey a realistic sample of employers, or is it dominated by a few large employers?
2. Is the data provided by other personnel specialists, not individual operating managers?
3. How old is the information?
4. How sound and experienced is the organization that prepared the survey?

If needed wage information is not already available, the organization can undertake its own wage survey. Figure 12–11 shows sample wage survey data from Arkansas on several jobs.

Developing a Wage Survey.   If an organization conducts its own survey, employers with comparable positions should be selected. Employers considered to be "representative of the community" should also be surveyed. If the organization conducting the survey is not unionized, the wage survey should examine unionized as well as nonunionized companies. Developing wages competitive with union wages may deter employees from joining a union.

Another decision the manager must make is what positions are to be surveyed. Not all jobs in all organizations can be surveyed and not all jobs in all organizations will be the same. An accounting clerk in a city government might perform a different job than an accounting clerk in a credit billing firm. Therefore, managers should select jobs that can be easily compared, that have common job elements and, represent a broad range of jobs.

The next phase of the wage survey is for the managers to decide what compensation information on various jobs is needed. Information such as starting pay, base pay, overtime rate, vacation-holiday pay and policies, and bonus plans can all be included in a wage survey. Requesting too much information may discourage survey returns.

The results of the wage survey may have to be made available to those participating in the survey in order to gain their cooperation. Some surveys specify confidentiality, but in others, organizations are identified along with what they pay for various jobs. Often different job levels are included and the wages are presented both in total and by cities to reflect cost differences. Sometimes included is a list of job descriptions to generally indicate the nature of the various job titles.

Figure 12–11. Sample Wage Survey Data.

CLERK-TYPIST II	TOTAL FIRMS	NUMBER EMPLOYEES	RANGE MINIMUM	RANGE MAXIMUM	ACTUAL MINIMUM	ACTUAL MAXIMUM	ACTUAL AVG SALARY
JOB CLASS ALL FIRMS	19	76	536	1014	647	724	679
100–250 EMPLOYEES	8	16	536	819	607	668	629
OVER 250 EMPLOYEES	11	60	568	1014	657	739	693
IN METRO COUNTY	13	58	536	1014	648	721	677
OTHER COUNTY	6	18	563	918	643	732	688
MFG. OF DURABLE GOODS	9	28	575	935	661	757	709
MFG. OF NON-DURABLE GOODS	5	17	563	914	697	795	738
SERVICE AGENCIES	5	31	536	1014	606	655	621

SENIOR SECRETARY	TOTAL FIRMS	NUMBER EMPLOYEES	RANGE MINIMUM	RANGE MAXIMUM	ACTUAL MINIMUM	ACTUAL MAXIMUM	ACTUAL AVG SALARY
JOB CLASS ALL FIRMS	22	42	600	1200	834	953	889
100–250 EMPLOYEES	9	10	600	1153	901	950	931
OVER 250 EMPLOYEES	13	32	685	1200	813	954	876
IN METRO COUNTY	17	36	600	1200	828	964	891
OTHER COUNTY	5	6	700	1045	872	888	881
MFG. OF DURABLE GOODS	10	12	700	1200	965	999	982
MFG. OF NON-DURABLE GOODS	4	4	710	1024	855	855	855
SERVICE AGENCIES	8	26	600	1156	771	947	851

SYSTEM ANALYST	TOTAL FIRMS	NUMBER EMPLOYEES	RANGE MINIMUM	RANGE MAXIMUM	ACTUAL MINIMUM	ACTUAL MAXIMUM	ACTUAL AVG SALARY
JOB CLASS ALL FIRMS	4	7	1112	2018	1341	1469	1409
100–250 EMPLOYEES	1	1	1112	1688	1536	1536	1536
OVER 250 EMPLOYEES	3	6	1157	2018	1308	1458	1388
IN METRO COUNTY	4	7	1112	2018	1341	1469	1409
OTHER COUNTY	0	0	0	0	0	0	0
MFG. OF DURABLE GOODS	2	3	1241	2018	1460	1560	1510
MFG. OF NON-DURABLE GOODS	0	0	0	0	0	0	0
SERVICE AGENCIES	2	4	1112	1777	1251	1401	1334

Source: Daniel R. Hoyt, Ph.D., Associate Professor of Management, Arkansas State University, NE Arkansas Wage Survey (April, 1981).

Pay Policies

Organizations must develop policies or general guidelines to govern the pay system. Uniform policies are needed for coordination, consistency, and fairness in compensating employees. One of the policy decisions that must be made is *the comparative level of pay* the organization tries to maintain. Specifically, if Arrow Stores has a policy such as "paying the going-rate" or "paying above area averages for similar jobs," the policy reflects the organization's philosophy as an employer. Arrow Stores, or any other employer, should try to follow the pay level policy, and not let it become a meaningless phrase in a company handbook.

Another policy decision involves specific company or organizational policies about the relationship between pay expenditures and productivity, sales, number of customers, and so on. The opening case illustrated a policy of maintaining wage and salary expenditures at 10% of gross sales volume. A policy such as this and the reasons for it should be explained to employees.

Pay Increases.   Another policy decision is how pay increases are to be distributed. Seniority or time with the company, time on a particular job, merit (performance), or some combination of time and merit should be identified. Similarly, many employers have policies that indicate the minimum time persons must be employed before they are eligible for a pay increase. If across-the-board or cost-of-living increases are to be given, this policy needs to be specified. Also, how often these or other automatic increases are given (for instance, once a year) should be identified.

Pay Structure

Once wage survey data are gathered, and pay policies determined, the organization's pay structure can be developed by combining that information with job evaluation data. One means for tying wage survey information with job evaluation data is to use a wage curve to establish pay grades.

Establishing Pay Grades.   Labor grades are determined by using a wage curve to chart job evaluation points to current pay or wage survey rates for all jobs. If current pay of employees is used, the employer is assuming that current pay generally is realistic and fair. Usage of wage survey data puts more emphasis on external market conditions. In this way the distribution of pay can be shown and a trend line using the least squares regression method can be drawn to plot a wage trend line. This line shows the relationship between job value or points and wage survey

Figure 12–12. Pay structure depicted graphically.

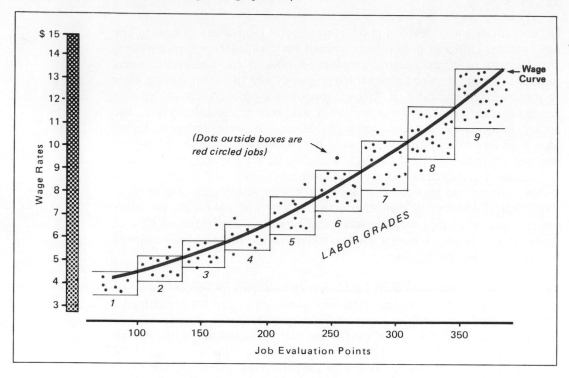

rates. An example is shown in Figure 12–12. Using all the information above, labor grades are developed.

LABOR GRADES are used to group individual jobs having approximately the same job worth together.

By using labor grades, an organization can develop a coordinated pay system. The intent is to avoid having to determine a separate pay rate for each position in the organization. A firm using a point method of job evaluation would group jobs having about the same number of points into one labor grade. As discussed previously, the factor comparison method uses monetary values. An organization using that method can easily establish and price the labor grades. A vital part of the classification method is developing grades, and the ranking method can be converted to labor grades by grouping several ranks together. Basic to setting up labor grades is deciding how many grades are to be established. Generally, 11 to 17 grades are used in small companies of 150–200 employees.[16] Labor grades can also have an overlap between grades, as those in figure 12–12 do.

Pricing of Jobs

Having established the labor grades, managers and/or personnel specialists must price them by establishing the monetary pay rate for each grade. A decision must be made if each job in a labor grade is to receive the same pay rate or if there is to be a range of pay. Figure 12–13 shows the labor grades determined through a typical point system and the pay for clerical employees that accompanies each grade for the same information presented in Figure 12–12.

Figure 12–13.   Example of priced labor grades.

Grade	Point Range	Hourly Pay Range*
1	100 and under	3.57–4.46
2	101–135	4.11–5.13
3	136–170	4.73–5.91
4	171–205	5.44–6.80
5	206–240	6.26–7.82
6	241–275	7.20–9.00
7	276–310	8.28–10.35
8	311–345	9.52–11.90
9	over 345	

* Note: 15% between grade minimums, with a 25% grade spread.

Pay Compression.   One major problem many employers face during the 1980s is *pay compression*. Such compression occurs for a number of reasons, but the major one is that labor market pay levels increase more than an employer's pay adjustments.

> PAY COMPRESSION occurs when pay differences between jobs of different evaluated worth become small.

To illustrate, assume that at Eastern Hospital physical therapist is a grade-8 job and X-ray technician is a grade-9 job. However, pay in the community for physical therapists has increased 20% in the past year because of a shortage of qualified therapists. But there is an adequate supply of X-ray technicians, so their pay levels have changed only 10%. If the hospital adjusts its pay structure 10%, the gap between a grade-8 job (physical therapist) and a grade 9-job (X-ray technician) has become reduced (compressed).

Pay compression is a difficult problem to confront. The major way to deal with it is to have wider pay grades and more grade overlaps. Another strategy is to have a policy of maintaining at best a 15%–20% differential (for example) if the compression occurs between supervisors' pay and the pay of those supervised.[17]

Individual Pay

Once rate ranges for pay grades are determined, the specific pay for individuals can be determined. Setting up a pay range for each labor grade provides flexibility by allowing individuals to progress in grade instead of having to be moved to a new grade each time they receive a raise. Also, a pay range allows some flexibility to reward more highly the better performing employees, while maintaining the integrity of the pay system.

As previously mentioned, job evaluation determines the relative *worth* of jobs. The evaluated worth of a job may be different from the pay an individual receives for that job. If skilled people are in short supply (for example, welders) the worth of a job may be evaluated at $6 an hour, but the going rate for welders in the community may be $8 an hour. In order to fill the position, the firm must pay $8 an hour.

"Red circle" rate.   A job whose pay rate is out of grade or range is identified as a *red circle rate*. A red-circled job is noted on the graph in figure 12–12. For example, assume Isaac Stein's current pay is $4.80 per hour, but the labor grade price is between $5.02 and $5.20. Isaac's job would be red-circled and attempts would be made over a period of time to bring Isaac's rate into grade.

A pay rate more than the determined pay rate is also red-circled. An attempt should be made to bring these rates into grade also. Occasionally managers may have to deviate from the priced grades to hire scarce skills or to consider competitive market shortages of particular job skills.

Standard Pay Raises.   One common pay raise practice is the use of a so-called cost of living adjustment. The theory underlying this approach is that giving employees a standard percentage figure enables them to maintain the same real wages in a period of economic inflation. Unfortunately some employers give across-the-board raises and call them "merit raises." If all employees get a pay increase as a minimum raise, the frequent reaction is to view this raise as a cost-of-living adjustment that has very little tie to "merit" and good performance. For this reason employers giving a basic percentage increase to all employees should avoid the term "merit" for it. The merit or performance part should be identified as that amount above the standard raise.

Performance and Pay Raises. Many employers profess to have a "merit" pay system that is based on performance as indicated by performance appraisal ratings. Reliance on performance appraisal information for making pay adjustments assumes that the appraisals are done well, especially for employees whose work cannot be easily measured. Some system for integrating appraisals and pay changes must be developed and applied equally.

In a true merit system no pay raises are given except for performance. Giving pay increases to people because they have 10–15 years' experience, even though they are mediocre employees, helps defeat a merit approach. Also, unless the merit portion of a pay increase is fairly significant, employees may feel it is not worth the extra effort. Giving an outstanding industrial designer making $20,000/year the "standard raise" of 8% + 1% for merit means only $200 for merit vs. $1600 for "hanging around another year."

Changing Pay Systems

An organization changing from an informal and uncoordinated pay system to a formalized pay structure should try to make the transition as smoothly as possible. The behavioral reactions of employees must definitely be considered. Clear communication to employees, a description of the new pay system, and an explanation of the need for change are all important actions to be taken. Whether or not the system is new, changes in the pay system should be phased in gradually. Attempts to institute radical and immediate changes in pay are likely to cause strong employee reactions.

Care must be taken to monitor a pay system once it has been implemented. A pay system that does not change after it has been established can become obsolete. Technological, social, product, or competitive conditions can all cause the need for a pay system to change. Internal changes including organizational shifts, expansion, and new products or services might also necessitate changes in a pay system.

Can you describe the process of developing a pay system?

REVIEW AND PREVIEW

The compensation provided by an organization is a major means of attracting and retaining employees. To determine whether the compensation has economic, psychosocial, and/or growth meanings to employees, managers should be concerned with providing adequate rewards in exchange for employees' inputs.

To ensure internal equity, job evaluation is necessary. Job evaluation is concerned with determining the relative worth of jobs, and it can be done through ranking, classification, point, or factor comparison methods.

Once the job evaluation process has been completed, an organizational pay system must be developed and administered. Wage survey data must be collected, pay policies identified, and the pay structure developed. To have an effective pay system, changes will have to be expected and made on a continuing basis.

This chapter has dealt with compensation as a major area of personnel management and has focused on the basic pay employees and managers receive. The next chapter examines two other types of compensation—incentives and benefits.

Review Questions

1. What did compensation mean to you in your most recent job? Why?
2. "Equity is the most important aspect of all compensation activities." Discuss how pay secrecy and pay openness relate to equity.
3. In what ways are the following laws different: (a) Fair Labor Standards Act, (b) Walsh-Healey Act, (c) Davis-Bacon Act?
4. People can be paid in three basic ways. What are they and what are the advantages of each?
5. What is job evaluation? Considering all methods, why do you believe the point method is the most widely used job evaluation method?
6. You have been named compensation manager for a hospital. How would you establish a pay system?

Case: Scientific Turmoil

Joan is the director of scientific computing at a large utility company. The people she supervises are all college graduates with backgrounds in science, engineering, or math. These people do systems work and computer programming that is more problem-oriented than other programmers in the company and the people in Joan's department are quite close knit.

Joan hired Fred into the group from the Engineering Department. Fred, who had worked for the company for seven years, learned the programming easily and was doing quite well. One year later Bob was hired into the group by Joan. Bob and Fred both assimilated into the group quickly.

About a month later, Joan's problems began. Information was quite freely shared by members of the group, especially job-related information such as salary. When Fred learned that Bob was making more money than he was, he was quite upset. Bob was doing the same kind of work with less experience at his new job. He also had less total working time with the company—only four years.

When Fred voiced his concern to his boss, he was told that the company had specific guidelines for raises and wide salary ranges for each job level. Bob was just on the high side of his old job's salary range and received a hefty raise when he was promoted to this new job. Fred was not pleased with the setup because he had received a raise just before Bob came and knew that it would be a year before he would get another one. In Fred's mind, he was now qualified, more experienced, had better knowledge of the company, and, if nothing else, more seniority than Bob. Fred's attitude and discontent was apparent in his work, and although Joan could not really prove it, Fred caused serious delays in projects. Also, new errors seemed to be cropping up in the computer programs that came out of Joan's section.

QUESTIONS

1. What role does equity play in this case?

2. Should companies demand that individuals not reveal their salaries? Why or why not?

3. Comment on the salary system and weaknesses you see in it.

4. As the director, how would you handle Fred?

NOTES

1. "Employee Payroll, Benefits Send Hotel Operating Costs Soaring," *Meeting News*, December 1979.

2. Gene Milbourn, Jr., "The Relationships of Money and Motivation," *Compensation Review*, 12, Second Quarter, 1980, pp. 33–44.

3. Ibid.

4. David W. Belcher, "Pay and Performance," *Compensation Review*, 12, Third Quarter, 1980, pp. 14–20.

5. William H. Wagel, "Bringing Salary Administration Out of the Closet," *Personnel*, July 1978, pp. 4–10.

6. Paul Thompson and John Pronsky, "Secrecy or Disclosure in Management Compensation?" *Business Horizons*, June 1975, pp. 67–74.

7. Wage and Hour Division, U.S. Department of Labor, *Handy Reference Guide to the Fair Labor Standards Act* (Washington, D.C.: U.S. Government Printing Office, 1978), p. 4.

8. *County of Washington* v. *Gunther*, 80-429 (1981).

9. Report to the Congress, Comptroller General of the United States, *The Davis-Bacon Act Should be Repealed*, U.S. General Accounting Office, HRD 79-18, April 1979.

10. Harold D. Jones, "Union Views on Job Evaluation: 1971 vs. 1978," *Personnel Journal*, February 1979, pp. 80–89.

11. David W. Belcher, *Compensation Administration*, 2nd Edition (Englewood Cliffs, NJ: Prentice-Hall, 1974), p. 155–156.

12. A detailed explanation of how to construct a factor comparison system can be found in Richard I. Henderson, *Compensation Management: Rewarding Performance*, 2nd. ed. (Reston, VA: Reston Publishing, 1979), pp. 491–497.

13. For more information on the Hay Plan see W. F. Younger, "The Hay-MSL System," in: Angela Bowey, ed., *Handbook of Salary and Wage Systems* (Epping, Essex, Great Britain: Gower Press, 1975), pp. 173–180.

14. Henderson, *Compensation Management*, is one possible source.

15. "Hiring at the Right Price," *Personnel Journal*, 59, December 1980, p. 968.

16. Warren E. Street, Dartnell's *Corporate Guide to Sound Compensation Practices* (Chicago: The Dartnell Corporation, 1980), p. 190.

17. Henderson, *Compensation Management*, p. 436.

CHAPTER 13

Incentives and Benefits

When you have read this chapter, you should be able to:

1. Define incentive and benefit and differentiate between them.

2. Explain two types of individual incentives and some problems with them.

3. Identify at least two types of group and organizational incentive systems.

4. List four guidelines to developing an effective incentive system.

5. Identify and briefly explain at least four of the major types of benefits.

6. Explain the cafeteria-style benefit system.

7. Discuss two general pension-related issues.

8. Describe concisely the requirements of the Employee Retirement Income Security Act of 1974 and the impact of changes in laws dealing with retirement.

9. Discuss the issues of early retirement and preretirement counseling.

How Can We Get Them to Work "Calls"?

Sarah Richards has been a nuclear medicine technologist at University General Hospital for five years. The only aspect of Sarah's job that she has found dissatisfying is having to "take call," that is, to be available to come in and work on short notice. She receives no compensation for her waiting time even though it limits what she can do. Two months ago Sarah accidently discovered a difference in compensation practices between her department and the other departments of radiology.

The policy for taking call in Sarah's department states that the technologist will be on call for one-week periods, either by telephone or electronic pager, and the technologist is not paid for the time spent being on call, but is compensated by receiving time-and-a-half for the hours actually worked when called in. The on-call policy for the other departments states that the technologist will take call for one-week periods and will receive 18 hours' straight pay for being on call and time-and-a-half for hours actually spent at the hospital if called in.

Sarah and the other technologists decided that the discrepancy between the two policies should be brought to the attention of the Nuclear Medicine administrative liaison, Mr. Kifer. When Mr. Kifer told Dr. Benson, head of the radiology department, that the technologists were very unhappy and that they might refuse to take call, Dr. Benson said that the department could not afford to pay them for call time.

The technologists are frustrated and disappointed in the response to their complaints. They do not feel that the "benefits" that accrue to others in the radiology area are being fairly distributed. They now feel that they have exhausted all their options and can see no other alternative but to stop taking call in an effort to force a decision. Although Sarah realizes the complications that refusing to take calls can cause, she can see no other alternative. As of February 23, there will be no call list and the pagers will be left at work.

Comments:

Inconsistent application of pay policies has led to conflict between the technologists and their superiors. The process of "taking call" might be a fertile one for the use of incentives to encourage technologists to take call. Monetary, as well as non-monetary, incentive systems on a group or individual basis are both possibilities. Use of extra compensation to reward performance beyond the normal should be explored by the manager and department head.

INCENTIVES and benefits are two types of additional compensation that an individual receives. However, incentives and benefits each have a different emphasis from the basic pay an individual receives.

DEFINING INCENTIVES AND BENEFITS

The major difference between a benefit and an incentive is that individuals receive benefits as long as they are employees of the organization. An incentive, however, is tied directly to performance and is only given for above-average performance. An individual who does not perform well will not receive as much in incentive compensation but will receive approximately the same benefit compensation as another employee who has been with the firm the same length of time and has the same general job responsibilities.

An INCENTIVE is *additional* compensation related to performance.

It provides additional compensation for those employees who perform well and attempts to tie additional compensation as directly as possible to employee productivity.

A BENEFIT is additional compensation given to employees as a condition of organizational membership.

As pointed out in the previous chapter, the personnel unit and other managers play varying roles in compensation. Figure 13–1 shows a typical compensation interface and identifies sample roles of each party concerning incentives and benefits. Notice the primary role of the personnel unit in the incentive and benefit areas. The role of the manager is more general supervision than direct involvement. The technical nature of many incentives and benefits gives the personnel unit a larger role to play. To more fully explore the various aspects of incentives and benefits, each is examined in a separate part of the chapter.

Can you distinguish between an incentive and a benefit?

Figure 13–1. Incentives and benefit portion of compensation interface.

Personnel Unit	Managers
Develops incentive systems	Assist in developing incentive systems
	Monitor attendance and productivity for incentive compensation
Develops benefit systems	Encourage and coach employees to obtain incentives
Answers employee's technical questions on benefits	Answer simple questions on benefits
Assists employees in claiming benefits	Maintain liason with personnel specialists on benefits
Coordinates special preretirement programs	Maintain good communications with employees near retirement

INCENTIVES

The main purpose of incentives is to tie employees' rewards closely to their achievements, which is done by providing more compensation for better performance. Whether or not an individual worker will strive for increased output or productivity and receive additional rewards that follow from the increased performance depends upon the individual. For example, some people may prefer some extra time off rather than earn more money. Consequently, organizations often use a combination of systems. As Figure 13–2 shows, there are three types of incentive systems: *individual, group,* and *organizational.*

Figure 13–2. Types of incentive systems.

INCENTIVE SYSTEMS		
Individual System	**Group System**	**Organizational System**
Piece Rate	Group Bonus	Profit Sharing

INDIVIDUAL INCENTIVES

Many different types of individual incentive systems are available, but they all attempt to relate individual effort to individual reward. For a salesclerk who works on a salary plus commission, the commission portion represents individual incentive compensation.

Individual incentive systems may have to be tailored to individual desires; thus, if a worker wants additional time off instead of additional take-home pay, the incentive system may have to provide that option to be effective. The discussion of Vroom's theory of motivation in chapter 3 implies that incentives will be most effective if the employees see that their extra work does lead to increased rewards. Also, it is important to provide employees with extra compensation as a reward for extra effort that has been given.

An individual incentive system may also be used as a means of measuring individual capabilities and initiative. Those who have special abilities and exert more effort can be identified for promotions or transfers to other more demanding and rewarding jobs. Two basic types of individual incentives are piece-rate systems and bonuses.

Piece-Rate Systems

The most basic individual incentive system is the piece-rate system. Under the *straight piecework system*, wages are determined by multiplying the number of units produced (garments sewn, customers contacted, etc.) by the piece-rate for one unit. As shown in figure 13–3, the incentive compensation for each piece does not change regardless of the number of pieces produced. The wage payment for each employee is easy to figure, and labor cost may be accurately predicted since the cost is the same for each unit.

Differential Piece-Rate.   Another type of piece-rate system, the *differential piece-rate system*, pays employees at one piece-rate if they produce less than a standard output, and at a higher piece-rate if they produce more than the standard. Developed by Frederick W. Taylor in the late 1800s, this system is designed to stimulate employees to achieve or exceed established standards of production. Managers often determine the quota or standard by using thorough time and motion studies. Using the example in Figure 13–3, assume that the standard quota is set at 300 gaskets/day. For all units over the standard the employee receives 20¢/gasket. Under this system, the worker who produces 400 gaskets in one day would get $62 in wages [(300 × 14¢) + (100 × 20¢)]. There are many possible combinations of straight and differential piece-rate systems. The specific system used by a company depends upon many situational factors.

Figure 13–3. Straight piece-rate system.

N (number of units)		R unit rate		W Gross Wages
400 gaskets produced in one day	×	14¢/each gasket produced	=	$56 earned in one day

Despite its incentive value, the piecework system is difficult to use. One reason is that for many types of jobs, standards are difficult and costly to determine. In some instances the cost of determining and maintaining the standard may be greater than the benefits derived from piecework. Jobs where individuals have little control over output or where high standards of quality are necessary may also be unsuited to piecework. However, in certain industries such as the garment industry, it is still widely used.

Bonus

Another type of individual incentive is the bonus. Although bonuses can be developed for groups and for entire organizations, the individual bonus is somewhat unique in that it rewards only high performing individuals. Providing the salesperson who sells the most new cars a trip to Las Vegas is an example of a bonus. Sales contests, productivity contests, and other incentive schemes can be conducted so that individual employees receive a bonus or something extra in the way of compensation.

Executive Bonuses. The bonus form of individual incentive compensation is often used at the executive or upper-management levels of an organization. Because of the broad nature of executive responsibilities, many executives have their individual bonuses based on corporate or divisional performance. Many bonuses are similar to profit-sharing plans except that the bonus incentives are usually limited to upper-level managers instead of being shared with many employees.

Because executive performance is difficult to determine, bonus compensation for executives must reflect some kind of performance measure if it is to be meaningful. One survey of the largest 100 companies in the United States found that 41 have bonus plans for executives. These bonuses are frequently tied to achieving company sales, earnings, or other performance goals. The sums received are often sizeable. For example, the chairman of Pillsbury Corporation received almost $550,000 in bonuses as part of a five-year plan. The chairman of Honeywell, Inc. received $242,775 as a one-year bonus.[1]

One method of determining an employee's annual bonus is to use a percentage of the individual's base salary. Though technically this type of bonus is individual, it comes very close to being a group or organizationwide system since it is based on group or organizationwide performance. To pay a division manager a bonus based on the profits of the division, the total performance of the division and its employees must be considered. A logical extension of this thinking is to offer group or organizationwide incentive systems.

What are two types of individual incentive
systems?

Problems with Individual Incentives

There are a number of problems with individual incentives that must be faced. One major concern with an individual incentive system is *keeping the system current.* A bonus payment to a salesclerk on the basis of the dollar value of sales may require changes to compensate for inflation or changes in the product line.

Another concern is that *employee competition* for incentives may produce undesirable results. Paying salesclerks in a retail store a commission may result in some clerks "fighting" over customers. Some salesclerks may be reluctant to work in departments that sell lesser valued items if their commissions are figured on the basis of total sales. For example, clerks in a department store may overconcentrate on selling major appliances without giving adequate attention to the small household appliances.

Any incentive system requires a climate of *trust and cooperation* between the employers and workers. If the workers believe that the incentive system is just a management scheme designed to make them work harder and that they ultimately will receive less pay, the individual incentive system *will not* be effective. The management of Citicorp, a large New York bankholding company, found out the hard way. Because of a weak corporate performance in 1980, employees did not receive bonuses. Previously individual bonuses had equaled 10%–15% of salaries. Someone at Citicorp sent out an anonymous letter blasting management, including the slogan, "Incentive is Just a Word—*You* Make it Work."[2]

Another problem is that an incentive system can lead to *overemphasis on one dimension* of a job; if you are not careful, you get more of what you emphasize than you wanted. An employee in a mattress factory who receives incentive compensation based on the number of units produced may turn out a large number of mattresses, but of lower quality. Another example of an overemphasized incentive system is rewarding a department store manager only for keeping costs down. As a result, the manager may not make some really necessary expenditures. Such problems have often occurred in Russia under its economic planning system.

Finally, individual incentive systems may be *resisted by unions.* Many unions are built on security, seniority, and group solidarity instead of the total productivity of an individual. Incentive systems may favor only the highly motivated, competent workers and actually depress the average workers' earnings.

What are some problems with individual incentives?

GROUP AND ORGANIZATIONAL INCENTIVE SYSTEMS

A group or organizational incentive provides rewards to *all* employees in a unit. This type is designed to overcome some of the limitations of the individual incentive system and to promote cooperation and coordinated effort within the group or organization.

Group Incentives

A group incentive system may be useful in overcoming the resistance of co-workers to an individual who produces more. A group incentive system, however, may not lead to higher productivity because individual effort is not as directly tied to the rewards. One critical factor in the group incentive system is the size of the group. If it becomes too large, employees may feel their individual effort will have little or no effect on the total performance of the group and the group incentive.

Small-group incentive plans are a direct result of a growing number of complex and interdependent jobs. Small-group plans may encourage teamwork in groups of as many as 40 employees; however, there is nothing to encourage cooperation between groups. Groups, like individuals, may restrict output, resist revision of standards, and seek gain at the expense of other groups.

Compensating individual employee groups with incentives may cause them to overemphasize certain efforts to the detriment of overall organizational good. For example, the conflict between the marketing and production branches of many organizations occurs because marketing's incentive compensation is based upon what is sold, while production's incentive compensation is based upon keeping unit production costs as low as possible. Marketing representatives may want to tailor products to customers' needs to increase their sales, but production managers want long production runs to lower costs. The overall company good may take second place. To deal with problems such as those, organizational incentive systems have been developed.

Organization Incentives

An *organizationwide* incentive system compensates all employees in the organization based upon how well the organization *as a whole* does during the year. Consider a simple example: If profits were up 10% over the previous year, all employees might receive an incentive payment of 10% of their regular monthly pay. The example cited earlier about conflict between marketing and production might be overcome by using an organizational incentive that emphasizes organizational profit and productivity.

The basic concept underlying organizationwide incentive plans is that overall efficiency depends on organization or plantwide cooperation. The purpose of these plans is to produce teamwork. To be effective an incentive program in a construction company should include everyone from hourly paid employees to managers and executives. Common organizational incentive systems include profit-sharing and Scanlon-type plans.

What is the purpose of group and organizationwide incentives?

Profit-sharing

As implied by its name, profit-sharing distributes a portion of profits of the organization to the employees. Typically, the percentage of the profits to be set aside for distribution to employees is agreed upon by the end of the year before profits are distributed. Profit-sharing plans distribute a substantial amount of extra compensation to employees.

The major objectives of profit-sharing plans are to make employees more profit conscious, to encourage cooperation and teamwork, and to involve employees in the organization's success. In some profit-sharing plans, employees receive their portion of the profits at the end of the year; in others, the profits are deferred and placed in a fund which is available to employees upon retirement or upon leaving an organization.

Employee Stock Option Plan. A common type of profit-sharing plan is the Employee Stock Option Plan (ESOP). An ESOP is designed to give employees some ownership of the company they work for, thereby increasing their commitment, loyalty, and effort. The chairman of Lowe's, a North Carolina retailer, feels that the reason Lowe's productivity is greater than competitors' is due to Lowe's ESOP in which Lowe's employees are also owners.[3]

In a typical ESOP, the employing organization provides a large block of stock for distribution to employees based on the length of service, salaries, and organizational performance during the fiscal year. According to one estimate, there were approximately 5000 ESOPs in existence in 1980, up from only 200 in 1975.[4]

The ESOP allows employees to purchase or accumulate stock in their employing organization. If the stock obtained has not increased in value because the company has not prospered, the employee may become disenchanted with the option as compensation. Also, setting up an ESOP to save a firm that would have otherwise gone bankrupt does not guarantee that the firm will survive.

Scanlon Plan.   A unique type of organizationwide incentive plan is the Scanlon plan. Since its development in 1927, Scanlon plans have been implemented in many companies; however, they have never been installed in a large company such as General Motors.

The basic concept underlying the Scanlon plan is that efficiency depends on teamwork and plantwide cooperation. The plan has two main features: (1) a direct incentive to employees to improve efficiency and (2) a system of departmental committees and a plant-screening committee to evaluate all cost-saving suggestions. Calculation of the standard and normal costs of production results in a formula upon which the Scanlon plan incentives are based. The incentive bonus is usually a ratio of past payroll to sales value of production (plus or minus inventory adjustment) compared to actual payroll. Any saving between actual and expected payroll is placed in a bonus fund. A predetermined percentage of this fund is split between employees and the company.

The departmental committees receive and review cost-savings suggestions. Suggestions beyond the level of authority of departmental committees are passed to the plant committee for review. Savings that result from submitted suggestions are passed on to members of the organization, as in the Quality Circle approach discussed in chapter 2. The Scanlon plan is not a true profit-sharing plan because employees receive incentive compensation for reducing labor costs, regardless of whether or not the organization ultimately makes a profit.[5]

Where the Scanlon plan has been implemented, some firms have experienced an increase in productivity and a decrease in labor costs. Also, employee attitudes have become more favorable, and there has been greater cooperation between management and workers.

What are two types of groups or organizational incentives?

GUIDELINES FOR AN EFFECTIVE INCENTIVE PROGRAM

As indicated in the above discussion, incentive systems can be complex and may take many forms. Managers should consider the following general guidelines when establishing and maintaining incentive systems:

Tie to Performance

Incentive systems should be tied as much as possible to performance. If an incentive is actually to spur increased performance and effort, employees must see a direct relationship between their efforts and their rewards. Further, both workers and managers must see the incentive rewards as equitable and desirable. If a group incentive system is to be used, it should be compatible with employees' desires and should reflect employees' efforts as a group of individuals.

Recognize Individual Differences

Incentive plans should provide for individual differences. Recognition of the complex view (chapter 3) requires that a variety of incentives systems may have to be developed to appeal to various organizational groups and individuals. Not everybody will want the same type of incentive rewards.[6]

Recognize Organizational Factors

The incentive system chosen should be consistent with the climate and constraints of an organization. A manager should recognize the basic incompatibility of attempting to devise a Scanlon plan for an organization in which there is strict adherence to traditional procedures and rules. The incentive plan should also be consistent with organizational resources and be developed in close consultation with the financial officers to determine how much incentive compensation an organization can afford.

Continue to Monitor

An incentive system should consistently reflect current technological and organizational conditions. Offering an incentive for clothing sales-clerks to sell outdated merchandise would be more appropriate than offering one for selling only current fashion items that are already good sellers.

Incentive systems should continually be reviewed to determine whether they are operating as designed. Follow-up through an attitude survey or other means will determine if the incentive system is actually encouraging employees to perform better. If it is not, then managers should seriously consider changing the system. Any incentive system should be based on performance; otherwise, it becomes a benefit.

What are four keys to an effective incentive system?

BENEFITS

Unlike incentive systems, *benefits* are available to all employees as long as they are members of the organization, regardless of differences in individual performance. For example, if an accountant is performing poorly but is still employed, he or she is entitled to the medical insurance and other benefits. Only when the employee resigns or is "dehired" does the individual lose benefits.

Types of Benefits

There are many different types of benefits provided employees, as shown in Figure 13–4. For ease of discussion, they are grouped into several types:

- required security
- voluntary security
- time-off related
- insurance and financial
- social
- recreational and miscellaneous other benefits
- retirement-related benefits

Benefit Costs

Although benefits are generally not considered part of an individual's compensation for tax purposes, they do represent a significant expenditure from the organization's point of view. Every two years the U.S. Chamber of Commerce surveys a large number of industries to determine

Figure 13–4. Examples of different benefits.

Required Security	Voluntary Security	Time Off Related	Insurance	Financial	Social & Recreational	Retirement Related
1. Worker's compensation 2. Unemployment compensation 3. Old age, survivors' and disability insurance 4. State disability insurance 5. Medicare hospital benefits	1. Severance pay 2. Supplemental unemployment benefits 3. Leave of absence	1. Birthdays 2. Vacation time 3. Company-subsidized travel 4. Holidays 5. Sick pay 6. Military reserve 7. Election day 8. Social-service sabbatical	1. Medical 2. Dental 3. Survivor benefits 4. Accidental dismemberment insurance 5. Travel accident insurance 6. HMO fees 7. Group insurance rates 8. Disability insurance 9. Life insurance 10. Cancer insurance	1. Credit union 2. Cash profit-sharing 3. Company-provided housing or car 4. Legal services 5. Purchase discounts 6. Stock plans 7. Financial counseling 8. Moving expenses 9. Tuition assistance	1. Tennis courts 2. Bowling league 3. Company Newsletter 4. Professional memberships 5. Club memberships 6. Counseling 7. Company-sponsored events 8. Child care services 9. Cafeteria 10. Season tickets 11. Service award jewelry	1. Social security 2. Pension fund 3. Early retirement 4. Preretirement counseling 5. Retirement gratuity 6. Retirement annuity plan 7. "In kind" benefits for retired employees 8. Disability retirement benefits

the extent of benefit payments. In the most recent survey, as of the writing of this book, an employer in American industry averaged paying 36.6% of total payroll in benefits. The significance of this average figure is that the average employee makes $15,191 per year and receives $5,560 in benefits per year. The amount of benefits provided varied significantly. An employee in the hospital industry averaged $64.60/week in benefits, while an employee in the chemical manufacturing industry received $135.79/week in benefits.[7]

Even more significant is the increase in benefits in a ten-year period. Benefits increased 1,971% from 1969 to 1979 while base pay grew only 107%. Figure 13–5 shows the types of benefits that are included in the U.S. Chamber of Commerce Survey.

Communication of Benefits

Some employees have instituted special benefit communication systems to deal with employee ignorance about the value of the benefits provided. Chicago Title and Trust Company holds periodic meetings, has prepared special literature, and uses its in-house employee publication to heighten awareness of benefits. Also, this firm, as well as many others, provides employees a "Personal Statement of Benefits" annually that translates benefits into dollars and cents.[8]

A unique approach to generating awareness of benefits has been used at the Samuel Moore Operations, Eaton Corporation location in Aurora, Ohio. A benefit awareness contest was held over a four-month period of time. Employees answered benefit quiz questions and each month those who got all the answers correct participated in drawings for prizes, including a one-week vacation trip. Over 80% of the employees participated and the program encouraged employees to learn about their benefits.[9]

Required Security Benefits

Some benefits are required by various federal and state laws. *Workers' compensation* and *unemployment compensation* are the most important of the required security benefits. Retirement funding through Social Security and pensions is discussed later in this chapter.

Workers' Compensation.   Starting with the Federal Employee's Compensation Act of 1908 and laws enacted by California, New Jersey, Washington, and Wisconsin in 1911, workers' compensation laws have spread to all the remaining states. Workers' compensation costs are borne entirely by the employer on the theory that industrial accidents should be considered one of the costs of production.

Figure 13–5.   Weekly Employee Benefits, per employee, 1969 & 1979.

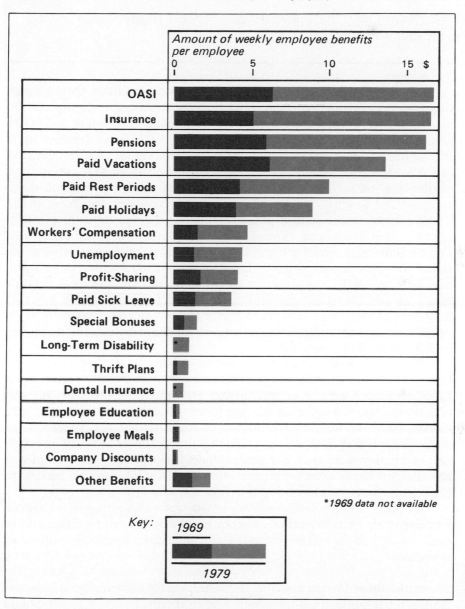

(Source: Fred D. Lindsey, "Employee Benefits Hit New Highs," *Nation's Business,* October 1980, p. 82. Used with permission.)

WORKERS' COMPENSATION provides cash benefits to any person injured on the job.

Employers pay premiums for workers' compensation through participation in a private insurance fund or in a state-operated compensation plan. Employer compensation rates are often related to job risk and safety records. The amount of compensation paid to employees depends upon the nature and severity of injury and varies from state to state. Because of the wide variation in state benefits, organized labor and others have pushed for the federal government to provide more control and more standardized benefits. As yet, these attempts have not been successful.

Workers' compensation plans originally provided only for physical injury. They have been expanded in many areas to cover emotional impairments that may have resulted from a physical injury. Also, emotional illnesses caused by job-induced strain, stress, anxiety, or pressure may be covered. In one situation in Rhode Island an employee became drunk at an office Christmas party and then fell and injured himself. Because the party was sponsored by the employer and employees were "expected" to attend, a court ruling made the company pay the employee as a workers' compensation claim.

Workers' compensation laws may be either compulsory or elective. Figure 13–6 indicates those states having *compulsory or elective laws.* Every employer subject to compulsory law must comply with its provisions for compensation of work injuries. Under an elective law, employers have the option of accepting or rejecting the act. If employers reject the act, they lose the customary common law defenses of assumed risk of employment and negligence. Under elective law, if an employer has rejected the act, an employee injured on the job may be unable to get compensation unless he or she sues for damages.

Workers' compensation provides two types of payments to injured workers or to a killed worker's next of kin. Payment can be either *direct cash* or it can be *reimbursement for medical expenses, pain, and suffering.*

Unemployment Compensation. Another legally required benefit is unemployment compensation, which was established as part of the Social Security Act of 1935. Each state operates its own unemployment compensation system, and the provisions differ significantly from state to state.

Employers finance this benefit by paying a percentage tax on their total payrolls to state and federal unemployment compensation funds. If an employee is out of work and is actively looking for employment,

Figure 13–6. Workers' Compensation: compulsory or elective?

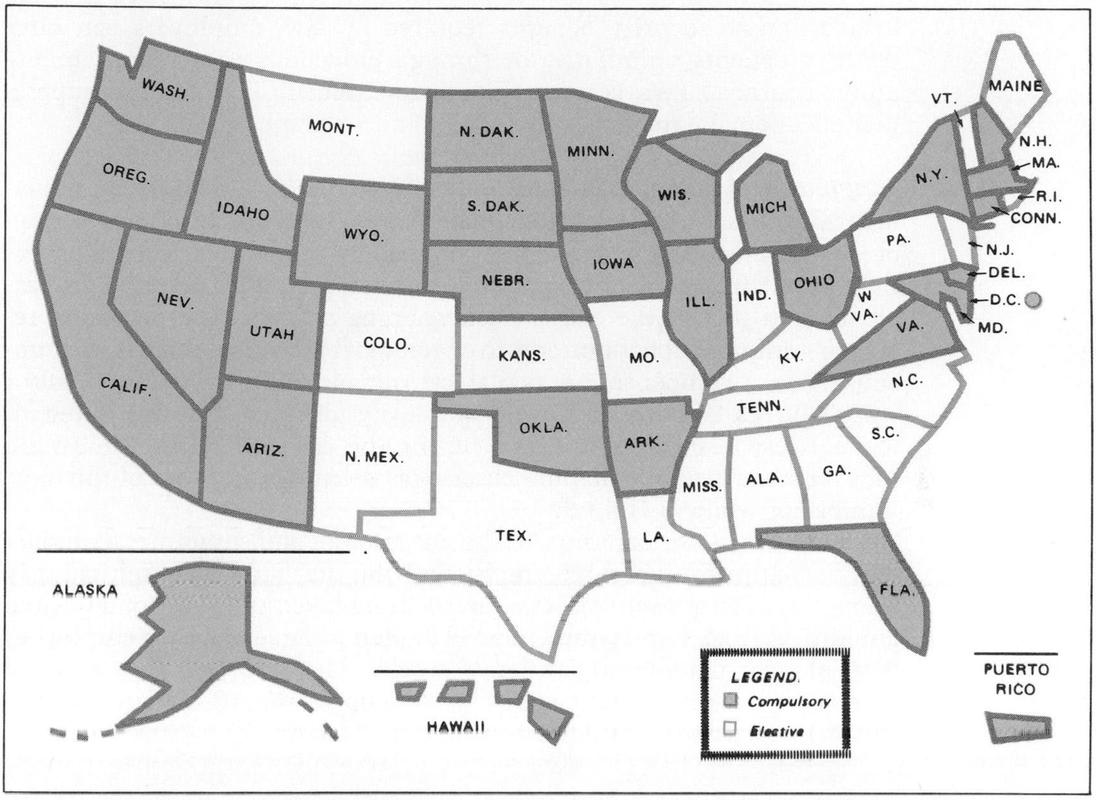

(Source: *State Workmen's Compensation Laws: A Comparison of Major Provisions with Recommended Standards*, Bulletin 212. Washington, D.C.: U.S. Department of Labor, 1971 rev., p. 3.)

he or she normally receives up to 26 weeks of pay, at the rate of 50% to 80% of normal pay.

Most employees are eligible. However, workers fired for misconduct or those who are not actively seeking work are generally ineligible. One problem is that some employees take advantage of the situation. In 1980, there were over 175,000 cases of fraud and abuse that involved $52.8 million. For example, an unemployed Ohio woman listed her canary as a dependent so that she received more money. She was caught when a state investigator called the school to check on the "dependent child."[10] Because of such abuses a number of dramatic changes have been proposed in bills introduced at both the state and federal levels. The push for change received active support by President Reagan following the 1980 election and it is likely that changes will evolve.

Voluntary Security Benefits

In addition to security benefits required by law, employers can offer security benefits voluntarily or through provisions in a management/union contract. Two common voluntary security benefits are supplemental unemployment benefits (SUB) and severance pay.

Supplemental Unemployment Benefits (SUB).   Supplemental Unemployment Benefits (SUB) are closely related to unemployment compensation but are not required by law. First obtained by the United Auto Workers in 1955, SUB is a benefit provision negotiated by a union with an employer as a part of the collective bargaining process. The provision requires company contributions to a fund, which supplements the unemployment compensation available to employees from federal and/or state sources or both. However, employers do not have unlimited financial responsibilities to SUBs; during the early 1980s the SUB fund for several automobile manufacturers was exhausted because of the large number of workers laid off.

SUB programs, common to the automobile and some metals industries, attempt to guarantee employees who are laid off or temporarily unemployed an amount close to their normal take-home pay for a limited amount of time. For example, one SUB plan provides laid-off employees 90% of their take-home pay for 26 weeks. The SUB payment is added to normal unemployment compensation up to the 90% figure. Figure 13–7 shows a sample calculation for a SUB plan.

Figure 13–7.   Sample supplemental unemployment benefit calculation.

Normal pay $5/hr and 40/hr week	=	$200/wk
90% of normal pay	=	$180/wk
State unemployment compensation	=	$ 82/wk
SUB pay		$ 98/wk

Severance Pay.   Severance pay is a security benefit offered by some employers. Employees who lose their jobs permanently may receive a lump-sum payment if they are terminated by the employer. For example, if a plant closes because it is outmoded and no longer economically profitable to operate, the employees who lose their jobs receive a lump-sum payment based on their years of service because their employment with that company is permanently severed. Severance pay provisions often appear in union/management agreements and usually provide larger payment for employees with longer service.

Time-Off Related Benefits

Holiday Pay.   Several benefits provide pay for time off: holiday, vacation, and sick pay are the most common ones. Pay for such established holidays as Labor Day, Memorial Day, Christmas, New Year's, and July 4 is well-established. Other holidays are offered to some employees by selected laws or union contracts.

According to one survey, the average number of holidays given is ten days per year. Almost half of the employers surveyed had "floating holidays" which can be selected by employees at their discretion or selected by management or management/union agreements.[11]

Vacations.   Paid vacations are a very common benefit. Employees often have graduated vacation time based on length of service. Figure 13–8 shows an example of graduated paid-vacation scheme. Some firms also allow employees to accumulate unused vacation.

Figure 13–8.   Sample graduated vacation plan.

Length of Service	Paid Vacation Time
At least 9 months to 2 years	1 week (5 days off)
2 years to 7 years	2 weeks (10 days off)
7 years to 15 years	3 weeks (15 days off)
More than 15 years	4 weeks (20 days off)

Sick Pay.   Another common type of pay is given for time not worked. Many employers allow their employees to miss a limited number of days because of sickness or illness without losing pay. Some sick-pay plans contain provisions whereby employees receive pay for sick days not taken. Also, some school systems, governmental units, and companies allow employees to accumulate sick-leave for future use.

Time off with pay is also given employees for coffee breaks, serving on jury duty, serving with the military reserves, assisting with elections, or voting. All of these time-off benefits add to employer costs.

Insurance Benefits

Another major group of benefits provided by employers is composed of various types of insurance coverage. Life, medical, disability, dental, legal, and auto insurance plans are all offered by some employers.

Life, Health, and Disability Insurance.   The costs of providing health-related insurance to employees have continued to increase significantly. Many employers pay the full cost of health insurance and long-term disability policies. Data gathered by the U.S. Chamber of Commerce (shown in figure 13–5) indicated that life, hospital, surgical, and medical insurance benefits averaged a cost of $16.56/per employee each week. For even a small employer with 200 employees, that sum is quite significant.

Because of the rapid increases in health-care insurance benefits, a growing number of employers have gone to self-funding.

SELF-FUNDING occurs when an employer sets aside funds to pay health claims, but the employer provides the insurance coverage.

Some employers even process their own claims, while others contract with a traditional insurance company to handle only the paperwork portion of the claims process.[12] Other efforts to contain health-care costs are made, including stressing preventive health and physical fitness programs, which are discussed in chapter 14.

Health Maintenance Organization.   A unique form of health care may be made available through a Health Maintenance Organization (HMO), an organized form of health care providing services for a fixed period and group on a prepaid basis. Unlike other health-care benefits, the HMO emphasizes prevention as well as correction.

An HMO is composed of a group of doctors and other professionals who provide basic and additional health care. Some employers offer this benefit because HMOs encourage broader health care services at a reasonable cost for employees. This form of health care is growing as an alternative to traditional health insurance systems. One review found that between 1978 and 1980 the number of HMOs increased by 20% and members covered by HMOs increased 22%. The review estimated that nine million U.S. workers have HMO coverage available to them as an option.[13]

Dental Insurance.   As an insurance benefit, dental insurance is highly desired by a growing number of employees. A 1980 study of 582 companies found that 59% of the companies provided dental benefits and another 15% were actively considering adding such a benefit.[14] Figure 13–9 shows the results of a government-sponsored study of dental benefits. Notice that of the 85 plans reviewed, 56 provided for orthodontic coverage, which is usually more costly.

Figure 13–9.   Dental insurance.

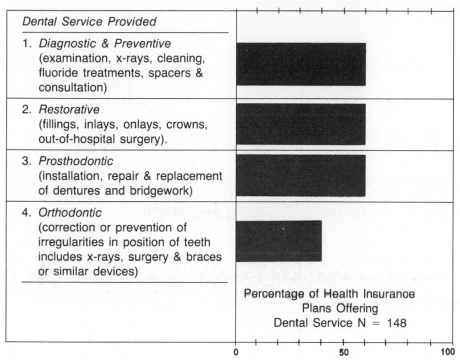

(Source: Donald R. Bell, "Dental and Vision Care Benefits in Health Insurance Plans," Monthly Labor Review, 103, June 1980, pp. 22–26.)

Legal Insurance.   As society becomes more complex, more people need legal assistance. However attorney fees have increased to the point that many who become involved with wills, contracts, divorces, and other situations cannot afford legal advice. Also, an insurance plan that pays a portion of legal fees saves the employee money because the legal fees are paid with pre-tax dollars, not out of the employee's take-home pay.

Auto Insurance.   Group auto insurance plans represent another new benefit for some employees. At Transnational Motors in Grand Rapids, Michigan, employees have 40% of their total auto insurance premium paid by the company. Because of group rates, employees also save money because the premiums are less than they would be on an individual basis. Rapid growth of such plans is possible if some state and federal insurance regulations are changed. Several large insurance firms such as Aetna and Prudential have started experimental plans also.[15]

In summary, a variety of group insurance benefits is offered by some employers: automobile insurance, dental insurance, health and disability insurance, legal insurance, prescription drug insurance, and eye-care insurance. The major advantage to employees is that many employers pay some or all of the cost of these plans. Also, cheaper insurance rates are available through a group program.

Financial Benefits

Financial benefits can include a wide variety of items. A *credit union* provides savings and lending services for employees. *Purchase discounts* allow employees to buy goods or services from their employer at a reduced rate. For example, a furniture manufacturer may allow employees to buy furniture at wholesale cost plus 10%. Or, a state bank may offer the use of a safety deposit box and free checking to its employees.

Employee *thrift, saving,* or *stock investment plans* may be made available. Some employers match a portion of the employee's contribution. These plans are especially attractive to executive and managerial personnel. To illustrate, in a stock-purchase plan, the corporation may provide funds equal to the amount invested by the employee to purchase that stock. In this way, employees can benefit from the future growth of the corporation. Another aim is that employees will develop a greater loyalty and interest in the company and its success.

Financial planning and counseling is a valuable benefit to executives. They may need information on investments, tax sheltering, and comprehensive financial counseling because of their higher compensation.

Numerous other financial-related benefits can be cited. The use of a company car, company expense accounts, and help in buying or selling a house when transferred are other common financial-related benefits. Those mentioned above reveal the variety of financial benefits that can be offered.

Other Benefits

Social and Recreational Benefits.   One group of benefits and services provided are social and recreational in nature, such as bowling leagues, picnics, parties, sponsored athletic teams, organizationally owned and provided recreational lodges, and sponsored activities and interest groups. Dances, banquets, cocktail hours, and other social events provide an opportunity for personnel to become better acquainted and strengthen interpersonal relationships. The employer should retain control of all events associated with the organization because of possible legal responsibility.

Strong emphasis on numerous social and recreation programs is designed to encourage employee happiness and team spirit. Employees may appreciate this type of benefit, but managers should not expect increased job productivity or job satisfaction to result.

Counseling services are an important part of many organizational benefit programs. Although supervisors are expected to counsel subordinates, most organizations recognize that there will be employees whose problems require qualified counselors. A more detailed discussion of such programs is provided in chapter 14.

Other benefits far too numerous to mention here are made available by various employers. Food services, child-care services (mentioned in the section opening information) paid professional memberships, lunch period entertainment, and organizationally provided uniforms are just a few. Applicable benefits must be developed into a coordinated and effective benefits program. A recent approach to benefit coordination is the cafeteria approach to benefits.

Can you identify and discuss at least four major types of benefits?

Cafeteria-Style Benefit System

The cafeteria-style approach to benefits is likely to be one of the next major steps in the evolution of employee benefits. It recognizes that individual situations differ because of age, family status and life-style. By allowing each employee to select an individual combination of benefits within some overall limit, the organization makes a variety of "dishes," or benefits, available. As shown in Figure 13–10 sometimes employees can even be offered the option of taking the cost of the benefits as part of their pay. Of all of the benefit options available to the 2,500 employees of Educational Testing Service of Princeton, New Jersey, the two most frequently selected options are medical insurance for dependents and supplemental retirement annuities. Accidental death insurance is the least popular choice.[16]

American Can Company is one employer who has made extensive

Figure 13–10.   Cafeteria benefit approach.

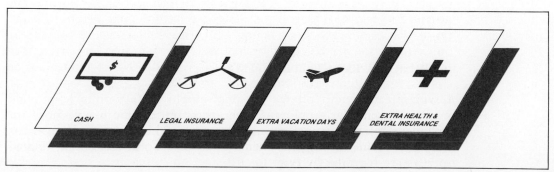

use of the cafeteria-approach to benefits for over 9,000 salaried employees at over 150 separate locations. Employees can use benefit credits to select options from medical and life insurance, additional vacation, disability income coverage, and additional retirement income accumulation credits. The program required the development of a very sophisticated computerized benefit system. Thus far the plan appears to be working satisfactorily.[17]

Advantages.   The cafeteria-style approach has several advantages. One is that this scheme takes into consideration the complex-view idea. Because employees in an organization have different desires and needs, they can tailor benefit packages to fit their individual life situations.

Another advantage to the variable-benefit approach is heightened employee awareness of the cost and the value of their benefits. By having to determine the benefits they will receive, employees know what they receive and what the trade-off options are.

Disadvantages.   The cafeteria-style approach to benefits is not without some drawbacks. One problem is the complexity of keeping track of what each individual chooses, especially if there is a large number of employees. Another problem is that employees may not always pick the benefit package that would be in their best long-term interest. A young male construction worker might not choose disability benefits; however, if he is injured, his family may suffer financial hardships. Part of this problem can be overcome by requiring employees to select a core set of benefits (that is, life, health, and disability insurance) and by offering options on other benefits.[18] A third problem is that as more benefits are made available, employees may not be able to understand the options because a benefit structure and its provisions can often become quite complicated. Overall, the cafeteria-style approach appears to offer an interesting way to tailor benefits to individual employees or employee groups.

Can you explain the cafeteria-style benefit system?

RETIREMENT-RELATED BENEFITS

A widespread benefit offered by most employers attempts to provide income security for employees when they retire. Few people have independent reserves to use when they retire. Thus, financial resources must be set aside throughout their work careers. Some retirement-related benefits are required *by law.*

Social Security

The Social Security Act of 1935, with its later amendments, established a system providing old-age, survivors', disability, and retirement benefits. Administered by the U.S. government through the Social Security Administration, this program provides benefits to previously employed individuals. Both employees and employers share in the cost of Social Security by paying a tax on the employees' wages or salaries.

Benefits.   Individuals may retire at age 62 with reduced benefits, or at age 65 or after with full benefits. In order to receive benefits under Social Security an individual must have engaged in some form of employment covered by the act. This act includes most private enterprises, most types of self-employment including farming, active military service, and employment in some nonprofit organizations and government agencies. Some groups of employees, including railroad workers and United States Civil Service employees who are covered by their own systems, generally are exempted from the act.

Potential Social-Security Changes.   Because the Social Security System affects a large number of individuals and is governmentally operated, it is a very politically sensitive program, and increases in Social Security benefits are often voted by legislators. Within the last few years, Social Security payments have been tied to the cost of living (through the Consumer Price Index). This action, plus the increasing number of persons covered by the Social Security System, has resulted in concern about the availability of future funds from which to pay benefits. Also, the changing makeup of the population and the increased longevity of many persons have placed severe strains on the system. To reduce this strain some have proposed that the age levels of 62 and 65 be changed to higher ages so that fewer payouts would be required.

"Universal" Social Security coverage is another proposed change. By universal, it means that all employees, especially government workers, would fall under Social Security instead of having separate systems. Because of the separate system, federal government employees receive significantly higher and more costly benefits. Whether universal coverage occurs depends upon changing political forces.[19]

Pensions

A second group of retirement benefits are provided through private pension plans established and funded by employers and employees. Pensions are considered rewards for long service and are not incentives to work more efficiently or effectively. They are deferred wages and are perceived as a right earned by employees, not as a gift given by the employer. The number of persons covered by private pension plans is expected to grow as the work force expands. A brief presentation of some of the basic terms and types of pensions requirements follows.

Pension Funding. Funds for paying pension benefits can be accumulated in two basic ways: funded and unfunded.

An UNFUNDED PLAN pays pension benefits out of current income to the organization.

Therefore, an unfunded plan relies on present income or sales dollars to generate the money necessary to pay pensions. Obviously, the unfunded plan depends very much on the economic conditions of the organization. Employees and former employees may be left without adequate pension benefits if current revenues are insufficient to pay these benefits.

The FUNDED METHOD provides pension benefits over a long period from funds accumulated ahead of time.

By amassing funds and interest prior to actual need, employers can insure employees that this pension will actually be available. For this reason, the funded plan is preferred and is more widely used.

Pension Contribution. Pension plans can be either contributory or noncontributory.

In a CONTRIBUTORY PLAN, the money for pension benefits is contributed by both employees and employers.

A NONCONTRIBUTORY PLAN is one in which the employer provides all the funds.

The noncontributory plan is preferred by employees and labor unions.

Pension Rights.   Certain rights are attached to employee pension plans, including vesting and portability. Vesting and portability are two common rights.

VESTING is the right of employees to receive benefits from their pension plans.

Typically, vesting allows employees to be assured of receiving a certain pension, providing that they have worked a minimum number of years. If an employee resigns or is terminated before he or she vests (that is, before an individual has been employed for the required time), no pensions rights accrue to the person except to receive the funds he or she has contributed. If employees stay the allotted time, they retain their pension rights.

Portability is another feature of employee pensions.

PORTABILITY allows employees to move their pension benefit rights from one employer to another.

For example, a plan that is portable within the paper industry will allow workers to move from one paper company to another without losing pension benefits. A commonly used portable pension system in colleges and universities is the Teacher Insurance Annuity Association (TIAA) System. Under this system, any faculty or staff member who accumulates pension benefits at one university can transfer those benefits to another university within the TIAA system.

Figure 13–11.   Pension portability.

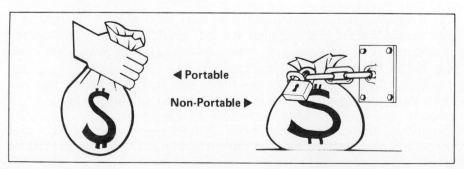

If individuals are not in a portable system, they must take a *lump-sum settlement* of the money they contributed to the plan plus accumulated interest on their contributions. The employee does not always receive the employer's contribution, however.

Pension Insurance.   If funds from a pension plan are accumulated in a trust fund or through a bank, it is often a "trusteed" or uninsured plan.

UNINSURED means that the benefits at retirement are determined by calculations that consider the age of the employee, years worked, and other factors.

An INSURED PLAN is one administered through insurance companies or similar institutions which buy retirement annuity policies.

Because pensions are so complex, employees often do not bother to learn about the provisions in their pensions and the advantages of various plans. Widespread criticism of pension plans led to the federal government passing a law in 1974 to regulate private pension plans. The underlying purpose of this law is to assure that employees who put money into pension plans, or depend upon a pension for retirement funds, will actually receive that money when they retire.

Can you discuss two general pension-related issues?

Employee Retirement Income Security Act of 1974

The Employee Retirement Income Security Act of 1974 (ERISA) is a technically worded and complex act that established a federal agency to administer its provisions. It covers six major areas, which are summarized in Figure 13–12.

The complexity of the law and the subject it deals with has resulted in much confusion for employers, banks, insurance companies, and other fiduciaries. However, ERISA provides employees increased security through regulation of pension plans. Employees who contribute to a pension plan can have more confidence that they will receive their benefits upon retirement.

Figure 13–12.   Employee Retirement Income Security Act of 1974: basic areas of coverage.

1. Fiduciary Standards

    A fiduciary is an entity controlling or holding property for someone else's benefit. The law established restrictions on fiduciaries and says that they must act as "a prudent man would."

2. Reporting and Disclosure

    Employers and fiduciaries are required to maintain extensive records and to disclose to employees and the regulating federal agency the status of pension plans.

3. Participation

    Generally the act states that an employee with one year's service and who is at least 25 years of age must be covered if a pension plan is offered by an employer.

4. Vesting

    Three types of vesting provisions are provided. Once the type is chosen by the employer and an employee vests, the employee is guaranteed the right to the appropriate pension benefits. Detailed provisions governing vesting provisions are also established.

5. Funding

    Minimum funding requirements are established for unfunded plans, and mandatory guides are set whereby employers must "catch-up" their unfunded pension liabilities.

6. Plan Termination Insurance

    The Pension Benefit Guaranty Corporation is set up to protect employees who might lose their benefits by their pension plan going out of existence. All plans covered by the law are required to purchase the insurance. If a plan fails, the Guaranty Corporation will pay vested benefits up to $750/month to the employees whose pension plan is terminated.

(Source: Adapted from information in Kenneth R. Huggins, "The New Pension Security Law," *Omaha Business Review*, 2, Spring 1975, pp. 1–3. Used with permission.)

Impact of ERISA.   By combining the benefits from government pensions, private pensions, and Social Security, many individuals are able to look forward to a reasonably secure retirement. Companies that terminated their pension plans because of ERISA requirements did so because compliance would have been too costly.

The most significant difficulty in complying with ERISA seems to be the voluminous paperwork involved in record keeping and reporting requirements. There are also problems with disclosure requirements, defining breaks in service, and with eligibility requirements and vesting.

Can you describe ERISA and what it requires?

Discrimination in Pension Plans

Pension plans which require that women contribute more because they live longer as a group have been found to be illegal by the Supreme Court because they violate the Civil Rights Act of 1964. Some think this ruling will force pension plan administrators to rely on "unisex" mortality tables instead of the separate tables for men and women that have traditionally been used. However, such "merged gender" mortality tables have been ruled against by some state insurance departments and the Equal Employment Opportunity has filed suit against them.[20] Once this federal vs. state conflict is resolved, the issue of "unisex" pension benefits and mortality tables will be clearer.

The 1978 Age Discrimination in Employment Act and Retirement

The 1978 amendment to an earlier age discrimination act stated that employees in private business having at least 20 persons on the payroll can no longer be forced to retire prior to age 70. Federal workers cannot be forced to retire at any age. Pension law, however, requires full vesting of pension rights no later than age 65 if the employee has at least ten years' service. Employees may continue to retire at age 65 with full benefits if they desire. Business can, however, retire high-level executives with retirement incomes of $27,000 or more at age 65, as long as he or she is in a "high-level policy-making position," and had been in that job for two years.

This act does not suggest that people over 65 cannot be terminated if they are no longer doing their jobs. Older workers who are poor performers can be terminated like anyone else. However, a person's ability to do a job does not necessarily decrease with increased age.

Unless the jobs require heavy, physical labor, workers from 65 to 75 generally perform as well as younger workers. Older workers tend to be more accurate, can compensate for age difficulties with experience, have increased responsibility, and tend to change jobs and be absent less frequently than younger workers. However, they have less ability to work at high speed, less capacity to memorize, and a slower rate of learning.[21]

Early Retirement

Provisions for early retirement are currently included in many pension plans and reflect a recent trend toward allowing employees to retire early and receive most or all of their benefits. There are numerous reasons for early retirement. Early retirement provides opportunities for people to get away from a long-term job. Individuals who have spent 25 or 30 years working for the same employer may wish to use their talents in another area. From the employers' viewpoint, replacing older and higher-paid workers with younger and lower-paid workers can be a way to cut costs in an economic slump. Sears, Roebuck, General Motors, United Airlines, and Caterpillar Tractor are just a few firms that have utilized such a strategy.[22] However, this tactic can turn out to be a disadvantage because a firm may lose a large number of skilled and loyal employees in a very short period of time.

A vital part of retirement is an awareness of the special needs and anxieties of managers and workers as they approach retirement. These problems may be dealt with through a preretirement counseling program.

Preretirement Counseling

Preretirement counseling is aimed at easing employees' anxieties and preparing them for retirement, and the benefits associated with it. The biological changes of aging may cause an individual concern, but suddenly not having a job as a basis from which to order one's life can cause even more anxiety. Preretirement counseling recognizes that retirement involves a mental adjustment for which employees need to be prepared. Good preretirement planning is twofold.

Financial Planning.   One aim is to have people begin their financial planning before they retire. Employees need to be aware of the amount of resources they will have, where these resources come from, their health and insurance benefits, and related assistance available through governmental and private sources.

Psychological Adjustment.   A second aim is to make older employees aware of the psychological changes caused by retirement. Employees should be encouraged to think about how they are going to use their time, the types of activities in which they will be involved, and employment and housing opportunities for older persons.

Preretirement counseling should not begin *immediately* before retirement, but should be a systematic process of gradual preparation. A good approach is to begin preretirement counseling several years before employees actually retire and to increase counseling opportunities as retirement approaches. Extensive counseling depends upon whether or not the organization is large enough to afford this type of program. If an organization cannot afford it, managers can encourage the preretiree to check state and federal agencies which might offer preretirement assistance and information. Also, associations such as the American Association of Retired Persons are available and helpful.

Can you discuss early retirement and
preretirement counseling?

REVIEW AND PREVIEW

Incentives and benefits are two types of additional compensation, each with a different purpose. Incentives attempt to tie increased performance to increased rewards. Benefits are available as part of organizational membership and are not directly related to performance.

Incentive systems that emphasize individual, group, or organizational performance rewards can be developed. Regardless of the system used, the incentives should be designed to actually reward extra effort.

A wide range of benefits can be offered by employers. Some are required by law; others, including voluntary security benefits, insurance and financial benefits, and social and recreational benefits, can be voluntarily offered to employees.

A final set of benefits are retirement-related. Through the federal Social Security System and private pensions, employees are provided financial benefits necessary during retirement. The increased regulation of private pension plans is designed to ensure that employees receive the retirement benefits they expect. Management should be aware of the concerns of a person who considers retiring early or who is approaching retirement by providing preretirement counseling.

An important part of personnel management is the maintenance of a healthy and safe work environment. This maintenance concern includes both the emotional and physical health and safety of employees. These concerns are covered in chapter 14.

Review Questions

1. Distinguish between an incentive and a benefit.
2. Identify two types of incentives and indicate some problems that can occur with each.
3. Why are group and organizational incentives used? What are several types?
4. Describe how you would establish an effective incentive system.
5. Which four types of benefits and services would you most prefer? Relate this answer to the "cafeteria approach" to benefits.
6. Describe two types of retirement-related benefits and indicate the impact the Employee Retirement Income Security Act might have on them.
7. What do you feel are the major issues in early retirement and in preretirement counseling?

Case: Benefit Budgeting

JDR Inc. is a New York-based company which is locating a new plant in Arkansas. This new plant which will be operated as a profit center, will have 300 employees (250 nonexempt and 50 exempt). It has been determined that wages at the plant will average $6.00 per hour and fringe benefits will equal 30% of the hourly wages. As the new personnel manager you are to determine the fringe benefits package. The costs of various benefits are as follows. Develop your benefit package.

SOCIAL SECURITY	6.70%
UNEMPLOYMENT INSURANCE	4.4%
WORKERS' COMPENSATION	1%
PENSION	11%
ONE HOLIDAY	2.4 Cents
REST PERIODS	3.6 Cents
SICK LEAVE 1 DAY/MONTH	1.2 Cents
ONE-DAY VACATION	2.4 Cents
FAMILY DENTAL CARE	9.8 Cents
DRUG INSURANCE PROGRAM	4.9 Cents
LIFE INSURANCE (3T SALARY)	4.9 Cents
HOSPITALIZATION 120 DAYS + MAJOR MEDICAL	27.9 Cents
CHRISTMAS BONUS	2.2 Cents
LONG-TERM DISABILITY SALARY CONTRIBUTIONS	1.1 Cents
VISION-CARE INSURANCE	2.4 Cents
GROUP AUTO INSURANCE	4.9 Cents
FUNERAL PAYMENT	.9 Cent
EMPLOYEE MEALS FURNISHED FREE	.1 Cent
ONE EMPLOYER/FAMILY PARTY	1.2 Cents
100% TUITION WAIVER-COLLEGE	1.1 Cents
DISCOUNTS ON COMPANY-PRODUCED GOODS	.8 Cent
RECREATIONAL PROGRAM	.3 Cent
PREPAID LEGAL SERVICES	.7 Cent
EMPLOYEE THRIFT PLAN	1.5 Cents
CREDIT UNION FACILITIES	.2 Cent
CHILD-CARE CENTER	2.2 Cents

Source: Daniel R. Hoyt, Ph.D, Associate Professor of Management, Arkansas State University, and J. D. Lewis, Division Personnel Manager, FMC Corporation, Cedar Rapids, Iowa, Fringe Benefit Case (May, 1980).

Notes

1. John Curley, "More Executive Bonus Plans Tied to Company Earnings, Sales Goals," *Wall Street Journal*, November 20, 1980, p. 29.

2. "Dear Mr. Citicorp: Thanks a Lot!" *Wall Street Journal*, February 4, 1981, p. 25.

3. G. Christian Hill, "Employee Stock Plans," *Wall Street Journal*, December 8, 1980, p. 1.

4. Ibid.

5. Herbert G. Zollitsch, "Productivity Time Study and Incentive-Pay Plans," in *ASPA Handbook of Personnel*, vol. 2, *Motivation and Commitment* (Washington, D.C.: Bureau of National Affairs, 1975), pp. 6–69.

6. A review of studies can be found in: Paul Tolchinsky and Donald C. King, "Do Goals Mediate the Effects of Incentives on Performance?" *Academy of Management Review*, 5, October 1980, pp. 455–457.

7. U.S. Chamber of Commerce, *Employee Benefits* 1979 (Washington, D.C.: U.S. Chamber of Commerce, 1980).

8. Robert Krogman, "What Employees Need to Know About Benefit Plans," *Personnel Administrator*, May 1980, pp. 45–47.

9. Betty J. Richards, "Benefit Exploration Contest Program," *Personnel Administrator*, October 1980, pp. 57–58.

10. "The Great Ripoff in Unemployment Pay," *U.S. News and World Report*, March 16, 1981, pp. 63–64.

11. *Paid Holidays & Vacation Policies*, Personnel Policies Jury #130, (Washington, D.C.: Bureau of National Affairs, November, 1980), p. 1.

12. J. Alex Wade, "Self-Funding: Is It Right for Your Company?" *Personnel Administrator*, November 1980, pp. 23–25.

13. Earnest W. Saward and Scott Fleming, "Health Maintenance Organizations," *Scientific American*, October 1980, pp. 47–53.

14. John J. Miller, "Trends and Practices in Employee Benefits," *Personnel Administrator*, May 1980, p. 50.

15. Robert Ricklefs, "Some Employers Help Pay Auto Insurance; Experts Suggest Benefit Could Catch On," *Wall Street Journal*, January 13, 1981.

16. "When Employees Choose," *Personnel Administrator*, May 1980, p. 20.

17. Sal J. Giudice, "Flexible Benefits Program," *Personnel Administrator*, October 1980, pp. 60–61.

18. David J. Thomsen, "Introducing Cafeteria Compensation in Your Company," *Personnel Journal*, 56, March 1977, pp. 124–131.

19. Richard J. Schulz, testifying for the American Society for Personnel Administration before the Ways and Means Subcommittee on Social Security, U.S. House of Representatives, March 23, 1981.

20. "Status Report on the Unisex Issue," *The Participant*, TIAA-CREF, March 1981, p. 1.

21. R. J. Paul, "Mandatory Retirement—Some Research Findings," Paper presented at 1978 Midwest Business Administration Association, Chicago.

22. Joann S. Lublin and Michael L. King, "More Employers Offer an Early Retirement; Some Workers Decline," *Wall Street Journal*, November 12, 1980, p. 1.

Organizational Maintenance

EAPS: "DO GOODING" OR SMART BUSINESS?

Healthy and safe employees are likely to be more productive than those who are affected by unhealthy or unsafe conditions. Every year, organizations lose money because of illnesses, accidents, and injuries on the job. A part of personnel management is to provide employees with working environments that are safe and to ensure that employees with health problems receive help.

EAPS, or Employee Assistance Programs, are attempts to help employees with the most difficult problems. Employee mental illness, whether related to alcoholism, drug abuse, emotional problems, or whatever, came out of the closet in the 1970s. The resulting rise of EAPS geared to getting troubled workers help before it's too late has been rather dramatic. From the early 1970s until today, over 2,000 EAPS have been instituted in the U.S.

Some personnel managers argue that EAPS make their other personnel programs more effective. For example, in one large company, the Vice-President of Personnel found that much of his people's time was being taken up by such problems as employee anxiety reactions, suicide attempts, alcohol- and drug-related absences, and family disturbances. Further, the Medical Department was not able to provide accurate information on whether or not affected employees could successfully return to work. The Vice-President decided an EAP might save a great deal of time and money.

It is no secret that every company of any size has employees with health and personal problems. Common problems are: personal crisis (marriage, family, legal, etc.); alcoholism and drug abuse; and emotional illness.

Part of the reason for companies' sudden increased interest in EAP is the increase in the incidence of these problems in the working population. Comparison of the survey results just mentioned with a similar survey done ten years earlier shows the incidence of these major problems has more than doubled.

Slightly less than half the companies responding to the survey offer in-house counseling for alcoholism or personal crises. About a third provide in-house counseling for emotional illness. The major problem in handling troubled employees is getting them to admit they are having trouble, then convincing them to accept advice or referral.

This section considers health and safety issues, personnel policies, and records associated with personnel management. Traditionally, safety received only minor attention in many organizations. The Occupational Safety and Health Act of 1970 has changed this outlook and added a new dimension to personnel management responsibilities. The regulations contained in the act are complex and sometimes compliance is difficult. Managers must also maintain an atmosphere of safety consciousness in the organization through continuous communication. Suggestions on dealing with the problems of health and safety and some details of the Occupational Safety and Health Act are included in chapter 14.

Coordination of personnel efforts requires policies and rules. However, if not well designed and enforced, policies and rules can be sources of irritation and may rightly be targets of criticism. Chapter 15 deals with organizational coordination as it is affected by personnel policies and rules and formal personnel communication.

Vital to personnel coordination efforts are adequate personnel records. These records are necessary for day-to-day monitoring of personnel activities. In addition, personnel records serve as a major source of personnel research data. Personnel research activities provide the organization with a more analytical perspective for decision making than just managerial intuition. Personnel records and research are discussed in chapter 16.

CHAPTER 14

Personnel Health and Safety

When you have read this chapter, you should be able to:

1. Define health and safety and explain their importance in an organization.

2. Discuss several factors affecting health and safety in organizations.

3. Explain the impact of four health problems in organizations.

4. Identify how organizations respond to alcoholism, drugs, and other health problems.

5. Identify the basic provisions of the Occupational Safety and Health Act of 1970.

6. Describe OSHA recordkeeping and inspection requirements including listing five types of OSHA citations.

7. Discuss both positive effects and problems associated with OSHA.

8. Identify and briefly explain the basic components of a systems approach to safety.

Near Proximity?

Peter Schultz is personnel director for Mid-Coastal Freight and Trucking, Inc. Recently Peter had a "visit" from Herman Medina, an OSHA compliance officer. On a tour of the warehouse Herman found no violations.

However, when Herman got to the loading dock he stopped to talk to two of the men loading a truck. Since the men had just finished loading some fairly heavy boxes, Herman asked them if they had ever gotten hurt loading boxes that size. Clyde Cutler, one of the loaders, said, "Sometimes we drop one and maybe we cut our hands or arms some. But some mercurochrome and a gauze bandage from the first-aid box usually stops the bleeding and it heals pretty quick."

Herman asked Peter if he was trained in first-aid and Peter said no. Herman then asked if anyone at the warehouse had been certified by the Red Cross in first-aid. Peter said no, primarily because a hospital was located about 15 to 20 blocks away. Herman said that was not sufficient because somebody injured would be at least ten minutes from treatment. Herman then described the OSHA standard 29,1910.151(b) on first-aid: "At least one employee must be Red Cross-certified if an infirmary, clinic, or hospital is not in near proximity to the work place." Peter groaned when Herman handed him a violation statement.

Comments:

This case is a narrative description of an actual OSHA case and illustrates the demands that OSHA can place on managers and personnel specialists. In the actual situation the company received a citation that was later overturned.

The impact of OSHA is clearly demonstrated in this case. The advantage of having a trained first-aid individual or very accessible emergency care is an important part of protecting workers. However, the language in the standard led to the employer and the inspector misinterpreting the compliance requirement.

O RGANIZATIONS are obligated to provide employees with a safe and healthful environment. Requiring employees to work with unsafe equipment or in areas where hazards are not controlled is a highly questionable practice. However, as the opening case points out, just providing safety equipment is not enough. Managers must also ensure that employees are safety conscious and maintain good health.

This chapter looks at ways organizations can maintain safe working environments for employees. Both managers and personnel specialists are involved in health and safety in an organization.

HEALTH AND SAFETY DEFINED

The terms "health" and "safety" are very closely related. Although they are often used in the same context, a distinction should be made.

> HEALTH refers to a general state of physical, mental, and emotional well-being.

Health is a broader and somewhat more nebulous term than safety. A healthy person is one who is free of illness, injury, or mental and emotional problems which impair normal human activity. However, exactly what is healthy or normal behavior is open to interpretation. Health maintenance or management refers to maintaining the overall well-being of an individual.

Typically, safety concerns physical well-being instead of mental or emotional well-being. The main purpose of effective safety programs in organizations is to *prevent* work-related injuries and accidents.

> SAFETY refers to protection of the physical health of people.

The focus of health and safety policies is the safe interaction of people and the working environment. Because many employers' efforts were inadequate, the federal Occupational Safety and Health Act of 1970 was passed. This act has had a tremendous impact and any person interested in personnel management should develop a working knowledge of the act's provisions and implications.

Can you define health and safety?

Health and Safety Interface

As Figure 14–1 indicates, the primary safety responsibility in an organization usually falls on supervisors and managers. A personnel specialist or safety specialist can help investigate accidents, produce safety program materials, and conduct formal safety training. However, department supervisors and managers are key in maintaining safe working conditions and a healthy work force. A supervisor in a ball-bearing plant has several health and safety-related responsibilities. Examples of some of his responsibilities are: reminding an employee to wear safety glasses; checking on the cleanliness of the work area; observing employees to see if any of them have alcohol, drug, or emotional problems which affect their work behavior; and recommending equipment changes (such as screens, railings, or guards) to specialists in the organization.

Figure 14–1.   Health and safety interface.

Personnel Unit	Managers
Coordinates health and safety programs	Monitor health and safety of employees daily
Develops safety reporting system	Coach employees to be safety conscious
Provides accident investigation expertise	Investigate accidents
Provides technical expertise on accident research and prevention	Observe health and safety behavior of employees daily

A personnel safety specialist in the same plant has other safety responsibilities: maintaining government required health and safety records; coordinating a safety training class for new employees; assisting the supervisor in investigating an accident in which an employee injured a hand; and developing plantwide safety communication and information materials. The interface between the supervisor and the personnel specialist is crucial to a coordinated maintenance effort.

NATURE OF HEALTH AND SAFETY

Every year employers lose an astounding amount of money and resources because of accidents. A Bureau of Labor Statistics Survey for a recent one-year period provides some rather startling statistics:[1]

1. On the average, about one of every 11 workers in private industry experienced a job-related injury or illness.
2. Work-related fatalities increased from 4,590 in the previous year to 4,950.
3. About 5.96 million work-related injuries and illnesses occurred.
4. Of this number, approximately 97% were injuries, 3% were illnesses.
5. Lost work days totaled 42.6 million days, equivalent to 66.2 lost work days/100 workers.

With problems of this magnitude, health and safety must be a prime concern in the management of human resources. Knowledge about factors affecting employee health and safety is important.

Worker Attitudes and Accidents

Because health and safety deal with individual well-being, employees' attitudes about safety should be considered in planning health and safety programs. Employees' attitudes toward their working conditions, accidents, and jobs should be analyzed when an organization's health and safety activities are examined. Many more problems are caused by careless employees than by machines or employer negligence. The safety director for a supermarket chain estimated that "80% of wholesale and retail-related accidents are due to unsafe acts by employees versus 20% due to unsafe physical conditions."[2]

At one time, it was thought that workers who were dissatisfied with their jobs would have a higher accident rate. However, this assumption has been questioned in recent years. One study of accident proneness found that younger and less-experienced employees were involved in more injuries and accidents. This same study suggested that there were some personality and emotional differences between people who had no accidents and those who had repeated accidents.[3] Another study found that biorhythm cycles were not significantly related to the occurrence of accidents.[4] All this information suggests that while employees' personalities and attitudes may have an effect on accidents, a cause-and-effect relationship is very difficult to establish.

Worker Boredom and Monotony. Employees doing the same job repeatedly each day can become bored. They either begin to pay less attention to the task or they develop bad habits which can cause accidents and injuries. One way to deal with worker boredom is to relieve the monotony by redesigning the job. Elements of job design such as job scope and job depth were discussed in chapter 6.

Engineering Approach to Health and Safety

Some accidents can be prevented by designing machines and equipment areas so that workers who daydream periodically or who perform rather mechanical jobs cannot injure themselves or others. This *engineering approach* tries to prevent accidents by constructing the working environment so that it is very difficult for employees to injure themselves. Providing safety equipment and guards on machinery and installing emergency switches are equipment changes which are often made to prevent accidents. To protect Martha Bernquist, a punch-press operator, from mashing her finger, a guard is attached to a machine so her hand cannot accidentally slip into the machine. Actions such as providing safety rails; keeping aisles clear; and providing adequate ventilation, lighting, heating, and air conditioning can all help make the work environment safer.

Ergonomics. A specialized field which has developed to engineer the work environment is *ergonomics*. Ergonomics comes from the word *"ergon"* meaning *"work"* and *"omics"* meaning *"management of."* An ergonomist studies the physiological, psychological, and engineering design aspects of a job. Other aspects such as fatigue factors, lighting, tools, equipment layouts, and placement of controls are also considered by an ergonomist.

What are some factors that may affect health and safety?

HEALTH

Employee health problems are inevitable in all organizations. These problems can range from illnesses such as a cold or flu to serious injuries on the job or elsewhere. Some employees have emotional problems; others have drinking or drug problems. All may affect organizational operations and individual employee productivity.

There are four major health problem areas which may have direct relevance to personnel management: physical illness, emotional illness, alcoholism, and drug abuse. As depicted in Figure 14–2, resolution of problems in all these areas is necessary for the development of healthy individuals.

Physical Health and Illness

Physical illnesses and problems may reduce an employee's ability to perform a job. As was pointed out in chapter 13, organizations help

Figure 14–2.   Major health problems.   *(4 major areas)*

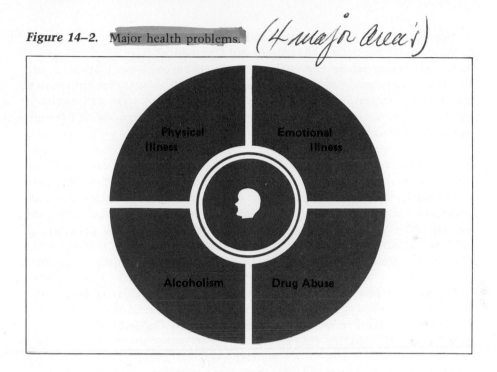

employees with physical illnesses and problems by providing hospital-ization and health insurance. However, sound health programs focus on preventing employees from getting sick, as well as helping employees get well.

Some organizations have staff medical professionals such as doctors or nurses to treat minor illnesses and job-related injuries. If a claims clerk at a large insurance company came to work feeling rather weak because he had a cold, the company doctor could prescribe some med-ication to help the clerk feel better. Many larger companies provide on-site medical assistance because the Occupational Safety and Health Act of 1970 (to be discussed later) requires certain first-aid treatment and health services to be available "in near proximity" to work stations.

Health Concerns and the Work Environment.   Many people have heard of the health problems developed by asbestos workers, coal miners, and some chemical workers. Cancer, black lung disease, and radiation poi-soning are all significant health concerns. One estimate is that over two million U.S. workers are disabled by occupational diseases.[5]

Other health problems can be caused by a work environment that exposes workers to excessive noise or harmful lighting. One example of how new health problems are developing because of technology in-volves employees who work at video display computer terminals. Ter-minal operators who were studied complained of dizziness and eye problems.[6]

Managers and personnel specialists must exhibit a heightened awareness of health problems; they must not just concentrate on safety problems. The engineering approach is likely to be used even more in the future to reduce the exposure of workers to health-damaging substances and environments. In cases of potentially hazardous jobs and environments, employers should continually monitor employee health through physical examinations.

Physical Exams.   Employers may sponsor general physical examinations yearly or on a regular basis. Organizations providing this service are investing in the physical health of employees who may not see a doctor regularly because of work schedules, personal reluctance, or lack of money. AT&T (the telephone company) has established a program of extensive health screening every five years.[7] This approach is used instead of the traditional annual physical which often is a "quickie exam." One physician has commented that the typical annual physical only tells that the person is alive, has blood circulating, and is breathing. Regardless of the type of physical given, organizations who offer them to employees believe that the employer benefits financially and organizationally if healthier employees are on the job.

Physical Fitness.   Another way that some employers assist employees in maintaining good physical health is by providing physical fitness programs. According to National Industrial Recreation Association data approximately 50,000 employees have physical fitness programs. Some programs are lunch-hour exercise classes or stop smoking clinics while others use complete gymnasiums provided by employers. Internorth, Texaco, IBM, Pepsico, and Merrill Lynch all are reported to have programs of varying degrees of complexity.[8]

Attempting to pinpoint potential health problems and deal with them early allows an employer to have the continued service of a valuable individual. Sometimes physical health and hygiene problems are caused by emotional or mental health factors.

Emotional Illness

Emotional or mental illnesses and hygiene problems can be caused by many complex and interacting factors. Causes can be related to an individual's personality, job, personal conduct, or contact with others. For example, extreme anxiety and emotional disturbance might be related to the death of a loved one, divorce, or physical changes due to age.

Stress.   The pressures of modern life, coupled with the demands of a job, can lead to emotional health concerns that are lumped together and labelled *stress.* The evidence of stress is ever present, from the 35-year-old executive who dies of a sudden heart attack to the dependable older worker who unexpectedly commits suicide. One indicator of stress is hypertension (high blood pressure). According to data provided by the Blue Cross and Blue Shield Association, 17 million U.S. workers suffer from hypertension, which results in $20 billion of lost wages and productivity every year.[9] Other problems such as alcoholism and drug abuse may be the result of severe emotional strain, as employees turn to them to help reduce stress.

When an emotional problem becomes so severe that it disrupts an employee's ability to function normally, the employee should be directed to appropriate professionals for help. Because emotional problems are very difficult to diagnose, supervisors and managers should not become deeply involved in them. If a quality control inspector is emotionally upset because of his marital difficulties, the supervisor should not get personally involved trying to solve the employee's problems. Even though most supervisors and managers are concerned about employees' problems, they should realize that appropriate professionals are better qualified to help troubled employees.

Why are physical and health concerns important considerations?

Alcoholism

Alcoholism is a costly health problem. It has been estimated by a U.S. governmental agency that the problem drinker on the payroll costs American industry approximately $20 billion a year in lost production, mishandling of resources, sick pay, absenteeism, and other costs, and up to 10% of the American work force suffers from various degrees of alcoholism.

Alcoholism Assistance Programs.   Because of the problems and costs involved, a growing number of organizations are sponsoring programs to deal with alcoholic managers and workers. Usually these programs are enthusiastically supported by unions. Some health insurance coverage includes alcoholism as a disease so that employees have help to pay for treatment of their drinking problems. By dealing with alcoholism, employers are able to retain otherwise good workers who are disabled by drinking problems. Insurance companies have been very active in providing comprehensive programs dealing with alcoholism. The Kemper, Equitable Traveler's, and Prudential Insurance companies have employee programs which consider alcoholism as a disease that can be treated. The director of an alcoholism assistance program for Union Pacific Railroad reports that more than 2,500 employees have used the program. The success rate has been about 86%.[10]

One process for dealing with problem drinkers is shown in Figure 14–3. Managers and supervisors should encourage employees with drinking problems to seek specialized treatment. This treatment can be made available through a company's program, a cooperative program between an employer and a union, a private agency, state or local health and social service agencies, or voluntary organizations such as Alcoholics Anonymous.

Assisting employees who have drinking problems is part of good personnel management. Although some alcoholic employees may resist treatment at first, alcohol rehabilitation programs generally have had a success rate of 50% to 75%.[11] Instead of immediately firing an employee with a drinking problem, many employers are recognizing their responsibilities in dealing with alcoholism.

Drug Abuse

The impact of drug abuse is evident throughout society—and in organizations. These problems cover the full range, from the use of minor drugs, such as marijuana, to the overuse of legal drugs, such as barbiturates and tranquilizers, and illegal hard drugs, such as heroin. Some firms have found employees selling drugs to other employees at work. One computer firm discovered a drug ring grossing $10,000 a week that involved over ten employees. In another firm in California some employees were observed drying cocaine in a microwave oven in the company cafeteria.[12]

Dealing with Employee Drug Problems.   Employers have responded to their employees' drug-related problems by including drug and other substance abuse within employee assistance programs. Managers attempting to deal with the problem of employee drug abuse should be aware of drug-induced changes in an employee's behavior. Possible tip-offs to drug abuse are excessive absenteeism, increased tardiness, decreasing job performance, and unexplained personality and behavior changes. However, a supervisor or manager can do little other than inform the company physician or counseling specialist about the problem and direct the employee to appropriate professionals.

Policies on drug abuse and how to deal with it are needed in many organizations. Improving selection procedures to screen out persons who abuse drugs is a possible solution. Some firms utilize urinalysis tests as a part of their selection process. This screening is very imprecise and may discriminate against persons who once had a drug problem but have overcome it. Another difficulty is defining exactly what constitutes a drug problem. Obviously, smoking marijuana occasionally is a different matter than being hooked on heroin. To deal with drug problems, organizations need to: (1) develop an awareness of drug problems and (2) develop organizational policies and responses to cope with drug abuse.

Figure 14–3. Policy on problem drinking.

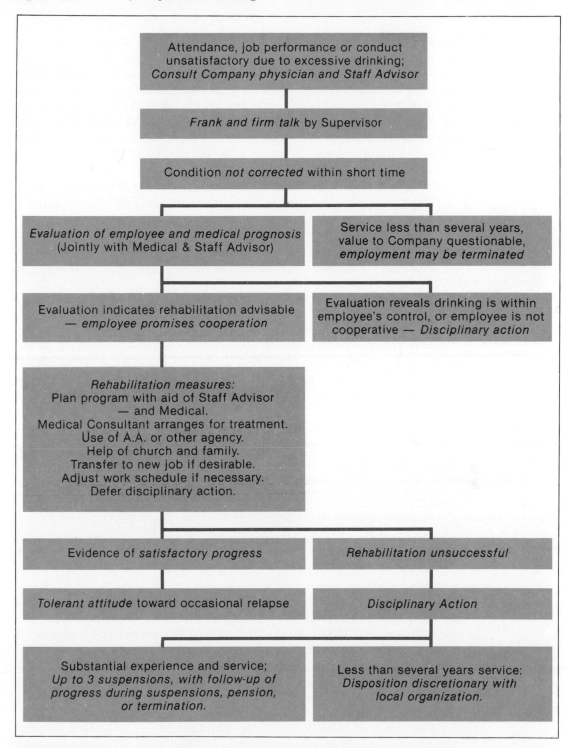

Attendance, job performance or conduct unsatisfactory due to excessive drinking; *Consult Company physician and Staff Advisor*

Frank and firm talk by Supervisor

Condition *not corrected* within short time

Evaluation of employee and medical prognosis (Jointly with Medical & Staff Advisor)

Service less than several years, value to Company questionable, *employment may be terminated*

Evaluation indicates rehabilitation advisable — *employee promises cooperation*

Evaluation reveals drinking is within employee's control, or employee is not cooperative — *Disciplinary action*

Rehabilitation measures:
Plan program with aid of Staff Advisor — and Medical.
Medical Consultant arranges for treatment.
Use of A.A. or other agency.
Help of church and family.
Transfer to new job if desirable.
Adjust work schedule if necessary.
Defer disciplinary action.

Evidence of *satisfactory progress*

Rehabilitation unsuccessful

Tolerant attitude toward occasional relapse

Disciplinary Action

Substantial experience and service; *Up to 3 suspensions, with follow-up of progress during suspensions, pension, or termination.*

Less than several years service: *Disposition discretionary with local organization.*

(Source: Adapted from August Ralston, "Employee Alcoholism: Response of the Largest Industrials," *The Personnel Administrator,* August 1977, p. 52. Reprinted with permission.)

Personnel Management and Health Maintenance

The various health problems discussed above are legitimate and real concerns in many organizations. At one extreme, responses can include ignoring or firing problem employees. At the other extreme, managers and organizations can provide special programs and services for employees with health problems. A survey of methods used in dealing with a variety of employee problems is capsuled in Figure 14–4.

Figure 14–4. Methods for dealing with problem employees.

	Alcoholism	Marijuana abuse	Prescription drug abuse	Hard drug addiction	Emotional illness	Personal crises
Consultation with supervisor	55%	40%	32%	26%	43%	55%
Discipline short of discharge	35(49)	15(17)	12	8(11)	9(16)	12
Discharge	29(15)	28(27)	15	25(33)	9 (7)	9
In-house counseling	45(67)	20(21)	22	15(18)	43(43)	55
Referral to outside agency	60(65)	38(21)	31	35(20)	55(67)	58
Other (please describe)	14	8	6	8	9	8
No response	12	37	48	48	28	18

Note: Figures are percentages of companies using specified method for each problem. Figures in parentheses are results of 1970 survey

(Source: "Counseling Policies and Programs for Employees With Problems," ASPA-BNA Survey #34, *Bulletin to Management*, March 23, 1978, Washington, D.C.: The Bureau of National Affairs. BNA Policy & Practice Series, The Bureau of National Affairs, Inc.)

Employee Assistance Programs. One method that organizations are using to deal with employee emotional problems is an *employee assistance program* (EAP). In such a program, an employer establishes a liaison relationship with a social service counseling agency. Employees who have problems may then contact the agency, either voluntarily or by employer referral, for assistance with a broad range of problems. Much or all of the counseling costs are paid for by the employer up to a preestablished limit.

The value of these programs is summarized in the section opening material. In one large corporation over 14,000 employees used the EAP in a three-year period of time.[13] Such a response rate indicates that firms that provide EAPs are truly responding to the health needs of their employees.

How do organizations deal with health problems?

Providing work conditions conducive to good employee health should be a prime concern for all managers and employees. The statistics mentioned earlier reflect the costs in lost productivity and human suffering. The Williams-Steiger Occupational Safety and Health Act of 1970 was passed to require employers to be more health and safety conscious.

OCCUPATIONAL SAFETY AND HEALTH ACT OF 1970

The Occupational Safety and Health Act, which became effective in 1971, is a part of the nation's labor law. The purpose of the act is "to assure so far as possible every working man or woman in the Nation safe and healthful working conditions and to preserve our human resources."[14] Every employer engaged in commerce who has one or more employees is covered by the act. Farmers having fewer than ten employees are exempt from the act. Covered under other health and safety acts are some employers in specific industries such as coal mining. Federal, state, and local government employees are covered by separate provisions or statutes.

Basic Provisions

The act established the Occupational Safety and Health Administration, known as OSHA. The act also established the National Institute of Occupational Safety and Health (NIOSH) as a supporting body to do research and develop standards.

Enforcement Standards.   To implement the act, numerous specific standards were established concerning equipment and working environment regulations. OSHA often uses national standards developed by engineering and quality control groups but they are not *voluntary* standards that the employer pledges to meet. Employers are *required* to meet the provisions and standards under OSHA. Figure 14–5 gives examples of some rather specific OSHA standards.

"General Duty" Clause.   Section 5a(1) of the act is known as the "general duty" clause. This section requires that in areas in which no standards have been adopted, the employer has a general duty to provide safe and healthy working conditions. Employers who know of or who should

Figure 14–5. Sample OSHA Standards.

§ 1910.151 Medical services and first aid.

(a) The employer shall ensure the ready availability of medical personnel for advice and consultation on matters of plant health.

(b) In the absence of an infirmary, clinic, or hospital in near proximity to the workplace which is used for the treatment of all injured employees, a person or persons shall be adequately trained to render first aid. First aid supplies approved by the consulting physician shall be readily available.

(c) Where the eyes or body of any person may be exposed to injurious corrosive materials, suitable facilities for quick drenching or flushing of the eyes and body shall be provided within the work area for immediate emergency use.

§ 1910.157 Portable fire extinguishers.

(a) *General requirements*—(1) *Operable condition.* Portable extinguishers shall be maintained in a fully charged and operable condition, and kept in their designated places at all times when they are not being used.

(2) *Location.* Extinguishers shall be conspicuously located where they will be readily accessible and immediately available in the event of fire. They shall be located along normal paths of travel.

(3) *Marking of location.* Extinguishers shall not be obstructed or obscured from view. In large rooms, and in certain locations where visual obstruction cannot be completely avoided, means shall be provided to indicate the location and intended use of extinguishers conspicuously.

(4) *Marking of extinguishers.* If extinguishers intended for different classes of fire are grouped, their intended use shall be marked conspicuously to insure choice of the proper extinguisher at the time of a fire.

. . .

(9) *Temperature range.* Extinguishers shall be suitable for use within a temperature range of at least plus 40° to 120° Fahrenheit.

Source: General Industry Standards USDOL-OSHA #2206 Nov. 7, 1978 OSHA S&H Stds (29CFR1910).

reasonably know of unsafe or unhealthy conditions can be cited for violating this clause. The existence of standard practices or a trade association code, which is also not included in OSHA standards, is often used as the basis for citations under the "general duty" clause.

Employers are responsible for knowing about and informing their employees of safety and health standards established by OSHA and for putting up OSHA posters in prominent places. In addition, they are required to enforce the use of personal protective equipment and to provide safety communications to employees so they are aware of safety considerations. Employees who report safety violations to OSHA cannot be punished or discharged.

Whirlpool Corp. v. Marshall.[15]   A major victory for employees and unions was won in this court case in 1980. The U.S. Supreme Court unanimously ruled that workers have the right to walk off a job if they believe it is hazardous without fear of reprisal by the employer. The criteria discussed by the court were that "employees have the right not to perform an assigned task because of a reasonable apprehension of health or serious injury coupled with a reasonable belief that no less drastic alternative is available."[16]

Can you discuss the basic provisions of OSHA?

Record-keeping Requirements

OSHA established a standard national system for recording occupational injuries, accidents, and fatalities. Employers are generally required to maintain an annual detailed record of the various types of accidents for inspection by OSHA representatives and for submission to the agency.

Summary Log.   Employers with good safety records the previous year who have less than ten employees are not required to keep detailed records. Figure 14–6 shows the OSHA summary log that employers must complete. The portion to the right of the dotted line must be posted for employee review during February of every year.

Criticism of OSHA's record-keeping requirements resulted in significant changes in 1977. Many small employers having less than ten employees were exempted from having to complete the summary records. Only those small firms meeting the following conditions must complete OSHA Form 200, the basic reporting document: (1) those firms having frequent hospitalization injuries or illnesses, (2) those firms having work-related deaths, (3) those firms included in OSHA's annual labor statistics survey.

Accident Frequency Rate.   Accident frequency and severity rates also must be calculated. OSHA regulations require organizations to calculate injury frequency rates per 100 full-time employees on an annual basis. The *accident frequency rate* is figured as follows.[17]

$$\frac{N}{EH} \times 200{,}000$$

where N = number of occupational injuries and illnesses
    EH = total hours worked by all employees during reference year
  200,000 = base for 100 full-time equivalent workers (working 40 hours per week, 50 weeks per year)

Accident severity rates are computed by figuring the number of lost-time cases, the number of lost workdays, and the number of deaths.

Figure 14–6. Log and summary of occupational injuries and illnesses.

Bureau of Labor Statistics
Log and Summary of Occupational
Injuries and Illnesses

U.S. Department of Labor

For Calendar Year 19 ______ Page ___ of ___

NOTE: **This form is required by Public Law 91-596 and must be kept in the establishment for 5 years. Failure to maintain and post can result in the issuance of citations and assessment of penalties.** ***(See posting requirements on the other side of form.)***

RECORDABLE CASES: You are required to record information about every occupational **death**; every nonfatal occupational **illness**; and those nonfatal occupational **injuries** which involve one or more of the following: loss of consciousness, restriction of work or motion, transfer to another job, or medical treatment (other than first aid). ***(See definitions on the other side of form.)***

Company Name

Establishment Name

Establishment Address

Form Approved
O.M.B. No. 44R 1453

Case or File Number	Date of Injury or Onset of Illness	Employee's Name	Occupation	Department	Description of Injury or Illness	Extent of and Outcome of INJURY: Fatalities — Injury Related	Nonfatal Injuries — Injuries With Lost Workdays				Injuries Without Lost Workdays	Type, Extent of, and Outcome of ILLNESS: Type of Illness — CHECK Only One Column for Each Illness *(See other side of form for terminations or permanent transfers.)*							Fatalities — Illness Related	Nonfatal Illnesses — Illnesses With Lost Workdays				Illnesses Without Lost Workdays
Enter a nonduplicating number which will facilitate comparisons with supplementary records.	Enter Mo./day.	Enter first name or initial, middle initial, last name.	Enter regular job title, not activity employee was performing when injured or at onset of illness. In the absence of a formal title, enter a brief description of the employee's duties.	Enter department in which the employee is regularly employed or a description of normal workplace to which employee is assigned, even though temporarily working in another department at the time of injury or illness.	Enter a brief description of the injury or illness and indicate the part or parts of body affected. Typical entries for this column might be: Amputation of 1st joint right forefinger; Strain of lower back; Contact dermatitis on both hands; Electrocution—body.	Enter **DATE** of death. Mo./day/yr.	Enter a **CHECK** if injury involves days away from work, or days of restricted work activity, or both.	Enter a **CHECK** if injury involves days away from work.	Enter number of **DAYS away from work.**	Enter number of **DAYS** of *restricted work activity.*	Enter a **CHECK** if no entry was made in columns 1 or 2 but the injury is recordable as defined above.	Occupational skin diseases or disorders	Dust diseases of the lungs	Respiratory conditions due to toxic agents	Poisoning (systemic effects of toxic materials)	Disorders due to physical agents	Disorders associated with repeated trauma	All other occupational illnesses	Enter **DATE** of death. Mo./day/yr.	Enter a **CHECK** if illness involves days away from work, or days of restricted work activity, or both.	Enter a **CHECK** if illness involves days away from work.	Enter number of **DAYS away from work.**	Enter number of **DAYS** of *restricted work activity.*	Enter a **CHECK** if no entry was made in columns 8 or 9.
(A)	(B)	(C)	(D)	(E)	(F)	(1)	(2)	(3)	(4)	(5)	(6)	(7) (a)	(b)	(c)	(d)	(e)	(f)	(g)	(8)	(9)	(10)	(11)	(12)	(13)
					PREVIOUS PAGE TOTALS →																			

INJURIES

ILLNESSES

OSHA No. 200

FOLD

Certification of Annual Summary Totals By ______ Title ______ Date ______

OSHA No. 200

POST ONLY THIS PORTION OF THE LAST PAGE NO LATER THAN FEBRUARY 1.

These figures are then related to total work hours/100 full-time employees, and compared to industrywide rates and other employers' rates.

Reporting Injuries/Illnesses.   There are several types of injuries or illnesses defined by the act:

1. *Injury or illness-related deaths.*
2. *Lost-time or disabling injuries:* disabling or job-related injuries which cause an employee to miss his or her regularly scheduled work on the day following the accident.
3. *Medical care injuries:* injuries requiring treatment by a physician but that do not cause an employee to miss a regularly scheduled work turn.
4. *Minor injuries:* injuries which require first-aid treatment and do not cause an employee to miss the next regularly scheduled work turn.

The record-keeping requirements under OSHA are summarized in Figure 14–7. Notice that only minor injuries do not have to be recorded for OSHA.

Managers may go to extreme lengths to avoid lost-time or medical care injuries. For example, if several managers are trained in first-aid, some injuries can be treated on the work site. In one situation an employee's back injuries were treated with heat packs by the plant personnel manager to avoid counting the accident as a medical care injury.

Until OSHA tightened regulations, many employers would move injured employees to other jobs to avoid counting an injury as a lost-time injury. Assume a seamstress in a clothing factory injured her hand on the job so that she could not operate her sewing machine. Her employer had her carry thread to other operators and perform other "make work" jobs so that she did not miss work, and the injury would not have to be reported. Current regulations attempt to control this kind of subterfuge by requiring employees to perform the same type of job.

There are several major reasons why employers try to make injuries appear less severe for reporting purposes. An abnormal number of lost-time or medical care injuries are warning flags to OSHA representatives and may lead to intensive investigations. Also, an employer's worker compensation and liability insurance rates may be affected by increased injuries and accidents.

Inspection Requirements

The 1970 act provides for on-the-spot inspection by OSHA agents, known as *compliance officers* or *inspectors.* In the original act an employer *could not refuse* entry to an OSHA inspector. Furthermore, the original act prohibited a compliance officer from giving prior notification of an inspection. This provision was included to allow inspection of normal

Figure 14–7. Guide to recordability of cases under the Occupational Safety and Health Act.

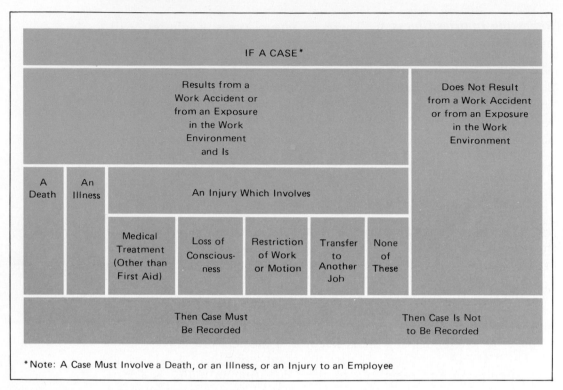

(Source: Bureau of Labor Statistics, U.S. Department of Labor, *What Every Employee Needs to Know About OSHA Record Keeping.* Washington D.C.: U.S. Government Printing Office, November 1978, p. 3.)

operations, instead of allowing an employer to "tidy up." This so-called no-knock provision was challenged in numerous court suits. Finally, in 1978, the U.S. Supreme Court made a definite ruling on this issue.

Marshall v. Barlow's Inc.[18]   In this case, an Idaho plumbing and air conditioning firm, Barlow's, refused entry to an OSHA inspector. The employer argued that the no-knock provision violated the fourth amendment of the U.S. Constitution, which deals with "unreasonable search and seizure." The government, through Ray Marshall, the Secretary of Labor, argued that the no-knock provision was necessary for enforcement of the 1970 act and that the fourth amendment did not apply to a business situation with employees and customers having access to the firm.

The Supreme Court rejected the government's arguments and held that safety inspectors must produce a search warrant if an employer refuses to allow an inspector voluntarily. However, the Court ruled that an inspector does not have to prove probable cause to obtain a search warrant. A warrant can be obtained if a search is part of a general enforcement plan.

Although this decision was initially viewed as a victory for employers, later analysis of the decision revealed that the Supreme Court took a middle-of-the-road position. Inspectors no longer must be admitted through the no-knock provision. However, warrants are relatively easy to obtain because of the "general enforcement plan" aspects of the decision. An employer can refuse admittance, but the process of obtaining a warrant for OSHA is not extremely restrictive.

A number of cases have been filed challenging the use of *ex parte* search warrants. This warrant can be obtained by OSHA without notice to the employer, and the employer cannot argue against granting of the warrant. Some lower federal courts have ruled against the use of the *ex parte* warrant while other courts have allowed them. Until a definite ruling is made by the U.S. Supreme Court, these warrants will continue to be used.

Conduct of Inspection.   When the compliance officer arrives, the manager should request to see the inspector's credentials. After entering, the OSHA officer typically requests a meeting with the top representative or manager in the organization. The officer also may request that a union representative, an employee, and a company representative be present as the inspection is conducted. The OSHA inspector checks an organization's records to see if they are being maintained and how many accidents have occurred. Following this review of the safety records, the inspector conducts an on-the-spot inspection and may use a wide variety of equipment to test compliance with the standards.

Figure 14–8 provides a list of some of the equipment that may be used by an OSHA compliance officer. Following the inspection, the compliance officer can issue citations for violations of standards and provisions of the act.

Safety Consultation.   OSHA, in conjunction with state and local governments, has established a safety consultation service. An employer can contact the state agency and have an authorized safety consultant conduct an advisory inspection. This consultant cannot issue citations or penalties and generally is prohibited from providing OSHA with any information obtained during the consultation visit. Such a visit provides an employer with an opportunity to receive a report useful in preventing future difficulties when OSHA does conduct an inspection.

What are key OSHA recordkeeping and
inspection requirements?

Figure 14–8. What the OSHA inspector carries.

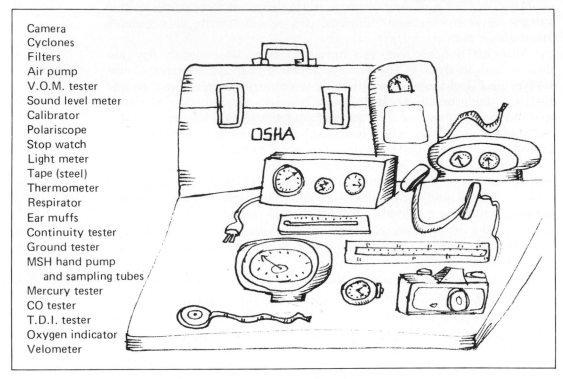

Camera
Cyclones
Filters
Air pump
V.O.M. tester
Sound level meter
Calibrator
Polariscope
Stop watch
Light meter
Tape (steel)
Thermometer
Respirator
Ear muffs
Continuity tester
Ground tester
MSH hand pump
    and sampling tubes
Mercury tester
CO tester
T.D.I. tester
Oxygen indicator
Velometer

(Source: *Factory*, August 1972, p. 28.)

Citations and Violations

The type of citations and violations issued depends on the severity and extent of the violation and the employer's knowledge of possible violations. There are basically five types, ranging from minimal to severe.

De minimis. A *de minimis* condition is one that does not have a direct and immediate relationship to the employees' safety or health. A citation is not issued but it is mentioned to the employer. For example, lack of doors on toilet stalls would be a *de minimis* violation.

Other-Than-Serious. This type of violation is one that could have an impact on employees' health or safety but probably would not cause death or serious harm. Having loose ropes in a work area on which people could trip and hurt themselves might be classified as a nonserious violation.

Serious. A serious violation is issued if there is great probability the condition could cause death or serious physical harm and the employer should know of the condition. Examples would be the absence of a protective screen on a lathe, allowing an employee to easily mangle a hand, or the lack of a blade guard on an electric saw.

Willful and Repeated. This type of violation is somewhat different from the others. Willful and repeated violations deal with employers who have been previously cited for violations. If an employer knew about a safety violation or had been warned for a violation and did not correct the problem, a second citation is issued. The penalty for a willful and repeated violation can go as high as $10,000. If death results from a willful violation, a jail term of six months can be imposed.

Imminent Danger. An imminent danger citation is a notice that is posted by an inspector if there is reasonable certainty the condition will cause death or serious physical harm if it is not corrected immediately. Imminent danger situations are handled on the highest priority basis. They are reviewed by a regional OSHA director, and the condition must be corrected immediately. If the condition is serious enough and the employer does not cooperate, a representative of OSHA may go to a federal judge and obtain an injunction to close down the company until the condition is corrected. The absence of any guard railings to prevent an employee from falling three stories into heavy machinery could be classified an imminent danger violation.

Penalties. In place of a rather rigid fine system, OSHA inspectors now use a regulated penalty calculation process. This process, which is somewhat complex, considers the probability of occurrences and the severity of possible injury. Then a penalty is calculated.

One significant change OSHA made in 1977 is that fines are levied only if there are more than ten conditions total (except *de minimis*) that are found. Thus, a machine shop owner who had eight "other-than-serious" violations would not be penalized if unsafe conditions were corrected by the next inspection.

What are the types of OSHA citations?

Effects of OSHA

OSHA has had a significant impact by making employers and employees more aware of safety and health considerations. In response to the query, "Has the act been effective?", the answer has to be discussed on several fronts. Although the effect on injury rates is still somewhat unclear, it appears that OSHA has been able to reduce the number of accidents and injuries in some cases. A study of the meat-packing industry in one state found that the application of OSHA standards in the meat and meat products industry was significant in reducing the frequency of employee injuries.[19]

OSHA has definitely increased the safety consciousness of employers and led to better reporting of safety and health injuries and illnesses. Because an organization must always be prepared for an OSHA inspection, managers are forced to serve as constant safety monitors. This safety awareness is evident in managers' attempts to improve the safety consciousness and orientation of their employees.

Criticisms of OSHA

Most employers agree with the act's intent to provide healthy and safe working conditions for all employees. However, criticism of OSHA has emerged for several reasons.

One reason is that *some standards are vague*, especially the "general duty" clause, and it is difficult to know whether or not one is complying. In the opening case a standard required that a plant having a certain number of workers have qualified medical personnel "in near proximity" to the work area. This standard has been the subject of several OSHA violations and cases; but what is "near proximity?" Is it in the work area? In the plant? Is it a hospital ten minutes away?

Secondly, the *rules are often very complicated and technical*. Often, small-business owners and managers who do not have a safety specialist find the standards very difficult to read and understand. The presence of many very minor standards also hurt OSHA's credibility. To counter such criticism, in 1978, OSHA revoked about 900 minor or confusing standards.

A third major criticism is that the OSHA *inspector cannot serve as a safety counselor*. However, with the establishment of the consultation program, this criticism loses some strength. Also, OSHA officials will meet with employees who are designing and building new facilities to review blueprints and plans. This review enables the employers to correctly design the facilities to comply with OSHA regulations.

A fourth concern is that the *cost of correcting violations* may be prohibitive for many employers. Requiring a small employer to make major structural changes in a building may not be financially possible. The cost of compliance may not be realistic given the cost of the violation. Saunders, Inc., a 60-employee foundry in Wichita, Kansas, went out of business rather than pay the $500,000 needed to comply with OSHA regulations involving extensive electrical work. Although OSHA was willing to negotiate, the owner refused to do so and closed the business, sold all the machines, and moved to Texas.[20]

In one case the U.S. Supreme Court indicated that OSHA regulations limiting the exposure of workers to cotton dust do not have to meet a cost/benefit test. The decision in the case indicated that Congressional intent of the 1970 Act establishing OSHA was to provide maximum worker protection. Use of a cost/benefit approach would lead to less protection, which would violate the law.[21]

As a result of this decision some efforts have been made to amend the 1970 act to include cost/benefit as a consideration. However such efforts have been strongly resisted by the AFL-CIO and other labor organizations.

A fifth problem with OSHA is different in perspective. With so many employers to inspect, many employers have only a relatively *small probability of being inspected*. Labor unions and others have criticized OSHA and Congress for not providing enough inspectors. One interesting study revealed that with the probability of being inspected and receiving a fine so low, many employers pay little attention to OSHA enforcement efforts.[22]

In summary, it can be said that OSHA has had a significant impact on organizations. However, not all the results have been of a positive nature. Some changes in the law and enforcement efforts are likely. As changes are made, continuing compliance with OSHA should be a major focus of any organization efforts. To do this, safety programs should be approached systematically.

What are some positives and negatives associated with OSHA?

A SYSTEMS APPROACH TO SAFETY

Effective safety management considers the type of safety problems, accidents, employees, and technology in the organizational setting. Furthermore, the systems approach to safety recognizes the importance of the human element in safety. Simply attempting to engineer machines, without dealing with the behavioral reactions of employees and without trying to encourage safe behavior, would compartmentalize the safety effort. There are several basic components in a systematic approach to safety.

Organizational Commitment

Any comprehensive and systematic approach to safety begins with an organization's commitment to a comprehensive safety effort. This effort should be coordinated from the top to involve all members of the organization and be reflected in their actions and work. One study of five plants that won safety awards found that "active management involvement in occupational safety makes the major difference between success and failure."[23] If the president of a small electrical manufacturing firm does not wear a hard hat in the manufacturing shop, he can hardly expect to enforce a requirement that all employees wear hard hats in the shop. Unfortunately, sincere support of top management for a safety program is often missing from many safety programs.

Coordinated Safety Efforts

Once a commitment is made to organizational safety, planning efforts must be coordinated with duties assigned to supervisors, managers, safety specialists, and personnel specialists. Naturally, the types of duties would vary according to the size of the firm and the industry. For this reason, it is inappropriate to suggest a single proper mixture of responsibilities.

Certainly, the focus of any systematic approach to safety is the continued diligence of workers, supervisors, and managerial personnel. Employees who are not reminded of safety violations, who are not encouraged to be safety conscious, or who violate company safety rules and policies are not likely to be safe employees.

Safety Committees. Involvement of workers in safety is often accomplished through the use of safety committees. These committees are often composed of workers of different levels and from a variety of departments. At least one member of the committee is usually from the personnel unit. A safety committee generally has a regularly scheduled meeting, has specific responsibilities for conducting safety reviews, and makes recommendations for changes necessary to avoid future accidents.

The safety emphasis must be consistently made and enforced. Properly coordinated efforts between the personnel unit and managers will aid in developing safety-conscious and safety-motivated employees.

Employee Safety Motivation

Encouraging employees to continually keep safety standards in mind while performing their jobs is difficult. Often, employees think safety measures are bothersome and unnecessary until an accident or injury occurs. For example, requiring employees to wear safety glasses in a laboratory may be necessary most of the time. However, the glasses are awkward and employees resist using them even when they know they should have protection. Some employees may have worked for years without them and think this new requirement is a nuisance.

Safety Discipline.   Enforcement of safety rules and disciplines of violations is important if safety efforts are to be meaningful. Frequent reinforcement of the need for safe behavior and feedback on positive safety practices have been found to be extremely effective in improving worker safety in a food manufacturing plant.[24]

Consistent enforcement has been used by employers as a defense with OSHA. In one situation a utility foreman was electrocuted while operating an overhead crane. However, the company was exonerated because it had consistently enforced safety rules and penalized violators. The employee who was killed violated a safety rule for grounding equipment even though the company had given him regular safety training, had posted signs prominently, and had warned all employees about grounding equipment. The OSHA district director ruled that the employee's action was an isolated incident unknown to management.

Safety Incentives.   Some firms have used safety contests and given incentives to employees for safe work behavior. Jewelry, clocks, watches, chain saws, and vacation trips have all been used to reward employees for good safety records. Safe driving awards for drivers in a trucking firm have been quite successful in generating safety consciousness. Belt buckles and lapel pins are especially popular with the drivers.[25]

Safety Training.   One way to encourage employee safety is to involve all employees at various times in safety training and committees. Another means to encourage safety is to hold frequent safety meetings with employees.

Safety Publicity.   In addition to safety training, continuous communication programs to develop safety consciousness are necessary. Posting safety policies and rules is part of this effort. Contests, incentives, and posters are all ways employers can heighten safety awareness.

One common way to communicate safety ideas is through safety films and videotapes. Viewing possible unsafe situations and the accidents that can result is good exposure to the need for safety. Changing safety posters, continually updating company bulletin boards, and attractively posting company safety information in high traffic areas are also recommended actions. Merely sending safety memos is a very inadequate approach to the problem.

Accident Investigation

When accidents or injuries do occur, a detailed investigation of the cause must be made and ways to prevent similar accidents from occurring in the future are studied. Accident investigation consists of three major parts: (1) the scene, (2) the interview, (3) the report.[26]

In investigating *the scene* of an accident, an attempt is made to determine the physical and environmental conditions that contributed to the accident. Poor lighting, poor ventilation, and wet floors are all possible considerations at the scene. Investigation at the scene of the accident should be done as soon as possible after the accident so that conditions have not significantly changed. One way to obtain an accurate view of an accident scene is to photograph or videotape the scene.

The second phase of the investigation is *the interview*. The injured employee, his or her supervisor, and witnesses to the accident should be interviewed. The interviewer attempts to determine what happened and how the accident was caused. These interviews may also generate some suggestions as to how to prevent similar accidents from occurring in the future.

The third phase of any good accident investigation is the accident investigation report such as the one in Figure 14–9. This report provides the data necessary to fill out the forms and records required by OSHA. One of the more humorous accident reports encountered is included as Figure 14–10.

As a part of an investigation, recommendations should be made on how the accident could have been prevented and what changes could prevent further accidents. Identifying why an accident occurred is useful, but identifying steps to prevent it from occurring again is the important part of systematic safety.

Accident Research

Closely related to accident investigation is accident research to determine ways to prevent accidents. Employing safety engineers, ergonomists, or having outside experts evaluate the safety of working conditions is useful. If a large number of the same type of accident seems to be occurring in an organizational unit, a safety education training program may be necessary to emphasize the importance of working safely. A publishing company reported a greater-than-average number of back injuries caused by employees lifting heavy boxes. Safety training on the proper way to lift heavy objects was then initiated to prevent back injuries.

Evaluation of Safety Efforts

Organizations need to monitor their safety efforts. Just as a firm's accounting records are audited, periodic audits of a firm's safety efforts should also be made. Accident and injury statistics should be compared to previous accident patterns to determine if any significant changes have occurred. This analysis should be designed to measure progress in safety management. A manager at a hospital might measure its safety

Figure 14–9. OSHA form.

OSHA No. 101   Form approved
Case or File No. _____   OMB No. 44R 1453

Supplementary Record of Occupational Injuries and Illnesses

EMPLOYER
1. Name _____
2. Mail address _____
   (No. and street)   (City or town)   (State)
3. Location, if different from mail address _____

INJURED OR ILL EMPLOYEE
4. Name _____ Social Security No. _____
   (First name)   (Middle name)   (Last name)
5. Home address _____
   (No. and street)   (City or town)   (State)
6. Age _____   7. Sex: Male_____ Female_____ (Check one)
8. Occupation _____
   (Enter regular job title, *not* the specific activity he was performing at time of injury.)
9. Department _____
   (Enter name of department or division in which the injured person is regularly employed, even
   though he may have been temporarily working in another department at the time of injury.)

THE ACCIDENT OR EXPOSURE TO OCCUPATIONAL ILLNESS
10. Place of accident or exposure _____
    (No. and street)   (City or town)   (State)
    If accident or exposure occurred on employer's premises, give address of plant or establishment in which
    it occurred. Do not indicate department or division within the plant or establishment. If accident oc-
    curred outside employer's premises at an identifiable address, give that address. If it occurred on a pub-
    lic highway or at any other place which cannot be identified by number and street, please provide place
    references locating the place of injury as accurately as possible.
11. Was place of accident or exposure on employer's premises? _____ (Yes or No)
12. What was the employee doing when injured? _____
    (Be specific. If he was using tools or equipment or handling material,
    _____
    name them and tell what he was doing with them.)
    _____
13. How did the accident occur? _____
    (Describe fully the events which resulted in the injury or occupational illness. Tell what
    _____
    happened and how it happened. Name any objects or substances involved and tell how they were involved. Give
    _____
    full details on all factors which led or contributed to the accident. Use separate sheet for additional space.)

OCCUPATIONAL INJURY OR OCCUPATIONAL ILLNESS
14. Describe the injury or illness in detail and indicate the part of body affected. _____
    (e.g.: amputation of right index finger
    _____
    at second joint; fracture of ribs; lead poisoning; dermatitis of left hand, etc.)
15. Name the object or substance which directly injured the employee. (For example, the machine or thing
    he struck against or which struck him; the vapor or poison he inhaled or swallowed; the chemical or ra-
    diation which irritated his skin; or in cases of strains, hernias, etc., the thing he was lifting, pulling, etc.)
    _____
16. Date of injury or initial diagnosis of occupational illness _____
    (Date)
17. Did employee die? _____ (Yes or No)

OTHER
18. Name and address of physician _____
19. If hospitalized, name and address of hospital _____
    _____
    Date of report _____ Prepared by _____
    Official position _____

Figure 14–10. Accident report.

Getting It Coming and Going

One hour after beginning a new job which involved moving a pile of bricks from the top of a two-story house to the ground, a construction worker in Peterborough, Ontario, suffered an accident which hospitalized him. He was instructed by his employer to fill out an accident report. It read:

"Thinking I could save time, I rigged a beam with a pulley at the top of the house, and a rope leading to the ground. I tied an empty barrel on one end of the rope, pulled it to the top of the house, and then fastened the other end of the rope to a tree. Going up to the top of the house, I filled the barrel with bricks.

"Then I went down and unfastened the rope to let the barrel down. Unfortunately, the barrel of bricks was now heavier than I, and before I knew what was happening, the barrel jerked me up in the air.

"I hung on to the rope, and halfway up I met the barrel coming down, receiving a severe blow on the left shoulder.

"I then continued on up to the top, banging my head on the beam and jamming my fingers in the pulley.

"When the barrel hit the ground, the bottom burst, spilling the bricks. As I was now heavier than the barrel, I started down at high speed.

"Halfway down, I met the empty barrel coming up, receiving several cuts and contusions from the sharp edges of the bricks.

"At this point, I must have become confused, because I let go of the rope. The barrel came down, striking me on the head, and I woke up in the hospital.

"I respectfully request sick leave."

(Source: R. J. Griffiths, Toronto Star, from *National Lampoon.*)

efforts by comparing the hospital's accident rates to hospital-industry figures and to the rates at other hospitals of the same size in the area.

Another part of safety evaluation is updating safety materials and safety training aids. Also, the accident investigation procedures and accident reporting methods should be evaluated continually to see that these are actually generating ideas useful in reducing accidents. Safety policies and regulations should be reviewed to be sure they comply with both existing and new standards set up by OSHA, state, and professional agencies.

A systematic safety program requires continual effort to maintain safe working environments. Managers and specialists should continually examine the organization's progress in developing a safe and healthful environment for its people.

What are the major components of a safety
system?

REVIEW AND PREVIEW

This chapter has examined the importance of personnel health and safety. Maintaining the general well-being of employees requires that an organization look closely at its working conditions and its workers' attitudes toward those conditions. General health and its more applied component, safety, are both important.

Health problems may be a result of off-the-job illnesses and problems. A manager becomes involved with employee health problems when they hamper the organization's operations. Physical illnesses, emotional illnesses, alcoholism, and drug abuse are common employee health problems. Responses by managers to these problems should be to direct employees to appropriate professional help, either inside or outside the organization.

Safety is a direct and applied process that has become more important since the passage of the Occupational Safety and Health Act of 1970. Through the enforcement of this act, the federal government has made personnel health and safety a mandatory concern for managers. OSHA appears to have been a factor in heightening safety awareness and in reducing work-related injuries and accidents, even though some valid criticisms of the act have brought about some modifications.

Meeting the safety requirements of OSHA can be accomplished by a systematic and comprehensive safety effort. An organization must be committed to safety and develop a coordinated safety effort to motivate its employees to be more safety conscious. Through investigation of accidents and evaluation of the organization's safety efforts, managers focus on preventing future accidents and injuries.

Actions aimed at maintaining the health and safety of personnel are one part of organizational maintenance. Another part is the development and maintenance of personnel policies and rules to achieve organizational consistency and coordination. Personnel coordination is facilitated by communicating matters dealing with personnel-related activities. Personnel coordination is examined in chapter 15.

Review Questions

1. Differentiate between health and safety as personnel activities. Then identify some factors that affect health and safety.

2. Discuss the following statement by a supervisor: "I feel it's my duty to get involved with my employees and their personal problems to show that I truly care about them."

3. Why should a firm be concerned about alcohol and drug usage by employees?

4. Describe the Occupational Safety and Health Act and some of its key provisions about standards, recordkeeping, and inspection requirements.

5. Discuss the following comment: "OSHA should be abolished because it serves to just harass small businesses."

6. Why is a systems approach to safety important?

Case: "What's Happened to Bob?"

"What's happened to Bob?" was the question asked Jack Otto, production supervisor, by one of his manufacturing workers, Clyde Fisher. Jack had been wondering the same thing for several weeks about Bob Hill, another of his welders.

Jack Otto is a 54-year-old production supervisor who has been with Store Fixture Manufacturing Co. (SFM) for 20 years. He is well liked and respected by his peers and subordinates and is very competent at the technical aspects of his supervisory job.

Bob Hill, 40 years old, has been a generally competent and productive welder at SFM for ten years. Bob has been popular with his co-workers. Although he periodically "blows up" at them, he always apologizes afterwards. His absenteeism rate has been higher than average for the last several years, with most absenteeism on Mondays. Also, it is not uncommon for Bob to be 10–15 minutes late at least once a week. But, because of a shortage of experienced welders and because Bob often cuts his lunch hour short to make up his tardiness time, Jack and other managers at SFM have decided to live with Bob's attendance problems as long as they don't become extensive.

It is not uncommon for many company employees to stop for a beer after work. Clyde told Jack that Bob has been staying at the neighborhood bar for several hours after work most nights. Clyde also said he had heard rumors that Bob Hill was having personal problems at home.

Jack doesn't like to pry into the lives of his workers, but he knows that he can't ignore the situation much longer, especially with the others beginning to talk about Bob's problems.

QUESTIONS

1. What actions, if any, should Jack Otto take?
2. Identify some ways that the company and Jack have contributed to the existing problem with Bob.

Notes

1. Bureau of Labor Statistics, U.S. Department of Labor, *Occupational Injuries and Illnesses in 1979: Summary*, (Washington, D.C.: U.S. Government Printing Office, March, 1981).

2. "The OSHA Tangle," *Chain Store Age Executive*, April 1975, p. 15.

3. John B. Miner and Mary G. Miner, *Personnel and Industrial Relations*, 3rd ed. (New York: Macmillan, 1977), pp. 433–438.

4. Davis W. Carvey and Roger G. Nibler, "Biorhythmic Cycles and the Incidence of Industrial Accidents," *Personnel Psychology*, 30, Autumn 1977, pp. 447–454.

5. Health, Safety, and Security Committee, American Society for Personnel Administration, *Occupational Safety & Health Review*, September 1980, p. 5.

6. *Wall Street Journal*, October 27, 1980, p. 1.

7. "Broader Health Checks," *Personnel Administrator*, August 1979, p. 46.

8. John Kondrasuk, "Company Physical Fitness Programs: Salvation or Fad?" *Personnal Administrator*, November 1980, pp. 47–50.

9. "High Blood Pressure," *Personnel Journal*, November 1980, p. 884.

10. Robert McMorris, "Workers and U.P. Benefit from Program to Aid Those Derailed by Drinking," *Omaha World Herald*, February 28, 1980.

11. Stanley E. Kaden, "Compassion or Cover-Up, The Alcoholic Employee," *Personnel Journal*, 56, July 1977, pp. 356–358.

12. "Drugs on the Job: The Quiet Problem," *Newsweek*, September 15, 1980, pp. 83–84.

13. Luis R. Gomez-Mejia and David B. Balkin, "Classifying Work-Related and Personal Problems of Troubled Employees," *Personnel Administrator*, November 1980, pp. 27–32.

14. Occupational Safety and Health Administration, U.S. Department of Labor, *All about OSHA*, OSHA #2056 (Washington, D.C.: U.S. Government Printing Office), p. 3.

15. *Whirlpool* v. *Marshall*, 78-1870 (1980).

16. Health, Safety, and Security Committee, American Society for Personnel Administration, *Occupational Safety & Health Review*, June 1980, p. 3.

17. Bureau of Labor Statistics, *Occupational Injuries and Illnesses in 1978:Summary*, p. 1.

18. *Marshall* v. *Barlow's, Inc.*, 76-1143 (1978).

19. Lawrence P. Ettkin and J. Brad Chapman, "Is OSHA Effective in Reducing Industrial Injuries?" *Labor Law Journal*, 28, April 1975, pp. 236–242.

20. Sanford L. Jacobs, "Rather Than Dicker with OSHA, 'Model' Foundry Closes Up Shop," *Wall Street Journal*, September 15, 1980, p. 31.

21. *American Textile Manufacturers Institute, Inc., et al.*, v. *Donovan, et al.*, 101 s.c.t. 2478, 69 LEd 2d 185(1981).

22. John M. Gleason and Darold T. Barnum, "Effectiveness of OSHA Sanctions in Influencing Employee Behavior: Single and Multi-period Decision Models," *Accident Analysis and Prevention*, 10, 1978, pp. 35–49.

23. "NIOSH: Management is the Key," *National Safety News*, September 1979, p. 41.

24. Judi Komaki, et al., "A Behavioral Approach to Occupational Safety," *Journal of Applied Psychology*, 63, April 1978, pp. 434–445.

25. Edward D. Dionne, "Motivating Workers With Incentives," *National Safety News*, January 1980, pp. 75–79.

26. W. G. Bufkin, "Accident Investigation," *National Safety News*, September 1971, pp. 49–51.

CHAPTER 15

Personnel Coordination

When you have read this chapter, you should be able to:

1. Define the purpose of personnel policies.

2. Describe the three stages in the life cycle of a rule.

3. Explain the nature of progressive discipline.

4. Identify and describe at least four different guidelines for developing effective personnel policies and rules.

5. List and briefly explain at least four forms of formal personnel communications.

I Want a Leave

Linda wanted to take a day's leave on the Friday after Thanksgiving; this leave would allow her a four-day weekend to visit relatives. Although Linda asked for the day off three weeks in advance, her supervisor, Ben, refused to grant her the leave. The main reason he refused her request was a heavy workload.

Linda complained that this action was unfair and discriminatory because another employee in the section was granted annual leave on that Friday. Furthermore, Linda felt that since she had the annual leave on the books, she was entitled to use it.

Ben replied that the employee who was scheduled to be off that Friday had asked for the leave time at the beginning of the year. Also, while Linda was a clerk/typist, the other employee was an accounting technician and the jobs were dissimilar. Ben stated that company policy gives him the authority to grant leave and, due to the heavy workload, he needed all his remaining employees.

Linda first complained to Ben's supervisor and requested annual leave, but the supervisor "washed his hands" of the situation by saying the decision belonged entirely to Ben. Next Linda talked with someone in the employee relations section, who also recited the supervisor's right to request a worker's presence whenever the work load required it.

Linda then requested an interview with the local union representative who, after listening to Linda's problem, agreed to speak to Ben and his supervisor. The discussion became quite heated and the union representative sided with Linda.

In the following weeks, Ben, his supervisor, and several employees of the section were repeatedly called into conference about Linda's situation. The basic issue of debate was whether or not Bob had the authority and the need to require Linda's attendance on the Friday in question.

Comments:

The actual outcome of the problem was that Linda *was required* to work on that Friday and she *did attend* work that day. This case illustrates the value of personnel policies and the importance of coordination. Giving Linda the day off on such relatively short notice could easily have triggered a multitude of requests for annual leave for that Friday.

The leave policy was flexible enough to allow Ben, the supervisor, some latitude in making leave decisions. However, a problem with the leave policy was that it did not indicate how far in advance requests had to be made. Addition of such a clause would aid supervisors by providing them adequate notice of a request and give them more time to adjust work schedules.

ACHIEVING personnel objectives in the organization requires a *coordination* of the efforts and actions of the departments and individuals involved. This coordination does not simply happen. It requires "coordinating mechanisms" and an appropriate communication climate if the activities of a number of different entities are all to be guided in roughly the same direction. If everyone went his or her own way, there would be a great deal of confusion.

The policies and coordination interface is shown in Figure 15–1. Overall organization policies require input from the personnel unit, and personnel policies require input from other managers as well.

Figure 15–1. Personnel policies and coordination interface.

Designs formal mechanisms for coordinating personnel policies	Help in developing personnel policies and rules
Provides advice in development of companywide personnel policies and rules	Review policies and rules with employees
Provides information on proper disciplinary procedures	Enforce employees' observation of rules through discipline
May help explain personnel rules and policies to managers	Serve as first source of explanation of rules and policies for employees

The personnel unit helps to achieve organizational objectives as well as its own objectives. For example, if the organization has a policy of nondiscrimination in its hiring practices and an objective of having as many minority individuals in the work force as their proportion in the general population, the personnel unit must design its selection, training, and other programs to help accomplish these objectives. Both *within* the personnel unit and in activities *between* that unit and others in the organization, coordination will be necessary to achieve the objective.

Because managers are the main users and enforcers of rules and policies, they should receive some training and explanation in how to use personnel policies and rules effectively. In the opening case, the personnel unit and Ben, the supervisor, took a unified and coordinated position on Linda's request. While it is not necessary for the personnel unit to always support other managers, it is critical that any conflict between the two entities be resolved so that employees receive a fair and coordinated response.

POLICIES AND PERSONNEL

Personnel policies may come from many different sources. Policies may be (in effect) imposed from outside the organization. For example, competition for skilled labor may lead to a policy to pay above the area wage for certain classifications of employees. Or, government regulations have led to EEO as a policy in organizations.

Long-run objectives of the organization may help dictate personnel policy too. For example, an objective of doubling the organization's size and output in ten years may dictate personnel policies regarding management development and recruiting practices. But, whatever the source of personnel policies, they serve to guide the actions of organizational members.

POLICIES are *general* guidelines that regulate organizational actions.

Policies are global in nature while *procedures* and *rules* are situation specific. The role policies play in guiding organizational decision requires that they be reviewed regularly. Obsolete policies can cause poor decisions and poor coordination. Policy proliferation must be carefully monitored. Failure to review, add to, or delete policies as situations change may lead to problems in the future. For example, some employers in the past followed policies that an employee having alcohol or drug problems should be fired. However, because of social changes and the practices of other employers, many organizations have changed their personnel policies regarding "troubled employees"—those with alcohol, drug, or emotional problems. Figure 15–2 shows a policy statement and supporting procedures for dealing with troubled employees.

What is the nature and purpose of personnel policies?

Formal Communication

A primary coordination tool is communication. Without effective communication of policies and rules, progress is difficult. Channels from manager to employee, from executive to subordinates, among managers, or among rank-and-file employees must be open. Our purpose in dealing with communication in this chapter is not to replace the kind of material usually covered in organizational behavior or interpersonal communication courses. Rather, the emphasis is on some formal communication means that are usually thought of as being specifically personnel man-

Figure 15–2.   Employee assistance program for the troubled employee (large northern manufacturer).

POLICY

The company recognizes that a wide range of human problems which are not directly associated with job functions can affect an employee's work performance. These problems include physical illness, mental or emotional upset, alcoholism, drug abuse, and other concerns. The company has several medical programs which address themselves to these problems with the intent of identifying them at the earliest possible moment and recommending appropriate treatment on an individual and confidential basis.

PROCEDURES
1. The initiation of any action with respect to an employee is contingent upon unsatisfactory job performance resulting from apparent medical or behavioral abnormalities. Judgments regarding unsatisfactory work performance remain the prerogative of cognizant supervision, which has the responsibility of seeking medical assistance through the Medical Department.
2. In the event an employee refuses to undergo diagnosis and treatment, the Employee Relations Division shall be notified.

(Source: ASPA-BNA Survey #34, "Counseling Policies and Programs for Employees with Problems," March 23, 1978p p. 9. BNA Policy & Practice Series, The Bureau of National Affairs, Inc. Used with permission.)

---

agement-oriented. They are: (1) employee newsletters, (2) employee handbooks, (3) employee communications committees, (4) suggestion systems, and (5) an ombudsman.

Rules and Discipline

Rules are coordination mechanisms. They provide more specific behavioral guidelines than policies. For example, one welding company has a policy that states management intends to provide the highest-quality welding service in the area. One of the rules that helps realize that policy is that a welder with fewer than five years of welder experience will not be hired. This rule constrains personnel selection decisions.

Finally, the need for rules leads to the need to enforce those rules. Discipline is a necessary part of every manager's job. Often personnel specialists become involved in either interpreting disciplinary procedures or, in some instances, doing some of the disciplining. Therefore, another coordinating mechanism to be considered is "progressive" discipline.

RULES AND DISCIPLINE

Rules serve several purposes in organizations. They are coordination mechanisms like those just discussed. But they serve other purposes as well because they maintain stability, and serve as handy decision guides so that routine decisions do not have to be made again and again. However, rules can pose problems as well. They can block new ways of doing work, can become excuses rather than reasons, and may add to the red tape in organizations.

RULES are specific guidelines that regulate and restrict the behavior of individuals.

Life Cycle of Rules

Like policies, rules need occasional audits and changes. It may be useful to think about rules in terms of a "life cycle." Figure 15–3 shows the life cycle of a rule.

In Stage I the rule-making process begins because of a need to limit behavior or coordinate activities. In Stage II the rule is accepted and obeyed because it is seen as fulfilling an organizational need. In Stage III the rule is rejected because situations have changed or it is no longer helpful in getting the job done. People start to deviate from the behaviors prescribed in the rule. This deviation may be accompanied by a reduction in the enforcement of the rule. Before a rule reaches this point in its life cycle, it should be changed to fit the current situation—hence rule #1_A in Figure 15–3.

Enforcement problems can result if policies and rules are completely unacceptable to employees. If a rule is not enforced, it will not be useful. For example, simply having a plant rule which prohibits smoking is insufficient. One factory has had a no-smoking rule for years, but the rule has not been enforced because the superintendent is a three-pack-a-day man. Other workers who feel they are in a safe area sneak a smoke when they can because they see the rule violated in the office. To be effective, rules must be enforced or changed.

When writing up a rule for distribution to employees the rule should be stated in an appropriate manner. The tone should not be threatening or patronizing. Care should be taken not to allow proliferation of rules. It is impossible to make a rule to cover every situation and therefore a certain amount of reliance on people's good judgment is inevitable.

What is the life cycle of a rule?

Figure 15–3.   The life cycle of a rule.

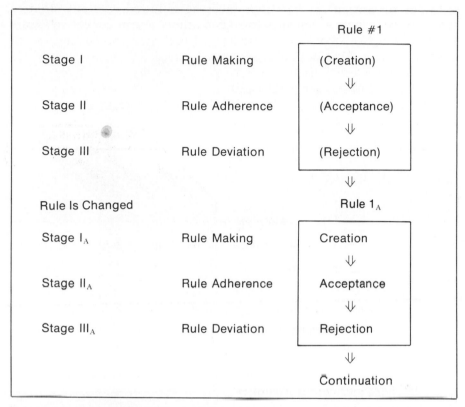

(Source: Adapted from J. H. Jackson and S. W. Adams, "The Life Cycle of a Rule," *Academy of Management Review* 4, April 1979, pp. 269–273.)

Nature of Discipline

Discipline is a form of training that enforces the organization's rules. It can be approached in two basic ways: *preventive* and *punitive*. Although these approaches may sound like conflicting terms, they are related. The purpose of *preventive discipline* is to heighten employees' awareness of company policies and rules in their work experiences. Knowledge of disciplinary actions may prevent violations. The emphasis on preventive discipline is similar to the emphasis on preventing accidents.

Counseling by a supervisor in the work unit can have positive effects. Many times people simply need to be aware of a situation, and counseling can provide that awareness. The best discipline is self-discipline. Developing an awareness of acceptable behavior through counseling is better than the punitive approach.

The punitive approach is used when violations or discipline problems occur. The hope is that, through punishment, employees will not repeat the undesired behavior. Most organizations use both these approaches to emphasize that rules must be followed. Certain offenses typically carry more severe penalties than others, as can be seen in Figure 15–4.

Figure 15–4. Offenses and penalty patterns.

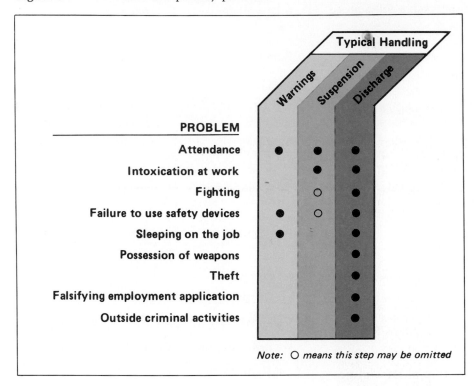

Employee Theft as Example. Employee pilferage and theft is a growing concern, especially for retailers. It has been estimated that employee theft costs over $10 million a year or more. As shown in Figure 15–4, theft most frequently leads to immediate discharge. Some interesting research has indicated that employee theft is related to job satisfaction, motivation, and alienation. Employees who have higher job satisfaction, are more motivated, and less alienated have more negative attitudes toward employee theft, as would be expected.[1] Consequently, it may be realistic to see employee theft as a symptom of broader personnel problems, not just as a discipline situation.

Equity, or fairness, must be considered in designing discipline systems to enforce rules. Few problems arise if employees understand the reasons and fairness behind policies and rules and if discipline is issued in different degrees of severity: *oral reprimand, written reprimand, formal written warning, suspension,* and *discharge.* The "progressive" nature of good discipline gives employees a chance to correct their ways. In this sense, discipline is training because for each failure to learn, the penalty is more severe.

Progressive Discipline

Progressive discipline is best viewed as the training or shaping of behavior in order to modify unacceptable behavior. This shaping may include punishment or it may not. Discipline is certainly not limited to punishment, as was noted earlier.

The concept of progressive discipline suggests that the attempts to modify behavior get more severe as the employee continues to exhibit improper behavior. Figure 15–5 shows steps in a typical progressive discipline system. As suggested above, any discipline is best viewed as training. An employee should be given an opportunity to correct deficiencies before being dismissed. This opportunity includes, at a minimum, steps 1, 2, and 4 in Figure 15–5. These steps ensure that both the nature and seriousness of the problem have been communicated to the employee.

Figure 15–5.   Progressive discipline.

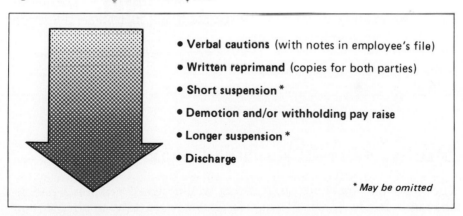

- **Verbal cautions** (with notes in employee's file)
- **Written reprimand** (copies for both parties)
- **Short suspension***
- **Demotion and/or withholding pay raise**
- **Longer suspension** *
- **Discharge**

* May be omitted

Defensible Dismissal

Special note should be made of the last step in the progressive discipline procedures—discharge or dismissal. While dismissing an employee is never a pleasant prospect, it sometimes must be done. However, defensible personnel practice demands that termination be properly done as the terminal point of a progressive discipline procedure.

In this sense, unionized organizations have an advantage over non-unionized organizations. A unionized organization almost always has a series of disciplinary steps as a part of its labor contract. These steps are agreed upon as fair by both union and management as a result of collective bargaining. Elements of the progressive discipline model described here are the basis of most union contract agreements on discipline and are widely accepted by management professionals as an appropriate route to dismissal.

Nonunion organizations may design a dismissal procedure in keeping with the models developed by unionized firms. They may use a procedure that is generally accepted as equitable, or they may act in some other fashion. Unfortunately, many poorly managed organizations, public and private, fail to consider the issue of an equitable dismissal system until a dismissal has been made and they are *forced* to consider it. Many firms do not have a formal discipline procedure at all.

A progressive discipline procedure is not designed to make it difficult to dismiss an employee who is not doing the job. Rather, it is designed to force the manager to document the efforts made to work with the employee's problem. When there is no third party to represent the employee, such as a union, this process also helps ensure that the employee is not the victim of arbitrary action on the part of a given manager.

Some companies have gone so far as to attempt rehabilitation for fired managers to help them deal with termination and find another job. Citibank of New York has an "outplacement" department where fired managers get counseling and make telephone calls to get new job referrals. In addition to Citibank, Celanese Corp. and General Electric Company have such departments.[2]

Can you explain the nature and importance of progressive discipline?

EFFECTIVE PERSONNEL POLICIES AND RULES

The following guidelines suggest that well-designed personnel policies and rules should be *consistent, reasonable, necessary, applicable, understandable,* and *distributed and communicated.*

Consistent

Rules should be consistent with the organization's policies, and policies should be consistent with the organization's goal. Managers should try to avoid having conflicting policies. The principal intent of policies is to provide written guidelines and to specify actions. If some policies and rules are enforced and others are not, then all tend to lose their effectiveness.

Reasonable

Ideally, employees should be able to see policies as being fair and realistic. Policies and rules which are so inflexible that individuals are penalized unfairly should be reevaluated. Apex Corporation has a policy that anyone to be promoted to vice-president must have a college degree. This policy might be seen as unfair and unreasonable for someone who began working for the company 20 years ago and knows how to handle the job. Adding a provision such as "Only in exceptional cases can experience substitute for formal education" might be perceived as more reasonable and fair.

A rule forbidding workers to use the company telephone for personal calls might be unreasonable because emergency phone calls are occasionally necessary. Limiting the amount of time the telephone can be used for personal business and the number of calls can make the rule reasonable. Figure 15–6 contains a list most people would agree is unreasonable.

Policies and rules should not be so inflexible that necessary exceptions are excluded. A company policy requiring all sales representatives to limit air travel to coach class may need exceptions. For example, an employee may need to fly to another city to confer with a client when no seats are available in coach class. Requiring the employee to pay the difference in fare would be unreasonable and unfair.

Some of the most ticklish company policies and rules involve employee dress. Dress codes are frequently attacked, and organizations that have them should be able to justify them to the satisfaction of both employees and outside sources that might question them. A great amount of time should not be required to check enforcement of such rules.

Necessary

Personnel policies and rules should be of value to employees; to this end, managers should confirm the intent and necessity of proposed rules and eliminate obsolete ones. If a railroad changes from coal-powered to diesel-powered engines, work rules for the engines should be changed to apply to diesel-powered engines. Policies and rules should be reviewed whenever there is a major organizational change. Unfortunately this review is not always done, and many outdated rules are still on the books in many organizations.

Figure 15–6. Policy change memorandum.

Memorandum
To: All Personnel
Subject: New Sick Leave Policy

It has been brought to my attention that the attendance record of this department is a disgrace to our gracious benefactor, who, at your own request, has given you your job. Due to lack of consideration for your jobs with so fine a department, as shown by such absenteeism, it has become necessary for us to revise some of our policies. The following changes are in effect immediately.

1. SICKNESS:
    No excuse . . . We will no longer accept your doctor's statement as proof, as we believe that if you are able to go to the doctor, you are able to come to work.

2. DEATH:
    (Other than your own) . . . This is no excuse. There is nothing you can do for them, and we are sure that someone else with a lesser position can attend to the arrangements. However, if the funeral can be held in the late afternoon, we will be glad to let you off one hour early; provided that your share of the work is ahead enough to keep the job going in your absence.

3. LEAVE OF ABSENCE:
    (For an operation) . . . We are no longer allowing this practice. We wish to discourage any thoughts that you may need an operation, as we believe that as long as you are an employee here that you will need all of whatever you have and you should not, under any circumstances, consider having anything removed. We hired you as you are and to have anything removed would certainly make you less than we bargained for.

4. DEATH:
    (Your own) . . . This will be accepted as an excuse, but we would like two weeks notice as we feel it is your duty to train someone else for your job.

ALSO, entirely too much time is being spent in the restroom. In the future, we will follow the practice of going in alphabetical order. For instance, those whose names being with "A" will go from 8:00–8:15, "B" will go from 8:15 to 8:30, and so on. If you are unable to go at your time, it will be necessary to wait until the next day when your turn comes again.

Applicable

Because personnel policies are general guidelines to action, they are applicable to a large group of employees in the organization. If this is not so, then the applicable areas must be identified. For instance, if a sick leave policy is applicable only to nonexempt employees, it should

be specified in the company handbook. Policies and rules that apply only
to one unit or type of job should be developed as part of specific guidelines
for that unit or job.

Understandable

Personnel policies and rules should be written so that employees can
clearly understand them. One way to determine if policies and rules are
understandable is to ask a cross-section of employees with various positions, education levels, and job responsibilities to explain the intent
and meaning of a rule. If the answers are extremely varied, the rule
should be rewritten.

To illustrate, at Environmental Products, a policy was drafted stating: "Employees will remain in the company's employ as long as their
work merits it." Another policy said: "If a layoff is necessary, *merit*
rating is the basis for deciding who remains." Conversations with a
number of different employees showed a variety of interpretations of
what would be done if a layoff occurred. Some thought that merit would
be considered only when a decision had to be made between two people
with equal seniority. The office workers thought the rule applied only
to workers in the plant. Supervisors had another interpretation. The
personnel manager decided that clarification was needed.

Distributed and Communicated

Personnel policies must be distributed and communicated to employees
to be effective. Employee handbooks can be creatively designed to explain
detailed policies and rules so that people can refer to a handbook at
times when someone is not available to answer a question. Supervisors
and managers can maintain discipline by reminding their employees
about policies and rules. Some major means used to formally communicate with employees are highlighted below.

*What are four guidelines for effective policies/
rules?*

COORDINATION THROUGH FORMAL
COMMUNICATION

To be effective, formal communication must allow information to flow
both up and down in the organization. Personnel information can be
formally communicated in several ways. *Employee handbooks, suggestion systems, employee communication committees,* an *organizational*

ombudsman, and numerous other publications, such as newspapers and magazines, are some that can be used.

Employee Handbook

Providing personnel information through a handbook gives employees a reference source for company policies and rules. The main purpose of an employee handbook is to help employees function effectively in an organization. Figure 15–7 indicates some items contained in a typical handbook.

Blue Cross of Southern California studied their internal communications and discovered some interesting facts about employee knowledge of the company. Most employees were not familiar with corporate policies and were confused about the organizational structure. To overcome this information deficiency, an employee handbook was published.

One problem with employee handbooks is that the specialists preparing them may not write on the reading level of those who will read them. A study comparing identical company handbooks showed only a small increase in their readability over a fifteen year period.[3] One solution is to test the readability of the handbook on a sample of employees before it is published.

Another important factor which should be considered in preparing an employee handbook is its use. Simply giving an employee a handbook and saying, "Here's all the information you need to know," is not sufficient. Some organizations distribute handbooks as part of their orientation process. One company periodically gives all employees a written test on the company handbook. Questions consistently missed become the focus of personnel communication efforts. These tests are also used to update the handbook.

Suggestion Systems

A suggestion system is a formal way to push communication upward through the organization. The opportunity for employees to suggest changes or ways to improve operations may develop loyalty and commitment to the organization. Often an employee in the work unit knows more about how waste can be eliminated or how hazards can be controlled than do managers, who are not as close to the job.

Making Suggestion Systems Work. A suggestion system should be publicized, and good suggestions should be used. The suggestions should be collected often and evaluated by a suggestion committee, usually composed of managers and nonmanagerial personnel. Suggestions selected by this committee are then passed on to upper management.

Figure 15–7. Employee handbook table of contents.

LETTER FROM THE MANAGER
ABOUT THE COMPANY
EQUAL EMPLOYMENT OPPORTUNITY
EMPLOYEE CLASSIFICATIONS
- FULL TIME
- PART-TIME
- TEMPORARY
- PROBATIONARY

EMPLOYEE RECORDS
PAY POLICY
WORKING HOURS
- LUNCH PERIOD
- BREAKS
- OVERTIME
- DEPARTURES

TIME CLOCK
ABSENCE FROM WORK
- PERSONAL TIME OFF
- JURY DUTY AND ELECTION DUTY
- DEATH IN THE FAMILY

SICK LEAVE
LEAVE OF ABSENCE
HOLIDAYS
VACATION
INSURANCE BENEFITS
- GROUP HEALTH INSURANCE PLAN
- DISABILITY INSURANCE
- LIFE INSURANCE
- WORKERS' COMPENSATION

HEALTH SERVICES
PENSION RETIREMENT PLAN
JOB POSTING
SAFETY
PARKING
DISCIPLINARY PROCEDURES
- FIRST OFFENSE—VERBAL AND/OR WRITTEN WARNING
- SECOND AND/OR THIRD OFFENSE—DISCHARGE
- FIRST OFFENSE—IMMEDIATE DISCHARGE

RULES OF CONDUCT
- CONFIDENTIALITY
- NO DRINKING RULE
- DRESS
- PERSONAL PHONE CALLS
- EMPLOYEE COMPLAINTS AND CONCERNS

TERMINATION OF EMPLOYMENT
- RESIGNATION
- DISCHARGE
- EXIT INTERVIEW

EMERGENCY PROCEDURES
- MEDICAL EMERGENCIES
- POWER FAILURES
- FIRE PROTECTION PROGRAM

Employees submitting useful suggestions should receive a reward. Some rewards are a flat fee such as a savings bond, or a percentage of the savings resulting from the suggestion. For example, a computer programmer whom the authors know works in a hospital. Noticing that the hospital was throwing away all the old computer printouts of patient rosters, she suggested that these printouts be sold to a paper recycling firm. Her suggestion was accepted and she now gets 5% of the $1,500 the hospital receives annually for the paper. G.E.'s space division offers "suggestion dollars" certificates that can be cashed in for $2 apiece whether or not the suggestion is adopted. There is no limit to the number of certificates an employee can acquire.[4]

The oldest continuously operating suggestion system in the United States is at Eastman Kodak Corporation. It began in 1898 with a $2 award to a man who pointed out the advantages of washing windows in a production department.[5] In one year Kodak received over 80,000 suggestions from 24,000 employees and 28,000 were adopted. Almost $2.8 million was paid out. Four awards of $50,000 were made and the average award was $90.43.[6]

A good suggestion system provides prompt feedback to all employees submitting suggestions. If employees are not told why their suggestions are accepted or rejected, much of the underlying momentum will be lost. The major reason for failure of suggestion programs is the inattention of management to feedback. Suggestions do not appear as fully developed plans. They are usually "ideas" that need some work on the part of management to succeed. Figure 15–8 summarizes some important dos and don'ts of suggestion systems.

Figure 15–8. Do's and Don'ts of suggestion systems

Do	Don'ts
*Commit management to answer every suggestion	*Reject a suggestion because it is not "polished"
*Publicize the program	*Allow the suggestions to get "lost" in the system
*Reward successful suggestions	*Fail to institute a suggestion system simply because it isn't a "sophisticated" system
*Respond to *all* signed suggestions	
*Use locked boxes, printed forms, and pick up routinely	

Employee Communications Committees

Some firms have established formal communication committees composed primarily of nonmanagerial employees. The General Electric Company has made effective use of what is called "an employee sounding board" at its large Maryland appliance complex. According to a G.E. spokesman, current personnel practices and work activities are the most frequent subjects covered by this group.[7]

An approach somewhat similar is in use at Norton Company, an industrial manufacturing firm in Massachusetts. In this firm, 21 in-plant "employee counselors" have been appointed who assist first-line supervisors by providing information to other workers on company personnel policies and practices. These communication counselors also provide some employee assistance counseling on personal job-related problems. The personnel director for Norton Company comments: "The In-Plant Counselor Program is eroding many barriers to effective communication that have existed and helped build a solid relationship between Norton Company and its employees."[8]

Both these programs further illustrate the advantage of involving nonmanagerial employees in formal personnel communications. Other formats are in use in other firms, and all are designed to enhance personnel coordination.

Organizational Ombudsman

The ombudsman, a concept originating in Sweden, is a person outside the normal chain of command who serves as a "public defender" or problem-solver for management and the employees. Providing an ombudsman in the organization gives employees a place to turn with complaints, problems, frustrations, and feelings of inequity or injustice.

Xerox Corporation uses an ombudsman to resolve complaints from employees which cannot be settled through the employee's supervisor or the personnel department. The ombudsman reviews the employee's information and complaint. After the problems are discussed with other individuals, such as the employee's supervisor or a representative of the personnel department, the ombudsman recommends a solution to the problem. Making this separate individual available gives employees the opportunity to talk freely about complaints and frustrations. Some of these complaints may not otherwise surface until they become serious problems.

The concept has been slow to gain acceptance in the United States, although General Electric and Boeing Vertol Company have also tried ombudsmen. A major problem has been finding an appropriate niche in the organizational structure for such a person. Some managers and supervisors may resent the ombudsman's privilege of hearing their employees' problems.

An ombudsman must have exceptional human-relations skills and training in behavioral sciences or counseling in order to improve communication and create a more open atmosphere. The ombudsman concept should not be a short-term program or gimmick. Establishing an ombudsman position may indicate the organization is aware of the long-range effect of good personnel relations on organizational effectiveness.

The most frequent problems faced by an ombudsman concern salary, performance, appraisals, intercompany job movements, layoffs, and benefits. General Electric's ombudsman estimated that in only about 10% of the cases could nothing be done to resolve the problem.[9]

Ombudsmen can provide a good source of information that can be used to revise policies and procedures. It is one way management can check to see if current policies are working properly. The complaints may indicate, for example, that a job posting system is required or that the performance appraisal system is not working, and changes then can be made.

Employee Publications

Organizations also communicate with employees through internal publications, sometimes called *house organs*. These include newspapers, company magazines, or organizational newsletters. These publications frequently contain feature stories on employees and their families, including news of promotions, retirements, and awards and news about the organization and its operations. Some very elaborate publications in larger companies require a full-time public relations staff. In smaller organizations a secretary in the personnel department may prepare a mimeographed newsletter.

Honesty is the Key.   The publication should be an honest attempt to communicate information employees need to know. It should not be solely a public relations tool to build the image of the company. Bad news, as well as good news, should be reported objectively in a readable style. Cartoons, drawings, and photographs improve the graphic appearance of publications and draw employee interest.

An airline publication has a question-and-answer section where employees anonymously submit tough questions to management. Management's answers are printed with the questions in every issue. Because every effort is made to give completely honest answers to these questions, this section has been very useful. This idea fizzled in another large company because the questions were answered with "the company line" and employees soon lost interest in the less-than-candid replies.

A column in Sun Company's publication, the *SUN NEWS*, illustrates the importance of openness and honesty. Robert Finucane's column raises questions of nepotism, indecisive middle managers, and sluggish elevator service. Among his biggest fans is the chairman of Sun Co. who notes that "Bob doesn't get nasty or mean."[10] But it is clear too that the column does not hesitate to chastise either side when it is wrong. Such reporting in a company publication makes it more than simply a management "mouthpiece."

Evaluate the Mission. Attention should also be paid to whether the newsletter is doing what management would like it to do. Two cases illustrate this quite clearly.[11] In a large pharmaceutical company, one entire division considers itself neglected by corporate management. This feeling is partially generated because the company's monthly newspaper fails to give this division the coverage it gives other divisions. In another company with six plants, the company paper had a lot of personal news about employees from all the plants. The objective was to provide the feeling of one "big happy family," even though the plants were far apart. A study showed that the workers did not care about people in other plants and simply were not interested in the newspaper. The solution was six separate newspapers, which increased the costs and time involved.

It has been suggested that the publisher of a house organ and the manager in charge must know:

1. What the publication is trying to achieve.
2. Exactly who is the audience being reached.
3. How the publication can involve the audience in its purposes.
4. Whether the cost of the whole process is worth the benefit.[12]

Other formal communications methods related to house organs are bulletin boards, posters, movies, and slides. Organizational communication is much broader than the above forms of formal personnel communication, although the formal techniques covered here can play a part in improving the coordination of personnel activities in the organization.

What are four forms of formal personnel
communication?

REVIEW AND PREVIEW

Personnel policies and coordination are vital parts of maintenance in an organization. Coordination efforts are partially accomplished by the development and enforcement of personnel policies and rules. Progressive discipline and equity underlie successful enforcement efforts. To be effective, personnel policies and rules must be developed following some general guidelines. Policies and rules should be consistent, reasonable, necessary, applicable, understandable, and distributed and communicated. Coordinating efforts are also accomplished through formal personnel communications. As a part of the broad organizational communications system, managers and personnel specialists can make use of several types of formal personnel communications. Employee handbooks, suggestion systems, employee communication committees, an organizational ombudsman, and employee publications are all means available to formally communicate with people in an organization.

Effective personnel coordination requires personnel research done to identify problems and changes needed in an organization. Chapter 16 focuses on personnel research.

Review Questions

1. What is the intent of personnel coordination activities?

2. You are a department manager in a discount store. Describe two situations: one in which you would use preventive discipline and one in which you would use punitive discipline.

3. Discuss the following statement: "Rules are always the basis for increased red tape in an organization."

4. Why might a progressive discipline procedure be seen as a logical extension of a policy of giving employees fair and equitable treatment while employed?

5. You have been assigned the task of writing a personnel policy manual. What general guidelines for writing policies would you use?

6. If you had to establish a formal means of communicating personnel policies in a community college, what means would you use? Why?

Case: "It's Time to Travel"

Eastern Valley State College is a regional state college with approximately 6,000 students. The Department of Business has seven faculty members. The policy manual for faculty contains the following statement: "Faculty members are expected to maintain their professional competence and the college affirms a policy of supporting faculty in this regard."

One of the main ways faculty maintain currentness in their professional fields is by attending professional meetings. When hired, Professor Hargraves was told that the college pays for a faculty member to attend one professional meeting each academic year. Because of his teaching responsibilities, Professor Hargraves waited until April 2 to apply to attend the Southern Business Meeting. He was told by his department chairman that the department was low on travel funds because another faculty member had attended two other meetings to present research papers. Therefore, the department chairman denied Professor Hargraves' request. Professor Hargraves was naturally upset, especially since there had been no written notice provided the faculty about the travel funding situation. Professor Hargraves returned to his office very disgruntled and started preparing his credentials sheet to use in applying for a job at another college.

QUESTIONS

1. Evaluate the policy statement about professional competence and the formal communication system relating to it.

2. Discuss the apparent inequity present in applying the policy and how the policy could be rewritten and better implemented.

Notes

1. Joe A. Cox and M. Ray Perryman, "An Empirical Investigation of the Relationship Between Employee Theft Perceptions and Other Attitudinal Variables," *Academy of Management Proceedings*, 1979, pp. 236–240.

2. R. S. Greenberger, "How CITIBANK Rehabilitates Those it Fires," *Wall Street Journal*, November 10, 1980, p. 31.

3. Keith Davis, "Readability Changes in Employee Handbooks of Identical Companies During a Fifteen-Year Period," *Personnel Psychology*, 21, Winter 1968, pp. 413–420.

4. "Idea Spur," *Personnel Administrator*, June 1979, p. 48.

5. A. W. Bergerson, "Employee Suggestion Plan Still Going Strong at Kodak," *Supervisory Management*, May 1977, pp. 32–33.

6. "Kodak Employees Awarded $2.8 Million," *Omaha World Herald*, April 2, 1981, p. 30.

7. Dougals G. Curley, "Employee Sounding Boards:Answering the Participants' Need," *The Personnel Administration*, May 1978, pp. 69–73.

8. P. B. Marshall, "Employee Counselors:Opening New Lines of Communication," *The Personnel Administrator*, November 1978, pp. 44–48.

9. "Where Ombudsmen Work Out," *Business Week*, May 3, 1976, p. 114.

10. Erick Larson, "Corporate Grapevine Produces Ripe Fruit for Robert Finucane," *Wall Street Journal*, March 9, 1981, p. 1.

11. Jim Mann, "Is Your House Organ A Vital Organ?" *Personnel Journal*, 56, September 1977, pp. 461–462.

12. Ibid.

CHAPTER 16

Personnel Research

When you have read this chapter, you should be able to:

1. Identify four methods for researching personnel problems.

2. Define and briefly discuss the concepts of a personnel audit and human resource accounting.

3. Describe why absenteeism is an important concern and how it might be controlled.

4. Discuss turnover concerns and control strategies.

5. Explain the importance of personnel recordkeeping.

6. Diagram a personnel information system.

7. List cautions to be observed in assuring the privacy of personnel records.

The New Personnel Director

Jerry Spence graduated a year and a half ago from a general business program at State University. He took a job that spring with Applied Systems Corporation, an organization of about 300 employees that designs and manufactures peripheral computer hardware. As part of the management training program Jerry was rotated from department to department, with his latest move to the personnel department for 3 months.

There he has acted as assistant personnel director to Ted Quantry who was 64 and approaching retirement. Ted was not particularly energetic or innovative and saw personnel as a recordkeeping and employment function. Last week, Ted had a massive heart attack and died. Yesterday after the funeral, Ted's boss called Jerry and informed him that he had been picked as Ted's replacement.

Jerry was a little overwhelmed with the responsibility involved, but his boss's encouragement made him feel he could handle the job. Jerry wishes now that he had taken a personnel management course or two in college, but the courses were not required. He has some vague ideas about areas that need some examination in the organization, but he is not sure how some of these areas tie together. For example, he knows that the turnover rate is about 30%, which he feels is above average for this type of operation. Also, he and his boss recognize that absenteeism is something of a problem. In addition, certain things in the organization that should be done have been put off, such as revising or, in most cases, preparing job descriptions. As he stares at the big picture on the wall across from his desk in his new office, Jerry wonders where to begin.

Comments:

Jerry is in the uncomfortable position of having landed in a situation with which he is not familiar. One suggestion would be for him to conduct a personnel audit to get a formal and fairly comprehensive reading on the current state of personnel activities in ASC. Then he might be able to determine the areas that really need immediate attention. Jerry's lack of knowledge of personnel management may hinder him, but there are many sources to which he can turn to learn about personnel: trade publications, professional publications, professional consultants, and personnel associations, to name some. Also, he has a number of personnel records available to him that have probably been kept because of government requirements. In summary, Jerry faces a challenging opportunity.

O NLY by studying personnel activities can managers determine program effectiveness, the quality and extent of employee performance, and the need for new practices and systems. Research on personnel management activities provides an understanding of what works, what does not work, and what needs to be done.

Such research is ongoing and requires that good records be kept. In addition, the government has imposed recordkeeping requirements on most business organizations. Auditing of personnel activities is a type of research that especially relies upon personnel records. These audits are not always well received, but it is a sign of a healthy organization when management allows and encourages detailed accounts of personnel activities.

In the personnel research and records interface shown in Figure 16–1, the personnel unit and operating managers share the responsibility for good personnel records and research. The personnel unit usually guides the design and collection of data, while managers provide assistance and necessary information. This chapter considers the basics of personnel recordkeeping and formal research and their importance in evaluating an organization's current personnel management operations.

Figure 16–1 Personnel research and records interface.

Personnel Unit	Managers
Designs personnel information systems	Have access to personnel information system as needed
Keeps required records	
Provides expertise to design and evaluate data gathering	Provide information on people in the work units
Provides overview of organization climate	Assist in gathering data on organizational climate
Evaluates turnover and absenteeism throughout the organization	Control absenteeism and turnover in own work unit
Conducts personnel audit	Cooperate in personnel audit

PERSONNEL RESEARCH

Personnel research is often the only way to solve personnel problems. Without accurate information poor decisions are likely to be made. Many managers are intimidated by the word "research" and its academic implication. However, much research is quite simple and straightforward.

For example, managers in a state education agency completed an attitude survey on job satisfaction in their unit. This survey pointed out problem areas which would not have been discovered otherwise, such as dissatisfaction with supervision and promotion policies.

There are numerous ways to research the status of personnel management in an organization. Some of the most important ones follow.

PERSONNEL RESEARCH analyzes past and present personnel practices through the use of collected data and records.

Employee Questionnaires

One type of research can be done by using an employee questionnaire. This device gives employees an opportunity to voice their opinions about rather specific personnel management activities. For example, questionnaires may be sent to employees regarding the organization's performance appraisal system to collect ideas for revising it. Or, employees may be asked to evaluate specific organizational communication methods, such as the employee handbook or the company suggestion system. Figure 16–2 shows a variety of possible questionnaire items.

Questionnaires can be distributed and collected by supervisors or surveys can be distributed with employee paychecks or mailed to their homes. Better information can be obtained if employees are not required to identify themselves on a questionnaire and if they can return completed questionnaires anonymously. For example, Linda Stice, a manager

Figure 16–2. Sample employee questionnaire items.

1. How would you describe the benefits in the organization?
   Excellent ____ Good ____ Average ____ Fair ____ Poor ____
2. How do you feel about the company policy of "buying back" sick leave?
   Like it ____ Dislike it ____ Don't know ____ Why?
3. Would you use a company tuition reimbursement plan at local educational institutions?
   Yes ____ No ____ Not sure ____
4. Would you be in favor of a flexible work week schedule?
   Yes ____ Undecided ____ No ____

in a large insurance company, was considered to be a very tough supervisor; her section consistently had more grievances than the others.
When the personnel department designed a survey to pinpoint problems
in the company, Linda was instructed to distribute and collect the questionnaires. The employees felt sure Linda would look at their answers
before returning the forms to the personnel department; consequently,
they did not answer the questions honestly.

Attitude Surveys.   Attitude surveys focus on feelings and motives to
pinpoint the employees' underlying opinions about their working environment. One source suggests three basic purposes for conducting
attitude surveys: (1) for use as a base for comparing other surveys, (2)
as a measurement of the effect of change before and after the change
occurs, and (3) to determine the nature and extent of employee feelings
regarding specific organizational issues and the organization in general.[1]

Surveys serve as a sounding board for employees' feelings about their
jobs, supervisors, co-workers, organizational policies and practices, and
the organization in general. Many prepared attitude surveys are available.
One should be careful, however, to see published reliability and validity
statistics before using a prepared instrument. Only acceptably valid and
reliable surveys really measure attitudes accurately. Often a "research"
survey that is self-developed by a manager is poorly structured, asks
questions in a confusing manner, or "leads" the employees to respond
in a manner to give the manager the "results" he or she wants.

Organizational Climate Surveys.   One useful survey technique is the
measurement of the organization's "climate."

> ORGANIZATIONAL CLIMATE is a composite view of the character-
> istics of an organization as seen by employees.

It attempts to determine how employees feel about the organization
or certain specific aspects of it. For instance, in one company, employees
liked the work they did, but problems with the company's structure and
policies hampered their job performances and satisfactions. In this particular case, employee satisfaction with their work differed from their
satisfaction with the company. The value of an organizational climate
study is that it can be used to diagnose the current state of an organization and indicate where changes are needed. An overall view of the
organization's climate can be displayed graphically, as in Figure 16–3.

It is important to remember that an organization's climate varies
from one unit to another. The climate of the housekeeping unit might
be different from the climate of the intensive care unit in a hospital.

Figure 16–3. Sales corporation organization climate.

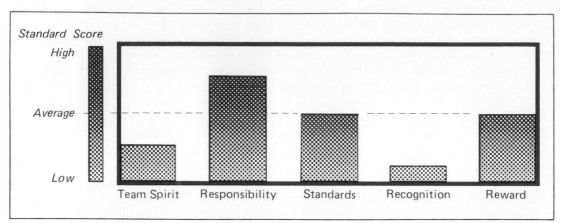

When researching organizational climate, the results should be identified both by subunits and as a whole to provide an overall organizational picture. Dimensions of organizational climate commonly measured include:[2]

1. *Structure*—feelings about rules, procedures, and constraints

2. *Responsibility*—feelings about the individual's decision-making freedom

3. *Reward*—degree to which employees perceive fairness in pay and other rewards

4. *Risk*—sense of challenge and risk

5. *Team Spirit*—feeling of group friendliness and identification with the organization

6. *Standards*—emphasis perceived on goal attainment and achievement of performance standards

Organizational climate may be measured and the results used as a diagnostic tool for managers or consultants. A large bank used organizational climate research to measure employees' feelings in one unit of the bank and recommended changes based upon the results. Climate surveys are action research devices used to intervene in an organization and provide a basis for making changes. They are typically conducted by external consultants. In this case it is often the role of the personnel department to recommend a consultant and to translate the consultant's recommendations into action.

Research Interviews

The personal interview is an alternative to the opinion survey and may focus on a wide variety of problems. One type of interview widely used is the *exit interview.*

Exit Interview.   In an exit interview, persons leaving the organization are interviewed and asked to identify problems that caused them to resign. This information can be used to correct problems so that others will not leave. Personnel specialists usually conduct exit interviews rather than supervisors, and a skillful interviewer can gain useful information.

One problem with the exit interview is that resigning employees may be reluctant to divulge their real reasons for leaving because they do not want to "burn any bridges." They may also fear that candid responses will hinder their chances of receiving favorable references.

The major reason an employee usually gives for leaving a job is an offer of more pay somewhere else. While this reason is considered to be acceptable, more pay may not be the only factor involved. Former employees may be more willing to provide more information on a questionnaire mailed to their home or in a telephone conversation sometime after leaving.

Experiments

Experiments can also provide useful data. Two formats for setting up experiments are: (1) measuring conditions before and after a change is made and (2) having some employees perform a job in a new way while others perform the same job in the old way and compare the results. Persons trained in experimental design and statistics are usually needed to conduct such studies and interpret the results.

Research Using Other Organizations

Personnel specialists can gain new insights from managers and specialists in other organizations by participating in professional personnel groups. The most prominent professional organizations are the American Society for Personnel Administration (ASPA) and the International Personnel Management Association (IPMA). These organizations publish professional journals and newsletters, conduct annual meetings and conferences, and provide many other services, often through local chapters. ASPA is primarily composed of private sector personnel administrators, whereas members of IPMA are primarily personnel managers from local, state, and federal government agencies.

Private management consulting firms and local colleges and universities also provide assistance in personnel research. These outside researchers may be more knowledgeable and unbiased than persons inside the organization. Consultants skilled in questionnaire design and data analysis can provide expert advice on personnel research. Appendix A contains a list of organizations and agencies having information useful to personnel specialists and other managers.

National or Area Surveys.   Surveys by other organizations can provide some perspectives on a company's internal research. Some professional organizations, like the Bureau of National Affairs and the National Industrial Conference Board, sponsor surveys on personnel practices in communities, states, regions, and in the nation. The survey results are then distributed to participating organizations. Or, an organization may conduct its own comparative outside surveys such as wage surveys.

Current Literature.   Professional personnel journals and publications provide useful communication between managers, personnel specialists, researchers, and other practitioners. Figure 16–4 is a list of journals which often publish personnel management information.

Importance of Personnel Research

Effective personnel management decisions are assisted by personnel research because there are no pat answers to personnel problems. Good personnel management comes through analyzing problems and applying experience and knowledge to *particular situations.* A manager who "supposes" that something may happen is not likely to be effective. In some organizations personnel research is formalized through a personnel audit. Such an audit provides an overall look at personnel activities and helps identify areas that need improvement.

What are four personnel research methods?

PERSONNEL AUDIT

A personnel audit is similar in purpose to the financial audit, which examines, verifies, evaluates, and investigates an organization's current financial status. Many of the research sources mentioned earlier are used in personnel audits. These sources can tell top executives, personnel specialists, and managers how well the organization is managing its human resources.

A PERSONNEL AUDIT is a formal research effort to evaluate the current state of personnel management in an organization.

Using statistical reports and research data, personnel audits evaluate how well personnel activities have been performed. A formal comprehensive audit can examine many areas (see Figure 16–5).

Figure 16–4. Current literature in personnel management.

A. Research Oriented Journals

(These journals contain articles that report on original research. Normally these journals contain rather sophisticated writing and/or quantitative verifications of authors' findings.)

Journal of Applied Psychology
Journal of Business
Journal of Business Communications
Journal of Communications
Journal of Industrial Relations

Academy of Management Journal
Academy of Management Review
Administrative Science Quarterly
American Journal of Sociology
American Sociological Review
Behavioral Science
Human Organization
Human Relations
Industrial & Labor Relations Review
Industrial Relations
Journal of Applied Behavioral Science

Journal of Management Studies
Journal of Social Pyschology
Journal of Social Issues
Management Science
Organizational Behavior & Human Performance
Personnel Psychology
Research Management
Sloan Management Review
Social Forces
Social Science Research
Sociometry

B. Management Oriented Journals

(These journals generally cover a wide range of subjects. Articles in these publications normally are aimed at the practitioner and are written to interpret, summarize, or discuss past, present, and future research and administrative applications. Not all of the articles in these publications are personnel-oriented.)

Human Behavior
Human Resource Management
Labor Law Journal
Management Review
Michigan Business Review
Michigan State University Business Topics
Monthly Labor Review
Nation's Business
Organizational Dynamics

Across the Board
Administrative Management
Advanced Management Journal
Business Horizons
California Management Review
Canadian Personnel
Columbia Journal of World Business
Dun's Review
Fortune
Harvard Business Review

Personnel
Personnel Administration
Personnel Journal
Personnel Management
Public Personnel Management
Psychology Today
The Personnel Administrator
Supervisory Management
Training and Development Journal

C. For assistance in locating articles, some of the following indices and abstracts contain subject matter of interest.

Applied Science and Technology Index
Business Periodicals Index
Dissertation Abstracts
Employee Relations Index
Index to Legal Periodicals
Index to Social Sciences and Humanities

Management Abstracts
Personnel Management Abstracts
Psychological Abstracts
Reader's Guide to Periodical Literature
Sociological Abstracts

Figure 16–5. Personnel audit checklist.

Personnel Audit checklist

Score **Work Analysis**

_____ Current job descriptions (at least 80% of jobs)

_____ Job specifications/qualifications

_____ Job design considerations

Staffing

_____ Human resource planning procedures and forecasts

_____ Use of internal recruiting sources

_____ Use of external recruiting media

_____ EEO compliance recruitment

_____ Legal application blank

_____ Validation of testing procedures

_____ Privacy concerns and reference checking

_____ Affirmative action plan

_____ Employment of women/minorities/ handicapped

_____ Training of interviewers (including supervisors)

Training and Development

_____ Orientation of new employees

_____ Job skill training programs

_____ Career planning programs

_____ Management development programs

Appraisal

_____ Job-related performance appraisal

_____ Appraisal feedback training for managers

_____ Internal equity of appraisal program

_____ Effective tie between appraisals and compensations

Compensation

_____ Formal wage and salary system

_____ Consistency with external wage/salary survey

_____ Incentive program

_____ Employee recognition program

_____ Benefit programs

_____ Retirement plan and counseling

Maintenance

_____ Safety compliance/investigation

_____ Discipline policies and procedures

_____ Turnover/absenteeism analysis and control

_____ Personnel records/employee privacy protection

_____ Employee-related activities and programs

_____ Exit-interview procedures

_____ Staffing and budgetary requirements

Union

_____ Formal grievance procedure

_____ Union problem prevention training

_____ Collective bargaining procedures

Scoring: Where you think your personnel department is doing a _very good_ job, give yourself a score of 3. For an _adequate_ job (one that needs some improvement) score 2. If you are _weak_ in an area (and need major improvement) score 1. Score a minus 1 (−1) where the activity is basically nonexistent. Typically, a small company's personnel department should score at least 90 if it is to be effective. How much work do you have to do?

(Source: Robert L. Mathis and Gary Cameron, "Auditing Personnel Practices in Smaller-Sized Organizations: A Realistic Approach," Reprinted with permission from the April 1981 issue of _Personnel Administrator_, copyright 1981. The American Society for Personnel Administration, 30 Park Dr., Berea, Ohio 44017, $26 per year.)

A beginning point for a personnel audit in any size organization is a determination by management of the objectives it wants to achieve in the personnel area.[3] The process then compares the actual state of personnel activities to the objectives.

Human Resource Accounting

Human resource accounting is similar in principle to an accounting statement. Just as financial accounting reflects the cost of capital assets such as machinery and buildings, human resource accounting, typically done either once a year or at regular intervals, attempts to place a value on an organization's human resources by formulating a human resource "balance sheet." This instrument demonstrates that human resources are an asset instead of a common expense and that they should therefore be computed as part of an organization's total worth.

HUMAN RESOURCE ACCOUNTING is a specialized personnel audit which continually attempts to quantify the value of an organization's human resources.

People as "Investments."   Human resource accounting shows the investment the organization makes in its people and how the value of these people changes over time—the acquisition cost of employees is compared to the replacement cost. The value of employees is increased by training and experience over a period of time. Upjohn, a large pharmaceutical manufacturer, has used human resource accounting to estimate that an employee represents a $2.34 million investment over a 30-year period.[4]

The importance of human resource accounting is illustrated by the effect a change in human resources has on the stock market. If a change occurs in a company's top management or key personnel, the price of that company's stock can go up or down. The board of directors of a large food company decided to remove the president, vice-president, and controller. When this news reached the stock market, the price of the company's stock soared because the market viewed this action as a major improvement in the company's operations. That illustrates the value placed on the top management team—in this case it was low.

Human resources accounting is not widely used because it is difficult to establish how much the value of organizations' human resources increase or decrease. Also, different accounting approaches can be used to measure human resources.[5] In sum, human resource accounting is a sophisticated way to measure the effectiveness of personnel management activities and the use of people in an organization. It is presented here as an illustration of attempts to measure the effectiveness of personnel activities.

Compare the concepts of personnel audit and human resources accounting.

ABSENTEEISM AND TURNOVER

Absenteeism and turnover are major concerns in most organizations. These two personnel problems are universally watched and studied by managers because they affect the organization's operations. If a manager needs 12 people to work in a unit to get the work done, and four of the 12 are absent most of the time, the unit's work will probably not get done. Research on the reasons for absenteeism should be done using an organization's own records.

Absenteeism

Employees can be absent from work for several reasons. Illness, death in the family, or other personal reasons are unavoidable and understandable; however, excessive absences may cause organizational coordination problems. Many employers have sick-leave policies which allow employees to be absent a certain number of paid days per year. Employees who miss fewer days are reimbursed with sick pay.

A formula for computing absenteeism rates suggested by the U.S. Department of Labor is as follows:

$$\frac{\text{Number of person-days lost through job absence during period}}{(\text{Average number of employees}) \times (\text{Number of work days})} \times 100$$

The rate can be computed based on the number of hours instead of days. In one study of 136 organizations the absentee rate ranged from 1.8% to 11.4%, with the average being 4%.[6]

Organizations have noted that there are consistently more absences on Fridays and Mondays than on other days. One reason for this is that some employees stretch the weekend to three or four days. Other causes for absenteeism can be suggested. A relationship between absenteeism and job satisfaction has been found. Employees with higher job satisfaction will probably be absent less often than those who are dissatisfied with their jobs.

Absenteeism Control

Dealing with absenteeism must begin with continuous monitoring of absenteeism statistics in work units. This monitoring will help managers pinpoint employees who are frequently absent and units with excessive absenteeism. Offering rewards for good attendance, giving bonuses for missing fewer than a certain number of days, and buying unused sick leave are all methods of reducing absenteeism. If absenteeism is excessive, the problem employees can be "dehired." Organizational policies on absenteeism should be clearly stated in the employee handbook and stressed by supervisors and managers. Employee counseling and discussion may correct some of the problems that make people reluctant to come to work and may suggest positive actions to be taken. Absenteeism control options fall into one of three categories: (1) discipline, (2) positive reinforcement, or (3) a combination of the two.

Disciplinary Approach.   Scott, a large paper company, used the disciplinary approach in their Mobile, Alabama, plant to good effect. People who were absent were first given an oral warning; subsequent absences brought written warnings, suspension, and finally dismissal. In five years under this system 70 workers were fired and the absentee rate dropped from 7% to around 4%.[7]

Positive Reinforcement.   Positive reinforcement includes cash for meeting attendance standards, recognition, time off, and other rewards. In one firm employees with perfect attendance records were given the "right" to participate in a lottery with a cash reward. The program reduced absenteeism markedly.

Combination Approaches.   Combination approaches ideally reward desired behavior and punish undesired behavior. At a Detroit architectural engineering firm each employee gets a time-off "account," against which vacation, holiday, and sick time is drawn. If employees run out of days in their accounts, they are not paid for the days missed. However, they can accrue sicktime yearly.

How can absenteeism be controlled?

Turnover

Turnover can be a very costly problem. One firm had a turnover rate of over 120% per year. It cost the company $1.5 million per year in lost productivity, increased training time, increased personnel selection time, lost worker efficiency, and other indirect costs.

TURNOVER refers to the process of employees leaving the organization and having to be replaced.

The turnover rate for an organization can be computed using the following formula from the U.S. Department of Labor (separations are people who left the organization):

$$\frac{\text{Number of employee separations during the month}}{\text{Total number of employees at midmonth}} \times 100$$

A national survey found that turnover ranged from 2% to 32.5% per year. The average turnover rate was about 3% per year.[8] It is important to note that turnover rates vary among industries. Organizations requiring little skill among entry-level personnel are likely to have a higher turnover rate among those employees than among managerial personnel. Therefore, it is important that turnover rates be computed by work units. One organization's companywide turnover rate was not severe. However, 80% of the turnover occurred within one department. This imbalance indicated that some action was needed to deal with problems in that unit.

Turnover is often divided into voluntary and involuntary segments. Involuntary turnover occurs when an employee is fired. Voluntary turnover occurs when an employee leaves by his or her own choice, and can be caused by many factors. The obvious ones are those that cause job dissatisfaction. Some other, not so obvious, causes of turnover are absenteeism, performance, and the competition for expected job openings.[9]

Turnover Control. Turnover can be dealt with in several ways. Because it is related to job satisfaction, matching an employee's expectations of rewards and satisfaction may help reduce turnover problems. A good way to eliminate turnover is to improve selection and matching of applicants to jobs. By hiring people who are more likely to stay through fine-tuning the selection process, managers can increase the possibility that fewer employees will leave.

Good employee orientation will also help reduce turnover. Employees who are properly introduced into the company and are well-trained tend to be less likely to leave. If people receive some basic information about the company and the job to be performed, they can determine early whether or not they want to stay. Another reason for turnover is that individuals believe there is no opportunity for career advancement. Career planning and internal promotion can help an organization keep career personnel.

A fair and equitable pay system can help prevent turnover. An employee who is underpaid relative to employees in other jobs with similar skills may leave if there is an inviting alternative job available. An awareness of employee problems and dissatisfactions may provide a manager with opportunities to resolve them before they become so severe that employees leave. Turnover problems can be pinpointed by researching personnel records.

How can turnover be controlled?

PERSONNEL RECORDS

The only function of many early personnel departments was record-keeping. It should be apparent by this point in the book that the contemporary personnel department has many more activities today, but the need for keeping personnel records has taken on much greater importance with increased government demands and such new sophisticated personnel techniques as human resources forecasting.

Personnel-related records and data provide an excellent source of information for auditing or assessing the effectiveness of a personnel department or any unit. They also provide the basis for doing research into possible causes of problems the organization may be experiencing. Figure 16–6 shows some of the kinds of personnel records and data that may be available in many organizations.

Figure 16–6. Examples of personnel records and data sources.

Accident Records	Termination Records
Employment Requisition Records	Job Specification
Personnel Inventories	Job Descriptions
Applicant Records	Salary Increase Records
Interview Records	Training Records
Turnover Records	Personal History Records
Transfer Records	Affirmative Action Records
Payroll Records	Medical Records
Work Schedule Records	Insurance Records
Test Score Records	Other Benefit Records
Performance Records	Committee Meeting Records
Grievance Records	Retired Employee Records
Arbitration Awards	Personal Interest Records
Occupational Health Records	Attitude/Morale Data
Job Bidding Records	Open Jobs Records
Exit Interview Records	Labor Market Data
Employee Expense Records	

Personnel records also serve as important documentation in certain cases. For example, a new employee stated on the application blank that he had a driver's license and was hired to drive a delivery truck. Examination later revealed the new employee did *not* have a driver's license and he was fired for falsifying the application. Without the record of the falsified application, proving he had lied would have been difficult because he claimed he had never said he had a driver's license.

Records and the Government

Federal, state, and local laws *require* that numerous records be kept on employees. The requirements are so varied as to exactly what should be kept and for how long that each specific case must be dealt with separately. Generally, records relating to wages, basic employment, work schedules, job evaluations, merit and seniority systems, and Affirmative Action programs should be kept by all employers who are subject to provisions of the Fair Labor Standards Act. The most commonly required retention time for such records is three years. However, this limit varies and should be carefully checked.

In addition, other records may be required on issues relating to EEO, OSHA, or the Age Discrimination Act. Such recordkeeping requirements have not been accepted easily by managers who must adapt to the additional paperwork. In addition to the time and expense of keeping records, many managers feel that records can be a source of major trouble by allowing the past actions of management to be questioned. There probably *is* a point beyond which it costs more to keep records than can be gained by doing so.

The major problem presented by personnel recordkeeping is more commonly the inability to retrieve needed information without major difficulties. For example, better personnel decisions can be made if good information is available on the nature, causes, and severity of accidents, the reasons for absenteeism, the availability of experience, the distribution of performance appraisals, and so forth. But for many organizations such information is not *readily* available. A solution to the problems associated with recordkeeping and getting useful information easily from the records that are kept is a well-designed personnel information system.

Why is personnel recordkeeping important?

Personnel Information Systems

> A PERSONNEL INFORMATION SYSTEM is an integrated computerized system designed to provide information to be used in making personnel decisions.

A personnel information system usually utilizes a computer, its attendant hardware and software, and a data base. Figure 16–7 shows a very simple model of a personnel information system.

Figure 16–7.   A simple model of a personnel information system.

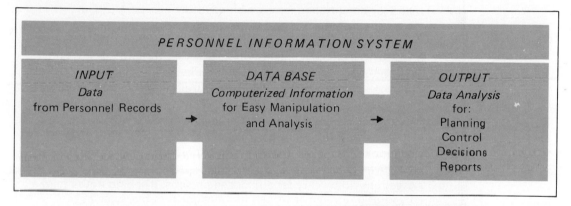

PERSONNEL INFORMATION SYSTEM

INPUT	*DATA BASE*	*OUTPUT*
Data	Computerized Information	Data Analysis
from Personnel Records	for Easy Manipulation	for:
	and Analysis	Planning
		Control
		Decisions
		Reports

Most of the records/data sources listed earlier lend themselves to quantification; that is, they can be stated in numerical terms. These numbers can then be combined or manipulated by the personnel manager or a computer programmer to provide the type of information necessary for planning, controlling, making decisions, or preparing reports.

The computer has vastly simplified the task of analyzing vast amounts of data and can be an invaluable aid in every aspect of personnel management from payroll processing to record retention. But it must be understood that the computer is only a machine. If it is given bad information, it returns in kind ("garbage in, garbage out"). Extracting useful information from raw data requires knowledgeable approaches and a good bit of common sense. In short, the computer is a tremendous aid to the personnel manager but can never replace the manager.

Uses.   Computers operating for personnel purposes are commonly used for: (1) payroll records and reports, (2) pay statistics and reports, and (3) personnel statistics and reports. Successful personnel information systems are commonly tied (at least initially) to the payroll system.[10]

Personnel information systems are used extensively in employee benefit programs. As these programs become more complex, computerization is necessary to maintain accurate records of the various benefits and options employees select. Another major use of computers is human resource planning and forecasting. Computers make it easier to build models and project work force demands and availability for the next five years.

Figure 16–8. Practical guides to development and use of a personnel information system.

---

1. Information has little value unless it can be used to make comparisons, ratios, or draw trends from which causality can be inferred.
2. Effective personnel information systems must emphasize the user of the information not the computer. The most elegant hardware and software available will not be of any use unless the end result is better decisions by the people using the information.
3. Both the users of the information and top management should be involved in the design of the system so it will meet their needs.
4. The system should have clear cut objectives and measures of effectiveness established from the start.
5. Changes to the system when needed should be made easily and quickly.
6. Access should be easy for authorized persons. It should not require a computer programmer to get information from the system.
7. Employees should know what information on them is on the system and should have at least an annual opportunity to see their files.**

(Source: Adapted from E. E. Burack and R. Smith, *Personnel Management.* St. Paul: West Publishing, 1977, p. 439. Used with permission.)

Computerization is not limited to use by large corporations. Smaller computer systems and desk-top computer units can be invaluable to small organizations which must store and quickly retrieve information. Figure 16–8 shows some practical guidelines for developing and using a personnel information system. All the guidelines underscore the importance of having a system that is flexible, responsive, and user-oriented. Ideally, the personnel department should be able to use the information system with very little help from computer programmers after it has been set up.

Can you diagram a personnel information system?

PRIVACY AND PERSONNEL RECORDS

As a result of governmental concern regarding the protection of individuals' rights to privacy, the Privacy Act of 1974 (Public Law 92-579) was passed. This law applies to federal agencies and companies supplying services to the federal government, but numerous state laws have also been passed. These states include California, Maine, Michigan, Oregon, Pennsylvania, Connecticut, and Ohio. There are also provisions affecting personnel records systems. One example of an organization attempting to deal with the spirit of the laws is IBM's establishment of four principles of privacy. These principles can serve as a guide in this area until more specific details are agreed upon:

1. Individuals should have access to information about themselves in recordkeeping systems.

2. There should be a way for an individual to correct or amend an inaccurate record.

3. An individual should be able to prevent information from being improperly disclosed or used for other than authorized purposes.

4. Reasonable precautions should be taken to be sure that data are reliable and not misused.[11]

Other pioneering companies include Bank of America, Aetna Life, Cummins Engine, Avis, TRW, G.E., Atlantic Richfield, AT&T, Control Data, Prudential, and General Motors. These companies have conducted information audits of their current practices and have eliminated unnecessary or objectionable information on employees.

A survey done by Sentry Insurance found that while most employees do not view their employers as engaged in improper collection of personal information, they do favor a new system of rules to handle sensitive information that is collected.[12] Further, they want decisions on promotions, job assignment, and discipline made on the basis of information that can be examined if a dispute arises. Employees and the public in the survey viewed fair information practices as a matter of good personnel management. But they are likely to see Congress and the law intervene if good judgment is not used.

These findings may require some rethinking and reorganizing of many existing recordkeeping systems in personnel units, but doing so is likely to minimize problems later. For example, in one firm no negative information on an employee is retained and used if it is more than two years old.

The records that are kept on personnel in organizations provide an excellent source for doing research inside the organization. Personnel research, as was suggested earlier, provides management with the information it uses to make adjustments or to continue with the status quo if adjustments are not needed.

How do privacy concerns affect personnel records?

REVIEW AND PREVIEW

In order to judge how effectively an organization is being managed, managers and personnel specialists attempt to evaluate how well the human resources have been used. This research provides information and insights for improving the effectiveness of personnel activities.

There are a number of research sources that can be used to evaluate personnel management actions. Internal sources such as employee questionnaires, research interviews, experiments, and personnel records are valuable. Others are other organizations, surveys, and current literature. In some organizations, personnel research has been formalized through a personnel audit and human resource accounting. These methods evaluate how well an organization's human resources have been managed. Absenteeism and turnover are two key areas for evaluation.

Personnel records are an important part of the research process. Personnel records contain a variety of information, but the government has mandated that certain records be kept. Personnel information systems can help greatly in managing great masses of personnel records. However, privacy of personnel records is becoming a greater concern.

The past section has considered activities that are part of the maintenance interface. Attention now turns to the interface with formal labor organizations which provides some special challenges to personnel management.

Review Questions

1. You are a personnel director for Consolidated Widgets. What means would you use to conduct personnel research on turnover and absenteeism problems in your firm?

2. A personnel audit and human resource accounting are somewhat different. Differentiate between them.

3. Why would you be concerned about turnover and absenteeism problems?

4. "Personnel recordkeeping is a necessary but mundane part of personnel management." Discuss.

5. What are the components of a personnel information system?

6. Discuss the following statement: "Privacy concerns will have a significant impact on personnel recordkeeping systems."

Case: George Must Guess?

George, the new department supervisor, wondered if he couldn't have spent his retirement from the Navy in a more relaxed atmosphere. He had just accepted a position at the Stevenson Company which had approximately 350 employees. He was replacing the original supervisor of the Transportation Department. The department had been created only five years before and was located at a site away from central headquarters. It started out employing only seven people and had steadily grown until 45 people were employed there. George had one assistant, two route managers, a dispatcher, an unfilled secretarial position, 23 full-time drivers, 17 part-time drivers, and a custodian. Job descriptions and department procedures had been established during the first few years of the department.

It didn't take George long to find out that the previous supervisor felt no one knew how a transportation department should operate except himself. Consequently, he had handled all the planning, organization, and operating of the department. He had delegated only minor duties to his staff and bailed out when he could no longer handle the increasing work load. To complicate the situation, the secretary who kept the books and department records left at the same time. Neither position was filled for six weeks.

The assistant supervisor, two route managers, and the dispatcher were apprehensive about the arrival of a new supervisor. All had assumed extra duties with which they were not familiar.

Many employees were disgruntled because several drivers had abused sick leave and were neglecting their job duties. This had resulted in an overall feeling that if others could get by with this type of performance, why should someone put forth any more effort than needed?

One week prior to George's employment, the supervisor had put Francine, a female minority driver, on probation for taking improperly requested vacation leave, excessive absenteeism, and neglecting her job duties. She filed a grievance with the Personnel Department against the supervisor. The company lawyer had requested the charges be dropped against the driver and the probation be rescinded to prevent an EEOC claim against the company. Employee records were so incomplete that no one could tell what had really happened. In addition, the assistant supervisor had been placed on probation for using improper procedures when putting an employee on probation and having inadequate accounts of the charges against the driver.

QUESTIONS:

1. What are the recordkeeping minimums that could have kept this from happening?
2. What can George do without records now?

NOTES

1. Rene V. Dawis and William Weitzel, "Worker Attitudes and Expectations," in: Dale Yoder and Herbert G. Heneman Jr., eds., *ASPA Handbook of Personnel and Industrial Relations* (Washington D.C.: The Bureau of National Affairs, 1979), pp. 6–40.

2. The dimensions in this form are suggested in an organizational climate instrument developed by George H. Litwin and Robert A. Stringer, *Motivation and Organizational Climate* (Cambridge, MA: Harvard University Press, 1981).

3. Robert L. Mathis and Gary Cameron, "Auditing Personnel Practices in Smaller-sized Organizations: a Realistic Approach," *Personnel Administrator*, April 1981, pp. 45–49.

4. Charles R. Day, Jr., "Solving the Mystery of Productivity Measurement," *Industry Week*, January 26, 1981, p. 66.

5. B. Jones, "Human Resource Accounting: A Need for Relevance," *Management Accounting*, March 1978, pp. 33–36.

6. Personnel Policies Forum, *Employee Absenteeism and Turnover*, PPF #106, (Washington, D.C.: Bureau of National Affairs, May 1974), p. 3.

7. T. H. Stone, "Absence Control: Is Your Company a Candidate?? *Personnel Administrator*, September 1980, p. 81.

8. Personnel Policies Forum, *Employee Absenteeism and Turnover*, p. 9.

9. S. A. Stumpf and P. K. Dawky, "Predicting Voluntary and Involuntary Turnover Using Absenteeism and Performance Indices," *Academy of Management Journal*, 24, March 1981, p. 148 and G. F. Dreher and T. W. Dougherty, "Turnover and Competition for Expected Job Openings: An Exploratory Analysis," *Academy of Management Journal*, 23, December 1980, pp. 766–771.

10. A. J. Walker, "The 10 Most Common Mistakes in Developing Computer-Based Personnel Systems," *Personnel Administrator*, July 1980, p. 40.

11. Virginia E. Schein, "Privacy and Personnel: A Time for Action," *Personnel Journal*, December 1976, p. 606.

12. A. F. Westen, "What Should Be Done About Employee Privacy?" *Personnel Administrator*, March 1980, pp. 27–30.

Organization/Union Interface

"THE WILLMAR 8"

Labor-management relations the world over have a speckled past. Labor history is full of accounts of murders and beatings, bombings, burnings, and so forth, as management and employees worked out the framework in which they would interact. But that stuff is all in the past now, isn't it? We have worked it out and institutionalized the framework. If you want a union, you can have one—no big deal. Right? Wrong.

In some industries and in some parts of the country, employees are at a clear disadvantage in dealing with employers. The Willmar 8 case is an excellent example. The Willmar 8 were 8 women who worked as bookkeepers and tellers at the Citizen's Bank of Willmar, Minnesota. The 8 were unhappy because they earned between $400 and $500 a month (in 1977) and had been repeatedly passed over for promotions. The promotions usually went to men *that they had trained*. When the women protested the promotion policies, the bank president told one of them, "We are not all equal, you know."

The women declared themselves the Willmar Bank Employees Association and demanded higher pay and fair promotions. When none of their demands were met, they went on strike. For 15 months (and two bitter Minnesota winters), they marched back and forth in front of the bank. They got a lot of publicity (national magazines, papers, and The Phil Donahue Show), but it did no good. In 1979, the National Labor Relations Board ruled against their Unfair Labor Practice request. The seven remaining strikers had to move on to other jobs.

While the Willmar 8 lost the strike, they may have made a point. A film made about the incident (a 50-minute documentary) is showing to packed houses of *bankers* around the country. Only 30 of the nation's 15,000 banks are unionized and the remaining 14,970 would like to keep it that way. Banks have traditionally relied on low-paid female clerical workers. Banking groups feel that if this situation can happen in Willmar, it can probably happen all over. Unions are interested in seeing the film, too, as you might expect!!

Although the banking industry does very little dealing with unions at this point, many organizations do formally interact with their employees through unions. To understand the basis of this relationship, the history of the labor movement and labor legislation must be studied. Chapter 17 provides a useful synopsis of the evolution of unionism and labor legislation in the United States. An understanding of the steps in the unionization process is an important part of a manager's knowledge.

If an organization is unionized, a labor contract is the basis for the relationship between an employer and a union. The process of reaching a contract agreement is known as collective bargaining, an important part of labor-management relations. The bargaining process and typical issues in collective bargaining are discussed in chapter 18.

Grievance procedures and arbitration are methods union members use to solve problems with the organization. In chapter 18, the daily administration of a labor agreement through the grievance procedure is discussed. If grievances cannot be settled, an arbitrator may be selected to decide what must be done. An analysis of some common problems arbitrators face and the relationship between a manager's behavior and grievance rates are also discussed in chapter 18.

CHAPTER 17

Nature of Union-Management Relations

When you have read this chapter, you should be able to:

1. Compare and contrast the philosophy of U.S. and European unions.

2. Describe two current and two future trends in unionism.

3. Depict the general structure of unions.

4. Trace the evolution of labor unions in the United States from 1800 to 1935.

5. Explain the acts which make up the National Labor Code.

6. Identify and discuss the stages in the unionization process.

*You Ungrateful *?!*

Art Gottlieb is the founder, owner, and president of Computer Service Bureau (CSB). Eight years ago Art started CSB as a time-sharing and computer services company. A combination of Art's sales ability and his hiring of several extremely good computer systems analysts resulted in CSB becoming very profitable and growing rapidly. Currently CSB has 200 employees, about half of whom hold clerical and keypunch jobs.

Most workers holding those lower-paid jobs are women under the age of 30, and fairly mobile. Because of the short training period and a very high turnover rate (100% per year), CSB starts new lower-level employees at 5% below the wage rate for similar jobs with other local employers. However, the local labor market is fairly loose, so CSB has had no difficulty hiring entry-level employees.

Currently, Art is angry. One of his supervisors just showed him a leaflet that an employee received at home. This leaflet urged the employee to sign a card indicating that the employee wants to vote on joining the International Office Workers Union (IOWU).

After a rather long tirade in which Art referred to the employees as "ungrateful * ?!," he told the supervisor he would send out a letter to all employees to say that anyone who signs a union card will be fired. Also, he plans to contact a labor attorney to help him "beat the union."

Comments:

The reaction exhibited by Art Gottlieb is typically seen in managers and entrepreneurs. However, Art would be better served if he realized that his employees might feel they need an outside force to deal with some of their problems. In addition, Art's ignorance of labor law may lead him to take illegal action by threatening employees with dismissal if they sign an authorization card.

Art should take action on two fronts. First, he should contact his labor attorney before taking any action so that he knows what he legally can and cannot do. Secondly, he needs to find out what problems employees have. However, employees may need a union or a unionization effort to effect necessary changes in wages and other job conditions.

 S OME people contend that unions represent an "outside force" caused by management neglect. Others argue that the union is an internal force because it is made up of employees from an employing organization. Regardless of the internal/external issue, one undeniable fact is that the existence of a union or unionization pressure presents additional challenges for managers and personnel specialists.

> A UNION is a formal organization that represents individuals employed in one organization, throughout an industry, or in an occupation.

Figure 17–1 shows a typical set of responsibilities the personnel unit and operating managers have in dealing with unions. This interface may vary in different organizations. In some organizations, the personnel unit does not become involved at all with labor relations because the operating management handles them. In other organizations, the personnel unit is almost completely in charge of labor relations. The breakdown of responsibilities shown in Figure 17–1 is a midpoint between these extremes.

This chapter takes a broad look at some of the trends and philosophies associated with unionism. The evolution and history of unions, current trends, union structure, and unionism in the public sector are all covered. Some specifics on how unions become employee representatives are then identified.

Once employees choose a union to represent them, formal collective bargaining between management and union representatives over certain

Figure 17–1. Union relations interface.

Personnel Unit	Managers
Deals with union organizing attempts at the company level	Provide conditions conducive to a positive relationship with employees
Monitors "climate" for unionization and union relationships	Avoid unfair labor practices during organizing efforts
Helps negotiate labor agreements	Administer the labor agreement on daily basis
Provides detailed knowledge of labor legislation as may be necessary	Resolve grievances and problems between management and employees/union members

Unions

issues must occur. Once these issues are included in a labor contract, management and union representatives must work together in managing the contract and preventing grievances. Grievances are formal complaints filed by workers with management. Collective bargaining and grievance procedures are two of the important interfaces between management and labor unions once a union has gained recognition as a legal representative of employee interests. Those two areas are examined in the next chapter.

UNIONISM CONCEPTS

Some concepts underlying unionism in the United States have come from philosophies and ideas about organized labor in Western Europe, especially England. The Industrial Revolution encouraged both employers and employees to seek personal advancement through collective action because individual effort was inadequate. However, unionism in the United States has developed its own philosophy and concepts.

Unionism in the U.S.

Unionism in the United States has followed a somewhat different pattern than unionism in other countries. In such countries as Italy, England, and Japan the union movement has been at the forefront of various political trends. For the most part this politicalization has not been the case in the United States. Perhaps the reason is that workers tend to identify with the American free enterprise system. Further, there is not the degree of class consciousness and conflict between the worker class and the management class in the United States that exists in many other countries. Ownership of private property by both management and union members is a further mediating influence in the United States.

Job-Centered Emphasis.   The primary emphasis of unionism in the United States has been the collective pursuit of "bread-and-butter" issues: higher wages, shorter working hours, job security, and good working conditions. To help protect workers' security, large unions in the United States have become politically active, although such activity was traditionally oriented more toward work-place issues than toward broad social concerns. However, since the mid-1960s unions have taken positions on economic issues, on full employment, and on some social issues.

Unions as a Countervailing Force.   Perhaps the most beneficial view of unions is as a countervailing force to help keep management "honest" and to make management consider the impact of its policies upon its employees. However, a rather delicate balance exists between management power and union power in an organization. It is very easy for this balance to be tipped one way or the other.

Management and unions, through their respective representatives, spend a great deal of time and effort disagreeing with each other. This disagreement is to be expected because of the nature of their built-in adversary roles. Yet, it is naive to suppose that either position or group is right all the time, nor is it correct to assume that there are always serious disagreements that lead to strikes. Figure 17–2 indicates that work stoppages because of strikes or lockouts are, and have been, a relative small percentage of total work time. The U.S. figures are considerably lower than those of many other countries.

Figure 17–2.   Work stoppages in the U.S. 1960–1980.

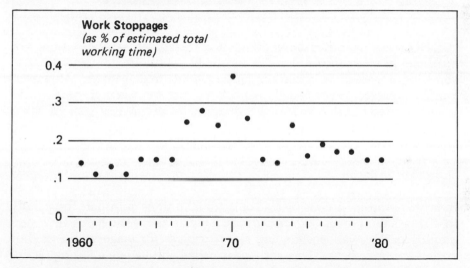

(Source: U.S. Department of Labor, Bureau of Labor Statistics, *Handbook of Labor Statistics, 1980.* Washington, D.C.: U.S. Government Printing Office, December 1980, p. 415.)

Unionism in Europe

Unions in a number of European countries have a somewhat different emphasis. They tend to be very ideological and political because they see themselves representing the working class. In several European countries political parties and trade unions merge together, and in some countries, such as Great Britain, one of the major political parties is actually called the Labour Party. One writer notes that European unions:

> embarked upon a course of advancing the entire working
> class by transforming the total society, in contrast to the

emphasis of the American movement on the immediate specifics of wages, hours, and working conditions for its members only.[1]

Extensive union involvement is demonstrated by statistics that indicate that almost all wage earners in Austria, Belgium, and Sweden are covered by collective bargaining agreements.[2]

Co-determination. Another facet of foreign unions that has not been widely adopted in the United States is the notion of worker involvement in managerial decision-making.

CO-DETERMINATION is a concept whereby union or worker representatives are given positions on a company's board of directors.

Different countries have different forms of co-determination. For example, in Germany workers sit on the board of directors and exercise some veto power over certain proposals by management. However, worker representatives usually cannot outvote management and stockholder representatives.[3] Co-determination is also a key part of labor relations in Sweden.

Unionism in Japan

In Japan company unions instead of national unions dominate, especially in firms having over 500 employees. During the spring of every year employees use wall posters and signs to press for wage increases, but strikes seldom occur.[4] This activity is called the People's Spring Offensive and includes other social groups as well as labor unions.

Many Japanese employers provide lifetime employment and emphasize paternalism and seniority. Companies often provide housing, vacations, and medical coverage for employees.

In the past Japanese workers rarely changed employers. However, some shifts began in the late 1970s as a result of a slowdown in the Japanese economy. Some layoffs of unneeded workers have occurred and a growing number of highly educated, younger workers are pushing for advancement. Such changes are expected to continue and will significantly change the labor/management scene in Japan during the mid- and late-1980s.

Merging Concepts of Unionism

It is becoming more apparent that unionism concepts from other countries are being adapted for use in the United States, and vice versa. As a result of widespread international trade and the growing number of international firms, cross-fertilization is increasing. International labor organizations may be labor's response to the multinational corporation. Already automobile workers' unions in Europe and the United States are discussing cooperative efforts. However, it is not likely that a labor party as such would be formed in the United States or that the labor unions in Europe and Japan will become less politically oriented. It would appear that some interchange and adaptations will occur, but the European and American unions will still retain some distinctly different characteristics.

Union/Management Cooperation

Worker participation through co-determination is not extensively developed in the U.S. However, in return for wage freezes and financial assistance, Douglas Fraser, president of the United Auto Workers, became a member of the Board of Directors of Chrysler Corporation. Such a highly visible step toward co-determination may be repeated in the future, probably on an individual situation basis. However, a number of U.S. unions have opposed co-determination as a goal of labor and it is unlikely that it will become widespread.[5]

An example of union/management cooperation that has been successful in the U.S. is *Labor-Management Committees*. These committees have been used to help attract industries to communities such as Evansville, Indiana, and Scranton, Pennsylvania.[6] Also, jointly supported programs dealing with employee absenteeism, vandalism, and alcoholism problems have been developed between individual companies and unions.

Can you compare U.S. and foreign unionism?

TRENDS IN UNIONISM

Reliable statistics on union membership in the United States are historically very difficult to obtain. Some unions tend to exaggerate membership reports to gain respect for themselves. Other unions have been known to report fewer members than they actually have for financial reasons, such as trying to avoid making higher payments to the labor federations to which they belong.[7]

Membership Trends

Figures available from the Bureau of Labor Statistics showed that membership in labor unions and public and professional employee associations headquartered in the United States, excluding Canadian members, was 22.3 million in 1980. What is revealing is that the number of union members as a percent of the total work force has declined from 24.7% in 1970 to 20.9% in 1980. Figure 17–3 shows this decline on the chart. What this decline indicates is that labor unions are not adding members as fast as new employees are added to the work force.

Figure 17–3. Union membership as a proportion of the labor force, 1970–1980.

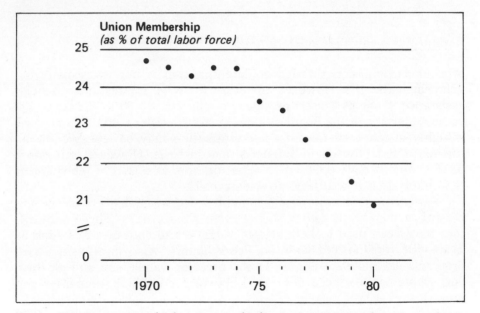

(Source: U.S. Department of Labor, Bureau of Labor Statistics, press release September 3, 1981.

Part of the slowness in total membership growth is the shifting character of the U.S. work force. The highly unionized manufacturing industries such as automobile and steel are those that have had layoffs and work-force reductions, causing union membership to shrink. At the same time the number of white-collar and women workers has been increasing.[8] These workers have traditionally been resistant to union membership efforts. Therefore, the overall figure that slightly more than 20% of the work force is unionized can be somewhat misleading. Certain industries are quite heavily unionized, whereas others are hardly unionized at all.

White-Collar Unionism

There are several reasons why white-collar unionization efforts are increasing. One is that advances in technology have boosted the number of white-collar workers in the work force. With total employees in white-collar jobs increasing relative to manufacturing jobs, unions have had to focus on white-collar areas in order to obtain new members.

Further, union leaders feel there is a growing realization among white-collar workers and professionals that their employment problems are not too different from those of manufacturing workers in the areas of pay, job security, and grievances. Also, professionals in areas such as nursing, teaching, and engineering are potential union members. For example, because of increases won by the Teamster's Union for other employees at Honeywell Corporation in Minneapolis, over 1000 engineers and technicians signed cards requesting a union representation election.[9] Unionization among such employees, who have not typically been union-oriented, presents a definite challenge for managers in a wide range of organizations.

Unionism in the Public Sector

Unions have been successful in obtaining members in the public sector. An increasing number of local, state, and federal government employees have joined unions. Figure 17–4 shows that total government union memberships have grown from 2.92 million in 1974 to 3.62 million in 1978, an increase of 17%. The growth has been greatest at the local level.

State and Local Government Unionism.   Unionism of state and local government employees presents some unique problems and challenges. First, many of the unionized local government employees are in exclusive and critical service areas. Police officers, firefighters, and sanitation workers all provide essential services in most cities. Allowing these workers to strike endangers public health and safety. Consequently, over 30 states have laws prohibiting public employee work stoppages. These laws also identify a variety of methods of impasse resolution including arbitration.

The impact of public employee wage increases on taxes is another concern. As taxpayers, the general public is increasingly critical of state and local government tax expenditures. Thus wage demands by public employees are often met with distrust and become political issues. In one metropolitan school district voters approved a spending lid of 7% increase on funding. Yet, a state court ordered a 16% increase in teacher salaries. The only course of action for the school board was to cut school programs such as junior high athletics, art programs, and the like.

Figure 17–4. Governmental union membership, 1974–1978.

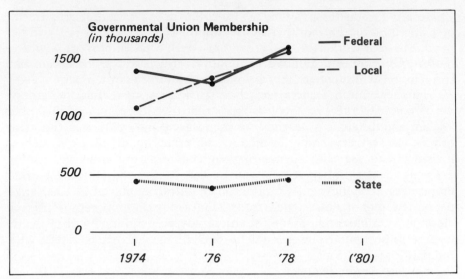

(Source: U.S. Department of Labor, Bureau of Labor Statistics, *Handbook of Labor Statistics, 1980.* Washington, D.C.: U.S. Government Printing Office, December 1980, pp. 407–408.)

Another problem is that state and local government unions often face widely varying laws and hiring policies from city to city and state to state. The widespread existence of civil service and so-called "merit systems" makes for a vastly different environment in the public sector. State and local laws take precedence, not federal labor laws, so unique situations are widespread. Also, lack of experience by local and state officials with unions and collective bargaining hampers union-management relations. Consider a farmer and a dentist serving on a city council and their limited knowledge of unionism activities and processes.

Unionism and the Federal Government. Although unions in the federal government hold the same basic philosophy as unions in the private sector, they do differ somewhat. Through past executive orders and laws, realistic methods of labor-management relations are established that consider the special circumstances present in the federal government. The Office of Personnel Management has considerable control over personnel policies and regulations. For example, because of limits on collective bargaining, federal government unions cannot bargain over wages. Allowing federal employees to organize and join unions definitely presents new problems and challenges for personnel administration in the federal government.

What is the current state of U.S. unionism?

Future Trends in Unionism

During the mid-1980s unions will face some interesting challenges. Several of the most prevalent ones are noted below.

Public Opinion and Unions. Numerous polls of public opinion have revealed that unions are increasingly being viewed in a negative light. In the 1980 elections, in which Ronald Reagan was elected President, an important number of labor-backed congressional candidates lost. Such results reduce labor's political power some. Consequently, many programs that were formerly backed by labor face modification or repeal. Labor unions are being seen as a major reason for inflation and decline in productivity. Also, wage increases tied to cost-of-living clauses in labor contracts that are not matched by other workers has created resentment, not a desire to join a union, in many Americans' minds. Unions will have to respond to such views effectively if they are to improve their public image.

Shifting Economic Factors. Another challenge facing unions is to halt the decline in their membership penetration of the work force. As mentioned earlier, shifts in the U.S. work force are causing an increase in workers in groups who traditionally resist unionization. Women, white-collar workers, and professionals have been reluctant to join unions. Yet, these groups represent the "market" segment with the greatest potential for union members.

Geographic shifts in population and industry also represent a challenge for unions. The greatest economic growth is occurring in the so-called Sun Belt states located in the Southwest, South, and West. Social and cultural values in those areas have traditionally been rather anti-union in nature. Yet, as facilities are closed in northern and eastern states in the U.S., union jobs are being reduced. Consequently, unions must follow the jobs to the new areas to maintain and grow in membership.

Emerging Issues in Unionism. In the future unions will be dealing with a number of issues that they have not yet had to face seriously. Concerns about foreign imports displacing American jobs and workers is one. It is no coincidence that the growth in Japanese automobile sales in the U.S. has seen an increase in the number of members of the United Auto Workers who have been laid off or lost their jobs. Similar job displacements have occurred in the electronics and textile industries. Unions will probably attack such problems by working with management to increase productivity, with government officials to push for import restrictions, and with foreign firms to attract foreign-owned industrial facilities to the U.S.

A number of other issues must also be confronted. Plant closings and pension fund investment policies are just two. A more pervasive issue is that union members are often younger and more educated than the national leaders of the labor movement. These members do not want to "do as they are told" and may view union leaders as "out of step" with them. This generation gap can only be resolved by a transition in leaders, which takes time and which is resisted by older union leaders. Because unions in the future may be forced to change to survive, it is helpful to look at how unions of today are structured.

What future challenges do U.S. unions face?

UNION STRUCTURE

Unions have become organizational structures with multiple levels. As Figure 17–5 illustrates, the American Federation of Labor and the Congress of Industrial Organizations (AFL-CIO) is composed of a number of individual unions.

The AFL-CIO is a rather loose confederation of national unions, each of which is semiautonomous. The AFL-CIO represents nearly two-thirds of the national unions in this country. Approximately one-third of the nationals, however, are not affiliated with the AFL-CIO. The largest unaffiliated union in this grouping is the Teamsters' Union. The United Mine Workers and the International Brotherhood of Longshoremen are also not members of the AFL-CIO.

Union Hierarchy

The national or international unions are autonomous from the federation (if affiliated). They have their own boards, collect dues, have specialized publications, and separate constitutions and by-laws. Such national/international unions as the United Steelworkers (USW) or American Federation of State, County, and Municipal Employees (AFSCME) determine broad union policy and provide services to local union units. They also help maintain financial records, provide a base from which additional organization drives may take place, and control the money for strike funds.

Intermediate union organizational units coordinate the activities of a number of local units. All the local unions in a state, or in several states, may be grouped together with some type of joint governing board. Such organizations may be city-wide, state-wide, or multi-state-wide.

Figure 17–5. Structure of the AFL-CIO.

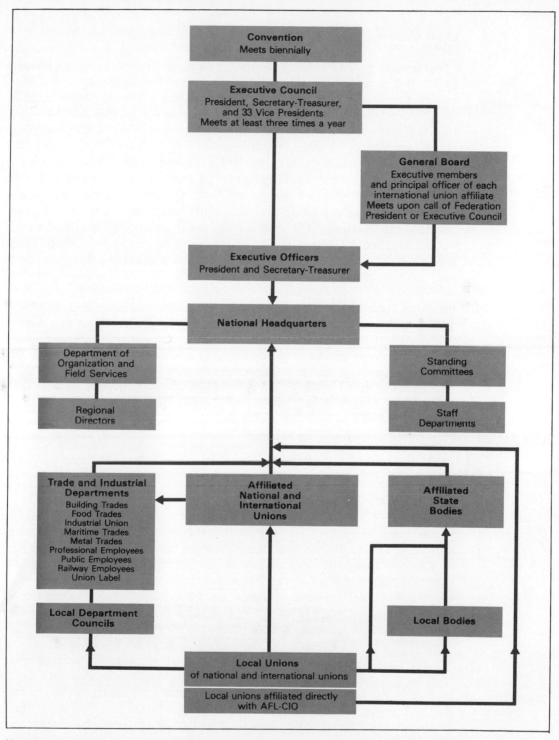

(Source: U.S. Department of Labor, Bureau of Labor Statistics, *Directory of National Unions and Employee Associations, 1977.* Washington, D.C.: U.S. Government Printing Office, 1977, p. 2.)

Local Unions

Local unions may be centered around a particular employer organization or around a particular geographical location. For example, the Communication Workers of America local for Dallas, Texas, might include all the nonexempt telephone company employees in Dallas. (As mentioned in chapter 12, nonexempt employees are subject to the overtime provisions of federal wage and hour laws).

The policy-making process of the local union is generally democratic in form. Members vote on suggestions by either the membership or the officers. Normally, secret ballots are used. Officers in local unions are elected by the membership and are subject to removal if they do not perform satisfactorily. For this reason, local union officers tend to be very concerned with the effect of their actions on the membership. They tend to react to situations much as politicians would react because they, too, are concerned with obtaining votes.

Business Agents and Union Stewards. Some unions have *business agents*, full-time union officials who are usually elected. The agent may run the local headquarters, help negotiate contracts with management, and may become involved in organization attempts. *Union stewards* are usually elected by the local union membership and represent the lowest elected level in the local union. They usually negotiate grievances with the supervisors and generally represent the workers at the work site.

How are unions in the U.S. typically structured?

EVOLUTION OF U.S. UNIONS

It has been suggested that the labor movement in the United States arose when craftsmen in similar occupations banded together voluntarily to protect their jobs.[10] Voluntary union membership is based on *job consciousness:* jobs are a scarce resource and union members must protect them. Under this line of reasoning, the union's chief concern is *job control:* a union must control the tasks making up the jobs under the union's jurisdiction, such as plumbing, electrical work, or carpentry. Job control has been one of the cornerstones of American unionism.

As early as 1794 in the United States, shoemakers organized into a union and conducted strikes and picketing. However, in the early days, unions in the United States received very little support from the courts. In 1805, when the shoemakers' union struck for higher wages, a Philadelphia court found union members guilty of engaging in a *criminal conspiracy* to raise wages.

Commonwealth v. Hunt

In 1842 a very important legal landmark, the case of *Commonwealth v. Hunt*, was decided. The Massachusetts Supreme Court ruled that: "For a union to be guilty of conspiracy, either its objective or the means used to reach it must be criminal or unlawful."[11] As a result of this decision, unions were no longer seen as illegal conspiracies in the eyes of the courts, and the conspiracy idea lost favor.

Post–Civil War Period

The end of the Civil War in 1865 was followed by rapid industrial expansion and a growth of giant business trusts. The 1870s were characterized by industrial unrest, low wages, long hours, and considerable unemployment. In 1877, great railroad strikes spread through the major U.S. railroad lines in protest against the practices of railroad management. Eight years earlier, a group of workers formed the Knights of Labor.

Knights of Labor.   The goals of the Knights of Labor were: (1) to establish one big union embracing all workers and (2) to establish a cooperative economic system to replace capitalism. They emphasized "political reform" and the establishment of "work cooperatives." However, the Knights, after their peak in 1885, soon faded from the labor scene.

American Federation of Labor.   In 1886, the American Federation of Labor (AFL) was formed as a federation of independent national unions. Its basic principle was to organize *skilled craft workers*, like carpenters and plumbers, to bargain for such "bread-and-butter" issues as wages and working conditions. Samuel Gompers was the AFL's chief spokesman and served as president until his death in 1924.

At first, the AFL grew very slowly. Six years after its formation, its total membership amounted to only 250,000. However, it managed to survive in the face of adversity while other parts of the labor movement withered and died.

While *craft unions* (made up of skilled craftsmen) survived and the AFL continued, the Civil War gave factories a big boost. Factory mass-production methods, using semiskilled or unskilled workers, were necessary to supply the armies. Though factories provided a potential area of expansion for unions, they were very hard to organize. Unions found they could not control entry to factory jobs because most of the jobs were filled by semiskilled workers who had no tradition of unionism. This difference ultimately led to the founding of the Congress for Industrial Organization (CIO) in 1938. Unionism outside the skilled crafts remained very uncertain, with the consequence that *industrial unions* were formed much later than *craft unions.*

Early Labor Legislation

The right to organize workers and have collective bargaining is of little value if workers are not free to exercise it. As historical evidence shows, management has used practices calculated to prevent workers from using this right, and the federal government has taken action to either hamper unions or protect them.

Sherman and Clayton Acts.   The passage of the Sherman Antitrust Act in 1890 forbade monopolies and efforts to illegally restrain trade. As a result of a 1908 Supreme Court Case (Danbury Hatters' case—*Loewe* v. *Lawlor*), union boycott efforts were classed as attempts to restrain trade.

Several years later, in 1914, the Clayton Act was passed which limited the use of injunctions in labor disputes, but it had little effect on the labor movement in the United States. The courts interpreted the Clayton Act to mean that the *activities* of a union determined whether or not it was in violation of the law. This interpretation never really changed labor's situation. As a result, union strength declined through the 1920s.

Railway Labor Act (1926).   The Railway Labor Act is significant because it represents a shift in governmental regulation of unions. As a result of a joint effort of railroad management and unions to reduce the possibilities of transportation strikes, this act gave railroad employees "the right to organize and bargain collectively through representatives of their own choosing." In 1936, airlines and their employees were added to those covered by this act. Both these industries are still covered by this act instead of by others passed later.

The act set up a rather complex series of steps to prevent work stoppages. Although a detailed explanation is beyond the scope of this book, it should be noted that many labor experts today feel that the airline and railroad industries should be covered under the same laws as all other industries. Because times have changed, they argue that the Railway Labor Act should be eliminated.[12]

Norris-LaGuardia Act (1932).   In 1932 Congress passed the Norris-LaGuardia Act which guaranteed workers' right to organize and restricted the issuance of court injunction in labor disputes. The Norris-LaGuardia Act substantially freed union activity from court interference and made the infamous *"yellow dog"* *contract* illegal. Under this contract, signed by the worker as a condition of employment, the employee agreed not to join a union upon penalty of discharge. It was called a yellow dog contract because, according to union sympathizers, only a "yellow dog" would take a job under such conditions.

In 1933 the National Industrial Recovery Act (NIRA) was passed. It contained, among other things, provisions extending the policies of the Railway Labor Act for railroad enployees into interstate commerce. Also, the act set up election machinery permitting employees to choose collective bargaining representatives. The NIRA was declared unconstitutional in 1935, and it was replaced by the Wagner Act.

Can you sketch U.S. labor history from
1800–1932?

The progress made by unions through the early 1930s provided the basis for the development and passage of several acts: (1) *Wagner Act*, (2) *Taft-Hartley Act*, and (3) the *Landrum-Griffin Act*. These later acts have the most direct and continuing impact on employers and unions today and form the *National Labor Code*.

NATIONAL LABOR CODE

Each of the acts in the National Labor Code was enacted to protect some entity in the union-management relationship. Figure 17–6 shows each of the segments of the code and which party received the greatest protection. The nature of this protection will become clearer as each of the acts is discussed.

Figure 17–6.   National Labor Code.

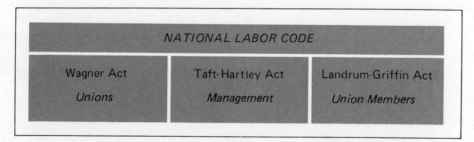

NATIONAL LABOR CODE		
Wagner Act	Taft-Hartley Act	Landrum-Griffin Act
Unions	*Management*	*Union Members*

The Wagner Act

The National Labor Relations Act (or Wagner Act) has been called the Magna Carta of labor and forms the first of the three parts of the National

Labor Code. The Wagner Act was, by anyone's standards, pro-union. It encouraged union growth in three ways:

1. It established the right to organize, unhampered by management interference;
2. It provided definitions of unfair labor practices on the part of management;
3. It set up the National Labor Relations Board to see that the rules were followed.

The act established the principle that employees should be protected in their rights to form a union and to bargain collectively. To protect union rights the act made it an unfair labor practice for an employer to do any of the following:

1. Interfere with, restrain, or coerce employees in the exercise of their rights to organize, bargain collectively, and engage in other concerted activities for their mutual aid or protection.
2. Dominate or interfere with the formation or administration of any labor organization or contribute financial or other support to it.
3. Encourage or discourage membership in any labor organization by discrimination with regard to hiring or tenure or conditions of employment, subject to an exception for valid union security agreement.
4. Discharge or otherwise discriminate against an employee because he filed charges or gave testimony under the act.
5. Refuse to bargain collectively with the majority of representatives of his employees.[13]

The Taft-Hartley Act

When World War II ended, the pent-up demand for goods was frustrated by numerous strikes. There were about three times the number of strikes as before the war. These conditions led to the passage of the *Taft-Hartley Act* in 1947.

The Taft-Hartley Act was an attempt to balance the collective bargaining equation. It was designed to offset the pro-union Wagner Act by limiting union tactics and was considered to be *pro-management*. It provided the second part of the *National Labor Code*.

The new law amended or qualified in some respect all of the Wagner Act's major provisions and an entirely new code of conduct for unions was established. The Taft-Hartley Act forbade a series of unfair labor practices by unions. It became unlawful for a *union* to:

1. Restrain or coerce employees in the exercise of their rights under the act; restrain or coerce any employer in the selection of his bargaining or grievance representative;

2. Cause or attempt to cause an employer to discriminate against an employee on account of membership or nonmembership in a labor organization, subject to an exception for a valid union shop agreement;

3. Refuse to bargain collectively in good faith with an employer if the union has been designated as bargaining agent by a majority of the employees;

4. Induce or encourage employees to stop work for the object of forcing an employer or self-employed person to join a union or enforcing an employer or other person to stop doing business with any other person (boycott provisions);

5. Induce or encourage employees to stop work for the object of forcing an employer to assign particular work to members of a union instead of to members of another union (jurisdictional strike);

6. Charge an excessive or discriminatory fee as a condition to becoming a member of the union;

7. Cause or attempt to cause an employer to pay for services that are not performed or are not to be performed (feather-bedding).[14]

"Right-to-Work."   One specific provision (Section 14B) in the Taft-Hartley Act deserves special explanation. The so-called right-to-work provision outlaws the closed shop, except in construction-related occupations and allows states to pass right-to-work laws.

A CLOSED SHOP requires employees to join a union before they can be hired.

Right-to-work laws are state laws that prohibit both the closed shop and the union shop. They were so named because they allow a person the right to work without having to join a union. Approximately 20 states have enacted these laws (see Figure 17–7). The act did allow the *union shop,* which requires that an employee join the union, usually 30–60 days after being hired.

The Landrum-Griffin Act

In 1959, the third segment of the National Labor Code, the Landrum-Griffin Act, was passed as a result of a congressional committee's findings on union corruption. The major union investigated was the Teamsters' Union headed by Dave Beck and James Hoffa. This law was aimed at protecting individual union members. Among provisions of the Landrum-Griffin Act are:

Figure 17-7. Right-to-Work states.

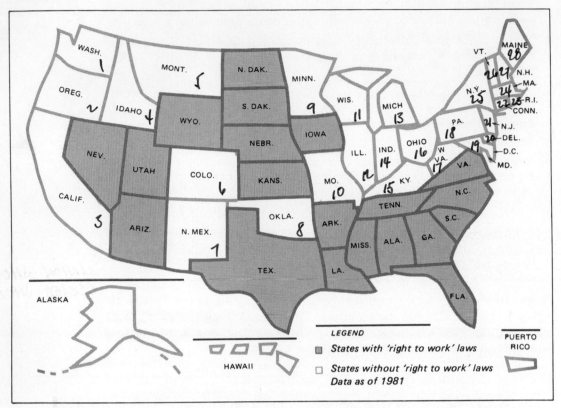

1. Every labor organization is required to have a constitution and by-laws containing certain minimum standards and safeguards.

2. Reports on the union's policies and procedures as well as an annual financial report must be filed with the Secretary of Labor and must be disclosed to the union's members.

3. Union members must have a bill of rights to protect their rights within the unions.

4. Standards are established for union trusteeship and union elections.

5. Reports on trusteeships must be made to the Secretary of Labor.

6. A fiduciary relationship is imposed upon union officers.

7. They are required to file reports with the Secretary of Labor on conflict of interest transactions.

8. The Secretary of Labor is made a watch-dog of union conduct. He is a custodian of reports from unions and their officers and he is given

the power to investigate and prosecute violations of many of the provisions of the act.[15]

Union Member Rights.   A union is a democratic institution in which union members vote on and elect officers and approve labor contracts. The Landrum-Griffin Act was passed to ensure that the federal government protects those democratic rights. Some of the important rights guaranteed to individual union members are:

1. Right to nominate and vote on officers.
2. Right to attend and participate in union meetings.
3. Right to have pension funds properly managed.

In a few instances union officers have attempted to maintain their jobs by physically harassing or attacking individuals who try to oust them from office. An extreme example occurred in the early 1970s when the president of the United Mine Workers had someone running against him murdered. In other cases union officials have "milked" pension fund monies for their own use. Such instances are not typical of most unions, but illustrate the need for individual union members to be protected.

What are the acts in the National Labor Code?

As society's needs change, the National Labor Code will continue to evolve. The collective bargaining relationship may need to be revised again. Proposed extensions of the National Labor Code include: compulsory arbitration; extended injunction powers for the President in national emergency situations; and some kind of extension of the price-wage control system to include management-union agreements. The important point is that this legal foundation of labor-management relations *does* change with time.

THE UNIONIZATION PROCESS

The following overview of the unionization process is designed to familiarize you with how unions become employee representatives. Today, most union contracts contain provisions for nine or more annual holidays, leaves of absence, sick leave plans, insurance, pension, supplemental unemployment benefits, and more. These provisions were not common benefits before unions became "protected" by federal law and used their resources to spread their representation of employees. Figure 17–8 shows the stages in a typical unionization effort. The first stage is handbilling.

Figure 17–8. Typical unionization process.

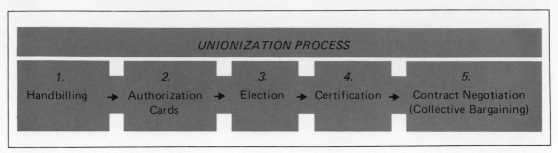

 Handbilling

This stage serves the same purpose that advertising does for a product: to create interest in "buying" the union. Brochures, leaflets, or circulars are all types of handbills. These items can be passed out to employees as they leave work, mailed to their homes, or even attached to their vehicles. Their purpose is to convince employees to sign an authorization card.

Authorization Card

This card, which is signed by an employee, indicates the employee's desire to vote on having a union. It does not necessarily mean that the employee is in favor of a union, but that he or she would like to have the opportunity to vote on having one. One reason employees who do not want a union might sign an authorization card is to attract management's attention to the fact that employees are disgruntled.

Conditions Favoring Unionization. One study found that employees who were dissatisfied with wages and benefits, job security, and supervisory treatment tended to vote for union representation. However, the type of work done did not seem to lead to a vote for unionization as much as working conditions did.[16]

A listing by the United Steelworkers of America of key factors leading to success in organizing white-collar workers reads like a checklist of "management don'ts." Important areas of employee discontent that can lead to unionization include:

1. A lack of communication between employees and management;

2. Management's ignorance of workers' problems;

3. Lower salary scales than most in the same geographical area;

4. Inequities in salaries, with people doing identical work receiving different rates;

5. Inequities in promotions with regard to seniority;

6. The absence of medical, surgical, sick leave, or pension plans for employees on a noncontributory basis;

7. Poor working conditions;

8. Overtime work without compensation;

9. Constant pressure and harassment for work completion;

10. Management's treating employees as if the employees were unintelligent.[17]

According to federal labor law, if 30% of the employees in the proposed bargaining unit have signed cards, the union may petition the National Labor Relations Board (NLRB) or a similar appropriate agency for an election. Disagreements between the employer and the union as to who should and who should not be included in the bargaining unit can lead to lengthy legal battles before the NLRB and in the courts. If the NLRB determines that an appropriate number of cards have been signed, it will order and supervise an election.

Representation Election

An election to determine if a union will represent the employees is supervised by the NLRB or another legal body. If two unions are attempting to represent employees, the employees would have three choices: union A, union B, or no union.

An employer can choose not to contest an election and have a *consent election*. However, frequently employers do contest an election and attempt to provide employees with information to convince them not to vote for a union. The unfair practices identified in both the Wagner Act and the Taft-Hartley Act place restrictions on the actions of both an employer and the union.

Dos and Don'ts.   There are a number of tactics used by management representatives to try to defeat a unionization effort. Such tactics often begin when handbills appear or when authorization cards are being distributed. Figure 17–9 contains a list of some of the more common tactics that management can and cannot use. A definite tactic to avoid was taken by the owner-manager of a small manufacturing firm who fired a worker for poor job performance who was soliciting authorization cards from other employees at lunch. The worker's poor performance was not adequately documented and the company was asked why the worker's performance became so poor so quickly. The result was that the em-

Figure 17–9. Management Dos & Don'ts in unionization process.

Do	Don't
1. Tell employees about current wages and benefits and how they compare to other firms	1. Promise employees pay increases or promotions if they vote against the union
2. Tell employees you will use all legal means to oppose unionization	2. Threaten employees with termination or discriminate when disciplining employees
3. Tell employees the disadvantages of having union (especially cost of dues, assessments, and requirements of membership)	3. Threaten to close down or move the company if a union is voted in
4. Show employees articles about unions and negative experiences others have had elsewhere	4. Spy or have someone spy on union meetings
5. Explain the unionization process to your employees accurately	5. Make a speech to employees or groups at work within 24 hours of the election (before that it is allowed)
6. Forbid distribution of union literature during work hours in work areas	6. Ask employees how they plan to vote or if they have signed authorization cards
7. Enforce in a consistent and fair manner disciplinary policies and rules	7. Urge local employees to persuade others to vote against the union (such a vote must be initiated solely by the employee)

ployee was reinstated, a representation election was ordered, and the company won the election 28 to 3. If hasty action had not been taken by management, the entire matter would have died down much sooner.

Some firms have experts who specialize in assisting management in using tactics to defeat a unionization effort. As the opening case illustrates, the first step a firm facing a unionization effort should take is to obtain expert advice from a labor attorney. But, as one writer points out, the most important action to reduce unionization threats is to listen to employees and respond to their real concerns.[18]

Election Process. Assuming an election is held, the union only needs to receive a *majority of those voting* in the election. For example, if a group of 200 employees is the identified unit and only 50 people vote, only 26 employees would need to vote "yes" in order for a union to be named as the representative of all 200. If either side believes that unfair labor practices have been used by the other side, the election results can be appealed to the NLRB. If the NLRB finds that unfair practices were used, it can order a new election. Assuming that no unfair practices have been used and the union obtains a majority in the election, the union then petitions the NLRB for certification. In a recent year unions won 44.5% of the elections held between one union and "no union."[19]

Certification

Official certification of a union as the legal representative for employees is given by the NLRB, or the relevant body, after reviewing the results of the election. Once certified, the union attempts to negotiate a contract with the employer.

Contract Negotiation (Collective Bargaining).   Negotiation of a labor contract is one of the most important methods used by unions to obtain their major goals. A general discussion of collective bargaining is contained in the next chapter.

Decertification.   Employees who have a union and no longer wish to be represented by it can utilize the same process, called *decertification*.

> DECERTIFICATION is a process whereby a union is removed as the representative of a group of employees.

The decertification process is very similar to the unionization process and requires that employees attempting to oust a union obtain decertification authorization cards signed by at least 30% of the employees in the bargaining unit. Then an election is called and if a majority of those voting in the election vote to remove the union, the decertification effort succeeds. One caution, however, is that management may not assist the decertification effort in any way by providing assistance and funding.

How does a union become a representative of
employees?

REVIEW AND PREVIEW

Labor relations in the United States reflect an emphasis on job-centered concerns in which unions serve as a countervailing force, which is unlike the role of unions in Europe and Japan. However, some concepts, such as co-determination and labor-management committees, have been adopted for use in the U.S.

Unionism as a movement has shifted and changed. Through its structure and leadership, unions must respond to future trends.

The conditions surrounding labor relations in this country reflect the historical development of U.S. unions and U.S. labor legislation. The National Labor Code provides a three-pronged base for current labor-management relationships in this country. The Wagner Act was pro-union; the Taft-Hartley, pro-management; and the Landrum-Griffin, pro-individual union members. Built on this legal base, the process of certification must be understood in order for management to respond to union efforts.

Labor-management relationships can span a spectrum from constant conflict to outright collaboration. Most relationships in this country currently fall between the two extremes, but examples of both extremes can sometimes be found. The next chapter looks at collective bargaining as another part of the management relationship. It also examines one of the most important interfaces between the union and management, that of the grievance procedure.

Review Questions

1. Discuss: "Unions in the United States and Europe are and always will be distinctly different."

2. Unionism in the United States is undergoing some changes. What are some of the current trends and changes?

3. What is the meaning of a "confederation" of unions? What are the levels within a union confederation?

4. List five key events that occurred in U.S. labor history before 1935.

5. Identify the three parts of the National Labor Code and the key elements of each act.

6. An employee has just brought you a union leaflet urging the employee to sign a card. What events would you expect from that point?

*Case: Witchcraft**

One of the most interesting cases in the history of the National Labor Relations Board involved a union election in Puerto Rico. The General Cigar Company (GCC) filed an unfair practices charge against the International Association of Machinists and Aerospace Workers (IAM). The final election results were 255 for the IAM, 222 for no union and 6 challenged votes, but the GCC asked the NLRB to void the election for several reasons:

1. An IAM supporter persuaded some other workers to smell the contents of a bottle of magic potion bought from a local "bujera" (witch or sorceress) and then told them they could not vote against the union without repercussions.

2. A publicly acknowledged witch was paid $150 by the wife of another employee to work for the union.

3. A male midget was hired by another pro-union employee to persuade employees to vote for the IAM.

4. The weather before and after the election was clear and sunny. However, during the election a torrential rainstorm hit.

The GCC also charged the IAM with threatening and bribing employees to vote pro-union. The IAM called the charges ludicrous and said the complaints showed the need for a union to protect employees from management.

QUESTIONS

1. If you were on the NLRB, what laws would you need to consider?
2. Would you rule for GCC or the IAM? Why?

* Adapted from information in *Business Week*, October 19, 1968, p. 132.

NOTES

1. Everett M. Kassalow, "The Development of Western Movements: Some Comparative Considerations," in: Richard Lester, ed., *Labor: Readings on Major Issues* (New York: Random House, 1965), p. 74.

2. Efren Cordova, "A Comparative View of Collective Bargaining in Industrialized Countries," *International Labour Review*, 117, July-August 1978, p. 424.

3. "German Labor Tensions Near the Danger Point," *Business Week*, December 18, 1978, pp. 75–76.

4. Robert C. Wood, "Japan's Multitier Wage System," *Forbes*, August 18, 1980, p. 57.

5. Kenneth A. Kovach, Ben F. Sands, and William W. Brooks, "Is Co-determination a Workable Idea for U.S. Labor-Management Relations?" *MSU Business Topics*, Winter 1980, pp. 49–55.

6. Urban C. Lehner, "Committees of Labor and Management Enjoying Resurgence in Communities," *Wall Street Journal*. August 8, 1979, p. 6.

7. A. A. Sloane and F. Whitney, *Labor Relations*, 2d ed. (Englewood Cliffs, NJ: Prentice-Hall, 1972), p. 6.

8. U.S. Department of Labor, Bureau of Labor Statistics, *Handbook of Labor Statistics, 1980* (Washington, D.C.: U.S. Government Printing Office, 1981), pp. 407–408.

9. Kathryn Christensen, "White Collar Blues . . .", *Wall Street Journal*, June 23, 1980, p. 1.

10. S. Perlman, *A History of Trade Unionism in the United States* (New York: Macmillan, 1929).

11. *Commonwealth of Massachusetts* v. *Hunt*, Massachusetts, 4 Metcalf 3 (1842).

12. For more details on the act, see Eugene C. Hagburg and Marvin J. Levine, *Labor Relations: An Integrated Perspective* (St. Paul, MN: West Publishing, 1978), chapter 10.

13. Reprinted by permission from *Primer of Labor Relations*, 17th ed., copyright 1969 by The Bureau of National Affairs, Inc., Washington, D.C. 20037.

14. Reprinted by permission from *Primer of Labor Relations*, 17th ed., copyright 1969 by The Bureau of National Affairs, Inc., Washington, D.C. 20037.

15. Reprinted by permission from *Primer of Labor Relations*, 17th ed., copyright 1969 by The Bureau of National Affairs, Inc., Washington, D.C. 20037.

16. Jeanne M. Brett, "Why Employees Want Unions," *Organizational Dynamics*, Spring 1980, pp. 47–59.

17. "White-Collar Unionization," *Generation*, September-October 1970, pp. 20–21.

18. Woodruff Imberman, "Union Avoidance Campaigns: You Need More Than Hocus-Pocus," *Management Review*, September 1980, pp. 45–49.

19. National Labor Relations Board, *Forty-Third Annual Report* (Washington, D.C.: U.S. Government Printing Office, 1967– 1978), p. 266.

CHAPTER 18

Collective Bargaining and Union-Management Relations

When you have read this chapter you should be able to:

1. Define collective bargaining and identify some bargaining relationships and structures.

2. Identify and describe a typical collective bargaining process.

3. Differentiate between a grievance and a complaint.

4. Describe the importance and extent of grievance procedures.

5. Explain the basic steps in a grievance procedure.

6. Discuss arbitration as the final phase of a grievance procedure.

7. Contrast the legal and behavioral approaches to grievance resolution.

The Clean-Up Grievance

The Willis Welding Company is a welding equipment supply firm whose nonmanagerial work force is unionized. Yesterday the union filed a grievance on behalf of Raymond Anzalone.

The union contract contains a clause that states: "Employees will be allowed at least ten minutes to clean up at the end of a work shift with pay." Two days ago Raymond's supervisor, Marshall Warren, found Raymond cleaning up 30 minutes before quitting time. Marshall said, "What are you doing quitting so early? If you don't get back to work, you'll be docked pay." Raymond replied, "I just finished filling the Acme order, which is a big job, and the next order is the Apex order, another big one. I didn't see any point in starting it for only a few minutes since I would probably have to start again tomorrow anyway to check where I was. Besides, our contract says we get clean up time." Marshall returned to his office and made a notation on Raymond's time card that 30 minutes should be deducted from Raymond's hours.

You are the plant manager and you are to meet with the shop steward this afternoon.

Comments:

This case points out how minor incidents can result in a grievance being filed. The vagueness of the contract provision is a major problem. A key factor in resolving the grievance is precedent. Questions that would be important include: What have been the past practices regarding clean-up time? Have there been other grievances filed on clean-up time? What were the final outcomes of those grievances?

The patterns established by precedents such as these would form the basis for resolving this grievance at some point. If the grievance reached arbitration, precedent factors would be the major grounds used by an arbitrator in making an award.

THE broad issues of unionism, as discussed in the previous chapter, become focused inside an organization following a successful unionization attempt. As noted in chapter 17, the final stage of the unionization process is the negotiation and signing of a contractual agreement between a union and an employer. This chapter discusses the process of contract negotiation through collective bargaining. Then it examines one of the most important areas of day-to-day union-management relations—grievances.

COLLECTIVE BARGAINING

In the United States collective bargaining is somewhat different than in other countries, due to different philosophical and political origins for the collective bargaining system. Different legal frameworks for collective bargaining also exist in different countries.

> COLLECTIVE BARGAINING is the process whereby representatives of management and workers negotiate over such items as wages, hours, and conditions of employment.

Collective bargaining is intended as a mutual give-and-take between representatives of two organizations for the mutual benefit of both. Although the power relationship contained in collective bargaining also involves conflict, the threat of conflict seems necessary to maintain the relationship. Perhaps the most important aspect of collective bargaining, however, is that it is *ongoing.* It is not a relationship that will end immediately after agreement is reached.

What is collective bargaining?

Types of Bargaining Relationships

One of the important factors determining the relationship between union and management is the attitude of management toward unions. This attitude plays a major role in determining the strategic approach used by management. The degree to which labor and management accept collective bargaining as an important institutional consideration has been found to be the most important element affecting union-management relations.[1]

Management-union relationships in collective bargaining can follow one of several different types. Figure 18–1 shows the relationships as a continuum, ranging from conflict to collusion. On the left side of the continuum, management and union see each other as enemies. However, the two entities join together illegally on the right end of the continuum.

Figure 18–1. Collective bargaining relationship continuum.

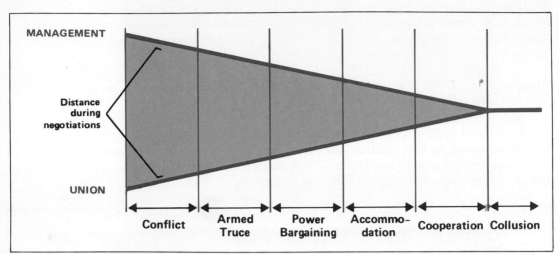

There are a number of positions in between. A discussion of the six strategies[2] follows.

Conflict. Under this strategy management takes a totally uncompromising view. An attitude of "busting the union" may underlie the use of the conflict strategy. Paraphrasing a phrase from an old western movie, management takes the approach that "the only good union is a dead union!"

Armed Truce. Management representatives take the position that they are well aware of the vital interests of the company and the union is poles away and always will be. The armed-truce approach does not mean that forcing head-on conflict is in the best interests of either and recognizes that the union is not likely to disappear. Many union-management relationships have not progressed beyond this stage, especially those in smaller businesses.

Power Bargaining. Managers engaged in a power bargaining relationship can accept the union and many pride themselves on their sense of "realism" which forces them to acknowledge the union's power. Management philosophy here assumes that management's task is to increase and then use their power where possible, to offset the power of the union.

Accommodation. Accommodation involves learning to adjust to each other and attempting to minimize conflict, to conciliate whenever necessary, and to tolerate each other. This strategy in no way suggests that management goes out of its way to help organized labor. However it does recognize that the need to reduce confrontation is helpful in dealing with common problems that are often caused by external forces, such as imports and governmental regulations. One industry executive identified accommodation as needed in a number of new areas during the 1980s.[3]

Cooperation.   This strategy involves full acceptance of the union as an active partner in a formal plan and is a relatively rare occurrence. In cooperation, management supports not only the right but the desirability of union participation in certain areas of decision-making. The two parties jointly deal with personnel and production problems as they occur. The labor-management committees and co-determination mentioned earlier are examples of cooperation.

Collusion.   This form of mutual interest monopoly is unconcerned with interests except its own. These situations, which are relatively rare in American labor history, have been deemed illegal. Under the collusion strategy union and management engage in material price fixing designed to inflate wages and profits, at the expense of the general public.

Bargaining Structures

Bargaining structures come in many forms. The *one-employer/one-union* structure is the simplest. A more complex model is the *multi-union* bargaining structure. This structure is common in the construction industry, where one employer may face several different building trade unions representing a number of different crafts.

Another variation, *multi-employer bargaining,* developed in the coal mining and garment industries. This structure has been used extensively in the steel industry, which uses a two-tier system: a "master contract" supplemented by a local contract dealing with individual company and/or plant issues.

Also, a bargaining structure may change over time as a result of unions attempting to stay up-to-date with changes in organizational or industry structure or technology. These changes are similar to those that often occur in corporate organizations.

> *What are some possible bargaining relationships and structures?*

PROCESS OF COLLECTIVE BARGAINING

The collective bargaining process contains a number of stages.[4] However, over time each union and management situation develops slight mod-

Figure 18–2. Typical collective bargaining process.

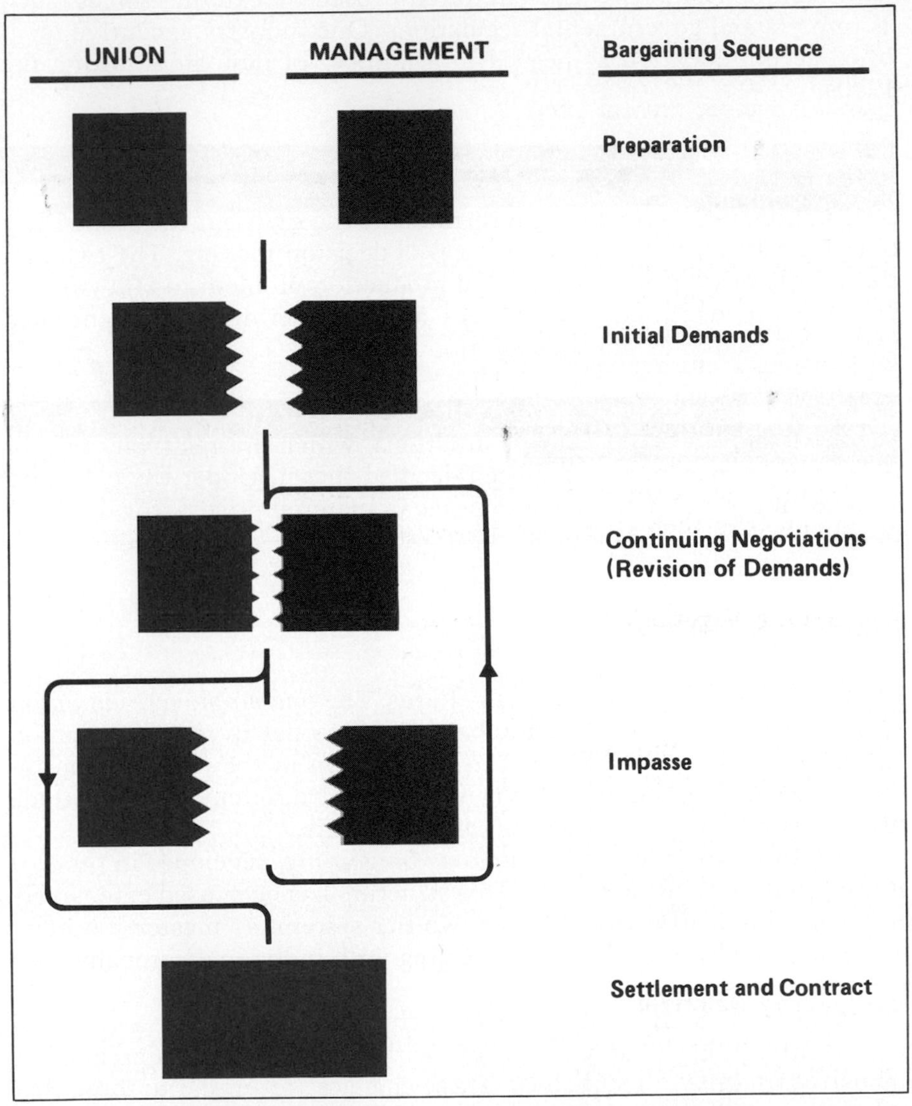

ifications that are necessary for effective bargaining to occur. The process shown in Figure 18–2 is a typical one.

Preparation

Both labor and management representatives spend extensive time preparing for the negotiations to follow. Both employer and industry data about wages, benefits, working conditions, management and union rights, productivity, and absenteeism are often gathered. Once the data are analyzed, each side identifies what their priorities are and what strategies and tactics to use to obtain what it wants. Each party tries to allow itself some flexibility in order to trade off less important demands for more critical ones.

Initial Demands

Typical bargaining includes an initial presentation of expectations (called *demands*) by both sides. The amount of rancor or calmness exhibited will set the tone for the future negotiations between the parties. Union and management representatives who have been part of previous negotiations may adopt a pattern that has evolved over time. In negotiations for the first contract between an employer and a union the process can become much more difficult. Management representatives have to adjust to dealing with a union and employees who are leaders in the union must adjust to their new roles.

Continuing Negotiations

After opening positions have been taken, each side attempts to determine what the other side values highly and to reach the best bargain possible. For example, the union may be asking for dental benefits to be paid by the company as part of a package that also includes wage demands and retirement benefits. However, the union is *basically* interested in the wages and retirement benefits and would be willing to trade the dental payments for more wages. The company, however, has to determine what the union wants most and decide just exactly what it must give up.

Bargaining Behavior. Collective bargaining is not just a logical and rational process. The behavior of the negotiators plays a critical role. Walton and McKersie have identified four types of behavior subprocesses present in collective bargaining.[5]

Distributive bargaining occurs when there is conflict over an issue and one party must win and the other lose. If a union wants a dues *check off*, through which employee union dues are deducted from paychecks by the employer, and the employer does not want a check off, only one side can win. There either will or will not be a check off.

Integrative bargaining occurs when both the management and union face a common problem and must work together for a solution. If a steel company and the United Steelworkers union (USW) are concerned because of employee absenteeism and discipline problems caused by worker alcoholism difficulties, under integrative bargaining the parties might negotiate a joint program that identifies how alcoholism-caused discipline problems are to be handled and require both parties to provide some funds to pay for alcoholism treatment activities.

Attitudinal structuring occurs when each side attempts to affect the "climate" of the negotiations. The climate created and the attitudes of the other party often result in the six bargaining strategies identified earlier in this chapter.

Intraorganizational bargaining occurs when disagreements exist within labor or management. Assume some union members felt that dental insurance should be included in a union proposal and other union members felt that higher retirement benefits were more important than dental insurance. Some consensus about dental insurance would have to be developed for the union negotiation team to take to the bargaining table.

"Good Faith." Provisions in federal labor law suggest that employers' and employees' bargaining representatives be obligated to bargain in "good faith." *Good faith* means that the parties *agree* to bargain and that they send negotiators who are in a position to make decisions, not someone who does not have the authority to commit either group to a decision. Good faith also means that the *decisions* are not changed after they are made and the *meetings* between the parties are not scheduled at ridiculous hours. In addition, it means not refusing to have a *written contract* and not using blatantly anti-union or anti-management propaganda during the bargaining process. The specifics of the collective bargaining "good faith" relationship are defined by a series of NLRB rulings and court rulings.

Settlement and Contract Agreement

After an initial agreement has been made, the two sides usually return to their respective constituencies to determine if what they have informally agreed on is acceptable. A particularly crucial stage is *ratification.* In this stage, the union negotiating team presents and explains the agreement to the union members for a vote. If approval is voted, this agreement is then formalized into the contract. Typical subjects for inclusion in a formal labor agreement, or contract, are shown in Figure 18–3. Notice that a wide range of issues are covered in the contract. The primary areas covered are wages, benefits, working conditions, work rules, and other necessary legal terminology. It is important for the contract to be clearly and precisely written. Just as in the opening case regarding clean-up time, unclear or imprecise wording often leads to grievances or other problems. It may even be advisable to do a readability test on the contract to ensure that it is understandable as well as legally accurate.[6]

Figure 18–3. Typical items in a labor "contract."

1. Purpose of agreement
2. Nondiscrimination clause
3. Management rights
4. Recognition of the union
5. Wages
6. Incentives
7. Hours of work
8. Vacations
9. Sick leave
10. Leaves of absence
11. Separation allowance
12. Seniority
13. Bulletin boards
14. Pension and insurance
15. Grievance procedure
16. Definitions
17. Terms of the contract (dates)
18. Appendices

Bargaining Impasse

Regardless of the structure of the bargaining process, labor and management do not always reach agreement on the issues. In such cases, a deadlock may result in *strikes* by the union or a *lockout* by management. During a strike union members stop work and often *picket* the employer by carrying placards and signs. One union tactic that is used to bring pressure on an employer during a strike is to persuade other unions to honor the picket line. At a trucking company in the South, some warehouse workers went on strike and set up a picket line that a truck drivers' union honored. Consequently, the employer could no longer ship goods even if members of management loaded them. In a lockout, management shuts company operations down to prevent union members from working to prevent possible damage or sabotage.

However, both strikes and lockouts are relatively rare occurrences, as Figure 17–2 illustrated in the previous chapter. Efforts to forestall such drastic actions on the part of either party can take the form of conciliation/mediation or arbitration.

Conciliation or Mediation. Conciliation or mediation efforts occur when an outside individual attempts to help two deadlocked parties continue negotiations and arrive at a solution. The mediator does not attempt to impose an external solution upon the parties but merely tries to keep them talking and may suggest compromise situations. A good example of this process is the work done by a federal mediator to help keep the professional baseball owners' and players' association at the bargaining table.

Arbitration. An arbitrator is an impartial individual whose job is to determine the relative merits of each argument and then make a decision, called an *award.* Contract arbitration is very rare except in parts of the public sector such as police and fire departments in some cities. Most arbitration is grievance arbitration.

Can you describe a typical collective bargaining process?

Complexity of Collective Bargaining

Collective bargaining is a subject with so many ramifications that it is a separate technical area of study at many universities. This brief discussion of collective bargaining presents some of the important issues involved.

Collective bargaining may or may not be handled by the personnel department and exactly what the personnel unit does handle varies from employer to employer. However, the study referred to in chapter 1 found that many managers felt that collective bargaining activities should be handled by operating managers rather than by personnel executives.

CONTRACT "MANAGEMENT" AND GRIEVANCES

Once a collective bargaining contract is signed, that contract is the main governing document. The typical contract details what management can and cannot do and what the responsibilities of the union are.

The day-to-day administration of a contract most often focuses on employee and employer rights. When a unionized employee feels his or her rights under the contract have been violated, that employee can file a grievance. The distinction between a grievance and a complaint is important.

A GRIEVANCE is a specific, formal dissatisfaction expressed through an identified procedure.

A complaint, on the other hand, is merely an employee dissatisfaction which has *not* taken the formal grievance settlement route. Man-

agement should be concerned with both grievances and complaints because many complaints can become grievances and because complaints
are good indicators of potential problems within the work force.

Can you differentiate between a complaint and
a grievance?

Alert management knows that an unsettled dissatisfaction, whether
real or imaginary, expressed or unexpressed, is a potential source of
serious trouble. Hidden dissatisfactions grow and soon arouse an emotional state which may be completely out of proportion to the original
complaint. Before long, workers' attitudes can be seriously affected.
Therefore, it is important that complaints and grievances be handled
properly.

Grievance Interface

Figure 18–4 shows a possible division of responsibilities between the
personnel unit and the managers. These responsibilities vary considerably from one organization to another, but the personnel unit usually
has a more general responsibility. Managers must live with the grievance
procedure as a possible constraint on some of their decisions.

In an organization where a union exists, grievances might occur over
several different matters: interpretation of the contract, disputes not
covered in the contract, and personal employee grievances. In non-
unionized companies, complaints also tend to relate to a variety of individual concerns: wages, benefits, working conditions, and equity.

Figure 18–4. Grievance interface.

Personnel Unit	Managers
Assists in designing the grievance procedure	Operate within the grievance procedure
Monitors trends in grievance rates for the organization	Attempt to resolve grievances where possible as "person closest to the problem"
May assist preparation of grievance cases for arbitration	Document grievance cases at own level for the grievance procedure
May have responsibility for settling grievances	Have responsibility for grievance prevention

Union

Importance of a Grievance Procedure

Grievance procedures are very important for effective employee-employer relations. The chance of a union successfully organizing a company's employees is much greater if a firm has no formal procedure to hear employee grievances.[7] Without a grievance procedure, management may not know about employee discontent in important areas, and therefore be vulnerable to organizing attempts.

Union organizers often conduct a careful survey before attempting to organize any company. A survey reveals more about the feelings of a company's employees than many managers are aware of through daily relationships with these people. Such information does not always *automatically* come to the attention of management. A great deal of it is dismissed at lower levels, and it never gets to levels where decisions can be made to rectify some of the problems. For these reasons, a formal grievance procedure can be a very valuable communication tool for management in providing workers a fair hearing for their problems.

Grievances and Job Security

Because many American workers are concerned with the protection of their jobs, many formal grievances can be viewed easily as job security problems. Suppose that Paula Goldberg filed a grievance when an employee with a lower job classification was promoted instead of her. Paula claimed that the contract stipulated seniority would be the first consideration in promotion. Paula really is not concerned about the meaning and intent of the contract. She knows employees in higher job classifications are less likely to be laid off during slack periods. The basis for her grievance is her own long-run security. People's need for security is a recognized behavioral fact and formal grievance procedures can be an aid in reducing security fears.

Individual Grievances and the Union

Individual union members do not always feel their best interests are properly served by the union. Workers and unions may not agree on the interpretation of a contract clause. For example, Craig Hensley feels strongly that the case of his suspension for drinking was not sufficiently represented by the union because the shop steward is a teetotaler. What is Craig to do?

If the individual does not feel the union has properly and vigorously pursued the grievance, he or she may have recourse to the federal court system. Such cases attempt to pinpoint individual rights inside the bargaining unit, and also to determine what those rights are if a person has been denied due process through the grievance procedure.[8]

Extent of Grievance Procedures

Grievance procedures are almost always included in labor-management contracts. One review found that 99% of contracts in all industries contained grievance procedures.[9] However, the pattern is significantly different when examining organizations whose employees are non-union.

Non-union Grievance Procedures.   Managers commonly insist they have an "open-door" policy—if anything is bothering employees, all they have to do is come to management and talk. However, employees are often skeptical of this approach, feeling that their complaint would probably be viewed as unnecessary "rocking of the boat." An "open-door" policy is not a sufficient grievance procedure. Ideally, grievance procedures should not be necessary. A "super manager" should be able to maintain open channels of communication and quickly spot and rectify any troubles that might become grievances. However, "super managers" who have this communication ability are very rare.

During the mid-1980s it is likely that an increasing number of employers will adopt formal "employee due process" procedures, as they are often called in non-union settings. One expert estimated that only a few hundred firms have such procedures out of 20,000 U.S. companies.[10] One reason some firms have "due process" procedures is the belief that the existence of some appeals mechanism helps maintain a non-union work force. Part of the federal privacy study, mentioned in chapters 8 and 16, advocated requiring "due process" procedures in order to protect employees. An electronics manufacturer in Oregon, TEKTRONIX, has voluntarily instituted such a process for its 20,000 employees. The procedure has five steps and each grievance is formally reviewed by higher level management at each step. However, the first step takes care of almost 90% of the employee grievances filed. McDonald's Corporation uses an ombudsman as a part of its "due process" procedures.[11]

What is the extent and importance of a grievance procedure?

GRIEVANCE PROCEDURE

Grievance procedures are usually designed so that grievances can be settled as close to the problem as possible. First-line supervisors are usually closest to the problem; however, the supervisor is concerned with many other matters besides one employee's grievance and may even be the subject of an employee's grievance.

Supervisory involvement presents some very real problems in solving a grievance at this level. For example, William Dunn is 27 years old and a lathe operator at Baker's Machine Shop. On Monday morning, his foreman, Joe Bass, approached him, told him that his production was lower than his quota, and advised him to catch up. William reported that there was a part on his lathe needing repair and requested that the mechanics examine and repair it. Joe informed William that the mechanics were too busy and that he must repair it himself to maintain his production. William refused and a heated argument ensued, with the result that Joe ordered William home for the day.

This illustration shows the ease with which an encounter between an employee and a supervisor can lead to a breakdown in the relationship. This breakdown or failure to communicate effectively can be costly to William if he loses his job, a day's wages, or his pride. It can be costly to Joe, who represents management, and to the owner of Baker's Machine Shop if production is delayed or halted. Grievance procedures can resolve such conflicts.

A GRIEVANCE PROCEDURE is a formal channel of communication used to resolve formal complaints (grievances).

Assume that Baker's Machine Shop had a contract with the International Brotherhood of Lathe Operators, of which William was a member. Further, the contract specifically stated that the company *plant mechanics* were to repair all manufacturing equipment. Then there is a clear violation of the union contract. What is William's next step? He may begin to use the appeals machinery provided for him in the contract. The actual grievance procedure is different in each organization. It depends on what the employer and the union have agreed upon and what is written into the labor contract.

Steps in a Grievance Procedure

As Figure 18–5 shows several basic steps exist in *most* grievance procedures. The grievance can be settled at any stage.

1. The employee discusses the grievance with the immediate supervisor.
2. The employee then discusses the grievance with the union steward and the supervisor.
3. The union *chief* steward discusses it with the supervisor's manager.
4. The union grievance committee discusses the grievance with the unit plant manager or the employer's industrial relations department.
5. The national union representative discusses it with the general company manager.

Figure 18–5. A grievance procedure.

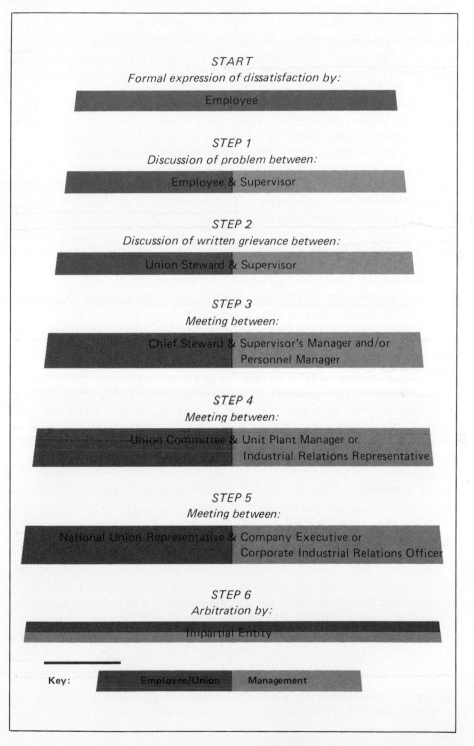

START
Formal expression of dissatisfaction by:

Employee

STEP 1
Discussion of problem between:

Employee & Supervisor

STEP 2
Discussion of written grievance between:

Union Steward & Supervisor

STEP 3
Meeting between:

Chief Steward & Supervisor's Manager and/or
Personnel Manager

STEP 4
Meeting between:

Union Committee & Unit Plant Manager or
Industrial Relations Representative

STEP 5
Meeting between:

National Union Representative & Company Executive or
Corporate Industrial Relations Officer

STEP 6
Arbitration by:

Impartial Entity

Key: Employee/Union   Management

6. The final step may be reference to an impartial umpire or arbitrator for ultimate disposition of the grievance.

Employee and Supervisor. In our example, William has already discussed his grievance with the foreman. This first step should eliminate the majority of gripes and complaints employees may view as legitimate grievances.

Supervisors are generally responsible for understanding the contract so that they can administer it fairly on a day-to-day basis. They must be accessible to employees for grievance investigation and must gather all the pertinent facts and carefully investigate the causes, symptoms, and results.

Union Steward and Supervisor. The second step involves the union steward. The main task here is to present the grievances of the union's members such as William to management. However, the responsibility rests not only with the individual steward but also, to a large degree, with the union membership as a whole. The effect of this grievance on the relationship between the union and management must be determined. One industry study found that the steward's need for dominance is related to the number of grievances filed.[12]

Assume the grievance remains unsettled after the second step. The steward takes it to the chief steward who contacts the supervisor's boss and/or the unit's personnel manager. In most grievance procedures, the grievance is documented and, until it is settled, much of the communication between management and the union is in writing. This written communication is important because it provides a record of each succeeding step in the procedure and constitutes a history for review at each subsequent step. The department manager (who is Joe's boss) backs Joe against the chief steward, so the grievance goes to the next step.

Union Grievance Committee and Unit Manager. Pressure tends to build with each successive step because grievances which are *not* precedent-setting or difficult are screened out earlier in the process. The fourth stage involves the local union-management grievance committee. In our case, the grievance committee of the union convinces the plant manager that Joe violated the contract and William should be brought back to work and paid for the time he missed. The plant manager gave in partly because he thought the company had a weak case, and partly because if the grievance continued past him, it would probably go to arbitration, and he did not feel the issue was worth the cost. Although in William's case a grievance committee was used, not all grievance procedures use committees. This step may be omitted in many procedures.

National Representatives and Arbitrator. If the grievance had remained unsettled, national representatives for both sides would have met to try to resolve the conflict. An arbitrator would have been selected and asked to make a decision on the matter. The manner of selecting an arbitrator varies but usually involves each party eliminating names from a list of potential arbitrator candidates until only one name remains.

What are the steps in a grievance procedure?

GRIEVANCE ARBITRATION

Grievance arbitration is a means of settling disputes arising from different interpretations of a contract. This dispute resolution is not to be confused with contract arbitration, which is arbitration to determine how a contract will be written. Grievance arbitration is a deeply ingrained part of the collective bargaining system, although it was not always so. For the most part, arbitration was not a useful part of the process of settling labor disputes in earlier times.

However, in 1957, another era began in the history of arbitration as a grievance-settling device. A court decision which established the right of unions to *sue* for specific performance of arbitration awards gave arbitration new strength. Later court cases added more strength to arbitration. It was ruled that a company had to arbitrate *all* issues not specifically excluded in the contract. Courts were directed *not* to rule on the appropriateness of an arbitration award unless misinformation, fraud, or negligence were involved.

Arbitration is very flexible. It can be applicable to almost any kind of controversy except criminal questions. Voluntary arbitration may be used either in the negotiation of agreements or in interpretation of clauses in existing agreements, or both. However, labor and management, for the most part, agree that disputes over negotiations of a new contract should not be arbitrated. So arbitration plays its most important part in labor relations as a *final point* in the grievance procedure.

Arbitration's Shortcomings.   Several problems exist in grievance arbitration. It has been criticized as being too costly, too legalistic, and too time-consuming. In addition, there are too few acceptable arbitrators.

Can you define and discuss grievance arbitration?

Arbitration and the Contract

The grievance procedure is the union member's most tangible contact with collective bargaining. The procedure set up in the contract is likely to have a visible, direct, immediate, and personal influence on the union member.

A very important part of arbitration is the wording of the contract clause which accurately expresses each party's intent relative to arbitration. It is important to spell out the types of disputes which may be taken to arbitration. Most collective bargaining contracts suggest that either party may start arbitration proceedings. Others, however, provide that only the union can initiate arbitration proceedings. Still others permit arbitration only when both parties agree.

Preventive Arbitration

Labor and management sometimes tend to ignore potential problem areas in the relationship until it is too late. The result can be an explosive dispute that does much more harm than good. However, preventive arbitration can minimize this sort of difficulty. The use of arbitration is sometimes advocated to settle disputes in non-union office situations.[13]

It is the duty of a preventive arbitrator to meet periodically, at least monthly, with union and management representatives to discuss areas of potential trouble between the parties. Although the use of a preventive arbitrator is not a panacea for resolving difficulties in labor-management relations, it can be a potentially useful tool. The plan calls for unilateral adherence to the arbitrator's recommendations during a 60-day period. During that time the problem is to be solved calmly and coolly.

LEGAL vs. BEHAVIORAL GRIEVANCE RESOLUTION

The inclusion of a union in a formal grievance procedure sometimes leads management to conclude that the proper way to handle grievances is to abide by the "letter of the law." This means management will do no more or no less than what is called for in the contract. Such an approach can be labeled the *legal approach* to the resolution of grievances. A much more realistic approach, the *behavioral approach*, recognizes that a grievance may be a symptom of an underlying problem which management might investigate and rectify.

The difference is apparent in the following example. At Acme Bolt Company a union has recently been voted in to represent the employees. One of the first actions the union took was to insist on having a formal grievance procedure recorded in the contract. One of the clauses in the grievance procedure states that a grievance cannot be reopened once it has been resolved to the satisfaction of both management and the union.

Ed Dysart, a custodian for the Acme Bolt Company, filed a grievance about the danger involved in working around some of the machinery. Dysart felt the machinery was not sufficiently safe so that he could get close enough to clean around it. As a result, the work place was not very clean. Dysart's grievance was that his performance was being hurt by the situation and had resulted in a warning for poor work from his supervisor. The grievance was resolved at the second level in the grievance procedure. The union "traded" Dysart's case for another, involving an employee who had taken extra days of leave for a funeral. The union felt that the second case was more important to the employees at large than Dysart's.

Dysart has *again* filed a grievance that management is rejecting under a contract clause which says a second grievance cannot be filed on the same issue. Management's *legalistic* approach in this case is hiding a very real problem: the employee is concerned about safety. Management has a duty to provide safe working conditions for its employees; if it fails to recognize that there is a problem here, the federal government can become involved through the Occupational Safety and Health Administration.

Management should consider a grievance a *behavioral* expression of some underlying problem. This statement does not mean that every grievance is symptomatic of something radically wrong. Employees file grievances over petty matters, as well as important concerns, and management must be able to differentiate between the two. However, to ignore a repeated problem and take a legalistic approach to grievance resolution is to miss much of what the grievance procedure can do for management.

Grievances and Leader Behavior

In a classic study done at International Harvester Company, two researchers discovered a relationship between the number of grievances filed and the leader behavior of the supervisors involved. In chapter 3, the two dimensions of leadership used in this study (consideration and structure) were discussed. But to review what each means:

1. *Consideration* includes behavior which indicates a mutual trust, respect, and certain warmth and rapport between the supervisor and the work group. This dimension appears to emphasize a deeper concern for group members' needs and includes such behavior as allowing subordinates more participation in decision-making and encouraging more two-way communication.

2. *Structure,* on the other hand, includes behavior in which the supervisor organizes and defines group activities in direct relation with the groups. The supervisor defines the role expected of each member. The leader assigns tasks, plans ahead, establishes ways of getting things done, and pushes for production. This dimension seems to emphasize overt attempts to achieve organizational goals.[14]

Figure 18–6 depicts the relationship between leader behavior and

Figure 18–6. Grievance rates and leader behavior.

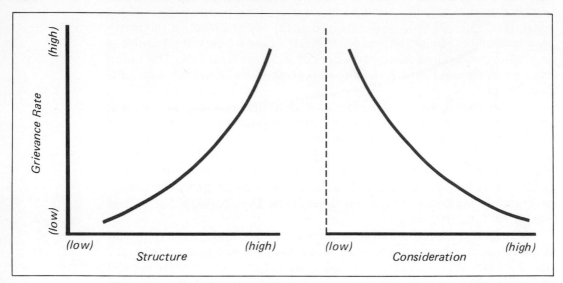

(Source: E. A. Fleishman and E. F. Harris, "Patterns of Leadership Behavior Related to Employee Grievances and Turnover," *Personnel Psychology,* 15, Spring 1962. Used with permission.)

grievance rates. The curves show that as the leader's behavior becomes more structured, the grievance rate tends to increase; as the leader's behavior becomes more considerate, the grievance rate drops substantially.

But how do different combinations of consideration and structure relate to grievances? Some supervisors score high on both dimensions, and some supervisors score low on both dimensions. Figure 18–7 shows the relationship between structure, consideration, and grievances.

In Figure 18–7, notice that for high-consideration supervisors (those represented by the lowest of the three lines), the amount of structure they use can be increased without substantially increasing the rate of grievances. However, *the reverse is not true.* For supervisors who were low in consideration (the top line), reducing structure did not reduce their grievance rate by very much. For those supervisors who were average or medium on consideration (middle line), grievances were lowest where structure was the lowest and increased as structure increased. Apparently, high consideration can compensate for high structure, but low structure will not offset low consideration.[15]

In summary, this study found that a supervisor's leader behavior can affect the number of grievances received from the work unit. High-structure supervisors receive more grievances, and high-consideration supervisors receive fewer grievances.

*Can you discuss the legal and behavioral
approaches to grievance resolution?*

Figure 18–7.   Combined effect of structure and consideration on grievance rates.

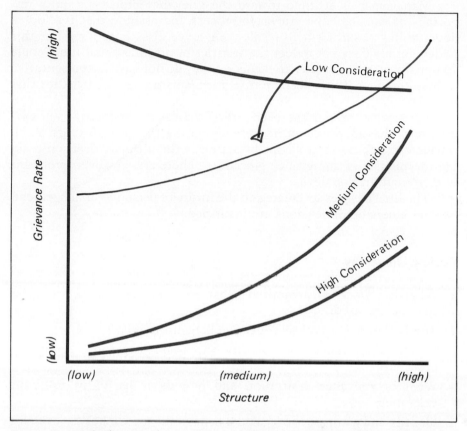

(Source: E. A. Fleishman and E. F. Harris, "Patterns of Leadership Behavior Related to Employee Grievances and Turnover," *Personnel Psychology*, 15, Spring 1962. Used with permission.)

REVIEW AND PREVIEW

The nature of union-management relations that follow certification has been examined in this chapter. Collective bargaining is a process in which management and union representatives attempt to reach a contractual agreement. An employer can take several approaches to collective bargaining. If these approaches fail, the firm must rely on conciliation/mediation or arbitration to reach a contract.

The second part of the chapter has dealt with the nature of the grievance procedure, its background, and specifics regarding its use. It is not necessary for employees to be represented by a union for an employer to have a formal grievance procedure. However, many employers wait to initiate one until they are forced to do so. The existence of a grievance procedure is viewed as a detriment to organizing employees by union representatives.

Management's attitude toward the grievance process is quite important. It can fight the grievance process and assume that its "open-door" policy is sufficient to resolve employee dissatisfactions. But this policy simply does not reflect the realities of organizational life. People do not always present their grievances if they do not have a representative to help them, or if they feel a formal mechanism does not exist for that purpose.

Arbitration, which has been called a form of "industrial self-government," has increased in importance during the past 35 years. Arbitration can help solve problems by acting as the ultimate decision-making mechanism in a grievance procedure. There are, however, problems with the arbitration device.

The final chapter speculates on the future of personnel management. Several emerging dimensions are identified.

Review Questions

1. What is collective bargaining? What are three bargaining strategies that can be used?
2. Briefly describe a typical collective bargaining process.
3. Define a grievance and identify the basic steps in a grievance procedure.
4. What is grievance arbitration and how is it useful in resolving grievances?
5. Identify and compare the legal and behavioral approaches to resolving grievances.
6. Discuss the statement: "A leader's behavior can affect the number of grievances."

Case: The Wilson County Hospital

The Wilson County Hospital has just recently seen its nurses organized after a long and bitter struggle that included dismissal and forced rehiring of some of the organizers. The nurses contended all along that the only reason that they needed to organize was to force the hospital administration to listen to important complaints. The complaints were primarily about poor working conditions and inappropriate patient care brought on by lack of proper facilities. The administration long ignored the nurses' pleas, claiming that available funds precluded them from doing anything about the facilities and working conditions.

The nurses have asked for a 7% cost-of-living increase in salary for each of the next three years. The hospital has steadfastly refused to offer any kind of increase in salary, claiming that it simply does not have the money available to pay for increased salaries. Further, since it has no money available, the hospital administration has declined to bargain with the nurses' union about salary. The nurses' union has been designated official bargaining agent for the nurses at Wilson County Hospital by the NLRB after the election. Vernon Cohn, the hospital administrator, was quoted as saying, "Hell, it makes no difference what they want to talk about. There's nothing I can do. We have no more money for salaries and therefore there's no sense in talking about it. I will not meet with the nurses to discuss salary."

Wilma Jones, the president of the local union, was reinstated in her job with the hospital after having been fired prior to the election. The NLRB found that Wilma had been fired for her organizing activities. In addition to a cost-of-living adjustment, Wilma feels very strongly that the nurses have several ideas on improving conditions and facilities for patient care (if only management would listen). Some method for presenting these ideas is needed because many of the nurses feel even more concerned about these issues than about salary increases.

QUESTIONS

1. Discuss the hospital administrator's refusal to bargain from both his viewpoint and a legal viewpoint.

2. If you were chairman of the board of directors for the hospital, what actions would you suggest to deal with the problems present in the case?

No Collective Bargaining

NOTES

1. James E. Martin and Lawrence L. Biasatti, "A Hierarchy of Important Elements in Union-Management Relations," *Journal of Management*, Fall 1979, pp. 229–240.

2. The six strategies are found in Arthur A. Sloane and Fred Whitney, *Labor Relations*, 2d ed., © 1972, pp. 32–37. Reprinted by permission of Prentice-Hall Inc., Englewood Cliffs, New Jersey.

3. Harry R. Gudenberg, "New Areas of Accommodation," *Labor Law Journal*, 33, August 1980, p. 462.

4. A realistic explanation of a detailed collective bargaining process can be found in Gary K. Himes, "Contract Negotiations—What Goes On?" *Supervision*, June 1980, pp. 12–16.

5. Richard E. Walton and Robert B. McKersie, *A Behavioral Theory of Labor Negotiations* (New York: McGraw-Hill, 1965).

6. Samuel C. Walker, "The Dynamics of Clear Contract Language," *Personnel Journal*, 60, January 1981, pp. 39–41.

7. James Wilson, "Thoughts on Union Avoidance," *The Personnel Administrator*, June 1977, pp. 14–18.

8. M. S. Wortman, C. E. Overton, and C. E. Block, "Arbitration Enforcement and Individual Rights," *Labor Law Journal*, 27, February 1974, p. 84.

9. "Basic Patterns: Grievances and Arbitration" in *Collective Bargaining Negotiations and Contracts* (Washington, D.C.: The Bureau of National Affairs, 1979), p. 51–1.

10. Lawrence Ingrassia, "Nonunion Workers Are Gaining Status, But So Far the Talk Outweighs the Action," *Wall Street Journal*, July 24, 1980, p. 36.

11. "The Antiunion Grievance Ploy," *Business Week*, February 12, 1979, pp. 117–120.

12. Dan R. Dalton and William D. Todor, "Manifest Needs of Stewards: Propensity to File a Grievance," *Journal of Applied Psychology*, 64, June 1979, pp. 654–659.

13. Robert Coulson, "An Informal Way to Settle Office Disputes," *Modern Office Procedures*, June 1980, pp. 182–186.

14. E. A. Fleishman and E. F. Harris, "Patterns of Leadership Behavior Related to Employees' Grievances and Turnover," *Personnel Psychology*, 15, Spring 1962, pp. 43–56.

15. Ibid.

Personnel
in the Future

WORK REVOLUTION?!

Revitalization, post-industrial society, information revolution, are all terms used to symbolize the major changes in work that are expected to occur by the year 2000. In a speech at USAA, a large insurance company based in San Antonio, Texas, an executive with a market research and opinion survey firm discussed some emerging trends. That executive is John Naisbitt, a Senior Vice-President with Yankelovich, Shelly and White. Some of his comments follow:

There are the beginnings of a job revolution in America, a basic restructuring of the work environment from top-down to bottom-up.

Whenever pressing economic trends converge with changing personal values, you get a change in a society. That's why we can start to look for some revolutionary changes in the workplace. A whole new attitude toward American workers is on the way. And it could result in a revitalization of the spirit of work and America's sagging productivity.

Here's the situation: The productivity growth rate is on a dismal downswing. Last year was the worst for productivity improvement in the nation's history.

At the same time, over the last two decades, personal values have been changing radically; there's a growing demand for more satisfaction from life. Workers feel it, too. Their psychic pain is reflected in their low productivity. They are sick of being treated like machines in the service of increased productivity. Workers refuse to produce and even deliberately sabotage the products they make.

They are no longer content with the traditional remedies offered up by labor unions, such as more pay, four-day weeks, better health benefits. What they really want, like everybody else, is deep human satisfaction from their work.

But industry had no compelling need to give it to them—until now. These dropping productivity figures will finally force industry, in economic desperation, to give more than token attention to the mental health of workers.

The workplace is in for a good shaking up. And the American worker is about to be saved by one of the most unlikely forces in society—call it humanization, "the human potential movement," participatory management. Call it whatever, it is about to converge with economic necessity to rescue the American worker from a deadened existence. For one thing, American industry is beginning to eye the way Japanese companies are run. Japan's productivity runs circles around ours.

It's often mistakenly thought that Japanese workers are so productive because they perform like robots, ever subservient to authority. The opposite is true. Unlike American workers, the Japanese are given enormous freedom to both plan and execute their work and solve problems alone without the help or interference of managers. The plants are run not from the "top-down" like ours where managers deliver orders, but from the "bottom-up" where the workers make many crucial decisions. Fully 90 percent of Japan's industrial work force is organized in work groups of 8 to 11 people. The whole theory is: the workers know their job better than anyone else, and given a chance, workers will be creative and self-motivated. Interestingly, the Japanese developed some of their management techniques from the theories of our own humanistic psychologists, such as the late Abraham Maslow.

When the Japanese use their techniques on American workers, the changes are astounding. The Japanese Matsushita Company several years ago took over a Motorola plant near Chicago and began to produce Quasar TV sets. The company retained 1000 on-line workers but dismissed half of the 600 supervisors and managers. Within two years, production *doubled* and the reject rate of sets dropped from 60 percent to 4 percent. Moreover, through good quality control, the company reduced its annual warranty costs from $14 million to $2 million.

Our workers are not stupid or lazy. They, like everybody else, want a chance for more personal satisfaction. And they are about to get it—even if the trigger is such an eyeglazing event as lower productivity figures. U.S. industry leaders may not understand such a trend as changing personal values, but they do understand dropping productivity. Because of how economically interlaced the U.S. is with the rest of the world, the only weapon it has against inflation that is in its full control is productivity improvement. As Peter Drucker says in his new book, "Managing in Turbulent Times," productivity improvement will be management's most important task for the '80s. And in this regard, creative management will be more important than creative technology.

Source: John B. Naisbitt, "Opinion and Trends: The New Economic and Political Order of the 1980's" *Aide*, Winter, 1980, p. 15.

CHAPTER 19

Personnel
and the Future

When you have read this chapter, you should be
able to:

1. Identify some reasons why more knowledgeable
   managers and personnel professionals will be
   needed in the future.

2. Discuss the nature of personnel as a career
   specialization.

"It's None of Her Business"

Jacob Mangren, new business manager for a medical clinic that has 30 doctors and 120 employees, has had a rotten Monday and it's only 10 A.M. He currently has a problem with Pam Ziegler that Pam really didn't cause.

Pam, 21 years old, is one of the best receptionists in the clinic. She is always cheerful when greeting patients, her attendance record is excellent, and she is well liked by the three doctors for whom she books appointments. Pam is a problem because of the supervisor for all the receptionists, Miss Trudy Prim. Miss Prim is 48 years old and has been with the clinic for almost 20 years. She started as secretary to the previous business manager and was named supervisor six months before Jacob started, even though she had no previous supervisory experience and did not get along well with the younger women in the clinic.

Yesterday, a very upset Pam came to Jacob's office carrying a copy of the performance appraisal Miss Prim had given her on the previous Friday. Pam was rated above average or outstanding on all individual job areas, but was given a "below average" on the overall. Miss Prim's explanation, according to Pam was as follows:

> "She told me I was one of the best receptionists she has, but she refused to rate me high overall or recommend me for a raise because I live with my boyfriend and have for eight months. Miss Prim said that once I got married or stopped 'living in sin', she would change the appraisal and recommend me for a raise. Just because she's an old maid, why take it out on me?"

After Pam left, Jacob remembered that Miss Prim had made similar comments to a former employee who quit the first week he was with the clinic. He must now decide how to handle this situation.

Comments:

This case illustrates how changing values and life styles affect managers. The receptionist was appraised legally using job duties, but the low overall rating would be difficult to defend or justify as being job-related. The situation is even more complicated because Jacob is new and Miss Prim is a long-service, loyal employee who probably should never have been promoted to supervisor. The promotion was probably the former business manager's attempt to reward Miss Prim with a "protected" job before he retired. Only by overriding Miss Prim's appraisal and giving Pam a raise can Jacob keep a good receptionist. However, by doing so he undermines Miss Prim with those she supervises. Jacob is experiencing one example of how personnel management is both complex and challenging.

T HE scope and complexity of personnel management have been emphasized throughout this book. Yet, only within the last decade has personnel management truly come into the mainstream of organizational life. The management of human resources in organizations is much more complex now than in the recent past because the external environment is placing more demands on managers and personnel specialists.

Organizations are in a continuous state of flux and must always be so if they are to remain in balance with a changing environment. As a result, an ongoing state of change must characterize the organization's structure, functions, work load, types of jobs, as well as employees and their qualifications, capacities, and behavior. Developments within the organization may necessitate promotions, transfers, demotions, layoffs, or other actions affecting personnel. Think, for example, of the many reorganizations necessitated by the widespread adaptation of computers as management tools.

FORCES OF CHANGE

Is continual change necessary? Can an astute manager avoid it? Certainly not everything needs changing all the time, but forces affecting the management of people in an organization dictate that change inevitably *does* and *will* take place. Some of the forces dictating change include:

1. Changing product life cycles and demand for products and services
2. Material shortages or surpluses and changing sources and forms of energy
3. International competition both domestically and abroad
4. Technological advances, especially computer-based equipment
5. Changing values and expectations of individuals in society
6. New knowledge of human behavior and ways of organizing
7. Varying levels of economic uncertainty that affect employees
8. Increasing government involvement in the employer-employee relationship
9. Shifts by unions in strategies and priorities
10. Increasing complexity of organizational life.

Some of these factors will affect *every type* of organization. The change forces mentioned above can be grouped into four categories: *social and work force changes, environmental change, personnel turnover,* and *technological change.* Each of these will be discussed in turn.

Work Force Changes

Because an organization is comprised of people, changes in work and what a job should be place more pressure on the management of people in work situations. Increasing concern about the "quality of life" at work is an indicator. Interest in flexible scheduling and the four-day work week reflects changing views about work scheduling and work's relationship to leisure.

Employee Expectations and Turnover.   Instead of attempting to force employees to conform to a "corporate mold," future managers may well have to allow for individual differences in people. Consider the problems caused by employers hiring more highly educated workers. Workers with more education may not be as willing to "mark time" in their jobs and wait patiently for promotions. Organizations that do not change their internal systems to accommodate this impatience may well see their turnover rates balloon. Because there will always be employee turnover, organizational change from this source is inevitable. An efficient organization will plan for, anticipate, and "manage" turnover through human resources planning and other managerial activities.

While some turnover is inevitable and even desirable, too much is an indication of organization problems. How much is too much? The answer is that "it depends." Some determining factors include the type of industry, historical trends, other employment opportunities in the community or geographical area, and the unemployment rate for the region.

In one organization, turnover has averaged 150% the last two years. That means that on the average, each job had to be filled one and one half times each year. This excessive turnover costs a great deal in training expenses alone, and keeps the company in a constant state of flux and turmoil. The turnover is basically a result of low wages, unpleasant work, and a low unemployment rate in the community, so discontented employees easily obtain other jobs.

Work Force Composition.   Another trend affecting personnel management is the shifting character of the work force. More and more occupations than ever before now include entry level educational qualifications. Those without a high school diploma are increasingly hard-pressed to find jobs. The continued importance placed on education, as well as the expansion in available educational opportunities, has resulted in a more educated labor force.

The changing age mix in the United States and its projection to 1990 means an ever-increasing number of older persons will be working. Some of these changes are already apparent with new retirement-age laws having been enacted.

The influx of women into the work force represents another major social value change that has a major impact on personnel management.

This shift leads to pressure to provide effective career paths for women and men and to reduce the distinction between "male" and "female" jobs. Hiring, training, and compensation systems are all affected.

Life-Style Changes and Mobility.   Other important changes relative to the work force include changes in life styles. As indicated in the opening case, many of today's employees have a different life style from the employees in the same age group only ten years ago and thus bring different values to the job now.

One change taking place over the last decade has had the net result of changing development policies and practices for many organizations. There has been a growing reluctance on the part of managers to accept relocation as a part of moving up in an organization. Employers have had to consider the costs of moving employees. Homequity, a large national relocation firm, estimated that the cost of a transfer of 1000 miles for someone who has a four-person family is $34,000! That figure represents a 70% increase in only two years. A large part of the cost is a mortgage differential payment to compensate for higher interest home mortgages.[1]

The effect of working spouses also hampers employer-initiated relocation efforts. Approximately half the work force now are women and many of them are not very willing to leave their jobs if their spouse is transferred. A number of firms help working spouses of employees, most frequently women, find jobs if a transfer occurs.

Environmental Changes

The social changes just described are one kind of environmental change. But the most direct environmental change for most organizations since 1960 has been the increasing involvement of government in organizational operations. A survey of over 300 executives listed government regulation as the biggest problems facing personnel executives during the 1980s.[2] Federal and state governments have agencies and statutes which can dictate wages that must be paid, certify the safety of working conditions, monitor the quality of the air surrounding many plants, provide minimum standards for hiring, and demand to see extensive records in order to scrutinize how organizations operate. This environmental change has forced managers to change personnel-related selection, recordkeeping, promotion, benefits, safety, and compensation practices, among others.

Governmental Regulation

Today, managers of organizations are confronted with an expanding and often bewildering array of governmental rules and restrictions that have a tremendous effect on the management of human resources. Government regulation of personnel activities has occurred for many years, and EEOC, OSHA, and ERISA are acronyms familiar to many managers. A brief comment on equal employment opportunities illustrates continuing changes affecting personnel management activities.

The Equal Employment Opportunity Commission (EEOC) can require employers to alter their hiring and promotion practices to assure that certain groups of people are provided equal chances for employment. With good reason, increasing emphasis has been placed on providing equal opportunities for women. The increasing concern about equal opportunities for women and the continuing concern for equal opportunities for racial minorities have had and will have a significant and vital effect on organizations in years to come.

The authors know one employer with 6,000 employees who has agreed to fill 15% of its management positions with women in the next five years. Currently the employer has only 25 women supervisors out of 800 managerial slots. To fulfill its promise in five years, the organization must have almost 100 more women in management jobs at a variety of levels. The pressure to provide women with greater opportunities has caused this organization to drastically restructure its recruiting, selection, and training practices.

EEOC has used its enforcement powers to such an extent that some EEOC officers now require organizations to tell them how many employees are of American Indian descent, including the tribal affiliation of each person claiming at least one-sixteenth Indian descent. Affirmative action programs to ensure meaningful equal opportunity and the related problem of "reverse discrimination" are destined to receive increasing attention in personnel management and probably resistance from non-protected male workers.

It is clear that governmental regulations currently have an important effect on personnel management. These pressures will continue to affect personnel management markedly in the future. More organization time, money, and effort will have to be allocated to comply with government regulations. The net effect of all these government interventions into personnel management will be to increase its importance in the organization.

PERSONNEL MANAGEMENT IN THE FUTURE: POSSIBLE CHANGES

This book has stressed the concept of "interfaces" between the personnel unit and other managers. As the changes noted above suggest, the days when personnel activities can be ignored or relegated to one part of the organization are gone. All managers will have to understand the basic issues and problems associated with personnel management if the organization is to be effective. A brief summary of each of these critical activities follows.

Work

A good working relationship between people and their jobs does not just happen. It requires analysis of the job to be done and proper design of the work people do. Job analysis, job descriptions, and job specifications will grow in importance in order to comply with EEO regulations and make validation of employment activities easier.

During the mid- and late-1980s greater emphasis on job redesign is likely to occur. The many different forms of redesign that have been and will be tried reflect consensus about improving productivity. Also the need to appeal to a more varied work force will lead to greater use of flexitime, job sharing, and other alternative work schedules and arrangements.

Staffing

Human resource planning, affirmative action, EEO, and test validity were terms lightly used 20 years ago. Yet, these concepts form the cornerstone of modern recruiting and selection practices. They affect personnel managers as well as production, marketing, and finance managers. All these managers have to staff their jobs with people in such a way as to live with current legal and social expectations.

A number of interesting trends appear to be developing. Increased use of a content validation approach will lead to a resurgence in testing for selection purposes. A growing emphasis will be placed on using structured interviews and training all who interview on effective and legal interviewing techniques. The shortages of skilled professionals such as nurses, engineers, and computer specialists will intensify and complicate recruiting efforts. Privacy protection regulations to outlaw polygraph (lie detector) testing and restrict background investigations will be passed unless employers "voluntarily" change their practices in these two areas.

Training and Development

Training needs assessment, training evaluation, and career planning have grown in importance. However, training costs—like everything else—are increasing, and management has a right to know whether or not it is receiving a dollar's worth of benefit for a dollar spent in this area. Further, as women and minorities with special training needs become more predominant in a broader range of jobs in organizations of all kinds, a greater need for specialized types of training and development will continue to grow.

A special concern is the retraining of employees who are "technologically obsolete." For example, a shortage of word processing specialists will force firms to retrain clerk-typists and secretaries to operate the more sophisticated word processing equipment.

The opposite situation is dismissal of employees who are no longer needed, combined with the closing of unneeded facilities. The layoffs and closings by such firms as Chrysler, Goodyear, U.S. Steel, and others have generated pressure for "outplacement." Through outplacement, firms assist their former employees to locate new jobs and/or to be retrained into new job skills. Continuing economic readjustments are likely to increase outplacement activities during the 1980s. Also legislation to regulate plant closings has been introduced in the past and is likely to be a continuing governmental attempt to force employers to assist affected employees.

The need for better management training and development programs and methods will probably continue unabated. Through increased managerial development activities organizations contribute both to their long-run effectiveness and to a more flexible organizational climate.

Appraisal

Performance appraisal has typically been very poorly done in most organizations. Yet, as the cost of keeping poor employees continues to grow, performance appraisal will increase in importance. The cost associated with having unrecognized excellence and potential is at least as great. Well-designed, properly implemented appraisal systems, perhaps more than any of the other activities, require the cooperative efforts of the personnel unit and operating managers in an organization.

Sound appraisals of job performance instead of personality traits continues to be a major concern. The American Society for Personnel Administration Foundation surveyed its local chapter leaders and found that managerial performance appraisal was the number one issue needing research in the early 1980s. Also, with the removal of automatic retirement at age 65, employers must develop legally defensible performance appraisals to use when making decisions about when individual older workers are no longer performing satisfactorily. In addition, more effective ways to tie performance appraisals to pay is necessary if true "pay for performance" systems are to be used.

Compensation

Productivity has been a national concern for some time. One possible way to increase productivity is to tie compensation to production. Yet, compensation administration is becoming increasingly complex. The Employee Retirement Income Security Act (ERISA) has greatly changed pension benefit plans, and increasing unionization in white-collar jobs will make the tie between productivity and compensation even more complex. New approaches, new ideas, and a professional approach to compensation and benefits are vital if strides are to be made in this area.

The rapid increase in benefit costs, especially health-related insurance benefits, will continue to be a major issue. At the same time employee and union pressure for new and improved benefit options is likely. One trend to observe is the extent to which firms attempt to use cafeteria-style benefit systems in order to offer employees more flexibility in using their benefit dollars. Preretirement counseling and retirement-related benefits will become even more prominent concerns.

At the same time organizations must develop and refine their basic wage and salary systems. It is much easier to administer a pay system when inflation is 4% than when it is double digit (over 10%). Various unique attempts such as keeping employee base pay stable but giving "merit raises" as lump sum bonuses have been experimented with by firms such as Scott Paper and others. Such efforts are likely to be attempted by a broad range of other organizations.

Public sector compensation systems are likely to change and become more similar to private sector practices. The old GS system, first established in the federal government, is being dropped by a growing number of governmental entities in favor of more sophisticated and realistic pay practices.

Maintenance

Largely because of OSHA, but also because of increasing management awareness of its social responsibilities to the public and its employees, personnel health and safety will continue to grow in importance. Further, the updating of personnel policies and rules must occur if organizations are to remain viable and competitive.

OSHA is likely to continue to change as a result of the many criticisms leveled at it. More emphasis will be placed on truly unsafe employers and problem industries, and less placed on small business and other firms with good safety and health records. In a broader health focus, increased interest in assisting troubled employees through Employee Assistance Programs (EAP) will be seen as a way to retain scarce skill and other employees.

Improved personnel communication and coordination systems will be needed to tap employee talents and improve productivity. Suggestion systems, used in conjunction with quality circle plans, represent an appealing strategy for a growing number of employers.

Privacy legislation, proposed or adopted, should have an impact on personnel recordkeeping systems. At the same time the development and usage of computerized employee information systems will enable firms to do a better job of human resource planning.

Union Relations

Finally, the interface with labor organizations will increase in importance for some organizations. In other organizations and industries a rethinking and reformulation of existing relationships may be necessary for the industries to grow and remain viable. The construction industry is an example of an industry where this reexamination appears to be occurring. Cooperative efforts between labor and management are likely in the steel and automobile industries and others hard hit by foreign competition.

Public sector and white-collar unions will continue to be fast growing segments of the labor movement. Employees who previously saw unions as villains are "seeing the light" and joining unions. School teachers, university professors, firefighters, police officers, and nurses are just a few of the professionals who have experienced the increased appeal of organizing.

Numerous managers in a variety of organizations will have to adjust to dealing with unionized employees. Also, established unions and their leaders will be facing internal challenges from younger workers. New bargaining relationships, such as the inclusion of no-strike clauses and compulsory arbitration in contracts, will have to be considered by both employers and unions.

A year-long study of future trends in the employee relations field focused on opinions of more than 100 leaders from industry, education, and government.[3] Among other interesting predictions this study forecasts is a stronger role in the public sector for arbitration/mediation services. This growth will be forthcoming because of a tremendous increase in unionization by public employees. The study also predicts growth in union members in all sectors and new and better-educated union leadership. The net result of such a trend will be to put additional pressure on personnel systems.

Non-union employers will try to stay that way by continuing to use sophisticated tactics and consultants. Also, adoption of employee "due process" and formal grievance systems will become another technique used by non-union employers to stay that way.

Unions typically have had the effect of causing organizations to be

more professional and careful about their personnel policies and practices. Especially in certain white-collar and professional occupations, a
major re-analysis of personnel management activities will be required
if the predicted trend does indeed occur.

Throughout this book it has been stressed that personnel management is a series of activities that must be performed in organizations.
Coordination between personnel specialists and other managers is vital.
The areas discussed earlier illustrate the challenges managers and personnel specialists are going to face in the future.

Emphasis on personnel management as a set of activities does not
ignore the fact that effective personnel management requires professional
personnel specialists. Personnel activities will become more and more
important, which will increase the demand for a greater number of
competent individuals to make personnel their career specialty.

What are some of the ways personnel will change
in the mid-1980s?

PERSONNEL AS A CAREER SPECIALIZATION

A wide variety of jobs are performed by career professionals. The common jobs and job titles listed in Figure 19–1 illustrate the number of
areas in which career personnel professionals can work. There are job
opportunities in specific personnel areas and for personnel generalists
who are knowledgeable in several areas.

Figure 19–1. Sample job titles of personnel professionals.

Personnel Director	Safety Coordinator
Director of Industrial Relations	Employee Relations Counselor
Employment Manager	Corporate Ombudsman
Compensation Analyst	EEO Compliance Manager
Benefits Coordinator	Training Director
Job Analyst	Manager of Organization
Personnel Interviewer	Development
Personnel Research Analyst	Pension Analyst
Labor Relations Specialist	Employee Services Coordinator
	Testing Consultant

Why will more knowledgeable managers in the
personnel area be needed in the future?

Career Opportunities in Personnel

Personnel as a career field is flourishing. One indication is that the number of personnel-related jobs is projected to grow faster than many other professional occupations. It is anticipated that between 15,000 and 20,000 new personnel jobs will be available each year from 1980 to the mid-1980s. As shown in figure 19–2, the number of personnel professionals is expected to grow from 405,000 in 1978 to 473,000 by 1990.

Figure 19–2.   Personnel-Labor Relations workers 1978–1990.

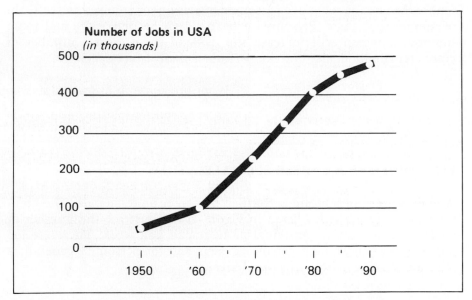

(Source: Occupational Projections & Training Data, 1980 Edition, U.S. Dept. of Labor, Bureau of Labor Statistics, Bulletin 2052.)

Another indicator is the importance of personnel issues. One survey of over 2,000 chief executives from leading business firms found that 40% of the respondents were spending between five and twenty hours per week on personnel-related matters. The same survey revealed that the pay for top personnel executives has increased to where those executives are paid relatively equal to top executives in other functional specialities.[4]

Personnel Salaries

The growth in personnel professional salaries is a reflection of two factors: (1) the importance of personnel activities to organizations and (2) the increase in education and professionalism of personnel practitioners. Figure 19–3 identifies the median salary level of some personnel jobs.

Figure 19–3. Typical personnel salaries, 1980–81.

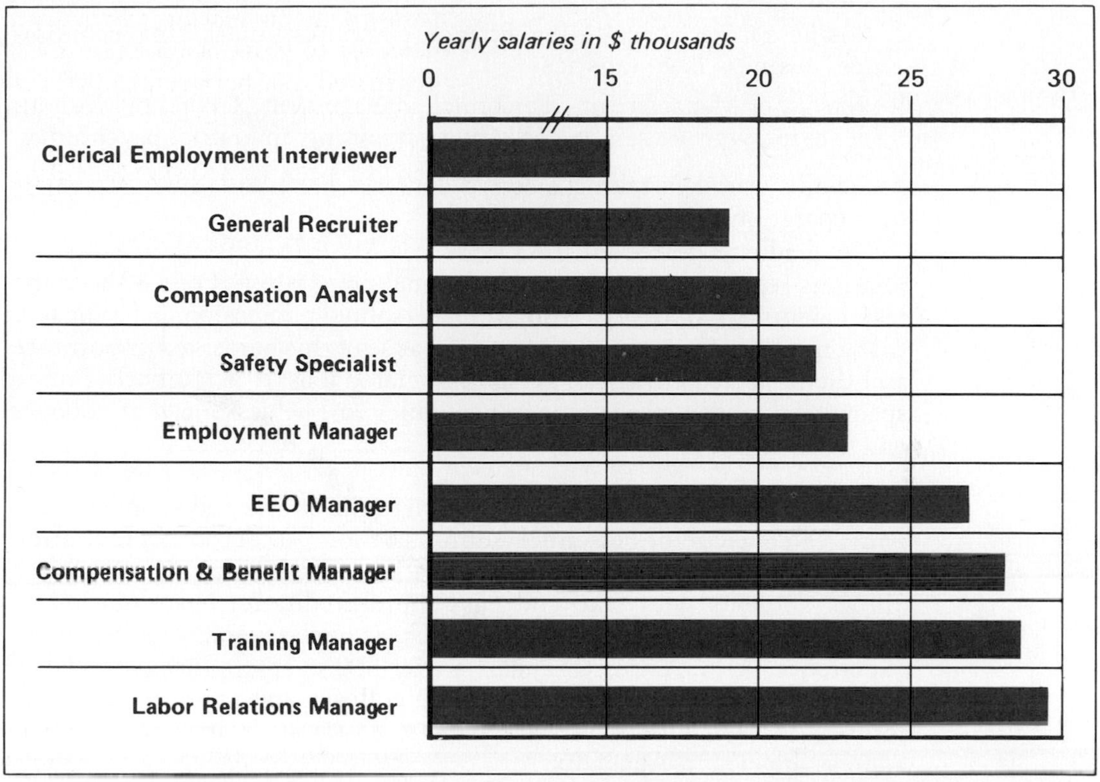

Yearly salaries in $ thousands

Clerical Employment Interviewer	
General Recruiter	
Compensation Analyst	
Safety Specialist	
Employment Manager	
EEO Manager	
Compensation & Benefit Manager	
Training Manager	
Labor Relations Manager	

(Source: Steven Langer, "Personnel Salaries: A Survey, Part I," *Personnel Journal*, 59, December, 1980, p. 984.)

According to one survey, personnel professionals in manufacturing organizations generally were paid more than those in non-manufacturing organizations. Also, as would be expected, personnel practitioners in small organizations made less than their counterparts in large organizations. Of particular interest is the finding that top personnel executives with MBA degrees made $2,000/year more than those with a B.A./B.S. degree, and $7,000/year more than those without a college degree.[5]

Career Preparation

There are several steps that appear to be helpful in preparing someone for a career in personnel. Education is a must.

Educational Preparation. The breadth of personnel issues to be faced means that future personnel professionals will need to be well-educated in a broad range of business and other courses. Three areas[6] have been suggested, with special emphasis noted:

1. General Education—English, mathematics, psychology, and social sciences
2. Business Core—Accounting, finance, computers, marketing, economics, business law statistics
3. Personnel Management—Personnel management, labor law, human behavior, wage & salary, collective bargaining, industrial psychology.

Especially useful is taking elective courses that have direct relevance to preparation for a personnel career.

A graduate degree (M.B.A., M.A., or M.S.) in personnel/industrial relations represents additional educational preparation. Over 80% of the respondents to a survey, who were personnel professionals, indicated that a master's degree is important.[7] Because of this perceived importance and the projected growth in personnel-related jobs, it is likely that more specialized master's programs in personnel will be developed at colleges and universities.

Accreditation and Involvement.   Through the efforts and support of the American Society for Personnel Administration (ASPA), an accreditation program for personnel professionals has been established. This program allows students who take and pass the accreditation examination to become fully accredited after they have gained several years of work experience. Also, ASPA, through its over 300 chapters, has established student personnel chapters at over 160 colleges and universities. More information on both these activities is available from ASPA, whose address appears in Appendix A.

Involvement in other professional organizations, such as the International Personnel Management Association (IPMA) and others listed in Appendix A, can also be valuable. Student and community groups in which an individual can demonstrate leadership are additional ways to prepare for a career in personnel.

Experience.   Personnel as a career field is not as easily entered without experience as some other fields, such as sales or finance. While this may not be as true in large metropolitan areas such as New York City or Houston, a realistic picture must be given. Consideration should be given to obtaining some part-time experience, summer internships, or other strategies to overcome the lack of experience. The ever-present situation of "I need experience, but how can I get it?" must be dealt with using non-traditional strategies. Some firms will not put anyone directly into a managerial job in personnel above trainee level, until that person has "gotten to know the territory" by working in sales, manufacturing, or some other operating area. Also, individuals hoping for a career in personnel must decide if they want to be personnel specialists (training, benefits, etc.) or generalists who deal with a broad range of personnel activities. Regardless of the career path taken, the need for personnel professionals certainly will not diminish in the next several years. Personnel as a career specialization is both attractive and challenging.

What are several aspects of personnel as a career field?

CONCLUSION

A major perspective of this book is that, to a certain extent, all managers are personnel managers. All managers, including career personnel professionals, must expand their knowledge of activities that focus on the management of human resources. In addition to a basic familiarity with the many ideas and issues contained in this text, managers and personnel professionals must continually develop their knowledge of general management and human behavior.

In the future, personnel management will play an increasingly important role in the destiny of organizations. This book has attempted to capture the essence and challenge of personnel management today, so that readers will be better prepared for the organizations of tomorrow.

Concluding Questions

1. What forces will be shaping personnel in the future? What will be their effects?
2. Why or why not would personnel be a possible career field for you? Would you prefer to be a specialist or a generalist? Why?

Case: Who Wears the Pants?

Martin Ward is a 60-year-old supervisor who has been with the company for 40 years, and does his job very, very well. He supervises a group of clerical employees, mostly women, working in an office. One of Martin's longstanding rules has been that women who work for him must dress in an appropriate fashion. For his women employees, this means neat grooming and wearing a dress. He does not tolerate pants of any kind in his unit; even expensive slack suits are unacceptable and anyone wearing this sort of attire on the job in the past has been sent home to change. This "dress code," as the employees call it, has never presented any problem for Martin until recently.

Over the past four years many of the older employees have retired and been replaced with younger employees. The turnover in the unit is not very high and, unless somebody retires, employees generally stay with the company. One of the main reasons for this low turnover is that the company pays quite a bit more than the prevailing wage rate in the community. Also, the company offers employee profit-sharing schemes and excellent benefits.

Recently, the rule about wearing a dress to work has become a point of contention among the younger group of clerks. Many of them feel that pant suits are acceptable attire anywhere today, and that it should be acceptable attire at work as well. The issue came to a head last Wednesday when Margaret Breland, one of the better clerks, came to work in a pair of fashion jeans and an expensive blouse and refused to go home when he suggested she do so. He told her she could stay but she would not be paid for the time she was at work in "those pants." Margaret wrote a letter to the personnel director criticizing Martin, contending that the rule was an infringement upon her freedom to dress as she chose and had nothing to do with her ability to perform the job. The letter is now on the desk of the personnel manager, Wayne Phillips, who must respond to it before the end of the week. On one hand, the personnel manager feels a need to support a management employee in his right to run his unit the way he sees fit. On the other hand, Wayne knows that societal attitudes toward dress have changed in the last ten years and that Martin is hopelessly behind the times. The personnel director mentally notes that this is the fifth problem he has had to deal with this year that in some way reflects new values and attitudes held by the employees. Wayne sighs and starts drafting his response.

QUESTIONS

1. How does a conflict in values enter into the case?
2. Discuss the company's role in causing the conflict.
3. If you were Wayne Phillips, what would you do?

NOTES

1. "Moving Events," *Forbes*, April 27, 1981, p. 166.

2. "Uncle Sam . . ." *Wall Street Journal*, February 12, 1980, p. 1.

3. M. R. Schiavoni, "Employee Relations: Where Will it be in 1985?" *The Personnel Administrator*, March 1978, pp. 25–27.

4. "People Power," *Wall Street Journal*, October 16, 1979, p. 1.

5. Steven Langer, "Personnel Salaries: A Survey, Part I", *Personnel Journal*, 59, December 1980, pp. 983–987.

6. Adapted from Daniel R. Hoyt and J. D. Lewis, "Planning for a Career in Human Resource Management," *Personnel Administrator*, October 1980, pp. 53–54.

7. "Higher Education for Personnel Managers," *Personnel Journal*, 60, March 1981, p. 154.

Comprehensive
Cases

COMPREHENSIVE CASE #1:
The Interview

Lenore Johnson responded to the following advertisement in a local newspaper:

> Repair Supervisor
> 12 repairmen,
> major brands
> LARGE RADIO & TV CO.
> address
> phone number
> An Equal Opportunity Employer

Lenore is a young, aggressive, black woman. She has been employed by an electronics manufacturing company as an assembly person for three years and as a line leader for the last year. She has a radio amateur operator's license and is studying for a commercial radio telephone license. Her work record at the ABC Electronics plant has been good. Her department manager's comments on her last performance appraisal indicated that she had good promotion potential.

The owner of LARGE RADIO & TV is an elderly gentleman who started the business many years ago. He has sixteen employees; four are salespeople and twelve are repairmen. He feels very proud of his accomplishments and is very much "his own man."

Lenore filled out the application blank (Figure 1) and was given an interview. The interview was held at the repair shop with several interruptions from customers' phone calls and questions from salespeople and repairmen. The owner described the job by making references to the previous supervisor in glowing terms (He was a great guy. He was always in here early to open up and make coffee, and he usually was the last one to leave). The previous supervisor was retiring because of bad health, and the owner did not want to run the shop by himself again. He was planning to go into semi-retirement and wanted someone who would keep the place going so he only had to "check in on things" once a day.

The owner asked her to take a four-page "electronics knowledge" test that had been developed by a local trade association. The owner left her to complete the test while he attended to another interruption. When she had completed the test, she waited for the owner to return. When he did so, he briefly scanned the test. He asked her who her boss was at the ABC Electronics Company because "I know most of the guys over

Figure 1. Large Radio and TV Co. Application for employment.

Large Radio and TV Co.

APPLICATION FOR EMPLOYMENT

1. Name: _____

2. Background in Radio/TV:

3. Your working habits:

4. What is your driving record?

5. Why do you want this job?

6. Do you realize if we get any collection calls or garnishment of wages on you, that you will be immediately dismissed? Yes ___ No ___

7. Do you use tobacco?

8. Are you in debt?

9. What are your hobbies?

I hereby affirm that my answers are true and correct.

Signed _____

---

there." She told him who her boss was and stated that he had written performance reviews which reflected her good work as a supervisor. When asked why she wanted to leave ABC Electronics, she stated that she wanted to advance herself and hoped to have a business like LARGE someday.

He asked her if she felt she would have any difficulty supervising twelve men. She replied that while most of the people she had been supervising were women, she had also supervised several men at the plant and felt that she would have no more problems than anyone else.

She asked what the normal working hours were for the shop. He replied that the shop was open from 7:30 A.M. to 4:00 P.M. every day except Sunday. "However," he said, "most of the men are still here at 5:00 or 5:30 P.M." He added that occasionally they would have a sale and the shop was open until 9:00 P.M.

Noticing the wedding band on her finger, he asked, "Will your husband mind if you have to work late once in a while?" She replied that she didn't think that had anything to do with the job, and that she expected to have to work some extra hours.

He asked if she was good with figures "since the previous supervisor had done almost all the paperwork," and added, "You women are usually good with numbers." She said that she felt her arithmetic skills were adequate and that she had been responsible for the assembly-line paperwork at ABC Company. "My line produced thirteen different models of television sets last year, and I was responsible for meeting production goals and making sure that the levels of inventory for my line were sufficient," she replied.

"Do you know anything about trucks?" he asked. "Glen used to take care of the little things with the service vans. Of course, we always sent the trucks to a repairshop if it was something serious." She replied that she had little automotive experience.

The owner concluded the interview by thanking her and indicated he would make his decision "soon."

After two weeks without word from the owner, she called to find out if she was still being considered. She was told that he had hired someone else.

When she inquired why she had not received the job, the owner said that he felt that the young man he had hired had stronger technical skills and that he would become a good supervisor. She pressed for details and found out that the young man was a recent graduate from an area technical school, but had no supervisory experience. The owner had interviewed the young man over lunch at a cafe and had accepted his technical school diploma as a substitute for the test she had taken.

QUESTIONS:

1. What grounds, if any, does Lenore have for an EEO complaint?
2. How should she proceed?
3. Characterize the professionalism of this selection process.

South-Eastern Life and Home Insurance Company (S.E.L.H.)[1]

The current success of S.E.L.H. is a tribute to a small group of dedicated business people and entrepreneurs who believed in the potential benefits of mass marketing and in the importance to individual and family security of "living protection" through life and home insurance. Although it is a relatively new company serving Florida, Georgia, Alabama, Mississippi, and Tennessee, in a comparatively short time S.E.L.H. has become one of the top companies providing this type of insurance in this area. Sales representatives, administrative personnel, clerical personnel, and even staff specialists in systems, accounting and the actuarial sciences work together as a team to contribute to the success of the company. People were at the heart of company successes and it was this recognition that was to spark an important area of inquiry into human resource planning for its own employees.

FORMULA FOR SUCCESS

Office inquiries were responded to courteously and promptly. Company representatives were seen as understanding individuals who tried to help potential clients plan well rather than simply to take on insurance and become burdened with more outflow of needed funds.

THE MASS MERCHANDISING APPROACH

All the key supervisors and managers had at one time attended special classes on merchandising and most had attended community colleges or universities; there was considerable expertise in the organization. At a very early point, a decision was made to see if book learning in marketing, merchandising, and technology would contribute to developing insurance sales and growth. In addition, company heads studied the techniques of mass merchandisers like K-Mart, Sears, Wards, and food chains, as well as the approaches of finance institutions and competitive insurance firms. The result of these analyses was a carefully balanced program of advertising and merchandising approaches backed up by a well-geared organization of dedicated people who really believed in their product and its importance to people. Also, computer procedures and information processing were so arranged as to take full advantage of an up-to-date, well-run computer system. Considering all this, the company's success is no surprise.

HUMAN RESOURCE PLANNING

Within a short time, S.E.L.H. was employing almost 2,000 people (see Figure 2) in a central headquarters facility, five regional offices, and 20 sales offices. Considering that the 20-year-old company began with only two offices and 25 people, its growth is truly impressive. Yet, at the same time, success is not without its problems. Anticipating people's needs and then securing and training personnel who could take a productive place in the organization, combined with the team concept of S.E.L.H., became critical to future expansion and success.

The employment figures shown in figure 2 reflect some of the growing pains of the company. For example, in the 7th and 13th years, the company was forced to cut back its operations because of numerous claims resulting from hurricanes, tornadoes, and floods. But company personnel learned well from these rather bitter experiences and their resilience and vitality for growth soon returned.

Emergence of Personnel and Initiation of Planning

The formation of a personnel and human resource department was a comparatively recent development, having been started only five years before when employment stood at 1,100. Office management and sales personnel were fully occupied with a complete range of operating problems, and the needs of personnel maintenance and planning were being done in sloppy fashion and only meeting regulatory and compliance needs. When the president learned of the poor state of personnel activity, it was immediately clear to him that the internal state of personnel and company plans for growth would simply not work out. The president learned that his executive secretary, Mary Murphy, who had innate business talent, had a minor in personnel from Georgia State College. The president talked to Mary of the need for filling the personnel slot. She was delighted to take on a new assignment.

Mary and the president, as well as all the key managers, had a series of meetings to determine the priorities for personnel and human resources. Mary had her own ideas but wanted to get all the key people involved in human resource procedures right from the beginning. It was finally agreed that the ordinary maintenance functions of personnel pertaining to payroll, taxes, ordinary records, and so forth, would remain with the office manager but that Mary would provide technical information as needed. Second, Mary and her department would assume full responsibility for various human resource planning activities including development, recruiting, forecasting, changes in the personnel data base, occupational health and safety, career planning, compensation and benefit planning, and recruiting for technical and professional personnel. The initial and first priority was a five-year plan reflecting needs for key and critical human resource categories, and compatibility of these plans with equal employment opportunity and affirmative action.

Figure 2. Employment Growth: 20-Year Experience.

A. Overall employment

Year	Overall employment	Year	Overall employment
1	25	11	600
2	100	12	800
3	150	13	750
4	200	14	900
5	250	15	1000
6	250	16	1100
7	225	17	1400
8	300	18	1600
9	400	19	1800
10	500	20	2000

B. Employment in key and critical categories

Recent employment experience—major occupational categories (figures rounded):

Number of people assigned*

Years	Supervisory	Managerial	Technical	Administrative	Total Employment
18	160	16	45	30	1600
19	190	25	50	35	1800
20	210	30	60	35	2000

C. Equal employment data

The most recent experience:

Supervisory			Managerial			Technical		
total	minority	female	total	minority	female	total	minority	female
210	5	5	30	1	1	60	3	1

Administrative		
total	minority	female
35	2	10

*Professional and semi-professional

Mary's Formulation of a Game Plan

When the meetings with the managerial groups and the president had been concluded, Mary started thinking about how to meet the human resource actions and priorities established through these meetings. Central to human resource planning would be the determination of future recruitment needs to complement internal development of various personnel categories. Consequently, it occurred to Mary that at least three different categories of human resource planning problems and issues were involved:

1. The total size of expected employment in five years.
2. The total development requirements for "key and critical" human resources.
3. The overall needs of S.E.L.H. for affirmative action and, in particular, for development of specific approaches within key and critical human resources categories.

She decided to turn her attention to devising a means of forecasting the various human resource needs in the organization and then formulating strategies for making these a reality.

QUESTIONS

1. Estimate the total increase in key and critical manpower from year #20 to year #25. Use the data of years 18, 19, and 20 as the best approximation of what is to be expected in year #25. *Hint:* What is the overall average of key and critical manpower (i.e., supervisory, managerial, technical staff, and administrative staff)?

2. If top management of S.E.L.H. has decided to double the percentage of women and minority groups among key and critical manpower by year #25, what will these percentages be?

3. Forecast S.E.L.H.'s need for women and minority recruitment and development by year #25 for key and critical manpower, if top management decides to double their proportion as a percentage of the total key and critical group.

4. Comment on the assumptions and conditions under which the forecasted figures for total employment, key and critical ("k and c") manpower, and minority/women among "k and c," are likely to be accurate or inaccurate. What factors will contribute to uncertainty regarding these factors? What new demands will be imposed on Mary Murphy? How should she cope with them?

---

[1] Reproduced from Elmer H. Burack, *Personnel Management: Cases and Exercises* (St. Paul: West Publishing Co., 1978), pp. 34–38. Used with permission.

COMPREHENSIVE CASE #3:

Northeastern Bank

Northeastern Bank, which is owned by a large multibank holding company, is the fourth largest bank in a moderately sized city. It employs 150 people and relies heavily on part-time employees, especially college students. Northeastern has three banking facilities in the city, the maximum allowed by law. Its main facility has the largest number of employees and contains all major departments of the bank.

There are two branch facilities. One is located in the major agricultural section of the city. This facility caters to the clients of the bank engaged in agricultural activities and is primarily oriented toward agricultural activities, such as auctions, commodities, etc. It accounts for a substantial portion of the bank's deposits. The other facility is located in the fast-growing western section of the city. The orientation of this facility is to attract new customers and "sell" the bank's services to them.

In the state where Northeastern Bank is located, the legislature is considering a bill that would allow banks in the state to open another branch facility. The banking community has lobbied for many years to get this bill passed, and last year the bill was narrowly defeated. This year, however, because of changes in federal banking laws, the bill is given a very good chance of passage. If the bill is passed, the banks in the state will be allowed to open an additional facility 30 days after the bill is signed by the governor.

The top management at Northeastern is very excited at the prospect of opening a new facility, and they want to be prepared to move quickly after the bill is passed. Therefore, they have directed the manager of the west branch facility to train a person for the position of bank representative/night manager and to prepare two tellers to be moved to the new facility once it is opened.

Although the manager of the new bank will be chosen from the staff at the bank's main facility, top management wants the other staff members to come from the west branch. They feel that employees of the west branch facility will be better prepared for the task of opening a new branch facility. Banks are restricted in the functions they can perform at their branch facilities. For example, branch facilities can only take loan applications and forward them to their main facility. They cannot approve loans.

John Wilson has been chosen as the person to be trained as bank representative/night manager. For the past three months, John has trained in this capacity and is now able to perform the duties expected of him with little supervision. John still works as a teller when the need arises because of illness or vacation, but this is not unusual, for all bank representatives at the west facility are expected to perform teller duties when the need arises.

However, in John's opinion, management is using this situation as a basis for not giving him a full promotion. Management still classifies John as a teller and not as a bank representative. There is a significant difference in responsibilities and salary between the two positions. Management says that they are not willing to fully promote John until he assumes his duties at the new facility. If the bill is not passed and the new facility not opened, John will reassume his job as a teller and be promoted to bank representative when a position opens up.

John is unhappy with this situation, and has had numerous discussions with management about his predicament. Management has not yet made a decision. John has decided to give management an ultimatum: either promote him fully to bank representative or he will look elsewhere for employment. John's boss does not want this to happen for John is an excellent employee and is already trained for the position. Furthermore, John is admired and well respected by nearly all the employees with whom he works. His leaving because of this situation would have a negative impact on other employees.

A second employee in the west branch facility, Mildred Pierce, is a part-time college student who has just been hired for a full-time job in the bookkeeping department at NEB. When she left the interview, Mildred thought it was going to be the perfect job. She was told the hours would be 8:30 to 4:30, four days a week, and 8:00 to 5:00, Saturdays. The duties of the job were filing checks, answering the phone, and operating a CRT. The bank provided full training and in a few months Mildred would have the opportunity to learn how to run proof or move into a teller position. She was also assured of a raise from $4.10 an hour to $4.25 or more after a review in three months.

During the first week, everything went well for Mildred. She filed checks, observed the other employees on the job, and learned her way around the bank. The second week she was given her own desk and told she was on her own. The check filing was simple, but when it came to the phone and the CRT, everything went wrong. Customers asked her questions about which she had no information, and many of the CRT procedures had been changed. When Mildred informed the supervisor of her problems, she told Mildred that she would help her "later." Later never came and Mildred ended up training herself by trial and error while upsetting quite a few customers along the way.

On the first Tuesday of the second month, Mildred came into work at 8:30 and was immediately called into her supervisor's office. She was told that everyone was expected to come in as early as possible on statement day (first Tuesday of each month) to help get the statements out on time. Because Mildred was a part-time student, it was very difficult for her to come in early. When she informed her supervisor, she was told to change her schedule if she wanted a good review. Mildred changed her schedule and began coming in early on statement day. When she went in for her review a month later, she was told that a new bank policy had gone into effect and it would be another three months before Mildred would receive a raise, and it would be impossible to train her for another position for a few months. Consequently, Mildred put in her two-week notice the next day.

Since Mildred quit two months ago, five other part-time employees have left and several of the bank's top management members have quit, including the personnel director.

QUESTIONS

1. Are there similarities in the way John and Mildred were handled?
2. What does the bank need to do to eliminate these difficulties?
3. Is the bank ready to expand from the standpoint of its human resources?

COMPREHENSIVE CASE #4:
Iona's Ire

Iona Eden worked in the Housekeeping Department of the Parker-House Hotel as an area maintenance specialist. The Parker-House Hotel is a large convention facility with several restaurants and meeting rooms in the downtown area of a large midwestern city. The hotel employs approximately 250 people in full- and part-time positions. The House-keeping Department includes approximately 100 employees with a manager, several assistant managers, and eight supervisors.

Iona, a woman in her late fifties, had been employed by the hotel for three years and was responsible for cleaning a specified area in the hotel as assigned by her supervisor, Reggie Hays. Iona was also a maintenance specialist trainer for new employees.

Because of rotating schedules there were several supervisors for each shift, although when a supervisor was gone, another on-duty supervisor would take responsibility for two or more areas. Each employee was assigned to a supervisor but when that supervisor was gone the employees of that area would report to the substitute supervisor.

Iona resigned from the hotel citing unfair treatment by Ralph Murphy, the substitute supervisor for her area. One month later Iona filed a charge of discrimination based on age against the hotel with the State Equal Opportunity Commission. In her suit against the hotel Iona claimed that she felt compelled to resign because of unfair treatment by Ralph Murphy over the three years she had worked at the hotel. She also stated that she had asked for her job back if the problems between herself and Ralph could be resolved but she was not allowed to tell her side of the story before the decision was made not to re-hire her. Furthermore, she claimed that Ralph had singled her out on several occasions for extra work rather than assigning extra work to other employees.

Investigation of the charge against the hotel indicated that Iona had threatened to resign on several occasions over misunderstandimgs and errors in her personnel file. In each of these misunderstandings the problem was resolved and Iona was satisfied. These incidents were minor in nature and not documented except for the changes made in her file—a change in her starting date and a change in her vacation hours. The starting date error went back to the time the hotel took over the house-keeping duties from a private contractor and hired their personnel.

Iona had worked for Ralph for several months right after the hotel assumed responsibility for its own housekeeping and had several encounters with Ralph during this time and over the three years she worked at the hotel. Usually the encounters involved the cleaning of guest rooms which were an addition to the regularly assigned rooms in Iona's area of responsibility as provided for in her job description. The housekeeping department's policy was that all empty rooms were to be cleaned by 3:30 P.M. and they took priority over other areas for cleaning. Iona had resisted being assigned additional rooms on several occasions when Ralph was the substitute supervisor in charge. None of these incidents had ever resulted in written action by a supervisor, however.

The event which caused Iona to resign began on a Friday when Reggie, her regular supervisor, was gone. Ralph observed Iona wearing her street clothes one-half hour before her scheduled quitting time which was against hotel policy. Ralph confronted Iona but took no action at that time. Instead, Ralph discussed the incident with Reggie for his action as her supervisor.

On the following Monday, Reggie met with Iona and discussed the incident as reported by Ralph. Iona's reason for the early change was that her son was picking her up after work to take her out to dinner for her birthday and she wanted to be ready when he arrived. She also indicated that she had finished her assigned work. She gave no reason for not asking Ralph for an exception to the policy.

Reggie re-emphasized the hotel's policy on street clothes but did not take further action since this was the first time Iona had violated the policy.

Iona left Reggie's office and immediately went to the assistant manager's office and resigned, citing unfair treatment by Ralph Murphy. She then proceeded to the manager's office and to the vice-president's office, each time giving her resignation and citing unfair treatment. All these actions were inconsistent with the hotel's established procedures for grievances and resignation.

Reggie Hays and the assistant manager of the department then met with Iona, discussed her desire to resign, and provided her with a resignation form which she completed.

Iona took an authorized day off and then called in sick on five consecutive days, using all her accumulated sick leave. This left her with four days of her two-week notice. On the last day of her notice, Iona went to Reggie Hays and asked to be re-instated on the condition that the unfair treatment by Ralph Murphy be stopped.

Reggie met with the assistant manager and then the manager of the department to discuss Iona's request. Their decision was to accept Iona's original resignation for the following reasons:

1. The temper outbursts displayed by Iona when she felt that the hotel's policies were wrong or that her records were not as they should be.
2. Iona had violated the hotel's procedure concerning grievances by resigning to three levels of management.

3. Iona had a problem accepting authority.

4. A replacement for her position had been hired during the two-week notice period and was to start the next working day.

QUESTIONS

1. To what extent is this case a case involving discrimination?

2. What mistakes were made by the managers and/or are due to organizational operating matters?

3. Identify and evaluate the personnel policies indicated in the case.

4. If you were the state investigator, what would be your ruling? Why?

COMPREHENSIVE CASE #5:
Compensating Oscar

Osmax Memorial Hospital (OMH) is located in the Northern U.S. and employs over 2,000 people in over 400 separate jobs. The job with the most positions is "Staff Registered Nurse," which has almost 300 incumbents. However, there are several jobs with only one incumbent. The jobs are classified as:

Professionals —Registered Nurses, Physicians, and Pharmacists

Technicians —Therapists, Laboratory Technicians, and Dieticians

Administrators—Department Heads, Supervisors, and Specialists in Accounting and Personnel

Support —Engineers, Security, Janitors, and Cooks.

The hospital environment is highly competitive. OMH has a shortage of registered nurses, and averages 35 to 50 positions open at all times. The same shortages are evident at other hospitals in the area. Shortages occur within other hospital jobs, especially in one-of-a-kind technical positions. Not only do area hospitals crave the services of these "healers," but facilities across the nation vie for the area's labor supply. Hospitals in Florida have been known to beckon experienced troops from the chills of Northern winters with posters and advertisements showing palm trees and sunny beaches.

In an effort to keep desirable help and discourage less competent employees, OMH uses a merit pay system developed for it by an international consultant firm specializing in compensation. The plan was very expensive to develop, but Fred Richards, OMH's Salary Administrator, is pleased with its day-to-day workings. Since the system was introduced six years ago there have been fewer disagreements between employees and the hospital over the worth of the positions held by the employees.

For years the hospital participated in semi-annual market surveys of compensation conducted by the Northern Hospital Personnel Association. The surveys provided the hospital with average compensation rates (but not ranges) for large groups of hospital jobs. The surveys are still used by other large hospitals and by hospitals not large enough to have a formal pay system. However, the surveys are neither precise nor formal and OMH no longer participates in this program.

Mr. Richards believes the merit pay system has helped keep the unions from needing to organize OMH employees. He claims that his problems with equity compensation from department to department have ceased, and adds that the system has shielded the hospital from comparable pay and legal wage and hour complaints.

Oscar Renta is a Respiratory Equipment Technician. This is one of four jobs in the Respiratory Therapy Department. There are 50 employees in the department, ranging from lowest to highest jobs as follows:

> Respiratory Equipment Technicians
>
> Non-Certified Respiratory Therapists
>
> Certified Respiratory Therapists
>
> Registered Respiratory Therapists.

The hourly wages for these jobs range from $4.25 to $9.00. Oscar has worked at OMH for two years, one of them as a Respiratory Equipment Technician, landing the job the summer after completing high school. He received two weeks of training at the hospital and is expected to keep up-to-date on the equipment used in the hospital. Oscar loves his work and takes personal pride in keeping the machines working at peak efficiency. He knows that both his work and the equipment help the respiratory therapy patients recuperate.

In spite of his love for his work and a promotion one year ago to Non-Certified Respiratory Therapist, Oscar has become disgruntled. In discussing his disaffection with his supervisor, Mike Maxey, Oscar says:

> "You guys didn't teach me everything I know, you know. When I started here two years ago, I brought plenty of knowledge about equipment with me. I just found out that a girl I went to high school with is starting out here next week as a Certified Respiratory Therapist. You know what she told me? She'll get more pay to start than I get after two years here! What gives? Why is she so special?"

Mr. Maxey asked Oscar to calm down. He explained that the new employee completed two more years of school to gain that certification. With the type of patient she would be dealing with and because of the medication and treatments required, education and training are required for this job. "Let's call the personnel department," Maxey said, "and see what's gone into the decision to pay a starting employee in that job more than a veteran employee in your job."

Maxey and Oscar discovered the following: In a formal system such as OMH has, points determine the salary range, using set criteria to determine the points for a job. OMH and Mr. Richards disclose the point structures of its job when asked to, but do not routinely disclose them at any other time. When a position opens, the hospital publishes the starting salary range only. Several employees at OMH were aware of the point system, but were concerned only with their current wage, not with the range or the points associated with the wage.

In this particular case, Oscar's job had 273 points. The job's wage range this year is $5.00/hour to $7.08/hour, with most incumbents earning the mean. The Certified Therapist job had 333 points. This translates to a $5.80 to $8.33 hourly wage range; however, the job is "red tagged" because of severe shortages of qualified people. Because of the red tagging, the job pays at the 368-point level with an hourly range of $6.20 to $8.96.

The time had come for Oscar's annual performance appraisal and merit pay increase. All he wanted out of life at this time was a raise. He didn't know what kind of an increase to expect, but he understood from reading the newspaper that the cost of living had increased about 12% in the past year, and that the hospital had given all non-exempt employees a 6% increase for inflation in June.

A month later, Oscar had an appointment with Maxey for his performance appraisal session.

> "Let's review what's happened here, Oscar," said Maxey, after completing the appraisal discussion. "Last year at this time you were appraised as meeting all standards, so you got a 5% merit pay increase on top of the cost of living increase. This year, you've surely met all the standards, and you've even exceeded some of them. Now, I'm not supposed to give you an 'exceeding all standards' rating for that, but I have because that's the only way I can pay you enough to survive inflation. What the heck, I've got to pay the Certifieds more than their job is worth; I won't discuss this with any of the other techs or therapists, and you have to promise to improve your performance even more in the next twelve months."

QUESTIONS:

1. Evaluate the wage and salary administration system in use at OMH as a general approach to compensation management. What is your opinion of the following specific features of the system:

   a. Disclosing points and salary ranges to those who ask.

   b. Paying an experienced employee below a new employee in a higher grade job.

   c. What is your evaluation of "red tagging" the Certified Respiratory Therapist job and the consequences of doing so versus not doing so?

2. What mistakes does Mr. Maxey made in dealing with Oscar and the salary system?

3. Is it realistic to expect Oscar to "keep the secret" of what Maxey did? Why or why not?

4. If you were Richards, how would you go about dealing with Oscar's problem and Maxey's efforts to distort the system?

COMPREHENSIVE CASE #6:
OSHA—Nuisance or Necessity?

The Bojo Corporation is composed of ten autonomous divisions and corporate headquarters. This case focuses on the Rural plant, which manufactures some chemical solvents.

The Rural plant is housed in a building erected in 1924 that is five stories high. The top two floors are not used as the floors are too dangerous, and the second and third floors have rotted places in them.

The third floor holds the laboratory and the marketing department. The second floor holds the rack shop, office, some warehousing, and some chemical compound production lines. The first floor contains the warehousing for heavier materials and the rest of the manufacturing lines. The rack shop is a support unit to make racks for drying chemicals. The plant is non-union.

The plant manager is Joe Allen, who has been with the Bojo Corporation for twenty years—all at the Rural plant. He has done almost everything at the plant. He started as foreman in the manufacturing unit, supervised the rack shop and the warehouse, and also sold the compounds. He has not, however, worked in the office or laboratory. The employees like Joe, although they are a bit afraid of him. Joe has wide latitude to run the plant as he sees fit, as the Rural plant is both geographically isolated and far from Bojo's headquarters in New York City.

Because the Rural plant consistently makes more money for Bojo than its budgets and forecasts call for, corporate headquarters lets Joe alone. Turnover and absenteeism are also lower than expected. The plant safety and health record is considered to be "average" for a Bojo operation. All in all, the Bojo Corporation and Joe Allen are satisfied with the operation of the Rural plant.

The local OSHA inspector, George Hlavecek, came to the Rural plant fairly regularly. In April, Mr. Hlavecek came to the Rural plant when Joe was at a meeting at Bojo Corporation headquarters. Hlavecek determined that part of the chemical-compound manufacturing process was producing toxic gases. As was his right, he shut down the plant that day. Joe promptly flew back and modified the gas filters himself. Mr. Hlavecek inspected the filters the next day, passed them, and the Rural plant resumed operation.

In May, Hlavecek came back and shut down the plant again, this time when Joe Allen was at another meeting. Once again the filters were cleaned and modified. By now, Joe Allen was beginning to become upset with these unannounced inspections and subsequent shutdowns.

The following month, the OSHA inspector again appeared at the Rural plant. Joe Allen instructed the receptionist to tell him that he was too busy to accompany him on his inspection tour and that he should come back the next day.

The rest of the day at the Rural plant was a "red alert." No work was done and the whole plant was cleaned up. Bottles in the laboratory that leaked toxic chemicals were secured. Handguards were put on the processing machines (they weren't used otherwise). Machines for which there were no handguards were covered up and moved to look as if they were out of service. The gas filters were cleaned. Dust masks were issued to the employees. The following day, Hlavecek came back, toured the plant with Joe Allen, and passed the operation.

In August, Hlavecek again appeared at the Rural plant. Joe Allen stalled him for 45 minutes when he asked to make the inspection. Finally, the inspector and a foreman inspected the plant but the foreman took Hlavecek to the warehouse first to give the rest of the plant time to clean up. It didn't help. The inspector issued four warnings and gave the Rural plant 24 hours to comply, or he would initiate action to have the plant closed permanently. By now, Joe Allen was quite angry, with the constant inspections, modifications, and procedural changes beginning to show up in declining output and rising expenses. He became angrier still when he heard that the OSHA inspector had referred to the plant, within earshot of the employees, as a "deathtrap," a "sweatshop," and an "accident waiting to happen." Joe Allen now became convinced that OSHA was "out to get him" and his operation.

The next day, Joe Allen contacted the office of Representative Smith, his congressman. He informed Smith's office that he was being harassed by OSHA with constant inspections and shutdowns, and that the OSHA inspector was out to make an example of him and his operation. He further informed the congressman that the OSHA inspector had conducted himself in an unprofessional manner in conducting his inspection. From that point, things moved swiftly. Smith contacted the head of OSHA directly, indicating that if things didn't change, he would request that the House Subcommittee on Occupational Safety and Health hold hearings on the matter. The OSHA Administrator promised him that action would be taken. The following week, Hlavecek was transferred to the OSHA regional office in St. Louis, halfway across the country.

About this time, Arthur Jackson, manager of the health and safety division of Bojo's corporate personnel department, received word (from the media) about the Rural plant's recent experience with OSHA. He thereupon decided to visit the Rural plant and make his own inspection. The day he arrived, Joe was ill. However, even though he had never been to the Rural plant, he went ahead and inspected anyway. He found numerous OSHA violations and several violations of Bojo's own safety and health regulations.

QUESTIONS

1. Evaluate the charge of harassment leveled at OSHA and how that charge was received in Washington D.C.

2. What responsibilities have been neglected by corporate headquarters and Arthur Jackson? Why did the neglect occur?

3. Discuss Joe Allen's approach to safety and contrast it with a systems approach to safety.

4. If you were Arthur Jackson, Corporate Safety Director, what would you recommend be done at the Rural plant?

COMPREHENSIVE CASE #7:
Hi Tech Plastic Company

In union-management relations, collective bargaining is essentially a power relationship. It is through the implied and actual use of power that parties are compelled to resolve their conflicts. This was the situation when the management of Hi-Tech Plastics Company sat down with the Amalgamated Plastics Workers to negotiate a new contract.

Allen Springer, the 35-year-old president and owner of Hi-Tech, was surprised at the list of demands presented by APW business agent, Tony Mattson. But Springer was completely taken aback by the union's tenacity. Throughout the six-hour session the union team refused to budge from their initial positions. It was not the first time the APW has caught Springer off guard; the organizing drive that brought the union into Hi-Tech had come unexpectedly.

Allen Springer took the reins of this midwest company following the untimely death of his father, the founder of the company. At that time, Detroit automakers needed plastic body parts, trim pieces, and fasteners to meet government-mandated high mileage standards. Allen took full advantage of this demand and shifted his company's output from consumer to industrial lines. Under this strategy, sales volume almost tripled and the employee roster doubled to its present size of 105 employees (although, measured against the industry leaders, Hi-Tech is still a small firm).

In the third year, a recession caused major setbacks in the auto industry; Hi-Tech's revenues declined and unsold inventory stacked up. In the midst of this bad news, Allen Springer was hit with another blow—his workers were signing cards and pressing for union certification.

Following the successful drive, the union represented 65 Hi-Tech employees. The first contract was hammered out easily with a 6% wage hike in a one-year pact, but in renewal the negotiations were more militant. Battlelines formed on three union demands.

1. A three year agreement with a 30% wage boost the first year of the contract and 13% for each of the following two years.

Because contract negotiations were time-consuming and expensive, Springer wanted the contract to run longer than the one-year term of the first contract, but not at the proposed wage increases. He offered what he believed was a generous 8% wage hike.

But Tony Mattson claimed that stingy wage hikes over the preceding five years had cut severely into the union members' standard of living. A 30% increase, he stated, was just bridging the gap between past wage increases and the inflation rate, as measured by the Consumer Price Index.

2. A dental health plan. On this point the talks became heated. Mattson pounded on the table, jumped to his feet, and shouted, "How can management claim to care about their workers while ignoring their health?"

3. Reinstate service pins. From the time Hi-Tech opened its doors, the elder Springer had acknowledged employee loyalty with 24-carat gold service pins for five, ten, fifteen, and twenty years of uninterrupted employment. But in the face of declining income and with gold prices at almost $500 per ounce, Allen Springer had halted the practice. The union was quick to respond with a grievance calling for the pins to be brought back. At contract negotiation time the issue was still unresolved, but the APW members were adamant—give us our pins, they said, or submit the entire issue to binding arbitration.

Aside from the specific demands, what troubled Allen Springer the most was the apparent willingness of the members to strike if their demands were not met. Throughout the session the power of a strike was implied. Several times Mattson hinted that the rank-and-file members had already voted for a strike if their demands were not met to the letter.

During a break in the negotiations, Mattson confided to Springer that, although he was personally against a strike, the members were prepared. His manner was in sharp contrast to the shouting and table pounding during the bargaining. Now he was speaking in low, even tones. "The local has already rented office space across the street from the plant for strike headquarters," he said. "The central labor union is giving advice and the other labor unions have pledged their support. I'm afraid they mean business."

This information disturbed Springer. If the union employees were on a picket line, he would be left with only clerical personnel, a sales staff, and six production supervisors.

As Springer reflected on the demands and the strike threat, he was at least grateful that this was only the first bargaining session with two more to go and the present contract had 15 more days before it expired. He had three days to prepare for the next bargaining meeting.

QUESTIONS

1. What information does Springer need to prepare for the next session? How would the information be useful?

2. What past practices of poor labor relations practices can you identify?

3. What strategy or strategies would you suggest Springer use? Should he "take a strike" or try to avert it? Why?

4. What could be done to develop more effective labor relations on a long-term basis?

Appendix A

Important Organizations in Personnel Management

1. AFL-CIO
   815 16th Street N.W.
   Washington, D.C. 20006

2. American Compensation
   Association
   P.O. Box 1176
   Scottsdale, Arizona 85252

3. American Management Association (AMA)
   135 West 50th Street
   New York City, New York
   10020

4. American Society for Personnel Administration
   (ASPA)
   30 Park Drive
   Berea, Ohio 44017

5. American Society for Training and Development
   (ASTD)
   Suite 305
   600 Maryland Avenue S.W.
   Washington, D.C. 20024

6. Bureau of Industrial Relations (University of
   Michigan)
   Ann Arbor, Michigan 48104

7. Bureau of Labor Statistics
   (BLS)
   Department of Labor
   3rd Street & Constitution
   Ave. N.W.
   Washington, D.C. 20210

8. Bureau of National Affairs
   (BNA)
   1231 25th Street, N.W.
   Washington, D.C. 20037

9. Department of Labor
   3rd Street & Constitution
   Ave., N.W.
   Washington, D.C. 20210

10. Equal Employment Opportunity Commission (EEOC)
    2401 E. Street, N.W.
    Washington, D.C. 20506

11. Internal Revenue Service
    (IRS)
    111 Constitution Ave.,
    N.W.
    Washington, D.C. 20224

12. International Personnel
    Management Association
    (IPMA)
    1850 K Street N.W.
    Suite 870
    Washington, D.C. 20006

13. Labor/Management Media-
    tion Service
    1620 I Street, N.W., Suite
    616
    Washington, D.C. 20006

14. National Association for the
    Advancement of Colored
    People (NAACP)
    1790 Broadway
    New York, New York 10019

15. National Association of
    Manufacturers (NAM)
    1776 F. Street
    Washington, D.C. 20006

16. National Association of
    Temporary Services
    1001 Connecticut Ave.
    N.W.
    Suite 932
    Washington, D.C. 20036

17. Occupational Safety and
    Health Administration
    (OSHA)
    200 Constitution Ave.,
    N.W.
    Washington, D.C. 20210

18. Office of Federal Contract
    Compliance (OFCC)
    200 Constitution Ave.,
    N.W.
    Washington, D.C. 20210

19. Pension Benefit Guaranty
    Corporation
    P.O. Box 7119
    Washington, D.C. 20044

20. U.S. Chamber of Commerce
    1615 H Street, N.W.
    Washington, D.C. 20062

Appendix B

Glossary

Adverse impact substantial underrepresentation of protected group members in employment decision.

Affirmative action efforts by organizations to identify problem areas in their minority employment and to identify goals to overcome those problems.

Arbitration process whereby an impartial entity determines the relative merit of different viewpoints and makes a decision called an *award*.

Authority the right to use resources to accomplish goals.

Benchmark job a standard type of job that is correctly priced and representative of major factors in most jobs in the organization.

Benefits additional compensation given to employees as a condition of membership. They are rewards available to employees or a group of employees as a part of organizational membership.

B.F.O.Q. (Bonafide Occupational Qualification)—legitimate reason why employment can be reasonably restricted to exclude persons on otherwise illegal bases of consideration.

Chronology a structured review of activities during a period of time.

Closed shop requires employees to join a union before they can be hired.

Co-determination a concept whereby union or worker representatives are given positions on a company's board of directors.

Collective bargaining the process whereby representatives of management and workers negotiate over items such as wages, hours, and conditions of employment.

567

Comparable worth   the concept that jobs requiring comparable knowledge, skills, and ability should be paid similarly.

Conciliation   process in which an outside entity attempts to help two deadlocked parties continue negotiations and arrive at a solution (also called *mediation*).

Consideration   behavior indicating warmth, trust, friendship and respect between the leader and the group members.

Contributory plan   a retirement plan in which money for pension benefits is paid by both employees and the employer.

Decertification   a process whereby a union is removed as the representative of a group of employees.

Discrimination   (E.E.O.C. definition)—the use of any test that adversely affects hiring, promotion, transfer or any other employment or membership opportunity of classes unless the test has been validated and is job related, and/or an employer can demonstrate that alternative hiring, transfer, or promotion procedures are unavailable.

Duty   a work segment performed by an individual composed of a number of tasks.

Equal employment   offering individuals regardless of race, creed, age, sex, religion, or handicaps, fair and equal treatment in all employment-related actions.

Equity   the perceived fairness of what a person does (inputs) compared to what the person receives (outcomes).

Ergonomics   field of study that examines the interaction among workers, jobs, and work environments.

Expatriate   an employee transferred out of his or her native country.

Extinction   refers to a situation in which no response is given the trainee.

Flex-time   refers to starting and quitting time variations but assumes that a constant number of hours (usually eight) are worked each day.

Four-fifths (4/5th) rule   discrimination generally occurs if the selection rate for any protected group is less than 80% of the selection rate of majority groups.

Funded method   provides pension benefits over a long period from funds accumulated ahead of time.

Grievance   a specific, formal dissatisfaction expressed through an identified procedure.

Grievance procedure   a formal channel of communication used to resolve formal complaints (grievances).

Halo effect   one characteristic or factor carries an inordinate weight when appraising or selecting an individual.

Health   a general state of physical, mental, and emotional well-being.

Human resource accounting   a specialized personnel audit which continually attempts to quantify the value of an organization's human resources.

Human resource planning   consists of determining what must be done to ensure the availability of employees required for an organization to meet its objectives.

Immediate confirmation   indicates that people learn best if reinforcement is given as soon as possible after the training response.

Incentives   additional compensation related to performance. They are rewards designed to encourage and reimburse employees for efforts beyond normal performance expectations.

Initiating structure   effort on the part of the leader to get the job done.

Interfaces   areas of contact between the personnel unit and other managers in an organization that occur within critical personnel activities.

Job   an organizational unit of work.

Job analysis   a systematic investigation of the tasks, duties, and responsibilities of a job, and the necessary knowledge, skills, and abilities a person needs to perform the job adequately.

Job depth   amount of planning and control responsibility in a job.

Job description   a summary of the tasks, duties, and responsibilities in a job.

Job design   refers to conscious efforts to organize tasks, duties, and responsibilities into a unit of work to achieve a certain objective.

Job enlargement   the concept of broadening the scope and/or depth of a job.

Job evaluation   the systematic determination of the relative worth of jobs within an organization.

Job rotation   a process of shifting a person from job to job.

Job scope   refers to the number and variety of tasks performed by the job holder.

Job specification   listing of the various knowledge, skills, and abilities an individual needs to do a job satisfactorily.

Labor grades   are used to group individual jobs having approximately the same job worth together.

Matrix organization   an organization in which two structures exist at the same time.

Motivation   an emotion or desire operating on a person's will and causing that person to act.

Negative reinforcement   when an individual works to avoid an undesirable reward.

Noncontributory plan   one in which the employer provides all the funds.

Norms   expected standards of behavior, usually unwritten and often unspoken, that are generally understood by all members of the group.

Open system   a living entity which takes energy from its environment, processes it, and returns output to the environment.

Organization   a set of stable social relations deliberately created with the intention of accomplishing some goal or purpose. It generally has an authority structure, and is influenced considerably by the technology and the environment in which it operates.

Organization design   results in a structure for the organization.

Organization development   a value-based process of self-assessment and planned change, involving specific strategies and technology, aimed at improving the overall effectiveness of an organizational system.

Organizational climate   a composite view of the characteristics of an organization as seen by employees.

Orientation   the planned introduction of employees to their jobs, their co-workers, and the organization.

Pay   basic compensation employees receive, usually a wage or salary.

Pay compression   occurs when pay differences between jobs of different evaluated worth become small.

Performance appraisal   determining how well employees do their jobs and communicating that information to them.

Personnel audit   a formal research effort to evaluate the current state of personnel management in an organization.

Personnel development   focuses on increasing the capabilities of employees for continuing growth in the organization.

Personnel information system   an integrated computerized system that is designed to provide information to be used in making personnel decisions.

Personnel management a set of activities focusing on the coordination of human resources in an organization.

Personnel research analyzes past and present personnel practices through the use of collected data and records.

Policies general guidelines that regulate organizational actions.

Portability a pension right allowing employees to move their pension benefit rights from one employer to another.

Position a collection of tasks, duties, and responsibilities performed by one person.

Positive reinforcement when a person receives a desired reward.

Punishment action taken to repel the person from the undesired action.

Recruiting process of generating a pool of qualified applicants for organizational positions.

Red circle rate a job whose current occupant's pay is out of grade or range.

Reliability the consistency with which a test measures an item.

Responsibilities obligations to perform accepted tasks and duties.

Reverse discrimination when a more qualified individual is denied an opportunity because of guarantees given to protected group individuals who may be less qualified.

Rules specific guidelines that regulate and restrict the behavior of individuals.

Safety protection of the physical health of people.

Salary compensation that is consistent from period to period and is not directly related to the amount of hours worked by the individual.

Selection process of picking individuals who have the relevant qualifications to fill jobs in the organization.

Self-actualization the striving of an individual to reach the highest level of potential.

Self-funding occurs when an employer sets aside funds to pay health claims, but the employer provides the insurance coverage.

Status the relative social ranking an individual has in a group or organization.

Structured interview is conducted using a set of standardized questions that are asked all applicants for a job.

System approach an organization is viewed as a whole comprised of subsystems.

Task a distinct identifiable work activity composed of motions.

Technology types and patterns of activity, equipment, materials, and knowledge or experience used to perform tasks.

Title VII that portion of the 1964 Civil Rights Act prohibiting discrimination in employment.

Training a learning process whereby people acquire skills, concepts, attitudes, or knowledge to aid in the achievement of goals.

Turnover process of employees leaving an organization and having to be replaced.

Unfunded plan pays pension benefits out of current income to the organization.

Uninsured the benefits at retirement are determined by calculations that consider the age of the employee, years worked, and other factors.

Union formal organization that represents individuals employed in one organization, throughout an industry, or in an occupation.

Validity a test carefully measures what it says it measures.

Vesting the right of employees to receive benefits from their pension plans.

Wages pay directly calculated on the amount of time worked.

Wage survey a means of gathering data on the existing compensation rates for employees performing similar jobs in other organizations.

Work group a collection of individuals brought together to perform organizational work.

Workers' compensation provides cash benefits to any person injured on the job.

Name Index

Subject Index